A Year with

American Saints

A Year with
American Saints

G. Scott Cady
and
Christopher L. Webber

CHURCH PUBLISHING
an imprint of
Church Publishing Incorporated, New York

Library of Congress Cataloging-in-Publication Data

Cady, G. Scott, 1948-
    A year with American Saints / G. Scott Cady ; Christopher L. Webber.
      p. cm.
    Includes index.
    ISBN-13: 978-0-89869-530-4
    ISBN-10: 0-89869-530-9
    1. Christian biography – United States. 2. United States – Church
history. 3. Devotional calendars. I. Webber, Christopher. II. Title.
BR1700.3.C33 2006
277.3′00922 – dc22
[B]
                                                     2006029170

Church Publishing Incorporated
445 Fifth Avenue
New York, NY 10016
www.churchpublishing.org

5 4 3 2 1

CONTENTS

INTRODUCTION

In the year 1607, the first permanent European settlement in the present territory of the United States was established in Jamestown, Virginia. Robert Hunt, their Chaplain, was a priest of the Church of England and the new colony quickly made the Church of England its established church. Thirteen years later, a second colony was established; this one in Massachusetts and this one establishing a reformed and congregational pattern of Christianity as the state church. Before long, Quaker and Scots Presbyterian and Dutch Reformed and Swedish Lutheran and Roman Catholic settlements had been made. In Europe, these various Christian Churches had often occupied separate territories and so, for a while, some of them did in the new world as well. But even where they did not, the colonial governments that created established churches seldom had the will or authority to enforce that establishment as had been done in Europe and many colonies had no official establishment in the first place.

Settlers in the new world brought their various churches and theologies with them, but those churches and theologies, in the radically different circumstances of the new world were inevitably changed. Even that largest and most centrally directed church, the Roman Catholic, found its American branch so transformed in the new atmosphere that at the end of the 19th century it officially condemned what it called "Americanism," an excessive adaptation to American ways.

Old churches were changed in America and new churches were created. The individuals who came to the new world, came seeking new and greater opportunity for themselves. Inevitably, however, those who wanted a new life for themselves were inclined to hope better things for their churches as well, and, if disappointed in their hopes, to separate themselves from the church that had disappointed them and create new bodies with higher, or at least different, standards. Soon there were literally hundreds of churches in competition with each other, some recognizably within the broad stream of Christian tradition, others departing so far from that tradition that it would seem necessary either to expand any traditional definition or to exclude some of these bodies from it.

As Americans migrated westward, they took their familiar churches with them. Yet once again, altered conditions engendered new religious bodies. At this same period, many denominations were beginning to send out missionaries — some to the native peoples of the west, but others to foreign lands. By the end of the 19th century, thousands of American missionaries were stationed in Asia and Africa, especially. The results of these relationships with the rest of the world brought about a number of changes. As American missionaries established schools and hospitals and spread their political ideals, they began to perceive their beliefs and allegiances in a new light. Some of their inherited divisions seemed irrelevant to the world in which they now found themselves. Missionary cooperation among denominations found common cause in the goal of spreading the gospel. This, in turn, fostered an interest in ecumenism. By the mid-19th century, various proposals for Christian unity were floated by one denomination or another in the United States. American missionaries played major roles in organizing the first World Mission Conference in Edinburgh in 1910 and the first world conference on Faith and Order in Switzerland in 1927.

Just as the conditions of American life reshaped churches, the churches strove to reshape society. The slavery question, the Civil War, and its aftermath dominated Christian thought and energies throughout the 19th century. Christians led the abolition movement as well as various attempts to incorporate freed slaves more fully into American society afterward. This effort came to a climax with the civil rights movement in the 1960s. Many Christians cooperated across denominational lines on these issues. But not invariably: at the same time, several major churches divided into northern and southern branches over slavery and segregation. On another front, as a once largely agrarian society turned increasingly industrial, the needs of immigrants and factory workers clamored for attention. Some religious groups threw themselves into the cause of economic justice and described themselves as "Christian Socialists," while others maintained that the business of the church was not social change but the conversion of individuals.

Over the centuries since the Jamestown settlement, Christians have witnessed to their faith in many ways. To single out a certain number of individual American "saints" for study is not to suggest that American Christianity deserves special consideration but rather to ask what American Christians have in common and what unites them. It is an exercise in ecumenicity, not nationalism. A sampling of lives over four centuries will naturally display diversity as well as unity and not every sentiment expressed will be congenial either to you, the reader, or to us, the compilers. Christianity is like a vast rainbow of colors, somehow united in one arc. St. Paul wrote to the Corinthian Christians about the diversity of roles we are given by the Spirit who works within us all as members of one body. In assembling these particular names, we sought signs of the unity of that body. The women and men included in this book sought to serve Christ according to their gifts and during the time and circumstances of their specific ministry. An old rhyme says:

> *Men's faces, voices, differ much;*
> *Saints are not all one size.*
> *Flowers in a garden various grow;*
> *Let none monopolize.*

This collection of flowers has been made in that spirit.

We should note at the outset that "American Saints" may not be the ideal title for such a compilation; all God's people are saints, set apart for God's purposes and called to be holy. It is not our intention to exclude these millions by limiting ourselves to 365 names. The individuals selected for this "honor roll" are men and women whose voices and witness were recorded for posterity. But, in the words of an ancient scribe, "some there be, which have no memorial." A book such as this, containing the best known (or perhaps the most easily discovered) bearers of the gospel ought to remind us of untold numbers who "were merciful men [and women], whose righteousness hath not been forgotten" (Ecclesiasticus 44:9–11). The body, St. Paul said, is one, yet it has many members and all play their part in the proper functioning of that body. Those not named here have also served according to the gifts they were given.

We have conducted no polls to test which 365 American Christians are most universally remembered and respected. No system we could imagine would be likely to win unanimous agreement, in any event. Some churches have a process for recognizing outstanding individuals. Others do not. However, we have not limited ourselves to officially recognized names. Undoubtedly we have overlooked some who may be more important than others we included. Yet the lives we chose reflect a significant part of the Christian story in this country. Their names and testimony provide insights into the impact of Christianity on America and of America on Christianity. In fact, many of these pilgrims of the faith are subtly connected to each other through their lives and ministries. Their connections are deeply woven into the fabric of American life and become clearer with historical perspective. To guide the reader, an asterisk (*) after a name mentioned in an entry indicates that that person also has an entry in this book.

We have pondered the definition of "American": should we exclude those not native-born or those whose career was primarily in overseas mission? In a nation of immigrants, too narrow a definition would exclude many who played critical roles in establishing Christianity on these shores. In the end, it seemed to make most sense to include people who spent the most significant part of their ministry in this country or who were raised and trained here before serving elsewhere as missionaries.

Whenever possible, we have tried to let individuals speak for themselves by providing a substantial quotation from their writings — sometimes, it is the words that live. But for others, even some preachers, writings have not survived. Others spoke through their actions. Therefore, while the majority of entries include both biography and a substantial reading, some entries have only brief quotations or none at all.

For variety's sake, most of the biographies have been arranged randomly. The exception is Dr. Martin Luther King, Jr., whose birthday is a national holiday, established by an act of Congress. Although ancient Christian practice celebrates the day of death as the "birthday into heaven," current national practice in this country honors heroes on their natal days. Initially, we thought of arranging our inclusions by their dates of birth, and have provided a calendar for anyone who wishes to remember them this way.

We have avoided clerical titles as an unnecessary barrier in this increasingly informal age. In a few cases — Father Flanagan, Sister Constance — the title has become almost inseparable from the name. However, had we decided to make exceptions, we would have been submerged in a plethora of forms of address, so it seemed best to let most names stand unadorned.

January

Robert Hunt

EPISCOPALIAN

1563?–1608

Almost nothing is known about Robert Hunt as a person. There is no certain date for his birth or his death. He left no documents except his will to help us judge his thoughts. What we do know is the impact he made on others, but from that evidence we see a faithful servant of God.

Robert Hunt was chaplain to the Jamestown colony, the first continuing English settlement in the western hemisphere. He served in that capacity for less than two years and only the last six or eight months were spent in Virginia. Yet in that time, Hunt played a vital role, conducting services, offering communion, preaching sermons, and working to resolve various tensions that arose among men far from home who felt threatened by disease and hardships. Captain John Smith and other members of the colony bore witness in their diaries and reports to the diligence with which Hunt ministered to them. When a memorial tablet was erected in his memory, those comments were collected into a eulogy:

> He was an honest, religious and courageous divine. He preferred the service of God in so good a voyage to every thought of ease at home. He endured every privation, yet none ever heard him repine. During his life our factions were oft healed and our greatest extremities so comforted that they seemed easy in comparison with what we endured after his memorable death. We all received

from him the Holy Communion as a pledge of reconciliation for we all loved him for his exceeding goodness.

Aside from this testimony, we know that Robert Hunt graduated from Magdalen College, Oxford, and served two small English parishes between 1594 and 1606: Reculver near Canterbury, and Heathfield in Sussex. Three years into his first parish, he married and he and his wife had two children. When plans were drawn up for planting an English colony in North America, Richard Hakluyt — famous for his writings on geography and voyages of discovery — was chosen to be rector of any parish established in Virginia. Hakluyt selected Hunt as his vicar, so it was Hunt who went out to the New World. Before leaving his home and parish, he wrote his will.

It had been more than 20 years since the first attempt to plant an English settlement in Roanoke had failed. Nevertheless, the Jamestown colonists were not much better prepared for the harsh conditions they faced. A hundred colonists arrived in May. By the end of the year, almost half had died, perhaps as many as 19 in August alone.

Among their difficulties were conflicts over leadership. Hunt worked to reconcile factions and, having done so, sealed the agreement among them by celebrating the Holy Communion. The furnishings for the service were described by Captain John Smith:

> When I first went to Virginia, I well remember we did hang an awning (which is an old sail) to three or four trees to shadow us from the sun, our walls were rails of wood, our seats unhewed trees till we cut planks, our pulpit a bar of wood nailed to two neighbouring trees.

There was a goblet of wine and a loaf of coarse bread. Around the little clearing men leaned on their guns, wary of the unknown dangers lurking in the vast wilderness beyond them. Later, Smith wrote, "We built a homely thing like a barn, set upon cratchets, covered with rafts, sedge, and earth; so also was the walls." In the bitter cold of the following January, a fire burned down the church, storehouse, and palisade. Hunt's library perished in the flames with the rest of his possessions, except for the clothes on his back. Yet he continued to hold daily prayer morning and evening, to preach two sermons each Sunday, and celebrate the communion every three months until he died. "Till he could not speak," Smith wrote, "he never ceased to his utmost to animate us constantly to persist." The little colony of adventurers — some of its members fixed on gaining a fortune, others on establishing their position, few thinking much beyond their own concerns — had a stable center to hold them together.

"You must die to self," said Jesus. The mark of his followers is not seen in the achievements they are credited with, but in the degree to which Jesus may be seen in them. Robert Hunt appears to perfectly embody that ideal. He left nothing of himself beyond the impact he made on others. He gave himself to them and they said, "We all loved him for his exceeding goodness." On the shore of the New World, in its first continuing English settlement, a high standard was set for those who would come after — who would be able to come because of the community Robert Hunt helped to endure.

✪ *January 2*

Mary Ignatia Gavin

ROMAN CATHOLIC

January 2, 1889–April 1, 1966

Those familiar with the Alcoholics Anonymous program usually recognize the names of the cofounders, "Bill W." and "Dr. Bob." Hardly anyone recognizes the name of the third member of the founding trinity. Mary Ignatia Gavin (Sister Ignatia) had no reason to protect her anonymity — unlike the other two, she wasn't an alcoholic. However, she hated publicity. When President Kennedy publicly recognized her work in 1961, she only agreed to accept the honor on behalf of her religious community and the nursing profession.

Ignatia had already begun a ministry to alcoholics in 1934, the year before Dr. Bob first approached her about caring for an alcoholic patient. The national experiment called "Prohibition" had ended the previous year. Alcoholism was still seen not as a disease but as a moral failure. Hospitals were reluctant to admit people who might be unruly, with problems they didn't know how to treat. In contrast to general attitudes, Ignatia saw alcoholics as people who needed care. Working with an intern in the emergency room, she had admitted patients who needed sobering up, sometimes hiding them in the so-called "flower room" where the bodies of the deceased were kept pending transfer to the morgue. When Dr. Bob approached her and requested a private room for his first patient, she told him, "We have no beds let alone private rooms... but I can make space in the flower room." To avoid difficulty with hospital administrators, they agreed on an official diagnosis of "acute gastritis," and brought the patient in. Hospital care and spiritual discipline, the doctor and the nurse both knew, were the essential ingredients of a recovery program.

Eventually St. Thomas Hospital in Akron, Ohio, began to see the importance of this ministry and became the first religious institution to recognize the right of alcoholics to receive hospital treatment. In 1939, St. Thomas opened a ward for alcoholics based on AA principles. When Ignatia's order transferred her to St. Vincent Charity Hospital, Cleveland, in 1952, she created another ward for alcoholics at St. Vincent's in that city. The hospital board was dubious about her proposal for a coffee bar, and tried to eliminate it. Ignatia explained that alcoholics are often undernourished and needed some place open around the clock to provide coffee, fruit juice, and food. She said that without a coffee bar there would be no alcoholics' ward. Ignatia prevailed.

A reading from Sister Ignatia from the October 1951 issue of *Hospital Progress*

We begin where reality begins for the alcoholic. Reality for the alcoholic is drinking. It is most important that the approach be made through another alcoholic — a sponsor. The sponsor speaks the language of the alcoholic. He knows "all the tricks of the trade," because of personal experience.

Those of us who have anything to do with admitting these patients would do well to have the humility to rely upon the judgment of the sponsor. Let him decide when the patient is ready for the program. We do not accept repeaters! Sponsors know this, hence they are very careful to qualify the person before bringing him into the hospital. Above all, he must have a sincere desire to stop drinking. Wives, relatives, friends, and well-meaning employers may try to high-pressure the alcoholic into accepting the program. Someone may even persuade the family doctor to use his influence with the hospital, so that the prospect may be admitted into the alcoholic ward. After registration the sponsor escorts his patient to the A.A. ward.... The alcoholic is ill, in body, mind, and soul; hence we begin with the physical care.

The physical condition of the patient is usually much improved on the second day. His mind is beginning to clear. He feels encouraged because everyone seems interested in him. Visitors call on him, telling him "This is how I made it." Some of the visitors may be men with whom he used to drink. The power of example is a great incentive to the patient. He begins to say to himself, "If he can do it — so can I. But how am I going to make it?" At this point he generally has a "heart to heart talk" with his sponsor. He acknowledges his utter powerlessness over alcohol. He honestly admits that he has tried innumerable times to drink normally and has always failed. He is finally ready, honestly and humbly, to admits defeat. His sponsor is delighted to know that his patient is really honest about his drinking. The sponsor says, "Good! We can help you since you are humble and honest."

This is the grace of God at work in the soul of the patient — to admit helplessness and to seek help outside of self. This may be the first time the patient has admitted the fact that he is powerless to help himself.

The next step is humbly to turn to God: "Ask and you shall receive." Patients have often said that is the first time they sincerely prayed. The "Our Father" takes on a new meaning at this point. They feel that they really *belong*.

❂ *January 3*

William Bradford

CONGREGATIONAL

March 1590–May 9, 1657

William Bradford's parents died when he was young. Though various relatives took him in for short periods of time, he had no real home until he happened on a Separatist congregation in a nearby town. When they fled from England to Holland, Bradford went with them. As a leader in his community, he moved on 12 years later when the first band of Pilgrims set sail for New England. "They knew," he wrote, "that they were pilgrims, and looked not much on those things, but lifted up their eyes to the heavens, their dearest country, and quieted their spirits."

Bradford's wife died on the voyage out and half the colonists, including John Carver their governor, died in the first winter. William Bradford was then chosen governor and continued in that position for all but five-year intervals until the time of his death. The journal he kept for the first 25 years remains one of our best sources of information on the Plymoth Colony. In the summer after "the starving time," the colonists learned how to farm the land and make use of the natural resources available so that by the fall of 1621, Bradford called for a celebration of the harvest: He recorded the event in his journal:

> They began now to gather in the small harvest they had, and to fit up their houses and dwellings against winter, being all well recovered in health and strength and had all things in good plenty. For as some were thus employed in affairs abroad, others were exercised in fishing, about cod and bass and other fish, of which they took good store, of which every family had their portion. All the summer there was no want; and now began to come in store of fowl, as winter approached, of which this place did abound when they came first (but afterward decreased by degrees). And besides waterfowl there was great store of wild turkeys, of which they took many, besides venison, etc. Besides, they had about a peck of meal a week to a person, or now since harvest, Indian corn to that proportion. Which made many afterwards write so largely of their plenty here to their friends in England, which were not feigned but true reports.

It should be noted that about half of these first settlers were not members of the Separatist congregation but had been brought along to fill up the number needed for a viable settlement. Thus many of the original colonists were not motivated by faith. Indeed, they often dissented from what the Pilgrims wanted to do. To resolve their differences, a covenant known as the Mayflower Compact was drawn up. It acknowledged the right of everyone who signed it to share in the making and administering of laws and the right of the majority to rule. This compact governed the colony's affairs during the early years.

As governor, Bradford made some allowance for different views, but there were limits to his toleration. In 1621, a number of the new individuals who had come to join the community wanted to celebrate Christmas. However, the Pilgrims had rejected all celebrations of ancient Christian festivals. On the day called Christmas-day, the governor called them out to work,

> but the most of this new company excused themselves and said it went against their consciences to work on that day. So the Governor told them that if they made it matter of conscience, he would spare them till they were better informed. So he led away the rest and left them; but when they came home at noon from their work, he found them in the street at play, openly; some pitching the bar, and some at stoole-ball, and such-like sports. So he went to them, and took away their implements, and told them it was against his conscience, that they should play and others work. If they made the keeping of it matter of devotion, let them keep [in] their houses, but there should be no gaming or reveling in the streets. Since which time nothing has been attempted that way, at least openly.

The balanced leadership Bradford provided helped the colony survive and prosper until it reached a point where some members moved out to new areas. He wrote in his journal that:

> [M]any were much enriched, and commodities grew plentiful; and yet in other regards this benefit turned to their hurt, and this accession of strength to their weakness. For now as their stocks increased, and the increase [saleable] there was no longer any holding them together, but now they must of necessity go to their great lots; they could not other wise keep their cattle; and having oxen grown, they must have land for plowing and tillage. And no man now thought he could live, except he had cattle and a great deal of ground to keep them; all striving to increase their stocks. By which means they were scattered all over the bay, quickly, and the town, in which they lived compactly till now, was left very thin, and in a short time almost desolate. And if this had been it, it had been less, though too much; but the church must also be divided, and those [who]had lived too long together in Christian and comfortable fellowship must now part and suffer many divisions. First, those that lived on their lots on the other side of the bay (called Duxberie) they could not long bring their wives and children to the public worship and church meetings here.

Though Bradford understood what was happening, he regretted the loss of the original sense of community. It had been a family to him since his teens and prospered through his guidance so much that ultimately it moved on, leaving him behind.

✪ *January 4*

Isaac Backus

BAPTIST

January 9, 1723/4 — November 20, 1806

The story of Isaac Backus marks an important chapter in the history of church-state relationships in the United States. His mother had been imprisoned for refusing to pay the church tax, and Isaac also refused to accept the prevailing pattern of church life without question. A conversion experience at the age of 18 made Backus unwilling to associate with the "lukewarm" Christians in the church his family attended. He and others therefore separated themselves from that "charnel house" and began to meet for prayer and exhortation in their own homes. This step brought them into conflict with the Connecticut authorities since they refused to pay the taxes levied to support the community church. Backus, like his mother before him, and many others were imprisoned for refusing to pay the church tax. He went on to play a vital role in the effort to separate church and state in New England. Backus came to believe in "believers baptism," and was baptized in 1751, when he was in his late 20s. Within five years, he organized a Baptist congregation which he served for over 50 years. During that time, Backus traveled constantly, estimating that he covered over 67,000 miles throughout the course of his ministry, preaching some 10,000 sermons. Backus has been called a leading orator of the "pulpit of the American Revolution." In 1773 he published *An Appeal to the Public for Religious Liberty, Against the Oppressions of the Present Day*, in which he asked, "Who can hear Christ declare, that his kingdom is, not of this world, and yet believe that this blending of church and state together can be pleasing to him?" Throughout the centuries, Baptists have preserved this commitment to the separation of church and state.

A reading from Isaac Backus's account of his conversion (preserving his spelling)

Although I was often warned and Exorted, (especially by my godly mother) To fly from the Wrath to come: — yet I Never was under any Powerful Conviction Till the year 1741, When it pleased the Lord to cause a very general awakening Thro' the Land; especially in Norwich.

Now about this time it pleased The Lord to Send many Powerfull Preachers To Norwich. The first that Preacht There was Mr. [Eleazer] Wheelock June 2, and in the latter end of The same week I heard Mr. Jedidiah Mills also Preach there two Sermons. I was something Affected But I Couldn't for my life get Such Convictions as I wanted and as I thought many others had. After this in the Summer I had oppertunity to hear Sundry awakening discources — but my case remained much The Same. About the begining of August Mr. [James] Devenport Came to Norwich and preached There three days going in an exceeding Earnest and Powerful manner: and I apprehend that his labours were the most blest For my Conversion of any one mans. Mr. [Benjamin] Pomroy and Wheelock met him Here at Norwich and we had a great Many powerfull meetings while they Were here; and a number I Believe were Converted but I seemed to be left: the thoughts of which Seemed dreadfull to my Soul.

Nothing now distresed me more Than to find that hearing the most Powerful preaching and also the Shreacks and Cries of Souls under Concern did not Affect me as I desired. But my heart Felt hard notwithstanding. But in Truth the Lord was then letting me in To see Something of the Plague of my Heart and the fountain of Corruption that was there. I Remember once in Particular that I had such a view of my Heart that I really Saw that there wan't a Sin In the whole World but I had the seeds of it In my heart. This Brought on distress Indeed, tho' not Such as I was seeking after. No; my tears and good desires that I was Seeking for were dryed up and instead of a Penitent frame I found a hard heart and a Blind mind and Instead of good desires I found Dreadful Qurelings against God, especially Against his Sovereingnty and the freeness of his Grace. That he was no ways obliged to give me His Grace, let me do as much as I would.

But then again to See that I had Such Corruptions in me brought on fresh distress That I knew not which way to turn. Sometimes I thought that my Convictions Were wareing off and that Gods Spirit would Leave me but that appeared dredfull indeed for I Still thought that this was the last Call That I ever should have — thus I worried Along for Some weeks. One Sabbath as our old minister [Benjamin Lord] was speaking to persons under Convictions he laid out a case much Like mine and then Said "if this be your Case don't be discouraged, but see if God don't Speadily appear for your help." Or words To that Purpose. Immediately the Tempter Clapt in, "There" Says he "is Incouragement for vou to be easey and not Trouble your Self So much; you may be Converted by and by." But I was made So Sensable that it was a Temptation that I was filled with more distress. Again one morning as I was thinking on my Case Them words seemed to be Spok into my mind in Mark 12:34 thou art not far from the kingdom of God. But no sooner did they come in But my Soul started for fear that 'twas The tempter that brought these words to try to Settle me down Short of Christ; which made me cry out more earnestly for help.

Not Long after this on August the 24, 1741 as I was mowing in the Field alone I was thinking of my case; and all my past Life Seemed to be brought fresh to my view And it appeared indeed nothing but a life of Sin. I felt so that I left work and went and sat Down under a Shadey tree; and I was brought to Look Particularly into my duties . . . and striveings. How I had tried to get help by awakening Preaching Taut found it fail. Had tried to

Mend my Self by my Tears prayers and Promises of doing better but all in vain — my heart was Hard and full of Corruption still. And it Appeared clear to me then that I had tryed Every way that Posibly I Could and if I perished Forever I Could do no more. And the Justice of God Shined so clear Before my eyes in Condemning Such a guilty Rebel that I Could say no more — but fell at his feet. I See that I was in his hands and he had a right To do with me just as he Pleased And I Lay like a Dead Vile Creature before him. I felt a calm in my mind — them tossings And tumults that I felt before seemed to be gone.

And Just in that Critical moment God who caused the light to Shine out of Darkness, Shined into my heart with such A discovery of that glorious Righteousness Which fully Satesfies the Law that I had Broken; and of the Infinite fullness that there Is in Christ to Satesfie the wants of just Such a helpless Creature as I was and these Blessings Were held forth So freely to my Soul — That my Whole Heart was attracted and Drawn away after God and Swallowed up with Admiration in viewing his Divine glories.

Never did his Word appear So before as It did now: — it appeared So glorious and Such Infallible Truth that I could with the greatest Freedom Rest my Eternal all upon what God hath Spoken. Now the way of Salvation appeared so excellent and glorious That I Wondered that I had stood out So long against Such a Blessed Redeemer. Yea I wondered that all the World didn't Come to him.

And now my Burden that was so dreadful Heavey before was gone: that tormenting fear That I had was taken away and I felt Sweet Peace and rejoiceing in my soul. But yet all This time I hadn't one thought that this was That Which is Called Conversion; it was so Different from the notion that I had of it before.

Yet afterward when I came to think of my Case I Couldn't get that distress Which I had Before, but I thought I should be Converted Hereafter. Thus I went on for Some days.

The first time that I thought I Was Converted was 2 or 3 days after at an Evening meeting when they read Mr. [George] Whitefields Sermon on Acts 19:2, Where he lays down Sundry marks of trial To know whether we are saints or not. I thought When they began to Read that, it wan't So Particularly for me for I never thought my Self Converted; and So I didn't need to try That point. But as they read along I was aware my Soul gave in that I had Felt what he there Lays down as marks of true grace: — as particularly a spirit of Prayer — a lothing and hatred of Sin — Love to the Bretherin etc. And then The Lord was Pleased to give me Some Sweet Sealings of the holy Spirit of Promise; and a Comfortable Season it was to my Soul. O Bless the Lord My Soul! And forget not all his benifits.

These mercies of the Lord are Greater than Tongue Can express. That He Should deliver my Soul from going down To the Pit and from the Clutches of the old Dragon. And that in the fore-part of my Days, Being then 17 years and 7 months old. O! For Strength always to live to The glory of God. Amen!

✪ *January 5*

William Adams Brown

PRESBYTERIAN

December 29, 1865–December 15, 1943

William Adams Brown was born into a well-to-do family and given the best education available, going from prep school to Yale where he earned a master's degree and doctorate. He earned a theological degree from Union Theological Seminary. A prolific writer, Brown's instincts were both social and ecumenical: addressing the crucial social needs of his day and giving of himself in causes related to a more united Christian witness. He participated in a variety of movements that dealt with such social needs as tenement housing, labor unions, free speech, and political corruption. In 1904, he joined his voice with others calling for reform of Tammany Hall corruption.

Brown called upon Christians of all persuasions to seek a deeper unity both in work and witness:

> We who have enlisted in the service of Christ's church have a cause which requires all and more that man can give. It is the cause of him who said to the young people of his day, and who is still saying to us today: "If any man will come after me, let him deny himself, and take up his cross, and follow me. For whosoever will save his life shall lose it: and whosoever will lose his life for my sake shall find it."
>
> It is to such service that the church invites. It is through such fellowship alone that it can achieve its end. Corporate unity is important; how important we are only beginning to realize. But in the last analysis it is a by-product of something deeper and more precious — a unity of spirit which makes the church in fact one. Where this inner unity is lacking we may have a body indeed, but it will be a body without a soul. Let this inner unity be achieved and the appropriate instrument for its effective expression will not long be lacking.
>
> At the first meeting of the World Conference on Faith and Order in 1927, Bishop Brent observed: "The world is too strong for a divided church." Were he physically present with us today as we know he is with us in spirit, we may be sure that he would not stop there. He would complete his sentence with this confident affirmation: "Against a united church no foe can prevail."

Brown's work in the ecumenical sphere centered on helping the church to become more effective in dealing with a broken in the world. The fact that his life and work straddled World War I gave him a greater sense of urgency to his call to bring Christians together. His labors helped establish the World Council of Churches in 1938. Brown was convinced that although our deeds do not bring about our own salvation, they are, nonetheless, the clearest evidence of our deepest beliefs. He wished to lead the church to a point where the cooperative efforts of believers in healing the world were clearly perceived as an outgrowth of our common claim to care for the world as Christ did. Nor did Brown limit his vision to those within the Christian fold. In *Church and State in Contemporary America,* he wrote:

> [The Church] holds up the ideal of universal brotherhood, yet it is itself divided. So as we have seen, our task, in this matter of determining the relation between church and state, is not simply, or even primarily that of adjusting the relations between the two institutions but of uniting the individuals both in church and in state who accept the Christian ideal for church and state alike and are willing to work for its realization.
>
> In this effort we may find allies among men of other names and faiths. While in this book we have been dealing with the responsibility of Christians we have not been unmindful of the fact that there are many who are not members of any Christian church who yet accept the principles which we associate with the name of Christ. With these we would gladly co-operate for the great end we have at heart — the achieving of a society that transcends the boundaries of individual nationality and class and through world-wide co-operation seeks to realize the maximum welfare for all men of whatever race or creed.
>
> Yet, while we welcome this co-operation and recognize that without it the ideal relationship between church and state can never be realized, we have a special responsibility as Christians for the effective discharge of the part of the task which belongs to us. For this we must set our own house in order. A church that preaches unity while it practices division will find its words fall on deaf ears.

Brown held a variety of positions throughout his life: professor of systematic theology at Union Theological Seminary, chair of the Missions Committee of the Presbytery of New York, Board of Home Missions of the PCUSA, and executive secretary of the General War-Time Commission of the Churches, which was part of the Federal Council of Churches. He chaired the Federal Council's Department of Research and Education and served on the Yale Corporation, the university's governing body. Brown was also chosen to be president of the Religious Education Association and was also the first to hold that office at the American Theological Society. In battles within his denomination, he took the modernist side but emphasized that it was not merely Presbyterians, but the unification of the whole church that offered hope to the world.

A reading from William Brown

So the test of our progress on the road toward brotherhood after which we aspire must be the extent to which we are able to unite with those who share our faith in common action. In our thinking we must expect often to part company; in the type of our religious experience we must be content often to go each his own way; but in common devotion to that task of achieving a social order worthy of free men we may be at one. Such devotion is easy to profess, but hard to achieve. It requires discipline, individual and corporate: discipline of mind that we may rid ourselves of prejudice; discipline of will that we may have done with sloth; above all, discipline of spirit as we strip ourselves of all that is irrelevant in order to concentrate on the one thing that matters.

It is such a disciplined church that the world needs today. Against the passionate conviction of the leaders of the rival faiths that challenge us, a complacent acceptance of conventional Christianity can avail little.

✪ *January 6* _____

Maisie Ward

ROMAN CATHOLIC

January 4, 1889–January 28, 1975

It is hardly unusual to see two names linked in the name of a publishing house or, for that matter, a law firm or retail store. It is more unusual for those two names to be husband and wife. However, such is the case with that well-known Roman Catholic publishing house, Sheed and Ward. Frank Sheed and Maisie Ward, the founders of the firm, represented a merger of skills and interests that is as rare in marriage as in business partnerships.

Maisie Ward was 37, with a well-established career, when she met and married Frank Ward. Her father and grandfather were intellectuals, influential in British Roman Catholicism since the 1840s. Maisie carried on the family tradition: writing, speaking, and involving herself in the world in practical ways. During World War I, she served as a nurse's assistant in military hospitals. After the Armistice, she became a founding member of the Catholic Evidence Guild, an organization whose members spoke on street corners and other public places about the fundamentals of their faith. It was through the Guild that she met Frank Sheed. It seemed only natural for them to found a publishing house within a year of their marriage, in order to do more effectively together what they had long been doing separately.

The firm of Sheed and Ward met a need. Soon a branch was established in New York. Ward and her husband moved there, and it was there that Maisie met Dorothy Day* and became involved in the Catholic Worker movement. Before long Ward was supporting the French worker priests movement, campaigning for the improvement of social services in India and attempting to provide low-cost housing in England and the United States. Both the lay apostolate and the role of the family continued to be major interests for her. With a publishing house at her disposal, she wrote biographies of major

Roman Catholic figures like G. K. Chesterton, whom she had numbered among her own friends, and a number of books on various aspects of the Christian faith and the Roman Catholic Church. As a publisher, writer, lecturer, and social activist, she exemplified in her own life the principles she espoused.

A reading from *Be Not Solicitous* by Maisie Ward

This book would be called in France *Temoignages.* For the French specialize in books in which the gathered experiences of many are brought together in rich illumination of some single theme. The theme of this book is God's Providence in relation to Catholic families who put their trust in Him....

Of special interest in the modern world is the degree to which the Christian family is aspiring to share both in the total trust and the practice of the counsels of perfection that for many generations were thought to be the prerogative of the monk and nun alone. The spirituality of the laity, the layman's — and more especially the family's — method of sanctifying and embracing poverty — these are topics today of frequent discussion and consideration.

In the history of the Church the spear-head of Christian effort has varied with the ages. At the beginning the tiny Christian community seems to act as one whole. But presently the martyrs stand out, then later it is the hermits who flock in their thousands into the desert. Presently the monks are tilling the wilderness and gathering around them the Christian people. Next come the great missionaries, so that a man like Saint Patrick is the creator of a new Christian nation — and that one of the greatest the world has ever known. Later, when faith and love need a fresh awakening, the Franciscan message, especially of love, the Dominican message, especially of truth, are brought by the friars.

In this last age of ours it would seem that the central place in penetrating modern paganism is held by the family. They are the chief Christian heroes of today and the stories in this book show a little of the greatness of their heroism.

You remember how Saint Theresa of Avila spoke one day to God. "No wonder you have so few friends, Lord, considering the way you treat them." The reward of trust often appears to be trial. If some of our stories tell of God's treats for His children, others tell of that "chastisement whereof all are made partakers" (Heb. xii, 8), "for what son is there whom the father doth not correct?" (v. 7). "Now all chastisement for the present indeed seemeth not to bring with it joy, but sorrow: but afterwards it will yield to those that are exercised by it the most peaceable fruit of justice (v. 11)."

A retreat master once said, "Christianity does not take away from us the burden of life, but it gives us a spirit to bear that burden." And no one looking back over a long life can fail to see in things hard to bear, in prayers that seemed unanswered, the very material out of which peace and happiness were later built. "Your sorrow shall be turned into joy," Our Lord said to the Apostles before His Passion — not simply followed by joy but *turned into* it. And sometimes we receive that joy here and now.

✸ *January 7*

Charles E. and Augusta Weltner

LUTHERANS

Charles: January 28, 1860–1917

Social ministry has always had passionate proponents within the Christian church, and Charles and Augusta Weltner found ample challenge for their compassion in the needs of the mill workers of South Carolina. Ordained in 1888, Charles served congregations in New York, Georgia, and South Carolina. His visual handicaps were such that it is surprising to learn that he was able not only to function as a pastor but also to become a moving force within the Synod and within the culture of the laborers of Columbia. The Rev. Dr. H. George Anderson (a former Presiding Bishop of the Evangelical Lutheran Church in America) wrote of him: "By memorizing the pericopes (segments of Scripture assigned to be read on Sunday mornings), announcements, and the sermon, he could lead the worship service so smoothly that visitors did not know he was nearly blind."

But it is for his social ministry that Weltner and his wife, Augusta, are most remembered. In the late 19th century, the new phenomenon of "mill villages" was developing across the south. The Industrial Revolution brought massive changes to American culture. We know the benefits of mass production — high volumes of goods of consistent quality, availability of new products, increased trade, and a global economy — but not everyone remembers the human toll of what we easily speak of as "progress." Long hours, low wages, unsafe work places, soul-numbing repetitive jobs, and complete dependence upon the corporation for livelihood were all part of the cost of the Industrial Revolution.

There were tight communities of rural people, mostly former farmers, living near and working in the spinning mills. The church saw them both as a challenge and an opportunity. The culture of the villages, whose inhabitants had been uprooted from an established pattern of life, was ripe for a myriad of social ills — alcoholism, gambling, social unrest, and domestic violence, to name but a few. They also presented an opportunity for service and evangelism. In 1909, a motion passed by the South Carolina Synod of the United Synod of the South (one of the predecessor bodies that eventually became part of the Evangelical Lutheran Church in America) made note of the fact that there were 130,000 souls living in mill villages in South Carolina alone, working in 180 mills. The Synod had ministries in only three of these villages. Two mills, Olympia and Richmond, were in Columbia, and a third, Mollohon, was in nearby Newberry. Olympia Mill had made an offer of land to the Synod and made a commitment to assist in establishing a church there. As a result, St. Luke's Lutheran Church was built, and, by 1906, it was ready for a full-time pastor.

C. E. Weltner was the choice. Born in Germany, and with experience living in poor immigrant conditions in his early years in America, Weltner was familiar with some aspects of the life of the working poor. He had also married a former deaconess, Augusta, whose assistance was invaluable to him in his ministry. With her help, and the support of the Synod, Weltner was able to address both the social and religious needs of the population. Believing that education was a stepping stone to more self reliance, greater opportunity, and wiser, more thoughtful living, he organized and superintended the "Central Night School," which allowed those with motivation to move beyond the limitations of their earlier education. The school enrolled over 200 mill workers.

In connection with the mill work, Weltner sought to found a deaconess training center to equip young women for work among the mill operators. This part of his vision did not come to full fruition, but three women did come through his training and go on to serve both church and world. Miss Josephine Copeland became a welfare worker in the mills, while Miss Gertrude Simpson and Miss Mary Lou Bowers became missionaries to Africa and Japan. The missionary outreach overseas was not especially unusual, except that women were still not very commonly sent to such locations, but a ministry of social outreach by a Christian deaconess to a population of factory workers remains even today a novel idea. We often assume that a worker has access to whatever he or she needs to deal with any issues in life, or to continue education, or seek a different vocation if they wish. This may not even conform to reality today, but with the long hours, harsh conditions, and lack of other social programs, it was difficult indeed for workers in the early 20th century. The Weltners perceived a need and were willing to try to meet it.

Major changes in social conditions bring such predictable responses as fear and retreat into the old ways on the one hand or an enthusiastic endorsement of the new ways on the other. Many of us focus our response on our expectation of the way in which the new order will affect us personally. But there are always some whose faith or ethics leads them to look carefully at the effect beyond themselves. What do these changes mean for others? What support is needed for those who may be struggling with the new ways? How can faith meet the practical needs of those whose lives are being torn apart or severely altered?

The Weltners understood it would be necessary to train people to ask and attempt to answer questions like these. They drew in others, like Copeland, Simpson, and Bowers to do the same. The very presence among us of such people challenges the rest of the church to ask itself if its ministry to any group truly addresses upheavals in their lives. Instead of just opening the doors of our congregations in the hope that a diverse group will gather, there are men and women like Charles and Augusta Weltner who have been willing to venture into unknown territory for the sake of the neighbor.

✪ *January 8*

Amanda Berry Devine Smith

AFRICAN METHODIST EPISCOPAL

January 23, 1837–1915

Amanda Smith was born into slavery in Maryland. Her father, however, was able to earn enough money to buy his own freedom and that of his wife and his children, so that she never personally experienced slavery. Nevertheless, with only three months of formal schooling, she gave her energy to her family until she was in her 30s. By that time, her husband had died and she was making a living by taking in washing. In 1870, she received a "divine call" to preach while attending a church in Brooklyn. Over the next several months, her exhortations in New York and New Jersey made over 150 converts in African American congregations. After that impressive beginning, she expanded her ministry to white congregations as well, preaching in camp meetings from Maine to Tennessee with such success that, in 1878, she was invited to travel to England to carry on her work there. Success in England led to an invitation to travel to India where she was again successful in drawing large crowds and leading many to be converted. After that, she spent eight years as an evangelist in West Africa, before returning to the United States in 1890. Reluctantly, the African Methodist Episcopal Church had decided to license women as nonordained evangelists because of the obvious gifts of Smith and others. However, few churches were willing to underwrite her work, so she moved to Chicago to found a school for black orphans. Unfortunately, her years of hard work and travel, along with rheumatism and recurring back pains, limited what she could accomplish. In 1911, she retired to Florida, where she died in 1915.

A reading from the autobiography of Amanda Smith

O, what a conflict. How the darkness seemed to gather around me, and in my desperation I looked up and said, "O, Lord, I have come down here to die, and I must have salvation this afternoon or death. If you send me to hell I will go, but convert my soul." Then I looked up and said, "O, Lord, if thou wilt only please to help me if ever I backslide don't ever let me see thy face in peace." And I waited, and I did not hear the old suggestion that had been following me: "That is just what you said before." So I said it again, "O, Lord, if Thou wilt only please to convert my soul and make me truly sensible of it, if I backslide don't ever let me see Thy face in peace,"

I prayed the third time, using these same words. Then somehow I seemed to get to the end of everything. I did not know what else to say or do. Then in my desperation I looked up and said. "O, Lord, if Thou wilt help me I will believe Thee," and in the act of telling God I would, I did. O, the peace and joy that flooded my soul. The burden rolled away; I felt it when it left me, and a flood of light and joy swept through my soul such as I had never known before. Then I sprang to my feet, all around was light. I was new. I looked at my hands, they looked new! I took hold of myself and said, "Why, I am new, I am new all over." There seemed to be a halo of light all over me; the change was so real and so thorough that I have often said that if I had been as black as ink or as green as grass or as white as snow, I would not have been frightened. I went into the dining room; we had a large mirror that went from the floor to the ceiling, and I went and looked in it to see if anything had transpired in my color, because there was something wonderful had taken place inside of me, and it really seemed to me it was outside too. As I looked in the glass I cried out, "Hallelujah, I have got religion; glory to God, I have got religion," O, what a day! I never shall forget it; it was a day of joy and gladness to my soul.

After I had been converted about a week I was very happy. One morning, I was so happy. I was singing an old hymn. Just then the enemy whispered to me, "There, you are singing just as if you had religion."

"Well, I have. I asked the Lord to convert me and He has done it."

"How do you know? "

"Well I know He did it, because it was just what I asked the Lord to do, and He did, and I know He did, for I never felt as I do now, and I know I am converted."

"You have a great blessing," the Devil said, "But how do you know that is conversion?"

Well," I said, "That is what I asked the Lord to do and he did it."

"You know, you don't want to be a hypocrite?"

"No, and I will not be, either."

"But you have no evidence."

"Evidence, evidence, what is that?" Then I thought, I wonder if that is not what the old people used to call the witness of the Spirit. "Well," I said, "I won't sing, I won't pray until I get the witness." So I began and I held this point; God helped me to hold this point. I said, "Lord I believe Thou hast converted my soul, but the Devil says I have no evidence. Now Lord give me the evidence," and I prayed a whole week. Every now and then the joy would spring up in my heart, the burden was all gone, I had no sadness, I could not cry as I had before, and I did not understand it and so I kept on pleading. "Lord, I believe Thou hast converted me, but give me the evidence,

so clear and definite that the Devil wilt never trouble me on that line again."
Praise the Lord, He did, and though I have passed through many sorrows,
many trials, Satan has buffeted me, but never from that day have I had a
question in regard to my conversion. God helped me and He settled it once
for all.

This witness of God's spirit to my conversion has been what has held
me amid all the storms of temptation and trial that I have passed through.
O what an anchor it has been at time of storm. Hallelujah, for the Lord
God Omnipotent reigneth. Ye shall know if ye follow on to know the Lord.
Amen. Amen.

✪ *January 9*

Lucretia Coffin Mott

QUAKER

January 3, 1793–November 11, 1880

"A new generation of women is now upon the stage," said Lucretia Mott.
She might well have added, "And I will lead them." Certainly no one else
could have provided more energy and leadership in the great causes of the
19th century than she did.

Born of Quaker parents and imbued with the doctrine of women's rights
from infancy, it seems never to have occurred to her that she could not be
a wife and mother and, at the same time, play a major part in the issues of
her day. After the third of her six children was born, Mott became a minister in the Society of Friends. After the birth of her sixth, she was elected
clerk of Philadelphia Woman's Yearly Meeting. Traveling widely through
the east and midwest, she addressed such reform organizations as the Non-
Resistance Society and the Anti-Slavery Convention of American Women
along with the quarterly and yearly Quaker meetings. She urged her listeners to boycott all products manufactured with slave labor, such as cotton,
sugar, or molasses. She and other abolitionists in Philadelphia supported
only stores that sold "free produce" goods.

In 1840, she became one of six women chosen to represent American
antislavery societies at the World's Anti-Slavery Convention in England. Unfortunately, however, the six were not recognized as delegates by that body,
so were seated with other women as observers. Mott encountered Elizabeth Cady Stanton,* another unseated delegate, and together they began to
make plans to hold a convention as soon as they returned home, and form
a society to advocate the rights of women.

That convention was not held for another eight years, but in 1848, when
it convened at Seneca Falls, New York, Lucretia Mott presided and became first to sign the "Declaration of Sentiments," which called for equal
treatment of women.

Through the 1850s, Mott remained deeply involved in the abolition movement. She and her husband took in fugitive slaves and they hosted John Brown's wife during his trial. Holding firmly to the principal of non-resistance herself, Mott could nevertheless affirm the moral principles of those who felt called to use force to overcome evil.

After the Civil War, Mott was elected the first president of the American Equal Rights Convention, worked to reconcile conflicting factions within the women's rights movement, and continued her involvement in causes for peace and equality through her later years, and made her last public speech at the thirtieth anniversary celebration of the Seneca Falls Convention just two years before her death.

A reading from a sermon delivered by Lucretia Mott at the Cherry Street Meeting in Philadelphia, September 30, 1849

It is time that Christians were judged more by their likeness to Christ than their notions of Christ. Were this sentiment generally admitted we should not see such tenacious adherence to what men deem the opinions and doctrines of Christ while at the same time in every day practise is exhibited anything but a likeness to Christ. My reflections in this meeting have been upon the origin, parentage, and character of Jesus. I have thought we might profitably dwell upon the facts connected with his life, his precepts, and his practise in his walks among men. Humble as was his birth, obscure as was his parentage, little known as he seemed to be in his neighborhood and country, he has astonished the world and brought a response from all mankind by the purity of his precepts, the excellence of his example. Wherever that inimitable sermon on the mount is read, let it be translated into any language and spread before the people, there is an acknowledgement of its truth. When we come to judge the sectarian professors of his name by the true test, how widely do their lives differ from his?

Instead of going about doing good as was his wont, instead of being constantly in the exercise of benevolence and love as was his practice, we find the disposition too generally to measure the Christian by his assent to a creed which had not its sign with him nor indeed in his day. Instead of engaging in the exercise of peace, justice, and mercy, how many of the professors are arrayed against him in opposition to those great principles even as were his opposers in his day. Instead of being the bold nonconformist (if I may so speak) that he was, they are adhering to old church usages, and worn-out forms and exhibiting little of a Christ like disposition and character. Instead of uttering the earnest protests against the spirit of proselytism and sectarianism as did the blessed Jesus — the divine, the holy, the born of God, there is the servile accommodation to this sectarian spirit and an observance of those forms even long after there is any claim of virtue in them; a disposition to use language which shall convey belief that in the inmost heart of many they reject.

Is this honest, is this Christ like? Should Jesus again appear and preach as he did round about Judea and Jerusalem and Galilee, these high professors would be among the first to set him at naught, if not to resort to the extremes which were resorted to in his day. There is no danger of this now, however, because the customs of the age will not bear the bigot out in it, but the spirit is manifest, which led martyrs to the stake, Jesus to the cross, Mary Dyer* to the gallows. This spirit is now showing itself in casting out the name one of another, as evil, in brother delivering up brother unto sectarian death. . . .

I desire to speak so as to be understood, and trust there are among you ears blessed that they hear, and that these principles shall be received as the Gospel of the blessed son of God. Happy shall they be, who by observing these, shall come to be divested of the traditions and superstitions which have been clinging to them, leading them to erect an altar "to the unknown God."

In the place of this shall an altar be raised where on may be oblations of God's own preparing. Thus may these approach our Father in Heaven and hold communion with him — entering his courts with thanksgiving, and his gates with praise, even though there may be no oral expression. He may unite in prayer and in praise, which will ascend as sweet incense, and the blessing will come which we can scarcely contain.

✸ *January 10* _____

Henry Sloan Coffin

PRESBYTERIAN

January 5, 1877–November 25, 1954

To be the moderator of the General Assembly of the Presbyterian Church in the U.S.A. or to be the president of Union Seminary in New York City provides the means to exert significant influence over American national life. Henry Sloan Coffin held both those positions at a critical time in American life and called his fellow Christians, fellow citizens, individuals, congregations, institutions, and the society as a whole to examine the strengths and flaws of their society and to respond with faith, hope, courage, and love to each historic situation.

A native of New York City, Coffin served as pastor of Madison Avenue Presbyterian Church in New York City (1905–26), and lecturer, associate professor, and president of Union Theological Seminary from 1926 to 1945. In 1943 and 1944, Coffin held the position of moderator of the General Assembly of the Presbyterian Church in the U.S.A. With his breadth of vision and depth of passion, Coffin was not content simply to administer an institution in his role as Union's president. He wanted the seminary to shape American Christian thought with his help. He entered the fray between liberals and fundamentalists, supporting Harry Emerson Fosdick,* then under attack by conservative forces. Coffin recruited the best Christian minds he could gather, hoping Union would set new standards of academic excellence and help lead the church to play a leadership role in American society. In this typical passage, Coffin brings a biblical perspective to bear on contemporary life:

> There is a depressing view of human history which keeps telling us that nothing much is accomplished in a single lifetime. But is that true? Was nothing permanent achieved when Abram went out from Ur, or when Moses led his people through the Red Sea, or when the prophets set before Israel and mankind the righteousness of God? Was nothing eternally significant completed when the Son of God bore men's sins in His own body on the tree? There have been days of the Lord whose effects continue transformingly through thousands of years. Why should we think that we, who have mysteriously been set down in a crucial generation, cannot, in our lifetime, yes in this very year, by what we under God and with his grace think, do and bear, bring to pass results in the relations of nations and races and of men one to another which shall render earth divinely better for whatever further ages it may pursue its course? One day with the Lord is a thousand years!

Born into a prominent New York family, Coffin studied the Westminster Shorter Catechism as a child. He learned to respect the ministry of the Presbyterian Church both at home and at the Fifth Avenue Church where the family worshiped. After private schools, he went off to Yale, where he was elected to Phi Beta Kappa and tapped for the Skull and Bones society. In addition, he served as president of the campus YMCA.

While Coffin was at Yale, he came under the influence of Dwight L. Moody.* This noted evangelist changed his life and made him seriously consider a call to ministry. Coffin traveled to Scotland to begin his theological studies, and finished them at Union Theological Seminary and Yale. Ordained to the ministry in 1900, he was called as pastor to Madison Avenue Church.

When he became president of Union Seminary in 1926, he used his inaugural address to articulate his vision of the worldwide kingdom of God. Reminding his constituency of the seminary's tradition, Coffin proclaimed, "We have taught here the gospel of Christ as the power of God not only for the salvation of individuals, but for the redemption of society — for the Christianization of industry and commerce, of education and statesmanship, of the relations of races and of nations." He committed himself to continuing that tradition.

For all his dedication to social and ecclesiastical issues, Coffin also recognized the individual hunger for spiritual growth:

It usually takes the experience of at least middle life to appreciate the graciousness of God. By that time we have had our disillusionments. Few of us have
been as useful as we hoped to be. The air-castles of our confident expectation
prove clay-hovels when we find ourselves in them. We are apt to grow cynical.
Most men and women need a rebirth in their forties.

The most serious peril of the middle years — "the destruction that wasteth
at noonday" — is conventionality. In youth we are rebels against things as they
are; but rebellion proves a hazardous and fatiguing enterprise, and before we
know it, we are accepting situations and fitting our ideals with considerable
whittling to the grooves and holes already cut. It is then that God's face shining forth on us throws the landscape again into its distinction of shade and
brightness. Bad is bad and good, good; and with a second morning of vitality
we go out to do battle. And it is not just the rebellion of protesting youth over
again, but a maturer, more clear-seeing, more patient and more resourceful
warfare. We fight not for ourselves only, but for our younger companions. A
Paul draws his sword for Timothy, and Titus and Mark and Luke. His veteran presence steadies and emboldens them. That's God's graciousness to the
middle-aged."

The ecumenical movement was high on Coffin's agenda, and especially the
rift between the northern and southern factions of the Presbyterian Church,
divided since the Civil War. He worked hard to resolve that schism and
also for a covenant between the Presbyterian and Episcopal churches. Both
efforts failed, though they laid the groundwork for later progress. Coffin
eloquent voice spoke out for some of the great causes of the 20th century.
He told the last graduating class of his presidential years at Union: "Ours is
a calling in which we share the joy of our Lord."

✪ *January 11*

John Carroll

ROMAN CATHOLIC

January 8, 1735–December 3, 1815

Missionaries from a variety of denominations were sometimes sent to cover
enormous areas on the western frontier. They were referred to by such titles as "bishop of all outdoors" and "bishop of all beyond." John Carroll,
the first Roman Catholic bishop in the United States, was given an even
greater jurisdiction. His diocese comprised the whole country, an area of
three million square miles — indoors and outdoors as well.

John Carroll's father was a merchant who came from Ireland, settled
in Maryland, and married Eleanor Darnell, the wealthy relative of Charles
Carroll* of Carrollton. Their son, John, was first educated in a Jesuit school
in Maryland, then at St. Omer's College in the French area of Flanders. At
18, he joined the Jesuit order and continued his studies at Liege until the age

of 34, when he was ordained to the priesthood. He remained in France for four more years teaching philosophy and theology, but in 1773 the Jesuit order was suppressed by the Pope. Carroll then returned to the United States as a missionary in Maryland and Virginia, supporting himself as the other Roman Catholic priests did.

At the outset of the American Revolution, John Carroll accompanied Charles Carroll on a mission to Canada to attempt to enlist Canadian support for the revolutionaries. After the war, he met with other priests to determine what the future of the Roman Catholic Church in the new country should be. Partly because they feared a bishop might make financial demands on them, they initially recommended against having one. Instead, they requested that a priest be appointed to supervise the church's work and nominated John Carroll for the position. The pope agreed and was much pleased with the report Carroll sent him on the condition of the church in the United States. Not long afterward, the same group of priests requested the pope to provide them a bishop, again nominating Carroll for the position. He was consecrated in England in 1790 and eighteen years later was made archbishop, with suffragan sees at New York, Philadelphia, Boston, and Bardstown.

Supporting and strengthening religious freedom in the United States became a basic principle of Carroll's ministry. He is considered to be one of the people responsible for the first amendment to the Constitution. When George Washington died, Carroll directed his clergy to observe February 22 as a day of mourning.

At his death in 1815, a Baltimore paper said of Carroll: "In him religion assumed its most attractive and amiable form...he was temperate yet compelling, considerate yet uncompromising."

A reading from John Carroll's first sermon as Bishop of Baltimore, November 6, 1789

In this, my new station, if my life be not one continued instruction and example of virtue to the people committed to my charge, it will become, in the sight of God, a life not only useless, but even pernicious. It is no longer enough for me to be inoffensive in my conduct and regular in my manners. God now imposes a severer duty upon me. I shall incur the guilt of violating my pastoral office, if all my endeavours be not directed to bring your lives and all your actions to a conformity with the laws of God; to exhort, to conjure, to reprove, to enter into all your sentiments; to feel all your infirmities; to be all things to all, that I may gain all to Christ; to be superior to human respect; to have nothing in view but God and your salvation; to sacrifice to these health, peace, reputation, and even life itself; to hate sin, and yet love the sinner; to repress the turbulent; to encourage the timid; to watch over the conduct of even the ministers of religion; to be patient and meek; to embrace all kinds of persons; these are now my duties — extensive, pressing, and indispensable duties; these are the duties of all my brethren in the episcopacy, and surely important enough to fill us with terror. But there are others still more burdensome to be borne by me, in this particular portion of Christ's church which is committed to my charge, and where everything is to be raised, as it were, from its foundation; to establish ecclesiastical discipline; to devise means for the religious education of Catholic youth — that precious portion of pastoral solicitude; to provide an establishment for training up ministers for the sanctuary and the services of religion, that we may no longer depend on foreign and uncertain coadjutors; not to leave unassisted any of the faithful who are scattered through this immense continent; to preserve their faith untainted amidst the contagion of error surrounding them on all sides; to preserve in their hearts a warm charity and forbearance toward every other denomination of Christians; and at the same time to preserve them from that fatal and prevailing indifference which views all religions as equally acceptable to God and salutary to men. Ah! when I consider these additional duties, my heart sinks almost under the impression of terror which comes upon it. In God alone can I find any consolation. He knows by what steps I have been conducted to this important station, and how much I have always dreaded it. He will not abandon me unless I first draw upon His malediction by my unfaithfulness to my charge. Pray, dear brethren, pray incessantly, that I may not incur so dreadful a punishment. Alas! the punishment would fall on you as well as on myself; my unfaithfulness would rebound on you and deprive you of some of the means of salvation.

✪ *January 12*

Caroline Louise Darling (Sister Constance)

EPISCOPALIAN

January 11, 1846–1878

Until the 20th century, yellow fever remained a deadly scourge. Its cause was unknown and there was no effective treatment. When, in 1878, an epidemic broke out in Memphis, approximately half the population — everyone with means to do so — fled the city. Some, however, stayed or returned, putting their lives at risk — often losing them — in order to minister to the sick and dying.

The Sisters of St. Mary, an order of nuns in the Episcopal Church, had come to the city five years earlier to establish a school for girls and run an institution known as the Church Home. Shortly after their arrival, yellow fever struck the city and they found themselves providing nursing care for the victims, though they had no previous experience in such work. Five years later, the fever hit again with a far more deadly impact. Sister Constance was staying at the mother house in New York when news came. She immediately returned to Memphis, emerging from the train station to find the city in a state of desolation: streets sprinkled with lime as a protection against the disease, mattresses of the dead burning in the streets, and wagons loaded with coffins rumbling past. Working with the other sisters and with a small team of clergy, doctors, and nurses, Sister Constance set out to organize the relief effort and to seek out those in need. There were orphans to provide for, sick people to be cared for, and the dead to be buried. One of her letters tells a typical story:

> Yesterday I found two young girls, who had spent two days in a two-room cottage, with the unburied bodies of their parents, their uncle in the utmost suffering and delirium, and no one near them but a rough negro drayman who held the sick man in his bed. It was twenty-four hours before I could get those two fearful corpses buried, and then I had to send for a police officer to the Board of Health before any undertaker would enter that room. One grows perfectly hardened to these things — carts with eight or nine corpses in rough boxes are ordinary sights. I saw a nurse stop one day and ask for a certain man's residence — the negro driver just pointed over his shoulder with his whip at the heap of coffins behind him and answered, "I've got him here in his coffin."

In the following days, first one member of the team, then another, sickened and died: one of the priests, then a sister, then a doctor and another sister. After three weeks of effort, Sister Constance herself caught the disease, dying the next day at the age of 32. Three of the other sisters, two of the priests, a doctor, and a nurse also died before the epidemic ended, as did a quarter of the remaining population of the city. Sister Constance and her companions who died are remembered in the Episcopal Church Calendar as "The Martyrs of Memphis."

A reading from the last letter of Sister Constance

Dear Bp. Quintard,

I was telegraphed for on Thursday of last week, and on my return, made such arrangements as I could for the safety of the Home, before exposing myself to any possible infection. I have sent Sister Frances to remain at the Home day and night, isolated the House as far as possible, and we may get through without any fever cases — but the disease is extremely contagious among children & very fatal this year. The markets are closed — nothing whatever is given to the children in the way of meat, bread, or vegetables — fresh meat cannot be bought, even if we had money — and I fear that there will be real suffering from improper or insufficient food, and overwork. No servant will do the washing at any ordinary price, and these little girls are really almost ill from their attempts to do it last week. Will you not make a special appeal to the managers — if you know where any of them are? In universal panic, letters from me would not be at all welcome, even if I had time to write them.

Sister Thecla, Sister Frances, and I are perfectly well, and the anxiety is so great that one has not difficulty in trusting both the present and the future — our nursing and our school — in GOD'S hands. You know a great trouble is often easier to bear than a little one! Sister Hughetta is far from well — I have, of course, kept her out of all nursing so far. She sleeps at Colonel Snowden's, but comes in every morning — there are little things that she can do.

I know that we shall have your prayers and your blessing on our work — but we are so helpless for want of means that we cannot yet attempt what we did before.

I see no reason to be more hopeful than we were in 1873 — in fact, there are some indications that seem to me to threaten even more serious results, and the form of the disease is undoubtedly worse.

We have the daily celebrations, and while we have that, there is nothing that really depresses me.

> Yours faithfully in our dear LORD,
> Sister Constance, S.S.M.

✪ *January 13*

Fannie Exile Scudder Heck

BAPTIST

June 16, 1862–August 25, 1915

In 1877, Fannie Heck's mother was invited to become president of a state-wide committee to encourage women to support mission work. A year later, she reported proudly that 17 societies had been formed and $300 raised. There then ensued such a storm of controversy over whether women were assuming too much that they discontinued their activities. Eleven years later, when Fannie Heck was 24, she was asked to take on such a job herself. The secretary-treasurer, Mrs. W. N. Jones, was only 18. With youthful optimism, tempered by her mother's experience, Fannie set to work with Jones. Believing that "missionary fires could not burn without missionary fuel," they began publishing a paper. *Missionary Talk* contained a news column, a children's corner, and articles about various aspects of foreign mission. In 1891, her home state of North Carolina joined with other states in a Southern Union. The following year, Fannie Heck, not yet 30, was selected to lead this larger endeavor.

A creative and tireless writer, Heck began immediately to compose for the *Foreign Mission Journal* and produced a steam of tracts on various subjects. She could be whimsical, as in an essay on whistling: did Adam and Eve whistle or was it the children, Cain and Abel, who first learned the art? She could also be methodical and practical. She reported that in one year she had written 1,438 letters, 300 postcards, and 3,000 mission cards, and sent out 14,000 copies of *Mission Talk* as well as 25,000 leaflets. There was no office in the early days; all work was done at home by the members of the committee, and "every chick and child" was pressed into service when mailings had to be sent. Heck served as president of the Baptist Convention's Woman's Missionary Union from 1892 to 1894, then from 1895 to 1899 and a final term from 1906 to 1915. These were transformational years for Southern Baptist mission efforts. In 1907, northern and southern Baptists met together for the first time since the Civil War, and the women met as well. Fannie Heck was chosen to preside. She was unable to attend the Edinburgh Conference on World Mission, three years later, but made certain that women of her denomination were represented. When Baptist women from around the world held a joint meeting at the World Baptist Alliance in Philadelphia in 1911, she was chosen to speak for all Baptists in America. She encouraged interdenominational cooperation, writing, "I am profoundly grateful we are not working at this task alone," and she encouraged exchanges with Methodists, Presbyterians, Episcopalians, and others.

The Woman's Missionary Union Training School (later renamed as the Carver School of Missions and Social Work) in Louisville, Kentucky, owes its existence in large part to Heck's work on its behalf, although the notion of females in the mission field was still controversial. Believing that prayer was the greatest priority of all, she said in one of her addresses: "Some of us, I know, could not have worked harder, but can it be that our very work has come between us and him for whom we work?" On another occasion, she insisted that "In the want of united fervent prayer lies the supreme need."

Some readings from the books and speeches of Fannie Exile Scudder Heck

When women began to feel within themselves the power to answer the cry which God had opened their ears to hear, Woman's Mission Work began to be a distinct feature in the lives of women everywhere. Here is work fitted to all the impulses of womanhood — love, pity, and tenderness for woman; obedience to and confidence in God. These are the motives that spur her to action; these are the forces which shall develop in her that which is highest and best; which shall lead her to wider visions of life and higher reaches of faith, these shall be God's pillars, of fire to guide her to her appointed place in the army which wages the long but always triumphant war for world-wide righteousness.

I wish we could get the idea that God is a reasonable God. Never was he more manifestly so than in the giving of money. He lays down some definite simple rules and takes the whole question of the amount of giving on his shoulders. If we do not have much, he does not expect much, but if we do have much, he expects his proportionate part of that. God is no beggar. He is the giver pre-eminent, but he asks and needs our co-operation. If you want to get rid of the constant worry and pull of this question, take God's definite plan and stand to it.

If any endeavor attempted in the name of Christ in its final outcome fails to bring living men in touch with the living Christ, it is not Christian.

If souls are immortal, while all else besides perishes, then soul-saving is the noblest work in the universe. I wish I might impress upon you the magnificent nobility of the work in which we as missionary societies, and more especially as individuals, are engaged. We who work are ennobled by the dignity of missions. Believe it, live it, glory in it, we are children of a King — laborers together with God. And it is not being laborers that ennobles, it is being together with God.

✪ *January 14*

Christian Newcomer

UNITED BRETHREN

January 21, 1749 (February 1, New style)–March 12, 1830

When John Wesley felt his heart "strangely warmed," he was responding to an experiential pattern of religion that had been gaining strength in Germany. Wesley and his colleagues, especially George Whitefield, carried that pattern throughout England, Wales, and North America. German settlers also brought experiential religion to North America. Eventually both English and German streams united, primarily in the Methodist Church. Experiential religion was ideally suited to the frontier, since it insisted on a personal experience of salvation and thus could be propagated by preachers without a sophisticated theological education.

Christian Newcomer, for example, was a farmer and carpenter who scheduled his missionary journeys in such a way that he could be back on his farm by harvest time. His background was in the German Mennonite settlement in Pennsylvania. Feeling the weight of sin, he formed resolutions to change his life, but failed to follow through until a serious illness convinced him that he could not delay longer. Nonetheless, he was reluctant to speak in public, feeling himself unqualified until, once again, an illness moved him to promise he would hold back no longer if he recovered. When he went to a meeting house on a subsequent Sunday and heard several speakers who seemed to him to have no experience of grace, he rose "with sorrowful heart" and told those present "what the Lord in mercy had done for me." He then joined himself with two preachers of the German Reformed Church, William Otterbein* and George Adam Geeting, who "preached the same doctrine which I had experienced." They "insisted on the necessity of genuine repentance, pardon of sin, and in consequence thereof a change of heart and renovation of spirit." This message made a powerful impression on those who gathered on the frontier in large groups and small to hear preachers like Newcomer who could verbalize their own experiences.

Additionally, Newcomer brought organization and structure. The German Reformed Church became the United Brethren in Christ, with him as a founding bishop of the new church. Over the last 35 years of his life, Newcomer estimated that he traveled 150,000 miles on horseback preaching, evangelizing, and organizing. During that time, he kept a journal that provides a unique picture of the work of evangelism at the beginning of the 19th century.

A reading from the journal of Christian Newcomer

November 12th (1803) — This morning my poor soul rejoiced in the God of my salvation; I am ready and willing to spend and be spent in the service of my Master. A great many people were assembled together today; I spoke to them from Hebrews 12:19 with great liberty. The Lord accompanied his words with power; many were the wounded and slain, some of the most stubborn sinners fell instantly before the power of God. The meeting continued the whole night, and before it closed several were enabled to rejoice in the pardon of their sins: glory be to God.

Significant Barn Meeting

Sunday, November 13th — Today we had indeed a little Pentecost, from three hundred to four hundred persons had collected, more than the barn in which we had assembled for worship, could contain. I preached to them from Titus 3, with great liberty and effect, for the salvation of souls. The congregation was remarkably attentive to the Word. Though it rained, those that had no shelter in the barn kept their stand in the rain without the least disturbance. It is indeed surprising, and to me somewhat mysterious, to behold the manner in which the power of God works here among the people. During the time of preaching, several persons fell to the floor, some laid as if they were dead, others shook so violently that two or three men could scarcely hold them; sometimes the excitement would be so great that I had to stop speaking for several minutes, until the noise abated; some few were praising God and shouting for joy. Br. Chr. Berger addressed the congregation. When I had concluded my discourse in the German, I then preached in the English language, from I Peter 1:3, and the effect was again the same. At night I preached at Mr. Swartz's; here also several persons of both sexes fell to the floor, others were crying for mercy; so it lasted till after midnight.

14th — This day we had the best time; I spoke short and concise. Presently crying and lamentations began; one fell to the floor on the right and another on the left. I felt such pity and compassion for poor mourning souls, that my heart was ready to burst with sadness, and yet I was rejoiced to behold such a work of grace: God grant that it may prove a work which shall endure throughout eternity. The time passed away as on eagles' wings; it was late in the day, and we had yet twelve miles to ride. Night came upon us, before we reached the place of our destination, and we lost our way. Ultimately we came to a house, where we received directions which enabled us to reach Mr. Abraham Overholtz's (at West Overton). Here we were kindly received, and entertained in the most friendly manner. I was very much fatigued, felt drowsy, and was surprised by a dark power. I immediately arose, went out of the house, drew nigh to God in secret prayer, and was quickly delivered: glory be to God for all His mercies.

✪ *January 15* _____

Martin Luther King, Jr.

BAPTIST

January 15, 1929–April 3, 1968

The legacy of Martin Luther King is almost too well known to need retelling. His inspired and courageous ministry was embodied in his commitment to a nonviolent confrontation with racial injustice. King was a complex man, too complicated to be represented by any one facet of his life or achievements. In common with many great church leaders, he began his odyssey locally, as a preacher. His early ventures into public conflict were sparked by personal or local incidents. His personality and speaking style, along with his message drew others to the causes he espoused, making him a natural leader, whether the issue involved the rights of garbage workers in one city, or a segregated lunch counter in another. Out of King's efforts came the call for African American voter registration throughout the south and greater participation for blacks in the American political process.

At each step, King was clear that his quest for justice was motivated by his profound belief in the gospels. Unapologetic about his Christian foundation, he never spoke ill of those who struggled with him, regardless of their religious affiliations or lack of them. He was bold to call on those in authority to change their positions when they displayed racial prejudice, and to insist they enact or enforce laws that would truly alter the lives of people of color, not just in the south, but in the entire nation.

King's positions developed dramatically during his lifetime, precisely because his local experiences taught him to understand the implications for the broader populace. Protecting local rights expanded into his call for national repentance and universal suffrage. He began to realize that political advances for blacks required changes in the economic structure as well. We can never be sure how he might have developed had he lived longer, yet it is clear that, in his final year, King began to link United States foreign policy in the Vietnam war with a national pattern of misused power. One of the most overlooked aspects of his ministry is his growing understanding of the need for universal liberation from the desire for power that enslaves us.

King's courage gave him strength to confront deeply entrenched hatred and systematic oppression with his insistence that love can overcome it. Those who are beaten must love those who beat them. The dispossessed must love those who deprive them. He had learned about the power of love from reading the New Testament, but also from watching the transformative effect of Gandhi's nonviolence movement in India. From these, King understood that no one is free so long as anyone is in bondage. Oppression takes a toll on the oppressors. King challenged his followers as much as his detractors. He never used his celebrity for personal gain, and premonitions of violence against himself only increased his sense of urgency in preaching his message of freedom for all.

The Southern Christian Leadership Conference (SCLC) was one of the outgrowths of King's work, providing him and his companions with the structure to advance and maintain the civil rights movement. In October of 1960, King was arrested at a lunch counter protest. Though not jailed for this action, he was nonetheless sentenced to Reidsville State Prison Farm for violating probation for an earlier traffic violation. John Kennedy, then in the final days of his presidential race, intervened to gain King's release, quite probably winning the White House by this move. Both Kennedy and his successor, Lyndon Johnson, supported some of the legal reforms King and the SCLC were seeking.

Though King's most loyal friends were Christian, so were many of his most ardent opponents. His willingness to unsettle the status quo, his "disturbing the peace," his involvement in "politics," and his use of protest techniques struck many white, and even some black clergy to be outside the calling of a pastor. Jailed in Birmingham, Alabama, in early 1963 for protesting unequal treatment of black and white customers as well as unfair hiring practices, King responded to critics with the now famous "Letter from Birmingham Jail":

> You may well ask: "Why direct action? Why sit-ins, marches and so forth? Isn't negotiation a better path?" You are quite right in calling for negotiation. Indeed, this is the very purpose of direct action. Nonviolent direct action seeks to create such a crisis and foster such a tension that a community which has

constantly refused to negotiate is forced to confront the issue. It seeks so to dramatize the issue that it can no longer be ignored.... We know through painful experience that freedom is never voluntarily given by the oppressor; it must be demanded by the oppressed.

In the summer of 1963, King worked with other leaders of the civil rights movement to organize a massive march on Washington, DC. Almost a quarter of a million people from all over America joined this peaceful demonstration calling for racial justice. Here King delivered his "I Have a Dream" speech, one of the most powerful orations in American history. Filled with biblical imagery, it anticipated a time when all people would be judged on their actions, and not by the color of their skin. Today, the justice of this may seem self-evident to most people. However, it must be remembered that it was not generally accepted at the time he said it. Thanks to King's witness, most of our society now understands racial stereotyping as clearly wrongheaded and unjust. Martin Luther King's assassination on April 4, 1968, left us a legacy of faith, vision, courage, and compassion that continue to inspire those who seek a just world for all.

✪ *January 16* _____

Eleanor Chestnut

PRESBYTERIAN

January 8, 1868–October 28, 1905

Great compassion can arise from great hardship. Eleanor Chestnut was alone from an early age; her father abandoned the family about the time she was born, while her mother died near the child's third birthday. She knew years of privation and loneliness in her childhood. Childless neighbors cared for her for a few years until she moved from her birthplace in Waterloo, Iowa, to Missouri to live with an aunt on a very rural, struggling farm. Somehow she heard of Park College (now Park University) in Parksville, Missouri, and saw it as a path out of her poor and limited life. She wrote to the president of the school when she was 12 and was invited to come. Though she resented her dependence on charity, she accepted whatever help others offered her to get the education she needed to develop and become independent.

Upon finishing college in 1888, Chestnut applied to the Chicago Woman's Medical College in order to become a physician. While in medical school, she also learned nursing, then went on to study pharmacology. She also took courses at the Moody Bible Institute. A somewhat restless and impatient student, Chestnut found her greatest contentment in caring for the poorest and most vulnerable patients. In 1893, she applied to become a missionary.

She was assigned to South China and, in 1894, sailed off with a group of other missionaries, filled with enthusiasm for the people, the language, and the work she had been sent to do. Using her own resources, she began building a small hospital and caring for her new charges. Medicines and other supplies were scarce and conditions were primitive. Yet Chestnut felt a deep attachment for the people she served in Lien-chou and wrote:

> The little hospital is nearly finished. I look upon it with admiring eyes and fancy myself within it administering "yarbs" and "essences" at a great rate. I have at present a young girl in my charge sick with a low fever. How I should like to remove her from her dark room to the hospital and look after her myself! Am afraid she will not recover, though I do hope for her sake and for the work's sake that she will.

On one occasion, she had to amputate a man's leg. The operation was successful, but the skin intended to cover the wound would not heal properly. Determined to give her patient the best chance at a life free from pain and infection, Chestnut realized he would need a skin graft. When one of her colleagues asked her why she was limping, she was evasive. Later a nurse explained how Chestnut had taken skin from her own leg under local anesthesia to repair her patient's leg.

Her facilities were cramped and Spartan, but she felt fortunate to be called to serve Christ and the Chinese people she had come to love. Yet many in China felt increasingly resentful about the presence of foreigners on their soil. What would come to be known as the "Boxer Rebellion" was brewing in the north. Violence became more frequent, and many missionaries were recalled to the United States or sent to safer mission stations. In 1902, Chestnut took a brief furlough, but was set on returning. She wrote:

> I concluded that it would be a mistake for me to leave Lien-chou. I am acquainted with the people there, their dialect, diseases, faults, virtues, and other points. Then I am so fond of them. I do not believe I could ever have quite the same feeling of affection for any other people. All my early associations in missionary life are connected to them. Moreover, Lien-chou has been so unfortunate in the matter of losing its missionaries that I fear it would be very discouraging to those at the station. The work is increasing every year. Before I left in the spring there was work enough for twenty missionaries instead of five.

Chestnut did return in 1903, but neither her compassion nor her effectiveness could protect her from the rising tide of antiwestern sentiment in the country. On October 28, 1905, mob violence broke out near her compound. When the hospital came under attack, Chestnut ran off to seek authorities who could control the riot. She located a police boat, on which she might have escaped, but decided instead to go back to help others. There were six other missionaries still in danger, a single woman, two couples, one with an eleven-year-old child. The situation was chaotic, with shouting, shoving, hitting, and general mayhem. During the melee, a boy's head was gashed and Chestnut tore off part of her own dress to cover the wound. It was her last act of compassion. Four men dragged her to the river and stabbed her to death. By the end of the riot, only two of the other six people at the mission station remained alive. The little girl, her mother, and another couple, in China for only forty-eight hours, had all been assassinated.

In New York City, on the wall of the Presbyterian Foreign Mission Board a plaque was placed which reads:

> In loving memory of the missionary martyrs of Lien-chou, China, Eleanor Chestnut, M.D., Mrs. Ella Wood Machle, and her little daughter Amy, Rev. John Rogers Peale and Mrs. Rebecca Gillespie Peale, who, for Christ's sake suffered cruel death at Lien-chou, China, October 28, 1905. "They loved not their lives unto the death." (Rev. xii 11)

✪ *January 17*

Alexander Schmemann

ORTHODOX

September 13, 1921–December 13, 1983

Centuries of growing hostility came to a climax in 1054 when the Pope and the Patriarch of Constantinople excommunicated each other and initiated the Great Schism between western and eastern churches. A wall went up that remained almost unquestioned until the 20th century when the traumatic events of the Russian Revolution and two world wars brought long-separated peoples together and encouraged them to wonder whether the church might once again be united. Among those who began to imagine new patterns of Christian living was the Orthodox scholar Alexander Schmemann.

Schmemann began his education in Paris, among the sizable Russian immigrant population there. At St. Sergius Orthodox Theological Institute, he received a sound foundation for his future role as a leader, not just in his own tradition, but in the wider church as well. His teachers included famous Orthodox theologians of the day like Anton Kartashev, Cyprian Kern, Nicholas Afanassieff, and Georges Florovsky.* Schmemann focused on liturgical theology. The dominant Christian tradition in France was Roman Catholic. In the aftermath of World War II, Rome was undergoing a period of theological and liturgical renewal, and France was in its vanguard. Denominationalism so dominated the religious landscape that developments in one church often had little impact outside their own communion. But Schmemann did notice this transformation. Like his teacher Florovsky, he was open to certain western ideas, and he began to question how much nationalism and nationalist images affected visions of Christianity. Despite a passion for Orthodox missionary work, Schmemann was willing to build relationships and connections with other churches.

Further west, the Orthodox Church in America was developing its own voice, and Florovsky invited Schmemann to teach at St. Vladimir's Seminary in New York City. When the former resigned as dean 11 years later, Schmemann took his place and developed the school into a site for panorthodox seminary training. He also introduced his interest in liturgical renewal, his zeal for Orthodox outreach, and his vision of a self-governing Orthodox Church in the Americas. In 1970, Schmemann took part in negotiations with the Patriarchate of Moscow, which resulted in autocephalous status for the Orthodox Church in America. Schmemann hoped this would ultimately pave the way for all Orthodox Christians in the United States to unite, including the Greeks and Oriental Orthodox, who are not currently part of the Orthodox Church in America.

His ongoing interest in other Christian traditions was expressed through activity on various commissions of both the World Council of Churches and the National Council of Churches. His contributions included his reaffirmation of the importance of baptism, a focus on regular reception of the eucharist, and the participation of laity in liturgical services. Schmemann was not interested in these questions for their own sake, but for the spiritual development of all God's people. A series of brief quotations from his writing will illustrate the direction of his thought.

Readings from Alexander Schmemann

More and more Christians tend to identify Christian love with political, economical, and social concerns; in other words, to shift from the unique *person* and its unique personal destiny, to anonymous entities such as "class," "race," etc. Not that these concerns are wrong. It is obvious that in their respective walks of life, in their responsibilities as citizens, professional men, etc., Christians are called to care, to the best of their possibilities and understanding, for a just, equal, and in general more humane society. All this, to be sure, stems from Christianity and may be inspired by Christian love. But Christian love as such is something different, and this difference is to be understood and maintained if the Church is to preserve her unique mission and not become a mere "social agency" which she definitely is not.

Christian love is the "impossible possibility" to see Christ in another man, whoever he is, and whom God, in His eternal and mysterious plan, has decided to introduce into my life, be it only for a few moments; to introduce, not as an occasion for a "good deed" or an exercise in philanthropy, but as the beginning of an eternal companionship in God himself. For, indeed, what is love if not that mysterious power which transcends the accidental and the external in the "other" — his physical appearance, social rank, ethnical origin, intellectual capacity — and reaches the *soul*, the unique and uniquely personal "root" of a human being, truly the part of God in him? If God loves every man it is because He alone knows the priceless and absolutely unique treasure, the "soul" or "person" He gave every man. Christian love then is the participation in that Divine knowledge and the gift of Divine love. There is no "impersonal" love because love *is* the wonderful discovery of the "person" in "man," of the personal and unique in the common and general. It is the discovery in each man of that which is "lovable" in him, of that which is from God.

In this respect, Christian love is sometimes the opposite of "social activism" with which one so often identifies Christianity today. To a "social activist" the object of love is not "person" but *man*, an abstract unit of a not less abstract "humanity." But for Christianity, man is "lovable" because he is *person*. There person is reduced to man; here man is seen only as person. The "social activist" has no interest for the personal, and easily sacrifices it to the "common interest." Christianity may seem to be, and in some ways actually is, rather skeptical about that abstract "humanity" but it commits a mortal sin against itself each time it gives up its concern and love for the person. Social activism is always "futuristic" in its approach; it always acts in the name of justice, order, happiness to come, to be achieved. Christianity cares little about that problematic future but puts the whole emphasis on the *now* — the only decisive time for love.

✪ *January 18* _____

Bertha Toni Agnes Carola Paulssen

LUTHERAN

January 15, 1891–April 2, 1973

Born into a prosperous and cultured family in Leipzig, Germany, Paulssen's early life was filled with all the best that German society had to offer. She had a fine education and was exposed to great music and art, architecture, and travel. A Lutheran by birth, Paulssen also received a classical German-Lutheran course of catechetical instruction. It did not sit well. As presented to her, the church seemed impersonal and dogmatic and far too fixated on confessional purity rather than the human heart and spirit. But she had also been involved in earlier years with a Moravian school. Their more pietistic and gentle approach would remain part of Paulssen's spiritual formation throughout her days.

Life in Germany had been good, but this was soon to change. World War I brought devastation to the entire nation. Paulssen lost a younger brother on the Western Front in 1915. Her father had died only two years before, so her own grief was intensified by the emotional upheaval that was part of being a German in the wake of that conflict.

Nevertheless, Paulssen was able to continue her education. She studied philosophy, psychology, and education at the University of Leipzig, and was awarded her Ph.D. in 1917. After working for a while as a librarian and teaching assistant, she moved, in 1919, to Frankfurt am Main to manage a home for young girls who needed practical training after dropping out of school. Then, for a few years, she worked with prostitutes, prisoners, and abused children in Kiel and Stettin. It was in this context that Paulssen reconnected with the Lutheran Church, whose social service arm was effective in some of the areas that aroused her passion.

Finally, in 1923, Paulssen was given a new position of great authority. Only 32 years old, she was put in charge of a state youth welfare organization with a staff of 800. Here, she brought her creativity to bear, introducing a case-work model of care that drew on the most up-to-date understandings of social work, medicine, and psychiatry. A less "top down" style replaced the older authoritarian mode, and smaller groups replaced large institutional populations as more personalized solutions were sought for individuals in need. She believed that the older ways of dealing with "human souls that have gone astray" had often failed to make the kind of "inner rapport" that would be needed to lead them to new lives. During this time, Paulssen became a regular lecturer and published author, also serving as an examiner for social workers.

But this promising career came to a sudden halt when the rise of Hitler and his Nazi party began to distort all German government and culture. Paulssen had been part of the government, but new rules did not allow women to hold positions like hers, so she was dismissed. It is not clear whether she had some Jewish lineage on her mother's side, but she decided that it would be best for her to leave Germany. She fled to friends in England and eventually to America. While in England she engaged in social work and became more proficient in English and then, at the age of 45, she came to New York City and immediately volunteered to become a youth group leader. Her work and expertise were noticed and soon she was invited to lecture and to teach, first at Gettysburg Seminary, then at the Deaconess Motherhouse in Philadelphia, and then at Wagner College on Staten Island.

But once again war disrupted her life. When America entered World War II, she was considered an "enemy alien" who needed official permission even to leave the county. Despite this, Paulssen wanted to become an American citizen. She went to Cuba for a short time so she could return as an immigrant rather than a refugee. In 1944, she received her citizenship.

Shortly thereafter, Paulssen was offered a chance to move to Allentown, Pennsylvania, and begin a joint teaching position with Muhlenberg College, Gettysburg College, and Gettysburg Seminary. Her training and experience gave her a fresh perspective on the importance of maintaining a close connection between psychology and sociology, and she was able to bring insights from both disciplines into the realm of theology. This new way of looking at the context of theology brought it closer to everyday human life. It excited her students and colleagues. Paulssen made lively personal connection to her students, who continued to rave about her impact on their lives years later.

Her style and her academic contributions were so profound that the seminary changed its constitution to allow a nonordained person to be granted full professorship. Paulssen was the first woman to become a tenured professor in any American Lutheran seminary. Her clear sense of the intersection between faith and life, theology and social science, and the theoretical and the human shaped the lives and thinking of a generation of students who were privileged to receive her wisdom.

Readings from Bertha Paulssen

How can the present-day church preach prophetically to a world in turmoil when its ministers and its teachers do not see clearly where in the present situation and in the cultural constellation the dangers and the temptations for humanity are found? The church stands in the human community and is part of it. But the church is also above the human community in that it must speak to it about its faults and sins from an existential plane; and to be able to do so, a realistic knowledge of our culture and its specific temptations is necessary. Modern men and women suffer most deeply from their inability to love their neighbors. How can they love their neighbors if they know nothing of God?

The catastrophic nature of our global life shakes humanity everywhere.... Somehow we stand again where Luther stood before he found grace... in a time of struggle and search, where century-old cultural patterns break down and new forms of social, economic and political life are coming. In such a time theology is not any longer a merely scientific enterprise but becomes a basis for the representation of Christianity to a world near the edge of being void of it.

✠ *January 19*

Francis Asbury

METHODIST

August 20, 1745–March 31, 1816

The Methodist movement arrived in America much later than many other churches, but it spread rapidly, soon outnumbering earlier arrivals. A primary force in its extraordinary growth was Francis Asbury — the first general superintendent or bishop in New World Methodism. Asbury was born in England and came under Methodist influence in the early days of the movement. Despite his limited education, he was accepted as a local preacher by the time he was 18 and was admitted to the Wesleyan Conference at the age of 21. For a few years, he served as an itinerant preacher, and then, in 1771, volunteered with four others to go to America. Within a year, John Wesley appointed Asbury to be his assistant in charge of all the work in America. When the American Revolution broke out, the other Methodist preachers returned to England, but Asbury remained and supported the fight for independence.

In 1784, Wesley consecrated Asbury as general superintendent of Methodism in the United States — a move that widened the separation between Methodists and the Church of England. Asbury tried to refuse, insisting that the position should be ratified by a vote of all his fellow preachers. After they elected him, he held the office jointly with Thomas Coke. For the next 30 years, he toured the eastern United States annually, crossing the Alleghenies 60 times and averaging 5,000 miles a year on horseback. He preached sermons wherever he went and ministered to the far-flung Methodist movement, organizing classes and directing the growing congregations. When he had first arrived in America, there were only three Methodist meeting houses and 300 members, but by the time of his death there were over 400 societies and well over 200,000 members. His journal carefully records his journeys and depicts the hardships of travel on the American frontier.

A reading from the journal of Francis Asbury

Tuesday [December] 29. At Mr. Sinclair's, found great peace of mind, and, thanks be to GOD, had power in preaching, though the people were dead and stupid. The next day at Mr. Chamberlain's, I had many people, and preached with freedom; then went to Galloway's, where we had great consolation.

January 1, 1773. My body has been weak for some time, but my mind has enjoyed a good degree of peace; and I have a strong desire to be kept in the meekness of Jesus Christ. My heart has been affected by reading, lately, part of Sewel's history of the Quakers; How great was the spirit of persecution in New England, when some were imprisoned, some had their ears cut off, and some were hanged! O that our GOD would arise, and bow the nations to himself!

January 2. After preaching to several people, at John Murray's, a new place, then rode back to Mr. Colgate's and preached in the evening.

January 3. Rode to Baltimore and had a large congregation at the house of Captain Patten, at the Point. Many of the principal people were there; and the Lord enabled me to speak with freedom and power. At night, I preached in town. The house was well filled with people, and we have a comfortable hope the work of the Lord will revive in this place. Bless the

Lord, O ye saints! Holiness is the element of my soul. My earnest prayer is, that nothing contrary to holiness may live in me.

Monday 4. Rode to S. Stevenson's, found life in my soul, and was much affected in preaching to the people. Then met and regulated the class.

Tuesday 5. They were kind enough to offer me the court-house in town; but judging it unfit, I preached in another house; then met and settled a class of men.

Wed. 6. We had a pretty good gathering at Nathan P—'s, about 6 miles from town. Then rode back to town, and after preaching with comfort in the evening, I formed a class of women.

Thursday 7. Rose with a determination to live for GOD. Preached twice in the country, met two classes and settled them as well as I could. The class at Mr. Simm's were lively and had the power of GOD among them. They were the fruit of Nathan P—'s labors, and many of them could give a good account of their experience.

Friday 8. My mind is fixed on GOD. I both desire and purpose to exercise fasting, prayer, and faith. After some exercise of mind, the Lord enabled me to preach with life and power at Mr. Merryman's, from these words "Be not ye partakers with them." I showed First, whom the words were spoken to. Secondly, with whom they were not to be partakers. Thirdly, how they were not to partake with them, viz. In spirit — in judgment — in practice.

Lord's day, January 10. Many people attended at Joseph Presbury's, to whom I preached twice, with some life, and then went 3 miles into the Neck, and felt much power while preaching on perfect love. The more I speak on this subject, the more my soul is filled and drawn out in love. This doctrine has a great tendency to prevent people from settling on their lees.

✪ *January 20* ───────────────────────────────────

Angelina Grimké Weld

QUAKER

February 20, 1805–October 26, 1879

Angelina was the youngest of 14 children born to a South Carolina slave-holder, the heir to a settled and comfortable way of life. Her older sister (sixth in birth order) rebelled against their inheritance and returned from the north to persuade her younger sister to come with her to freedom. But it was Angelina who emerged first as a public figure when her letter to the abolitionist leader William Lloyd Garrison was published. Angelina had not given consent to this publication but refused to retract it when ordered to do so by the Society of Friends. On the contrary, she proceeded to publish "An Appeal to the Christian Women of the South," calling on her sex to use their moral influence to overthrow slavery. Copies of the document were burned by the South Carolina post office and both sisters were threatened with arrest should they return to their home state. When Angelina spoke in Philadelphia, mobs attacked the building and burned it down the next day. Not daunted, she even expanded her subject to include women's rights. When the sisters condemned racial prejudice, they were criticized even by other abolitionists for going too far and denounced from Congregationalist pulpits in New England. Never one to retreat, Angelina wrote, "Whatever is morally right for a man to do, it is morally right for a woman to do. I recognize no rights but human rights — I know nothing of men's rights and women's rights; for in Christ Jesus there is neither male nor female."

Although she married a noted abolitionist and feminist, Theodore Weld, even her husband found his wife's position a bit too advanced. He suggested that the sisters might best concentrate their attention on the cause of abolition alone.

The duties of a wife and mother did in fact make such demands on Angelina's time that her public activity was limited after her marriage. Nonetheless, she, Weld, and her sister collected articles written by southern newspaper editors, publishing them under the title, *American Slavery As It Is: Testimony of a Thousand Witnesses*. These firsthand accounts are said to have provided Harriet Beecher Stowe* with much of the raw material for her famous novel, *Uncle Tom's Cabin*.

A reading from a speech delivered by Angelina Grimké in Pennsylvania Hall

Men, brethren and fathers — mothers, daughters and sisters, what came ye out for to see? A reed shaken with the wind? Is it curiosity merely, or a deep sympathy with the perishing slave, that has brought this large audience together? [A yell from the mob without the building.] Those voices without ought to awaken and call out our warmest sympathies. Deluded beings! "they know not what they do." They know not that they are undermining their own rights and their own happiness, temporal and eternal. Do you ask, "what has the North to do with slavery?" Hear it — hear it. Those voices without tell us that the spirit of slavery is here, and has been roused to wrath by our abolition speeches and conventions: for surely liberty would not foam and tear herself with rage, because her friends are multiplied daily, and meetings are held in quick succession to set forth her virtues and extend her peaceful kingdom. This opposition shows that slavery has done its deadliest work in the hearts of our citizens. Do you ask, then, "what has the North to do?" I answer, cast out first the spirit of slavery from your own hearts, and then lend your aid to convert the South. Each one present has a work to do, be his or her situation what it may, however limited their means, or insignificant their supposed influence. The great men of this country will not do this work; the church will never do it. A desire to please the world, to keep the favor of all parties and of all conditions, makes them dumb on this and every other unpopular subject. They have become worldly-wise, and therefore God, in his wisdom, employs them not to carry on his plans of reformation and salvation. He hath chosen the foolish things of the world to confound the wise, and the weak to overcome the mighty.

As a Southerner I feel that it is my duty to stand up here tonight and bear testimony against slavery. I have seen it — I have seen it. I know it has horrors that can never be described. I was brought up under its wing: I witnessed for many years its demoralizing influences, and its destructiveness to human happiness. It is admitted by some that the slave is not happy under the worst forms of slavery. But I have never seen a happy slave. I have seen him dance in his chains, it is true; but he was not happy. There is a wide difference between happiness and mirth. Man cannot enjoy the former while his manhood is destroyed, and that part of the being which is necessary to the making, and to the enjoyment of happiness, is completely blotted out. The slaves, however, may be, and sometimes are, mirthful. When hope is extinguished, they say, "let us eat and drink, for tomorrow we die." [Just then stones were thrown at the windows, — a great noise without, and commotion within.] What is a mob? What would the breaking of every window be? What would the levelling of this Hall be? Any evidence that we are wrong, or that slavery is a good and wholesome institution? What if the mob should now burst in upon us, break up our meeting and commit violence upon our persons — would this be any thing compared with what the slaves endure? No, no: and we do not remember them "as bound with them," if we shrink in the time of peril, or feel unwilling to sacrifice ourselves, if need be, for their sake. [Great noise.] I thank the Lord that there is yet life left enough to feel the truth, even though it rages at it — that conscience is not so completely seared as to be unmoved by the truth of the living God.

We may talk of occupying neutral ground, but on this subject, in its present attitude, there is no such thing as neutral ground. He that is not for us is against us, and he that gathereth not with us, scattereth abroad. If you are on what you suppose to be neutral ground, the South look upon you as on the side of the oppressor. And is there one who loves his country willing to give his influence, even indirectly, in favor of slavery — that curse of nations? God swept Egypt with the besom of destruction, and punished Judea also with a sore punishment, because of slavery. And have we any reason to believe that he is less just now? — or that he will be more favorable to us than to his own "peculiar people?" [Shoutings, stones thrown against the windows, &c.]

We often hear the question asked, "What shall we do?" Here is an opportunity for doing something now. Every man and every woman present may do something by showing that we fear not a mob, and, in the midst of threatenings and revilings, by opening our mouths for the dumb and pleading the cause of those who are ready to perish.

✪ *January 21*

Charles Hodge

PRESBYTERIAN

December 28, 1797–June 9, 1878

The Presbyterian Church, along with other denominations in the Reformed tradition, is grounded in a specific theological system. John Calvin's *Institutes of the Christian Religion* are a detailed and complex exposition of the nature of the faith. Reformed theologians must always come to grips with it. No American theologian has done this better than Charles Hodge. It has been said that his six-volume *Systematic Theology* is probably the best of all modern expositions of Calvinistic dogmatic.

No one should imagine, however, that theology was only dry doctrine for Charles Hodge. He saw it as a description of the faith by which he lived, and it was expressed in every aspect of his life. He said,

> As far back as I can remember, I had the habit of thanking God for everything I received, and asking him for everything I wanted. If I lost a book, or any of my play things, I prayed that I might find it. I prayed walking along the streets, in school and out of school, whether playing or studying. I thought of God as an everywhere-present Being, full of kindness and love, who would not be offended if children talked to him. I knew he cared for sparrows. I was as cheerful and happy as the birds and acted as they did.

Though conservative in his theological outlook, Hodge was warm and affectionate toward individuals regardless of their views. "The experience of one Christian," he said, "is the experience of all. This is the conscious bond of their union."

Born in Philadelphia, Charles Hodge graduated from the College of New Jersey (Princeton University) and Princeton Seminary and then was a member of the seminary faculty for 56 years. His interests, however, were far larger than this might suggest. He served for one term as chair of the Presbyterian Board of Foreign Mission and had important things to say about the relationship between church and state. Here Hodge was in the broad tradition of Calvinism that sees the ruler or state as a "nursing father." The state's role is not simply to do the will of the church but to enable the church to do its work effectively. Thus, "as [government] cannot violate the moral law in its own action, or require the people to violate it, so neither can it ignore Christianity in its official action. It cannot require the people or any of its officers to do what Christianity forbids, nor forbid their doing anything which Christianity enjoins."

A reading from Charles Hodge's *Systematic Theology*

We have now completed our exposition of Presbyterianism. It must strike every one that it is no device of man. It is not an external frame-work, having no connection with the inward life of the Church. It is a real growth. It is the outward expression of the inward law of the Church's being. If we teach that the people should have a substantive part in the government of the Church, it is not merely because we deem it healthful and expedient, but because the Holy Ghost dwells in the people of God, and gives the ability and confers the right to govern. If we teach that presbyters are the highest permanent officers of the Church, it is because those gifts by which the apostles and prophets were raised above presbyters, have, in fact, ceased. If we teach that the separate congregations of believers are not independent, it is because the Church is, in fact, one body, all the parts of which are mutually dependent.

If this is so — if there is an outward form of the Church which corresponds with its inward life, a form which is the natural expression and product of that life, then that form must be most conducive to its progress and development. Men may, by art, force a tree to grow in any fantastic shape a perverted taste may choose. But it is at the sacrifice of its vigour and productiveness. To reach its perfection, it must be left to unfold itself according to the law of its nature. It is so with the Church. If the people possess the gifts and graces which qualify and entitle them to take part in the government, then the exercise of that right tends to the development of those gifts and graces; and the denial of the right tends to their depression. In all the forms of despotism, whether civil or ecclesiastical, the people are degraded; and in all forms of scriptural liberty, they are proportionably elevated. Every system which demands intelligence tends to produce it. Every man feels that it is not only one of the greatest advantages of our republican institutions that they tend to the education and elevation of the people, but that their successful operation, demanding popular intelligence and virtue, renders it necessary that constant exertion should be directed to the attainment of that end. As republican institutions cannot exist among the ignorant and vicious, so Presbyterianism must find the people enlightened and virtuous, or make them so.

It is the combination of the principles of liberty and order in the Presbyterian system, the union of the rights of the people with subjection to legitimate authority, that has made it the parent and guardian of civil liberty in every part of the world. This, however, is merely an incidental advantage.

The Church organization has higher aims. It is designed for the extension and establishment of the gospel, and for the edification of the body of Christ, till we all come to the unity of the faith and knowledge of the Son of God; and that polity must be best adapted to this end, which is most congenial with the inward nature of the Church. It is on this ground we rest our preference for Presbyterianism. We do not regard it as a skilful product of human wisdom; but as a divine institution, founded on the word of God, and as the genuine product of the inward life of the Church.

✪ *January 22*

William Howard Bishop

ROMAN CATHOLIC

December 19, 1886–June 11, 1953

The wave of immigration that brought many Roman Catholics to the United States brought them chiefly to the great cities. Rural America was largely neglected by Rome. William Howard Bishop had grown up in the city himself. After ordination, he was assigned to a suburban parish outside Baltimore. The pastor under whom he served, however, found the young priest deficient in many ways. In particular, he said Mass too slowly — a practice the senior pastor considered unfair to busy parishioners who needed to get on with their lives. After two years of escalating conflict, Bishop asked for a transfer and was assigned to a small rural parish in Clarksville, Maryland. That assignment changed the focus of his life.

His advocacy for rural mission developed slowly. First, he needed to build a school and convent to serve the parish. Though the community's resources seemed inadequate at first, Bishop managed to accomplish the project in four years. Then he heard about a conference on rural ministry in the Midwest. After attending it, he organized a society to support rural mission in Maryland. Finally, when he was 52, the Archbishop of Cincinnati supported him in the establishment of a religious order of priests whose primary mission would be to rural communities throughout the United States. Two years later, he founded a similar order for women, and by the time of his death 14 years later, he had established a seminary to train clergy and a magazine to provide mutual support and communication. By that time, there were 21 priests in the Glenmary order, 51 candidates for ordination, and 16 members of the women's order with 26 novices.

William Bishop spoke often of the vast areas of the country without Roman Catholic clergy as "No Priest Land." He displayed maps and charts at conferences showing 1,000 counties without a resident priest. His vision extended to the 65 million Americans who professed no creed. To him, the priestless counties and creedless Americans were a vast mission field:

If the children of India and China are worth the sacrifice of vast sums and the consecrated toil of unselfish missioners to save, what about the farm children of our own Maryland who will be its citizens of a future day? When the Savior said, "Go and teach all nations," He did not say that we should omit our own.

Bishop planned to "accept as bases of operation the little border-line parishes that nobody wants and from them to build up little outposts and parishes where now no hope of them exists." Two priests would be sent to such places. One would have primary responsibility for making contact with the unchurched, to call on every house, find out who might be interested, and gradually draw them into contact with the life of the parish. This was not merely to make converts, but

> to make all of them better people and bring them nearer to God. Whether he ever makes a convert to the Church or not, the town, the county, the lives of the people must be better because of his example, his preaching, his activities among the poor, the sick, and the sinful of all creeds and none.

Lay people were to be trained to be missionaries as well:

> They must be ready to answer questions, to find and cultivate interested persons, to bring them to the priest and above all things, always to set the best example, and pray in season and out of season for conversions.

Borrowing an idea from the Protestant evangelists of rural America, Bishop organized outdoor preaching missions:

> These campaigns are held every summer. In some of our areas we use a trailer chapel, in others a station wagon. Loud-speaker equipment, phonographs, and moving pictures are pressed into service when and if the campaigner finds them advantageous.

The focus on neglected rural areas brought Glenmary missioners into contact with rural prisons, and they began to make justice a focus of their ministry. Bringing the gospel to people who have been overlooked remains the calling of the Glenmary mission. In a typical speech, Bishop defined his vision this way:

A reading from William Bishop

If we may be permitted to do a bit of wishful thinking and dreaming — a favorite indoor sport with most of us Americans — we would indulge the image of the Church all over America, stepping out of doors and adopting the entire public for its audience. Not in every case physically out-of-doors, but outside the confined circles of its own membership.

If this were so, not *some* parishes, but *all* parishes would have a convert-making program. Not *some* but *all* dioceses would have street-preaching and open-air meeting programs in their cities and towns. They would also go as far as possible toward carrying on this work in the villages and open country.

Not *some* religious communities, but *all* religious communities would give some of their men for this work. And every religious house located in rural sections would carry on a program of neighborhood instruction in religious matters while taking care not to conflict with but rather to cooperate with the work of nearby parishes.

✪ *January 23*

John Bachman

LUTHERAN

February 4, 1790–February 24, 1874

The story of John Bachman is intertwined with the story of the South Carolina Synod of the Lutheran Church in America, but his life began in New York State. He grew up in Rensselaer County and was educated at Williams College, where he found great joy in both religion and science. Bachman was an avid naturalist and later contributed to the expanding fields of botany and zoology. His early career led him to teaching and studying in Philadelphia, and then, in 1813, he was licensed to serve his first parish in Centre Brunswick, New York. But the climate in the Hudson Valley can be harsh. Health problems became an issue, so Bachman decided to move south for a time, to see if he could regain his strength before returning north to continue his service. He went first to the Caribbean and then, returning home, he was asked by two of his mentors to consider service at St. John's in Charleston, which had a pastoral vacancy. Bachman accepted the call and was ordained by the New York Synod in 1814. At the beginning of the following year, he began what would become a half-century ministry in South Carolina.

In those early days of Lutheran church life, Bachman offered significant leadership in the development of the Synod of South Carolina, Southern Seminary, and Newberry College. He also contributed to a renewal of church life in a number of congregations in Georgia. There were opportunities to minister to African Americans in that region, and Bachman responded to them. He is credited with work that encouraged several important black Americans to seek ordination and make their own contributions to the church. The careers of Daniel Payne* and Braxton Drayton* are described elsewhere in this volume. Both were shaped by Bachman's ministry and encouragement.

In addition to his formal ecclesiastical work, Bachman's interest in the natural world also bore fruit. He labored together with his friend John J. Audubon, publishing works on plants and animals. Out of these studies, he produced a book arguing that all human beings are a single species with a single origin, molded and guided by place and time. Bachman was not an abolitionist, though his writings were used by some who were. He did not oppose slavery, and though he grieved the separation of the Union, supported the Confederacy. Still, his vision of a single human race, his support for African Americans — not just in their personal faith, but in their quest for professional training — and his contributions to the development of the Lutheran Church in the south reveal a man whose beliefs were utilized for the wider good of his neighbors.

Bachman's essay titled *The Doctrine of the Unity of the Human Race Examined on the Principles of Science,* published in 1850, demonstrates his use of the scientific method to address an issue most often looked at through the lens of either philosophy or theology. While references to the size of the "brain of the negro" sound offensive to us, we must remember that these were terms commonly used at the time to defend the supposed superiority of European Americans. Bachman, however, employs them to refute separate origins for races and help lay the foundation for our modern assumption of the equality of all humans. Quoting from earlier studies, Bachman summarizes findings related to African neurobiology:

1. The brain of the negro is upon the whole quite as large as that of the European and other human races, — the weight of the brain, its dimensions, and the capacity of the cavum cranii prove this fact. Many anatomists have also incorrectly asserted that Europeans have a larger brain than negroes.

2. The nerves of the negro, relatively to the size of the brain, are not thicker than those of the Europeans, as Soemmreing and his followers have said —

3. The outward form of the spinal cord, the medulla oblongata, the cerebellum, and the cerebrum of the negro, show no important difference from that of the European.

4. Nor does the inward structure, the order of the cortical and medullary substance, nor the inward organization of the interior of the negro brain show any difference form that of the European.

Beyond the data, Bachman turns again to his religious tradition and draws the conclusions we now take for granted:

We have now placed before our readers the outline of our views on this intricate subject of inquiry. The true solution of this problem will no doubt in time be found. When this shall have been effected it will be seen, that like all other discoveries, the plans of the Great Creator were uniform, simple and wise, and that all the difficulties arose from the short-sightedness and imperfections of the human mind. It would however, in our conception, enlarge our views of the power and the benevolence of the Deity and strengthen our sentiments of philanthropy and charity could we all be permitted to regard the Great Creator as having "made of one blood all nations of men for to dwell on the face of the earth." Influenced by such exalted conceptions of the Deity, all the races of men, the bond and the free, in the various gradations of society, would be bound in closer bonds of brotherhood, and could with filial confidence worship together at the footstool of the Universal Parent of Mankind who had given Immortality and offered Salvation to all men, of every grade, every colour every nation, who obey his law, whether emanating from his inspired word, or written on the tables of the heart.

Although Bachman was not entirely free of all the unjust presuppositions of his culture, he was both able and willing to nudge his contemporaries to a broader view. That his words were more than mere intellectual theorizing is evident in his very concrete and practical ministry to and with the African Americans in Charleston, long before the wisdom or justice of this work was clear to the culture as a whole.

✪ *January 24*

John Clarke

BAPTIST

October 8, 1609–April 20, 1676

In the popular imagination, the Pilgrims and Puritans are said to have come to America to establish religious liberty, but the credit really belongs to John Clarke, Roger Williams, and the Baptists of Rhode Island. John Clarke had a broad education and diverse skills. An advanced student of Hebrew and Greek, Clarke was a student of theology and educated in law, but he made his living in the practice of medicine. Obviously he would have been an asset to any community, but Clarke's religious convictions did not fit comfortably into the England of the early 17th century. Therefore, in 1637, he went to New England seeking freedom to worship in accordance with his conscience — and failed to find it.

What Clarke found in the Massachusetts colonies looked remarkably similar to the religious restrictions he had left behind. Citizens paid a church tax. Those who refused were subject to the civil authorities and threatened with fines, punishment, and prison. As Clarke saw it, men "were not able to bear each with other in their different understandings and consciences as in these utmost parts of the world to live peaceable together." His solution to the problem was to gather other men and women of similar views and lead them off to Rhode Island, as Roger Williams had done. In 1638, a church was established with Clarke as its pastor — now considered the first Baptist Church in America.

Putting the colony on a secure footing was difficult. The territory was considered English, but was subject to pressure from the Puritan colony to the north. In 1641, Roger Williams and John Clarke traveled back to England to secure a charter. They were successful, although enemies of its principles continued to attempt to modify or abolish it. Clarke stayed in England for some years to represent Rhode Island interests. Finally, in 1663, after the

accession of Charles II, he managed to obtain a new charter that provided a
greater degree of religious freedom in Rhode Island than in Massachusetts
or England. Quakers had been executed and Baptists had been whipped in
Boston, but Rhode Island's charter provided

> that no person within the said colony, at any time hereafter shall be any wise
> molested [harassed], punished, disquieted, or called in question, for any dif-
> ferences in opinion in matters of religion, and do not actually disturb the civil
> peace of our said colony; but that all and every person and persons may, from
> time to time, and at all times hereafter, freely and fully have and enjoy his and
> their own judgments and consciences, in matters of religious concernments,
> throughout the tract of land hereafter mentioned, they behaving themselves
> peaceable and quietly.

This landmark document, obtained by John Clarke, remained in force in
Rhode Island for almost 200 years.

A reading from *An Answer to the Question, Why Are You a Christian?* by John Clarke

Not because I was born in a Christian country, and educated in Christian
principles; — not because I find the illustrious Bacon, Boyle, Locke, Clarke,
and Newton, among the professors and defenders of Christianity; — nor
merely because the system itself is so admirably calculated to mend and
exalt human nature: but because the evidence, accompanying the gospel has
convinced me of its truth. The secondary causes, assigned by unbelievers,
do not, in my judgment, account for the rise, progress, and early triumphs
of the Christian religion....

That there once existed such a person as Jesus Christ; that he appeared
in Judea in the reign of Tiberius; that he taught a system of morals, superior
to any inculcated in the Jewish schools; that he was crucified at Jerusalem;
and that Pontius Pilate was the Roman governor, by whose sentence he was
condemned and executed, are facts which no one can reasonably call in
question. The most inveterate deists admit them without difficulty....

But, I confess, my creed embraces many more articles. I believe, that Jesus
Christ was not merely a teacher of virtue, but that he had a special commission to teach. I believe, that his doctrines are not the work of human reason,
but divine communications to mankind. I believe, that he was authorized by
God to proclaim forgiveness to the penitent; and to reveal a state of immortal glory and the blessedness to those who fear God, and work righteousness.
I believe, in short, the whole evangelic history, and by consequence, the divine origin of Christianity, and the sacred authority of the gospel. Others
may reject these things as the fictions of human art or policy: but I assent to
them from a full conviction of their truth. The grounds of this conviction,
I shall sign in the course of this work; and I shall undertake to show, why

the objections of infidelity, though they have often shocked my feelings have never yet shaken my faith.

To come into the question: Why are you a Christian? I answer, because the Christian religion carries with it internal marks of its truth; because not only without the aid, but in opposition to the civil authority, in opposition to the wit, the argument, and violence of its enemies, it made its way, and gained an establishment in the world; because it exhibits the accomplishment of some prophecies, and presents others since fulfilled; and because its author displayed an example, and performed works which bespeak, not merely a superior but divine character. Upon these several facts, I ground my belief as a Christian; and, until the evidence on which they rest can be invalidated by counter evidence, I must retain my principles and my profession.

❂ *January 25*

August Gottlieb Spangenberg

MORAVIAN

July 15, 1704–September 18, 1792

Originally raised as a Lutheran, August Spangenberg seemed destined for a successful academic career and had become an assistant professor of theology at the famed University of Halle, in Germany. But Spangenbert had begun to learn of the Moravians, a group of early reformers exiled from their native land (what is now the Czech Republic) and relocated in Germany, where they found refuge and hospitality on the estate of Nicholas Lewis, Count Zinzendorf. The faculty at Halle disapproved of the Moravians — their theology and origins were neither Lutheran nor Calvinist and did not fit neatly into traditional German understandings of the faith. Therefore, Spangenberg was told to sever his contact with them or forfeit his teaching post. He chose the latter option, and, in 1733, moved to Herrenhut — the Moravian colony associated with Zinzendorf.

Spangenberg was both a scholar and a leader, capable of inspiring as well as dealing with very practical matters of finance and commerce. He was persuaded to lead a group of Moravian emigrants from Germany to Georgia. Other Moravians had already moved to the New World and had settled in North Carolina and Pennsylvania. Their industriousness and willingness, even eagerness, to work among Native Americans and African slaves made them good candidates for establishing European outposts. There was little money for this journey, and most lending sources thought the risks too high to finance, but under Spangenberg's leadership the company managed to reach Georgia and immediately began to establish a settlement on a small tract set aside for them in Savannah by the trustees in England. Here again, as in their earlier settlements, Moravians in general, and Spangenberg in particular, became valued neighbors. Other colonies nearby, even a small Jewish group, got on well with them.

When the language barrier became a problem, Spangenberg decided to find an English-speaking youth to help them learn to converse. He heard of a boy whose father had been executed. His mother, upon remarrying, had abandoned him to caretakers who treated him cruelly. Spangenberg offered to take him in to his own household, where his nurture was assured. In turn, the Moravians improved their English with the boy's help. Spangenberg met John Wesley during Wesley's sojourn in Savannah, and the two men developed a fondness and appreciation for each other. Both were interested in missions to the Indians and offered one another mutual encouragement in that work. In 1745, now a bishop, Spangenberg went to Pennsylvania to assist a mission in that colony. His oversight contributed to the Moravian colony in and around Bethlehem. He also traveled to the Virgin Islands to visit Moravian missionaries there.

Spangenberg's own life is a testament to seeing the hand of God in a gracious outreach to neighbors of different cultures. He represents the servant whose devotion to his Master overcomes trials and fears that would otherwise seem insurmountable, except for his strong faith and passionate commitment.

A reading from August Spangenberg

Now one and then another nation of the heathen, was recommended to the service of the Brethren in the gospel. This called for their attention, and made them resolve on the one hand, never to go to any heathen without a call, in which the hand of God was evident to them; and on the other hand, never to refuse any call among the heathen, in which they could perceive the finger of the Lord, though they should see beforehand that such a call might endanger their lives, and be otherwise connected with many things very difficult to human nature; and this is actually their intention to this very hour.

[The Moravian missionaries] had at the same time a well grounded hope, that our Lord Jesus Christ himself, would always find and prepare such people, whom he might make sure of in executing his thoughts of peace toward any heathenish country or nation. This he hath also done hitherto in great mercy among the brethren's people. When any body was wanted here or there among the heathen, he touched now the heart of this, and then of that brother, by his gracious operation, and encouraged and made them willing for that purpose. If any place could be suitably served by brethren that were not brought up to study, but to a different way of life, the Lord suffered us not to want people who were willing to that end. But whenever circumstances required a learned brother, God was also please to stir up such of this class, who heartily devoted themselves to the service of our Saviour among the heathen.

Often I have been astonished at the willingness and desire of the brethren for this service. Having once made known on a prayer-day, at Bethlehem in North America, that five persons were departed from this life in a very short time at St. Thomas, where the difficulties of our brethren were then very great, not less than eight brethren voluntarily offered themselves on that very day, to go thither to replace them. We have certainly cause to thank the Lord our Redeemer alone for this; especially as the service of the gospel among the heathen is no easy matter.

✠ *January 26*

Dorothea Dix

CONGREGATIONAL

April 4, 1802–July 17, 1887

In the 19th century, America underwent a period of immense and turbulent change. Upheavals caused by the Civil War, the Industrial Revolution, the westward migrations and floods of new citizens migrating to our shores are well-documented. At the same time, church conflicts and revivals stirred Christians out of complacency, while political intrigues called into question the very institutions of government. Minds were preoccupied by currency, trade policy and international relations. All these and other factors were forging the culture and personality of the new nation.

Far down the list of most people's concerns came the treatment of prisoners in jails or the mentally ill in asylums. But a few people found their consciences burdened by these issues, remembering that Jesus tells us to care for "the least of these." Dorothea Dix was one such believer, and her heart was troubled by the dismal treatment of those who were locked away, often to be forgotten or abused. Her extensive travels familiarized her with the laws and policies of most states and major cities as well as the actual application of policies within specific jails and prisons.

Dix was not given to theorizing about human nature in general or life in captivity in particular. Her interests focused on bringing about a general reform of incarceration polices and practices. In an article called *Remarks on Prison Discipline &c.* she provided an insight into her approach to the issues, and her firm faith-based response to the men and women whose lives were lived behind bars:

> Heretofore the exceeding importance of selecting officers by their moral gifts and fitness, not merely to maintain outward discipline, but to promote the sub-

stantial, lasting good of the prisoner, has been often overlooked, or regarded as a secondary consideration. But that character is not, in its general, social acceptation lost sight of, is revealed in the fact that, for at least fifteen years past, the standard for the choice of the head officer of prisons in the United States has been rising, and it is mainly to this that the progressive improvement in prisons, gradual as it has been, may be ascribed. In proportion as these offices are made honorable and respectable, — I mean not only the offices of the chief warden, but those of second and third rank, — in both the penitentiaries and county jails, will competent and respectable men be found to conduct these institutions. I would not have the officers become preachers; I would not have them much interfere with the religious teaching, so called, of the prisoners; but I would have them all moral guides; and, while I would not desire to see them always, nor very often, be engaged in discoursing and formal lecturing, I would have all they both say and do produce an encouraging, awakening, and enlightening effect upon the prisoner. A few words are more likely to do good, than a tedious lesson; the too little regarded influences of manner, tone, and expression, are the most efficient help to all prisoners, whether among the "silent," "the separate," or "the congregated classes." In order to do good, a man must be good; and he will not be good except he have instruction by counsel and example. Now who have the power of exercising these direct hourly influences, except the officers who have charge of the prisons and prisoners? It is the word in season, and fitly spoken, which may kindle a desire in the degraded to retrieve himself. The faint desire becomes quickened into a living purpose; this passes into the fixed resolve; and this creates a sentiment of self respect. Self-respect implanted, conducts to the desire of possessing the respect and confidence of others; and through these paths grow up moral sentiments, gradually increasing and gaining strength; and, in time, there is the more profound and soul-saving sentiment of reverence for God, acknowledgment of his laws, and a truer perception of that sanctifying knowledge which causeth not to err.

Her respect for the feelings of prisoners stands in sharp contrast to the attitudes of society in general, both in her day and in ours. Dix's concern extended beyond what happened within prison walls to what came afterwards. In this same article, she discussed what might follow a prisoner's release:

At the expiration of a sentence, it is customary, in all the States, to discharge the prisoner decently clothed, and supplied with a small sum of money, usually varying from three to five dollars. If a prisoner have friends and home near, this is sufficient; but this is not oftenest nor often the case; and this usual provision is quite inadequate to convey the convict to a distant home, to a place of business, or long to support him honestly while he seeks employment; and which, as a graduate from a State prison, he obtains not without encountering many difficulties and repulses, if indeed his efforts do not end in total disappointment; so that, discouraged and tempted, he returns to old associates and associations, and betakes himself again to those law-deriding modes of life that shortly subject him to misery and disgrace, if not to a speedy incarceration in the county jail.

As reasonable as this sounds, Dix was then, and remains even today, far ahead of society at large in her concern for the men and women who many regard only as objects of fear and suspicion. Her faith told her that all people were to be given every chance to know a life of dignity.

✱ *January 27*

Isaac Thomas Hecker

ROMAN CATHOLIC

December 18, 1819–December 22, 1888

As late as the mid-19th century, Roman Catholics in the United States were primarily immigrants, standing on the fringes of the mainstream culture. The "Know Nothing Party" was formed to oppose further Catholic immigration, while, for their part, Roman Catholics isolated themselves by establishing their own schools and social organizations.

Isaac Hecker (who took the name Thomas when he was confirmed) was the child of Protestant immigrants. He left school early in his teens to work in the family bakery. Through involvement with a political organization for the workers, he met Orestes Brownson who was forming an experimental community at Brook Farm outside Boston. This little community was formed to explore whether or not it was possible to create a society without the divisions and conflicts that were so much a part of life in the early years of the Industrial Revolution. Hecker lived for a while at Brook Farm, where he mingled with Ralph Waldo Emerson, Nathaniel Hawthorne, and other Boston-area intellectuals. He was searching for spiritual guidance and a new purpose for his life.

Brook Farm did not satisfy his longings, nor did conversations with clergy from various churches. Eventually, he joined the Roman Catholic Church and was baptized at 25, in 1844. He studied for ordination in Europe, then returned to the United States, hoping to commend Catholicism to Americans. To that end, he formed the Paulist Fathers, a new religious community, and started *The Catholic World,* a magazine to help spread his ideas. In all his writing and teaching, he dedicated himself to integrating his church with the American spirit of freedom and reason. Hecker believed that his early years as a Protestant, his experience in the labor movement, and his contact with the New England Transcendentalists gave him a unique ability to commend Catholicism to citizens of the United States. The Paulist order continued to grow long after Hecker's death and the spirit of renewal which he advocated foreshadowed some of the changes called for by Pope John XXIII a century later.

A reading from the diary of Isaac Hecker

I strive to follow my spiritual director or else I should be fearful of my state. All my difficulties sins & temptations I make him acquainted with. It is said by many of the most renowned spiritual writers it never has been known at any time that a Soul has been lost that has obeyed its director. I fear that I do not sacrifice more and more daily and without which there can be no progress towards God. I am not at all desirous to consider where I am but what is still before me. Oh that I gave more of my time to silence and divine abstraction. That I would not consider this time so devoted as lost. That I could free myself from all vanity pride and self-esteem. Oh Holy Mary Mother of God who was untouched by sin tho' tempted as we all are do thou pray for me that I may be given such grace as was given to thee. I am sinful and would speak to all of my sins even in this I fear that my vanity would feed itself on. Even my desire for goodness is not free from selfishness. Oh where shall I fly in order to get free from sin? Oh that I could break through these unreal difficulties that beset me. That I could form new resolutions and keep them. If I am rewarded for my prayers then I think how much greater it is to live by faith. And if I am not rewarded then I think it is because I am so evil. Well well I see no way for me to get free from these trials. They must be born. It is the lot of us all. If we should be freed from uncertainty then we would fall into presumption immediately. O what a thing is Man! How far from settled peace and rest.

Oh Lord free my Soul from the burthen & travail which now rests upon it in its desire for the peace and salvation of those who are dear to it. Bring them to the light and give them Thy grace that they may be strong and embrace the eternal truth. Lead them oh Lord in thy way. Fill their hearts with the desire of Thee. Let them not rest untill they shall have found and united themselves to Thee. Lord if thou lookest with delight on the soul that seeketh the salvation of another do thou answer its call as thou hast promised thou wilt do. How can I rest and be at peace if these shall be lost and find Thee not. Oh all ye powers intercede to the Lord for their salvation. Ye ministering spirits inspire their hearts with holy thoughts and firm resolutions. Oh all ye saints martyrs prophets and virgins pray for them. May all that they see quicken their hearts towards thee oh God. May the prayers of the faithful here oh Lord be effectual. Lord take from me and give to them, Lord let me suffer and they rejoice. What may I oh Lord do for them. Thou who art all give answer to my weak desire. Relieve and Release me oh Lord. My Soul is troubled and all the day is wrestling before Thee for them. Thou knowest oh Lord this is my desire but how far short do I come from it. Oh that my asking was effectual and could not be repulsed. I will hope and never despair.

Pray for my soul and be always with me my blessed and good Guardian Angel.

✪ *January 28*

Benajah Carroll

BAPTIST

December 27, 1843–November 11, 1914

American Christianity is replete with stories of the rebellious child who rejects the faith of his pious parents, then experiences a dramatic conversion and devotes his life to preaching the gospel. Benajah Carroll followed that path to extremes. He bitterly rejected Christianity and went so far as to write a book expressing his views. When the Civil War began, Carroll joined the Texas Rangers and was wounded in battle. On his return from the war, he was persuaded to go to a revival meeting, and he agreed to attend one last time, expecting it to affect him no more than previous ones. But this time, the preacher exhorted the congregation to "make a practical, experimental test" of Christianity, to give Jesus Christ a fair trial. Carroll thought that was reasonable and went forward. Later, he described the affect the service had on him:

> Suddenly there flashed upon my mind, like a light from heaven, this Scripture: "Come unto me, all ye that labour and are heavy laden, and I will give you rest." I did not see Jesus with my eye, but I seemed to see Him standing before me, looking reproachfully and tenderly and pleadingly, seeming to rebuke me for having gone to all other sources for rest but the right one, and now inviting me to come to Him. In a moment I went, once and forever, casting myself unreservedly and for all time at Christ's feet, and in a moment the rest came, indescribable and unspeakable, and it has remained from that day until now...my soul was filled with such a rapture and such an ecstasy of joy as I had never before experienced. I knew then as well as I know now, that I would preach; that it would be my life work that I would have no other work.

He was ordained the following year and, after assisting in camp meetings and revivals around the state of Texas and serving as pastor of several small congregations, was called to be pastor of the First Baptist Church of Waco. He served there for 28 years and taught at Baylor University for 33 years, becoming a major figure among Texas Baptists. His *An Interpretation of the English Bible* eventually totaled 17 volumes. Carroll helped found Baylor Seminary in 1905, and in 1908, at the age of 64, he was one of the founders of the Southwest Baptist Theological Seminary, where he was president until his death.

Readings from Benajah Carroll

Benajah Carroll speaks of his life and invites others to come

What unjust ideas I once had about God! What ideas I have now about God since I studied Jesus! I now know the Father; I know His approachableness.

I know that He is not confined to Jerusalem, nor the mountains of Samaria, but everywhere on the face of the earth, a soul, any soul, no matter how sinful, may for itself come directly to Jesus and say, "God be merciful to me, a sinner," and salvation comes to that soul. Will you try it? I know that if any poor prodigal, homeless, helpless, ragged and wretched, will but arise and go to the Father, from afar off the Father will see him and run to meet him, and tenderly embrace him and kiss him much and welcome him with joy to light and home and melody and happiness.

Let no man dare to block the way to God. Let neither priest, apostle, nor devil forbid any petitioner direct access to God through Christ. Stand back, thou self-appointed peddler of the divine favors! Withdraw thy baneful shadow from the path of the comer to God! Come on, ye supplicants! Hear the Master:

"Come unto me all ye that labour and are heavy laden, and I will give you rest." "Him that cometh to me I will in no wise cast out." Come on, mothers, with your babies! Come, blind Bartimeus! Come, thou prodigal! Come, Zaccheus and Matthew! Come, ye Magdalenes! Come, dying thieves! The door is wide open by day and night. No sentinel blocks the way. No disciple may forbid. Come yourself to God Himself. O sinner, dying sinner, do come!

Benajah Carroll speaks of his role as a preacher

I magnify my office, oh, my God, as I get nearer home. I can say more truthfully every year, "I thank God that He put me in this office"; I thank Him that He would not let me have any other; that He shut me up to this glorious work; and when I get home among the blessed on the bank of everlasting deliverance and look back toward time and all of its clouds and sorrows and pains and privations, I expect to stand up and shout for joy that down there in the fog and mists, down there in the dust and in the struggle, God let me be a preacher. I magnify my office in life; I magnify it in death; I magnify it in heaven; I magnify it, whether poor or rich, whether sick or well, whether strong or weak, anywhere, everywhere, among all people, in any crowd. Lord God, I am glad that I am a preacher, that I am a preacher of the glorious gospel of Jesus Christ.

✹ *January 29* _____

Phoebe Worrall Palmer

METHODIST

December 18, 1807–November 2, 1874

A pioneer in the role of women in the church, Phoebe Worrall married Walter Palmer when she was 19. A decade later, her conversion experience prompted her to start evangelizing. One of her early ministries was in a poor section of New York City, where she visited and distributed tracts in cellars, garrets, and attics and also carried on a prison ministry. Later, she spoke every summer at revival meetings and published a series of popular books. She conducted revivals in Chicago, New Orleans, and California as well as the British Isles. These meetings were often under the auspices of other denominations, Baptist, Congregational, and Anglican. Working sometimes with her husband, and sometimes by herself, she expanded by word and example the role of women in ministry.

A reading from *The Devotional Writings* of Phoebe Palmer

At another time, about a year subsequent to the period just alluded to, the Lord again greatly comforted her soul during the night season. She had again, as on the former occasion, been for a long time wrestling earnestly with God, till nature had become wearied; when, on falling asleep, she dreamed she was standing without. The canopy of a beautiful midnight sky was spread out above her; the firmament was cloudless, and the full moon was silently walking the heavens. A stillness, that seemed hallowed to something unusual, reigned, but her eye was intently fixed, and her mind all absorbed by the attraction of a bright star. Presently it began to enlarge its circle, wider and yet wider, when (as she continued to keep her eye fixed on the point where it first began to rest) the form of the infant Saviour was presented, and these words were proclaimed, "For unto us a child is born, unto us a son is given. . . . And his name shall be called wonderful, counselor, the MIGHTY GOD, THE EVERLASTING FATHER, THE PRINCE OF PEACE."

In the mean time, while these words were being proclaimed, the circle rapidly widened, until the whole heavens had become encircled in one glow of glory.

The happy experience of succeeding years, when, by keeping her eye steadily fixed upon the Day-star from on high, her spiritual horizon had become enlightened, and, as she had continued to gaze, had rapidly taken in yet wider and still wider circles of glory, until the whole firmament of her soul had become radiant with its blissful beams, assured her that this communication was intended to convey a greater infinitude of meaning than her feeble capacities comprehended at the time.

Though this was in a measure blest to her soul, at the time when given, and tended to assure her heart more confidently of the gracious designs of Infinite Love toward her, yet the impression soon passed away, and she relapsed into her former habits of reasoning and unbelief.

One day, after having given to a friend a narration of the way by which the Lord had brought her, and stated a variety of experience, trials by the way, and the manner in which she had been enabled to overcome them, the friend remarked something expressive of surprise and gratitude in reference to the Lord's instructive dealings. "O," said she, in return, "this is the way the Lord takes to instruct and discipline his children. That which is learned by *experience* is much more deeply written upon the heart than what is learned by mere precept. By this painful process, the lessons of grace remain written in *living* characters upon the mind, and we are better able to tell to travelers coming after us, just how and where we met with this and the other difficulty, how we overcame, and the peculiar lessons learned by passing through *this* and *that* trial, and thus be not only advantaged in our own experience, but helpful to our fellow-pilgrims."

Scarcely had she finished speaking, when the prayer that she might be made a monument of the extent of saving grace to transform the heart and life was brought by the Spirit to her remembrance, and the inquiry was presented whether she would be willing that the petition should be granted, if, in order for its accomplishment, it were needful that she should be called to pass through trials unheard of in magnitude and duration?

An unutterable weight of responsibility rested upon her mind, and she hastened to prostrate herself in solitude before God. She felt that it was an inquiry proposed by the Spirit that searcheth all things, and was assured that the decision of that hour would tell momentously on her eternal destiny.... Prostrate on her face before the Sovereign of heaven and earth she said, "O Lord, I now renewedly give myself into thy hands, as clay in the hands of the potter, in order that thy whole will and pleasure may be accomplished in me. Let the petition be answered. Let thy power be manifested to transform and save to the uttermost. Though trials of inconceivable magnitude may await me, I rely upon thy faithfulness. Thou hast promised that I shall not be tempted above that which I am able to bear. But if thou seest, at any time, my faith about to fail, remove the trial, or cut short the work in righteousness, and take me home to thyself; suffer me not to live to dishonor thee."

The seal, proclaiming her wholly the Lord's was now more deeply enstamped, and she realized from that hour that she was taken more closely to the embrace of Infinite Love, and had cast anchor deeper within the veil. Ever afterward, in passing through the most painful, complex trials, she found a blessed satisfaction in referring to this period when she had so fully counted the cost.

✸ *January 30* _____

Sarah Platt Doremus

REFORMED

August 3, 1802–January 22, 1877

It took 27 years for the seed to sprout, but when it did, it grew rapidly and proved worth the wait. David Abeel* planted that seed. In 1834, he returned from his work in China to speak in New York about the need for women in the mission field. Chinese women, he said, were asking for members of their sex to come and share their faith. Sarah Doremus was in the audience, and she attempted to create a female missionary society, but strong opposition to the notion of single women serving in that way thwarted her early efforts.

So Doremus found other things to do. In addition to raising her nine children and finding time to paint and do embroidery, she took charge of a tract society and an organization to return women prisoners into society; she organized relief efforts for Greek Christians and distributed Bibles to the destitute; she helped found a children's hospital and a separate women's hospital in New York State; she visited the women's ward of the city prison and organized services for them; she started a nursery where women who worked could leave their children; and, during the Civil War, she helped distribute supplies among city hospitals. She learned how to make things happen.

By 1861, conditions were greatly changed. The Civil War had drastically reduced the number of men available to work in any field, while women had proved they could face hardship by nursing on the battlefields. Doremus's second attempt to organize a female mission society germinated rapidly. The Women's Union Missionary Society was the first organization of women in America dedicated to helping women in Africa and Asia. For 15 years, it operated out of the Doremus home. The first missionary they sponsored, Harriet Britain, went out to India in 1862. Twenty years later, the society was supporting over 100 missionaries at 12 stations. By the time she died, Doremus had directed over 1,000 female teachers, doctors, evangelists, and relief workers to mission work all over the world. Other denominations had followed her example and created their own mission societies supported by the particular churches. Forty years after the Women's Union Missionary Society was created, there were 52 Women's Boards with annual combined budgets of over $2.5 million

Still looking for new challenges, Doremus helped organize a home for elderly women in 1866; when the Irish potato famine struck in 1869, she organized relief efforts; and when Italian immigrants began flooding into New York, she joined a committee in 1876 to create Italo-American schools.

A reading from a column "Famine Orphans" by Sarah Platt Doremus in the Women's Union Missionary Society magazine

"Famine Orphans! What a funny name," methinks I hear some of our little readers say. Yes, it is a strange name, but a very sad one, too, for it was given to some poor, helpless little children, living the other side of the world, whose fathers and mothers had been starved to death.

A long time ago, in India, it did not rain for nearly *two* years! which made the ground so dry and parched, that nothing could grow there. Then there came a most terrible famine, just like the one we read of in the Bible, when Joseph lived, and thousands upon thousands of people died, because they could get nothing to eat. Numbers of little children died too, but a great many were left alone in the world, without any one to care for them. Some good people felt so sorry for them, that they gave them a home where they could be clothed and fed, and then they called them "Famine Orphans." You cannot think how it made the hearts of these good people ache, when they heard these poor little outcasts cry all the time for "Bread, bread," and often they found them eating soap, and tallow candles, just as you would enjoy cake or candy. By-and-by, these children were sent to school, but they were so naughty that they did not tell the truth, and then would steal, and do a great many wicked things, for which, we know "God is angry every day...."

But I want tell you of one thing more about these poor orphans, to show you how they had improved. Some time after this the famine grew worse, so that every one who had any money, had to send to another country for food. These children, who knew what a dreadful thing it was to be starving, thought they would like to give some money to those who, unlike them had no kind friends to care for them.

Now, you must know this was a great deal for them to do.... But there were many very little children in the school, who could not earn anything, and so had no money to give away. What do you think they did? They asked the teacher if he would not buy less every day for them to eat, and then give all the money he saved, to those people who had no food at all. This he was willing to do, so for two months the children had to practice great self-denial, but not once did he ever hear a word of regret or complaint from them.

And now, dear little readers, do you not think you can learn some beautiful lessons from these "Famine Orphans?" You must remember, they were not born, as you were, in a happy land, where dear ones help you to be good, and teach you about God; but in their far-off country people are very unhappy, because they are so wicked, and think the gods they worship permit them to be. Do not forget that it is your pennies which help to send some kind teacher to them, that they may learn about the loving Saviour who has died for them, as well as for us.

✺ *January 31* _____

Richard Allen

AFRICAN METHODIST

February 14, 1760–March 26, 1831

Born in slavery, Richard Allen had a conversion experience in his early 20s and then led his master to conversion and the conviction that slavery was wrong. As a result of this, Allen's master allowed him and his brother to buy their freedom for the equivalent of $2,000. Finding work as a wagon driver and wood cutter, Allen began to preach and so impressed the great Methodist evangelist, Francis Asbury,* that he invited Allen to travel with him. Allen declined the invitation, but was often invited to preach in churches in the area of Philadelphia.

With Absalom Jones,* Allen worked to attract African Americans to St. George's Methodist Church in Philadelphia. The two were so effective that white members of the congregation felt threatened and decided that black members should be sent to sit in the gallery. When the ushers tried to move them during the service, Jones, Allen, and the other black members left. Jones and the majority of the black members decided to organize themselves as an Episcopal parish, but Allen felt indebted to the Methodists for his conversion, and decided he could be nothing else.

As a result of this decision, Allen opened a small church in 1794 with the help of Asbury. He became the first African American ordained by the Methodists. Conflict with Methodist authorities continued, however, as they consistently placed restrictions on Allen and his congregation. Finally, in 1816, a gathering of delegates from Baltimore and other places in the area resolved to "become one body under the name of the African Methodist Episcopal Church" and chose Allen to serve as their first bishop.

A reading from "An Address to the People of Color in the United States of America" by Richard Allen

Feeling an engagement of mind for your welfare, I address you with an affectionate sympathy, having been a slave, and as desirous of freedom as any of you; yet the bands of bondage were so strong that no way appeared for my release; yet at times a hope arose in my heart that a way would open for it; and when my mind was mercifully visited with the feeling of the love of God, then these hopes increased, and a confidence arose that he would make for my enlargement; and as a patient waiting was necessary, I was sometimes favored with it, at other times I was very impatient. Then the prospect of liberty almost vanished away, and I was in darkness and perplexity.

I mention experience to you, that your hearts may not sink at the discouraging prospects you may have, and that you may put your trust in God, who sees your condition, and as a merciful father pitieth his children, so doth God pity them that love Him; and as your hearts are inclined to serve God, you will feel an affectionate regard towards your masters and mistresses, so called, and the whole family in which you live. This will be seen by them, and tend to promote your liberty, especially with such as have feeling masters; and if they are otherwise, you will have the favor and love of God dwelling in your hearts, which you will value more than anything else, which will be a consolation in the worst condition you can be in and no master can deprive you of it; and as life is short and uncertain, and the chief end of our having a being in this world is to be prepared for a better, I wish you to think of this more than anything else; then you will have a view of that freedom which the sons of God enjoy; and if the troubles of your condition end with your lives, you will be admitted to the freedom which God hath prepared for those of all colors that love him. Here the power of the most cruel master ends, and all sorrow and tears are wiped away.

To you who are favored with freedom, let your conduct manifest your gratitude toward the compassionate masters who have set you free; and let no rancour or ill-will lodge in your breast for any bad treatment you may have received from any. If you do, you transgress against God, who will not hold you guiltless. He would not suffer it even in his beloved people Israel; and you think he will allow it unto us? Many of the white people have been instruments in the hands of God for our good even such as have held us in captivity, are now pleading our cause with earnestness and zeal; and I am sorry to say, that too many think more of the evil than of the good they have received, and instead of taking the advice of their friends, turn from it with indifference. Much depends upon us for the help of our color — more than many are aware. If we are lazy and idle, the enemies of freedom plead it as a cause why we ought not to be free, and say we are better in a state of servitude, and that giving us our liberty would be an injury to us; and by such conduct we strengthen the bands of oppression and keep many in bondage who are more worthy than ourselves. I entreat you to consider the obligations we lie under to help forward the cause of freedom. He who knows how bitter the cup is of which the slave hath to drink, O, how ought we to feel for those who remain yet in bondage! Will even our friends excuse — will God pardon us — for the part we act in making strong the hands of the enemies of our color?

John Meyendorff

ORTHODOX

February 17, 1926–July 22, 1992

Formally separated from the western Christian church since 1054 AD — in practice, separated even before that — the Orthodox Church brings a unique and valuable perspective to ecumenical dialogue. As Christian immigrants from eastern Europe became more numerous in America and comfortable in their new setting, Orthodox voices like that of John Meyendorff began to make a significant impact.

John Meyendorff was born of Russian émigré parents in France and came to New York to teach at St. Vladimir's Seminary in 1959. He remained there until his death but also taught at Fordham, Columbia, and at Union Theological Seminary. An Orthodox theologian neither born nor educated in one of the east European countries, Meyendorff was able to view the divisions within the Orthodox community more objectively than those with more cultural baggage. He devoted much of his energy to trying to overcome those differences. He was instrumental in the negotiations that led to self-governing status for the Orthodox Church in America. He also worked to establish a standing committee of bishops and an Orthodox theological society, and was deeply involved in the years before his death in discussions looking toward the creation of a more unified Orthodox body in America. The time was ripe, in his opinion, for American Orthodox Christians to assert themselves as an independent and mature voice within Orthodoxy. As he explained,

> In America, both by their numbers and by the quality of many among its clergy and laity, the Greek Orthodox community deserves a position of leadership. ... [T]he mission to all Americans regardless of ethnic background (as required by the Gospel itself) cannot wait for changes occurring in Istanbul, Turkey.

Perhaps because Orthodox Christians were accustomed to a united church in their countries, Orthodox theologians have been deeply involved in the ecumenical movement from the beginning. John Meyendorff's concern for Christian unity was not limited to unity among the Orthodox; he often represented the Orthodox Church on the Central Committee of the World Council of Churches and its Faith and Order Commission, and was Moderator of that Commission from 1967 to 1975. He also served for a number of years on the Orthodox-Roman Catholic Consultation in the United States. "It would be a spiritual mistake," he wrote, "to settle for a new form of American sectarianism." The Orthodox tradition was one of unity and they must work for that in America as well. "She (the church) has a missionary responsibility for all men. She can never identify herself with a political ideology or an ethnic group.... Let us respect and cultivate everything which is precious in our ethnic cultures. But let us also remember that the Church is not an instrument or tool for earthly causes, but a foretaste of God's kingdom for all men."

Meyendorff's writing and lectures on the Orthodox perspective made him a nationally known figure. As editor of the *St. Vladimir's Theological Review* for almost twenty years, as well as the *Orthodox Church,* a monthly newspaper, he devoted himself to clarifying and propagating the Orthodox perspective so as to enrich ecumenical dialogue. He understood that Christian unity was not an end in itself but a means by which the church could witness more effectively to society as a whole. Believing that the Orthodox emphasis on the "parousia" or second coming of Christ brought a critical balance to the church's witness, he wrote that "a Christian solution of social issues is never either absolute or perfect as long as the *parousia* has not taken place, and ... an Orthodox Christian can live with that imperfection because he knows that the *parousia* will eventually come; but he cannot be reconciled with imperfection as such.... Orthodoxy will always maintain that the starting point, the source, and the criterion for solving social issues are found in the uninterrupted, mysterious, and in a sense transcendent communion of the ecclesiastical gathering."

With that perspective, John Meyendorff made an invaluable contribution to American Christianity, helping draw together its millennial concerns and its passion for social justice.

✪ *February 2*

Braxton Drayton

LUTHERAN

c. 1800–1866

African American men in the south rarely received Lutheran ordination in the early 19th century, but St. John's Lutheran Church of Charlestown, South Carolina, developed an interest in a Lutheran mission to Africa and hoped to send a black pastor there to conduct it. First to go was Jehu Jones, a member of the congregation who had gone to New York in 1832 to become the first black man ordained by a Lutheran body in America. He approached the Lutheran Ministerium of New York with his dream of a mission to Africa, but their inaction allowed the plan to die.

There was intense debate about the wisdom of African Americans returning to Africa. Some felt it would be best for blacks to be restored to their own continent for their own sake. Others felt it would be a good idea for the sake of white Americans to be free from racial tensions. Still others felt this would be nothing more than a kind of deportation for men and women dragged here against their will several generations before. Indeed, Daniel Alexander Payne,* the second black ordained by Lutherans, had entered Gettysburg Seminary in 1835 with the clear understanding that he would not be trained for African colonization.

Nevertheless, a substantial migration of ex-slaves to West Africa occurred and Liberia was formed for these immigrants. Since a number of Liberians had been exposed to Christianity while in America, a Christian missionary effort to that new colony seemed a sensible idea. Both white and black missionaries were dispatched. Braxton Drayton had been a lay leader at St. John's for several years before he sought and received permission to become a Lutheran missionary to Africa. He became the third black man ordained by the Lutherans in America, and the first to be sent as an African missionary. In 1845, he went to a new colony there called Maryland, just to the southeast of Liberia. Drayton wrote in a letter to the states:

> I have been blessed by the Lord to find a field of labor not in competition with any others, that the Lord has reserved for us. The governor has told me that I can have as much land as I want to build on in the name of the Lutheran Church in America. I will begin a school . . . I will build it large enough that it may be used as a church. We shall call it the Lutheran Missionary School.

Though the mission did not go well — the indigenous population was unresponsive to Christian outreach — Drayton did not abandon his hope for the region. He decided to remain in Africa in another capacity and became governor of the colony until its annexation by Liberia in 1857. At that point, he became the Chief Justice of the Liberian Supreme Court. He died in 1866 in a drowning accident.

Perseverance and determination are powerful assets in mission work, but so is adaptability. While the ministry of Word and Sacrament is a high calling, so is secular public service when done with integrity and in the service of God. Drayton might have left the Maryland colony in Africa embittered by failure. He might have returned to St. John's to be among supporters and old friends. Instead, he shifted his office, but not his commitment to those he came to aid.

Drayton's story not only reflects on his life and work, but also reminds us of the difference a single congregation can make in national and even international affairs. St. John's was very much out of step with most Lutheran congregations in their region, yet their decision to reach out to the black community changed Lutheranism. Who could have realized that their actions would produce a future Chief Justice of Liberia? What may seem like a simple act of welcome, or even an expedient technique for church growth, often proves to be an opening for God to raise up a new generation of leaders — not just for that congregation, but potentially, for lands and peoples far away. For Lutherans, the role of civil authority is considered second only to the gospel as God's way of blessing humanity. The church, armed with the Good News of God's mercy, is how salvation is offered. But the state, armed with wise and good leaders, is how God gives peace, security, and prosperity to us. Together, the sacred and secular authorities make a joyful, humane life possible. Drayton offered both in turn, serving his new land in the various roles to which he was called.

✪ *February 3*

Louise Cecilia Fleming

BAPTIST

January 10, 1862–June 20, 1899

Born in slavery, she never knew her father who had gone off to fight with the Union Army, but Louise Cecilia Fleming grew up listening to stories of how her paternal grandfather had been captured in Africa and brought to America as a slave. From childhood, Louise Fleming knew that someday she too wanted to go there. "The Lord had need of me in Africa," she said, "and the happiness that I used to enjoy in the work at home was marred from time to time with the shadow of the darkness of the Dark Continent." With the end of the Civil War, new opportunities opened for black people in the south. A visiting pastor from Brooklyn saw Lulu (as she was called) teaching in her church and found support within his congregation to send her to Shaw University in Atlanta.

American Baptists had taken responsibility for the Livingstone Inland Mission and were actively recruiting black missionaries for it. Fleming volunteered, becoming their first female worker in the Congo. She was assigned work as a teacher in Palabala, Congo (now Zaire). Her letters home read like those of any other western missionary of the era. She exclaimed over "picturesque scenes" and contrasted them with the "benighted minds of the inhabitants." "Their religion," she wrote, "consists of all kinds of superstitions. They have a different fetich for nearly everything. Those for medicine being worn as is the one to keep off the bad man, whom they call *ndoki*."

Fleming was deeply committed to her work and her epistles reveal the intensity of her struggle to claim her own identity, as she experienced conflict with male missionary leaders and compared the differences between her circumstances and those of the native Africans. She worked hard to teach them, evangelizing and recruiting young African women to send to the United States for training. When she became ill and had to return to America, she took the opportunity to acquire the medical education she knew was needed in the Congo. Beginning her work at Shaw, Fleming went on to study at the Woman's Medical College of Philadelphia. In 1895, she returned to Africa as a medical missionary under the auspices of Russell Conwell's* Grace Baptist Church. Unhappily, after only four years, she contracted a fatal form of sleeping sickness. She returned to the United States for treatment, hoping to come back as soon as she was better, but died in 1899 at the age of 37.

A reading from a letter by Louise Fleming

Palabala Station,
L.I. Mission of the A.B.M. Union,
Congo Free State, S.W.A.
October 6, 1887

Would that I could describe the picturesque scenes of the Congo River and country. The limited portion, seen by my admiring eyes, to more beautiful than anything I have before seen in nature. The evergreen bluffs of the mighty river and the gigantic peaks of the mountainous valleys are truly grand. What a contrast to the benighted minds of the inhabitants!... The climate seems quite like that of my own State, with that exception. We are never more than a few weeks without rain there. I cannot see what it can be that steals away the vital powers of foreigners in this delightful climate, save the excessive growth and decay of vegetation. This I think poisons the air. There is no other way of accounting for the death rate of foreigners. If the country is ever cleared up, as Florida is being cleared, the climate will be even superior to that of Florida. I have been as well as I would have been at home. Have not had a single fever as yet.

The English Baptist Society have lost six of their Congo missionaries this year. The people in this great valley are for the most part peaceful on the lower rivers; vary much in features, form and color. They have marks, such as taking out the center upper front teeth, notching the same, sharpening all the upper fronts to a point, picking certain shaped marks In their foreheads and temples, and making animals, or a great many small marks, on their chests or backs to distinguish the different tribes. Their dress is very simple, consisting only of a loin-cloth for the common people, while the royal family and the rich wear long choice skirts down to the ankle and a shoulder wrap besides; they also wear in abundance heavy brass rings on their waists and ankles, the women wearing strings of beads around their waists and up and down their chests and backs. The stiff bristle from the tail of the elephant is also considered a fine article of jewelry, being worn as are the brass rings.

Their religion consists of all kinds of superstitions. They have a different fetich for nearly everything. Those for medicine being worn as is the one to keep off the bad man, whom they call _ndoki_. The first one of the women about our station to give up her _minkisi_ (fetiches) gave them to me last month. They numbered three, and were for use as follows: the greatest and first to keep her pulse beating, the second to keep Satan off, and the third to cure her headaches and such like. She willfully took them off from her neck and said she wished no longer to trust in them, but in Jesus. She has been hearing the blessed story of the cross, doubtless, for years, and was quite prepared to answer any question respecting His death for sinners. Our hearts were made glad by the demonstration of the beginning of the work of the Holy Spirit in the hearts of the women....

Yours in Africa,
Lulu C. Fleming

✪ February 4

Benjamin Rush

PRESBYTERIAN

December 24, 1745–April 19, 1813

An enemy of strong drink, tobacco, slavery, capital punishment, and war, Benjamin Rush had an opinion on almost everything. He favored blood-letting as a cure for many illnesses long after others had abandoned the practice, but he was far in advance of his time in his opposition to slavery and capital punishment and in his ideas about how to treat the mentally ill. He has been portrayed as impulsive, indiscreet, wildly popular, fallible, with a limitless zeal for the public good. It must be acknowledged, however, that few other Americans of his time had thought so deeply about so many things and formed their opinions in the light of the Bible and Christian faith.

Rush was trained as a doctor and had studied in London, Edinburgh, and Paris. Benjamin Franklin assisted him and, in turn, Rush came to America to work for independence. He was made surgeon general of the Revolutionary army but, impatient of military administration, he made indiscreet remarks about General Washington that forced his resignation. This turned out to be a temporary setback in a career that made him one of the most respected citizens of his country. Yet he remained an independent thinker. Pondering the organization of the new American government, for example, he asked why there was a War Department and not a Peace Department, since surely peace was more desirable and required at least as much concern.

Rush founded the Philadelphia Dispensary for the relief of the poor, the first institution of its kind in the United States. For many years he provided his services there without charge. He founded Dickinson College and was one of the charter trustees of Franklin College, which later became Franklin and Marshall. Rush also helped incorporate the Young Ladies Academy in Philadelphia because he thought women should be educated as well a men. At that time, slavery was a generally accepted institution even in the north, but Rush eloquently opposed it in these words:

A reading from Benjamin Rush

And now, my fellow countrymen, what shall I add more to rouse your indignation against slave-keeping. Consider the many complicated crimes it involves in it. Think of the bloody wars which are fomented by it, among the African nations, or if these are too common to affect you, think of the pangs which attend the dissolution of the ties of nature in those who are stolen from their relations. Think of the many thousands who perish by sickness, melancholy and suicide, in their voyages to America. Pursue the poor devoted victims to one of the West Indian islands, and see them exposed there to public sale. Hear their cries, and see their looks of tenderness at each other upon being separated. — Mothers are torn from their daughters, and brothers from brothers, without the liberty of a parting embrace. Their master's name is now marked upon their breasts with a red hot iron. But let us pursue them into a sugar field, and behold a scene still more affecting than this — See! the poor wretches with what reluctance they take their instruments of labor into their hands. — Some of them, overcome with heat and sickness, seek to refresh themselves by a little rest, — But, behold an overseer approaches them. — In vain they sue for pity. — He lifts up his whip, while streams of blood follow every stroke. Neither age nor sex are spared.... But let us return from this Scene, and see the various modes of arbitrary punishments inflicted upon them by their masters. Behold once covered with stripes, into which melted wax is poured — another tied down to a block or stake — a third suspended in the air by his thumbs — a fourth obliged to set or stand upon red hot iron — a fifth, — I cannot relate it — Where now is law or justice? — Let us fly to them to step in for their relief. — Alas! — The one is silent and the other denounces more terrible punishments upon them.... O! God! Where is thy vengeance! — O! humanity — justice — liberty — religion! — Where, — where are ye fled. —

But chiefly — ye ministers of the gospel, whose dominion over the principles and actions of men is so universally acknowledged and felt, — Ye who estimate the worth of your fellow creatures by their immortality, and therefore must look upon all mankind as equal; — let your zeal keep pace with your opportunity to put a stop to slavery. While you inforce the duties of "tithe and cummin," neglect not the weightier laws of justice and humanity. Slavery is an Hydra sin, and includes in it every violation of the precepts of the Law and the Gospel. In vain will you command your flocks to offer up the incense of faith and charity, while they continue to mingle the sweat and blood of Negro slaves with their sacrifices. . . . Remember that national crimes require national punishments and without declaring what punishment awaits this evil, you may venture to assure them, that it cannot pass with impunity unless God shall cease to be just or merciful.

✪ February 5

John LaFarge

ROMAN CATHOLIC

February 13, 1880–November 24, 1963

At the time John LaFarge was born, the United States was only beginning to recover from the trauma of the Civil War. Two days before he died, John F. Kennedy was assassinated. LaFarge spent 15 years as pastor of a rural parish in Maryland, including the period of World War I. He moved to New York City to serve on the editorial staff of *America* while the country was in the midst of the Depression and World War II. He was still there when the Brown vs. Board of Education decision triggered the civil rights movement. During all this time, he remained an eloquent voice for human justice, the Christian faith, and the Roman Catholic Church.

Trained as a Jesuit, LaFarge spent the first few years of his priesthood as an instructor in Jesuit colleges, but when he was assigned to serve a community of rural whites and African Americans he began to apply his faith to social problems. In 1924, he founded an industrial school for African Americans in Ridge, Maryland, to provide agricultural training for those whose educational opportunities were limited. When he came to New York, he founded the Catholic Laymen's Union, an African American association that evolved before long into the first Catholic Interracial Council of New York and ultimately became part of a national movement to work for interracial justice. He encouraged the formation of other such groups by giving speeches across the country and by writing frequently on racial issues.

Racial equality, in LaFarge's view, was not an end in itself, but part of the larger working-out of God's purpose for humanity. That purpose was unity. The means to it were not merely appeals to justice or equal opportunity for all, but in the receiving of the ancient sacraments of the church:

Since the Spirit of God fashions human unity. He must have a workshop in which to do the fashioning. That workshop is the world as He has created it, its material as well as its spiritual aspects, even the physical aspects of man. This means that the Spirit, the transcendent, divine Spirit, uses for His purposes in dealing with mankind the "elements of the world," those humble, natural, even material circumstances that form the context of our earth-bound life....

Food, too, is our language, and drink, the rites and fellowship that accompany them. Yet these, too, can be the language and the instruments of the Spirit. I do not know any more complete denial of a materialist concept of society — and racial prejudice is a form of materialism — than when men are united in the sharing of the Body of the Lord.

Christians could not effectively promote unity if they were divided among themselves. Long before Vatican II espoused the ecumenical cause, LaFarge was writing:

Christianity is essentially a religion of unity. Christ our Lord placed unity above all attributes of the supernatural society which he founded: when individual Christian people, or when large bodies of Christian people, or Christian nations as a whole, embrace disunity, they suffer a wound in their very souls....

Patience, humility, and freedom are critical to the struggle for unity, as LaFarge understood. Unity cannot be imposed; it must be freely chosen. The fact that the Roman Church had so often coexisted with, even collaborated with nondemocratic countries has sometimes brought its commitment to human freedom into question. LaFarge nevertheless was convinced that freedom was consistent with the Church of Rome and it had no more to fear from democracy than democracy from the church:

[Roman] Catholics have no fear of reason nor of honest democratic frankness; they do fear the rule of prejudice and the suppression of reason in the name of democracy or for any other cause. They believe that God's cause flourishes in the full light of day, and they are convinced that all true Americans, whatever be their personal beliefs, are determined to keep that light shining.

Freedom of religion is a right of all Americans, who hold many different personal beliefs. LaFarge insisted that Roman Catholics also provided a spectrum of opinions. One needed only to drop in on a meeting of a church association devoted to rural life problems, the press, race or labor relations, international peace, juvenile guidance, or family life, or a local parish forum to see that. Stronger faith was forged by the interplay of minds, but that interplay, to be successful, required humility. "Humility," LaFarge wrote, "is the guide. And...humility, though often beaten in the short-term contest, invariably wins out in the long run." In that spirit, he asked the readers of *America* for their "thoughts...ideas...prayers...suggestions... comprehension, tolerance, initiative — all those things which we demand of ourselves."

Ultimately, of course, what matters is love. Asked to speak at a banquet celebrating the 50th year of his ordination, LaFarge spoke of love, not as a disembodied emotion but as something that "permeates all our thoughts, our inspirations. It wells up and flowers in our actions; it directs and guides us; it brings us together . . . (and) impels us to go forth and spread that same love abroad."

✪ *February 6* —————————————————————————————

Adelaide Teague Case

EPISCOPALIAN

January 10, 1887–June 19, 1948

The word "liberal" has been defined in so many different ways that it has become almost useless as an adjective to describe either a person or a movement. Persons seen as liberal in certain respects can be quite conservative or orthodox in their theology. Adelaide Teague Case considered herself a liberal and worked hard to define what she meant by the term. As a woman in a leadership position in the church in the first part of the 20th century, she was inevitably seen as liberal in the sense of one who is pressing for change in the church's structures. Case's own definition, however, concerned the role of the church within society and the way in which it prepared its members to carry out that role. It was her belief that "the heart of the Christian message is in its belief in radically transformed relationships, in its insistence on human brotherhood." To work for that transformation, Case became a leading authority on Christian education in the Episcopal Church as well as the first woman to be a professor in an Episcopal or Anglican seminary. In order to take that position, she gave up, in mid-life, a secure professorship at Columbia University to move to the Episcopal Theological School in Cambridge at a much lower salary. Resented by some and boycotted by others, she nonetheless won a place for herself by her commitment to high standards and her deep devotional life. One student said of her, "She was a true believer in Christ and you saw him living in and through her."

Adelaide Teague Case began her career teaching mathematics and Latin at an Episcopal boarding school in Poughkeepsie, New York, but poor health limited her ability to work regularly for several years. Enrolling in the doctoral program at Columbia in 1917, she received her Ph.D. in 1924, became a faculty member at Columbia's Teachers College, and eventually a full professor and chair of her department. It was her belief that "education, when it becomes socially dangerous, is surely beginning to be socially useful." The liberal, she wrote "expects that through experience and instruction" Christians will gain new insights into "the Bible, theology, Jesus, social welfare, the reconstruction of society, the political state, international and interracial problems, human nature, and education." These insights were available, she believed, even to children in church school. "Children can take part in the search for truth. A church school cannot evade the task of showing its pupils that our country is rich and our people are poor." Believing that Christian faith should transform society, Case was a pacifist and a member of the Church League for Industrial Democracy.

A reading from *Liberal Christianity and Religious Education: A Study of Objectives in Religious Education* by Adelaide Teague Case

The movement for reconstruction is impatient with the restrictions of ecclesiasticism but it desires no break with historic Christianity, holding that liberalism represents the inevitable next step in Christian progress. Its point of view involves a series of shifts in emphasis, the full significance of which is just beginning to be felt. In general, it is less concerned with the restatement or rejection of traditional dogmas — though much has been attempted along this line — than with the recognition of Christianity as a dynamic factor in the moral progress of humanity.

It tends to define its concepts less in theological terms than in terms of social psychology and ethics. Its standards are social standards and its goal the creation of a new human society, the *democracy* or the *commonwealth* of God. It is even interpreted as not primarily a reform movement, not remedial, but radical and creative. The word "radical" has however somewhat confusing connotations; so too with the word "modernist." "Progressive" means little or nothing. In spite of their awkwardness, the terms "liberal Christianity" and "the liberal movement" are probably the most clearly understood....

The aspects of the liberal movement noted in this chapter — involving as they do standards of method, items of knowledge, and individual and social attitudes — carry with them numerous educational objectives. While these objectives have been implied in the foregoing analysis, it remains necessary to state them in such a way that they may serve as standards for the religious education of children and youth in the issues here mentioned. They are not special or final ends but directions of effort that we may expect to find running through all educational activities characteristic of liberal Christianity. These objectives include:

1. Knowledge of the facts of our present civilization — accurate information on living conditions, on social institutions including the church and the state, and on the make-up of human nature.

2. The desire and the ability to relieve suffering and to work toward the reform of un-Christian social conditions.

3. An evaluation, on a Christian basis, of the institutions with which the groups under instruction come into contact, and active efforts for whatever reconstructions are found to be needed.

4. Mutual appreciation and cooperation between groups where there are racial, occupational, national or other differences; and the attempt to destroy "special privilege" due to age, sex, race, wealth, etc.

5. Activity in abolishing war as a means of settling disputes, and participation in efforts for reconciliation between individuals, classes, and nations.

6. Active faith in humanity and in the gradual transformation of society into what is commonly called "the kingdom of God." This is always taken to mean a brotherly society and usually involves the acceptance of a democratic ideal and experiments in democratic organization.

7. Efforts to develop the Christian church as an effective agency for the reconstruction of society.

✪ *February 7*

Henry McNeal Turner

AFRICAN METHODIST EPISCOPAL

February 1, 1834–May 9, 1915

Born free in South Carolina, Henry McNeal Turner learned to read from a white playmate and from clerks in the law office where he worked as a janitor. Married at the age of 22, he and his wife moved to Baltimore. Turner had been licensed to preach at age 19 but later, having joined the African Methodist Episcopal Church, he worked with others to persuade Lincoln to appoint black chaplains in the army and himself became the first to serve in that capacity.

Turner saw the Civil War as a second Exodus from Egypt and a turning point for black Americans. Trusting the promise of that era, he walked to Georgia to organize the African Methodist Church in that state and to lead the way for African Americans to enter the political process. By some counts, Turner organized over a hundred congregations in Georgia and became the presiding elder. In politics, he served as a member of the state's Constitutional Convention and then was elected to the Senate of the Georgia legislature.

Turner's high hopes for a new day in the south, however, were disappointed. He and other black members were ejected from the legislature in 1868, and Turner became involved in schemes for settling American blacks in Africa. Those hopes also were disappointed when those who went were not adequately prepared or funded. Many died, while others returned. Booker T. Washington, who argued that the future of American blacks was in America, had been proved right, which eroded Turner's leadership.

Turner died in Canada, disillusioned with the United States, isolated and embittered. Nonetheless, his leadership during the Civil War and the creation of the African Methodist Church in the south and in parts of Africa remain among his enduring achievements. He was ahead of his time in trying to build bridges with the Baptists, giving women a larger role — including ordination — encouraging the use of African American spirituals in worship, and in working to create racial pride. Proclaiming his people's need to see themselves in their God, he announced that, "We have every right to believe that God is a Negro."

A reading from a letter of Henry McNeal Turner concerning a Supreme Court decision refusing to intervene against state laws segregating the races

God will some day raise up another Lincoln, another Thad Stevens and another Chas. Sumner. In my opinion, if Jesus was on earth, he would say, when speaking of eight members of the Supreme Court, and the decision which worked such a cruel wrong upon my people, "Father forgive them; they know not what they do."

God would have men do right, harm no one, and to render to every man his just due. Mr. Justice Harlan rightly says that the Thirteenth Amendment intended that the white race should have no privilege whatsoever pertaining to citizenship and freedom, that was not alike extended and to be enjoyed by those persons who, though the greater part of them were slaves, were invited by an act of Congress to aid in saving from overthrow a government which, theretofore by all of its departments, had treated them as an inferior race, with no legal rights or privileges except such as the white race might choose to grant. It is an indisputable fact that the amendment last mentioned may be exerted by legislation of a direct and primary character for the eradication, not simply of the institution of slavery, but of its badges and incidents indicating that the individual was once a slave. The Supreme Court must decide the inter-State commerce law to be unconstitutional on account of interference with the State's autonomy, for it must be remembered that Mrs. Robinson, a citizen of Mississippi, bought a ticket from Grand Junction, Tennessee, to Lynchburg, Virginia, and when praying for satisfaction for rough and contumacious treatment, received at the hands of the company's agent, she was informed by the Court, that the Court was without power to act. Congress had constitutional power to pursue a runaway slave into all the States by legislation, to punish the man that would dare to conceal the slave. Congress could find the poor fellow seeking God's best blessing to man, liberty, and return him to his master, but Congress cannot, so say our honorable Court, give aid sufficient to the poor black man, to prove beyond all doubt to him that he is as free as any other citizen.

Mr. Justice Harlan says: "The difficulty has been to compel a recognition of the legal right of the black race to take the rank of citizens, and to secure the enjoyment of privileges belonging under the law to them as a component part of the people for whose welfare government is ordained. At every step in this direction, the Nation has been confronted with class tyranny, which is of all tyrannies the most intolerable, for it is ubiquitous in its operation, and weighs perhaps most heavily on those whose obscurity or distance would draw them from the notice of a single despot. Today it is the colored race which is denied by corporations and individuals wielding public authority, rights fundamental in their freedom and citizenship. AT SOME FUTURE TIME IT MAY BE THAT SOME OTHER RACE WILL FALL UNDER THE BAN OF RACE DISCRIMINATION." This last preceding sentence sounds like prophecy from on high. Will the day come when Justice Bradley will want to hide from his decree of the 15th day of October, 1883, and say non est factum? I conclude with great reluctance these brief lines, assuring you that the subject is just opened and if desired by you, I will be glad to give it elaborate attention. I ask no rights and privileges for my race in this country, which I would not contend for on behalf of the white people were the conditions changed, or were I to find proscribed white men in Africa where black rules.

A word more and I am done, as you wish brevity. God may forgive this corps of unjust judges, but I never can, their very memories will also be detested by my children's children, nor am I alone in this detestation. The eight millions of my race and their posterity will stand horror-frozen at the very mention of their names. The scenes that have passed under my eyes upon the public highways, the brutal treatment of helpless women which I have witnessed, since that decision was proclaimed, is enough to move heaven to tears and raise a loud acclaim in hell over the conquest of wrong. But we will wait and pray, and look for a better day, for God still lives and the LORD OF HOSTS REIGNS.

I am, sir, yours, for the Fatherhood of God, and the Brotherhood of man.

H. M. TURNER.
Atlanta, Georgia, January 4th, 1889.

✪ *February 8*

Phineas Franklin Bresee

CHURCH OF THE NAZARENE

December 31, 1838–November 13, 1915

Two competing instincts are often at war within the Christian church. One desires to offer God the best humanity can create in music and art and architecture, and to build strong organizations to preserve and propagate the church's mission. The other instinct fears that all these things subvert the need to rely solely on the power of the Holy Spirit and to carry the gospel to the poor. When Constantine gave official status to the early church, some Christians responded by fleeing to the desert to become monastics. When the medieval church acquired too much power, one result was the Franciscan revolution. When the Church of England was securely established in the 18th century, John Wesley's Methodist revival swept the nation. When Methodism left behind its modest, late 18th-century beginning to become the largest American denomination only 100 years later, there was a pentecostal call for renewal.

Phineas Bresee began his ministry in the Methodist Church, serving for 25 years in Iowa and then for 12 more years in southern California. In both areas, he was a presiding elder for a term, as well as a delegate to the General Conference. He was a member of several General Conference committees. But despite his successful ministry, he was not satisfied. It seemed to Bresee that Methodists had lost the Wesleyan insistence on personal holiness and had failed to follow John Wesley in carrying the gospel to the poor. Once Bresee began to insist on these principles, he felt himself increasingly frozen out by his colleagues.

In 1884, Bresee broke with the Methodists. A year later, he formed the First Church of the Nazarene in Los Angeles, California. "It has been my long cherished desire," he said, "to have a place in the *heart of the city,* which could be made a center of holy fire, and where the gospel could be preached to the poor." The Nazarene movement spread along the Pacific coast and merged with other holiness movements. By the beginning of the 20th century, it had become a national church movement at a time when many denominations, including the Methodists, remained divided between north and south. By the time of his death, the Church of the Nazarene had 800 American congregations, colleges and universities, and mission work in many areas of the world

A reading from a sermon by Phineas Bresee on divine power

There is nothing so gentle, so humble, so unassuming as a Christian. There is nothing — divine paradox — so powerful as a Christian. Not of himself; he of himself, is but weakness. It is the Holy Ghost who is with and in him who bears all power. The Christian prays

> Now let me gain perfection's height,
> Now let me into nothing fall!
> As less than nothing in thy sight;
> And feel that Christ is all in all.

The answer to that prayer, puts the excellency of power into earthen vessels. Every Christian is to be empowered. A weak Christian, a weak church, a weak gospel is a disgrace to Jesus Christ. This does not refer to weakness of body; neither to weakness of intellect; but to weakness of Spiritual life and power — weakness in faith, in that which is supernatural in salvation — not having that strength which God supplies through His eternal Son. To be trying to work out our own salvation in this sinful earth; to be trying to do His work without equipment, is to have defeat, and does not properly represent Him who says, "all power is given unto me...go ye, therefore, and make Christians of all nations."

It is evident that the baptism with the Holy Ghost is the conveyance into men and through men of the "all power" of Jesus Christ — the revelation of Him in the soul. All earth power is only the conditions for heaven power in this work. And the best conditions of manhood whether brought about by earthly or heavenly power form but a basis for the efficient, sufficient power of God in this work. All that possibly can be done for a man or woman in the way of education or intellectual development — the greatest cultivation of the best natural gifts, does not give power to live godly or to do the work of God.

Human nature at its best, under the blessed remedial power of the blood of Jesus, is but a dwelling place from which, or an avenue through which God acts. Of course the dwelling place or avenue is glorified by His presence, as the water in the river-bed makes its banks fresh with life and beauty. There must be conditions of power, but the conditions are utterly useless without the added power....

A human soul can be nothing more than conditions. It may be clean and pure, it may be strong and perfect, but to be kept so and to be enabled to help others, to bring dead men to life — to open blind eyes, and unstop deaf ears — it must have the power of God.

✪ *February 9* ————————————————————————

Eleazar Wheelock

CONGREGATIONAL

April 22, 1711–April 24, 1779

Most of the early New England colleges were founded to train men for the ministry. Dartmouth College is exceptional, in that it was established to train Native Americans so they could be evangelists for their own people. Eleazar Wheelock, its founder, had a lifelong concern for Native American conversions. In 1743, he was approached by a converted Indian, Samson Occom, who had learned about Wheelock's school to prepare young men for college. He asked whether he could be accepted as a student. Wheelock took Occom into his home for four years, arranging for church members to support him, and providing for medical attention when the young man fell ill.

Having educated Occom for ministry, Wheelock looked about for other candidates. He took in two Delawares from New Jersey at the end of 1754 and three others a year later. They studied with the other students already enrolled in the academy. Later, the school was moved to the New Hampshire frontier and renamed to honor William Legge, Earl of Dartmouth, who had responded generously to an appeal brought to England by Occom and another minister. In 1770 Wheelock left the parish he had been serving for many years in Lebanon, Connecticut, to move to Hanover, New Hampshire. The wilderness around the land had to be cleared and log cabins built to house the college. Its first students graduated in 1771. In declining health, the founder held the post of president until his death eight years later. Wheelock's tombstone, in the Dartmouth College cemetery, reads:

> By the gospel he subdues the ferocity of the savage;
> And to the civilized he opened new paths of science.
> Traveler,
> Go, if you can, and deserve
> The sublime reward of such merit.

A reading from letters of Eleazar Wheelock

Tho' my Straitn'd circumstances in the World forbad My doing much for them (Native Americans), Yet I could not but be plotting for them, and devising Some Methods, to Spread the Knowledge of the true God, & only Saviour among Them. And when I have considered the Difficulties attending an English Mission among them, arising from . . . the deep-conceived Prejudices against the English, arising partly from the unrighteous Dealings of Many bad men with them . . . but principally from the Subtle Insinuations of great Numbers of Jesuits, industriously employ'd for that Purpose. And also the almost insuperable Difficulties in learning their Languages, And the Difficulty, if not Impossibility of getting Interpreters, who are capable, & faithfull to communicate Spiritual things in their True Light. And many more, and great Impediments, in the Way of an English Mission among them, which can Scarcely be represented, and Set in a Light Strong enough, to one who is not personally acquainted with the Affair, or intimately acquainted with those who are in it. I say when I have considered these things, it has been Settled in my Mind, the Most likely Expedient, for accomplishing the great Design, is to take of their own Children, (two or more of a Tribe, that they may not Loose their own Language) and give them an Education Among ourselves, under the Tuition, & Guidance of a godly, & Skillful Master; where they may, not only, have means to Make them Schollars, but the best Means to Make them Christians indeed . . . to fit them for the Gospel Ministry among their respective Tribes. It seems to me, the Acquaintance they will get in Such a School, with one another's Person, and Languages (for it is not in general hard for them to learn one-another's Language) and the Friendship they will contract who belong to Tribes. 2, 5, 10, 20, a hundred Miles distant, will probably greatly Subserve the great Design. And besides this it will be a most likely Expedient to remove their Prejudices, attach them to the English & to the Crown of Great Brittain.

And I was not a little Encouraged in this Affair by the Success of the endeavors I us'd . . . in ye Education of Samson Occom who has been usefull . . . beyond what could have been Reasonably expected of an English man & with less than half of the Expence.

AND there is good Reason to think, that if one half which has been, for so many Years past expended in building Forts, manning and supporting them, had been prudently laid out in supporting faithful Missionaries, and School-Masters among them the instructed and civilized Party would have been a far better Defence than all our expensive Fortresses, and prevented the laying waste so many Towns and Villages: Witness the Consequence of sending Mr. Sergeant to Stockbridge, which was in the very Road by which they most usually came upon our People, and by which there has never been one Attack made upon us since his going there.

✪ *February 10*

Penny Lernoux

ROMAN CATHOLIC

January 6, 1940–October 8, 1989

When the United States first enunciated the "Monroe Doctrine," it was advertised as a refusal to allow European power to be projected into the western hemisphere. That may have been so; however, even where European power has been absent, the United States has frequently been present, not so much to protect democratic governments as its own U.S. business interests. The one European power that continues its involvement in Latin America is the Roman Catholic Church. Often it has been a friend of the Latin American ruling class and dictatorial governments, but sometimes it befriends the poor and the oppressed. In the middle of the 20th century, the powers of the Roman Catholic Church and the United States collided dramatically when a generation of Roman Catholic bishops, priests, and activists proclaimed a "liberation theology" and took the side of the poor. North Americans have seldom shown much interest in this subject, but Penny Lernoux spent her life attempting to tell the story.

Lernoux was a journalist and a deeply committed Roman Catholic who initially went to Latin America to work for the United States Information Agency. She stayed on as a freelance writer, sending back articles and books describing South America as she saw it daily. One of the new realities she depicted was the creation of "base communities" in which clergy lived with the poor, explaining the gospel in their terms. This, Lernoux wrote "is an entirely new stance, rejecting the church's old ties to the landed aristocracy and industrial elite for a more critical, even defiant attitude towards existing power groups."

Of course, the church was not alone in challenging the established powers; Communist movements had done so for some time. Christian clergy and lay people often joined with Communists when their aims coincided. This encouraged conservatives to appeal for help from Europe and the United States to confront "atheistic communism," so that sharp divisions widened within the church. Lernoux, however, believed the church leaders in the new movement were not identified with any particular social doctrine, quoting a Brazilian priest, Dom Helder Camara, who said, "We have no objection to private property, provided that each person can own it." She also cited the words of a Uruguayan Jesuit, Juan Luis Segundo, who said, "If Christianity is to withstand the Marxist challenge, we must stop reducing it to a ritualized 'bribing of God' with Masses, sacraments and good intentions. There must be a genuine political and social commitment to Christianity's basic values, particularly love of fellow man."

As elements within the church raised voices of protest against the oppression of the poor, military governments increasingly resorted to violence. Lernoux reported:

> All political parties, labor unions and student federations are outlawed. Anyone critical of the regime is considered a traitor to the state. Punishment ranges from imprisonment or exile to loss of job and/or smear campaigns by the government-controlled press. Following Argentina's example, several of the regimes have eliminated the complications of police arrest. "Enemies of the state" are now kidnapped by a group of unidentified men, never to be seen again. Attempts by family or friends to trace the victim are futile since the police deny all knowledge of his or her existence.

As an American writing for Americans, Lernoux was sensitive to the ways in which, as she reported, "U.S. taxpayers' dollars have not been spent." Often, instead of providing aid, American dollars were used "to train and arm the Honduran military and police, and always with the same objective: to crush any expression of popular aspiration that might endanger the 'stable' business climate in which United Brands and its Honduran partners could exploit the people."

When reporters asked questions about this, government spokespeople acknowledged it, but argued that a stable climate was essential. Lernoux quoted one American official who said, "It is obviously not our purpose or intent to assist a head of state who is repressive. On the other hand, we are working in a lot of countries where the governments are controlled by people who have shortcomings."

Increasingly, Lernoux moved from reporting to harshly criticizing her country's policies. She became a passionate advocate for the poor, and a supporter for members of her church who were committed to the same cause, writing:

> Three decades after World War II, it must again be asked if the support by bribery of right-wing totalitarian governments that have killed thousands of innocent people is morally defensible because "if I don't do it, my competitor will." Or whether it is acceptable to teach Latin-American paramilitary organizations how to make bombs or to instruct governments in press censorship and the persecution of the Catholic Church. That is the United States' record in Latin America since World War II.

On the policy of the Roman Catholic Church in Latin America, she said:

> The choice between a prophetic and a traditional Church also calls into question the cherished ideal of a Church so united that it can speak to and for all people. This ideal denies the existence of class conflict, a reality in Latin America, and neutrality is thus an illusion: either the Church takes a critical position in favor of the poor, or it silently supports existing structures.
>
> The Catholic Church has been severely persecuted in Latin America for denouncing the Defense Department and the immoral business practices of a host of U.S. corporations, yet it is merely asking the American people to respect their own ideals.

In 1989, after 25 years, Penny Lernoux returned to the United States with her husband and child, but in early September of that year she discovered she had cancer. The primary cancer began in her lungs, then spread into her bones and liver where it resisted chemotherapy. Two weeks before her death at the age of 49, she wrote:

> I feel like I'm walking down a new path. It's not physical fear or fear of death, because the courageous poor in Latin America have taught me a theology of life that, through solidarity and our common struggle, transcends death. Rather, it is a sense of helplessness — that I who always wanted to be the champion of the poor am just as helpless — that I, too, must hold out my begging bowl; that I must learn — am learning — the ultimate powerlessness of Christ. It is a cleansing experience. So many things seem less important, or not at all, especially the ambitions.

✪ *February 11* _____

Kamehameha IV

EPISCOPALIAN

February 9, 1834–November 30, 1863

Royal saints are not uncommon on the church calendar. Margaret of Scotland, Elizabeth of Hungary, and Louis of France are a few examples. But they are rather unexpected among Americans. Kamehameha IV of Hawaii did not, in fact, want to be American, using every means at his command to avoid the fate that overtook his island 35 years after his death. In the middle of the 19th century, Hawaii was coveted by England, France, and the United States. Kamehameha, who had traveled both to England and the United States as a young man, had been impressed with the orderly structure of British society. English society also seemed more congenial to a monarch than did the United States. And Kamehameha had had an unfortunate experience with racial prejudice in America. He had no desire to see Hawaii become simply another province of the British Empire, but he believed England could be a useful counterweight against undue American influence.

Part of the English influence that Kamehameha accepted without reservation was the Church of England. He had been educated to the age of 14 by American missionaries, but the solemn dignity of the services he witnessed in England made a lasting impression. He hoped to build an Anglican Cathedral in Honolulu and would have done so had he lived longer. As it was, his successor laid the cornerstone of St. Andrew's Cathedral in his honor six years after his death.

Kamehameha's faith was not a mere matter of political strategy. Central to his vision of an independent kingdom was his concern for his subjects. The influx of English and American merchants and sailors had brought new diseases to ravage the population. The king saw that better health care was essential. When appeals to the legislature for support for hospitals and homes for the elderly produced little response, he turned to the merchants. There he met with greater success. So important was this cause to him that he went door to door himself soliciting funds from his subjects. He succeeded in establishing Queen's Hospital, still the largest civilian hospital in the islands, to provide free medical care for Hawaiians and part Hawaiians. He also sponsored a home for sailors and an agricultural program to foster interest in farming as a way of life. To make his faith accessible to the native population, the king himself translated the Book of Common Prayer and an English hymnal into Hawaiian. But Kamehameha's ambitious vision for his country and people was cut short by his sudden death at the age of 29.

A reading from Kamehameha IV in the Hawaiian Book of Common Prayer

If we are Christians according to the teaching of the Holy Scriptures, we cannot withhold our belief in the Holy Catholic Church established on earth by Jesus Christ our Lord. There are branches of this church in every land. How the church has come down from the times of the apostles to these days in which we live is not a matter about which the generality of men are ignorant. It were useless perhaps to set forth how she has taken root sooner or later all over the world. She is planted in America, in Asia, in Europe, in Africa, in the islands which stud the ocean, and now, behold! She is here with us in these islands of our own.

Let us see how she felt her way and reached us at last. Our ancient idols had been dethroned, the sexes ate together, and the prohibition upon certain articles of food was held in derision by the females to whom it had been a law, the temples were demolished, the *kapu* had become no more than a memory of something that was hateful before, and the priests had no longer any rites to perform — indeed, there were no priests, for their office had died out. These changes came no doubt by the inspiration of the Holy Spirit, acting through blind, unsuspecting agents. These revolutions were greatly furthered and helped along by those devout and devoted men who first brought here and translated into our mother-tongue God's Holy Word, and we, while these lines are being written, see the complete fulfillment of what the Bible enjoins in the establishment here of Christ's church complete in all her functions.

The church is established here in Hawaii through the breathings of the Holy Spirit and by the agency of the chiefs. Vancouver, long ago, was requested to send us the True God; Iolani (Liholiho, the king who, as Kamehameha II, died in London in 1824) then your King, went to a distant and powerful country to hasten the advent of that which our eyes now see and the spirit within us acknowledges, the very church, here planted in Hawaii — but how long we had waited! It is true that the representatives of the various forms of worship had come here, and there had been many controversies, one side generally denying what some other sect had laid most stress on. Now we have grounds to rejoice, and now we may hold fast to the hope that the true Church of God has verily taken root here. In this *Book of Common Prayer* we see all that she prescribes; we see what she rules and enforces; what her offices, her creeds, her system, her support in life, her promises in death; what things we ought to do and leave undone; which things being constantly before our eyes and dutifully followed, we may humbly hope to be indeed her children, and be strengthened to fulfill all the commandments of our blessed Lord, the one Head of the One Church, which we now gladly behold and gratefully acknowledge.

✴ *February 12* _____

Luther Rice

BAPTIST

March 25, 1783–September 25, 1836

The question of free will versus predestination has divided Christians from the early centuries to the present. If we have free will, how can our future be determined? But if God is omnipotent, how can anything be out of the divine control? Congregationalists, as the heirs of John Calvin, inherited a bias toward predestination, but in the rational and liberal atmosphere of the 18th century, that doctrine was often challenged.

Luther Rice grew up a Congregationalist and struggled long with the question, "Whether I would be willing to give Deity a blank and let Him fill up my future destiny as He should please!" Finally, at the age of 22, he decided to "give myself up to the eternal Jehovah, soul and body, for time and eternity to be dealt with as he should see fit." While studying at Williams College and Andover, he, along with a small group of friends, decided to offer himself for foreign mission work.

Fulfilling this commitment, Rice sailed for India in 1812. Among his fellow travelers were Baptist missionaries from England. The long voyage out was filled with theological discussions and searching of Scripture. Adoniram Judson,* a friend who traveled with a second group, was convinced and, arriving in India, was baptized by immersion. Rice soon followed his example. But since Congregationalists could not be asked to support a Baptist missionary, Rice's decision required him to return to New England to seek support from the Baptists. Though for many years he hoped to return, it turned out to be the end of his overseas mission activity.

Back in New England, where the Congregationalists asked for their money back, Rice quickly saw that foreign mission needed a stronger base of support. Traveling to spread this message among Baptist congregations, he became convinced that domestic missionaries were just as necessary. Among those responding to his vision was John Mason Peck,* who became one of the most effective Baptist missionaries in the midwest. In one year, Rice reported,

> I have traveled 6,600 miles — in populous and dreary portions of country — through wilderness and over rivers — across mountains and valleys — in heat and cold — by day and by night — in weariness, and painfulness, and fastings, and loneliness; but not a moment has been lost for want of health; no painful calamity has fallen to my lot; no peril has closed upon me; nor has fear been permitted to prey on my spirits; nor even inquietude to disturb my peace.

In the two decades of ceaseless activity that followed, Rice established a magazine and a college and inspired dozens to offer themselves for the work abroad. When he attended his last Triennial Convention in 1835, membership in the mission society had grown from 8,000 to 600,000. The Convention supported 25 missions and 112 missionaries and now recognized 15 institutions of higher learning within the Baptist camp. No one individual could take credit for all this, but Luther Rice's work had certainly helped make it happen. Rice, himself, found great comfort in the belief that God had shaped all this in carrying out a predetermined plan that enters into the very ground-work of the hope of immortality and glory, that has become established in my bosom; and constitutes the basis of the submission and joyfulness found in my religious experience.... Why should it not be the very joy of our bosoms, that he 'has foreordained whatsoever come to pass?' What can real benevolence desire, but that every thing should 'come to pass,' in the wisest and best manner, to the wisest and best ultimate end? Could not an infinitely wise and good God ordain everything to come to pass in this very way, and to this very end? Such, too, being the fact, is it not evidently the duty and happiness of every one to give up himself in absolute submission to the will of God; and to be pleased that all things are at the disposal and under the control of this infinitely wise and good Being.

I am persuaded that we lose much, very much, of the comforts in religion, which we might otherwise enjoy, by our very negligence in these respects. To be decided Christians — to live for heaven daily, hourly — to be constant, and undeviating, and prompt in the path of duty — to keep a conscience void of offense towards God and towards man; this, this is the way, I doubt not, to let our light shine to glorify God, to enjoy comfort ourselves, and to do good to others. If we fail of this, the fault must be our own. By sincere watchfulness, by serious and attentive consideration, by earnest prayer, and by careful circumspection and diligence, this elevated and happy condition may undoubtedly be attained.

God grant that while I write these things — hoping they may prove acceptable, and perhaps in some degree, even beneficial to you — my own course, and conduct, and conversation, may be, by the effectual operation of the Holy Spirit, in view of these things, modified more and more by the stamp of truth and goodness: "Whatsoever things are true, whatsoever things are honest, whatsoever things are just, whatsoever things are lovely, whatsoever things are of good report." May I be assisted by the grace and good spirit of the Lord, evermore to "think on these things." How happy, how impressively excellent, must be the character that is modified, and molded, and constantly governed, by the enlightening and purifying influence of "The glorious gospel of the blessed God."

Luther Rice trusted God beyond the point many others could understand. It was said he "had great weaknesses. One was excessive hopefulness...." But how could one fail to be hopeful, knowing that God had planned everything for the best?

✪ *February 13*

Emily Greene Balch

QUAKER

January 8, 1867–January 9, 1961

In 1913, Wellesley College made Emily Balch a professor of economics and sociology after she had already spent 17 years on the faculty. But the college made an even more important contribution to her career in 1918 when they terminated her contract. Emily Balch had never been able to draw a sharp line between her academic career and the needs of the world around her. She insisted that her students back up their library research by going to see the conditions they were describing for themselves. She herself served on state and municipal commissions on children, urban planning, industrial education, and immigration. She had participated in movements for women's suffrage, racial justice, control child labor, and for better wages and working conditions.

With the advent of World War I, Balch expanded her horizons by joining the peace movement. In 1915, she served as a delegate to the International Congress of Women at The Hague. She prepared peace proposals for consideration by the combatants and was sent as a delegate by the American Congress to the Scandinavian countries and Russia to urge their governments to initiate mediation offers. She also drew up a position paper on the European colonies that influenced the mandate system later adopted by the League of Nations. However, when she asked for a leave of absence from her college position to work against American involvement in the war, Wellesley fired her instead — thus freeing her to become secretary general of the Women's International League for Peace and Freedom with headquarters in Geneva. She took a staff position at the *Nation* and became a member of the council of the Fellowship of Reconciliation. In the ensuing years she was involved with governments, international organizations, and commission of various sorts and worked on such matters as disarmament, the internationalization of aviation, drug control, and conditions in Haiti which was then garrisoned by American marines.

Brought up as a Unitarian, Emily Balch became a Quaker in 1921, because of their strong pacifist stance. In the '30s, she helped victims of Nazism. In 1946, Balch was awarded the Nobel Peace Prize and finally found herself unable to maintain her pacifist convictions in the light of World War II. The Chairman of the Nobel Committee, Gunnar Jahn, cited her own words in making the presentation: "International unity is not in itself a solution. Unless this international unity has a moral quality, accepts the discipline of moral standards, and possesses the quality of humanity, it will not be the unity we are interested in."

A reading from "An Exploration of the Infinite" by Emily Greene Balch

By a personal God, I mean a being not limited by the attributes of human persons, but a being whose nature is not less than personal. I mean a being adequate to the cosmic immensities of space and power but one, also, certainly not inferior to the intelligence of the greatest intellect we can imagine and not poorer than the purest and strongest love and goodness. How this is possible is difficult to explain or even conceive, but I believe I find evidence of the reality of such a God — the God of the astronomer and the God of the saint. This evidence is what teachers call the "inner light."

Another common position is denial of the possibility of "the supernatural." Like the word "personal" this needs definition. Few "intelligent" or "educated" people today believe in miracles in the old sense. In another sense we may well say that we not only live in the midst of continuous miracles but are miracles ourselves.

Whether this miracle is "supernatural" depends on what we mean by supernatural and what it would be to be above or beyond it.

To a modern mind, it is inconceivable that anything can be contrary to reason, inconsistent with experience or involving a self-contradiction in the universe.

For our own fathers to sit and enjoy music being sung on the other side of the planet would have seemed to call for a supernatural explanation. Yet without even connecting wires the "wireless" brings this about.

To our fathers, the facts that we know about radioactivity and the transformation of elements would have seemed contrary to the law of nature, yet we have had to widen our conceptions to accept these novel revelations of research.

In the field of "psychic" experiences, scientific minds are no longer content with a universal denial but endeavor to investigate them as objectively as any other problem. There is much sober evidence in the field of telepathy or paraphysical perception of which Professor Rhine, at Duke University, is trying to test certain aspects.

As the Curies were baffled by something in their results that did not tally with their equations, so in the curious and often sordid world of mediums, spiritualists and all this tribe — a world clouded with deliberate fraud as well as with emotional states of mind and other deceptive influences — it is by no means clear that there is not a residue which accepted explanations do not cover.

Science suffers whenever there is a refusal to face evidence or accept results, however revolutionary.

There is, however, one thing of which modern man is sure: however much he may have to modify his idea of what is possible in this strange and complex world, he will not have to admit as an explanation for things any type of supernatural causation that is inconsistent with the whole orderly universe.

If Messiah should arise bodily from death, it would mean there was more for us to learn in our efforts to understand than we had expected. It would not overthrow any truth that we had ever truly reached, whatever adjustment our thought might have to make.

Thought and will and emotion, as we know about them, are bound up with the brains and nerves. They are as physical as a beefsteak.

Yet the courage which a beefsteak may help to refresh in an exhausted man is not to be explained in physical terms alone.

Thought and will and emotion are as different, when experienced, as a toothache felt is from a toothache described. Scientific knowledge, however far it is carried, does not even tend to make known to us aspects of facts as experienced. There are worlds with which science does not deal, the world of values being one.

To speak for myself, most of what is commonly called supernatural I believe to be superstition and unreality. But to affirm that nothing is supernatural, in a sense which would limit reality to these dimensions of experience that are all we, in a scientific sense, know, would seem to me "brash" in the extreme. Let us beware of positing barriers in a world as yet so incompletely understood.

✪ *February 14* ———————————————————

Charles Colcock Jones

PRESBYTERIAN

December 20, 1804–March 16, 1863

In the years leading up to the Civil War, while southern Christians exerted themselves to defend their "peculiar institution" against the growing vehemence of the northern abolitionists, a few southerners simply concentrated on evangelizing the black population. Charles Colcock Jones was one of them. A native of Georgia, he grew up on a plantation but went north to study at the Presbyterian seminaries in Andover and Princeton. After graduating, he was licensed to preach in 1830 and spent a year as pastor of the First Presbyterian Church in Savannah, Georgia, before he returned to Liberty County where he was born. At that time, educating black people was often prohibited by law, but Jones took it on himself to teach them anyway.

His talents were such that he was twice called on to serve as professor of church history in the Columbia Seminary in South Carolina, yet each time he returned to missionary work and educational ministry in his home county until, in 1850, he became secretary of the Board of Domestic Missions of the Presbyterian Church and moved to Philadelphia. After seven years in that position, his health began to fail, so he returned to Georgia for the last six years of his life.

In addition to many tracts and papers, Jones wrote *Religious Instruction for Negroes in the Southern States* (Savannah, 1837), *Suggestions on the Instruction of Negroes in the South* (1855), and a *History of the Church of God*, which was edited by his eldest son and published after his death.

A reading from the work of Charles Colcock Jones

We are prepared now to take up the obligation of the church of Christ in the slave-holding States to impart the Gospel of Salvation to the Negroes within those States. That obligation is imposed upon us in the first instance by the providence of God.

This follows undeniably from all our previous statements, in the history of their religious instruction, and in the sketch of their moral and religious condition. But it may be of some service to be particular under this head. It was by the permission of Almighty God, in his inscrutable providence over the affairs of men, that the Negroes were taken from Africa and transported to these shores. The inhabitants of the Colonies at their first introduction had nothing to do with the infamous traffic, and were, we may say, universally opposed to it. The iniquity of the traffic and of their first introduction, rests upon the Mother Country.

Being brought here they were brought as slaves; in the providence of God we were constituted masters; superiors; and constituted their guardians. And all the laws in relation to them, civilly, socially, and religiously considered, were framed by ourselves. They thus were placed under our control, and not exclusively for our benefit but for theirs also.

We could not overlook the fact that they were men; holding the same relations to God as ourselves — whose religious interests were certainly their highest and best, and that our first and fundamental duty was to provide to the extent of our ability, for the perpetual security of those interests. Our relations to them and their relations to us, continue the same to the present hour, and the providence of God still binds upon us the great duty of imparting to them the Gospel of eternal life.

There has been neglect — shall it be said, a criminal neglect? I feel it. Others feel it. The whole country sees it. Can there be no reformation? Shall the ministers of Jesus Christ never be moved with compassion on the multitudes who faint and are scattered abroad as sheep having no shepherd? Shall their hearts' desire and prayer to God never be that this people may be saved? Shall they never be attracted and drawn towards this people by their very spiritual destitution and miseries, and spend and be spent for them, constrained by the love of Christ, towards their own souls? Alas! it is the darkest feature in all this dark scene that the ministers of the Gospel, taken as a body, feel no more and do no more for the salvation of the Negroes in the United States! Let no one suppose that we wish the church thrown into a state of excitement on the subject; and the good that has been done, and now is doing, and the many able and efficient ministers in this field to be overlooked and buried in oblivion. Let no one suppose that we wish this work to be represented and urged before the country, as the great work to be done, to which all other works of benevolence are to contribute, and in comparison with which they are nothing worth. Let no one suppose that we desire ministers to form great societies and distribute agents over the land, to arouse their brethren to their duty. Far, very far from any thing of this kind are our views of propriety and our impressions of duty. On the contrary, there are organizations and associations enough in existence through which every thing can be done, necessary to be done by them in the religious instruction of the Negroes. What is required is that every minister do his own duty in his own sphere of ministerial action; let him begin with himself first, and then if opportunity offers, let him seek to influence others, in some of the ways already pointed out.

I would commend the work also, to the Members of the Church of Christ.

You are expected to be forward to every good word and work. Here is an abundant opportunity for doing good opened before you. Enter into it for the improvement of your own graces, as well as for the salvation of souls. All your zeal for missions may find ample scope for exercise here. Be forward to superintend schools, to take classes, to act on committees of instruction, and be not weary in well doing, for in due season you shall reap if you faint not.

I would commend the work also to every Lover of his Country.

The moral and religious improvement of two millions eight hundred thousand persons, must be identified with our individual peace and happiness, and with our national prosperity and honor. "Righteousness exalteth a nation, but sin is a reproach to any people."

✪ February 15 _____

Mev Puleo

ROMAN CATHOLIC

January 26, 1963–January 12, 1996

The power of pictures is well known. One of them, we are often told, is worth a thousand words. Mev Puleo didn't write many words, but the pictures she took spoke volumes and changed lives. Her own life had been changed early on by what she saw. At 14, she went to Brazil with her parents and rode up the hill overlooking the harbor at Rio de Janeiro to see the world-famous statue of Christ holding out his arms. On one side, as she looked, she saw opulent homes with swimming pools but on the other side were shacks of the poorest sort and children dressed in rags begging for coins. What does it mean, she asked herself, to be a Christian in a world of such contradictions? As a Christian, raised by Roman Catholic parents, she was able to understand that part of the meaning was to be found in suffering — by embracing it, not avoiding it. She wrote:

> When I was in my early teens, a thought took hold of me: Jesus didn't die to save us from suffering — he died to teach us how to suffer.... I'd rather die

young, having lived a life crammed with meaning, than to die old, even in
security, but without meaning.

"Sometimes," she added with brutal honesty, "I actually mean it."

The priest who presided at her funeral said, "Such are the dangers of our
high and holy thoughts," because Mev Puleo did die young, having lived
a life crammed with meaning. As the sight of poverty first aroused her to
think about life's meaning, she made her greatest impact on others through
her pictures.

In college, Mev Puleo worked at the St. Louis Catholic Worker House,
where she saw the effect of poverty in her own country. She earned graduate
degrees in theology, but everything she learned convinced her more deeply
of the power of images. She said, "I believe less in theology and more in
God, because I believe that in theology there is only so much you can say
about God."

After graduation, Puleo became a photographer, traveling the third world
to conduct interviews and take pictures. In 1994, she published a collection
of these pictures and interviews under the title, *The Struggle Is One: Voices
and Visions of Liberation.*

A well-known Protestant theologian, Robert McAfee Brown,* wrote in
the introduction:

> If I were to choose a single book by means of which to introduce North Amer-
> icans to the real meaning of liberation theology, it would be this book. For
> liberation theology is not about dogmas or documents or church councils or
> even social analysis, nearly so much as it is about people. God's people.

Mev Puleo said, "This book gives voice to the struggle and puts a face on
those who struggle." She continued,

> Here we will meet the world famous and the often anonymous midwives of
> change. Here we will meet the persons behind the personalities — the pilgrims,
> pioneers and prophets of our day.
>
> Here we will meet poets and mystics who know that God is dreaming with
> the community for a new world of justice and joy.
>
> Here we will meet the martyrs and saints who, like the prophet Ezekiel, are
> blowing the spirit of hope and life into the brittle bones of suffering and death.
>
> Hear, then, their voices and their visions.
>
> Hear their journeys, their turning points, their choices. Hear their insights
> and understandings. Hear their interpretations of church conflicts. Hear their
> hopes for the future of liberation theology, for women in the church, for the
> birth of an ecologically-grounded spirituality.
>
> Hear from the poor their word for the rich.
>
> Hear from the privileged, who have opted for the poor, their message for
> those who wish to make that same choice.
>
> Hear the personal invitation to solidarity from your sisters and brothers
> South of the border. Hear the prayers and desires of this hopeful, struggling
> people.

> Hear in their words the echo of your own struggles and desires. And see in their faces a reflection of your own.

Newly married, she died just before her 33rd birthday of a malignant brain tumor. Fr. John Kavanagh, with whom she published a second book, *Faces of Poverty, Faces of Christ,* said, "She had wanted to give the poor a face, a voice. She always wanted to be identified with them. And so it came to pass: by the time of her last days, you could see them all in her face — the poor of Bosnia, the hungry of Haiti, the powerless of Brazil.... She became the poor she loved."

✸ *February 16*

Friedrich Konrad Dietrich Wyneken

LUTHERAN

May 13, 1810–May 4, 1876

"Although I wasn't supposed to begin my missionary activity in Ohio," wrote Friedrich Konrad Dietrich Wyneken, "I was forced by luck, as the world speaks of it, to minister in Allen and Putnam Counties, because I found a few German settlers who hadn't heard a sermon in years. They tearfully begged me to stay with them awhile. I stayed in two settlements for eight days. I preached every day, one of the days I preached twice. I confirmed a young husband, who had been instructed, but hadn't as yet received Holy Communion. I baptized 13 children, (ten of them at the same time, most of them almost fully grown up) a mother of two children, and a grown up, 18-year-old girl."

Wyneken had come to America from Germany in 1838 to serve new regions as settlers began moving there. He began his ministry in Baltimore before heading west on a missionary journey for the Pennsylvania Synod. They intended to send him somewhat beyond the Mississippi. However, the conditions he encountered in Ohio, Indiana, and Michigan were so difficult that he felt compelled to offer his help to German settlers there. There were simply not enough pastors to provide the most basic pastoral care for the people of these areas. Their hunger for religious leadership was deep; resources were few. Wyneken set out to do what he could but, once again, he was "forced by luck, as the world speaks of it" to alter his plans. Illness compelled him to return to Germany, where he corresponded with church leaders there, telling them about the great need he had witnessed. He requested clergy from Germany to minister to German settlers in the upper midwest in an appeal called *The Distress of the German Lutherans in North America.*

Not all settlers had been eager for Wyneken's ministry. He described rejection as well in *Distress,* yet this did not deter him:

After being rebuffed by a settler, and because I had no one to direct me, I had to pass up a whole settlement which for seven years had been without Word or Sacrament. A native of Hamburg, whom I soon found working in front of his house, calmly left me standing in the rain and went into the house muttering only "Is that so" when he heard why I had come. In a town on the Wabash Canal, on a Sunday afternoon, I almost had to drag the men out of whiskey bars, in which I succeeded only after haggling with them for a long time, although the majority of them had not heard a German sermon as long as they had been in America and they understood no English. I could still cite some, though not many, additional examples of such gross indifference.

Perhaps you, dear Christian, would say; "Forget about them, if they want it that way"; but, dear soul, ask yourself and see how it was with you before the Lord touched your heart. Did he win with one stroke? Look at the Lord! Did He wait until we came to Him, or did he not rather come down to us? Was He not the fire in His Word which softened our hearts? Where would you and I and all Christians be, had not the Lord searched for the lost?! Should it not rather soften our heart when we see the terrible danger of the hardening of the heart before our very eyes, to which all our brothers must finally come if they do without the Word and the Sacraments still longer? Who is to blame? Would not the church long since have been obliged, like a good mother, to bestir herself, and with the help of her servants to go after the languishing children who are so miserably dying away? But now imagine thousands of families spread out over this wide stretch of land — and parents go on and die without hearing God's Word; no one awakens them or warns them, no one consoles them. Behold, young and old are lying on their deathbeds, the soul does not even possibly think of preparing itself for the serious judgment; but the servant of the Lord could direct the lost one to the Holy God Who, without Christ, is a consuming fire, but, with Christ, is a forgiving Father. . . . Oh, what a blessing the messenger of peace would be, who would come with words of absolution for the repenting soul and with the Sacrament of the body and blood of Christ, the sacrament which could secure the doubting, wandering soul and direct its eyes to the body which was broken and the blood which was shed for the sinner for the forgiveness of his sin. How many thousands die unprepared and go unconsoled into eternity?

The response to his appeal was gratifying. A pastor named Wilhelm Loehe recruited dozens of pastors who migrated to the United States to serve the German communities across the expanding frontier. Twenty-two of them were personally trained by Loehe.

After recovering from his illness, Wyneken came back to America to serve in Fort Wayne, Indiana. At about this same time, a band of German Lutherans arrived in Missouri, refugees from an edict merging various Protestant groups in Germany. They were founding a new ecclesiastical body which would become the Lutheran Church–Missouri Synod. Wyneken offered important assistance in the formation of the LCMS and was elected its second president, serving between 1850 and 1864. During those years, Wyneken continued to travel widely among the congregations supporting their ministries. His pastoral instincts for the spiritual needs of the settlers left their mark on the formative years of Lutheranism in frontier America.

❂ *February 17*

Clara Swain
METHODIST

July 18, 1834–1910

In 1869, most women in America were trapped within the limited sphere assigned to them by a male society. Clara Swain was not to be so constrained. She became a physician, and, as if that were not enough, went on to become the first fully qualified female missionary in a place where she had to develop her own medical facilities. The youngest of ten children, Swain was a willful child. She had been pampered, and expected to get what she wanted. At the same time, however, she showed compassion for neighborhood animals, especially those that were hurt or seemed lost. She loved attending Sunday worship and the opportunity to hear noted preachers of the day. Listening to their sermons, she felt moved to devote herself to others. She often took notes, reflecting deeply on how she might apply these messages to her life. Driven by that vision Swain, attended medical school and prepared for her life as a Christian missionary.

She was called to India because there was an orphanage there, supported by the Methodists. In addition to providing a home, they also instructed people about hygiene and physiology. Mrs. Thomas, the director, dreamed of it becoming a full-fledged medical mission and had solicited the support of both Indian and English officials. At length, an Indian agreed to defray the cost if a woman from America could be found to manage it. Thomas wrote to a Mrs. Gracey, herself a former missionary, with the request, and Gracey went to the Philadelphia Woman's Medical College to seek a suitable person for the job. Clara Swain's medical and Christian credentials seemed to fill the bill. After much prayerful consideration, she accepted.

Swain found Indian women were neglected, so devoted attention to some of the most underserved — especially those whose caste kept them from getting proper care available to others. Ironically, the higher-caste women were the most secluded, therefore not free to seek medical help. When women received treatment at all, it was usually from untrained female barbers.

Swain's initial journey to India was harrowing and exhausting. She wrote: "The latter part of our voyage was very rough and I was too sick to write, and I had five sick ones to look after besides myself . . . I cannot bear to think of the sea, it treated me so badly." Yet her determination remained unshaken despite so many obstacles: baggage containing many of her medical supplies was delayed; the horse that was to take her from Bombay would not move; tigers roamed the outskirts of the village; she missed her train to her next stop and was often unable to procure food. Nevertheless, she finally arrived at her destination, Bareilly, in January, 1870.

Swain began work immediately. There were Christian women there, some Indians, and one missionary. The missionary knew the language, which got the medical work off to a quick start. In that first year, Swain treated over 1,000 patients and trained more than a dozen new medical students to engage in the work. Within four years, she had constructed the Women's Hospital and Medical School — the only institution of its kind in all Asia. This accomplishment was almost miraculous in itself. There was some available land, but it was owned by a devout Muslim who vowed to allow no Christian missionaries in the city. Since timidity was not in Swain's nature, she prayed, then went to him and requested a gift of land for her hospital. He is reported to have received her with courtesy and said: "Take it, take it; I give it to you with much pleasure for that purpose."

In addition to her medical work, Swain was always looking for opportunities to share her faith. She found women in India whose religious knowledge was so limited that they worshiped her sewing machine. To such women she brought her message of Christian love and grace. Danger, near death, and disease did not stop her from proclaiming Christ's presence among the people of India, and to serve them in his name with all her skill. But she often considered the cost of her choice. Writing home, she observed,

> After eighteen months of the religious life of America and the many precious privileges enjoyed there, it seems harder to settle down to the life here. I miss the church services much more than I did when I was here before.

She also said:

> I have sometimes felt tempted to give up my work here, but then the thought comes to me that I can do more by remaining here....

In 1909, Swain's letters were published as *A Glimpse of India.*

Too rarely do we witness the kind of Christian commitment that seeks the needs of others before one's own. Swain's service to the world and the church is a reflection of the grace she herself received, and does honor to Him in whose name she served.

✪ *February 18* _____

Alexander Campbell

DISCIPLES OF CHRIST

September 12, 1788–March 4, 1866

Unity among Christians based on the Bible alone has been a beguiling dream of divided Christians for centuries. Many have proclaimed this standard, only to discover they have merely created yet one more division. The "Campbellite" movement, or Disciples of Christ, began with just such a goal, yet it too has become simply another voice on the American religious scene. Alexander Campbell was born in Ireland, the son of Thomas Campbell, who had first been an Anglican and then a Presbyterian. Thomas worked for peace in his turbulent country, particularly striving to reunite two warring Presbyterian groups. His efforts damaged his heath, and he was advised to go to America to recover, which he did in 1807. Alexander followed two years later. Before that, he had attended the University of Glasgow, where he was exposed to the writing of John Locke, Isaac Newton, David Hume, Rousseau, and others.

Meanwhile, his father had begun a ministry to some small Presbyterian congregations in Pennsylvania and caused trouble by inviting non-Presbyterians with no church of their own to share in the communion service. Rebuked by the Presbytery and Synod, the Campbells entered into a relationship with the Baptists. Finally, 17 years later, they created a new church. They hoped to bring about a new Reformation and "to rid the world of denominationalism" by a complete restoration of primitive Christianity. In 1832, the Campbells, who called their association the "Disciples of Christ," or the "Reformers," united with a similar movement headed by Barton Stone.* Stone's followers called themselves simply "Christians." In 1906, the Disciples of Christ divided again. The smaller group adopted "Churches of Christ" as its title, but in some sections of the country, both use "Churches of Christ" and "Christians" interchangeably with "Christian Church."

Although various significant figures shaped the early movement, Alexander Campbell had the most commanding personality; but he lacked the temperament to provide stability. It was said of him that "his weakness was his ambition" and that he would rather have been "first man in a village than the second man in a city." The elder Campbell, Stone, and a former Baptist, Walter Scott,* all possessed humility and sympathy to balance Alexander Campbell's intellect and gifts of leadership. Alexander Campbell produced 60 volumes of writings, including a version of the New Testament and a hymnal. In 1840, he founded Bethany College, serving as its president until his death. He was a member of the Virginia Constitutional Convention of 1829 and became wealthy through his managerial abilities and methods of scientific farming.

A reading from *The Christian System* by Alexander Campbell

The Bible alone is the Bible only, in word and deed, in profession and practice; and this alone can reform the world and save the church. Judging others we once judged ourselves, there are not a few who are advocating the Bible alone, and preaching their own opinions. Before we applied the Bible alone to our views, or brought our views and religious practice to the Bible, we plead the old theme, "The Bible alone is the religion of Protestants." But we found it an arduous task, and one of twenty years' labor, to correct our diction and purify our speech according to the Bible alone; and even yet we have not wholly practically repudiated the language of Ashdod. We only profess to work and walk by the rules which will inevitably issue in a pure speech, and in right conceptions of that pure, and holy, and celestial thing called Christianity — in faith, in sentiment, and in practice.

A deep and an abiding impression that the power, the consolations, and joys — the holiness and happiness — of Christ's religion were lost in the forms and ceremonies, in the speculations and conjectures, in the feuds and bickerings of sects and schisms, originated a project many years ago for uniting the sects, or rather the Christians in all the sects, upon a clear and scriptural bond of union — upon having a "thus saith the Lord," either in express terms, or in approved precedent, "for every article of faith, and item of religious practice." This was offered in the year 1809, in the "Declaration and Address" of the Washington Association, Pennsylvania. It was first tendered to the parties that confessed the Westminster creed; but equally submitted to the Protestants of every name, making faith in Christ and obedience to him the only test of Christian character, and the only bond of church union, communion, and co-operation. It was indeed approved by all; but adopted and practiced by none, except the few, or part of the few, who made the overture.

None of us who either got up or sustained that project, was then aware of what havoc that said principle, if faithfully applied, would have made of our views and practices on various favorite points. . . . We flatter ourselves that the principles are now clearly and fully developed by the united efforts of a few devoted and ardent minds, who set out determined to sacrifice everything to truth, and follow her wherever she might lead the way: I say, the principles on which the church of Jesus Christ — all believers in Jesus as the Messiah — can be united with honor to themselves, and with blessings to the world; on which the gospel and its ordinances can be restored in all their primitive simplicity, excellency, and power, and the church shine as a lamp that burneth to the conviction and salvation of the world: — I say, the principles by which these things can be done are now developed, as well as the principles themselves, which together constitute the original gospel and order of things established by the Apostles.

✪ *February 19* _____

Edward Taylor

CONGREGATIONAL

1642?–June 24, 1729

Very little is known about the life of Edward Taylor. Even his verse lay unread for two centuries until the manuscripts were discovered in Yale's library. Now he is acknowledged to have been one of the most prolific and creative poets in colonial America. Evidently, he was born in England and may have been educated at Cambridge University. He would have grown up in the days of Oliver Cromwell's Commonwealth. With the restoration of the monarchy, however, clergy were required to sign an Act of Uniformity with the established church. As a Puritan, Taylor would have been unable to teach or preach in England. A diary records his Atlantic crossing in 1668 and his arrival in New England, where he enrolled at Harvard as an upperclassman.

For one accustomed to English life and academic surroundings, it must have seemed like a radical change to find himself in Westfield, Connecticut — a frontier settlement in the midst of the virgin forest. Indian attack was an ever-present threat, settlers were called to worship by drums instead of church bells, while the clergy farmed to earn their living. It took Taylor eight years to get the first church organized, but it was evidently a mutually satisfactory relationship since Taylor served that congregation until his death 50 years later.

Few parishioners realized at the time that the farmer and clergyman was turning his experience into poetry. Among Taylor's early subjects were the changing face of nature ("The Ebb & Flow") and tragedies of private life ("Upon Wedlock, & Death of Children"). He produced metrical paraphrases of the psalms and a metrical history of Christianity 20,000 lines long. His best works were meditations inspired by preparation for his sermons and for administering the sacraments. Though he opposed liberalizing tendencies that would permit all members to take part in the Lord's Supper, Taylor's meditations revealed his own deep humility. Often, he confesses his unworthiness as he prepares himself to receive God's gift of grace.

A reading from *Christographia* by Edward Taylor

It is natural for persons to Honour and advance such as honour and advance them. Everyone is a friend to him that gives gifts: this is testified to us by the Holy Ghost (Pro. 19. 6). The Law of Nature teacheth us to love them that love us (Matt. 5. 46). And Grace doth not debilitate, or disgrace, but regulate, and exalt the Law of Nature, and improove it, to attend matters not Contrary to, but above the Precepts of the Law of Nature. And here is Such an improovement of it to be made, viz, in Admiring and Honouring God, and Christ, for Honouring, and advancing us and our Nature unto this Personall Union to Christ. What greater argument to move thereto, than what our text affords us? Here is God preparing our Nature, and fitting of it for union to the Seconde person of the Godhead. Here are laid out the Wonders of Divine Operation. Further here is expresst the Highest Divine Love, and Honour, I thinke, that is possible to be expressed to any Creature. For it is the highest Glory, and Elevation, that Created nature can be advanced unto, to be personally united to the Godhead. And so to exalt a person onely by the Personality of the Son, So that the person of the Son of God, is the Proper, and onely person of this Manhood or Individual

Embodied Humanity assumed in which is no humane personality. I judge it impossible for Created nature to be advanced to higher honour, and Glory than this, unless it were possible for Created Nature to be Deified, and made Deity itselfe. But this is as absolutely impossible, as it is for Godhead to be made, or Increated Nature to be Created. Hence this Honour is higher, and brighter, than any that either was, or shall be Conferred on any other Creature. Whether Fraile man, or fulgent Angell. But yet it is Conferrd on our nature, and so on us. Angell nature never had it; nor shall any other have it (Heb. 1. 16). Hence then here being Conferred the Highest Honour, and Glory, that God Confers on any, it necessitates the greatest Love, and Grace in God to be the reason, and ground of it. Now where the Greatest Love, and Favour, Honour and Glory are in truth bestown, there the argument cometh most forceably to Constrain to the returns of the Highest Honour, and Praise, Glory, and Advancing that can be given. And so we see by this rule, that this Worke, and Duty falls on us. And therefore it Should press us on so to lay out ourselves to Honour, and advance the Glory of God, and Christ for the Same.

✠ *February 20*

Henriette Delille

ROMAN CATHOLIC

March 11?, 1813–November 17, 1862

Six weeks before Abraham Lincoln signed the Emancipation Proclamation, the following obituary appeared in a New Orleans newspaper:

> Last Monday died one of these women whose obscure and retired life was nothing remarkable in the eyes of the world but is full of merit before God. . . . Without ever having heard speak of philanthropy, this poor maid had done more good than the great philanthropists with their systems so brilliant yet so vain.
>
> Worn out by work, she died at the age of 50 years after a long and painful illness borne with the most edifying resignation.

It had taken a lifetime to win that recognition, and there had been countless obstacles along the way. The obstacles were freely embraced. Henriette Delille was born into one of the oldest families of free people of color in New Orleans. Her great-great-grandmother Nanette had been a slave, but she and her daughter and granddaughter were mistresses of aristocrats. Like most young women of this background, Henriette was given the best education available. She read French literature, played music well, and learned to dance with grace. From her mother she also learned nursing skills and the use of herbs for medicinal purposes.

With her light skin and cultured taste, Henriette Delille could have married well or chosen the same comfortable life as her mother, as mistress to one of the New Orleans elite. Henriette's sister, Cecilia, chose her mother's path, but Henriette met a French nun, Sister St. Martha Fontier, whose life of faith and charity in the black community so impressed the young woman that she set out to imitate her. By the time she was 14 years old, Delille had become a lay catechist, teaching slaves on the plantations about the Christian faith. Several like-minded friends gathered with her on Sundays to pray at the bishop's chapel and at St. Louis Cathedral. During the week, they would visit the sick and the aged, feed the hungry, and travel up and down the levees of the Mississippi River to conduct catechism classes wherever opportunities presented themselves.

As a person of color, Delille was barred by law from joining a white religious community. When she sought to establish one for women of color, the bishop initially denied her request. Delille was undeterred, however, and when her mother died, she sold her property and with several other free black women formed the Sisters of the Presentation of the Blessed Virgin Mary. They began a ministry to the sick and poor in the black community, living in a small, rented house with five elderly women and supporting themselves by begging. Often they went to bed hungry. Sometimes they would give their own meals to those poorer than they. The hardships discouraged some of the little community and they left to seek a community in France or return to secular life. It was at that point that Delille wrote in her diary the simple prayer that continued to guide her life: "I believe in God. I hope in God. I love and I want to live and die for God."

In 1842, impressed by the strength of her determination, the bishop permitted Delille to create a new order to be known as the Sisters of the Holy Family. Official recognition did not make life easier. Ridicule, hard work, and extreme poverty remained the sisters' lot. Nonetheless, more women joined the community, and they were able to expand their work. In 1850, the order founded a school for girls. In 1860, they opened a home for sick and needy black people, some of them slaves who had been cast off by their owners as no longer useful to them. Delille was also able to purchase a home the order could use as a community center where slaves and free black people could come to socialize and to learn the Christian faith

Remarkably, all this was accomplished within a slave-owning society that Delille attempted to reshape into a more Christlike image. Having rejected the role of a Creole mistress to a wealthy white man, Delille and her order campaigned against the New Orleans custom of plaçage, in which wealthy white men and light-complexioned young women of color entered into extramarital partnerships. Delille made efforts to enable sacramental marriages between black slaves, which were illegal in slaveholding states because slaves were not considered human beings, but property.

When Henriette Delille died, worn out by incessant work and privations, she was not yet fifty. The Civil War had not yet been won, so abolition had not been declared in the south. At the time of her death, there were still only 12 sisters in the order and they had not yet been permitted to wear a distinctive habit. But the foundations were well laid. The order grew to include 250 members and to work in several states, along with countries in South America and West Africa. Their work in New Orleans continues, and the Lafon Nursing Home of the Holy Family, now 153 years old, may well be the oldest nursing home in the United States.

✪ *February 21* _____

Emily Malbone Morgan

EPISCOPALIAN

December 10, 1862–February 27, 1937

When Henry VIII dissolved religious orders in England, his motive was less their supposed corruption than his desire to break their power and take their lands and property for the crown. Anglicanism did not reestablish religious orders until the 19th century, but when they did so, their structure continued to follow the medieval pattern. Monks and nuns again lived in communities, where they took the traditional vows of poverty, chastity, and obedience. Although they engaged in good works such as teaching and nursing, they continued to live separated from "the world" in monasteries and convents.

Although raised in the Anglo-Catholic tradition in the Episcopal Church, Emily Malbone Morgan envisioned a different model — a community not set apart from the culture, but centered on intercessory prayer and a ministry of hospitality. At 22, she formed the Society of the Companions of the Holy Cross as an order for lay women who would take lifetime vows but come together only during the summer for a shared retreat at the community house in Massachusetts. Members of the order pledged themselves to six ideals: the Life of Intercession, Social Justice, Christian Unity, Simplicity of Life, Thanksgiving, and the Way of the Cross. The commitment to social justice was worked out in creating hospitality houses for female mill workers and their children. Morgan gave lectures and wrote to earn money for these houses. By the beginning of the 20th century, the order had grown to include more than 250 members around the world and by the beginning of the 21st, it included some 800 members. The order made a significant impact on the social consciousness of the Episcopal Church, but there is no way to measure its accomplishments through its deep commitment to intercessory prayer.

Excerpts from the letters of Emily Malbone Morgan to the Society of the Companions of the Holy Cross

We are an order of women living in the world with a desire for the stronger development of the spiritual life in ourselves and others, and we must develop that life along the lines of the world in which we live and with a sympathetic sense of the needs of the nineteenth century. Any pseudo-nunlike life would be at best but a weak imitation of those who possess a sacred vocation to which most of us have not been called. What we must try to understand by our association together is our own vocation as that of women living in the world and having individual influence, social or otherwise, banded together to meet the serious religious, educational, and social problems of our age, first by prayer and then by battle. We are distinctly called to understand intelligently the great yearning needs of the century so nearly gone and the century just dawning. Emphasis should be laid therefore on the intellectual as well as on the spiritual life of such a house, by a study of great movements, of Church history, of social problems and conditions. We might elaborate indefinitely on the possibilities of such a house, and on that which might grow into a larger work than just the summer months of association together, to interpret the life of the Church to a larger number of people and to grow in that power which makes for righteousness. It is always far better, however, to leave God and the future to settle our plans and the details of them. . . .

Indeed the breaking of bread at the ordinary meal is one of the loveliest symbols of human fellowship. I can remember some years ago at one of my houses when twenty of us sat down at table and nine different nationalities were represented. At my right hand was one of great promise who I feel will do much for her race, the African race in the United States, and on the left hand sat one of the simplest of human souls, yet from a world's point of view rich beyond the dreams of avarice. The feeling came to me so naturally and delightfully as I sat there that we represented a fragment of the Kingdom of Heaven when we shall all sit down together at the Heavenly banquet. It cannot come all at once, because we are shortsighted and very human and particular, and condemn even a woman's soul because she eats with her knife, and think others strange because they prefer chopsticks to knives and forks. These funny little human shibboleths that prevent us so often from looking into the real faces of each other and make us cheat ourselves of real friendships because we are so proper and other people are so queer!

I think during the past four years at Adelynrood we have laid the right accent on our life in relation to our hospitality toward others, but I am hoping each year our prayers may pass into more and more loving actions of social graciousness that shall give them a living reality. St. John the Baptist in preparation for the mission of a great prophet must stand as the type of the ascetic, the recluse, the dweller in solitude, the type of monasticism. We learned during the Retreat that it is only the exceptional person who is called to the special mission of prophet-reformer or religious, and that the calling of most of us is to the highest living out of life under ordinary circumstances and to follow Christ in all the varied social relations of life; therefore, that the cultivation of all social gifts on our part lies in the line of ordinary duty.

✪ *February 22*

Luther Lee

METHODIST

November 30, 1800–1889

In the years leading up to the Civil War, Presbyterians and Baptists were divided, north and south, by the question of slavery. Methodists, on the other hand, were divided internally in the north as well, with Free Methodists and Wesleyan Methodists refusing to belong to a body that countenanced slave-holding among any of its members. Feelings ran high on the subject and northerners were by no means of one mind. Luther Lee was one of those who left the Methodist Church to join the Wesleyan Methodists because of the slavery issue and although his ministry was in New York and New England, he was attacked several times by angry mobs. Nevertheless, he declared, "My life would appear imperfect indeed if nothing should be said about my connection with that wonderful institution, the 'Underground Railroad.'" His home in Syracuse was a major station of the railroad and he challenged the authorities to stop him. He wrote in his autobiography:

> I planted my feet on the rock of eternal right. I affirmed that slavery is wrong — a moral wrong, a violation of every commandment of the decalogue, that no law can make it right to practice it, or support it, or to in any way aid and abet it; that the Fugitive Slave Law is a war upon God, upon his law, and upon the rights of humanity; that to obey it, or to aid in its enforcement, is treason against God and humanity, and involves a guilt equal to the guilt of violating every one of the ten commandments. I never had obeyed it — I never would obey it. I had assisted thirty slaves to escape to Canada during the last month. If the United States authorities wanted any thing of me, my residence was at 39 Onondaga Street. I would admit that they could take me and lock me up in the Penitentiary on the hill; but if they did such a foolish thing as that I had friends enough in Onondaga County to level it with the ground before the next morning. The immense throng rose upon their feet and shouted, "We will do it! We will do it!

For many, the phrase "underground railroad" was a figure of speech. For Lee, at least, the "railroad" part of the phrase was quite accurate. "The fact was," Lee wrote, "I had friends, or the slave had, connected with the railroad at Syracuse, of whom I never failed to get a free pass in this form: 'Pass this poor colored man,' or 'poor colored woman,' or 'poor colored family,' as the case might be. The conductors on the route understood these passes, and they were never challenged." He added, "My name, the name of my street, and the number of my residence, came to be known as far south as Baltimore, and I did a large business." The president of the railroad was a supporter of Lee's work and provided free tickets to the fugitives so they could safely ride to Canada. As many as 30 a month passed through Lee's hands in this way. He noted with some satisfaction that one of the fugitives he assisted came from a plantation owned by a noted slave-driver named H. F. Slater, who "owns the choicest pew in the big M. E. Church in Baltimore" and who took slaves on speculation for the southern market.

In the same way that Lee campaigned against slavery, he also campaigned against Unitarianism. On one occasion, he and his opponent debated the doctrine of the Trinity for 11 nights at the city hall, each giving two speeches per evening. "Mr. May was a remarkable man," wrote Lee, "not so much for his profound erudition, as for his gentlemanly bearing and benevolence. He was better known in the city than I was, but I offset his prestige by a frank, open, honest, and earnest manner." Lee could recognize his opponent's strengths because his approach was always reasoned, so much so that he was known as "Logical Luther Lee." His lectures in theology are unusual among evangelicals for their appeal first to nature and then to Scripture. Lee took logic as far as it would go before turning to revelation for fuller insights.

A reading from "The Right to Personal Liberty Is Recognized, by Reason, as a Natural and Universal Right" by Luther Lee

1. Liberty, like life, may be forfeited. When a man so abuses his liberty as to endanger the rights of others, his liberty is forfeited, and may be rightfully taken from him. But this proves nothing against the right of personal liberty as natural and universal....

The cringing slave feels not only the love, but the right of liberty within him. While his limbs are bound, his mind, his thoughts, are free; and within he reads his right to be free written in the elements of his own conscious soul...."

5. Nature, with all her lights and tongues, is dark and silent on the great mediatorial system, which the Gospel reveals. Nature cannot teach on this subject, because her lights were all created, and her tongues all commenced their play before this system of grace was developed or needed. The science of salvation through a Mediator, having its necessity in the apostacy and corruption of humanity, which occurred after the creation, cannot be revealed in and through nature. This is revealed only in the Gospel, and here Revealed Religion triumphs over Natural Religion, without subverting it, as far as it goes. Here the end is reached, and if all that has been said shall by the means of leading one human wanderer through the channels of

truth which nature reveals, to the altar of Christianity, where the fountain of salvation is ever open, and ever flows full and free, the end will be gained and the labor more than paid beyond computation.

✪ *February 23*

Theodore Sedgewick Wright

PRESBYTERIAN

April 1797–March 25, 1847

Theodore Sedgewick Wright was born to a free African American family. He was only the second man of color to be admitted to an American institution of higher learning, and the first to be awarded a theological degree. He entered Princeton Seminary in 1825, graduated in 1828, and was called as pastor to the First Colored Presbyterian Church in New York City, the second largest church there at the time. His service lasted 17 years, and he became a leading voice calling for institutions to aid youth. Wright founded the Phoenix Society and the Phoenix High School for Colored Youth to address the spiritual and moral needs of the young people of the city.

Vigorous, often bitter, debates about slavery were part of the social environment in those years, and Wright was no stranger to them. He was a vociferous champion of the antislavery cause, and an outspoken opponent of plans to resettle people of African descent on that continent. Wright believed African Americans should be fully integrated into the broader society. In a 1837 speech to the New York Anti-Slavery Society, he said: "It is an easy thing to ask about the vileness of slavery in the South, but to call the dark man a brother, to treat all men according to their moral worth . . . that is the test."

Wright died at 50, possibly from exhaustion due to overwork. He had been a close colleague of other black leaders like James Pennington,* Henry Highland Garnet,* and Louis Tappan,* Wright poured his seemingly limitless energies into his several passions: the development of youth, including enabling them to acquire a first-rate education, the spread of the Gospel, and the destruction of slavery. Organizations he either founded or helped develop and lead included the American Anti-Slavery Society, the New York Anti-Slavery Society, the Union Missionary Society, and the American Missionary Association.

Despite his involvement in so many outside interests, Wright devoted himself to his pastoral responsibilities as well. At some time in the early 1830s, Henry Garnet joined one of the Christian Education classes sponsored by the congregation, and Wright became Garnet's mentor. It was Wright who baptized his friend and, through his influence, set the stage for Garnet to come into his own as a major figure in the African American church and in the abolitionist movement. The two men remained close, and Garnet delivered the sermon at Wright's funeral service.

Wright understood that in order to remake the culture so that all people could be treated as God intended, this conviction would need to take root in the souls of ordinary people. He proclaimed, "Let every man take his stand, burn out this prejudice, live it down, talk it down, everywhere consider the colored man as a man, in the church, the stage, the steamboat, the public house, in all places, and the deathblow to slavery will be struck." In church pulpits, lecture halls, antislavery conventions, and progressive newspapers and magazines, he expressed his dedication to a new society free from color boundaries. He wanted all African Americans to have the educational opportunities he had been given.

Wright's dream was not even partially fulfilled until long after his untimely death. He did not live to witness the Emancipation Proclamation, and its consequent reforms, much less the civil rights movement of the 1960s. Inequalities still exist between whites and blacks, even in our own time. As the battle for equal rights continues, the themes of Wright's ministry will remain relevant. But Wright's labors continues to bear fruit, whether in integrated neighborhoods, fairer hiring practices, legal recourse to antidiscrimination laws, or admission to public and private schools. Wright's name may not be as well known as those of more recent Civil Rights leaders like Martin Luther King, Jr.,* but King's generation built on his efforts in the ongoing struggle for a more just nation.

✪ February 24

Pierre-Jean De Smet

ROMAN CATHOLIC

January 30, 1801–May 23, 1873

Among the converts made by the early Jesuit explorers of North America were members of the Iroquois tribe, whose respect for the "black robes" was such that their descendants continued to talk about them. A century and a half later, some Native Americans in the Rocky Mountain area heard their story and sent emissaries to St. Louis to ask for "black robes" to come to them. The first three delegations found no one willing to come, but the fourth, in 1839, discovered a young Belgian priest who had come to the United States at the age of 20 specifically to offer himself as a missionary among the Indians.

Pierre-Jean De Smet had been trained in the Jesuit novitiate in Whitemarsh, Maryland, and sent to St. Louis. He had already been on a missionary trip to the Pottawatamies at Council Bluff in 1838 and visited the Sioux to arrange a peace between them and the Pottawatamies. Now he began a trip to the Pacific northwest that would cover nearly 5,000 miles and would bring him into contact with a number of tribes. Well received everywhere, De Smet returned to St. Louis and went back the following year to establish a permanent mission in Montana. Now having a better idea of the work involved, he journeyed the next year to Europe to raise money and to bring back additional helpers.

Such was De Smet's relationship with the various tribes that he was often called on by the United Sates government to assist them in their peace-making efforts. He was willing to do this, except when he felt the purpose of the mission to be punitive. In relations with the federal government as well as with European nations, De Smet became an advocate for the Native Americans, and he is said to have traveled over 180,000 miles in his lifetime visiting popes, kings, and presidents on their behalf. There seems to have been an instinctive rapport between De Smet and the Native Americans so that he had their complete confidence and could often go alone to negotiate with a hostile tribe where no other white man would been safe.

Much of his work in building missions among the many tribes west of the Mississippi was swept away by the tide of white settlement, yet his journals and letters provide a record of permanent value of their dialects, stories, and poems.

A reading from a letter of Pierre-Jean De Smet to the editor of the *Catholic Herald* from the Steamboat *Oceana*, Missouri River, May 1, 1841

On my arrival at St. Louis, I gave an account to my superior of my journey and of the flattering prospects which the mission beyond the Rocky Mountains held out. You will easily believe me when I tell you that my heart sank within me on learning from him that the funds at his disposal for missionary purposes would not enable him to afford me scarcely the half of what would be necessary for the outfit and other expenses of an expedition. The thought that the undertaking would have been given up, that I would not be able to redeem my promise to the poor Indians, pierced my very heart and filled me with the deepest sorrow. I would have desponded had I not already experienced the visible protection of the Almighty in the prosecution of this great work. My confidence in him was unabated. Whilst in this state of mind one of my friends encouraged me to appeal to the zealous and learned coadjutor of Philadelphia [Francis Patrick Kenrick] and to his indefatigable clergy. I immediately acted upon the thought. I did appeal and with what success the Catholic public already know. To the Bishop who gave his sanction to the plan of a general and simultaneous collection throughout his diocese; to the clergy of the different churches of the city who so kindly interested themselves in this good work and proposed it to their congregations; to the generous people of Philadelphia who so liberally responded to the call of their pastors, I return my sincere thanks and will daily beg the father of mercies to reward them with his choicest blessings.

I must not omit to make mention of other generous contributors. After having written to Philadelphia I was advised to visit New Orleans and recommend the cause of the Indians to the good Bishop [Antoine Blanc] of that city and to his clergy and people. I did so. The Bishop received me with great kindness; gave his approbation to a collection, and placed his name first on the list. His clergy followed his example. As I had only a few days at my disposal, I thought it best to solicit subscriptions through several generous ladies who offered themselves for this purpose. In the space of three or four days, they collected nearly $1,000. You have no idea with what spirit the pious portion of the people entered into the affair. Almost every moment of my stay persons came to offer me something for the Indian mission. Several ladies gave me various trinkets, such as earrings, bracelets, and ornaments of every description; others brought implements and articles, which will be of great use in the Indian country. In a word, Reverend Sir, I left New Orleans with $1,100 in cash and six boxes full of various and most useful articles. From the Reverend Mr. Durbin of Kentucky I received $300, and the Reverend Jno. O'Reilly remitted $140, the amount collected in St. Paul's Church, Pittsburg. St. Louis supplied the balance of what was necessary for the outfit, the expenses of the journey and the commencement of the establishment in the Indian country. To the Bishops and to the zealous clergy and laity of Philadelphia and New Orleans; to the clergy and laity of other places who aided the good cause; in a word, to all the benefactors of the mission beyond the Rocky Mountains, I again return my sincere thanks....

✪ February 25

Ruth Youngdahl Nelson

LUTHERAN

1904–April 6, 1984

Proverbially, American grandmothers sit in rocking chairs, knitting for grandchildren, or stand at the stove cooking Thanksgiving dinner for them as they arrive by horse-drawn sleigh "over the river and through the woods." Ruth Youngdahl Nelson was such a grandmother, but with a difference. Married to a Lutheran pastor, she had raised seven children, three of them foster children. She was also a speaker, Bible teacher, preacher, and author. At the grandmotherly age of 78, she was arrested for disturbing America's peace.

As a student at Gustavus Adolphus College, Ruth Youngdahl demonstrated energy and endurance in sports competitions, becoming the first woman chosen for the school's Hall of Fame. Dedicated to raising appreciation for woman's sports programs, she helped organize the first local chapter of the National Women's Athletic Association and became its first president. In addition to swimming and diving, Nelson played basketball, softball, volleyball, and even fullback on the first co-ed football team, a feat that made national headlines in 1923. She was the first woman elected to the Gustavus Adolphus Board of Directors and later served on the board of Luther Seminary in Minneapolis.

This energy and drive stood her in good stead in her professional pursuits, as well. She worked side-by-side with her pastor husband in diverse congregations from Minnesota, Illinois, and Washington, DC, to Saudi Arabia, and Switzerland. In addition, she pursued her own interests, giving speeches about poverty, elder care, prison ministry, and the plight of poor urban youth in Europe and Asia, as well as in the United States. Nelson wrote ten inspirational books, several of which were also autobiographical. She was named "Church Woman of the Year" in 1960 and "Mother of the Year" in 1973 — indicating how highly she was esteemed.

Nelson was particularly committed to peace and justice, whether in the inner city, the household, or in wider society. She could not remain silent about the Cold War's nuclear weaponry, which threatened annihilation of the human race. For her, church teachings about peacemaking and love of neighbor were not just unattainable ideals but a practical way of life. In 1982, at the age of 78, Nelson and her son, Jonathan, were arrested for trying to block a nuclear Trident submarine headed for the naval base at Bangor, Washington. Their little armada of protestors sailed out to create a makeshift blockade to show their opposition to the American arms race. The charges against her were dismissed, yet even without a trial, the activist grandmother had made her point. Jesus calls us to be "peacemakers," and our decisions and actions ought to embody this call.

Nelson did not consider herself a major figure in American religious life, nor did she ever overstate her contribution. She proclaimed, "I am no theologian. I can only speak and write about what Christ can do in my everyday life." Her last book was titled *A Grandma's Letters to God*. She challenged her readers to consider the children who would grow up to inherit a society adults had shaped: "It's a messy situation my generation handed down to them. We're constantly hearing about economic disaster and, more awfully and realistically, the threat of nuclear annihilation. Some of them are very discouraged. What can I say to them? How can I be helpful?"

Is it hard to reconcile our images of a traditional grandmother with an advocate for women's sports and nuclear protestor? Nelson combined a variety of roles in her life because they all reflected her concern for people. Her family needed her to be a loving mother and grandmother. Her church and college needed her service. The impoverished, rejected, and elderly needed her advocacy. A world on the brink of nuclear incineration needed her, so she acted. Nelson's faith connected her various spheres into a unified Christian discipleship. Following Christ manifests itself in many ways, yet compassion and a redemptive vision form the foundation for each action. Nelson's example inspires us not to compartmentalize our lives, but unite them in love and service to others.

✪ *February 26*

Harry Emerson Fosdick

BAPTIST/ PRESBYTERIAN

May 24, 1878–October 5, 1969

Truth commonly emerges out of a contest between viewpoints, and such contests have been a part of Christian life from the beginning. Because of the variety of currents flowing into American Christianity and arising out of it, such contests have been a recurrent phenomenon — and not often resolved. Harry Emerson Fosdick was a central figure in the conflicts of the 1920s and 1930s between factions called "fundamentalist" and "liberal." Born in Buffalo, New York, Fosdick, a graduate of Union Theological Seminary, was ordained to the Baptist ministry and served a parish in Montclair, New Jersey, until 1915, though he began teaching at Union Seminary in 1908 and combined the teaching ministry with parish work first in New Jersey and then at the First Presbyterian Church in Manhattan. As preaching minister of the Manhattan Church, Fosdick moved to the center of the growing controversy between fundamentalists and liberals. Fosdick had begun his ministry on the fundamentalist side, but his reading led him to reject a stance that he came to believe had "held up the progress of mankind." He said, "I no longer believed the old stuff I had been taught. Moreover, I no longer merely doubted it. I rose in indignant revolt against it."

In 1923, Fosdick preached a sermon entitled "Shall the Fundamentalists Win?" that called on churches to be open-minded and tolerant. The ensuing controversy led the General Assembly of the Presbyterian Church to demand that New York Presbytery make its pulpits conform to their denomination's Confession of Faith. Fosdick's congregation tried unsuccessfully to resolve the dispute but failed to do so, and Fosdick finally resigned in 1925. Soon afterward, he received a call from the First Baptist Church of New York, but he could no longer accept baptism by immersion and disapproved of the church's location in a wealthy area of the city. The congregation therefore relocated itself to a new building, constructed with the help of John D. Rockefeller. The new Riverside Church made no requirements, either for baptism or creed. Fosdick occupied its pulpit until his retirement in 1945, and became one of the best-known preachers of his time. He strongly supported the growing movement to provide pastoral counseling as an aspect of pastoral care.

Fosdick called preaching "personal counseling on a group scale," arguing that "every sermon should have for its main business the head-on constructive meeting of some problem which was puzzling minds, burdening consciences, distracting lives, and no sermon which so met a real human difficulty, with light to throw on it and help to win victory over it, could possibly be futile."

A reading from Harry Emerson Fosdick's sermon "Shall the Fundamentalists Win?"

Just now the Fundamentalists are giving us one of the worst exhibitions of bitter intolerance that the churches of this country have ever seen. As one watches them and listens to them he remembers the remark of General Armstrong of Hampton Institute, "Cantankerousness is worse than heterodoxy." There are many opinions in the field of modern controversy concerning which I am not sure whether they are right or wrong, but there is one thing I am sure of: courtesy and kindliness and tolerance and humility and fairness are right. Opinions may be mistaken; love never is.

As I plead thus for an intellectually hospitable, tolerant, liberty-loving church, I am, of course, thinking primarily about this new generation. We have boys and girls growing up in our homes and schools, and because we love them we may well wonder about the church which will be waiting to receive them. Now, the worst kind of church that can possibly be offered to the allegiance of the new generation is an intolerant church. Ministers often bewail the fact that young people turn from religion to science for the regulative ideas of their lives. But this is easily explicable.

Science treats a young man's mind as though it were really important. A scientist says to a young man, "Here is the universe challenging our investigation. Here are the truths which we have seen, so far. Come, study with us! See what we already have seen and then look further to see more, for science is an intellectual adventure for the truth." Can you imagine any man who is worthwhile turning from that call to the church if the church seems to him to say, "Come, and we will feed you opinions from a spoon. No thinking is allowed here except such as brings you to certain specified, predetermined conclusions. These prescribed opinions we will give you in advance of your thinking; now think, but only so as to reach these results."

My friends, nothing in all the world is so much worth thinking of as God, Christ, the Bible, sin and salvation, the divine purposes for humankind, life everlasting. But you cannot challenge the dedicated thinking of this generation to these sublime themes upon any such terms as are laid down by an intolerant church....

The present world situation smells to heaven! And now, in the presence of colossal problems, which must be solved in Christ's name and for Christ's sake, the Fundamentalists propose to drive out from the Christian churches all the consecrated souls who do not agree with their theory of inspiration. What immeasurable folly!

Well, they are not going to do it; certainly not in this vicinity. I do not even know in this congregation whether anybody has been tempted to be a Fundamentalist. Never in this church have I caught one accent of intolerance. God keep us always so and ever increasing areas of the Christian fellowship; intellectually hospitable, open-minded, liberty-loving, fair, tolerant, not with the tolerance of indifference, as though we did not care about the faith, but because always our major emphasis is upon the weightier matters of the law.

✪ *February 27*

Lillian Trasher

ASSEMBLIES OF GOD

September 27, 1887–December 17, 1961

To listen to a call from God requires putting our own plans aside. This is what Lillian Trasher learned when she prayed her childhood prayer: "Lord, if ever I can do anything for You, just let me know and I'll do it." Her upbringing in Georgia exposed her early on to a simple piety, and it became her lifelong intention to listen to God's call and follow it. As Trasher grew old enough to work, she was invited by a Miss Perry to assist her in caring for the children at her orphanage. Without realizing it, she was starting what would become a lifetime vocation. Through the daily chores of the orphanage, she learned how to cook, sew, care for large groups of children of different ages, and, most importantly, trust in God.

Chronically short of money, Trasher was content to live on donations. If her shoes wore out and only men's shoes arrived in a box of donated clothing, then men's shoes were what she wore. But her ability to find contentment with whatever came her way did not prevent her from seeking more effective forms of service. She attended a Bible College in Ohio, led a church, and did evangelistic outreach in Kentucky. In time, she became engaged and planned to marry. With the wedding less than two weeks off, Trasher attended a talk by a missionary to India. Hearing about the needs of the people and the importance of Christian work abroad moved her to tears. She felt that God's voice had spoken to her through this address, beckoning her to the foreign mission field. She broke off her engagement and, without any resources or definite plan, went off to a missionary convention in Pittsburgh. One thing led to another until Trasher and her sister, Jenny, found themselves preparing to leave New York City for Africa. Along the way, someone had suggested that Trasher look to the Bible for a word from

God. She opened to Acts 7:34 where she found: "I have seen, I have seen the affliction of my people which is in Egypt, and I have heard their groaning, and am come down to deliver them. And now come, I will send thee into Egypt." So off they sailed, with what little money they had, to begin serving in Egypt.

The sisters traveled to Assyut, a town south of Cairo on the Nile. Ragged, undernourished children were everywhere, poverty was rampant, and services were few. Trasher's main work really began when she was summoned by a local citizen to pray for a dying woman in 1911. Using a translator, she went to the home where she was stunned to find a three-month-old child trying to drink spoiled milk from a dirty can. Her tenderness toward the infant was so evident that the dying mother asked Trasher to care for her child. Of course she agreed. She and her sister tried to tend the baby at the missionary compound. Weak as she was, the child cried almost ceaselessly. Finally, after 12 long days and nights, the other staff could take no more. Trasher was instructed by her supervisor to return the child. She had been taught to be obedient to elders and was willing to remove the baby from the compound, but to where? Rather than abandon it, she decided to stay with the little girl herself. This meant she would be an unwed, single mother with no financial support living alone in an Arab culture. Even her sister decided to return to America. No one could see how any good could come of the situation.

Yet Trasher had lived on charity before and was not afraid to do so now. She begged for food and clothes and managed to have just enough. She felt God's own providence was carrying her through each day. Securing a place to stay, she traveled about on a donkey searching for basic daily needs. The scorn and ridicule of the local people turned into admiration for her persistence and stamina. Life began to get just a bit easier once her mission was taken on by the Assemblies of God. Clothes arrived in barrel loads, and money too, from time to time. So did the children. By 1915, she was running an orphanage of 50. Eight years later, it had grown to 300. A Scottish philanthropist named Lord Maclay heard of her in the 1930s, and began to send her money. Thanks to his generosity, Trasher was able to improve her facilities and programs. By the time of her death, she felt blessed to be able to look into the faces of 1,200 children.

During her years in Egypt, Trasher and her orphans survived an uprising against the British, a cholera epidemic, and all the more normal trials of building, expanding and maintaining an institution of such size. The Lillian Trasher Orphanage remains to this day, and its web page boasts it is one of the largest orphanages in the world. This simple Georgia girl gained her desire: to serve God. In answering this call, thousands of children were given security and compassion. Lillian Trasher had offered her life, and so became the conduit for new lives for her children.

✲ *February 28* _____

A. J. Muste

DUTCH REFORMED, QUAKER, AND PRESBYTERIAN

January 8, 1885–February 11, 1967

The survival of democracy depends on the renunciation of violence and the development of nonviolent means to combat evil and advance the good.
— A. J. Muste

Only the nonviolent can apply therapy to the violent.
— A. J. Muste

There is no way to peace; peace is the way.
— A. J. Muste

Pacifism and nonviolence have never been popular in North America, even among Christians. Yet Abraham Johannes Muste found in his faith the courage to advance the cause of peace through the means of peaceful action. Born in the Netherlands, Muste was brought to Michigan at age six and raised in the Calvinist tradition. In 1909, he graduated from Union Theological Seminary in New York and was ordained to the ministry of the Dutch Reformed Church. World War I brought his pacifist commitments to the fore, convincing him that he could no longer serve a church that did not espouse nonviolence. So, in 1918, he enrolled as a minister of the Society of Friends (Quakers) at Providence, Rhode Island. In Boston, Muste found support among fellow pacifists and also involved himself with the struggles of local laborers at the cloth mills in Lawrence. These strikes could become violent and would be a proving ground for Muste's advocacy of nonviolent change. First he raised cash to make a strike possible for the 30,000 workers who were set to walk off the job. Then he took a place at the front of the line, to experience fully what the workers themselves had to endure.

Muste was severely beaten by the police and placed under arrest. When police spies tried to persuade the strikers to attack a line of machine guns along the strike route, Muste wrote:

> I told them, in line with the strike committee's decision, that to permit ourselves to be provoked into violence would mean defeating ourselves; that our real power was in our solidarity and our capacity to endure suffering rather than to give up the right to organize; that no one could 'weave wool with machine guns;' that cheerfulness was better for morale than bitterness and that therefore we would smile as we passed the machine guns and the police on the way from the hall to the picket lines around the mill. I told the spies, who were sure to be in the audience, to go and tell the police and the mill managers that this was our policy.

The strike lasted almost four months and was brutal. The protesters suffered break-ins and beatings from would-be strike breakers. Just as the will to continue was weakening, and Muste decided the fight had been lost, he was called in by managers and told that the workers' demands would be granted. The strikers had won, and the use of nonviolent tactics had proved effective even in the face of bloodthirsty opposition.

Later, Muste served in several capacities in the labor movement, coordinating a number of strikes and sit-ins to gain ground for workers. Following a period of involvement in radical left-wing politics, he returned to his roots as an ardent proponent for a Christian pacifist perspective. He was enrolled in the ministry of the Presbyterian Church in 1937, though he never served in a pastoral role. In his book of 1941, *Non-Violence in an Aggressive World,* he examined the whole area of international conflict and proposed strategies to move beyond the cycle of wars and retributions. In an essay called "The World Task of Pacifism," he wrote:

> Christian realism would lead us to renounce war preparation and war as obviously suicidal; to offer to surrender our own special privileges; to participate in lowering tariff walls, in providing access to basic resources on equitable terms to all peoples; to spend the billions we shall otherwise squander on war preparations, and war, for the economic rehabilitation of Europe and Asia, for carrying a great "offensive" of food, medicine, and clothing to the stricken peoples of the world; to take our full share of responsibility for building an effective federal world government.

In 1942, as World War II raged on, Muste boldly called for a negotiated settlement initiated by the United States that would incorporate the following points:

1. the U.S. will help build a federal world government;

2. the U.S. will invest billions for the economic rehabilitation of Europe and Asia;

3. no attempt shall be made to fasten *sole* war guilt on any nation or group of nations;

4. subject nations such as India, Philippines, Puerto Rico, Denmark, Norway, France, Belgium, and Holland must be granted full self-determination;

5. all peoples should be assured of equitable access to markets and to essential raw materials;

6. to further democracy the U.S. should provide decent housing, adequate medical and hospital service, and equal educational facilities for all its people, including Negroes and Orientals;

7. the U.S. must repudiate racism and call on Germany and other countries to do the same;

8. drastic reduction of armaments by all nations should move all rapidly to an economy of peace.

Undeterred by widespread rejection of his outlook and specific suggestions, Muste continued to bring his nonviolent vision to bear on issues of the day. Wars between nations were not the only signs of a moral crisis of the time. Muste offered a nonviolent solution for racial tensions in America in his capacity as executive secretary of the Fellowship of Reconciliation (FOR). His commitment to pacifist principles moved James Farmer and Bayard Rustin,* — both FOR Staff members at the time — to take nonviolence seriously in their demands for racial equality. The young Dr. Martin Luther King, Jr.,* also adopted Muste's tactics and viewpoint.

Over time, Muste extended his areas of protest. He helped conscientious objectors, burned draft cards, challenged the McCarthy investigations, and withheld income tax from 1948 on. He spoke out against the Korean War, refused to participate in a civil defense drill in New York, and opposed nuclear testing in Nevada by the U.S., in the Sahara by the French, and in Leningrad by the Soviet Union. In 1961, Muste helped form an experimental World Peace Brigade in Beirut, Lebanon, in cooperation with other like-minded reformers from around the world. His resistance carried on into the Vietnam era with protest marches, calls for civil disobedience, and visits to both Saigon and Hanoi seeking ways to end the conflict. He died in early 1967, just a month after his second trip to Hanoi to demonstrate for peace. Tireless, courageous, compassionate, faithful, and hopeful, A. J. Muste's life was a gift to both the church and the nation in the search for a world free from violence.

March

Frances Xavier Cabrini

ROMAN CATHOLIC

July 15, 1850–December 22, 1917

Frances Cabrini grew up in Italy wanting to become a nun but was rejected by the two religious communities she applied to on the grounds of her fragile health. Her parish priest, however, needed someone to teach children and visit the poor so she took on those responsibilities, and when a smallpox epidemic broke out, she ministered to its victims. In 1874, Cabrini was asked to be director of a school for orphans. Six years later, the bishop asked her to found a religious order of missionary sisters. With a few companions, she took up residence in an abandoned monastery and inscribed "Institute of the Missionary Sisters of the Sacred Heart" over the door.

The Institute grew rapidly and established a number of houses in Italy. When she traveled to Rome to seek approval of the order's rule by the Vatican authorities, she learned about the hardships of Italian immigrants in America. Like the saint whose name she had taken — Francis Xavier — she longed to go to China. Like him, she was sent elsewhere. The Pope told her, "Not to the East, but to the West," so two weeks later she was on her way to New York. Even New York was too narrow a field to contain her prodigious energy. Before long, Cabrini established centers in New Jersey and Pennsylvania, then Louisiana, Mississippi, Illinois, Colorado, Washington, and California. The order founded schools, hospitals, and orphanages and provided prison visitations and social services. Soon, they were in Nicaragua,

Chile, and Argentina. Cabrini crossed the Andes on a mule and sailed the Atlantic over 30 times, enduring storms that "tossed the ship about as if it were a mere shell." Yet despite so much travel, she somehow managed to put down roots in the New World and become an American citizen. Her concern for the poor and the needy was balanced by administrative and financial skills that enabled her to supervise the burgeoning ministry she had founded. By the time of her death, the Missionary Sisters of the Sacred Heart had 67 communities with over 4,000 members.

A reading from a letter of Frances Xavier Cabrini written on a voyage from New York to Havre

However difficult a work may be, I always place it in the Adorable Heart of our sweet Jesu, and thus I rest sure and tranquil, even though I am far away, for I know well that He can do and complete the work I desire for His glory.

When I am on the spot I shall work with might and main, but when Obedience calls me away to work elsewhere, I must leave without anxiety the previous work, trusting in Jesus that He will give help and energy to the Sisters who have to continue the work which I have left interrupted. Oh, the law of love is so beautiful and amiable! He has given it Himself to His creatures. But we cannot love Him if we are not first loved by Him. Having given such a law, He has communicated to us the grace with which to love Him. What shall we not do, then, for love of a God so amiable and generous towards us, that He has called us to follow Him closely and to continue His Mission on this earth?

Let us correspond to His Love. Let us be generous, remembering always that the salvation of many souls is entrusted to our charity. We can do nothing of ourselves, for we are poor and miserable, but if we have faith and trust in Him Who comforts us, then we can do all things. Let us open wide our hearts, let us help those souls lying under the yoke of the king of darkness.

Let us break, by the fire of ardent charity, the heavy chains that bind these poor souls to the terrible slavery of the devil, and we shall see that our efforts are not in vain. Let us fall at the feet of Jesus, and, sorrowing over the iniquity of the world, supplicate the Divine Heart to open the treasures of Its infinite Mercy. Then let us begin anew, never allowing ourselves to be overcome by fatigue. Difficulties should never frighten the Spouse of Christ; but render her stronger and more steadfast. Do not be discouraged by repulses and contradictions, but always go forward with the serenity and strength of the Angels, keeping to your path despite every contrary influence.

When things are easy, everything appears to smile, but difficulties prove where there is fidelity and consistency. Remember, daughters, you are the tutelary Angels of the earth, therefore you should always be ready when holy obedience calls, to fly over the vast fields which charity lays before you. Let your lives be a perennial sacrifice of yourselves in behalf of the human race. Let your joy consist in working much and praying much. Always renew your offering as victims of expiation and reconciliation between Heaven and Earth.

✪ *March 2*

Henry Melchior Muhlenberg

LUTHERAN

1711–October 7, 1787

Henry Melchior Muhlenberg is considered the foundational figure in American Lutheranism. Born in Einbeck, Germany, in 1711, he studied at Göttingen and at Halle. In the early 18th century, Lutherans in America lived in widely scattered communities. Their varied national and cultural backgrounds and the lack of any kind of central organization put severe limitations on their ministries. When he first came to the New World, Muhlenberg found many self-appointed leaders, many of whom had no formal calling and lacked even the most basic qualifications for ministry. There was no one to exercise oversight or discipline in Pennsylvania when Muhlenberg arrived there. In his journal Muhlenberg wrote:

> I learned forthwith that Mr. Kraft had traveled through the whole province of Pennsylvania, appointed deacons and elders here and there, and established a general presbytery in the whole country and a special presbytery, as he called it, in Philadelphia. And besides all this, he had organized a consistory of which he was the president and Mr. John Caspar Stoever, the assessor. The assessor, Stoever, is a bookbinder whom the scoundrelly collector, Frederick Schultze, appointed a so-called Lutheran preacher here in a barn and thus conferred the dignity of ordination upon his disreputable behavior. The purpose of the presbytery was to make it possible for Valentine Kraft and his assessor to travel around the country and carry on their trade with the holy sacraments. The consistory served the purpose of letting him ordain a few more lazy and drunken schoolmasters and place them as preachers in vacant places. He enjoys great respect because our poor, ignorant Lutherans are pushed into the corner by the Moravians on the one hand, and on the other are duped by his windy boasting.

And again:

> Our host received a visit today from a German family of our religion who live in Old Indian Swamp, fifty miles away in the country. The man's name is Philip Eisenmann and he has a plantation of his own, but no Negroes. He and his wife cultivate the place by themselves in the sweat of their brows and prove thereby that a man can live and find food and clothing without the use

of black slaves, if he be godly and contented and does not desire to take more out of the world than he brought into it.

They lamented the great lack of schools and religious services in their neighborhood. They have been using their barn for public worship and have taken on as a preacher a young man who recently arrived from Germany and spent some time teaching in a school in Charleston. The man said that the pastor works the whole week on a sermon, gathering it together from books and writing it all out, and then on Sunday dryly reads it from the paper without the slightest expression in his voice. He even has to read the Lord's Prayer, not knowing it from memory, and gives as his excuse the fact that the Lord did not give him the gift of a good memory. The good Lord is always the one to be blamed when these sluggards remain uncircumcised in heart and ears. The only credentials he brought with him from Germany were a pair of black breeches.

Conditions such as these had prompted several congregations to contact Halle University, asking for a pastor to take charge. One of the Pietist leaders at Halle, Hermann Francke, chose Muhlenberg and charged him with a mission to colonial America. He arrived in Charleston on September 23, 1742, but moved quickly up to Pennsylvania. It took Muhlenberg little time to assess the situation, and to begin to rectify it. His reputation grew among German, Swedish, and other Lutherans. His clear vision, forthright manner, creative spirit, and desire to pull together a more functional Lutheran Church that remained true to its heritage, while effective in the new land, all contributed to his reputation. Muhlenberg developed liturgical resources as well as organizational models that helped Lutherans make the transition from Europe to America.

Having been authorized to serve the parishes in Wicaco (the original Swedish settlement on the Philadelphia waterfront) in 1745, Muhlenberg's skills were quickly put to use. Just over the river, in the colony of New Jersey, other Lutheran congregations were having their own troubles. In 1714, Justus Falckner* had founded the first parish there (now known as Zion, Oldwick). But all was not smooth as the new church developed. Bachman provides one telling example:

> Twenty years later, the then two congregations in the Raritan valley, having called a pastor from Germany, had a falling out with him. John August Wolf's behavior occasioned the calling of a synod-like meeting in 1735 by a new generation of New York pastors. But the attempt to settle the bitter dispute failed. The leading pastor, William Christopher Berckenmeyer, serving the German congregation in the Hudson valley, was too unbending in his orthodoxy and in dealing with people. For the ensuing decade the conflict continued. The Raritaners verged on despair spiritually....

> By August Muhlenberg was free to act and respond to the elders in New Jersey. Almost since his arrival in America, they had been importuning him to come and settle the quarrel between the now four small congregations in

the Raritan valley....The story is as follows: Muhlenberg succeeds in settling the decade-long dispute between Pastor Wolf and the congregations. Wolf
receives his back salary and leaves. The people rejoice. The Raritan congregations ask Muhlenberg to be their pastor. He accepts their call to him as
pastor-in-chief, or rector, which enables him thereafter to send assistant pastors or vicars in his stead. His instructions to the first of these assistants are a
model of ministerial responsibility and the exercise of pastoral concern. These
instructions reflect Muhlenberg's own experience gained during a second trip
to the Raritan in November of 1745. At that time the elders of the four small
congregations...would unite and build a church centrally located....In less
than five years Zion Church was dedicated.

It is hard to imagine what shape Lutherans in America would have found
themselves in after another few decades of unqualified leadership of the kind
described above. Muhlenberg dealt quickly and effectively with fly-by-night
preachers and shoddy standards afflicting the colonial congregations in the
northeast. Muhlenberg also understood that too little structure can cause
damage. He brought his best efforts to bear to rectify the church's life, and
left a more vigorous Lutheran Church to future generations.

✪ *March 3* _____

James Mills Thoburn
METHODIST
March 7, 1836–November 28, 1922

James Mills Thoburn was not a man to be defeated by technicalities. He had
dreamed for years of beginning work in the Philippines. When the Spanish-
American War broke out, he was in Manilla conducting services before the
firing stopped. One of his primary concerns was to find Filipinos to carry
on the missionary effort. Not until his second trip to the Philippines, a year
later, did he find the candidate he was looking for. He determined that the
man must be ordained, but Methodist polity required the candidate first to
be accepted by an Annual Conference which would then elect him. However,
the Conference that included the Philippines had already adjourned and no
Conference in Asia was in session. Thoburn knew, however, that the South
Kansas Annual Conference was meeting, so he sent a cable to Chanute,
Kansas, asking them to receive his candidate, elect him to deacon's orders
"under the Missionary Rule," transfer him to the Malaysia Conference for
ordination, then send an immediate reply to him at Manila when they had
done so. Such was Thoburn's reputation that they acted as he had requested.
Shortly thereafter, the first Filipino was ordained by the Methodist Church.

Thoburn had gone to India at the age of 23, having already spent two
years preaching in Ohio after graduating from college. He served briefly
in Garhwal, Moradabad, Sambahl, Rae Bareilly, and Lucknow. When he

moved on to Calcutta in 1874, he followed St. Paul's example by supporting himself without a missionary salary. Before long he had built up the
largest church in the country and was referred to as "the most influential
religious figure in India." Thoburn founded the *Indian Witness* in 1871 and
worked with another missionary to establish churches in Burma and Singapore. Returning to the United States in 1886 to recover from an accident,
he was made Bishop of India and Malaysia before being sent back. But the
new responsibility was too narrowly defined for Thoburn. In 1896, he was
able to expand the title to include "Burmah, the Malay Peninsula, and all
adjacent islands inhabited by the Malay race." The Philippines were such
islands, but under Spanish rule they had been inaccessible to missionaries.
When the Spanish-American War opened the door, Thoburn journeyed there
at once, put clergy in place, and, in 1900, reported that there was already a
Filipino church with 200 members, and weekly services attended by about
600 Filipino adherents.

It was said of Thoburn that he "put India on America's heart." John R.
Mott* described him as "possibly the greatest ecclesiastic of the 19th
century."

A reading from *The Church of Pentecost*
by James Mills Thoburn

The power of prayer, the very meaning of united prayer, can never be fully
understood by the Christian world, till the unity of the Church of Pentecost
becomes a common experience among multitudes of those who bear the
Christian name. While it is still blessedly true that one lonely prophet on
the mountain-top may summon the winds and the storm cloud by calm
prevailing prayer, yet the praying power of the Christian world must be that
which goes up from united hearts. The supplicants must "agree," must be of
one heart in desiring, of one purpose in asking, and of one faith in expecting
a response to their petition. If added power attends the prayer of two or
three, what transcendent power may we not expect to attend the prayer
of a hundred, a thousand, a million believers? If all true believers on earth
could only unite, not in repeating the words merely, but in uttering from the
heart and bearing it as a daily burden on the heart, the first petition of our
Lord's Prayer — "Thy kingdom come," — the nations would be shaken, and
the kingdom of God would begin to advance with mighty strides towards
universal triumph.

The attainment of the unity of Pentecost would duplicate, — nay, add
ten-fold, to the working efficiency of any company of associated believers,
who have become accustomed to the ordinary experience of mingled accord
and discord which too generally exist in the modern church. If my missionary brethren will pardon the personal reference, I will venture to say that it

has of late become deeply impressed upon my mind, that the weakest spot in their work is found here. I do not intimate that they are more defective than other Christians, but they have abundant need to be in advance, and to rise above the low standard which prevails in the home churches. They of all men need to be of one heart and one soul. The comparative isolation in which many of them live and the close personal association with fellow missionaries into which they are brought have a tendency in many cases to call attention to personal peculiarities in an unpleasant way, and the result is that while a measure of love and unity prevails in the several little communities, it is not wholly after the pattern of the Church of Pentecost. The missionaries preach and teach, and do what they regard as their duty faithfully enough, but their testimony cannot impress the multitudes around them as it would if the conditions laid down were fully met. The mission station, of all places, should be a miniature of Pentecost. Its little community should live in personal fellowship with Christ; they should breathe an atmosphere of love, they should walk in the light of God, and ever impress those who know them best as belonging to a kingdom which is not of this world. If all the missionaries of the world could to-day be made of one heart and one soul according to the standard of the Church of Pentecost, the change would be equivalent to an immediate reinforcement of a thousand, or perhaps I ought to say of ten thousand, fully equipped new workers.

✪ *March 4*

John Winthrop

CONGREGATIONAL

January 12, 1588–March 26, 1649

John Winthrop was born in comfortable circumstances, unlike many of his fellow Separatists who were typically merchants and tradespeople. Winthrop's father was the lord of Groton Manor and the son was educated by a private tutor until his father sent him to Cambridge. Although the Winthrops were sympathetic to the Puritan teaching, it was apparently not until John Winthrop married into a strongly Puritan family that he began to take their views seriously and apply them to himself. Even afterward, he continued on his apparently destined course, learning to manage the family estate and studying law until at least the age of 30. Then, as he records in his diary, he went through a time of dryness in which God

> showed me the emptiness of all my gifts and parts, left me neither power nor will, so as I became as a weaned child I could now no more look at what I had been or what I had done nor bee discontented for want of strength or assurance mine eyes were only upon his free mercy in Jesus Christ. I knew I was worthy of nothing for I knew I could do nothing for him or for my self. I could only mourn, and weep to think of free mercy to such a vile wretch as I was. Though

I had no power to apply it yet I felt comfort in it. I did not long continue in this estate, but the good spirit of the Lord breathed upon my soul, and said I should live. Then every promise I thought upon held forth Christ unto me saying I am thy salvation. Now could my soul close with Christ, and rest there with sweet content, so ravished with his love, as I desired nothing nor feared anything, but was filled with joy unspeakable, and glorious and with a spirit of Adoption. Not that I could pray with more fervency or more enlargement of heart than sometimes before, but I could now cry my father with more confidence.

It was after this, at the age of 42, that Winthrop began to believe that the reforms he and others hoped for were unlikely to be accomplished in his native country, and that he would have more freedom to practice his faith in the New World. He and other Seperatists secured a charter as the Massachusetts Bay Company and Winthrop was chosen governor. The expedition set sail in April of 1630, arriving in Massachusetts quite unprepared for life in a wilderness. Many died, while others returned to England. Winthrop's own son was one of the fatalities. Nonetheless, the governor's leadership managed to hold the colony together. He supported the settlement until it was secure and flourishing, often using his own resources. Except for two intervals, he continued as governor until his death in 1649.

On board the ship, as they approached the New World, Winthrop delivered a sermon that continues to be quoted, calling on his fellows to establish a "city set on a hill." Toward the end of his sermon he said the following:

A reading from a sermon by John Winthrop

We must entertain each other in brotherly affection. Wee must be willing to abridge ourselves of our superfluities, for the supply of other's necessities. Wee must uphold a familiar commerce together in all meekness, gentleness, patience and liberality. Wee must delight in each other; make other's conditions our own; rejoice together, mourn together, labor and suffer together, always having before our eyes our commission and community in the work, as members of the same body. So shall we keep the unity of the spirit in the bond of peace. The Lord will be our God, and delight to dwell among us, as his own people, and will command a blessing upon us in all our ways. So that we shall see much more of his wisdom, power, goodness and truth, than formerly we have been acquainted with. We shall find that the God of Israel is among us, when ten of us shall be able to resist a thousand of our enemies; when he shall make us a praise and glory that men shall say of succeeding plantations, "the Lord make it like that of New England." For we must consider that we shall be as a city upon a hill. The eyes of all people are upon us. So that if we shall deal falsely with our God in this work we have undertaken, and so cause him to withdraw his present help from us, we shall be made a story and a by-word through the world. We shall open the mouths of enemies to speak evil of the ways of God, and all professors for God's sake. We shall shame the faces of many of God's worthy servants, and cause their prayers to be turned into curses upon us till we be consumed out of the good land whither we are going.

✪ *March 5* _____

Sophie Koulomzin

ORTHODOX

December 3, 1903–September 29, 2000

One of Sophie Koulomzin's earliest memories was of running barefoot across the grass of her family's estate near St. Petersburg in Russia. She was 13 at the time and World War I was already raging. Her father was the last vice president of the Czarist legislature. With the collapse of the Czarist regime and the victory of the Communists, there was no longer any place for the Shidlovsky family in Russia and they fled, first to Estonia and later to Paris. To gain an education under such conditions was not easy, but she won a scholarship to the University of Berlin, then to Columbia University in New York, where she became the first Orthodox woman to receive a Masters Degree in Religious Education. Returning to France, she married a Russian engineer, Nikita Koulomzin, and worked with Russian émigré priests and lay people to edit two volumes of church school lessons: *My First Book about the Orthodox Faith* and *My Second Book about the Orthodox Faith*.

In 1949, the Koulomzins and their four children came to the United States and settled just north of New York City in Nyack. Sophie's work in Christian education was already well known, and she was immediately invited to join the Metropolitan Council Church School Committee. In the following years she dedicated her energy to Christian education, translating and editing materials from Russian and writing new works herself. She traveled widely through the United States to lecture, conduct workshops, and organize church school conferences. She also ran the church school in her home parish in Nyack, where she taught three classes every Saturday for many years.

Concerned that Orthodox Christians in the United States were trying to teach the old faith in the old language, Koulomzin recognized that various eastern traditions ought to cooperate more closely, share resources, and find ways to teach Orthodoxy to a new American-born generation. She took the leading role in creating the Orthodox Christian Education Commission with members from nine different Orthodox Churches, became its executive secretary, and edited its first publication, *The Bulletin*. Later she helped produce three magazines, one each for young children, for teenagers, and for college students and teachers. Moving beyond the world of the Orthodox Church, she wrote articles for the World Council of Churches and served as a delegate to two of their conferences: in Toronto in 1949 and Evanston in 1954. In 1956 she was appointed to the staff of St. Vladimir's Seminary, where she taught future priests and bishops, not only from the United States, but also from Japan and the Middle East. She said that Christ did not "look for baby-sitters or separate the children" but called them to come to him. She believed that their spiritual needs were as real as those of adults and that the church should understand and provide for them.

A reading from *Our Church and Our Children* by Sophie Koulomzin, 1975

For many centuries educational philosophy, whether secular or Christian, took for granted that each child's soul is a "tabula rasa." Protect the child from exposure to bad influences, punish misdemeanors, recompense good actions, and the end product will be a good person.

Though one of the main points of Christian spiritual guidance — as seen, for example, in the *Philokalia* — is that each soul is absolutely unique and that the spiritual father's task is precisely to discern what is right for the spiritual growth of each particular person, this approach was not reflected in the general practice of the religious education of children. Individual spiritual fathers and saints had a remarkable measure of this personal insight, but the effort to understand the individual child, to recognize his inborn talents and traits, to encourage his creativity and self-expression, to understand the "reason why" of his behavior, was not part of the religious educational program of the Church as a whole.

The principle of man's freedom under God has gained great importance in recent times. It is *the* concept that distinguishes our Christian world-view from modern anti-Christian dictatorial philosophies. The act of Christian faith is a free act. Faith does not impose itself with the obviousness of something you cannot deny. It is a "conviction of things unseen" (Hebrews 11:1). There can be no faith without freedom, you can truly believe only if you are free to doubt. All this was implicit in Christian theology of all ages, but it is only fairly recently that it has become such a part of man's Christian conscience.

This has a deep influence on our entire approach to Christian education. It means that we can expose a person to what we believe, to the reality of faith in our life, but we cannot *make* anyone believe, and, by extension, we cannot *make* anyone believe correctly. The ultimate act of faith has to be a person's own free act. This insight lies behind the generally accepted principle of religious toleration, and this is why we cannot accept the principle of authoritarianism as a method of religious education. It does not mean that we do not accept authority. Obviously a great part of our faith is based on trust in the authority of someone — of saints, of the Church, of the Holy

Scriptures. But this very trust is an act of free choice and cannot be imposed. Authoritarianism as a method of religious education simply does not work any more. We cannot tell our children and young people: "You must believe thus and so became I say so, or because it says so in the catechism, or because it is in the Bible...." We can and must say: "I believe...," "the Church teaches...," "It is written in the Gospels...." But our educational work should be based on the presupposition that any child or young person can attain faith only in an authentic free act of his own. This is why we need to understand our children, their emotional and intellectual development, their motivation. The child's way of thinking and his imagination must become part of Christian education in a way not considered in the past.

✪ March 6 _____

James DeKoven

EPISCOPALIAN

September 19, 1831–March 19, 1879

When an individual makes a decision to serve God, we often call this a "life-changing" event. The New Testament presents this change in radical terms: "once you were darkness, now you are light" (Ephesians 5:4). It is natural, then, for believers to attempt to change every aspect of life and to look for detailed guidance about the most trivial act. When asked for guidance by new Christians at Corinth, St. Paul suggested this concern could be carried too far. Some converts were worrying about what kinds of food they might eat and when they could eat it. But Paul told them, "Whether you eat or drink, or whatever you do, do everything for the glory of God" (10:31).

Nonetheless, Christians continue to make issues out of secondary matters of behavior to this day both inside the church and outside. The Reformation left most Protestants convinced that almost anything done in the Middle Ages was wrong. Therefore, they reasoned, those who continued to use patterns of worship from the pre-Reformation church or from contemporary Roman Catholic practice must have forsaken the true, Reformed faith and have become Roman Catholics. Such controversies emerge from time to time in various forms. In the latter part of the 19th century and first part of the 20th, what was called "the ritualist controversy" divided opinions in the Episcopal Church. Some Episcopalians found vestments and candles, bowing and genuflection helpful to their devotional life. Others condemned such practices and attempted to outlaw them by action of the church's General Convention.

Among the leaders of the so-called "Ritualist" party in the Episcopal Church was James DeKoven, an Episcopal priest who had gone to the Wisconsin frontier to help create academic institutions and to train young people for positions of leadership. He taught at the church's Wisconsin seminary,

Nashotah House, served as headmaster of a college preparatory school, and became warden of a college. All these endeavors thrived under his leadership. At the General Conventions of 1868 and 1877, he became the spokesman for the "Anglo-Catholic" position, defending ceremonial practices with good humor and fervor. He always insisted that such practices were secondary to the central importance of faith in Christ and the salvation of souls.

Four times James DeKoven was nominated to serve as a bishop, yet each time he was denied on grounds of "unsound doctrine." Although the General Convention had agreed that Anglo-Catholic practices were only of secondary importance to the faith, nevertheless, prejudice against them was enough to deny him the episcopate. Worn down by his labors and constant controversy, DeKoven died suddenly at the age of 48.

A reading from James DeKoven's address to the General Convention of 1874

In order to get the force of my argument you will have to follow the Canon, and I believe the argument to be one which, if I can set it forth, will convince the House that at least that specification, "the use of incense," is an utter piece of nonsense. Let us see. It says, "Ceremonies, or practices during the celebration of the Holy Communion not ordained or authorized in the Book of Prayer, and setting forth or symbolizing erroneous or doubtful doctrines, have been introduced into a parish within his jurisdiction; and, as examples, the following are declared to be considered as such.

That is, it does not simply forbid the use of incense — I wish that were all. What it does is to say that the use of incense symbolizes erroneous or doubtful doctrines, which is a dreadful thing to commit this House to. For this House to forbid the use of incense is a very proper thing, perhaps; but for this House to say that the use of incense symbolizes false doctrines, is for this House to put itself in utter and total opposition to the Holy Scriptures; for, remember, what does David say? "Let my prayer be set forth in Thy sight as the incense, and let the lifting up of my hands be an evening sacrifice." In other words, David says that the use of incense, to which that holy prophet and king was accustomed — having not lived in our own day — symbolized prayer; and will this church say — is it prepared to say, — that the use of incense, which symbolizes prayer, symbolizes false doctrine?

I pass over the second specification, although I must say that I do not think the iconoclasm goes quite far enough; for when, in St. Thomas' Church only yesterday morning, I witnessed the great statues of the Apostles standing all around, I am free to say that, had I not been as much of a Protestant as I am, as I bent and bowed, I might have been led into the Roman error of wor-shipping images or something of that kind. [Laughter.] I do not think that thing goes quite far enough. Cut out the crucifix from the stained windows, put it out of your prayer-books, forbid pictures as well as images, if it be necessary; but do not let us believe, in this day, that the mere looking at the image of the human nature of our Divine Redeemer, and exciting our emotions by his thorn-crowned brow and his bleeding head and pierced hands, can possibly be said to symbolize false doctrine!

Mr. President, we live in troublous times, and around us are all sorts of terrible questions. It does seem to me the need of the day is not now to legislate on nice points of doctrine, or to prescribe exactly the measure of a genuflexion, or the angle of inclination which can express an orthodox devotion. The answer to all this panic and all this outcry is one, and one only. It is *Work;* work for the cause of Christ; work for the souls of men; and a fuller, deeper, more noble sense of the obligation of the Church, developing its powers, and sending it forth to mould and form this mighty nation, and to give new life and vigor to every effort that is made for the salvation of men. I see the storm-cloud gathering. I see the lightnings flash. I hear the thunder roll afar. I hear the trumpet call. In my ears the bugle blast is ringing. And I call you, brethren, in a time like this, not to narrow-hearted legislation, but broad, Catholic, tolerant charity, and to work, as never men worked before, for the souls of those for whom the Saviour died.

✹ *March 7*

Maria W. Stewart
AFRICAN BAPTIST
1803–1879

Maria Stewart was among the earliest black voices to call for justice for African Americans. In 1831, she responded to William Lloyd Garrison's request for contributions from black women for his newspaper, *The Liberator.* Stewart's eloquent essay was published, and she was invited to speak publicly — the first black woman to be asked to do so. Her initial talk was given on April 28, 1832, before the African-American Female Intelligence Society of America. On September 21 of that same year, she addressed a New England Anti-Slavery Society meeting in Boston's Franklin Hall, describing the evils of slavery and the oppression of free blacks.

Stewart (née Maria Miller) was born free in Hartford, Connecticut, but when she was orphaned at five, she was bound out as an indentured servant in the home of a clergyman. There is no evidence that she had formal schooling, but she may well have had opportunities to learn in the household where she served. At 15, when her indenture ended, she supported herself as a domestic servant. She moved to Boston at some point and married James W. Stewart in the African Baptist Church. Stewart was a veteran of the War of 1812, an independent shipping agent, and member of the black middle class, but when he died three years later, white businessmen managed to take over his estate, depriving Maria of her inheritance. Once again, she worked as a domestic for a few years until a religious experience inspired her to be a "warrior" for her people. With that intention, she responded to the call for articles from William Lloyd Garrison.

A few years after making her public witness in Boston, Stewart moved, first to New York, then Baltimore, and finally to Washington, working as a schoolteacher. In the final year of her life, she published the speeches and essays on freedom, equality, and women's rights for which she is still remembered.

A reading from Maria Stewart's first public address, delivered at the Franklin Hall in Boston in 1832

God has fired my soul with a holy zeal for his cause. It was God alone who inspired my heart to publish the meditations thereof; and it was done with pure motives of love to your souls, in the hope that Christians might examine themselves, and sinners become pricked in their hearts. It is the word of God, though men and devils may oppose it. It is the word of God; and little did I think that any of the professed followers of Christ would have frowned upon me, and discouraged and hindered its progress.

Ah, my friends, I am speaking as one who expects to give account at the bar of God; I am speaking as a dying mortal to dying mortals. I fear there are many who have named the name of Jesus at the present day, that strain at a gnat and swallow a camel; they neither enter into the kingdom of heaven themselves, nor suffer others to enter in. They would pull the motes out of their brother's eye, when they have a beam in their own eye. And were our blessed Lord and Saviour, Jesus Christ, upon the earth, I believe he would say of many that are called by his name, "O, ye hypocrites, ye generation of vipers, how can you escape the damnation of hell." I have enlisted in the holy warfare, and Jesus is my captain; and the Lord's battle I mean to fight, until my voice expire in death. I expect to be hated of all men, and persecuted even unto death, for righteousness and the truth's sake....

It appears to me that there are no people under the heavens, so unkind and so unfeeling towards their own, as are the descendants of fallen Africa. I have been something of a traveller in my day: and the general cry among the people is, "Our own color are our greatest opposers"; and even the whites say that we are greater enemies towards each other, than they are towards us. Shall we be a hissing and a reproach among the nations of the earth any longer! Shall they laugh us to scorn forever! We might become a highly respectable people; respectable we now consider ourselves, but we might become a highly distinguished and intelligent people. And how? In convincing the world, by our own efforts, however feeble, that nothing is wanting on our part but opportunity. Without these efforts, we shall never be a people, nor our descendants after us. . . .

I have sometimes thought, that God had almost departed from among us. And why? Because Christ has said, if we say we love the Father, and hate our brother, we are liars, and the truth is not in us; and certainly if we were the true followers of Christ, I think we could not show such a disposition towards each other as we do: for God is all love. . . .

O woman, woman! upon you I call; for upon your exertion almost entirely depends whether the rising generation shall be any thing more than we have been or not. O woman, woman! your example is powerful, your influence great; it extends over your husbands and over your children, and throughout the circle of your acquaintance. Then let me exhort you to cultivate among yourselves a spirit of Christian love and unity, having charity one for another, without which all our goodness is as sounding brass, and as a tinkling cymbal. And O, my God, I beseech thee to grant that the nations of the earth may hiss at us no longer! O suffer them not to laugh us to scorn forever!

✪ *March 8*

Cyrus and "Nettie" (Nancy Fowler) McCormick

PRESBYTERIAN

Cyrus: February 15, 1809–May 13, 1884
Nettie: February 8, 1835–July 5, 1923

Cyrus and Nettie McCormick grounded their marriage firmly in their Christian faith. Both their public and their private lives were lived in accord with the principles of their religion. Cyrus McCormick had had a conversion experience in his youth. Once he passed up a chance to witness to his faith in his local congregation and was told by his father that silence amounted to a denial of Christ. McCormick took that to heart and sought advice on how to become a serious Christian. The next Sunday he did stand to give testimony and the rest of his life bore its fruit.

Known most widely as inventor of the threshing machine, McCormick was industrious, clever, determined, and eager to put his talents to use for others. The fortune he amassed from business enabled his philanthropy, which provided support for Christian work near and far. His labors were only intensified when he met and married "Nettie."

Cyrus and Nettie met in 1856, when she was 21 and he was 46. She was reluctant to marry him at first, but he told her: "I do not think there is a man in the world who would strive more to please you than I should do — no one whose disposition and manner would be more under your control and influence than mine as your husband." They were married on January 26, 1858.

Nettie's life and faith were even more serious and focused than her husband's. Orphaned at the age of seven, she had been reared by grandparents. Never given to extraneous frivolity, she sought from her earliest years to live a useful life as a follower of Jesus. Nettie had always been active in her church, involved in music and Sunday School. Though brought up in a secure and comfortable environment, her sense of responsibility would not allow her to take such blessings for granted. She was affected by the pains and problems of others. While a 17-year-old student at Troy Female Seminary, she wrote her brother, "It has been very, very cold here today. Oh my heart bleeds for those who are turned out of house and home this stinging cold night." Her attitude toward the meaning and purpose of life was summed up in these words: "Usefulness is the great thing in life; to do something for others leaves a sweeter odor than a life of pleasure."

Nettie's marriage to Cyrus was not easy. Though a good husband, his business took him away from her often. Two of their offspring died very young, Nettie had two miscarriages, and two of their remaining five children were diagnosed with mental illnesses. Her grief and loneliness were difficult crosses for the McCormicks to bear, but bear them they did. Cy built a prosperous farm machinery business in Chicago. When the Great Fire of October 23, 1871, destroyed the factory, he resolved to retire, but she insisted that he rebuild and continue. As he aged, she took a more active role in running the enterprise. The factory continued to be profitable, and the McCormick's generosity continued to flow.

In 1859, Cyrus had given $100,000 to move Hanover Seminary to Chicago where it was renamed McCormick Theological Seminary. In later years, Nettie maintained her connection with the school, offering buildings, equipment, upkeep, and scholarships. In 1905, well after Cyrus's death, Nettie was still giving to the seminary, setting up an endowment to pay the president's salary. Over the years, the family donated over $4,000,000 to the school.

Another academy benefiting from the McCormick's generosity was Tusculum College in Tennessee. Cyrus had given them financial support, and Nettie continued it. Involvement with that college aroused her interest in southern institutions. Other schools, churches, and Sunday Schools became her beneficiaries. John Mott* of the Student Volunteer Movement called her "Christianity in action." Her generosity benefited all kinds of people and projects. Individuals in need received help with medical or dental bills or were provided with funds that allowed them rest and renewal before resuming demanding work. Institutions supported by Nettie included the Moody Bible Institute, Princeton, Alborz College of Teheran, a Siamese hospital, pastoral schooling in Korea, and the first women's hospital in Persia. Between 1890 and her death in 1923, Nettie McCormick's fortune provided $8 million to medical institutions, relief projects, schools, youth programs, and churches.

Nettie is quoted as saying, "Yes, money is power, as you have said, but I have always tried not to trust in it, but rather use it for the glory of my Master." She added: "We plan and God steps in with another plan for us, and He is all wise and the most loving friend we have always helping us."

Cyrus and Nettie McCormick shared the view that our lives are best lived in service to God and neighbor. Whether in business, personal life, or public philanthropy, the McCormicks lived their faith. Their understanding is in stark contrast to those who say that religion is purely personal, not to be confused with public and professional commitments. Nettie and Cyrus demonstrated that it is possible to be prosperous and creative while remaining faithful and generous. These are not two compartmentalized ways of life. A Christian's faith leaves its mark on every decision made.

✪ March 9

James Anthony Walsh
ROMAN CATHOLIC
February 24, 1867–April 14, 1936

When James Anthony Walsh was ordained to the priesthood, the Roman Catholic Church still considered the United States to be a mission field, and church members in America gave hardly any thought to mission work elsewhere. Most of the material on missions available to the ordinary Roman Catholic was imported from England, where it had been translated from the French. It was not widely read. When James Anthony Walsh was asked in later years how he became interested in mission, he had no ready reply. He recalled, however, that a German Jesuit had visited the parish where he grew up, distributing cards that would hold twelve pennies. Walsh took a card and went around the neighborhood collecting coins for orphans in China. Maybe that planted a seed. Later, a seminary teacher from France who had friends in missionary work in Japan attracted his interest. Walsh and the professor together raised $15 a month to support a catechist in Japan.

As a young parish priest, Walsh continued to have a special interest in mission. He supported the Society for the Propagation of the Faith, and in 1903, was asked to become director of the Boston branch office. Lacking materials to rouse interest in mission, he joined with two others to produce a small magazine on the subject. He was already thinking about creating a seminary to train men for mission. Approval for that project was given in 1911. With the support of the American Roman Catholic leadership, it was designed to create a religious society of priests dedicated specifically to foreign missionary work. In 1918, the first Maryknoll priests left for China and before long there were Maryknoll sisters as well. Asia was the first focus of Maryknoll attention, but by the time Walsh died in 1936, World War II was disrupting that area. As Maryknoll priests were driven out of Asia, they shifted attention to Latin America. Their priests and sisters were soon caught up in the social conflict there. Walsh's seminary professor once showed him a letter from a colleague discouraged by his lack of success in mission, who was convinced that progress would not be made until missionary blood was shed. The possibility of such an outcome was a frequent theme in Walsh's talks to seminarians, and Maryknoll priests and sisters have witnessed with their lives over the years. James Anthony Walsh understood that the work of mission is God's work. God may "crush us to the ground," he said. "He may make us feel spiritual desolation. We do not know. We only know that He will give us the strength to bear whatever he sends."

A reading from a letter from James Anthony Walsh to "All Maryknollers"

My beloved Maryknollers,

I make no distinction among you, since we are all missioners. Whether our daily tasks are in the homeland or in the field, we are of one heart and one mind — pledged to the converting of the world, with special interest in the people entrusted to our care by Rome.

The sands are going down in the glass, and my days are evidently numbered, I write in the expectation of my departure, with God's grace, for the life that changes not.

It has been my privilege — a rare one for a cofounder — to see the work of Maryknoll developed to a promising maturity. I thank God for the bountiful Providence which from the beginning has been so strikingly manifest.

I am far from thinking that our development is perfect. No one has been more conscious of weakness than I, who for all these years have been at the head of our society. I have often lamented my own shortcomings and my limitations. All I can say for myself is that I have tried to be the willing instrument of God, who has urged me forward, leaving to me the duty of watching that I should not trip....

There are many counsels and admonitions I would leave with you, but above all else, take care that your work for Maryknoll brings you closer to Christ and increases your desire to seek His will in all things — be it life or death! Let Him be your tower of strength! Cultivate reliance on His Divine Providence! "I can do all things in Him which strengthens me."

To work for Christ is a great privilege. To labor with Him, and in Him and through Him, mindful always that we are His willing instruments, is the assurance of our success, spiritual especially, and often material. Learn to be familiar with Christ as an elder brother. Speak to Him as if His presence were visible, and, in the silence of the tabernacle, or in your own room — listen!!!

Let His humility and that of our Blessed Lady and St. Joseph mark your lives! — I cannot urge you too strongly to be humble. The self-opinionated person accomplishes little and is a disturbing influence. Try to see the other person's point of view, and remember that arguments, unless sincerely employed to get at the truth, are of little or no use....

Be generous, self-forgetting and patient — then your life will be as happy, holy and successful missioners will be assured....

May each of you persevere in your holy vocation, and fight courageously to the end against worldliness and the powers of darkness! My wish is that you remain simple, generous, cheerful and selfless, loving God and His saints with a strong personal affection, as little children love good parents. May God keep you faithful to the highest ideals of those who would follow Christ!...Keep me in filial remembrance, and know that if God finds me worthy, I will be your helper until we meet merrily in heaven.

> Affectionately in Christ,
> James Anthony Walsh

✪ *March 10*

John Tietjen

LUTHERAN

June 18, 1928–February. 15, 2004

Though relationships between Christian traditions can be tense, major differences within a tradition are often ferocious. In the history of 20th-century controversies among Lutherans in America, the Rev. Dr. John Tietjen played a heroic role. Yet his early career showed no signs of anything but the usual progress of a successful church leader. As a member of the Lutheran Church–Missouri Synod, he took his BA from Concordia Collegiate Institute in Bronxville, New York, then a master of divinity from Concordia Seminary in St. Louis. He went on to earn his master of sacred theology and doctorate from Union Theological Seminary in New York. Tietjen served a parish before becoming what might be called a bureaucrat as the executive secretary of the Division of Public Relations for the Lutheran Council in the USA. This organization was formed by the various Lutheran denominations in the United States to work together on a number of projects, in the hope of achieving greater unity among themselves.

In 1969, a career change put Tietjen in a position to make some momentous decisions. He became President of Concordia, the premier seminary of the Lutheran Church–Missouri Synod, in St. Louis. In that era, many members of its faculty were noted scholars, embracing the some of the best methods of biblical, historical, and theological research. The seminary had become celebrated beyond its own denomination for its rigorous theological discourse and solid academic discipline. Yet one faction of the LC–MS disapproved of their methods and conclusions. A very conservative cleric, J. A. O. Preus, was elected president of the Synod. Intent on eliminating what he considered "liberalism" from the seminary, he demanded that Tietjen, as its president, put a stop to the teaching of historical criticism, which analyzed the Bible with the same rigor as any other historical book. Tietjen refused to comply and was fired in 1974. Far from settling the controversy, a church-dividing war erupted from Preus's action. Most of the other faculty and student body quit in support of their former president, moving across town to set up a new school called the "Seminary in Exile."

The split at the seminary was mirrored in hundreds of congregations around the country and resulted in a new Lutheran body called the Association of Evangelical Lutheran Churches (AELC). In 1987, Seminex, as it had come to be known, merged with the Lutheran School of Theology in Chicago. In 1988, the AELC merged with the American Lutheran Church (ALC) and the Lutheran Church in America (LCA) to form a new Lutheran body, the Evangelical Lutheran Church in America (ELCA).

Some people regarded John Tietjen as the leader of a schismatic faction, but others continue to honor his steadfast commitment to the gospel for the good of the whole Body of Christ. He refused to save his job by participating in the dismantling of a great scholarly seminary that would have condemned faculty and students to one narrow interpretation of Holy Scripture. Tietjen's integrity, academic qualifications, theological insights, pastoral instincts, and passion for unity under the gospel have helped have helped shape the current expression of American Lutheranism.

A reading from a sermon by John H. Tietjen entitled "Peter's Confession — and Ours"

Peter's confession makes it clear who Jesus is. He is everything I have said this morning, everything others have said about him, but he is more. He is the Messiah, the Son of the living God. Son of God tells us who he is; Messiah tells us what he does. As Son of God he did the Messiah's work of bringing God's gracious rule into people's lives. Peter made his confession out of the living faith of the people of Israel. They were waiting and longing for the Messiah to come, as many Jews do to this day. Peter was convinced he had found him.

We could use other language to confess the substance of Peter's confession. With the apostle John we could say Jesus is the eternal Word of God, who creates new life in us. With the apostle Paul we could say Jesus is the embodiment of God through whom we become a new creation. The point is the same. Jesus makes all the difference in how we see God and God's relation to us, what we do with our lives, and what we can expect God to do for us.

God is a very present help in trouble, as I am ready to witness. God gives the strength needed for the problems each new day brings. I have placed my life in God's hands. Therefore I know all will be well, including what happens at death. No, death is not the end of it all. Jesus is the Messiah, the Son of the living God. God raised Jesus from the dead. Because He lives, I too will live. The Messiah said so.

✸ *March 11*

Isabella Thoburn

METHODIST

March 29, 1840–September 1, 1901

In the middle of the 19th century, the women of India remained, as someone put it, "unwanted at birth, unhonoured in life, unwept in death." It was still customary in many areas for a widow to be cremated alive on her husband's funeral pyre. James Thoburn,* an early Methodist missionary in India, felt someone was needed to reach out to these women. Initially, he hoped his wife could begin such a ministry, but when she died that dream could no longer be realized. The one other woman he knew who had the skills and dedication for such a ministry was his sister, Isabella, a schoolteacher in Ohio. On an impulse he wrote to her. Isabella was willing to try, but only under Methodist auspices, and there was no Methodist missionary society as yet prepared to send a woman abroad. Three years passed before a society was organized and Isabella could go. With her, in 1869, went Clara Swain,* a doctor, the first medical missionary sent by the Methodist Church.

The idea of sending women as missionaries to foreign countries was still new in the United States, and not accepted by all. But this was nothing compared to the resistance in India, where the culture was unprepared for women as teachers or the notion of instruction for female children. When Thoburn organized her first school, she had difficulty coaxing seven frightened girls to come in. Such was the opposition that a man with a club had to be hired to stand at the door to prevent intruders from trying to disrupt the program.

Isabella was much more than a teacher. She went out into the villages to share the gospel with women, traveled across India to speak up for woman's education, and published a semi-monthly journal in Hindi titled *Women's Friend* (Rafiq-i-Niswan). Slowly the school grew from a one-room establishment to include a high school, then a boarding school, and finally a college. In 1893, a teacher's program and a kindergarten were added. By 1903, it had been named the Isabella Thoburn College, and is now the women's college of Lucknow University. When President Harrison met Thoburn, he remarked that if she alone had been the result of all the money spent on missions, she was worth the entire sum. One of her students said of her, "Again and again the thought would come to me, that, just as Jesus came to show us the Father, she had come to show us Jesus."

A reading from reports made by Isabella Thoburn on her work in India

When we can not go to the village women; we may bring them to us in the persons of their daughters. Teachers can not always, or often, be placed in remote villages; but the girls can be brought to boarding-schools in central stations; and while they live in a manner as nearly like their home as possible, they may be taught elementary knowledge of books, and practical wisdom of the kind that Lemuel's mother commended to her son. There are girls in the middle classes of such schools, in the province of Rohilkhand, who have not only cooked but ground the grain that made their food throughout the school course: there is a school in Kumaun where bright intelligent girls have passed the examinations that admitted them to the Agra Medical School, who not only ground their own grain, but helped to plant and reap it in the terraced fields on the hillside. These girls are good Bible students, and before they leave school they have opportunity to teach in Sunday-schools and visit in mohullas near by, doing just the evangelistic work which is needed in their native villages. They return, not only as teachers, but to build up the Christian family lives of their homes, whether with their parents or husbands, and to aid in developing the spiritual life and work of the village Churches.

We have sometimes forced growths, and sometimes prevented development. We have not always remembered that education is indigenous. Given the right impulse, surrounded by the right influence, restraints, and encouragement, character of mind and heart will have a healthy growth, and habit and custom will form around character. We have tried sometimes to train the women and girls committed to our care to our customs, but oftener to our ideas of their customs. They may not arrange their homes according to our taste, nor dress as we would choose, but if they have that within them which delights in "whatsoever things are true . . . and whatsoever things are lovely," they will not make serious mistakes.

We should lay the duty of bringing India to Christ upon every heart that we can touch. One lesson will not be sufficient. Like the study of English, or science, or any other subject, this requires a daily living contact with missionary work and interests. Its lessons must be well learned in order to pass tests of time, and trial, and discouragement, and the learner must be filled with the power that is only given by the Holy Spirit. Organization is the present-day method, and this missionary effort should be given the form and permanent force of organization. The Young Women's Christian Association, the Society of Christian Endeavor, or something similar, should find place in all our schools.

And so education comes back to evangelization. All that is done or planned in any department of the service has but one Object, to extend the kingdom of Christ and to glorify his name.

✪ *March 12*

Levi Coffin

QUAKER

October 28, 1798–September 16, 1877

A slave-catcher on the trail of fugitive slaves remarked, "There's an underground railroad around here, and Levi Coffin is its president." Indeed, there were many who played their part in the operation of smuggling slaves to freedom, but Coffin was particularly successful and persistent. Brought up on a South Carolina farm without slaves, he spent so much time working with his father in their fields that he was unable to spend much time in school. But he inherited from his parents and grandparents a hatred of slavery, and those feelings were confirmed when a group of slaves in chains passed by his home and he heard them tell his father that they were being separated from their families to be sold in another state. Young Levi wondered how he would feel to be separated from his parents. As a teenager, he acted for the first time to assist a slave in gaining his freedom. Despite his limited education, Coffin attempted to start a school for slaves, but opposition from their owners soon forced it to close.

When Coffin married and moved to the new state of Indiana, he quickly learned that the route being followed by fugitive slaves passed through his community. He began hiding them and helping them on their way. Three principal lines from the south converged at his house. As Coffin put it: "The roads were always in running order, the connections were good, the conductors active and zealous, and there was no lack of passengers. Seldom a week passed without our receiving passengers by the mysterious road." Eventually it was estimated that over 3,000 slaves passed through the simple eight-room house in Wayne County. Later Coffin moved to Cincinnati and opened a store selling goods made exclusively by freed slaves. He visited England to raise funds for the cause and served as a delegate to an International Anti-Slavery Conference in Paris.

A reading from the *Reminiscences of Levi Coffin*

In the winter of 1826–27, fugitives began to come to our house, and as it became more widely known on different routes that the slaves fleeing from bondage would find a welcome and shelter at our house, and be forwarded safely on their journey, the number increased. Friends in the neighborhood, who had formerly stood aloof from the work, fearful of the penalty of the law, were encouraged to engage in it when they saw the fearless manner in which I acted, and the success that attended my efforts. They would contribute to clothe the fugitives, and would aid in forwarding them on their way, but were timid about sheltering them under their roof; so that part of the work devolved on us. Some seemed really glad to see the work go on, if somebody else would do it. Others doubted the propriety of it, and tried to discourage me, and dissuade me from running such risks. They manifested great concern for my safety and pecuniary interests, telling me that such a course of action would injure my business and perhaps ruin me; that I ought to consider the welfare of my family; and warning me that my life was in danger, as there were many threats made against me by the slave-hunters and those who sympathized with them.

After listening quietly to these counselors, I told them that I felt no condemnation for anything that I had ever done for the fugitive slaves. If by doing my duty and endeavoring to fulfill the injunctions of the Bible, I injured my business, then let my business go. As to my safety, my life was in the hands of my Divine Master, and I felt that I had his approval. I had no fear of the danger that seemed to threaten my life or my business. If I was faithful to duty, and honest and industrious, I felt that I would be preserved, and that I could make enough to support my family. At one time there came to see me a good old Friend, who was apparently very deeply concerned for my welfare. He said he was as much opposed to slavery as I was, but thought it very wrong to harbor fugitive slaves. No one there knew of what crimes they were guilty; they might have killed their masters, or committed some other atrocious deed, then those who sheltered them, and aided them in their escape from justice would indirectly be accomplices. He mentioned other objections which he wished me to consider, and then talked for some time, trying to convince me of the errors of my ways. I heard him patiently until he had relieved his mind of the burden upon it, and then asked if he thought the Good Samaritan stopped to inquire whether the man who fell among thieves was guilty of any crime before he attempted to help him? I asked him if he were to see a stranger who had fallen into the ditch would he not help him out until satisfied that he had committed no atrocious deed? These, and many other questions which I put to him, he did not seem able to answer satisfactorily. He was so perplexed and confused that I really pitied the good old man, and advised him to go home and read his Bible thoroughly, and pray over it, and I thought his concern about my aiding fugitive slaves would be removed from his mind, and that he would feel like helping me in the work. We parted in good feeling, and he always manifested warm friendship toward me until the end of his days.

✪ *March 13*

Mary Katherine Jones Bennett
PRESBYTERIAN

November 28, 1864–April 11, 1950

The two great social issues debated by 19th-century Americans were slavery and women's suffrage. The former was settled by the Civil War. Women could then concentrate on winning the right to vote and taking an equal place in society. The generation of women who came of age after the Civil War remained disenfranchised, but were increasingly able to make their voices heard through various women's organizations. Then, after World War I, the women's suffrage amendment to the Constitution was adopted, allowing them to become equal partners in other social institutions.

Mary Katherine Jones Bennett was born as the Civil War was drawing to a close, graduated from Elmira College with high honors, and settled into a traditional career as a teacher. Seeking to serve her church, she became involved in social service and, by 1894, was national secretary for the Women's Board of Home Missions of the Presbyterian Church, U.S.A. She was also active in the College Settlements Association, founded to create centers for social work following the pattern of Jane Addams's Hull House in Chicago.

Married in 1898, Bennett stepped back from her national positions for about ten years and then returned to serve from 1909 to 1923 as president of the Women's Board of Home Missions. When the Presbyterian Church decided not to keep women's work separate, Bennett became the vice president of a merged Board of Home Missions, serving in that capacity from 1923 to 1941.

During these years, the church started using new methods of analysis to determine how best to serve the needs of society. Bennett joined with Walter Rauschenbusch* and others to issue a collection of studies of the church's role "In City Industries," "In Mountains and Mills," "Among Negro Laborers," and "In Lumber Camps and Mines." Later she wrote position papers on "Causes of Unrest Among Women of the Church" and on the status of women in the Presbyterian Church. She served ecumenically on committees of the Federal Council of Churches and was present at the founding of the interdenominational Council of Women for Home Missions in 1908.

A reading from Mary Katherine Jones Bennett's essay "The Call to Service"

Statistics . . . show that church membership is steadily declining in proportion to population. Such figures prove conclusively that the great work to be done by the church among the large groups of people affected by the present labor difficulties, must be done largely with those who have lived apart from the church, careless of their own needs or of the help that church could give. To these groups the church has at this time a definite ministry — in welcoming them into the communities to which economic need may take them, in attaching them to the local church body, in heartening them for their tasks, in showing to them that "No nation is safe without Jesus. The America of the future, like America of the past, must be a spiritual reality, or we are doomed."

There are doubtless many reasons, springing from innumerable sources, for the lack of church attendance — some due to indifference, some to positive antagonism but the one great general cause, it is certain, is that for multitudes of people attention is concentrated on the problems of physical existence; the rapid increase of material things to the few raises hope in the minds of many that they, too, may be among those who will share largely in the wealth of the country. This hope directs thought and energy into the channel of commercialism. Whatever tends to bring about the realization of the hope is keenly sought to the exclusion of other things which seem of less immediate importance. This position is emphasized by the great increase of secular literature in the form of newspapers and cheap magazines, which provide a reading supply that directs the attention still further toward material things and away from the contemplation of matters relating to the spirit. Travel increases and Sunday travel especially. Church attendance suffers thereby, and more and more the Church seems a thing apart from the problem of life.

While a few are actively antagonistic to the church for one reason or another — a few because of persecution suffered in other lands, the great mass of non-church goers are frankly indifferent, if that can be called indifference which is without thought, i.e., the church does not appear on their horizon except as the agency of marriage and death — they ignore it because they never think of it....

To command the attention of the great throng that is apart from the church, that body must present an aggressive program of service; it must preach a gospel of justice, of brotherliness, of love; it must translate its preaching into daily practice in large things and in small; it must concern itself with this world's relationships as well as with those of a future life; with clearness and directness it must convince all that "man cannot live by bread alone."

✪ March 14 _____

Fulton John Sheen

ROMAN CATHOLIC

May 8, 1895–December 10, 1979

In recent years, religion on television has all too often been identified with those televangelists whose priority seems to be raising funds and supporting right-wing causes. Yet one of the first church people to make use of this new medium was a Roman Catholic bishop. In a purple-trimmed black cassock, with his piercing deep-set eyes, Msgr. Fulton Sheen was a commanding presence on the small screen as he preached a very traditional Christianity. Sheen's pioneering broadcasts used none of the current techniques such as vast, theater-like auditoriums, hand-waving choirs, PowerPoint "praise" lyrics, or plexiglass lecterns beloved of the current flamboyant preachers we see when we surf channels. Instead, he sat alone on the small set, using only a simple blackboard along with his winning charm. His effectiveness lay in bringing classic Christian perspectives to current issues and the struggles of his generation. While acknowledging his Roman Catholic perspective, Sheen delivered a Christian message that might be affirmed by most church people, providing thoughtful, theological reflection on their lives.

Born in El Paso, Illinois, Sheen graduated from that state's St. Viator College in Bourbonnais. He studied at St. Paul Seminary in Minnesota and was ordained in September 1919, becoming an instructor in religion at the Catholic University of America. Eventually, he preached on WLWL Radio in New York, which, by 1930, led to his becoming the regular preacher on NBC radio's "The Catholic Hour." His familiarity with broadcasting made him a logical choice to preside over New York's first televised religious service in 1940 and to serve as director of U.S. activities for the Society for Propagation of the Faith (1950–66). He understood that television offered a pulpit that could evangelize an increasingly secular culture. Sheen's long-running program, "Life is Worth Living," started in 1952. When he was made an Assistant Bishop of New York, then Bishop of the Diocese of Rochester, it seemed somehow like a demotion.

A reading from a presentation by Fulton Sheen on compulsions

How We Are Torn: Compulsion I

"I am a compulsive drinker."
"She is a compulsive eater."
"I don't know what made me do it; I just heard a voice."

These are the excuses one hears daily, implying that the will is no longer free, but as if under the direction of another.

Is there such a thing as compulsion? Definitely. How does it come about? Generally through three stages: consent, act and habit. Every person has buried in his subconsciousness certain powers, capacities or impulses given for his perfection. One refers to our body, the other to our mind, and the last to things outside the body and mind. The first is sex or the creative impulse; the other is a desire for power, e.g., through a search for truth or the pursuit of a talent or the right use of power. But outside of the body and the mind, there are things. The person is finally driven to possess property. Just as the will is free because a man can call his soul his own, so property is external and an economic guarantee of human freedom.

Each of these impulses is capable of being perverted. Fire on the hearth is good, but fire in the clothes closet is not. The sex instinct can be distorted into license and perversion. In that case, the other person is really not loved, but is used. One drinks the water; one forgets the glass. Hidden in our nature is a lot of flammable material which is not ignited except by some suggestion from without, with the consent of the will. External influences only tempt; they do not compel. There is no inseparable connection between the two. When Joseph was tempted by Potiphar's wife he said, "How can I do this great wickedness and sin against God?"

The mind's desire for knowledge and truth can be perverted by each person saying to himself, "There will be no measure of truth or knowledge outside of me. Whatever I decide to be true is true. I make the truth. I make the law. I am my own creator. I am my own savior." The drive for the possession of things can be turned into avarice, greed, selfishness and the refusal to help the poor.

When does the good impulse become tempted? It becomes tempted generally by a solicitation from without. For example, the sex impulse might be perverted by a picture, a book, a person. There is no perversion at this particular point; there is only a suggestion. This is what is called temptation to do something immoral. No temptation to do evil is wrong in itself; it is only the consent which is wrong.

It has been said that it is wrong to repress our impulses. No! Repression is not always wrong. As a matter of fact, every expression of something good, e.g., to give food to a hungry person, is a repression of selfishness.

When an outside evil pleasure is presented, our nature exaggerates the proportions of everything; it shows the pleasure or the profit through a magnifying glass, multiplied by desire and expectation. One can imagine a mountain of gold, but one can never see a mountain of gold. What the imagination does is to present things to the mind not as they are, but as the mind would have them to be. Notice that all love songs are songs of expectation. Nothing cheats a man as much as expectation, which promises high but performs nothing.

The desire to pervert our good impulses means that the subjective and the objective meet; that which before was only within the heart now begins to feel the touch and the allure of something outside. As Shakespeare said:

> How oft the sight of means to do ill deeds
> Make deeds ill done!

After the consent of the will to do what is wrong, comes the deed. As the boy grows into a man, so the will grows into the act. Once the wrong act is done, there follows the uneasiness and remorse which is actually God calling the soul back to itself. The act repeated many times turns into habits. They are like tiny strands of silk, any one of which can be readily broken, but when woven day after day, they become a great chain which no giant can break. Habits tend to create or strengthen an attitude and disposition. They become so very natural that we are hardly conscious of them, whether good or bad. All the good things lie downstream, and all we have to do is just float like a log. When finally the habit creates a rut in our brain so that we automatically respond to any temptation, we have what is called "compulsion."

✪ March 15

William Stringfellow

EPISCOPALIAN

April 26, 1928–March 2, 1985

World War II and its aftermath produced a rare sense of unity in American society. A common foe had been defeated, and heroic soldiers returned to build suburban homes and elect a president most often seen by the public playing golf. But William Stringfellow found no comfort from this peaceful interlude. He perceived underlying and unresolved tensions in American life and devoted himself to calling people's attention to them, and helping others who shared his vision.

Work and scholarships enabled Stringfellow to enter Bates College at age 15. Afterward he studied at the London School of Economics, following this with a period of service in the Second Armored Division of the US Army. Upon earning his law degree from Harvard, Stringfellow moved to Harlem to live. He opened an office there and involved himself in the local community. Stringfellow joined the East Harlem Protestant Parish, where he taught Bible study for the youth of the neighborhood, showing his students that the New Testament has power to transform lives and communities when thoughtfully read.

Never given to parochial thinking, Stringfellow also worked in the World Christian Student Federation and the World Council of Churches. Nor did he have any aversion to being a faithful disturber of the peace. He once stood up in the National Cathedral in Washington, DC, to plead for the ordination of women before the Episcopal Church had made up its mind on that subject. His home on Block Island became a kind of sanctuary of hospitality to other prophetic Christians, like his friend, Daniel Berrigan,* the Jesuit antinuclear activist.

Much-traveled, and the author of many books, Stringfellow was persistent in his attempts to call the church to a deeper awareness of the aggressive and destructive power of the "principalities of this world" and the need for

Christians to confront them with the life-giving gospel. His belief that God is active in the world and engaged with our lives animated his efforts to assert unpopular truths, both to religious and secular institutions. Stringfellow argued that only a return to the prophets' radical call to repentance, together with a complete allegiance to Christ's new life could offer hope to our nation. Karl Barth called him "the most conscientious and thoughtful" mind he encountered during an American visit.

A reading from the preface to *An Ethic for Christians and Other Aliens in a Strange Land*

My concern is to understand America biblically. This book — which is, simultaneously, a theological statement and a political argument — implements that concern.

The effort is to comprehend the nation, to grasp what is happening right now to the nation and to consider the destiny of the nation within the scope and style of the ethics and the ethical metaphors distinctive to the biblical witness in history.

The task is to treat the nation within the tradition of biblical politics — to understand America biblically — not the other way around, not (to put it in an appropriately awkward way) to construe the Bible Americanly. There has been much too much of the latter in this country's public life and religious ethos. There still is. I expect such indulgences to multiply, to reach larger absurdities, to become more scandalous, to increase blasphemously as America's crisis as a nation distends. To interpret the Bible for the convenience of America, as apropos as that may seem to be to many Americans, represents a radical violence to both the character and content of the biblical message. It fosters a fatal vanity that America is a divinely favored nation and makes of it the credo of a civic religion which is directly threatened by, and, hence, which is anxious and hostile toward the biblical Word. It arrogantly misappropriates political images from the Bible and applies them to America, so that America is conceived of as Zion: as the righteous nation, as a people of superior political morality, as a country and society chosen and especially esteemed by God. In archetypical form in this century, material abundance, redundant productivity, technological facility, and military predominance are publicly cited to verify the alleged divine preference and prove the supposed national virtue. It is just this kind of Sadducean sophistry, distorting the biblical truth for American purposes, which, in truth, occasions the moral turmoil which the nation so manifestly suffers today and which, I believe, renders us a people as unhappy as we are hopeless. It is profane, as well as grandiose, to manipulate the Bible in order to apologize for America.

✪ March 16 _____

George Washington Truett

SOUTHERN BAPTIST

May 6, 1867–July 7, 1944

People recognized gifts in George Washington Truett that he was slower to notice in himself. While he planned to be a lawyer, others saw his call to ministry. He was offered a church before he was ordained, and ordained before he had a parish to serve. When a congregation first approached him, his first instinct was to turn it down. Yet when he finally accepted a call, he proceeded to serve that congregation for 47 years, building it into the largest congregation not only in America but in the world at that time.

Born on a mountain farm in North Carolina, Truett was 19 before he made a personal profession of faith in Christ. He joined the local Baptist Church, was baptized, and began to teach church school. To pay his way through college, he decided to open a school and soon had 300 students and three assistant teachers. He began to preach also and was offered a congregation but turned it down to move with his parents to Texas. After he spoke on Sunday in his new church there, the oldest deacon stood and called on the congregation to ordain him. Truett protested, asking for six months to consider, but the people of Wainwright, Texas, were unwilling to wait. "But there I was," he said, "against the whole church." So he was ordained but, lacking a place to serve, accepted a position as chief financial officer of Baylor University. He eliminated the institution's considerable debt in less than two years. He was later offered the presidency of the university but turned it down, recognizing at last that pastoral ministry was his calling.

He was 30 years old when — after a first instinct to turn it down — he accepted a call from the First Baptist Church of Dallas. Over the next 47 years, the congregation grew from 715 members to over 7,000. Truett's preaching was a major factor. He always preached for decision. But an excellent training program for Sunday School teachers was also an important factor.

A reading from a sermon by George Washington Truett on religious liberty

We shall do well, both as citizens and as Christians, if we will hark back to the chief actors and lessons in the early and epoch-making struggles of this great Western democracy, for the full establishment of civil and religious liberty — back to the days of Washington and Jefferson and Madison, and back to the days of our Baptist fathers, who have paid such a great price, through the long generations, that liberty, both religious and civil, might have free course and be glorified everywhere.

Years ago, at a notable dinner in London, that world-famed statesman, John Bright, asked an American statesman, himself a Baptist, the noble Dr. J. L. M. Curry, "What distinct contribution has your America made to the science of government?" To that question Dr. Curry replied: "The doctrine of religious liberty." After a moment's reflection, Mr. Bright made the worthy reply: "It was a tremendous contribution."

Supreme Contribution of New World

Indeed, the supreme contribution of the new world to the old is the contribution of religious liberty. This is the chiefest contribution that America has thus far made to civilization. And historic justice compels me to say that it was preeminently a Baptist contribution. The impartial historian, whether in the past, present or future, will ever agree with our American historian, Mr. Bancroft, when he says: "Freedom of conscience, unlimited freedom of mind, was from the first the trophy of the Baptists." And such historian will concur with the noble John Locke who said: "The Baptists were the first propounders of absolute liberty, just and true liberty, equal and impartial liberty." Ringing testimonies like these might be multiplied indefinitely.

Not Toleration, but Right

Baptists have one consistent record concerning liberty throughout all their long and eventful history. They have never been a party to oppression of conscience. They have forever been the unwavering champions of liberty, both religious and civil. Their contention now, is, and has been, and, please God, must ever be, that it is the natural and fundamental and indefeasible right of every human being to worship God or not, according to the dictates of his conscience, and, as long as he does not infringe upon the rights of others, he is to be held accountable alone to God for all religious beliefs and practices. Our contention is not for mere toleration, but for absolute liberty. There is a wide difference between toleration and liberty. Toleration implies that somebody falsely claims the right to tolerate. Toleration is a concession, while liberty is a right. Toleration is a matter of expediency, while liberty is a matter of principle. Toleration is a gift from God. It is the consistent and insistent contention of our Baptist people, always and everywhere, that religion must be forever voluntary and uncoerced, and that it is not the prerogative of any power, whether civil or ecclesiastical, to compel men to conform to any religious creed or form of worship, or to pay taxes for the support of a religious organization to which they do not believe. God wants free worshipers and no other kind.

✪ March 17 _____

Jupiter Hammon

CONGREGATIONAL

October 17, 1711–1806?

Jupiter Hammon was born a slave and died in slavery. As a child, he was sold to the Lloyd family of Long Island, and he remained in their possession for three generations. Today, however, he is remembered while they are forgotten, since he is known as the first published African American poet. The Lloyds were relatively kind owners, providing their slaves with an education and the opportunity to earn money for themselves. Jupiter Hammon took full advantage of these opportunities, learning to read and write. He maintained a garden plot to sell produce, so that at 21, he was able to purchase a Bible. Recognizing his abilities, the Lloyds made him a clerk in the family business. He worked also as a farmhand and craftsman.

In 1760, Hammon's first poem was published as "An Evening Thought: Salvation by Christ with Penitential Cries." Seventeen years later, he wrote a tribute to Phillis Wheatley — also a slave and poet. Born free, Wheatley had been enslaved at seven and brought to Boston where she also managed to study and develop literary skills. Hammon managed to publish two more poems and four prose pieces, though only seven examples of his work have survived. It is believed that Hammon preached, at least occasionally. His last published work is an "Address to the Negroes of the State of New York" delivered before their African Society on September 24, 1786. In this address, he says he has no desire to be free himself but imagines freedom is a good thing and that those who are able to should seek it. It should be remembered that nothing written by a slave would have been published without the approval of the master. Nevertheless, it is quite possible that Hammon was indeed satisfied with his lot. Nothing is known of the last years of his life.

A reading from an address "to the Negroes of the State of New York" by Jupiter Hammon

Now I acknowledge that liberty is a great thing, and worth seeking for, if we can get it honestly; and by our good conduct prevail on our masters to set us free: though for my own part I do not wish to be free, yet I should be glad if others, especially the young Negroes, were to be free; for many of us who are grown up slaves, and have always had masters to take care of us, should hardly know how to take care of ourselves; and it may be more for our own comfort to remain as we are. That liberty is a great thing we may know from our own feelings, and we may likewise judge so from the conduct of the white people in the late war. How much money has been spent, and how many lives have been lost to defend their liberty! I must say that I have hoped that God would open their eyes, when they were so much engaged for liberty, to think of the state of the poor blacks, and to pity us. He has done it in some measure, and has raised us up many friends; for which we have reason to be thankful, and to hope in his mercy. What may be done further, he only knows, for *known unto God are all his ways from the beginning*. But this, my dear brethren, is by no means the greatest thing we have to be concerned about. Getting our liberty in this world is nothing to our having the liberty of the children of God. Now the Bible tells us that we are all, by nature, sinners; that we are slaves to sin and Satan, and that unless we are converted, or born again, we must be miserable for ever. Christ says, except a man be born again, he cannot see the kingdom of God; and all that do not see the kingdom of God, must be in the kingdom of darkness. There are but two places where all go after death, white and black, rich and poor; those places are Heaven and Hell. Heaven is a place made for those who are born again, and who love God; and it is a place where they will be happy for ever. Hell is a place made for those who hate God, and are his enemies, and where they will be miserable to all eternity. Now you may think you are not enemies to God, and do not hate him: but if your heart has not been changed, and you have not become true Christians, you certainly are enemies to God, and have been opposed to him ever since you were born.

Many of you, I suppose, never think of this, and are almost as ignorant as the beasts that perish. Those of you who can read, I must beg you to read the Bible; and whenever you can get time, study the Bible; and if you can get no other time, spare some of your time from sleep, and learn what the mind and will of God is.

But what shall I say to them who cannot read? This lay with great weight on my mind, when I thought of writing to my poor brethren; but I hope that those who can read will take pity on them, and read what I have to say to them. In hopes of this, I will beg of you to spare no pains in trying to learn to read. If you are once engaged, you may learn. Let all the time you can get be spent in trying to learn to read. Get those who can read, to learn you; but remember, that what you learn for, is to read the Bible. If there was no Bible, it would be no matter whether you could read or not. Reading other books would do you no good. But the Bible is the word of God, and tells you what you must do to please God; it tells you how you may escape misery, and be happy for ever.

✷ *March 18* ───────────────────────────────

Catherine de Hueck Doherty

ROMAN CATHOLIC

August 15, 1896–December 14, 1985

Perhaps it was the chaotic life she lived that convinced Catherine Doherty of the central importance of prayer. She was born into a wealthy Russian family but was married at the age of 15 and found herself and her husband caught up in the First World War. She served at the front as a nurse and he as an engineer, but when the communist revolution followed the war, they escaped to England and then to Canada. In Canada her husband's health failed, and Catherine went to work to support herself, her husband, and their child, but they endured grinding poverty and the marriage failed. Later it was annulled by the church. Catherine discovered she had a talent for public speaking and made a successful career for herself, traveling across Canada to lecture.

Through these troubled years, her spiritual life deepened. She had been baptized in the Orthodox Church, but became a Roman Catholic in England. In 1930, after spending a year in prayer, she discerned a vocation to serve the poor. With the blessing of the Archbishop of Toronto, she made provisions for her son, sold all that she had, and went to live in the poorest part of the city. Others joined her, and a Friendship House apostolate was created, similar to the Catholic Workers Houses being established by Dorothy Day* at the same time in the United States. Catherine moved to New York in 1937 and established a Friendship House in Harlem where, for a time, she was joined by Thomas Merton.* Catherine married Eddie Doherty in 1943 and in 1958 they returned to Canada and developed a ministry to the rural poor at Combermere in Ontario. Others joined them, and they began the Madonna House movement, devoted to prayer and serving the poor. In 1955, members of the community took the three-fold vows of poverty, chastity, and obedience. Catherine and her husband took the same vows and lived celibate lives thereafter. Today the Madonna House movement has nearly 200 members with an apostolate in 16 cities in Canada and the United States as well as seven other countries in Europe and Africa.

From the writings of Catherine de Hueck Doherty

On the eucharist

The simplest things that a man could give his friends were bread and wine. Christ made these elements a vehicle of his love, of his strength, so that his followers could live his law of love. It is in the mystery of the Eucharist that we acquire the strength to live this law of love.

On the church

From the very beginning of my apostolate, when I sold all that I had, God gave me a tremendous love for the church and for priests. This church cannot perish. When you love the church, you even love those in the church who do evil. You know that over the centuries the church has been ruined over and over again, and each time she has risen anew more splendid than ever. God has given me an overpowering love for the church. Call me a fool. I am a fool. I see Christ in the church.

On poverty

You cannot be paternalistic toward the poor, that is, live somewhere else and just drop in once in a while and do some kind of social work. You have to become poor. Identification with the poor is identification with Jesus Christ. True, he did say that "the poor you will always have with you." But he also said, "I was in prison. . . . I was hungry, etc." We cannot forget this judgment that awaits us, I pondered very seriously that judgment.

Again, this kind of thinking was radical and unique. We were pioneers. Women just didn't live in storefronts with hoboes! Certainly not! However, it worked! It worked for the hoboes, and it worked for the many, many people who came to join us. I understood that begging and being one with the poor was (and always will be) a crying need of the church.

On prayer

We have forgotten how to pray. We have forgotten that there must be a time when we are silent so we can hear what God wants to say to us. Yes, my friends, we must pray. It must be the prayer of two people in love with each other who cease to talk. Their silence speaks. This is the kind of prayer that the *poustinia* [desert of the soul] will teach you. Resting in God's love, you will understand the *sobornost,* the unity, he wishes for his children. Then, as a *strannik,* a pilgrim, you will go forth and shout and sing about this to all peoples.

Two people in love! When you are in love with God you will understand that he loved you first. You will enter into a deep and mysterious silence and in that silence become one with the Absolute. *Sobornost!* Your oneness with God will overflow to all your brothers and sisters. My friends, this is the kind of prayer we need today. If you pray like this you will be overshadowed by the wings of a dove, the symbol of the Holy Spirit. On those wings your prayer of silence will be lifted into the hands of the Woman Wrapped in Silence, and she will lay it at the feet of the Most Holy Trinity. The answer today to the salvation of mankind lies in prayer.

On living the gospel

What is the essence? Christians who love one another and who form communities of love. Humanity today is the Doubting Thomas who wasn't there when Christ appeared for the first time after his resurrection. Humanity today is a man who must touch the wounds of Christ in order to believe, to be converted. Then he will come to the Lord in thousands, perhaps in millions.

The only way to show these wounds of Christ to others is to live the gospel without compromise. Does that mean that we must turn our lives upside down? Does it mean a complete change of values? Does it mean the breaking up, the demolition of our comfortable way of life? Quite simply, yes, it does.

✖ *March 19* _____

Barbara Andrews

LUTHERAN

May 11, 1935–March 31, 1978

On December 22, 1970, Barbara Andrews became the first woman ordained in the American Lutheran Church. Those who missed the era of debate leading up to this decision and the mixed reception given to those brave representatives of their sex may not fully appreciate their courage and stamina. It is true that women had been ordained in certain other denominations for some time, and notable examples had served in various traditions as pastors for well over a century. Still, the practice had not become widespread and most Christian bodies were simply not open to females as ordained clergy. In the 20th century, the movement toward full gender equality in the church began to gain momentum. Still, the weight of ancient tradition, narrow readings of some of Paul's statements in his epistles, along with stubborn convictions about the role of women in general made the conversation about their ordination difficult. Long after most other careers were open to women, the clergy remained nearly all male.

Many who advocated change were labeled heretics, unsettlers of the divine order, blasphemers, and apostates. These are just some of the more polite labels that were hurled. Suggesting that women could lead a congregation as pastor was enough to lose a position in some church bodies. The fights were heated and bitter. Even after prohibitions on female clergy were lifted, opportunities for service after ordination remained limited, while reception by colleagues, Lutheran or otherwise, could be icy and tense.

Nonetheless, in western culture, vocation had come to be understood as a combination of the individual's deep, inner, personal sense of a call and the community's prayerful ratification of that calling. Therefore some, Barbara Andrews among them, were willing to follow, even in the face of intense opposition, a belief that God was calling them into official ministry. She held firm to the vision of a church in which there is "no more male and female, but all are one in Christ." It seemed an audacious claim of increasing numbers of women in the middle third of the 20th Century that God intended to use them as clergy. But their unwavering trust in the validity of that call eventually enabled their communities of faith to be moved to open the vocation of clergy to women.

Andrews's call was to campus ministry. Countless women barred from ordination had found an outlet for their service in hospital and academic chaplaincies. Their ministry is particularly pastoral, one-on-one encounters or small-group conversations as opposed to liturgical or sacramental functions. Baptisms, weddings, funerals, and weekly communions are not always necessary in such settings to make the love of Christ real to students or patients. At the University of Minnesota, Andrews first served as a campus pastor from 1962 to 1969. She took this position upon graduation from Gustavus Adolphus College, and became one of only three women enrolled in Luther Seminary on the ordination track. Her desire was to serve as a medical chaplain, but one who was able to bring the sacramental aspect of the Christian faith to bear for the sake of the patients she would encounter.

She earned her M.Div. degree in 1969, and by the end of 1970, the ALC had made the decision to ordain women. She had received her call and been approved for ordination by December of that year. After ordination, she was assistant pastor at Edina Community Lutheran Church, then served as chaplain of a nursing home run by Lutheran Social Services of Michigan from 1974 to 1977. She was interim pastor of Resurrection Lutheran Church in Detroit for the final year of her abbreviated life.

In addition to the "normal" difficulties faced by pioneers in a new field — entering a previously all-male domain — Andrews was also physically challenged. Born with cerebral palsy, she used a wheelchair for mobility. Her determination to serve in the church and her decision to seek ordination even before her church was ready are testimony to her unflagging spirit. She served with dedication and care. Her own physical struggles helped her understand what it meant to be on the receiving end of medical care, and to need the constant assistance of others.

In 1978, Pastor Andrews died in a fire in her apartment. She was posthumously awarded the Faithfulness in Ministry Cross from Luther Seminary in Minneapolis. She had carried her burdens with dignity both in the struggle for women's ordination and the struggle for the rights of the physically challenged. In living up to a skeptical world's reservations, she proved that a woman, indeed a woman with serious physical limitations, could be a messenger of God's grace in Christ and an effective pastor in the church. Barbara Andrews opened doors so that many other faithful servants of Christ have entered.

✱ *March 20* _____

John Raleigh Mott

METHODIST

May 25, 1865–January 31, 1955

Americans have tended to be optimistic people, and John Mott rode the high tide of American optimism and idealism in the first half of the 20th century when it seemed to many that such goals could be reached in a not too distant future. It was Mott who invented the slogan, "the evangelization of the world in this generation." "My life," said John Mott toward the end of his life, "might be summed up as an earnest and undiscourageable effort to weave together all nations, all races, and all religious communions in friendship, in fellowship, and in cooperation."

Born in New York State but brought up in Iowa, Mott had a Methodist conversion experience early in his college career. He discovered his vocation when a speaker at Cornell University challenged his hearers with three sentences: "Seekest thou great things for thyself? Seek them not. Seek ye first the Kingdom of God." Responding to that challenge, Mott involved himself with the Y.M.C.A. during his last two years of college and made it his life's work after graduation.

Beginning as national secretary of the Intercollegiate Y.M.C.A. of the U.S.A. and Canada, Mott served also with the Student Volunteer Movement, helped organize the World's Student Christian Federation, and worked for the creation of the World Council of Churches. Eventually, he became general-secretary of the International Committee of the Y.M.C.A. and, from 1926 to 1937, president of the Y.M.C.A.'s World Committee. His international travels and contacts led to various diplomatic missions on behalf of the American government and activities on behalf of prisoners of war in various countries. Although the uniqueness of Christ remained central to Mott's vision, he also worked successfully with Jews, Muslims and Buddhists, seeking common understandings and ways to cooperate. He was awarded the Nobel Peace Prize in 1946. Few if any others have succeeded as well as Mott at combining a deep commitment to evangelism with ecumenical and interfaith activity. "While life lasts," he said, "I am an evangelist."

A reading from John R. Mott's Nobel Prize Lecture, December 13, 1946

There is an irresistible demand to strengthen the leadership of the constructive forces of the world at the present momentous time. This is true because of stupendous, almost unbelievable changes which have taken place in recent years on every continent. Extreme nationalism and Bolshevism have broken up the old world, a new world is in the making. It is literally true that old things are passing away; all things may become new, granted we have wise, unselfish, and determined guides.

What should today and tomorrow across the breadth of the world characterize the leadership of the forces of righteousness and unselfishness?

It should be a comprehending leadership. It should reveal a vivid awareness of the present expansive, urgent, and dangerous world situation. The leaders must understand its antecedents and background. They must know the real battleground, therefore the forces and factors that oppose, and those that are with us. They must indeed know our world, our time, and our destiny. In discovering the leaders of tomorrow we must become acquainted with the unanswered questions of ambitious youth and the possibilities of human nature. Above all, we must rely upon the superhuman resources.

The leadership so imperatively needed just now must be truly creative. The demand is for thinkers and not mechanical workers. Bishop Gore, one of the most discerning leaders of his day, summed up our need in an aphorism as apt today as yesterday: "We do not think and we do not pray"; that is, we do not use the principal power at our disposal — the power of thought — and we do not avail ourselves of incomparably our greatest power — the superhuman power of prayer. Well may we heed the injunction of St. Peter to "gird up the loins of your mind." How essential it is that those who tomorrow are to lead the constructive forces should give diligent heed that the discipline of their lives, the culture of their souls, and the thoroughness of their processes of spiritual discovery and appropriations be such as will enable them to meet the demands of a most exacting age.

The leadership must be statesmanlike. And here let us remind ourselves of the traits of the true statesman — the genuinely Christian statesman. He simply must be a man of vision. He sees what the crowd does not see. He takes in a wider sweep, and he sees before others see. How true it is that where there is no vision the people perish.

The most trustworthy leader is one who adopts and applies guiding principles. He trusts them like the North Star. He follows his principles no matter how many oppose him and no matter how few go with him. This has been the real secret of the wonderful leadership of Mahatma Gandhi. In the midst of most bewildering conditions he has followed, cost what it might, the guiding principles of non-violence, religious unity, removal of untouchability, and economic independence.

In closing, let me emphasize the all-important point that Jesus Christ summed up the outstanding, unfailing, and abiding secret of all truly great and enduring leadership in the Word: "He who would be greatest among you shall be the servant of all." He Himself embodied this truth and became "the Prince Leader of the Faith," that is, the leader of the leaders.

✠ *March 21*

William J. Seymour

PENTECOSTAL

May 2, 1870–September 28, 1922

William Seymour was one of those who challenged and changed the life of the church, though he himself was rejected. Raised as a Baptist in Louisiana by parents who had been slaves, he received very little formal education. Nevertheless, he taught himself to read and write and began to study the Bible, convinced that the Holy Spirit's gifts could still be experienced in the present-day church.

He also believed that wherever this came to pass, Jesus would be proclaimed with power, and a unity of Christian worship and work would replace the factions in the church, whether denominational or racial. Seymour was influenced in his convictions by the teachings of a man named Parham in Houston, who expected the Holy Spirit to move in some mighty way in the near future. Seymour began to preach, not with great oratory, but with a simple, quiet conviction of the trustworthiness of God's promises as he read them in Scripture.

In 1906, he was invited to become the pastor of the vacant Second Baptist Church in Los Angeles, but what seemed like a great opportunity came to an abrupt end. After his first sermon, Seymour was locked out of the church. The call had come as part of intense prayer for an outpouring of the Holy Spirit, but when Seymour proclaimed his understanding that this outpouring would be accompanied by the gift of tongues, his new flock would not hear it. Whatever sign of the Spirit's presence they had been praying for, it did not include glossolalia. Parham had taught, and Seymour had come to believe, that speaking in tongues would accompany each outpouring of the Spirit. It was clear to both Parham and Seymour that the speech would be for the purposes of praising Christ and spreading the word of God, not simply as a kind of sensationalism or competition among believers. Still, Seymour's preaching caused more controversy than joy, and his ministry at Second Baptist Church ended.

Seymour was not to be defeated, however, by a single congregation's rejection. He found an unused church on Azusa Street and began to lead worship there. Rough furnishings did not detract from the enthusiasm experienced by those who gathered to hear him. The Azusa Street Mission, as it came to be known, abolished racial segregation — still the norm at the time, and not uncommon even through the 20th century. Seymour envisioned that the Spirit would bring together people of all races, nationalities, and classes in a new age of Christian faith, and denominationalism would become a thing of the past. Women were also fully included in worship and leadership. Seymour preached: "No instrument that God can use is rejected on account of color or dress or lack of education. This is why God has built up the work [at Azusa]."

From 1906 to 1908, Azusa Mission offered services three times each day, and hundreds filled the building while hundreds more listened from outside. By 1908, over 24 missionaries had been sent to Liberia, South and North China, and Japan. People came from all over the world to attend the Azusa meetings. It was a glorious time for Seymour and the church. Inevitably, however, Azuza's unusual, largely spontaneous services upset more traditional leaders. Even more troubling to some was the easy camaraderie between blacks and whites. Seymour was violating cultural norms by preaching that traditional church order and worship, along with separation of black and white Christians had come to an end. The Holy Spirit would move to replace old ways with a new day and a new promise.

This was too much for many Christians to accept. Even Parham, when he came to see his student's work, did not approve. It was too wild and unorthodox, even for someone who taught that the Holy Spirit would move in a mighty new way. At the same time, other leaders of what would become known as the Pentecostal movement went further than Seymour, insisting that the gift of tongues was the only valid sign of the Spirit's outpouring, while Seymour believed there were other signs of the same gift.

Accounts of Seymour are not in agreement. To some, he is a great hero of Pentecostalism. Others regard him as having taken a powerful movement, only to distort it beyond recognition. Seymour's African roots, together with his message that racial barriers are inconsistent with God's word cost him much needed support. His mission continued until his early death from heart disease, but the initial enthusiasm waned and numbers of worshipers dwindled. Nevertheless, the movement continued. The gift of glossolalia was given to others, even Episcopalians and Roman Catholics. Speaking in tongues remains controversial, yet the Pentecostal revival has unquestionably become a significant force in the contemporary church, with the Azuza Street Mission recognized as its birthplace.

Some value Seymour's emphasis on the gift of tongues, while others only honor his vision of a church undivided by race or nation. Yet there can be no question that William Seymour's vision, like the Spirit on the Day of Pentecost, shook the church of his day and sent out a new message to the world. He summed up his beliefs in these words:

> Let us be deeply sensible (from what we have known) of the evil of a division in principle, spirit or practice, and the dreadful consequences to ourselves and others. If we are united, what can stand before us? If we divide, we shall destroy ourselves, and the work of God, and the souls of our people (Gal. 5:15–17). In order to have a closer union with each other: (1) Let us be deeply convinced of the absolute necessity of it. (2) Pray earnestly for and speak freely to each other. (3) When we meet let us never part without prayer. (4) Take great care not to despise each other's gifts. (5) Never speak lightly of each other. (6) Let us defend each other's character in everything so far as is consistent with truth. (7) Labor in honor each to prefer the other before himself. We recommend a serious perusal of the causes, evils and cures of heart and church divisions.

✪ *March 22* _____

Pearl S. Buck

PRESBYTERIAN

June 26, 1892–March 6, 1973

China with its vast area and population has always fascinated Americans, and Pearl Buck could write about it from a deep familiarity. Best known for her Pulitzer Prize–winning book, *The Good Earth*, she helped Western audiences acquire a more sympathetic and informed view of Chinese people and culture.

Buck was born in West Virginia, but grew up in China where her parents were missionaries. She learned Chinese before English and developed a deep appreciation for Chinese life and a growing concern about the attitudes of some western Christian missionaries toward the people among whom they ministered. Buck attended college in America, but returned to China in 1914. There she married her first husband, himself a missionary, and both of them took teaching posts in the University of Nanking.

Her first book, *The Good Earth,* was published in 1931. Not only did it win the Pulitzer Prize, but it was the best-selling book of both 1931 and 1932. It was awarded the Howells Medal in 1935 and was made into a movie in 1937. In 1938, not even ten years after its publication, Buck was awarded the Nobel Prize in Literature — the first American woman to be so honored. Over the course of her life, she wrote more than 70 other books, including novels, collections of stories, biographies and an autobiography, poetry, drama, children's literature, and translations from Chinese.

At the peak of her fame as a novelist, Buck found herself in the middle of a theological controversy. As a woman of letters, she published a favorable, extended review of an article in the *Christian Century* called "Re-Thinking Missions." The article considered the Hocking Report — an interdenominational committee's study of foreign missions and their effectiveness. The report recommended a sensitive approach to other religious traditions. It also suggested that Protestant missionaries ought to be more inclusive and take into account more liberal theological traditions.

The report was like a call to arms for the more conservative Presbyterians. Neither Buck's fame, nor her experience in China, shielded her from the ire of those whose methods were critiqued in the report. In the face of the challenge, Buck did not back down, but went on to write another article for *Harper's,* in which she offered her opinion that Christian foreign mission work was justifiable, but only if Christianity made its new adherents "kinder and more compassionate" people. Such views flew in the face of the powerful fundamentalist movement within American Christianity at the time. The Presbyterian Church forced her to resign as a missionary.

Buck continued to believe that justice and compassion form the core of Christianity. She labored for civil rights and women's rights as part of her dream of a kinder world. In 1949, Buck established Welcome House, the first international, interracial adoption agency. She was furious that the adoption services of her time refused to place Asian and mixed-race children with white parents. Over the years, Welcome House found homes for thousands of children with adoptive parents. In 1964, she also established the Pearl S. Buck Foundation to assist Amerasian children not eligible for adoption.

Buck's appreciation of Asian culture and people is illustrated in these opening lines of her first published novel *East Wind: West Wind* (1930). In it, a Chinese woman, caught between her beloved traditions and the rising influence of the west, speaks as follows:

> These things I may tell you, My Sister. I could not speak thus even to one of my own people, for she could not understand the far countries where my husband lived for twelve years. Neither could I talk freely to one of the alien women who do not know my people and the manner of life we have had since the time of the ancient empire. But you? You have lived among us all your years. Although you belong to those other lands where my husband studied his western books, you will understand. I speak the truth. I have named you My Sister. I will tell you everything.
>
> You know that for five hundred years my revered ancestors have lived in the age-old city of the Middle Kingdom. Not one of the august ones was modern; nor did he have a desire to change himself. They all lived in quietness and dignity, confident of their rectitude. Thus did my parents rear me in all the honored traditions. I never dreamed I could wish to be different. Without thinking on the matter, it seemed to me that as I was, so were all those who were really people. If I heard faintly, as from the distance outside the courtyard walls, of women not like myself, women who came and went freely like men, I did not consider them. I went, as I was taught, in the approved ways of my ancestors. Nothing from the outside ever touched me. I desired nothing. But now the day has come when I watch eagerly these strange creatures — these modern women — seeking how I may become like them. Not, My Sister, for my own sake, but for my husband's.
>
> He does not find me fair! It is because he has crossed the Four Seas to the other and outer countries, and he has learned in those remote places to love new things and new ways.

Through her novels, Buck was able to bring the humanity and the common struggles she had encountered in China to American ears, and thus to erode the pervasive chauvinism of the west. Buck longed for a world less bound by stereotypes and prejudice. Her sense of Christian mission was to lift up the humanity of all people in her writings, moving beyond narrow images of cultural superiority. To that quest, she dedicated her life.

✪ *March 23*

Peter Maurin

ROMAN CATHOLIC

May 9, 1877–May 15, 1949

Aristode Pierre Maurin — known as Peter Maurin — founded the Catholic Worker movement with Dorothy Day.* Although her name is more familiar, he was the primary source of its vision.

Born in France, Maurin entered the Christian Brothers order at only 16. This community emphasizes simplicity of life, piety, and service to the poor. In 1898 and '99, he was required to do military service. This experience convinced him that the demands of civic and religious duties were at odds with one another. Maurin decided to follow the urging of his faith and seek a path of nonviolence and humble living. For a time, he became active in a French Catholic lay movement that promoted Christian democracy and improved conditions for laborers. In 1909, Maurin moved to Canada, which did not require military service. He worked at a series of jobs in factories and on farms, eventually ending up in the United States. In the early 1930s, he was a jack-of-all-trades at a Roman Catholic boys' camp in rural New York State, receiving, in exchange for his food, the privilege of using the chaplain's library and sleeping quarters in the barn. While many people would become resentful or depressed by such a life, Maurin saw his poverty as a blessing from God. Stripped of the normal burdens of home, family, and career, he had ample time to reflect and pray. He began to envision a society based on the tenets of the gospel "in which it would be easier for men to be good."

The camp's location made it possible for Maurin to travel to New York City from time to time. There he spent time in low-income areas and in the public library. He was eager to discuss his ideas and share his vision with anyone willing to converse with him. Maurin had no desire for isolation. He wanted his reading and research to be of concrete assistance to those who lived on the margins of society. In a city already filled with self-proclaimed prophets and visionaries, not many took Maurin seriously. But some did. George Shuster, who worked for *Commonweal* magazine, found his ideas worth further exploration. He gave Maurin Dorothy Day's address. The two met in December of 1932. She was a journalist and recent convert to Roman Catholicism. They saw in each other a source of mutual support and inspiration. Maurin taught Day to contemplate the lives of the saints as a means of understanding God's will in history. He argued that familiarity with their trials and victories could provide powerfully relevant insights into the problems of early 20th-century America.

Maurin also suggested that Day begin a newspaper. Rather than just one more vehicle for factual reporting, it was to disseminate the best Roman Catholic social teaching, so that people could come to envision a different way of life. Maurin believed this could help remake the whole culture in a bloodless revolution that would bring into being the kind of world Jesus taught his followers to create.

At first, the *Catholic Worker* did not fulfill Maurin's hopes. In a period of radical protest movements, it looked like just another publication promoting its own ideals. He did not see the point of producing one more catalog of gripes and human solutions. Why fight about the length of the work week or the hourly pay rate if the work place was still treating laborers as one more expendable resource? Nor was he interested in trying to adjust a system that, in his opinion, dehumanized society. It would crumble on its own, he believed, and he wanted to create a community with a new vision that would take over once it did.

But even bad jobs put food on the table, so in order for Maurin's vision to be practical, it must provide sustenance for workers and their families. His experience farming had led him to the conclusion that "there is no unemployment on the land." So the *Catholic Worker* began to advocate a society in which mutual assistance and interdependence replaced classes, hierarchies, and social divisions. Artists, craftspeople, and scholars would labor side-by-side in small worker-owned industries or farms. The root of these communities would not be economic, but religious. Maurin did not merely want to create a different source of income for people, but to help them realize a renewed image of themselves as witnesses to Christ. Hospitality — an ancient Christian virtue — would lie at the heart of these new communities. Maurin wrote:

> People who are in need and are not afraid to beg give to people not in need the occasion to do good for goodness' sake. Modern society calls the beggar bum and panhandler and gives him the bum's rush. But the Greeks used to say that people in need are ambassadors of the gods. Although you may be called bums and panhandlers you are in fact the ambassadors of God. As God's ambassadors you should be given food, clothing and shelter by those who are able to give it.

Family homes, he wrote, should have "Christ Rooms," while parishes should have houses ready to offer hospitality to any "ambassadors of God." Soon, houses of hospitality became a trademark of the Catholic Worker movement, some with more success than others. As in most transformational movements, disputes arose and some factionalism developed. Nevertheless, houses of hospitality did open. Some functioned well, as did some farms and retreat centers. Maurin's travels and teaching had found willing listeners and effective colleagues.

Maurin suffered a stroke in 1944, and for the next five years lived at the Maryfarm Retreat Center in the vicinity of Newburgh, New York. Upon his death, he was laid to rest in a secondhand suit in a borrowed grave. His vision, together with the humble life he chose to live based on the gospels, continue to suggest a compelling alternative to a world of mass production and mass consumption.

✪ March 24

David Pendleton Oakerhater

EPISCOPALIAN

c. 1846–August 31, 1931

Christianity is a corporate faith. Baptized into the body of Christ, most Christians come to understand what St. Paul meant when he said, "There are many members, yet one body. The eye cannot say to the hand, 'I have no need of you,' nor again the head to the feet, 'I have no need of you.' On the contrary, the members of the body that seem to be weaker are indispensable...." Nevertheless, there have been times in Christian history when Christians have been obliged to live without the support of other, stronger members of the body. The story of the "hidden Christians" in Japan during two centuries of persecution is one example. The story of David Pendleton Oakerhater is another. Converted to Christianity and ordained a deacon in the Episcopal Church, he spent most of his ministry in an isolated area, without help from the larger church. Yet he remained faithful, and his work survives.

"Oakerhater" is an Anglicized version of the Native American name, "O-kuh-ha-tah," which means "Making Medicine." Oakerhater was a leader among the Cheyenne, born on a reservation in Oklahoma, a warrior in the last conflict between the invading white settlers and the Indians. After the 1874 battle of Adobe Walls in Texas, Oakerhater and a group of 27 other leaders in the uprising were arrested and taken to a military prison in Florida for what might now be called "re-education." Government policy removed the leadership of warlike tribes in order to provide white settlers with greater security. In Florida, Oakerhater was put in the charge of an army captain who believed that schooling and good treatment would promote better relations between conflicting societies.

While in Florida, Oakerhater was introduced to Alice Pendleton, the daughter of Francis Scott Key and a vacationer from Cincinnati who spoke with him about the Christian faith. As a result of these conversations, Oakerhater and three others decided to be baptized and to seek ordination in the Episcopal Church. With the assistance of a deaconess from the Diocese of Central New York, the little group was released from prison and traveled to New York State to study theology. Oakerhater was baptized at St. Paul's Church, Syracuse, in 1878 by the Rev. John B. Wicks, the rector, and took the name David Pendleton in honor of his benefactor and her husband. In 1881, he was ordained a deacon and returned to Oklahoma with Wicks. Together, they founded a successful mission. Oakerhater's preaching was well received by the Cheyenne, and one of his first converts was Whirlwind, the chief of the Cheyenne tribe. As time went on, however, support from the diocese and national church was reduced, then eliminated. There were "higher priorities." Nonetheless, Oakerhater continued to minister to his people, though he was never ordained a priest and thus could not preside at the eucharist. Even after his retirement, he continued as a Cheyenne peace chief and "holy man," preaching, performing baptisms, marriages, and funerals, and training lay readers. By the time he died in 1931, he had served longer than any priest in the diocese.

Oakerhater was not replaced, however, and for more than 30 years no one carried on his work. Then, in the early 1960s, a family of Episcopalians moved to the area of Oakerhater's mission and, finding no Episcopal congregation, placed an ad in the local paper announcing a meeting at their home. Over 30 Cheyenne, taught by Oakerhater or his lay readers, responded. Thus, the old mission was revived. The only recorded words of David Pendleton Oakerhater are from his first address at the beginning of his ministry:

> Men, you all know me. You remember when I led you out to war I went first and what I told you was true. Now I have been away to the East and I have learned about another captain, the Lord Jesus Christ, and He is my leader. He goes first, and all He tells me is true. I come back to my people to tell you to go with me now in this new road, a way that makes all for peace....

✇ *March 25*

John Mason Peck

BAPTIST

October 31, 1789–March 14, 1858

John Mason Peck began to teach school when he was 18, founded a seminary before he was 40, and was awarded a doctorate by Harvard University when he was 63. Nonetheless, he felt his own education had been inadequate, so he dedicated his life to providing better opportunities for others. Peck was a pioneer missionary in the west and is considered possibly the greatest missionary to serve the Missouri area.

Born in Litchfield, Connecticut, Peck was converted in a revival in the Litchfield Congregational Church, but he and his wife became Baptists when they had to consider whether to have their first child baptized and came to the conviction that baptism was for believers. When they settled in New York State, the local minister only came once a month, so Peck began to preach on the other Sundays. Two years later, he was ordained and soon decided that the west needed missionaries. It took a year to persuade the Baptist mission board to appoint a domestic missionary, but in 1817 he and a colleague were appointed "as missionaries to the Missouri Territory." They reached St. Louis before year's end. Soon, Peck established the United Society for the Spread of the Gospel, the first such organization in the west.

Peck was a constant organizer and promoter. To overcome opposition from "antimissioners," he organized Bible societies — he felt no one could oppose them — then Sunday Schools. He founded churches throughout the territory, a seminary in his home, traveled east to raise funds for his work, and finally organized the American Baptist Home Mission Society to coordinate and support the domestic missionary work. His focus was not narrow. Peck helped lead the struggle to keep Illinois from becoming a slave state and ordained the first African American preacher in Missouri. He promoted settlement in the territory, lectured on agricultural practices, published a guide for immigrants to the west, and edited a gazetteer of Illinois.

A reading from the journal of John Mason Peck

On Monday, January 25th (1819), I gave the parting hand to my traveling companion, whom I left to perform missionary labor in the Boone's Lick country, and rode to Franklin. My horse being lame I had left him in Booneville, and hired one for the late tour. Finding his disease was the swinney, and that it would require many months to recover, I was compelled to leave him and buy another to take me to St. Louis. On my way down I had appointments for frequent preaching.

During the period of my visit to the Boone's Lick settlements the winter was unusually mild and open; no snow of consequence, light showers of rain, and for one-third of the nights no frost. I reached St. Louis on the 5th of February.

February, 1819. It now became expedient to make such arrangements in the Western Missouri enterprise, as would save expense and promote its objects more effectually. It had been in our plan at first, even before we left Philadelphia for this region, to establish a seminary for the common and higher branches of education; and especially for the training of school-teachers and aiding the preachers now in office, or who may hereafter be brought forth in the churches. The education of the ministry is of primary importance in all new countries. A classical and scientific education, such as academies and colleges furnish, has never been regarded by Baptists as an indispensable requisite to entrance on the gospel ministry, or to perform the duties of a Christian pastor. But there are certain branches of education that are indispensable to ministerial usefulness.

The mind must be trained to habits of thinking; to logical reasoning, to readiness of speech; to systematical arrangement of gospel truth, and to a practical application of Christian duties. Mere declamation is not preaching the gospel. A man may stand up, rattle off words, tear his voice to tatters, and foam at the mouth, and yet not communicate one Scriptural idea, nor excite one spiritual emotion in his hearers. We have a very poor opinion of a man who has to write all his discourses, and read them off on the Sabbath. If he has not, and cannot acquire the gift of "aptness to teach," he had better let this work alone. And yet the writer has written out in full, and read from the platform not a few discourses in early times through the old settlements of Illinois and Missouri. This was done, in part, on special subjects, that seemed to require a cluster of facts, and sometimes dates, to produce the desired impression; and partly to counteract the violent prejudices that prevailed against preparatory study and written outlines in pulpit discourses. The Puritans (Presbyterians and Congregationalists) since their origin, about three hundred years ago, have gone to the extreme in their reading lessons. Baptists and Methodists, until late years, may have erred on the other hand; and for lack of concentrated thought, and writing out their thoughts in logical and consecutive order, became mere declaimers; or, rather, like the blind horse in a mill, go round and round on the few Scriptural ideas they profess.

Our aim was not to establish a regular theological institution, or lay the foundation and build up a college. The writer never had the gift of anticipating and attempting great things. It has been his rule through life to do what he could for the present, and trust to Providence for the future,

✪ *March 26*

William Ladd

CONGREGATIONAL

May 10, 1778–April 9, 1841

William Ladd was an optimist who set out to improve the world. It was an optimistic period in the United States. Victory over England in the War of 1812 unleashed a wave of exuberant self-assurance in the new nation, with advocates working for every kind of reform. Ladd felt caught up in the spirit of the times, convinced that only a little serious attention to gospel teachings could set society on the right path. He spoke against slavery; he battled for temperance; he strove for peace. Not much changed, and yet today he is seen as one of the important early advocates of international organizations to work for peace.

Ladd was born in New Hampshire to a father who became a successful merchant. The son graduated from Harvard, sailed with some of his father's vessels, and, at 20, commanded one. He married in England and settled in Georgia where he attempted to manage a plantation without using slave labor. He failed miserably, losing most of his property. Returning to his first career, he followed the sea until the War of 1812 made this undesirable. He then retreated to Maine, where he farmed on scientific principles.

The life of a gentleman farmer agreed with him, as it provided the leisure necessary to advocate his ideas. Ladd wrote essays on peace and had them published in a Portland, Maine, newspaper. These were subsequently collected and published in two volumes. Some of his writing was published in England, as well. In 1828, he became the first president of the newly formed American Peace Society. He continued to write about his favorite subject in essays and books for children. Eventually his church licensed him to preach, though his primary focus remained the lecture hall where he was still arguing for peace even when he could no longer stand.

The Peace Society sponsored a competition for essays. When the best of them were published, Ladd added one of his own, an "Essay on a Congress of Nations," which is believed to be the first American suggestion for such an international organization. Ladd's ideas were debated in Europe and America, and before long Peace Congresses were held in Brussels, Paris, London, and the Hague. The 20th century saw the creation of the League of Nations and the United Nations. The reality of peace remains elusive, but the search for structures of peace began with men like William Ladd, who was known in his day, and remains, as "The Apostle of Peace."

A reading from "A Solemn Appeal to Christians of All Denominations in Favor of the Causes of Permanent and Universal Peace" by William Ladd

Christians should labor and pray for the abolition of war, because God has chosen them to be the instruments of accomplishing his gracious purposes.

But if any should ask, what are Christians to do? I answer, just the same that they do for the conversion of the heathen. Let every minister of the gospel labor to undeceive his people as to the true nature of war, and show its absolute inconsistency with the religion of Christ. We have no need to send peace missionaries ten thousand miles. Their work is nearer home. Christian nations must *first* be converted from this sin. All its abominations should be clearly pointed out; the whited sepulcher should be laid open: and the exceeding sinfulness of war should be clearly brought to light. Next, let the churches unite in humble and hearty prayer to Almighty God, that he would remember his promise, and "do as he hath said." Let them pray, and pray fervently, that wars may cease to the ends of the earth.

The day for an annual concert of prayer recommended by the American Peace Society, is the 25th of December, or some convenient day near it, not from any idea of the peculiar sanctity of that day, but because the associations connected with it by Christians generally, are favorable to the object. Now, suppose that a majority of the churches in the United States should agree in observing some part of that day, perhaps the evening, with a concert of prayer for God's blessing on the cause of peace, might we not expect that the churches of England — where the peace cause has many more efficient friends than it has in this country — would imitate our example, as they have in the temperance cause? If the churches generally in Great Britain and the United States should engage in this concert, would it be possible for the rulers of either country to declare war against the other? When this concert of prayer has been established in the United States and Great Britain, it is reasonable to expect that the evangelical churches on the continent of Europe will join in it, and indeed all over the world. Christians of every sect would be praying for deliverance from the scourge of war. Who, that has any faith in the efficacy of prayer, can doubt for a moment that these prayers would be answered, not only because God has promised to answer prayer, but the very fact, that Christians everywhere were generally engaged in a concert of prayer for the abolition of war, would cast such a damp on the spirit of war as would extinguish it. Christian rulers would not dare to declare war, when they saw the best part of their subjects engaged in prayer against it. War would begin to be considered as a sin — a relic of barbarism, and would be abandoned by all Christian and civilized people.

✪ *March 27*

Paul Hanly Furfey

ROMAN CATHOLIC

June 30, 1897–June 8, 1992

"We ought constantly to emphasize the fact," Paul Furfey wrote, "that no important problem can be solved without taking the supernatural into account." It is hard to imagine a more revolutionary statement, but Paul Furfey took these words seriously and attempted to live them. Nearly 2,000 years after Christ first set a new model for human beings to follow, most of his followers continue to attend services, read the Bible, and say their prayers, yet few lead transformed lives

Furfey was an academic sociologist who taught at Catholic University in Washington for 41 years. He had earned his doctorate there and served as chairman of the sociology department for 32 years. But Paul Furfey was convinced that the key to a transformed society was not in academic research but in a community of truly Christ-centered individuals. He dismissed those who "pin their faith entirely on social legislation, organizations, publicity, committees, lectures, pamphlets, and such 'devices of merely human prudence,' forgetting that these means of propaganda become effective only when used as subordinate devices to further our real social action which centers in the Mass." He wrote that, "The man who has comprehended the reality of that mysterious love which drew down God to earth, a love hot as the sun's fire and strong as death, will not be attracted by those human affections which often masquerade so guiltily under the name of love. . . . A scale of values built upon contemplation will. . . . lead to a contempt for the things which this world values."

Social justice was Furfey's passion, and sociology was simply a tool to be used toward that end. He traveled to South America to witness the liberation theologians and their followers in action. He lived out his beliefs by sharing the life of the poor while working with others to establish institutions in Washington, DC, where he lived to carry out experiments in interracial living. During the Vietnam War, he established Emmaus House as a center for antiwar activity.

A reading from *Fire on the Earth* by Paul Hanly Furfey

Life in a truly Christian society is therefore not only fundamentally right; it is also fundamentally exciting. It calls for the full exercise of every power. It is a life in which the individual strains every faculty, in the pursuit of a good so deeply satisfying that this panting pursuit becomes a joy like the thrill of an exciting race. The intellect is overwhelmed with the contemplation of the deepest reality in the universe; and human science seems pale by comparison. The will is satisfied with an enormous love, the love for Pure Beauty, Pure Goodness; and human love fades into insignificance. Even the body is not unimportant, but is called upon to cooperate in its degree in this exciting quest. Finally, all this dynamic life is whipped to a high pitch of intensity by the interaction of the members of the Christian community.

The social group then which practices the Christian ideal discovers a thrilling life. It reflects Christ's desire, "I am come to cast fire on the earth" (Luke 12:49). The pagans believed in a pale stoicism. Everything was to be moderate, balanced. Christianity has a balance too, but it is a balance between mighty coexisting extremes. The pagans preached a philosophical detachment from the sweaty multitude. Christianity preaches a life of accomplishment in the midst of the excitement of life. It was St. Ignatius who dared to pray to be made drunk with the blood of Christ. *Sanguis Christi, inebria me.*

How foolish, then, are those cautious Catholics who want to compromise and to share the unimaginative life of worldly men. Let the world live its humdrum life. Let it worry about the childish things which seem to it so important — stock margins, table manners, the technique of golf shots, or the latest Paris fashions. We have more important things to do. The life of the Kingdom of God is our eternal concern. This Kingdom offers us a high degree of satisfaction here below. It offers us perfect fulfillment in the after life.

When the pride of this earth shall pass away, when from our death beds we shall contemplate the transitory nature of these earthy affairs which seem so important to contemporary thought, then we shall be able to look forward to the consummation of our Christian society, of this same Kingdom of God which we learned to love on earth — a consummation which shall be a flawless society of deep, mutual love. Love of God first of all; love of each other in God. This life in Heaven will be a life of exciting activity in which all our powers will find their satisfaction and fulfillment. There we shall find perfect self-realization for ourselves and perfect self-realization for human society. The city of God which we have loved on earth is only the faint beginning of that perfect future society, for "our country is in the heavens" (Phil. 3:20, Westminster Version).

✪ March 28

John Christian Frederick Heyer

LUTHERAN

1793–November 7, 1873

In the turbulent days of the Napoleonic era, John Christian Frederick Heyer was born in Germany. His parents decided to send him to America after his confirmation to live with an immigrant family. When he arrived in Philadelphia, he continued his studies and began to concentrate on theology. Completing his studies, he served for two years as an instructor at Zion School in Southwark, Pennsylvania, before going back to Germany in 1814 to attend the University in Göttingen.

Returning to the United States in 1817, he was licensed as a lay preacher by the Pennsylvania Ministerium. He began his work by proclaiming the Word around Pennsylvania, in an area that included Crawford and Erie in Pennsylvania, and Cumberland in Maryland. Married in 1819 and ordained to the Ministry of Word and Sacrament in 1820, Heyer spent the next two decades preaching, starting up Sunday Schools, and teaching at both the Lutheran college at Gettysburg and its neighboring Lutheran Seminary. He held pastorates in Somerset and Carlisle, Pennsylvania, and was elected to be president of the West Pennsylvania Synod.

Heyer's energy and skill were noticed, and in 1837 the Central Mission Society of the Evangelical Lutheran Church in the United States asked him if he would be willing to go off to explore mission opportunities in the Mississippi Valley. He accepted the call and began to see his ministry as bringing the gospel to places where it had not been fully heard. While serving in the Mississippi mission field, Heyer's wife died. As often happens in major life transitions, he began rethinking the direction and focus of his ministry. Thus, when approached by the Foreign Mission Society of the General Synod in 1840, he agreed to serve abroad as the first American Lutheran missionary in the foreign field.

He studied Sanskrit and medicine in Baltimore (at what would become Johns Hopkins) in preparation, and when he felt ready, he was dispatched to India. Lutheran missionaries from Europe were already at work in the areas around Tinnevelly, Tranquebar, and Madras. Heyer's work between 1842 and 1857 concentrated on the Andhra region. He served at Guntur, Palnad, and Rajahmundry and earned a medical degree during a brief return to America in the late 1840s.

The work and the environment were both demanding, and Heyer's health suffered. For medical reasons, he traveled back to North America, where he set about founding congregations in Minnesota. He was instrumental in establishing the Minnesota Synod in 1860. In 1869, he returned to India for two years. His presence in Andhra, together with his personal charisma, gave a much needed boost to the ongoing mission work. Back again in the States, Heyer took a position as chaplain and house father of the newly founded Lutheran Theological Seminary at Philadelphia, a position he held until his death in 1873. Known to many as "Father Heyer," he left his mark on the church on three continents and countless lives.

What is it that takes a person so far from the comforts of home and the securities of a settled existence? For Heyer, it was the longing to bring the gospel message of hope and comfort to those who had never heard it. While the church needs people to maintain settled congregations, along with other duties of a stable Christian community, she also always requires men and women to "seek and save the lost." The Body of Christ needed St. James to stay in Jerusalem to tend the faithful there. But where would we be without St. Paul and his companions, driven to spread the Word as far as possible?

Missionaries are not stirred by a desire for fame or numbers — many remain unknown, and few have been well-paid. There has never been any assurance that they would make large numbers of converts. But the very act of traveling so far and undertaking so many difficult tasks is itself a testimony to the passion of Christians for their neighbors.

Jesus commissioned the church to "go into all nations." We are grateful for people like John Heyer who took this call literally. Because of missionaries like him, we have Christian partners in all parts of the globe. Building upon the foundations they laid, we are able to continue critical ministries in those lands in both good times and bad. Empowered by Christ's Spirit, and directed by his call, we pray that, like John Heyer, we will find our own ministries and be his willing servants to the world.

✪ *March 29*

Orange Scott

FREE METHODIST

February 13, 1800–July 31, 1847

Orange Scott's story began like many others of his time. Part of a large family with few resources, he received a limited education and had scant involvement with the church before he experienced a conversion as a young adult during the early 19th-century revivals. With his conversion, Scott became a serious Christian, deeply committed to the faith he had finally accepted. Only six months after a revival meeting in Barre, Vermont, and still in his early 20s, Scott began to "exhort" in the Methodist Episcopal Church and was accepted as a "class leader."

Before long, Scott became an itinerant preacher with a circuit of 200 miles and 30 stops, which he often covered on foot. Filled with enthusiasm for the gospel and youthful energy, he attracted the notice of leaders in the ecclesiastical structure. By the time he was 30, he had become a Presiding Elder, a high office in the Methodist Episcopal Church of the day. His influence was felt across much of New England. Had Scott determined to do so, he could have risen far in the denomination and gained the respect of his colleagues.

So it might have been, except that his attention was increasingly drawn to the issue of slavery. Scott did not set out to be an advocate for a political cause; he was content to preach the gospel and serve the parishes and pastors within his district. But just as he had experienced a passionate conversion to Christ in his earlier years, his heart was now captured by the pain and brutal injustice of American slavery. He began to read abolitionist literature and have it sent to the elders under his direction. By 1835, he was preaching about the need to do away with slavery as part of his understanding of what a Christian nation needed to do.

Of course, most church bodies were just as divided on the issue of slavery as the nation was. Many Christians disagreed about the role preachers should play in the debate. Some believed that slavery was a purely political issue that had no place in Christian pulpits. For others, anything involving justice, freedom, equality, or the promise of human betterment lay at the heart of Christ's teachings and must be given voice by faithful preachers of his word.

Scott was clearly of the latter persuasion. Had he been a man of less importance, it is possible he could have simply continued his course without attracting much notice. But noticed he was. His Bishop told him that if he continued to raise the issue of abolition, he would not be reappointed to his post. It was not in Scott's nature to put aside so deeply held a belief as the need to end slavery. So it was that Orange Scott gave up his prestigious position. By 1837, he was released from his duties in the church so that he could devote all his time and energy to spreading the antislavery position.

Scott's life bears witness that sometimes we can be called away from official positions within the church, especially if those positions are securing for us privileges that our neighbors are blocked from attaining. Scott abandoned neither the church nor his Christian faith, but broke from the Methodist Episcopal Church of his day to exercise his faith as part of the "Free Wesleyan Society." His journey took him from a personal concern for his own salvation to becoming a leader among his fellow Methodists, and finally to be an advocate for people he did not know and who might never know him. In the widening circle of his concern, we see the biblical vision of a kingdom of God that includes "all tribes and nations." We see also something of the dimensions of the claim the gospel places on our lives if we are to forsake all and follow a Lord "whose service is perfect freedom."

✪ *March 30*

Theodore Weld

QUAKER

November 23, 1803–February 3, 1895

The abolition movement in the United States was strongly influenced by the parallel English movement. In both countries, the fight against slavery was strongly supported by evangelical Christians. William Wilberforce was the principal leader of the movement in Great Britain. Charles Finney* was its American champion. These two men combined to convert Theodore Weld. Charles Finney's preaching drew him to the ministry, while Charles Stuart, an Englishman, supported his studies and convinced him to commit himself to the abolition movement.

Weld joined The Anti-Slavery Society in 1834, three years after it was founded, and abandoned his studies to work as an agent for the society. It was not a popular cause in upstate New York. Weld's meetings were often broken up by hostile crowds. In Troy, he was stoned by a mob. But he was a powerful speaker and attracted others to the cause, Harriet Beecher Stowe* among them. Moving to Ohio to study for the ministry at Lyman Beecher's* Lane Seminary in Cincinnati, Weld organized debates on the slavery issue. These led to his expulsion, but almost the entire student body resigned in support. They all went to the newly founded Oberlin Institute, now Oberlin College, which agreed to admit students without regard to color.

From Oberlin, Weld moved to New York to serve as editor of the abolition society's newspaper, the *Emancipator.* He also wrote antislavery articles for other newspapers and periodicals and directed a national campaign of petition to the government, opposing slavery. When the Congress accused John Quincy Adams* of violating its rules by reading such petitions, Weld moved to Washington to assist in his defense. In Washington he became an advisor to the antislavery Whigs, converting such leaders as Ben Wade and Thaddeus Stevens to the cause.

A prolific writer, Weld published a number of books and pamphlets including *The Bible against Slavery* (1837) and *Slavery As It Is* (1839), but his name did not appear on them. *Slavery As It Is* provided material for *Uncle Tom's Cabin* and is generally considered almost as influential. After his marriage to fellow abolition campaigner, Angelina Grimké,* Weld joined the Society of Friends and settled in Belleville, New Jersey, with Angelina's sister, Sarah Grimké,* where they opened a school. Weld returned to the campaign trail during the Civil War in support of Republican candidates and the Union cause.

A reading from *The Bible against Slavery* by Theodore Weld

The spirit of slavery never takes refuge in the Bible *of its own accord*. The horns of the altar are its last resort. It seizes them, if at all, only in desperation — rushing from the terror of the avenger's arm. Like other unclean spirits, it "hateth the light, neither cometh to the light, lest its deeds should be reproved." Goaded to phrenzy in its conflicts with conscience and common sense, denied all quarter and hunted from every covert, it breaks at last into the sacred enclosure, and courses up and down the Bible, "seeking rest, and finding none." THE LAW OF LOVE, streaming from every page, flashes around it an omnipresent anguish and despair. It shrinks from the hated light, and howls under the consuming touch, as demons recoiled from the Son of God, and shrieked, "Torment us not." At last, it slinks away among the shadows of the Mosaic system, and thinks to burrow out of sight among its types and shadows. Vain hope! Its asylum is its sepulchre; its city of refuge, the city of destruction. It rushes from light into the sun; from heat, into devouring fire; and from the voice of God into the thickest of His thunders. . . .

Enslaving men is seducing them to articles of property, making free agents chattels, converting *persons* into *things*, sinking intelligence, accountability, immortality, into *merchandise*. A *slave* is one held in this condition. He is a mere tool for another's use and benefit. In law "he owns nothing, and can acquire nothing." *His right to himself is abrogated.* He is another's, property. If he say *my* hands, *my* feet, *my* body, *my* mind, *my* self, they are figures of speech. To *use himself* for his own good is a CRIME. To keep what he *earns* is stealing. To take his body into his own keeping is *insurrection*. In a word, the *profit* of his master is the END of his being, and he, a *mere means* to that end, a *mere means* to an end into which his interests do not enter, of which they constitute no portion. Man sunk to a *thing!* the intrinsic element, the *principle* of slavery; MEN sold, bartered, leased, mortgaged, bequeathed, invoiced, shipped in cargoes, stored as goods, taken on executions, and knocked of at public outcry! Their *rights* another's conveniences, their interests, wares on sale, their happiness, a household utensil; their personal inalienable ownership, a serviceable article, or plaything. as best suits the humor of the hour; their deathless nature, conscience, social affections, sympathies, hopes, marketable commodities! We repeat it, *the reduction of persons to things;* not robbing a man of privileges, but of *himself;* not loading with burdens, but making him a *beast of burden;* not *restraining* liberty. but subverting it; not curtailing rights, but abolishing them; not inflicting personal cruelty, but annihilating personality; not exacting involuntary labor, but sinking him into an *implement* of labor; not abridging his human comforts, but abrogating his *human nature;* not depriving an animal of immunities, but *despoiling: a rational being of attributes*, uncreating a MAN to make room for a *thing!* ...

This is American slavery. The eternal distinction between a person and a thing, trampled under foot — the crowning distinction of all others — their center and circumference — the source, the test, and the measure of their value — the rational, immortal principle, embalmed by God in everlasting remembrance, consecrated to universal homage in a baptism of glory and honor, by the gift of His Son, His Spirit, His Word, His presence, providence, and power; His protecting shield, upholding staff, and sheltering wing; His opening heavens, and angels ministering, and chariots of fire, and songs of morning stars, and a great voice in heaven, proclaiming eternal sanctions, and confirming the word with signs following.

✪ *March 31* _____

Louis Tappan

PRESBYTERIAN

1788–1873

Louis Tappan was born in Northampton, Massachusetts, in a conservative religious home, but he did not find his parents' faith captivating and so, at 15, he moved to Boston with a few dollars to begin an independent life. There he began to attend the Federal Street Church, where he found the liberal teachings comfortable. It was a center of Unitarian teaching, but such views did not go unchallenged in those times. Lyman Beecher,* a gifted Congregational preacher from Connecticut, moved to Boston to try to counter Unitarianism with Trinitarian views. Tappan attended Beecher's meetings and fell under their influence. He met with Beecher and discussed the Trinity, the nature of Christ, and other matters with him. He studied his own Bible to try to make sense of the different ideas he was hearing from the two congregations.

This process of reflection led Tappan to conclude that there was a real need for repentance, a Redeemer, deeper prayer, greater generosity, and a sense of God's mysterious nature. He reported that this studious examination of spiritual issues led him to a new sense of God. "I felt a constraining influence to address God in three persons, and then pray to Jesus. I was unwilling to rise until the scales had fallen from my eyes."

Such a conversion was not unusual, especially during this period of religious enthusiasm in America, but for Tappan a real life change occurred. Comfort and success were no longer his goals. Instead, service and philanthropy became his life's goal. Tappan moved next to New York to join his brother Arthur in a business partnership. He worked hard and well and the business prospered. Arthur Tappan & Co. made over a million dollars annually, which in the early 1800s was an immense sum. But the Tappan brothers lived very simply, believing that their wealth was to be put to God's gracious purposes. Some of the organizations and agencies that benefited from their gifts were the American Bible Society, the American Tract Society, the American Home Missionary Society, the American Education Society, the American Temperance Society, the American Sunday School Union, the American Board of Commissioners for Foreign Missions, and the American Seaman's Friend Society.

Tappan's religious zeal is obvious, but his was not a religion blind to wider social issues. He found racial injustice a major scandal because slavery and discrimination against African Americans offended his sense of God's purposes. Nor was he reticent about speaking out for racial equality. It was this commitment that led him to support Oberlin College, recently founded, because it admitted both black and white students.

In 1834, Tappan decided to try to elevate the celebration of "Emancipation Day." At this time, New York celebrated it as a rather rowdy festival on the Fourth of July each year, commemorating the freeing of all the state's slaves on that day in 1827. Tappan opened his chapel at Chatham Street to give a religious and political dimension to the festivities. Crowds came, including a number of African Americans, but also a number of proslavery whites. His strong reading of the abolitionist's "Declaration of Sentiments" increased the tensions, which spilled over into several days of violence, vandalism, and arson. Tappan's home was seriously damaged in the uproar. "When my wife saw the large chimney glass — which we purchased eighteen years ago and which I often said looked too extravagant — was demolished, she laughed and said, 'you got rid of that piece of furniture that troubled you so much.'" Tappan seized the chance to make a point. He left his home in ruins that summer. This would serve, he thought as a "silent Anti-Slavery preacher to the crowds who will flock to see it."

Believing that apathy was the only real obstacle to eventual victory, Tappan decided to use a direct-mail campaign to clergy, educators, and political leaders both northern and southern. He said, "If you wish to draw off the people from a bad or wicked custom, you must beat up for a march; you must make an excitement, do something that everybody will notice." Just at this time, the now famous *Amistad* event occurred (see also John Quincy Adams*). Some slaves had taken over the ship on which they were being transported and found themselves in New Haven. No legal precedent governed what to do with them. The Spanish crew argued that they were to be treated as any other cargo and returned to their "owners." Others thought they should be returned to Africa, still others that they should be welcomed to stay in America. Tappan saw the event as a great drama that could open people's eyes to the evils of slavery. He and two colleagues, Joshua Levitt and Simon Jocelyn, became a committee to help the Africans. Together, they published the following appeal:

Thirty-eight fellow men from Africa, after having been piratically kidnapped from their native land, transported across the seas, and subjected to atrocious cruelties, have been thrown upon our shores, and are now incarcerated in jail to await their trial for crimes alleged by their oppressors to have been committed by them. They are ignorant of our language, of the usages of civilized society, and the obligations of Christianity. Under these circumstances, several friends of human rights have met to consult upon the case of these unfortunate men, and have appointed the undersigned a committee to employ interpreters, able counsel, and take all necessary means to secure the rights of the accused. It is intended to employ three legal gentlemen of distinguished abilities, and to incur other needful expenses. The poor prisoners being destitute of clothing, and several having scarcely rags to cover them, immediate steps will be taken to provide what may be necessary. The undersigned, therefore, makes this appeal to the friends of humanity to contribute for the above objects. Donations may be sent to either of the Committee, who will acknowledge the same, and make a public report of their disbursements.

> SIMEON JOCELYN, 34 Wall St.
> JOSHUA LEAVITT, 143 Nassau St.
> LEWIS TAPPAN, 122 Pearl St.
> New York, September 4, 1839

The *Amistad* affair ultimately was decided by the Supreme Court. It ended in the return of the freed slaves to Africa and helped galvanize public sentiment against slavery, especially in the north. Tappan's passion to support those in need was emblematic of his view of faith, active in love.

April

Herman of Alaska

ORTHODOX

1756–December 13, 1837

As the nations of western Europe moved out during the 18th and 19th centuries to build empires in Africa, Asia, and the Americas, Russia moved eastward across Asia into Alaska and down the west coast of North America, establishing a chain of trading posts and missions. The Russian Orthodox Church sent its first missionaries to Alaska in 1794, and among them was a young priest known only as Herman. Settling in the Aleutian Islands, Herman built a small cell to live in, and remained there for the rest of his life, living in extreme simplicity, ministering to the native people, and teaching the Gospel by word and example.

Herman was born in the Moscow area and showed a great interest in the religious life from childhood. At 16, he entered a monastery near St. Petersburg and after five or six years moved to another monastery on an island in Lake Ladoga, where he was allowed to live as a hermit about a mile from the community. He continued this pattern of life in the Aleutian islands, wearing a heavy chain around his waist, eating little more than wild berries, dried mushrooms, and fish caught in the streams. Herman and his fellow missionaries quickly converted several thousand natives and founded a school to educate the children, but the mission aroused opposition from the shamans of the local religions as well as officials of the Russian trading companies who were upset when the missionaries protested oppression of the native people. Some of the missionaries were killed, and there was constant harassment. After five years, the head of the mission and several companions were drowned. Before long, only Father Herman was left to carry on the work.

When an epidemic broke out, he worked tirelessly to care for the sick. Father Herman would sit late into the night to teach the Christian faith to any who would listen. Stories were told of how even the animals came to hear him speak and when he died, witnesses in several locations saw a pillar of light extending up into the sky. They say that the grass is still green on his grave, summer and winter.

A reading from *The Way of a Christian* by Father Herman

Without exalting myself to the rank of teacher, nonetheless, fulfilling my duty and obligation as an obedient servant for the benefit of my neighbor, I will speak my mind, founded on the commandments of Holy Scripture, to those who thirst and seek for their eternal heavenly homeland.

A true Christian is made by faith and love of Christ. Our sins do not in the least hinder our Christianity, according to the word of the Savior Himself. He said: I am not come to call the righteous, but sinners to repentance; there is more joy in heaven over one who repents than over ninety and nine just ones. Likewise concerning the sinful woman who touched His feet, He said to the Pharisee Simon: to one who has love, a great debt is forgiven, but from one who has no love, even a small debt will be demanded. From these judgments a Christian should bring himself to hope and joy, and not in the least accept the torment of despair. Here one needs the shield of faith.

Sin, to one who loves God, is nothing other than an arrow from the enemy in battle. The true Christian is a warrior fighting his way through the regiments of the unseen enemy to his heavenly homeland. According to the word of the Apostle, our homeland is in heaven; and about the warrior he says: we wrestle not against flesh and blood, but against principalities, against powers, against the rulers of the darkness of this world, against spiritual wickedness in high places (Eph.6: 12).

The vain desires of this world separate us from our homeland; love of them and habit clothe our soul as if in a hideous garment. This is called by the Apostles the outward man. We, traveling on the journey of this life and calling on God to help us, ought to be divesting ourselves of this hideous garment and clothing ourselves in new desires, in a new love of the age to come, and thereby to receive knowledge of how near or how far we are from our heavenly homeland. But it is not possible to do this quickly; rather one must follow the example of sick people, who, wishing the desired health, do not leave off seeking means to cure themselves.

✪ April 2

Vida D. Scudder

EPISCOPALIAN

December 15, 1861–October 9, 1954

The radical transformation of society is most often accomplished in small steps. Those who lead the way are seldom the ones who attain the goal. American society, in particular, changes slowly as the major parties accept proposals made by minority groups that can never gain power themselves. Yet often, the few, glimpsing the kingdom beyond the existing order, see their vision gradually accepted by the majority.

Vida Scudder took stands that would still seem radical today, long after her death. She called herself a Socialist, spoke of the spiritual relationship between Marxism and Christianity, and contemplated the possible "overthrow of the social order as we know it." It was unacceptable to her that children should be employed in factories and that the wealthy few should enjoy their profits at the expense of the many in need. Unwilling to wait for the slow process of evolutionary change, she joined with others in 1890 to organize a "Church of the Carpenter" in Boston to create the nucleus of a new world order in which Mary's song would be realized as the mighty were put down from their seats and the poor and lowly lifted up. As she recalled that era:

> Not only did we worship together, singing with special zeal the Magnificat, but we had wonderful suppers, true agape, when the altar at the back of the little room was curtained off and we feasted on ham and pickles and hope of an imminent revolution.

Not many saw that vision, but Vida Scudder, the daughter of a Congregational missionary in India, found in the Anglo-Catholicism of the Episcopal Church a vision of the world that offered hope. The doctrine of the incarnation and a sacramental outlook on life took the needs of the material world seriously, providing a realistic alternative to the kind of Protestant individualism that gave unlimited opportunity to some while showing no real concern for others. Scudder taught English literature at Wellesley College from 1910 until her retirement but was deeply involved in the settlement house movement, the Fellowship of Reconciliation, and the Society of the Companions of the Holy Cross, an organization for women in the Episcopal Church practicing intercessory prayer (Emily Malbone Morgan*). The particular goals she strove for failed or were brought to fruition by others, but society has changed and it was her belief that God's purpose was being accomplished through prayer. She wrote that "there is one sure...way of directly helping on the Kingdom of God. That way is prayer. Social intercession may be the mightiest force in the world."

A reading from "Social Problems Facing the Church" by Vida Scudder

We have never run or knowingly patronized sweat shops, or underpaid workers; the struggle between organized labor and company unions is wholly out of our picture. Indeed, we have really no direct contact with these great abuses and injustices which wise men are denouncing. We live within the capitalistic order, to be sure; and we are being taught not to approve of it; yet we can not run away. We could not escape the profit system for that matter, even if we wove cloth for our own garments on Gandhi's spinning wheels. There are always a few interesting idealists who are trying to run away but they are very partially successful. We can not escape; we do not feel responsible for the system; we agree with our spiritual guides that it is a very bad system. Then they tell us that "we" must change it, and we inevitably ask them, "how?" No answer comes....

There is one sure outlet for our sluggish inertia, one way of directly helping on the Kingdom of God. That way is prayer. Social intercession may be the mightiest force in the world. And here is something which the simple, the sick, those wholly removed from active life, can practice as effectively as any one else. The whole Church should be on her knees these days praying quite concretely for definite ends: for the peace of the world; for wise agricultural policies; for financial reform. If prayer is the deep secret operative force that Jesus tells us it is, we should be very busy with it. He meant us to pray for definite things; He pointed to a real mountain when He said that prayer could dislodge that mass and cast it into the sea. Now He did not want that foolish thing to be done; but He did and does mean that prayer is a force as real as electricity, and competent to overthrow all piled up evils which interrupt our vision of the heavens.

The responsibility for social intercession is not satisfied by vague aspiration, "Thy Kingdom Come." That petition, to be sure, covers all our desires; but if we pray specifically for the recovery to health of a beloved friend, for example, we should be equally specific in our prayers for the health of the body politic. Now we can not be specific unless we have some conviction and some intelligence. There is a type of purely formal prayer; not wholly useless, we hope. But most Christian people have some little experience at least of another kind of prayer, the prayer of power. That kind of a prayer must be enlightened; it must be lit at the torch of knowledge. The chief reason why all Christian people should be making themselves intelligent about the great issues of the day, is that they may learn to pray with fervor and to use the prayer of power.

To cultivate social imagination; to study; to pray; here even if no practical activity is possible to us, are outlets for that need of action native to men, here is sure release from bewildered and unworthy private-mindedness.... But let us not suppose that what lies before us will be easy. To evolve that "new economic order" which the Churches desire, will mean heavy cost to every single man. Let us rejoice; for tests of heroism and of readiness for sacrifice await us. The fate of our whole Western civilization hangs today in the balance; and on the Church, that is, on the body of her children, this fate may well depend.

✪ April 3

Ralph David Abernathy

BAPTIST

March 11, 1926–April 17, 1990

For black people in America, the 1940s and 1950s were both a time of hope and disappointment. Civil Rights legislation passed in 1956 seemed to indicate that legal segregation would cease to exist during the lifetime of those who had longed for such a day. There was also a fainter but real promise of a time when more subtle and, in many ways, more dangerous and degrading forms of racism would fade from the culture. Yet at the same time, bitter court battles and lynchings continued, along with a fierce increase of activities by the Ku Klux Klan. African Americans needed leadership to see them through a time of peril and fear. The black church, which for generations had listened to the charismatic voices of black preachers, provided a natural source for such leaders. During those difficult days, Ralph Abernathy was one of the central leaders of the Southern Christian Leadership Conference and the civil rights movement as a whole.

Ordained as a Baptist minister in 1948, Abernathy began his ministry in 1950 at the First Baptist Church in Montgomery, Alabama. As the '50s unfolded, racial tensions in America increased. Abernathy's vision and courage called him to address the issue as directly as he could. During that same period, Martin Luther King, Jr.,* was beginning his ministry, and the two men shared a passion to see racial prejudice ended. Abernathy and King joined forces to organize a boycott of the Montgomery bus system, which led to its desegregation in 1956 and demonstrated that a nonviolent protest could be victorious.

Seeing the need for a more effective structure to carry on the struggle, Abernathy collaborated with King to create the Southern Christian Leadership Conference (SCLC). The year was 1957, and many parts of the nation continued to believe that it was possible to have a just society segregated by race. The SCLC confronted the falsehood inherent in segregation and worked to build a society in which skin color would no longer be a factor in the treatment of human beings. The purpose of the SCLC was to help various smaller, local organizations that were working for full equality for people of color in every facet of American society. It also provided a strong foundation for the development of black leaders during these decades of intense racial unrest. King was the first president of the SCLC and Abernathy the secretary/treasurer.

The tactics they employed included nonviolent actions such as sit-ins and marches. They also met with legislators and the media and helped with court cases, as well as leadership-training programs, citizen-education projects, and voter-registration drives. As a result, public sentiment shifted, new laws were passed, civil rights laws already on the books were enforced, and new recruits for the cause of justice were raised up to continue the work. SCLC projects were influential in the passage of the national Civil Rights Act of 1964 and the Voting Rights Act of 1965. The SCLC was not the only organization at work on these issues, but it was one of the most consistent and effective.

As the movement grew, Abernathy moved to Atlanta, Georgia, in 1961 and became the vice-president-at-large. With the office came the assumption that at some future time, Abernathy would follow King as president. Tragically, King's assassination in 1968 brought this about. Along with the sudden and sorrowful loss of his friend and colleague, other social factors made the transition a difficult one. The slow pace of change in many places and institutions drew criticism from the black community. The murder of King by a white killer provided ammunition to those who doubted the efficacy of a totally nonviolent approach.

Others argued that injustices stemmed primarily from economic inequality. Black businesses, better jobs, and education leading to respected careers would topple the structures of inequality. Desegregation laws were fine, but would not necessarily provide all the needed advances. Jesse Jackson took such a view and left the SCLC in 1972 to begin a new project called Operation Breadbasket. As often happens, once a founding leader is gone, disagreements and schisms can undermine the founder's work, even as all the squabbling parties seek to honor his memory. The SCLC went through such a period, although Abernathy continued on the path that he and King had set out on almost two decades before. Though weakened, there is no doubt that the SCLC, with Abernathy at the helm, continued to be a vital part of the quest for justice in America.

Abernathy, like King before him, was accused of embracing a process that was too slow, too conciliatory, and uncertain to achieve its goals. In spite of criticism, however, he managed to stay the course, faithful when even some of those he fought for disapproved of his methods. He remained head of the SCLC until his resignation in 1977.

A reading from Ralph Abernathy's eulogy to Martin Luther King, Jr., on January 15, 1969

Many people thought he was out of his mind when he led an army, not armed with guns or bricks or stones, 50,000 strong in Montgomery, Alabama, in

1955, and said to his followers: "Love your enemies, pray for them that curse and despitefully use you." Some of us may have wondered about him when he led us without physical weapons in the battles of Albany, Georgia; St. Augustine, Florida; and Danville, Virginia. And we knew something must have been wrong with him when defenseless we stood before Bull Connor in Birmingham facing vicious and hungry dogs, fire hoses and brutal policemen.

He was the redeemer of the soul of America. He taught the nation that "an eye for an eye, and a tooth for a tooth," if followed to its ultimate conclusion, would only end in a totally blind and toothless society. He discovered that the most potent force for revolution and reform in America is nonviolence. He knew, as the eminent historian Arnold Toynbee has written, that if America is saved, it will be through the black man who can inject new dimensions of nonviolence into the veins of our civilization.

✪ April 4 _____

Jonathan Edwards

CONGREGATIONAL

October 5, 1703–March 22, 1758

Although Jonathan Edwards is often remembered only for his sermon "Sinners in the Hands of an Angry God," students of American society continue to single him out as the first great American theologian in many ways — and one in many ways ahead of his time. Born and brought up in Connecticut, Edwards studied at Yale and became deeply involved in the controversy between the orthodox Calvinism of his Puritan ancestors and the proponents of the dawning "Age of Reason." Edwards attempted to recast his Calvinist heritage in a way that would take account of Newtonian physics and John Locke's psychology. His efforts to reconcile theology with new ideas in science are said to anticipate modern theoretical physics. Similarly, the 20th-century theologian, H. Richard Niebuhr, suggested that Edwards's analysis of free will and the human propensity to sin was essential for our understanding of the devastation and wars of the modern world.

Edwards served as pastor of the congregation in Northampton, Massachusetts, for over 20 years. He had already been there some time when the Great Awakening began, a revival movement that swept the colonies in the 1740s. Edwards's description of these events, called *A Faithful Narrative of the Surprising Work of God* (1738), won him an international reputation. Yet when he tried to impose a higher standard for membership, he was forced out by his congregation. Edwards then served for several years in Stockbridge, a western settlement in Massachusetts. There, he also ministered to a congregation of Native Americans. During this time, he wrote many of his major theological works. He was chosen to serve as the first president of the College of New Jersey (later Princeton University) but died after only a few months in that position.

A reading from "Sinners in the Hands of an Angry God," a sermon by Jonathan Edwards

The bow of God's wrath is bent, and the arrow made ready on the string, and justice bends the arrow at your heart, and strains the bow, and it is nothing but the mere pleasure of God, and that of an angry God, without any promise or obligation at all, that keeps the arrow one moment from being made drunk with your blood. Thus all you that never passed under a great change of heart, by the mighty power of the Spirit of God upon your souls; all you that were never born again, and made new creatures, and raised from being dead in sin, to a state of new, and before altogether unexperienced light and life, are in the hands of an angry God. However you may have reformed your life in many things, and may have had religious affections, and may keep up a form of religion in your families and closets, and in the house of God, it is nothing but his mere pleasure that keeps you from being this moment swallowed up in everlasting destruction....

The God that holds you over the pit of hell, much as one holds a spider, or some loathsome insect over the fire, abhors you, and is dreadfully provoked: his wrath towards you burns like fire; he looks upon you as worthy of nothing else, but to be cast into the fire; he is of purer eyes than to bear to have you in his sight; you are ten thousand times more abominable in his eyes, than the most hateful venomous serpent is in ours. You have offended him infinitely more than ever a stubborn rebel did his prince; and yet it is nothing but his hand that holds you from falling into the fire every moment. It is to be ascribed to nothing else, that you did not go to hell the last night; that you was suffered to awake again in this world, after you closed your eyes to sleep. And there is no other reason to be given, why you have not dropped into hell since you arose in the morning, but that God's hand has held you up. There is no other reason to be given why you have not gone to hell, since you have sat here in the house of God, provoking his pure eyes by your sinful wicked manner of attending his solemn worship. Yea, there is nothing else that is to be given as a reason why you do not this very moment drop down into hell.

O sinner! Consider the fearful danger you are in: it is a great furnace of wrath, a wide and bottomless pit, full of the fire of wrath, that you are held over in the hand of that God, whose wrath is provoked and incensed as much against you, as against many of the damned in hell. You hang by a slender thread, with the flames of divine wrath flashing about it, and ready every moment to singe it, and burn it asunder; and you have no interest in any Mediator, and nothing to lay hold of to save yourself, nothing to keep off the flames of wrath, nothing of your own, nothing that you ever have done, nothing that you can do, to induce God to spare you one moment.

✪ *April 5*

Mary Elizabeth (Maura) Clarke

ROMAN CATHOLIC

January 13, 1931–December 2, 1980

Central America, for most North Americans, is a mosaic of small states, a source of bananas and coffee, but which of the seven states is which most would be hard put to say. For a long time, the economies of these small countries have been dominated by North American companies whose concern has been to keep conditions stable and wages low. Any local government capable of providing those conditions would find supporters in the United States administration. During the Cold War years, if the local government was simply not communist, that provided further credentials.

Yet, in those same Cold War years, Pope John XXIII and the Second Vatican Council aroused hopes of a new day in some of the most underprivileged countries in the western world. Native leadership and American missionaries made common cause with the poorest of the poor, supporting their efforts to develop base communities, study the Bible, educate their children, and develop their economies. Prominent among the missionaries were women from Maryknoll, a Roman Catholic order dedicated to mission and focusing its efforts in Latin America.

Maura Clarke grew up in a typical Queens neighborhood in New York City, attended parochial elementary and secondary schools, and went off to St. Joseph College for Women intending to be a teacher. In her freshman year, however, this goal took on a slightly different focus, so that at the age of 19, she entered Maryknoll with the idea of teaching in Africa. Once Maura finished the Maryknoll teachers' college, however, she was assigned to different mission territory: the Bronx. Five years in that environment proved her commitment and ability, winning her the long-hoped for assignment abroad, in Nicaragua.

Over the next twenty years, Maura Clarke developed deep relationships with the Nicaraguan people. She worked in a rural village centered on a gold mine owned by Canada, then in a destitute neighborhood in Managua, the capital city. Though the sisters understood their work to be nonconfrontational, simply being with the poor and finding ways to help, they couldn't help being aware of the gulf between the rich and the poor and between the government and the people. Gradually they became aware also of how complicit the United States government was in the oppression they saw around them.

In 1980 the sisters began new work in El Salvador, and Maura Clarke returned from a three-year assignment in the United States to join the new work. She was well aware of the danger. Archbishop Oscar Romero, who had written American President Jimmy Carter to protest American support for the repressive government, had recently been shot down in his cathedral, but she had found a ministry she loved with people she cared for. Stopping in Nicaragua on her way to El Salvador, she found people celebrating the first anniversary of the overthrow of the Somoza dictatorship, and reported:

> In the one year that has passed since the end of the war there have been some very significant advances. The program of alphabetizacion in which thousands of young students and teachers have gone to very isolated and difficult areas in order to teach those who never had the opportunity to learn to read and write has been very well organized and is having a lot of success. Parents speak with pride about their fourteen- and fifteen-year-olds not only teaching but helping the farmers with their work and sharing in their family life. There are many Sisters and priests involved in this crusade. Another very notable step has been the provision of work and needed benefits for the poorest class. The effort to raise food production, communal farms, the construction of roads and housing is gradually providing more jobs. The creation of neighborhood grass roots groups in which all have a voice is an effort to have all Nicaraguans participate in the new government.
>
> Since the country was so devastated by the war I expected to find it much worse but the general spirit is one of a new freedom and hope for the future. There are also nice signs like a lovely children's park in the middle of the earthquaked city of Managua, the supermarket once only for the wealthy now filled with the working class and the type of foods they need and the new billboards about the heroes of the revolution as well as towns and streets named after them.
>
> I have heard so many stories of suffering, death and heroism from the people of the Christian communities. There are monuments everywhere to each one of the thousands that died in the revolution. In the middle of this mystery of pain there is at the same time such a belief in resurrection — in something new being born....
>
> What is very hopeful is the role the Church has played and continues to play in being very close to the people in their suffering and struggle.

Hoping that a similar new birth could take place in war-torn El Salvador, divided as it was between guerilla insurgents and a ruthless government, she traveled to her new assignment in July of 1980. That was a year of assassinations and the arrest of church personnel, bombings and machine gunnings of church property. When the sisters returned from a December conference of Central American Maryknoll missioners, they were followed from the airport by government soldiers in plain clothes, stopped on a remote road, raped, murdered, and buried in an unmarked grave beside the road. Maura Clarke had understood the situation she had chosen and its dangers. She had seen people cut up with machetes and bodies floating in a lake. She wrote that "the courage and suffering of these people never ceases to call me." Archbishop Romero had said, "Those who are committed to the poor must share the same fate as the poor."

✪ *April 6*

Frederick H. Knubel

LUTHERAN

May 22, 1870–October 16, 1945

Sometimes Sunday School really makes a difference! Frederick Knubel's father was a successful businessman who encouraged his son to get an education and follow in his footsteps. But the boy felt drawn in another direction. The family attended a German congregation in Manhattan where he became well-grounded in Lutheran tradition. Both the pastor and his Sunday School teacher profoundly affected his outlook, so that by the time he was 19, Knubel decided to seek ordination.

Among the seminaries scattered up and down the east coast was Gettysburg, in Pennsylvania. Knubel's pastor had graduated from that seminary and served on its board of trustees. It introduced Frederick Knubel to an academic community that focused on teaching how to think rather than what to think. Though it held the Lutheran confessions in high esteem, the seminary was not afraid to engage with other kinds of theology, or the society at large. As a result, Knubel was trained to embrace the catholicity of the Lutheran Church, and to believe in Christian unity as something to be pursued. But before Lutherans could be effective ecumenical partners with others, they needed to make progress on issues that were separating Lutherans from each other. Knubel would come to play important roles in both these areas.

He was a bright student, so when the faculty decided to establish connections with some of the great European universities, the young theologian was chosen to go to Germany to attend Leipzig. This major German city was steeped in Lutheran history: a place where Martin Luther had debated John Eck, and Johann Sebastian Bach had been organist and choirmaster. Goethe's "Faust" was partly set in Leipzig. The community boasted a great Lutheran choral tradition. Germany enabled Knubel to view America with a new perspective and broadened his view of both ecclesiastical and secular society. His stay strengthened his understanding of Lutheran tradition, while also helping him better understand its future possibilities.

Returning to America, Knubel was ordained and charged with establishing a parish in upper Manhattan. Thanks to his energy, the Evangelical Lutheran Church of the Atonement grew quickly, and he served there for over 20 years. But though the duties of a home mission pastor were many and the rapidly growing parish required much of his time, Knubel remained engaged with larger trends within American Lutheranism. Over the years several merger proposals had met with success, while others failed. Lutherans had experienced some painful separations like the one between northern and southern churches during the Civil War. Strict confessionalists distrusted those who favored more openness. Fears of overcentralized structures sometimes inhibited effective leadership. Knubel saw these developments and was drawn into them. His insight, strength of character, and skills as administrator, orator, theologian, and pastor all made themselves felt in the attempt to forge some new and better form of American Lutheranism.

Knubel himself belonged to the body known as the General Synod. He served on its Inner Mission Board and the Deaconess Board, both of which helped him form relationships within the synod, while also cultivating networks with his counterparts in such other bodies as the General Council and the United Synod in the South. His contributions were noteworthy enough that he was awarded an honorary Doctor of Divinity degree by Gettysburg in 1912. Knubel also followed developments in the wider church beyond America's shores. The Ecumenical Missionary Conference was held in 1900 in New York, spurring enthusiasm for greater partnerships. The World Missionary Conference in Edinburgh in 1910 led to the Faith and Order Commission of the World Council of Churches. When an American regional meeting of this group was held, Knubel was one of five representatives from the General Synod.

As 1917 approached, Lutherans looked forward to the 400th anniversary of the Ninety-Five Theses, and a new spirit of cooperation was in the air. In part, they may have drawn together because the United States entry into World War I fostered American suspicion of Lutherans. Even Scandinavians members were branded as potential German sympathizers because of their church's Germanic roots. Pressured to prove their loyalty to their adopted country, in conjunction with a need for mutual support, Lutherans looked forward to a more unified, more clearly American Lutheranism. Finally, in mid-November of 1918, the General Council of the Evangelical Lutheran Church in North America, the General Synod of the Evangelical Lutheran Church in the USA, and the United Synod of the Evangelical Lutheran Church in the South came together to establish the United Lutheran Church in America. Frederick Knubel was elected its first president. Although the office ran only two years, no limits were placed on terms, so he continued to serve until 1944. His diplomacy and vision guided the new denomination through many difficult times, including inner tensions and the national traumas of the Depression and World War II. The ULCA grew into a strong church body, keeping the spirit of Christian unity alive into yet another merger. In 1962, they became the Lutheran Church in America (LCA) and later still, in 1988, the Evangelical Lutheran Church in America (ELCA). Knubel's contributions at each new stage were critical. His influence remained significant in the full-communion agreements between the ELCA and five other major church bodies, developed between 1997 and 2003.

Doubtless, the skills Knubel brought to church leadership would have made a great contribution to the family business as well, but an unsung Sunday School teacher and pastor motivated a vision that helped shape a far larger church.

✠ *April 7*

Samuel Hopkins

CONGREGATIONAL

September 17, 1721–December 20, 1803

At the time of the American Revolution, New England society was torn between conflicting forces: the Calvinism that was its Puritan heritage, and the newer ideas of the Age of Reason. One worldview saw a God intimately involved in human affairs and acting without perceivable reason to save one person and damn another. The other saw God as a distant and benevolent ruler, concerned in a general way for human freedom and happiness, but indirectly involved with his creation. For one side, sin was an obvious part of God's purpose; for the other, a mystery hard to explain. A long line of New England theologians, Samuel Hopkins among them, labored to reconcile these differences.

Samuel Hopkins was a student of Jonathan Edwards* who worked closely with him early in his ministry. From 1770 to 1803 he lived in Newport, Rhode Island. There, his support of the Revolution forced him to abandon his church until the war was over and his abolitionist views angered Newport merchants involved in the slave trade. All of this, however, fit neatly into Hopkins's understanding of God's working: he had no doubt that God's intentions were wholly benevolent, yet human beings were sinful by nature, totally dependent on God for salvation. But the individual who is saved may not necessarily be happy. God is concerned for the general good. Individuals may need to suffer in order for that general good to be achieved. Though Hopkins's congregation could pay him very little during and after the war, and though his wife was an invalid for 20 years, he did not consider this evidence of God's disfavor. Perhaps it was all necessary to accomplish the divine purpose for humanity.

Hopkins's views about slavery fit into this theology. Slavery was an evil and should be eradicated, but yet this evil might serve some larger purpose if it resulted in the evangelization of Africa or the salvation of freed American slaves. In a rational world, Hopkins could appeal to human reason to see the need to abolish slavery. Not only should Africans be set free, but they should be paid reparations for their years of bondage.

Strangely, Hopkins put his principles into action not by setting free a slave he owned but by selling him and contributing the money he received to the abolitionist cause.

Hopkins taught that, as a benevolent deity, God was concerned that human beings should be like him. Right reason would discern true holiness, and true holiness is the greatest good in the universe. Yet God alone could produce holy human beings. "Hopkinsianism," as his theology awkwardly came to be called, was a major influence in the evolution of the Calvinist tradition. It called on Christians to examine their lives not just in fear of future punishment, but also in terms of their immediate impact on the world around them.

Readings from Samuel Hopkins

On holiness

Holiness is that in which the highest enjoyment or happiness consists, and is really the greatest good in the universe. That therefore which gives true enjoyment, intending the highest, perfect, universal good of intelligent beings, is true holiness and nothing else can be worthy of that name.

It is true that holiness may be the occasion of misery and a perfect holy being may not be perfectly happy in certain particular circumstances. As the imperfect holiness of the saints in this life is the occasion of pain and distress of mind, which no unholy person can have; and Christ in his human nature, though perfectly holy, was subject to great pain and suffering. But this is not properly owing to any thing in the nature and tendency of holiness, but the peculiar circumstances which attend it. Therefore those exercises of mind which give a being the highest enjoyment his nature is capable of, and put him in possession of all possible good, and at the same time promote the greatest happiness of the whole, is true holiness. And those exercises which have not this nature, but the contrary, are opposed to holiness.

On slavery

And shall this shameful practice, this evil, which has got such deep root, and is spread so far and wide, never have an end? Can no stop be put to those wicked men who are devouring their fellow-men who are more righteous than they? Must this gross and open violation of the rights of man, of the laws of God, and the benevolent religion of the Savior continue forever? Shall the horrid scene of unrighteousness, violence, cruelty, and misery, which has so long taken place in the West Indies and Africa, never be abolished?

Thanks be to God! He has assured us that all these works of the devil shall be destroyed, and that the time is hastening on, when all the people shall be righteous and benevolent, and there shall be none to destroy or hurt in all the earth; and what has taken place of late, gives reason of hope and confidence that this sore evil will soon be made to cease. The attention of thousands and millions has been awakened and turned to this subject; much has been written upon it, and light and conviction have had a rapid and extensive circulation. Numerous societies have been voluntarily formed wholly to abolish this evil; and there is reason to conclude that this light and conviction, and these exertions, will continue and increase till the slave traders shall be utterly destroyed.

✪ April 8

Prudence Crandall

QUAKER

September 3, 1803–January 27, 1890

Whatever words Prudence Crandall spoke have been lost to history, but her life speaks for her. Indeed, it spoke so loudly in her own day that twice she was placed on trial and threatened with mob violence. Yet what could be wrong with starting a school? How could this simple act so inflame normally peaceful New Englanders?

The difficulty began when Prudence Crandall, a Quaker born and educated in Rhode Island, was asked by the wealthy citizens of Canterbury, Connecticut, to open an academy for young ladies. Crandall, who had taught in Rhode Island, was happy to comply and all went well at first. But the following year, 1832, she admitted Sarah Harris, a black woman. The 20-year-old had attended district schools in Norwich, Connecticut, but hoped that by attending the academy she could qualify as a teacher. Her presence upset some of the sponsoring families of the school so much that they withdrew their daughters. Crandall's reaction was to recruit more black women to take their places. Soon, 15 or 20 new students arrived from Boston, New York, and even as far away as Philadelphia.

The people of Canterbury were not prepared to support this intrusion. They attempted by boycott, insult, abuse, and attempts to enforce an obsolete vagrancy law, to remove the students and close the school. When a town meeting was called, a clergyman from a nearby town came to represent Crandall, though warned it was not safe for him to do so. Arriving at the Meeting House, the Rev. Samuel Mays found that over a thousand citizens crammed the building to its capacity. Resolutions detailed "the disgrace and damage that would be brought upon the town if a school for colored should be set up there." Leading citizens spoke vehemently. The Rev. Mr. Mays reported in his journal that one speaker

> twanged every chord that could stir the coarser passions of the human heart
> and with such success that his hearers seemed to be filled with the apprehension

that a dire calamity was impending over them, that Miss C. was the author or instrument of it, that there were powerful conspirators engaged against them in the plot and that the people of Canterbury should be roused by every consideration of self-preservation as well as self-respect to prevent the accomplishment of the design. . . .

Mays attempted to intervene on Crandall's behalf, saying that she would gladly move her school to a less central location if only they would pay off the debt on the building she was using, but other speakers showered him with invective for interfering in their local affairs. The meeting was adjourned, and not long afterward, the state legislature passed a so-called "Black Law" that banned any school established to educate nonresident African Americans without the consent of the local authorities. When that consent was refused and Crandall continued to teach, she was arrested, jailed, and brought to trial.

The case against Crandall was dismissed for lack of evidence, but a mob attack on the academy before the next school year could begin persuaded her to close for the safety of her students. She moved to Illinois with her new husband, a Baptist clergyman, then, after his death, to Kansas. She remained an outspoken champion for equality of education and the rights of women for the rest of her long life.

"Time," says a familiar hymn, "makes ancient good uncouth." Fortunately it can also produce the reverse affect, justifying those vilified in their own era, and illuminating the church and society so that they abandon their previous errors of judgment. Four years before Crandall died, Mark Twain and others persuaded the Connecticut legislature (which had long since repealed the "Black Law") to grant her an annuity in recognition of her courage. Over a century later, legal arguments used by her 1834 trial attorney were submitted to the Supreme Court during their consideration of the historic civil rights case of Brown vs. Topeka Board of Education. Today Prudence Crandall is recognized as Connecticut's "State Hero."

✪ *April 9*

Reinhold Niebuhr

EVANGELICAL AND REFORMED

June 21, 1892–June 1, 1971

Few mid-20th century Protestants wielded more influence than Reinhold Niebuhr, who worked tirelessly to relate theology to the realities of the world and influenced so many within and beyond the institutional church.

Niebuhr was born in Wright City, Missouri. His father was a pastor in the German Evangelical Synod, a Lutheran denomination that merged with

another church in the Reformed tradition to form the Evangelical and Reformed Church and, still later, joined with Congregationalists to form the
United Church of Christ.

After graduating from Elmhurst College and Eden Seminary in Illinois,
Niebuhr earned an M.A. from Yale Divinity School, then became pastor of
a middle class Detroit parish for 13 years. As a liberal and pacifist, he found
the harsh conditions in Detroit factories horrifying. They convinced him
that prophetic witness to sin and judgment remained necessary after all. His
first book, *Moral Man and Immoral Society,* drew widespread attention and
led to his appointment as professor of Christian ethics at Union Seminary
in New York City, where he stayed until he retired. The Depression, World
War II, and the Cold War only confirmed his pessimistic view of human nature, a position that came to be called "neo-orthodoxy," though he disliked
the term. He wrote books and articles taking a pragmatic attitude toward
political matters, both national and international, and served sometimes as a
consultant to the State Department and other governmental agencies. With
John Bennett, his colleague at Union Seminary, he founded the magazine
Christianity and Crisis, which offered a Christian perspective on political
and ethical issues of the day.

A posthumous collection of his sermons and prayers revealed a man of
deep personal faith who had been unknown except to close friends and
family.

A reading from an essay entitled "Working While It Is Still Day"

Perhaps our generation will fail. Perhaps we lack the humility and charity
for the task. There are ominous signs of our possible and even probable failure. There is the promise of a new life for men and nations in the gospel, but
there is no guarantee of historic success. There is no way of transmuting the
Christian gospel into a system of historical optimism. The final victory over
man's disorder is God's and not ours; but we do have responsibility for prox-
imate victories. Christian life without a high sense of responsibility for the
health of our communities, our nations, and our cultures degenerates into
an intolerable other-worldliness. We can neither renounce this earthly home
of ours nor yet claim that its victories and defeats give the final meaning to
our existence.

Jesus wept over Jerusalem and regretted that it did not know the things
that belonged to its peace (Luke 19:41). In the Old Testament, we have the
touching story of Abraham bargaining with God about the size of the saving
remnant which would be needed to redeem the city (Gen. 19:22–23). Would
fifty or forty or thirty be required? He and the Lord finally settled for twenty.
Only a small leaven is needed; only a little center of health can become

the means of convalescence for a whole community. That fact measures the awful responsibility of the people of God in the world's cities of destruction.

But there is a climax in this story which is frequently disregarded. It is a terrible climax which has relevance for our own day. However small the saving remnant which God requires for the reconstruction of our communities, it was not forthcoming in Sodom and Gomorrah. Perhaps it is valid to express the surmise that the leavening minority in Sodom may have been quantitatively adequate but that its righteousness was irrelevant for saving Sodom and Gomorrah. One has the uneasy feeling that we are in that position. There is so little health in the whole of our modern civilization that one cannot find the island of order from which to proceed against disorder. Our choices have become terribly circumscribed. Must we finally choose between atomic annihilation or subjection to universal tyranny?

If such a day should come, we will remember that the mystery of God's sovereignty and mercy transcends the fate of empires and civilizations. He will be exalted though they perish. However, He does not desire their perdition but rather that they turn from their evil ways and live. From us He demands that we work while it is day, since the night cometh when no man can work.

✵ April 10 _____

Pierre Toussaint

ROMAN CATHOLIC

1766–June 30, 1853

"In lowliness of mind," wrote St. Paul, "let each esteem other better than themselves" (Phil. 2:3). Pierre Toussaint seems to have taken this advice into the very center of his being. Born in slavery in Haiti, he came with his master, Jean Berard, to New York in 1787. Berard apparently feared a possible slave uprising, so he decided to move his family and servants out of harm's way. His fears were fully justified: in 1791, a revolution in the country brought killing and devastation. Berard subsequently returned to Haiti to secure his property, leaving Toussaint in charge of the household. He contracted pleurisy, however, and died not long after his return to New York.

Berard had always urged Toussaint to learn a trade, so he became an expert hairdresser. In an age when women spent as much as $1,000 a year on hair styles, this was a remunerative trade. Toussaint's manner encouraged people not only to chat with him (as many do with a hairdresser or barber), but to confide in him and ask his advice. The wealthiest women in the city patronized him for the latest styles as well as his own creations. He had, it was said, a "natural wit and gaiety," but he would also quote the Beatitudes and *The Imitation of Christ*, advising his clients to pray and submit their anxieties to God. In spite of his popularity, however, Toussaint was forced to walk to his appointments, since carriages would not pick up a black person.

With Berard's death, the family was left with scant resources and no income. Toussaint decided he would support them himself rather than save his money to purchase his freedom. Working a 16-hour day, which he always began by attending the 6 o'clock Mass at St. Peter's in Barclay Street, Toussaint managed to purchase his sister's freedom and the freedom of others, but also gave generously to charities, constantly putting off any thought for himself. He noticed black orphan boys on the street and brought them home with him to feed them, clean them up, and give them a place to stay until he could find them a position with one of the wealthy patrons whose hair he styled.

At last, when he was 41, the dying Mme. Berard gave him his freedom. Free at last to do so, he married Juliette Noel, a Haitian woman whose freedom he had purchased. Together, the couple continued the charitable work that Pierre had begun, helping refugees find jobs and caring for orphans. To provide a more lasting remedy to the problem of poverty, they opened a school to teach black children a trade. When the plague struck New York, Pierre personally cared for the victims. In an era before hospitals, it was important to have people sit with those who were ill and he was always willing to fill that role. After city authorities quarantined a part of the city in an attempt to prevent the spread of an epidemic, Toussaint crossed the quarantine lines to bring assistance to a woman who had been abandoned by everyone else. His own sister said to him, "You think of everyone but yourself. Now that you are free, you are still acting like a white man's slave." But Toussaint replied, "I have never felt I am a slave to any man or woman but I am a servant of the Almighty God who made us all. When one of His children is in need, I am glad to be His slave." Toward the end of his life, he was asked why he continued to work rather than retire. He answered, "Madam, I have enough for myself, but if I stop work, I have not enough for others."

Toussaint was always generous with the church and its institutions. He and his wife gave financial help to the Oblate Sisters of Providence, founded by another Haitian refugee, Mary Elizabeth Lange.* When the Roman Catholic diocese began to build the first St. Patrick's Cathedral, Toussaint gave generously to the construction fund. Yet once the building was finished, he was denied entrance because of his race. He was buried in its churchyard. Over a century after his death, his remains were finally moved to the crypt of the present St. Patrick's. He is the only lay person to have received this honor.

During his final illness, Toussaint was asked whether there was anything he needed. He replied, "*Rien sur la terre* — Nothing in earth." The pastor who preached at his funeral did not mention his race, accepting him at last simply as a human being.

✪ *April 11*

Hiram Bingham IV

EPISCOPALIAN

July 17, 1903–January 12, 1988

"Formation" is a new, or recently recovered, word in the Christian vocabulary. It is, however, a primary goal of Christian living from church school and earlier to the end of this mortal life. It is the objective of teachers, reformers, monastics, evangelists, and the ordinary individual at prayer. Christian lives are to be formed in the pattern of Christ so that the Christian man or woman will act instinctively, unthinkingly, as Christ would act. To hesitate when faced with a moral choice is to reveal a life not yet fully formed, not yet fully committed. The Christian should be one who asks, "What else could I have done?" In Jesus' parable of the separating of sheep and goats at the last judgment, neither sheep nor goats seem to be aware of what they have done. Both groups ask, "Lord, when did we see you sick or hungry or in need and did (or did not) care for you?" What was done was done because of the character that had been formed already in part by deliberate choice, in part by the influence of others. In the critical choices of his life, Hiram Bingham IV seems to have acted in just that way: by a character formed to allow him no other choice. In a reminiscence written at the age of 80, he put it quite simply:

> We had to learn (the Beatitudes) by heart in Sacred Studies during my First Form year at Groton.
>
> They made a tremendous impression which I've never forgotten.
>
> Of all Christian teachings they were my favorites — and just as rich in meaning as the two Commandments to love God and neighbor and the Lord's prayer as the foundation of all Christian ethics.
>
> The great services in Battell Chapel in our early days in New Haven and the sermons at Groton of the Rector...did a lot to stimulate my belief in the importance of Christianity and helped to satisfy my hunger and thirst for righteousness. —
>
> "Blessed are they who hunger and thirst after righteousness for they shall be filled."
>
> Of course I didn't understand exactly what this meant and I still don't — but in my days in Groton I was teased unmercifully for being "Righteous." Why I was called "Righteous" I never could understand because I didn't think of myself as self-righteous at all. But it must have been partly because I judged others for not being perfect and for not believing as strongly as I did in Christian principles.
>
> While still at Groton I learned that religion by one definition was "giving the best that you have to the best that you know."
>
> The best I knew were the beatitudes — especially the one about hungering and thirsting for righteousness.

Bingham graduated from Groton and Yale, joined the foreign service, and, after service in China, Poland, and England, was sent to Marseille in 1937. When the Germans overran France and established a puppet government in the south, thousands of refugees, among them Jews fleeing the Holocaust, flooded into the south of France. An American Rescue Committee sent Varian Fry, a journalist, to see what could be done to help the exodus. Meanwhile the American State Department's visa division had sent instructions to keep the number of immigrants as low as possible. When Fry came to Bingham looking for help and Bingham had to choose between career and conscience, his early formation left him no choice. Nor was his career the only thing at stake; other diplomatic personnel were arrested and jailed by the Nazis for helping the refugees. But Bingham issued visas, affidavits in lieu of passports, and other travel documents, many blatantly fraudulent, and provided a meeting place and shelter for many in his home. It seems likely that he used his own money in these activities, since consular salaries were not generous. Those who knew him then said he "seemed filled with an endless despair about his powerlessness," but a colleague said that Bingham "broke every rule in the book" to do what he could. But what else, having responded to Jesus' teaching, could he have done?

Among those who made their way to safety with Bingham's help were such famous artists as Marc Chagall, Marcel Duchamp, and Max Ernst, the writers Thomas Mann, Jr., Leon Feuchtwanger, and Arthur Koestler, the Nobel Prize–winning scientist Otto Meyerhoff, architect Walter Gropius, and philospher Hannah Arendt. While Bingham understood the importance of such people to western civilization, he also issued visas to numerous refugees with no such claim to fame simply because it was the "righteous" thing to do. Over 2,500 — perhaps twice that number — escaped as a result of his work and with his signature on their documents.

The Nazis learned eventually what was happening and complained to the American State Department, which issued orders for Fry to return. Bingham's superior told him, "The Germans will win the war. Why should we do anything to offend them?" When the French Vichy police arrested Fry, Bingham personally intervened to secure his release. But the State Department, still intent on neutrality, transferred Bingham first to Lisbon and then to Argentina. When the war was over, Bingham discovered that the Argentine government was harboring Nazi war criminals, but the State Department closed off his efforts to investigate the matter and he resigned in protest.

"What turned this man's hair white within the period of a year and carved ineradicable furrows on his brow," wrote a member of his family, "was the knowledge of those he could NOT save. This haunted him for the rest of his life; so we must understand his silence as eloquent testimony to a sadness that never quite left him." Returning to his family home in Salem, Connecticut, Bingham spent the rest of his life struggling to make a living as a small businessman and never speaking of the events that had cost him his career. Five years after he died, in 1988, his family came upon the papers that gave evidence of his courage and self-sacrifice in the way of righteousness. In 2002, Secretary of State Colin Powell issued a posthumous "constructive dissent" award to Hiram Bingham IV and spoke of how he "risked his life and his career" and exemplified a "proud tradition of service" with "deep roots in American history and in the Foreign Service."

❽ *April 12* _____

Matthew Vassar

BAPTIST

April 29, 1792–June 23, 1868

Matthew Vassar had lots of money, no children, and a feeling that the wealth he had earned should be of benefit to others. Born in England, Vassar came to America as a child with his father, and settled in the Poughkeepsie area on the Hudson River about 60 miles north of New York City. There James Vassar bought some land and began farming. The senior Vassar had learned to make beer back in England. In his new home, he began to brew it, first for his own family, then for his neighbors to augment his farming income. By 1801, his brewing business was moved to Poughkeepsie, where a busy brewery soon flourished. In time, Matthew Vassar took over the enterprise and amassed a substantial fortune.

In 1845, Vassar took some time off from his years of diligent toil to travel through Europe and reflect on how he might leave a legacy that would bene-fit society. From these meditations, and influenced by his niece, Lydia Booth, who operated a small female seminary in Poughkeepsie, Vassar determined to build and to fund a college for women that would be for their gender what Yale and Harvard were for men. In January of 1861, Vassar Female College was incorporated. By March, Matthew Vassar had transferred to the Board of Trustees the sizable sum of $400,000, representing half of his personal wealth, along with a deed for 200 acres of land. Upon his death, his will more than doubled the endowment.

When Vassar College formally opened its doors in September of 1865, it had 353 students and 30 faculty members, most of them women. Vassar College continues to be a center of fine education for generations of women, and a century after its founding, it opened its doors to men, as well. Famous alumnae include Edna St. Vincent Millay (1917), the first woman to win a Pulitzer Prize for poetry; Helen C. Putnam (1878), one of the first woman gynecologists; and Vicki Miles-LaGrange (1974), the first African American woman to be sworn in as a U.S. attorney. Vassar recruited its faculty from the best-educated women of the time. One example is Maria Mitchell, who had discovered a previously unknown comet on October 1, 1847. The king of Denmark awarded her a gold medal, and she became a noted astronomer.

Matthew Vassar invited her to become the first professor of astronomy in the United States at Vassar College in 1895.

Vassar's generosity was not limited to educational philanthropy. During his lifetime, he donated substantial sums to the Baptist Church in Poughkeepsie to which he belonged. His offerings covered most of the cost of a fine church building for the congregation. His giving was subsequently emulated by several other family members. Poughkeepsie became the home of the Vassar Brothers' Hospital, the Vassar Brothers' Home for Aged Men, the Vassar Brothers' Scientific and Literary Institute, and a branch of the New York Society for the Prevention of Cruelty to Animals. The family endowed two professorships at the college, and continued to build facilities there. Thousands of lives have directly benefited from Vassar's vision, and countless others from the highly educated women who studied at the school. To this day, Vassar College continues to develop minds and serve the wider society.

Vassar and his extended family could certainly have found more personal uses for their wealth, but their faith convinced them God's blessings brought responsibilities to those who received them. In Luke 12:48, Jesus says: "From everyone to whom much is given, much will be required; and from the one to whom much has been entrusted, even more will be demanded." Matthew Vassar took this teaching seriously, as a joyful opportunity to share with others for their benefit.

His decision to fund an institution of higher learning that held women to the highest expectations demonstrates a vision ahead of his time. Not content to add to the endowments of pre-existing schools, Vassar sought to use his gift to raise up American women, preparing them for new levels of knowledge and service. He had seen evidence that they could handle the rigors of serious study and was convinced that highly educated women would be a boon to the emerging American nation. Vassar women have played an important part in the struggle for women's rights in a variety of areas.

Vassar's own sentiments about this were set out forcefully in a letter of April 28, 1868, written to a student thanking him for bringing a woman speaker to the college to lecture on women's rights. His own educational shortcomings are demonstrated by his spelling, preserved in this excerpt:

> The subject of "Womens Suffrage" or "Idiots and Women," was correctly quoted from the Laws granting the right of them to the ballot Box, and when I first read the Law some years ago I was equally surprised to find our Fair sex placed in so shamefull category as "criminals, paupers, Idiots &c," which if the Law was right by this Classification I think it is full time that my 300 Daughters at 'Vassar' knew it, and applied the remedy.
>
> The truth is it is all *nonsense* and irreconcilable with Divine truth in regard to the Mental Capacity of Woman, nothing but long prejudice with the dominering spirit of Man has kept Woman from occupying a higher elevation

in literature & art, but mans *tyrany,* jelousy, and willful usurpation of her normal rights &c.

✪ *April 13*

Althea Brown

PRESBYTERIAN

December 17, 1875–1937

Heading out from London with her newly gathered supplies in 1902, Althea Brown was eager to bringing the gospel to the people of the Congo. Raised in the deep south when few African Americans were able to obtain a good education, she had been lucky enough to attend Fisk University in Nashville, Tennessee, an institution with a strong liberal arts emphasis. She took full advantage of her time there, determined to prepare for a life of service. To pay her expenses, she took in sewing and even made fudge to sell. Brown graduated with honors and began a teaching career in Pikesville, Tennessee, but in spite of her success, and the deep affection her students had for her, she was feeling another call. In 1901, she applied for a position with the American Presbyterian Congo Mission. The Bantu tribe there had not yet been evangelized. The continent was particularly unsettled by a mix of colonial problems, intertribal warfare, and religious conflicts. Christian missionaries from North America, even those with African roots, were sometimes in the center of the conflict. Brown's own ethnic background provided no protection from the resentment some indigenous peoples felt toward missionary workers in their land.

Brown stepped into just such a conflict between rival Congolese factions. The government allowed missionaries and traders to work in the country, but rebel forces wanted both driven out. At the Ibanche mission, she and her colleagues found tensions boiling over. King Lukenga, a local tribal chieftain, had called on his followers to destroy all homes of white people and bring him the traders' hearts and the missionaries' heads. Although this ran against official policy, his words provoked violent attacks on some colonial and missionary outposts. Brown and her coworkers knew that a confrontation was immanent. A messenger to Ibanche brought a stick dipped in the blood of a murdered Christian as a warning that the rebels were advancing, burning all colonial compounds on the way. On the evening of November 2, 1904, fighting erupted nearby. As the night came on, the Ibanche missionaries prepared for the worst. Brown wrote, "None of us expected to see the rising of another sun. Every breath we took was a prayer for deliverance or of fitness to stand before the King [God]." "The hours until dawn seemed endless. Then we sang the doxology." The besieged mission entrusted their lives into the hands of the One whose call they had followed and in whose Name they served.

The long night passed, and their prayers for deliverance seemed to have been answered. But with nightfall, uncertainty and fear returned. Next morning, government soldiers arrived to remove the missionaries from danger. Brown recalled, "There must have been five hundred of us. It was a pathetic sight. Small children four and five years old were walking and even bearing burdens. The native soldiers, fearing an attack along the road ordered us to march at full speed." Snatched from almost certain death, the missionaries thanked God and made for safer territory.

After this terrifying experience, no one would have thought less of Brown if she then decided to focus her efforts in a less conflicted place, or even return to the United States. But she had fallen in love with one of her companions at Ibanche, and they made other plans. Alonzo Edmiston and Brown married in Africa. She sewed her own wedding clothes because they had left everything behind when they were evacuated from the mission. Later, they did return to America but only long enough to spread the word about the work in Africa and raise funds for a new mission. After the birth of their child, all three returned to Africa to continue spreading the gospel of Christ's love and grace to the people.

With no formal linguistic training, Brown nevertheless compiled the first dictionary and grammar of the Bakuba language. Eventually, she contracted sleeping sickness and died in Africa, entering the church victorious in 1937.

✠ *April 14* _____

Mary Josephine Rogers

ROMAN CATHOLIC

October 27, 1882–October 9, 1955

"I never cared for nuns," said Mary Josephine Rogers. "They wore black habits, and I thought, 'I certainly wouldn't want to go around dressed that way.'" Mollie Rogers grew up in a faithful Roman Catholic family but chose to go to Smith College. She had no intention of trying a religious vocation, but the college was much influenced by the Student Volunteer movement that recruited students to do mission work in China and elsewhere. A number of classmates volunteered, so Mollie began to wonder whether, as a Roman Catholic, she too might devote her life to some such purpose. After graduation, she came back to Smith to teach zoology, and it was when another member of the faculty asked her to organize something for Roman Catholic students, that Mollie Rogers found herself drawn toward the life she had thought to avoid.

To give focus to a gathering of Roman Catholic students, Rogers sent to Boston for materials on foreign mission and met James A. Walsh,* who would become the co-founder of Maryknoll. Walsh was attempting to arouse interest in foreign mission through his magazine, *The Field Afar.*

"Can I help you, Father, in my spare time?" asked Mollie Rogers. By 1911, she and a colleague had full responsibility for the magazine, and by 1912, she was the leader of a group of seven who had moved to Maryknoll to form the nucleus of a new woman's order to work with the Maryknoll priests.

It took eight years and three petitions before authorities in Rome recognized the new order. Rogers reported that they thought "American girls would not make good missioners. They thought we were too soft, too inured to luxury, that we didn't have the right kind of faith." Over the following years, Maryknoll nuns proved that assessment wrong. "Ours are to be the labors of the apostolate," wrote Rogers; "unflagging, continuous; we are to expect reproach, ingratitude, weariness of soul and body; to be betrayed — to have our own passion — and in the end, death. All with joy, eagerness, and exhilaration." It was a grimly realistic prophecy. Two sisters lost their lives in the turmoil of World War II; two more became martyrs in Central America in the 1960s. By the time Rogers died, the order had grown to over 700 and worked in China, Japan, the Philippines, Africa, and Central America as teachers, catechists, doctors, nurses, and social service workers. No longer merely assistants to the Maryknoll priests, they established a new pattern of monastic life — led by a woman "who never cared for nuns."

A reading from Mother Mary Joseph (Mollie Rogers)

"What is the Maryknoll spirit?" we ask ourselves again. I like to have people see in us real simplicity devoid of all subterfuge and hypocrisy — that simplicity of which our Lord spoke when He saw Nathaniel approach Him — "Behold a man without guile." I like to feel that people see reflected in our eyes the charity of Christ, and hear from our lips words that bespeak the charity of Christ; that they find our ears closed to gossip and scandal, but ever open to the griefs and sorrows and joys of others. I like to feel that they see in us the spirit of mutual love and tenderness which certainly existed in the early ages of the Church when the pagans were forced to say, "See how they love one another! ... "

We have tried from the beginning to cultivate a spirit which is extremely difficult, and which for a long time was in danger of being misunderstood even by those who were nearest to us; that is, the retention of our own natural disposition, the retention of our own individuality, correcting, of course, what is wrong in it, and supernaturalizing all.... We think of religious women in this country and we know the love, the esteem and respect in which they are held. It is the natural thing for them to stand aloof, to wait for people to come to them, to be sought out and to be sought after, but our work in its very nature is absolutely opposed to that. We are seeking souls. We expect to go out and live amongst those who will be suspicious of us, who will not like us, who will respect us only when we have proven our virtue, our sincerity and our usefulness to them. Why should they come to us? For no reason at all except for what they can get from us.

Therefore it is necessary that we should make the advances to seek and find the lost sheep and bring them home. For this we need all our individuality, all our generosity, all our graciousness and sweetness and simplicity, all our powers of gentle persuasiveness, in fact, all of the things which the good God has given to us. Each one of us in her own work, with her own particular attractiveness, which is to be used by God as a particular tool for a particular work in saving particular souls, must cultivate her natural gifts on a spiritual plane. That explains our spirit. It is an attempt to keep our individuality, casting out what is objectionable in it, using and finding what is good and beautiful in it, and supernaturalizing this, and then using it — not for ourselves, not for any honor or distinction — but only with the desire to promote God's honor and glory and to accomplish His will.

✪ *April 15*

Rosa Young

LUTHERAN

1890–1971

Rosa Jinsey Young grew up as the daughter of a Methodist circuit rider. Few black women of her time were able to go to college, but Rosa attended Payne University. She saw in education the hope of advancement for early 20th-century African Americans. She felt passionately about the spiritual and intellectual welfare of her people, and, in 1912, opened a private school in Rosebud, Alabama, to address these needs. Her seven pupils met at first in a Methodist Church, but within only three terms, she was educating over 200 students.

Finances were a constant problem so, at the suggestion of Booker T. Washington, Young sought help from the Lutheran Synodical Conference of North America. They saw the potential for an important ministry. The Rev. Nils Jules Bakke came to Rosebud and on Palm Sunday, 1916, he performed 58 baptisms and 70 confirmations. Out of this work came 20 new congregations.

Young joined the Lutheran Church–Missouri Synod and continued her educational labors. One of her pupils noted, "Miss Young was married to the education of her people and to the Lutheran Church. She was a superb communicator, an excellent teacher, and she spoke two languages: English and Christianity. She went the fifth and sixth mile for the church, mortgaging everything she had, including property, to carry on the work."

Young founded schools for the church throughout rural Alabama — most notably the Alabama Lutheran Academy and Junior College (later, Concordia

College) in Selma. Her autobiography, *Light in the Dark Belt*, tells of her life and work. She died in 1971 at the age of 81.

A reading from the address entitled "Serve the People" by the 19-year-old valedictorian, Rosa Young, at the Payne University, Selma, Alabama, June 1, 1909

There rests upon mankind a moral obligation, the highest law, by which they are mutually bound to aid each other. This is the highest conception of duty both to God and man.

The demand of the civilized world has ever been for efficient service, and the man who has learned the art of serving is the man who will succeed best in life.

It is by this philosophy one creates his own atmosphere and makes his life yield its best and rarest fruits. Every vocation in life implies service. Those who are aspiring for high positions should seek to become the servants of all. So let us come to the rescue of the people and seek to introduce new methods, by which they can better their condition and thereby become public benefactors.

The talent we possess is for the service of all. The truth we hold is the truth of all mankind. Truth has been the same in all ages and is the common property of all mankind. Human estimates of truth may change, but truth itself is invariable. Truth is the written Word of God. It should be a guiding principle in our lives. It should mold our characters and shape our destinies.

The work of life is placed before us. The best service only can accomplish satisfactorily the duties that now await us. The men and women whom we delight to honor are those who spent their lives in the service of others. The altruistic spirits buried the thought of themselves in their ambition to benefit others.

"He that is greatest among you shall be your servant," is the language of the Great Teacher. To serve is regarded as a divine privilege as well as a duty by every right-minded man. Do something worthy for mankind, is the cry of the civilized world. Give light to those who are in darkness; sustain the weak and faltering; befriend and aid the poor and needy....

As we go from these university halls into the battle of life, where our work is to be done and our places among men to be decided, we should go in the spirit of service, with a determination to do all in our power to uplift humanity....

Abraham Lincoln, whose praises are sung by millions to-day, recognized the fact that he could perform a service to four million slaves and his country by issuing the Emancipation Proclamation. He possessed the moral courage to strike off the shackles of those held in bondage and declared them free.

The founders of this university have rendered an immeasurable service by providing an excellent school in which the colored youth can prepare itself for the great work of life.

We must carry to others the blessings which we have received here. The purpose of education is not personal enjoyment. It is a preparation for the most efficient service. It sends us out to do something for the masses.

The people are looking to us for strength and help. They need our best efforts, our bravest words, our noblest deeds, our tenderest love, and our most helpful sympathy. This is a needy world; outstretched hands may be seen by the thousands asking for aid. It is our duty to relieve human wants. Let us place our standard high, but be willing to do the lowest task, the most distasteful labor, be ever helpful and generous, and be ready to lend a helping hand....

It makes no difference how circumscribed opportunities may be, show yourself a friend to those who feel themselves friendless. Do not sit with idle hands, but take up the first task that offers itself to do — work in the field, at the desk, at the washtub, tending to customers behind the counter, or whatever it might be, and be faithful in the task at hand.

There is no greatness in material things of themselves. The greatness is determined by the use of them. When we go out into the world and offer our service to the people, we must give to the world something that we feel mankind needs. Cast your bread upon the waters, and you will find it many days hence.

✪ *April 16* _____

Anna Howard Shaw

METHODIST

February 14, 1847–July 2, 1919

Anna Shaw began to teach before she had been to high school and was licensed to preach before she had attended either college or seminary; but from an early age, she learned that she could handle a challenge. Growing up on an isolated frontier farm in Michigan, Anna found herself effectively in charge by the age of 12. Her father was absent, her mother had a nervous breakdown, and her older brother was ill, so Anna worked at clearing the land, planting the crops, finishing the cabin, and caring for the family. Somehow she made her way through college and then the divinity school at Boston University, where she was the only woman in a class of 40. It took two more years to find in the Methodist Protestant Church a body willing to accept her as a woman in ordained ministry.

During the next six years, Anna Shaw served congregations in Cape Cod while earning a medical degree from Boston University. Then she resigned her pastorates to devote her time to woman's suffrage and temperance causes. She became vice president, under Susan B. Anthony, of the newly formed National American Woman Suffrage Movement, and served as president herself from 1904 to 1915. In 1919 she became the first woman to receive the highest civilian Presidential citation, the Distinguished Service Medal, for her international efforts on behalf of world peace.

A reading from *Women in the Ministry* by Anna Howard Shaw

Many young women come to me for counsel in regard to entering the ministry as a life work, but I am unable to encourage them, because I know how unwelcome they will be to the orthodox churches and how difficult every step of the way will be made. Men find it hard to contend with "the world, the flesh, and the devil," and it is asking too much of women to add to these the church also. I think, however, it would be as undesirable to have only women ministers as it is now to have only men in that position. The church needs the two, and both can do better work together than either can do alone.

It is commonly observed that the parishes over which women preside are like a large family in their oneness of interests and the harmony of their meetings. It is said of one city where for many years a woman has been minister that the young men of her congregation can be distinguished anywhere on the street or in society by their beautiful deference to women. To listen to the teaching of one who leads a high spiritual life tends to inspire a respect and reverence for the teacher; and where men are accustomed to this week after week from a woman, it cannot fail to create in them a respect and reverence for all womankind.

I realize how impossible it is to predict, with any degree of accuracy, what will be the ultimate result of women's ministerial work. Their power in the pulpit and their especial fitness for the pastorate will be developed and shown in proportion as the church makes them free. So long as they are permitted to officiate only in small and poor parishes; so long as many denominations continue to oppose their preaching as contrary to the Scriptures and antagonistic to the best interests of the church; and so long as both internal and external influences combine to limit and dwarf to its greatest possible insignificance all that women do in this office — just so long will their real value as pastor and preacher remain unknown. In exact proportion as the church limits the usefulness of its women along the lines of its own spiritual development and misdirects them into so-called "domestic duties," the spiritual advance of the kingdom of Christ will be hindered and delayed.

It will require many years of loyal and unflagging service in barren and untried fields before women will be able to prove to cold and skeptical denominations their capabilities for the ministry. Not only will they have to do the work fully as well as men, but they will be compelled to prove themselves superior before just recognition will be accorded them. They have had to stand this crucial test in every other department of the world's work, and the church will prove no exception to the rule. The last of the learned professions to accord women equal opportunities with men will be the ministry; and yet the church is founded upon the sublime declaration, "God is no respecter of persons." and, "There is neither male or female, for ye are all one in Christ Jesus the Lord."

✪ *April 17*

Anne Hutchinson

QUAKER

1591–1643

"Mrs. Hutchinson," said Governor John Winthrop,*

> you are called here as one of those that have troubled the peace of the commonwealth and the churches here; you are known to be a woman that hath had a great share in the promoting and divulging of those opinions that are the cause of this trouble, and to be nearly joined not only in affinity and affection with some of those the court had taken notice of and passed censure upon, but you have spoken divers things, as we have been informed, very prejudicial to the honour of the churches and ministers thereof, and you have maintained a meeting and an assembly in your house that hath been condemned by the general assembly as a thing not tolerable nor comely in the sight of God nor fitting for your sex, and notwithstanding that was cried down you have continued the same. Therefore we have thought good to send for you to understand how things are, that if you be in an erroneous way we may reduce you that so you may become a profitable member here among us. Otherwise if you be obstinate in your course that then the court may take such course that you may trouble us no further.

When the Puritans had lived in England, it was clear who they were: they were not the established Church of England. They held up the Bible as the pure word of God and preached faith as the central requirement in the human relationship with God. They saw no need for bishops and Prayer Books. In old England, John Winthrop and Anne Hutchinson would have been united in their dissent, but in New England, where the old authorities were an ocean away, the unity among themselves that they had taken for granted was no longer so evident. The habit of questioning authority had not been left behind, and the chosen leaders of the people struggled to stifle the voices that questioned them and to create a community at peace with itself.

As Anne Hutchinson struggled to ground her faith in the Scripture, she found she could not allow others to do her thinking for her or tell her what she should believe. She pleaded her case before Governor Winthrop:

If you please to give me leave I shall give you the ground of what I know to be true. Being much troubled to see the falseness of the constitution of the Church of England, I had like to have turned Separatist. Whereupon I kept a day of solemn humiliation and pondering of the thing; this scripture was brought unto me — he that denies Jesus Christ to be come in the flesh is antichrist. This I considered of and in considering found that the papists did not deny him to be come in the flesh, nor we did not deny him — who then was antichrist? Was the Turk antichrist only? The Lord knows that I could not open scripture; he must by his prophetical office open it unto me. So after that being unsatisfied in the thing, the Lord was pleased to bring this scripture out of the Hebrews. he that denies the testament denies the testator, and in this did open unto me and give me to see that those which did not teach the new covenant had the spirit of antichrist, and upon this he did discover the ministry unto me; and ever since, I bless the Lord, he hath let me see which was the clear ministry and which the wrong. Since that time I confess I have been more choice and he hath left me to distinguish between the voice of my beloved and the voice of Moses, the voice of John the Baptist and the voice of antichrist, for all those voices are spoken of in scripture. Now if you do condemn me for speaking what in my conscience I know to be truth I must commit myself unto the Lord.

But the court was more comfortable with community consensus than with individual conscience. The judges asked Hutchinson, "How do you know that was the spirit?" How, indeed, could you be sure of such things once you step outside inherited tradition and declare your right to challenge it? Hutchinson had no clear answer, except she realized that others before her had been forced to rely on their own judgment. "How did Abraham know," she asked, "that it was God that bid him offer his son, being a breach of the sixth commandment?" The court rashly replied, "By an immediate voice." "So to me," said Anne Hutchinson, "by an immediate revelation. . . . By the voice of his own spirit to my soul."

At the end of the trial, Hutchinson and a small group of followers were exiled to Rhode Island, moved to Connecticut, and then to East Chester, New York, where she was killed in an Indian raid in September 1643. Seldom has the essential contradiction at the heart of American life been expressed so clearly as it was in her trial. Individuals must be free to choose, to follow the light they are given; but then what becomes of community? What is to bring together those who have come to these shores for so many reasons and in pursuit of such diverse visions and goals? The question is still to be answered, but sooner or later Americans have usually honored those like Anne Hutchinson, who "troubled the peace of the commonwealth and the churches," believing that in some paradoxical way it is that very dissent that lies at the heart of our unity.

✪ *April 18*

Horace Bushnell

CONGREGATIONAL

April 14, 1802–February 17, 1876

In the age-old struggle between emotion and reason as the primary source of religious knowledge, 19th-century New England was a major field of battle. The deism and rationalism of the 18th century had emerged in new forms as Unitarianism and Transcendentalism, but the Second Great Awakening powerfully reasserted the claims of emotion. Horace Bushnell felt the influence of both but managed to maintain a balance that recognized the force of both sides while maintaining a relatively orthodox Christianity.

Born and raised on a farm in northwestern Connecticut, Bushnell made a late decision to go to college, then emerged from the experience with no clear sense of direction for his life. He tried teaching and journalism but, finding no satisfaction in either, he returned to Yale to study law. Then, toward the end of his legal studies, the Second Great Awakening hit New Haven, prompting Bushnell to change careers again and study theology. It was clear to him that reason was an inadequate guide to a faith that worked so powerfully through the emotions, yet reason still seemed to hold a place in the world of faith. Therefore, he set out to create a rationale for an understanding of God based largely on experience.

Becoming pastor of the Third Congregational Church of Hartford, Bushnell remained there for the rest of his life, building a reputation as one of the country's foremost preachers. He published a series of theological studies that helped reshape the Congregational tradition and liberal Christianity in America. These studies gained him an international reputation, and he is considered by some to be a worthy successor to Jonathan Edwards. Bushnell preached of "The Gentleness of God" and the mystery at the heart of religion. He rejected, on the one hand, the simple rationalism of the Unitarians and, on the other, the dry dogmatism of his New England heritage. Though he approached God as a mystic, distrustful of logic and language that attempted to contain the deity; the Trinitarian God of traditional Christianity remained at the center of his beliefs.

Bushnell was a man of amazing versatility. He led the way in urging the Christian training of children, arguing that their experience of conversion differed from adult experience yet might bring them to Christ even at a young age. He founded a college that eventually grew into the University of California. He laid out railroad routes and was a pioneer in city planning. He was involved in the abolition movement and the campaign for women's suffrage. He played a significant part in the Hartford business community and Connecticut politics. The Bushnell Center for the Performing Arts and Bushnell Park, "America's oldest public park," are still Hartford landmarks.

A reading from an essay by Horace Bushnell entitled "Our Gospel: A Gift to the Imagination"

The Christian gospel is pictorial. Its every line or lineament is traced in some image or metaphor, and no ingenuity can get it away from metaphor. No animal ever understood a metaphor. That belongs to man as a creature of intelligence, by virtue of his power to see in all images the faces of truth and to read their meaning. All the truths of religion are given by images; all God's revelation is made to the imagination: and all the rites, and services, and ceremonies of the olden times were only a preparation of draperies and figures for what was to come, — the basis of words sometime to be used as metaphors of the Christian grace.

Christ is "God's last metaphor!" "the express image of God's person!" and when we have gotten all the metaphoric meanings of his life and death, all that is expressed and bodied in his person of God's saving help, and new-creating, sin-forgiving, reconciling love, the sooner we dismiss all speculations on the literalities of his incarnate miracles, his derivation, the composition of his person, his suffering — plainly transcendent as regards our possible understanding — the wiser we shall be in our discipleship.

Nothing makes infidels more surely than the spinning, splitting, nerveless refinements of theology. This endeavor, to get the truths of religion away from the imagination, into propositions of the speculative understanding, makes a most dreary and sad history.... They were plants alive and in flower, but now the flavors are gone, the juices are dried, and the skeleton parts packed away and classified in the dry herbarium called theology....

Scientific theology will be completely thought out about the same time that words are substituted for algebraic notations, and poetry reduced to the methods of the calculus or the logarithmic tables.

All attempts to think out the cross and have it in dogmatic statement have resulted only in disagreement and distraction. If we undertake to make a science out of the altar metaphors, it will be no Gospel, that we make, but a poor, dry jargon rather — a righteousness that makes nobody righteous, a justice satisfied by injustice, a mercy on the basis of pay, a penal deliverance that keeps on foot all the penal liabilities.

✪ *April 19* ⎯⎯⎯⎯⎯⎯⎯⎯⎯⎯⎯⎯⎯⎯⎯⎯⎯⎯⎯⎯⎯⎯⎯⎯⎯⎯

Thea Bowman

ROMAN CATHOLIC

December 29, 1937–March 30, 1990

One collection of her speeches and writings was entitled *Thea Bowman: Shooting Star,* and that seems an accurate description. Like a bright star, she flashed all too briefly across the American skies and then was gone, leaving a luminous memory of a special kind of joy. Born in Canton, Mississippi, in the days of segregated schools, Bowman's parents were a teacher and a doctor. When they discovered Thea still could not read after five years in the black public school, they sent her to a Roman Catholic school. They hoped that their daughter would like it and do well, and she did. What they had not expected was that she would like it so well that, at the age of 12, she would decide to become a nun. Unlike many such decisions made at this age, this commitment was kept. Thea entered a Franciscan community in Wisconsin at the age of 16, became a teacher at the age of 25, and then, after ten years of teaching in Roman Catholic schools in Wisconsin and Mississippi, began graduate studies and earned a doctorate in English literature in 1972. Returning to Wisconsin, she taught at Viterbo College and eventually became chair of the English Department and director of a school chorus called the "Hallelujah Singers."

But her roots were in the south, and in 1978 she was called back to Mississippi to work with a diocesan intercultural program. In 1980, she helped establish the Institute for Black Catholic Studies at Xavier University in New Orleans and began to design courses and liturgical celebrations to assist clergy and religious education directors. These proved so popular that she was asked to speak at numerous events across the country and became a kind of traveling evangelist, preaching and singing, giving workshops and lectures, and urging people to celebrate their particular ethnic heritage. She taught people not to complain that the liturgy did nothing for them but to ask what they had done for the liturgy. She urged participation and involvement and "a sense that joy is the important spiritual good." Diagnosed with cancer in 1984, she continued to travel, even to Africa, to speak, teach, and sing, speaking from a wheelchair to the National Assembly of Catholic bishops and getting them to dance only months before she died. Her final days bore witness to the power of love to overcome weakness and to reach across human barriers.

A reading from a speech by Thea Bowman on reclaiming black history

It seems to me that our ancestors had a "Mary and Joseph way of looking at things." It didn't matter to our ancestors that their children were born in the stable of a hostile society. They shared their belief in a God who could make a way out of no way. It didn't matter to our ancestors that their children would be ridiculed by those who couldn't appreciate their heritage. They taught us to walk tall anyway.

It didn't matter to our ancestors that their children would have to journey toward a life worth living on a perilous road. They focused our eyes on the victory anyway. They encouraged our dreams anyway. They sparked our imagination anyway. They forgave us our wrongs anyway. They celebrated our successes anyway.

And it didn't matter to our ancestors that most often they were the only ones who recognized the presence of God in black life. They didn't need the approval of somebody else to know that we, too, are made in the image and likeness of God.

Just like our ancestors, we got to hold on to a "Mary and Joseph kind of faith." We've got to hold on to a "Mary and Joseph way of looking at things." We've got to stop being ashamed that our history included slavery. We didn't enslave ourselves. Somebody else enslaved us. Let the people who created slavery answer to God for it, and let us thank God for the cultural and faith traditions that enabled us to overcome.

You can be sure that Mary and Joseph were not ashamed of the stable in Bethlehem. They didn't choose it. They didn't ask for it. They knew they didn't deserve it. They let somebody else answer to God for the stable while they thanked God for their child.

We've got to stop assuming all the blame and guilt for the failures of our people. We didn't shape human history by ourselves. For every opportunity we missed, another one was denied. And for every opportunity that was handed to us, we created another one ourselves. Oh, yes, we have plenty of reasons to plead for forgiveness, but we also have plenty of reasons to praise God with thanks.

We've got to stop forgetting the contributions that nonblacks have made to black life. There is truth and goodness in the heritage of every cultural group. As we gather to celebrate the best in ourselves, we welcome and acknowledge the best in all humanity. Our celebration does not profess that we are better than other people. Our celebration is a way of joining hands with every person who seeks the Lord with an open heart.

At the same time, let us not be so awed by the gifts of others that we forget to marvel at the gift of ourselves. We present our history and our lives before the altar with gratitude and thanks. For it was through us that God gave the world Martin Luther and Coretta Scott King, whose vision and sacrifice have shown the power of good over evil. Through us, God gave the world Eubie Blake and B. B. King, whose jazz and blues mark the time to the seasons of all human life. Through us God gave the world Langston Hughes and Alice Walker, whose poetry and praise have given a voice to what is noble in every human heart. Through us, God gave the world Booker T. Washington and Mary McLeod Bethune, who taught us that we can make a better tomorrow for everybody by making the most of ourselves today.

God has spoken to the world through us. He has made him present, to the world through us. So we gather in God's house, just as Mary and Joseph did to give praise with our thanksgiving. Knowing the wisdom of our ancestors who did with us what Mary and Joseph had done, we present our history and our lives before the altar and say thank you to God.

✠ April 20

James Lloyd Breck

EPISCOPALIAN

June 27, 1818–March 30, 1876

As the tide of settlement moved westward across the United States, churches sent missionaries to minister to them, developing a variety of methods to meet the challenges of the frontier. Methodists and Baptists relied largely on itinerant preachers and revivalists, but Episcopalians and Roman Catholics often established mission stations with schools and seminaries from which to reach out to the surrounding area. One of the most noteworthy examples of this approach was created by an Episcopal priest, James Lloyd Breck, and his companions in Wisconsin.

Breck was born in Pennsylvania and studied at the University of Pennsylvania and the General Theological Seminary in New York City. He was interested in the growing Anglo-Catholic movement that had recently come to the United States from England. While in seminary, he heard an inspiring address by Bishop Jackson Kemper,* the first Episcopal bishop in the western territories. When Breck graduated, he and two classmates traveled to Wisconsin to plant a seminary and mission center. On a 500-acre tract in the middle of a forest, they set out to establish Nashotah House, where a monastic pattern of life was lived by students and faculty together. They rose at 5, said Morning Prayer at 6, then students worked from 7 to 9 in the morning and from 1 to 3 in the afternoon. Evening Prayer was said daily at 3 and Vespers at 6:30 or 7 p.m. The four hours of work done daily by the students paid for their board and laundry, while a six-week "vacation" at the time of the fall harvest enabled them to earn enough money to cover other expenses. The clergy also worked four hours a day to support themselves, spending the rest of their time teaching and doing missionary work in the neighborhood.

Having established Nashotah primarily to minister to white settlers, Breck moved on to Minnesota in 1850, where he tried a similar pattern among the Ojibwe and Dakota tribes. Once again, he built a seminary (Seabury), boarding schools, and missionary centers. Finally, in 1867, he moved on to California with a party of 17 clergy, candidates for ordination, and female church workers. By the time of his death, nine years later, he had established five congregations, and a college with a grammar school and seminary.

A reading from a report by James Lloyd Breck describing his ministry among Native Americans

From what I have now written you, you will learn, Christian brethren, that plants are ripening here for the harvest that comes on apace, before the reapers can be prepared to enter in. But you will like to know something further, viz., in what have the two years promised fruit, where we have been laboring? Seeds of glorious light have been sown, and they are even now shooting forth branches which promise, in due time, an abundant harvest.

Enter with me now, please, the neat squared-log church. It is the very picture of simplicity and solemnity. Ever kept sacred to the *Divine homage*, it is always in that perfect order which becometh his sanctuaries. These Indians call Christians the "praying people," and the church building the "Wigwam of Prayer." About eighteen months since we began connecting a simple form of religious worship, with the daily instruction of an advanced class of native youth. This attracted a few adults into the Mission House, which continuing through the winter, grew into a habit, and when the church was ready for consecration, we transferred the prayers to it and built a distinct house for the school; so that now every day, at half past 4 P.M., the bell rings and tolls for an Ojibwa service, whereupon the laboring Indians and others come up in their native dress (where they have not adopted our own habit,) and here they conduct themselves with the utmost propriety....

I have asked you, Christian friends, to enter the church. It is a week-day; fifty-six natives are present. The average number of daily attendants is over forty — quite frequently there are fifty; as large a number as you would see at their *medicine dance*, which occurs but twice in the year! Pagan is well translated into Ojibwa by one word, which signifies *the people who do not pray!* The small handful of whites you observe in the church, are my fellow missionaries in the Lord, who have, male and female, come thither to instruct the heathen in the better way of things, both temporal and spiritual....I am thankful to say I am able to read the liturgy in their own tongue, and thus appear before them in the true light of a clergyman. The interpreter gives the sermon and other instructions by word of mouth to the people, and also leads in the Ojibwa responses, which the people commit to memory and say orally....

How exceedingly thankful then, should we be, in this remote corner of the wilderness, to see not only a Christian temple built, but a body of *daily* worshippers in it, to the number that I have stated; nor only so, but amongst them three Indians and one white young man actually going through a course of preparation for the ministry; whilst from the white mission in Minnesota we have already sent three young men to Nashotah to prepare for holy orders! How thankful, I say, should we be for all this evidence of *life* in the use of all those divers helps which the Lord hath appointed in his church on earth.

✹ *April 21*

Marian Anderson

BAPTIST

February 27, 1897–April 8, 1993

In America's long and often painful journey from segregation and racism to a multicultural society there have been many symbolically important moments. One of them was Marian Anderson's concert on the Washington Mall on Easter Day, 1939. The Daughters of the American Revolution had built a concert hall in a central Washington location and inserted a "whites only" clause in contracts for its use. When they rejected an application for a concert by Marian Anderson on Easter Day, Eleanor Roosevelt and a number of leading government figures joined to support an alternative concert site on the Washington Mall. Anderson sang from the steps of the Lincoln Memorial for a crowd of 75,000 who came, not only to hear her but to bear witness to their disapproval of the DAR's policies.

Anderson was a quiet trail blazer. For the crowds that came to hear her, she was a great artist with a memorable voice. Her quiet dignity and marvelous artistry helped Americans learn that skin color was irrelevant

Singing and faith were part of Marian Anderson's life from the beginning. She joined her church choir as a child. She took her faith and her voice as gifts from God, without questioning either. When friends urged her to develop her voice with lessons, she did; but her faith remained undeveloped. A distinction is often made between "once-born" and "twice-born" Christians. Marian Anderson was once-born. Her faith was simple, an integral part of who she was. Her mother had taught her to pray, so it was quite natural for her to say in a letter home, "You know mother dear, the Lord is so good to me." When she sang the words, "Great is Jehovah, the Lord, for heaven and earth proclaim his power," from Schubert's *Die Allemacht,* listeners noticed how her own deep faith enabled her to interpret the words and music with special feeling. Her admirers realized that a shared faith, like our shared humanity, need not put up with the artificial divisions of race. By the time Marian Anderson died at 96, most of the legal and social barriers between the races were gone, and black people were more generally accepted and played a larger role in American life. Anderson's deep faith and the power of her music played an important part in that change.

A reading from Marian Anderson's autobiography, *My Lord, What a Morning*

I believe in the basic things Mother believes in. Her God is my God. I would not condemn people who do not believe as we do. I feel, however, that each one of us must have something in which he believes with all his heart, so that he need never be absolutely alone. Mother was wise not to try to persuade us to be as she is or to do as she does; her example was such that we wished to follow in her footsteps.

My religion is something I cherish. I am not in church every Sunday, but I hope and believe that I am on good speaking terms with Him. I carry my troubles, and I don't sit back waiting for them to be cleared up. I realize that when the time is ripe they will be dissolved, but I don't mean that one should sit inert, waiting for all things to come from above. If one has a certain amount of drive, intelligence, and conscientiousness, one must use them. Having made the best effort, one is more likely to get a hearing in an extremity.

I believe that I could not have had my career without the help of the Being above. I believe, as Mother does, that He put it in the hearts of many people to be kind, interested, and helpful, and to do things that needed to be done for me and that I could not have done for myself. It would have happened anyhow, some might say. I don't believe that it would have happened anyhow.

One Sunday recently I went to church in Danbury, Connecticut, where my home is. I felt more impelled than usual to go that Sunday, I could not say why. During the service the minister said, "I have been praying since I came here to substitute for your minister that one Sunday before I left a certain person might arrive, and my prayer has been answered." He believed that his prayer was answered, and I had not known that he had prayed. I just had to go to church. All-seeing God had put things together.

I suppose you can always find manifestations if you are a believer, and if you don't believe you can find reasons to prove that the believer is wrong. But you can only travel the spiritual way you believe to be best for you, regardless of whether it is good for anyone else.

It is well that there are different roads to faith. Mother's faith has lighted the way for us in all the days of our lives, even the hardest we have gone through. Her day-to-day living and the way she accepted and greeted life and its meaning were the forces that guided us.

✪ *April 22* _____

Marcus and Narcissa Prentiss Whitman

PRESBYTERIANS

Marcus: September 4, 1802–November 21, 1847
Narcissa: March 14, 1808–November 29, 1847

Marcus Whitman had trained as a physician and was practicing in upstate New York when he began to feel called to another kind of service. He presented himself to the Presbyterian American Board of Foreign Mission in January of 1835. About the same time, Narcissa Prentiss, a schoolteacher, felt called to work with Native Americans. The board hesitated to send an unmarried woman to a post this difficult and dangerous. Providentially, she and Marcus met and were married in 1836. They were teamed up with Henry and Eliza Spaulding to go to the Oregon Territory to minister to the tribes in that area.

Narcissa and Eliza were the first white women to travel to such a remote part of the northwest. The demanding journey took them to Fort Vancouver. Then, the couples split up to evangelize two different groups. The Whitmans worked in Waiilatpu with the Cayuse Indians. Ten years of labor yielded scant results. They made some converts, but their successes were few. Other white settlers were moving to the territory and the diseases they brought, together with their conflicts with the native populations, made the Whitman's work even more difficult.

The mission faced troubles from the beginning. The attitudes and tactics employed by the Spauldings were harsh — it was not uncommon for them to whip even young children as a punishment. Marcus was a pacifist who did not use corporal punishment. But the Indians became increasingly suspicious of white settlers, lumping the missionaries together with the deceptive and greedy men and women encroaching on native lands. In addition, denominational conflicts among Methodist, Roman Catholic, and Presbyterian missions, all active in the same area, created confusion and conflict among the missionaries and the natives alike.

Personal hardships also weighed down the Whitmans. Their young daughter drowned, Narcissa was often not well, and Marcus was absent, getting supplies or advocating for the mission for months at a time. The tension between natives and newcomers grew. Marcus Whitman describes a confrontation in which he was threatened by an Indian named Sakiaph with an ax:

> After I took away the ax, he held my collar & struck me with his fist on the mouth & tore my clothes. Mrs. W. took the ax from me & Mr. G[reene] put both the ax & hammer up stairs & we sat down again. Sakiaph soon returned with a club and advanced upon me. As I arose to take hold of the club, I avoided the blow he was leveling at my head. For this I was much ridiculed by the Indians as fearing death. [Then Sakiaph returned with a gun.] They persisted in saying because I said I was not afraid to die that I challenged them to kill me, but I told them no — I did not challenge them nor did I want to suffer pain but still I did not fear to die.

Despite all this, the couple never seriously considered leaving the mission field. Finally, an outbreak of measles among the Indians led to an uprising of the tribe in which both Marcus and Narcissa were killed, along with 12 of their companions. Years later, the tribe handed over five men who were involved in the killings. They were executed, but requested Christian prayers before their deaths.

Not all good effort is rewarded with good results. In the parable of the sower, Jesus teaches that some seeds grow better than others. Marcus and Narcissa dedicated their lives to bringing medical care and the gospel to the northwestern tribes when even the journey to that part of the continent was too hard for most people. But the Whitmans had committed themselves to this tribe and its future. Hardship and danger would not deter them. In the end, they paid for their devotion with their lives. Narcissa describes a particular Sunday service with the Nez Perces that reflects some of the joy and sense of purpose that gave them the courage to remain in such a risky environment:

> Sab. at Tukanon. Jan. 27, 1839. This has been a day of peculiar interest here. Could you have been an eye witness of the scenes you would, as I do, have rejoiced in being thus privileged. . . . Husband talked to them of the parable of the rich man and Lazarus; all listened with eager attention. After prayer and singing, an opportunity was given for those who had heavy hearts under a sense of sin, and only those, to speak if they wished it. For a few moments all sat in silence; soon a prominent and intelligent man named Timothy broke the silence with sobs weeping. He arose, spoke of his great wickedness, and how very black his heart was; how weak and insufficient he was of himself to effect his own salvation; that his only dependence was in the blood of Christ to make him clean and save his soul from sin and hell.
>
> He was followed by a brother, who spoke much to the same effect. Next came the wives of the first and of the second, who seemed to manifest deep feelings. Several others followed; one in particular, while confessing her sins, her tears fell to the ground so copiously that I was reminded of the weeping Mary who washed her Saviour's feet with her tears. . . . You can better imagine my feelings than I can describe them on witnessing such as scene.

C. S. Lewis wrote that we are not called to calculate and plan for the results of our work, but simply to be obedient and let God determine the end result. This attitude is exemplified in the Whitmans story. They went to a place and people where they believed God had called them to bring the gospel to life. "One sows and another reaps, but it is God who gives the increase."

✸ *April 23* _____

John Baptist Lamy

ROMAN CATHOLIC

October 11, 1814–February 13, 1888

For nearly 200 years, the present state of New Mexico belonged to the Spanish empire in the New World. Then, in a series of rapid changes, it first became part of the Republic of Mexico (1821), then finally, after the Mexican-American War that began in 1846, a territory of the United States (1846). By that time, a once flourishing mission field for the Roman Catholic Church had been largely abandoned in the midst of all the turmoil.

To deal with this situation, the Vatican authorities appointed John Baptist Lamy as Vicar Apostolic in 1850. In 1853, he was made the first Bishop of Santa Fe. Born and educated in France, Lamy volunteered for mission work and, at 25, came to the United States not long after his ordination in 1838. He served first in Ohio, then Kentucky, before being posted to the new southwestern state. Since he traveled on horseback, it took him nearly a year to get there. No bishop had visited the area in 80 years. The Franciscans, who had served the Spaniards and Indians for over two centuries, had been sent elsewhere, and all their schools had been closed.

Lamy's first priority was to obtain the cooperation of the priests remaining in the area. Having been on their own for so long, they were not accustomed to taking orders. The vicar set off by mule on a 2,000 journey to gain the support of the area's former overseer, the Mexican Bishop of Durango. Next, he needed new, well-qualified assistance. The Sisters of Loreto opened an academy in 1853, the same year Lamy visited Europe and came back with four priests, a deacon, and two subdeacons. Soon afterward, he obtained the assistance of the Brothers of the Christian Doctrine, the Sisters of Charity, and, in 1867, the Jesuits, who opened a college at Las Vegas and also established a journal. In 1875, Bishop Lamy was made archbishop of a newly created archdiocese.

The rough frontier was a transforming challenge for the French priest and bishop, but he adapted well to his new surroundings while, at the same time, bringing a bit of the Old World to the New. The cathedral he built reflects the style of the south of France, where he grew up. Willa Cather's novel *Death Comes for the Archbishop* is loosely based on the colorful life of John Baptist Lamy.

A letter to the Archbishop of New Orleans from John Baptist Lamy, written while returning from a plenary council of bishops in Baltimore

Blue River Camp [Mission], August 6, 1852.

Monseigneur:

I am writing to you from under a tree twenty miles west from Independence. The first time I went to New Mexico I met with some *contretemps;* but it seems that the Divine Providence has been pleased to send me this time more severe trials, disappointments and troubles than at my first start. A good priest from the diocese of Cleveland was coming with me to share the labor of our mission in New Mexico, but he died of the cholera at St. Louis on the 11th of July. His name was Rev. Mr. Pendesprat [sic]. From St. Louis to Independence the Mother Superior of the Sisters of Loreto died also of the cholera, on board the steamboat *Kansas*, the 16th of July; the same day another Sister was taken sick and is yet very low. I have been obliged to leave her at Independence to my great regret. Two more Sisters were also attacked by the same dreadful epidemic, but thank God, they got over it. My Mexican priest has been very sick, and now he is just able to travel in a carriage; besides, I have lost nine of my best animals. You know that we have to travel through the plains with caravans, and that everything has to be brought by wagons. Besides some animals I had here, I bought a few more, but I have lost a great number of them. I have been very much fatigued myself, but still God has given me the grace to bear all with patience, and my strong constitution has stood the labor and the care I had on my mind. I hope to take a fair start tomorrow for the plains; we are only two or three miles from the boundaries between the State of Missouri and the Indian Territory. I have twenty-five persons in my company, ten wagons or other conveyances. My expenses are very great; but still, with God's help, I hope to meet all in one or two years. Recommending myself to your prayers, I have the honor to be,

> Your most grateful friend and ob't serv't.
> JOHN LAMY, Vic. Ap. of N. Mexico.

✪ *April 24*

Samuel Simon Schmucker

LUTHERAN

February 28, 1799–September 26, 1873

As a 21-year-old student at Princeton, Samuel Schmucker dreamed great dreams. He told a friend that he had three urgent desires. The first was to translate an important German theological book into English, the second to found a seminary, and the third to found a college. Within 12 years, he had accomplished all three. Schmucker translated a German book on Christian Dogmatics (1826), was the moving influence in the formation of Gettysburg Seminary (1826), and helped found Gettysburg College (1832).

Schmucker was one of the organizers of the General Synod (1820), one of the early attempts among Lutherans to build a more cohesive and effective ecclesiastical body in North America. During the foundational years of the synod and seminary, Schmucker attempted to restore interest in the formative document for worldwide Lutheranism: the Augsburg Confession. He advocated a distinctly American Lutheranism that nonetheless remained loyal to its traditional roots. He assisted other synods and congregations with model constitutions and helped put together hymnals, liturgies, and fresh editions of Luther's Catechism. His work within the General Synod helped launch the Home Missionary Society, the Foreign Missionary Society, the Parent Education Society, and others. More than 60 books, articles, and addresses are credited to his pen.

But Schmucker's commitment to his own tradition did not blind him to the harm that sectarianism did to the Christian church and its mission to the world. Nowhere was this more evident than in the freshly liberated colonies of America. With no state church to set standards, there was little sense of denominational commitment. Self-proclaimed prophets and preachers emerged on the frontier, streams of immigrants brought new religious leanings, while the ideal of independence in all aspects of life helped further fragment Christian life in America. It was obvious to Schmucker that the mission of the church to the world was being eviscerated by a lack of understanding and cooperation between its differing bodies. Few of his contemporaries felt any urgency to work for Christian unity, nor had they a vision of how it might be accomplished. Instead, each church tradition assumed it had a good handle on what the true faith looked like.

Schmucker insisted that if all Christians would look to the organization of the early church — the first three or four centuries of Christian life — they would discover a style of Christian unity still applicable for the current age. It would focus on the Scriptures and the summary of Apostolic teaching as found in the Apostles' Creed. This model would allow the liberty to hold divergent views on subjects not central to the faith, to acknowledge one another's members and clergy, and accept one another's discipline and joint efforts in mission work. Taking into consideration the practical, historical, and psychological issues, Schmucker did not foresee the end of denominations. Indeed, he urged even greater loyalty to them, but did believe that Christian churches could and should adopt a position of full mutual recognition and common work as long as the basic truths expressed in the Apostles' and Nicene Creeds were maintained.

Schmucker's six points for reunion are:

1. The several Christian denominations shall retain each its own present ecclesiastical organization, government, discipline, and mode of worship.

2. Let each of the confederated denominations formally resolve for itself not to discipline any member or minister for holding a doctrine believed by any other denomination whose Christian character they acknowledge, provided his deportment be unexceptionable, and he conform to the rules of the government, discipline, and worship adopted by said denomination.

3. Let a creed be adopted including only the doctrines held in common by all the orthodox Christian denominations, to be termed the Apostolic, Protestant Confession, and let this same creed be used by all the denominations as the term of sacramental, ecclesiastical, and ministerial communion.

4. There should be free sacramental, ecclesiastical, and ministerial communion among the confederated churches.

5. In all matters not relating to the government, discipline, and forms of worship of individual churches but pertaining to the common cause of Christianity, let

the principle of cooperation regardless of sect be adopted so far as the nature of the case will admit and as fast as the views of the parties will allow.

6. The Bible should be as much as possible be made the textbook in all religious and theological instruction.

Each of these was followed by several pages offering a rationale and ways to deal with potential difficulties.

Schmucker's plan did not meet with much enthusiasm or success during his lifetime. Most Lutherans were so worried about the implications of his suggestion that he lost his credibility as a leader. Now, however, recent developments toward Christian unity turn out to be very close to his vision.

A reading from Samuel Simon Schmucker's *Fraternal Appeal*

When the sincere and unsophisticated Christian contemplates the image of the church as delineated both in theory and practice by the Saviour and his apostles, he is charmed by its delightful spirit of unity and brotherly love. When he hears the beloved disciple declare, 'God is love, and they that dwell in love dwell in God,' and again, 'Beloved, let us love one another, for love is of God, and every one that loveth is born of God and knoweth God,' 'He that loveth not, knoweth not God; for God is love,' and again, 'Beloved, if God so loved us, we ought also to love one another.' 'If any man say I love God, and hateth his brother, he is a liar; for he that loveth not his brother whom he hath seen, how can he love God whom he hath not seen? And this commandment we have from him, that he who loveth God, love his brother also' — when the Christian listens to such declarations as these and numerous others of similar import, when, forgetting things as they exist around him, he brings his whole soul under the influence of this love to God and the brethren, he perceives the moral beauty of these sentiments and finds his heart vibrate in delightful unison with them. But when he awakes from this fascinating dream and beholds the body of Christ rent into different divisions, separately organized, professing different creeds, denouncing each other as in error, and oftentimes hating and being hated, his spirit is grieved within him and he asks: how can these things be among the brethren?

✪ *April 25* ――――――――――――――――――――――――――――――――

Florence Spearing Randolph

AFRICAN METHODIST

August 9, 1866–December 28, 1951

John Wesley dreamed of renewing the Church of England, but the established church was comfortable with the status quo, and Wesley's message was more attractive to people like Welsh coal miners who had no place in the established order. In the same way Methodism's emotional call to personal renewal and holiness found a ready audience among settlers on the frontier of the New World and the newly freed African Americans. Revival preachers brought excitement to otherwise bleak lives, assuring them that although they might be unimportant to powerful people in society, they were eternally important to God.

Yet the notion that a woman could speak with authority, even among the least-esteemed, did not gain acceptance easily. Florence Spearing Randolph, herself, was not enthusiastic about women preachers. Born in South Carolina to a family that had been free for two generations, Randolph attended local schools and a "normal school" intended to train teachers, but moved north in search of better opportunities. She settled in New Jersey to build a career as a dress maker.

Raised in the Methodist Church and converted at age 13, Randolph became active in her local AME Zion Church, taught church school, and was a youth leader. Eager to learn more, she began studying the Bible under the guidance of the Rev. George E. Biddle, an AME Zion Holiness minister and Yale graduate known as a scholar of Greek and Hebrew. With Biddle's encouragement, Randolph began to exhort and finally, in 1888, agreed to take one afternoon a week from her business to devote to missionary efforts in the city. White and black churches alike began to invite her to speak, but she resisted the idea of being a "preaching woman." She asked God to give her a sign of a call by letting her business fail in one year, then providing spiritual success in the next. When her business collapsed, while opportunities to preach continued to increase, she spent a night struggling in prayer, then resolved to give up "husband, home and baby and all" if need be, and "to go out homeless and penniless alone with Christ."

She encountered intense opposition from the Presiding Bishop and other clergy, but after a lengthy and bitter debate, she was ordained a deacon in 1901 and an elder in 1903. Other women had been licensed to preach, but none had been called to be pastors. Randolph was assigned to small, struggling, "problem" churches. When they became successful under her leadership, they were reassigned to a "nice young man" and Randolph was sent on to another difficult assignment. In the early 1920s, at her own expense, she spent nearly two years as a missionary in Liberia and the Gold Coast. At last, in 1925, she was sent to the Wallace Chapel in Summit, New Jersey, where she presided over the building of a new church and oversaw the growth of a large congregation. She remained pastor there until her retirement in 1946. Beyond her local church, she served as an official lecturer for the New Jersey WCTU, was founder and first president of the New Jersey Federation of Colored Women's Clubs, was on the executive board of the New Jersey State Suffrage Association, a chaplain of the Northeastern

Federation of Colored Women's Clubs (1918–1919), and was elected national president in 1916 by the denomination's General Conference. Florence Spearing Randolph spoke often about holiness and renewal, but her vision extended to the whole of national life.

A reading from a sermon entitled "If I Were White" by Florence Spearing Randolph

If I were white I would speak in no uncertain language to my own people what I believe to be right, or in other words the truth as I see it respecting the American Negro. If I believed in Democracy as taught by Jesus I would preach and teach it, no difference who differed with me. If I really loved my country and believed that she, because of her high type of civilization, her superior resources, her wealth and culture, should lead the world into a just and durable peace — a peace that would bind all nations together so that wars should forever cease, then I would stress the fact that charity must begin at home. From my pulpit I would say as Jesus said in that wonderful sermon on the Mount, Matthew 7:3–5, "And why beholdest thou the mote that is in thy brother's eye, and considereth not the beam that is in thine own eye? Or how wilt thou say to thy brother, let me pull out the mote out of thine eye; and behold, a beam is in thine own eye? First, cast out the beam out of thine own eye and then thou shalt see clearly to cast out the mote out of thy brother's eye."

On Race Relations Sunday and during the entire Brotherhood Month, I would recommend as far as possible that Negro speakers of thought and education be invited to speak from white pulpits and that white ministers and other workers, who believe the Gospel they preach, be invited to speak from Negro pulpits. I would urge that Missionary Societies, Clubs, Young People's Groups, give some study to fourteen million black Americans in our own country, to their contributions to American culture, to their loyalty to the Country in every war. . . .

If I believed in skin superiority rather than fineness of personal character I would be much embarrassed in what happens in my own Country and many times in my own town when I looked at my white skin.

In the city of Summit, in which we are most interested, I would speak of the unjust housing problems affecting Negroes, the school problem, the movies, the hospital and certainly the Negro physician; the lack of Negro books in the library, the ignorance of Negro history because it's not taught in our schools. Whether my argument availed or not, I would be conscience free before him with whom I have to do.

✪ *April 26*

Aiden Wilson Tozer
CHRISTIAN AND MISSIONARY ALLIANCE
April 21, 1897–May 12, 1963

Many churches stress the value of an educated ministry, but there is also a long tradition in the United States of clergy who have been raised up with no special training or learning who, nevertheless, become wise teachers and valued pastors. Such a one was A. W. Tozer. Born in rural Pennsylvania, Tozer became serious about the Christian life when he was in Akron, Ohio. There, he was challenged by a street preacher to call upon God to find salvation. Tozer was in his early teens, but he went home, knelt in prayer, and began a spiritual journey that would affect not just himself but thousands of other people.

Lacking much formal education, Tozer began to read extensively, and developed into a gifted orator and writer, motivated by his conviction that "Apart from God, nothing matters. We think that health matters, or knowledge, or art or civilization. And but for one insistent word, they would matter indeed. That word is eternity." At 22, Tozer began preaching in a West Virginia congregation. After a few years, he moved to Indianapolis, where he established a successful pastorate and his reputation as a preacher spread. He started writing down his ideas, beginning what would become a distinguished career as an author.

A congregation on the south side of Chicago heard about him and solicited him to become their pastor. He resisted for a while, because he did not feel called to move, but he did agree to preach for these Chicagoans on a few occasions, which only increased their determination to have him. After long negotiations, Tozer accepted the call to the Southside Gospel Tabernacle in 1928 and spent the next 30 years in its service. At the time of his coming, the congregation was small — about 80 people. Under his leadership, it quickly grew to over 800. In 1950, Tozer was put in charge of the Christian and Missionary Alliance denominational magazine, *Alliance Weekly,* and doubled its circulation. His editorials reflected the same homespun, heartfelt, biblical message that marked his sermons, indeed his life from his first conversion.

A man of simple needs, Tozer never owned a car and donated most of his books' proceeds to charity. He looked on material wealth as just one more worldly temptation. Witty, passionate, focused, and thought-provoking, Tozer challenged everyone he encountered to seek and to follow the gracious God that he had found. His final ministry was in Toronto, Canada, where he died from a heart attack at age 66. His epitaph sums up his simple and faithful life; it reads "A Man of God."

A reading from A. W. Tozer's *The Pursuit of God*

It is a spiritual grace to help people without putting them under obligation, without humiliating them and without establishing a superior-inferior relationship. It is an art that can do good casually instead of formally or, as the teenagers say, "making a production out of it."

The world has a saying that if you want to lose a friend, do him a favor. Without doubt this saying is the crystallization of many and bitter experiences in the give and take of human relations.

But could the fault be all on one side? Maybe when we did our friend a favor we adopted a patronizing attitude that struck at his self-respect and stung him to the quick.

Surely of all people we Christians should best know how to receive favors without servility and do good without arrogance. Our Lord was a master of this art; we can learn from Him.

There is today no lack of Bible teachers to set forth correctly the principles of the doctrines of Christ, but too many of these seem satisfied to teach the fundamentals of the faith year after year, strangely unaware that there is in their ministry no manifest Presence, nor anything unusual in their personal lives. They minister constantly to believers who feel within their breasts a longing which their teaching simply does not satisfy. I trust I speak in charity, but the lack in our pulpits is real. Milton's terrible sentence applies to our day as accurately as it did to his: "The hungry sheep look up, and are not fed."

It is a solemn thing, and no small scandal in the Kingdom, to see God's children starving while actually seated at the Father's table. The truth of Wesley's words is established before our eyes: "Orthodoxy, or right opinion, is, at best, a very slender part of religion. Though right tempers cannot subsist without right opinions, yet right opinions may subsist without right tempers. There may be a right opinion of God without either love or one right temper toward Him."

The meek man is not a human mouse afflicted with a sense of his own inferiority. Rather he may be in his moral life as bold as a lion and as strong as Samson; but he has stopped being fooled about himself. He has accepted God's estimate of his own life. He knows he is as weak and helpless as God has declared him to be, but paradoxically, he knows at the same time that he is in the sight of God of more importance than angels. In himself, nothing; in God, everything. That is his motto. He knows well that the world will never see him as God sees him and he has stopped caring. He rests perfectly content to allow God to place His own values. He will be patient to wait for the day when everything will get its own price tag and real worth will come into its own. Then the righteous shall shine forth in the Kingdom of their Father. He is willing to wait for that day.

In the meantime he will have attained a place of soul rest. As he walks on in meekness he will be happy to let God defend him. The old struggle to defend himself is over. He has found the peace which meekness brings.

✪ *April 27*

Mary C. Collins

CONGREGATIONAL

April 18,1846–May 25, 1920

Even in the days when women were not permitted to serve as ministers in an established parish, they could nonetheless be missionaries, even in areas of great danger. Mary Collins first resisted a call, but finally offered herself for the work in Micronesia. When she was asked, instead, to work among Native Americans, she reluctantly agreed to go where she was most needed. As her wagon train moved deeper into the Great Plains, her sense of loneliness drove her to hug a telephone pole one night, as a symbolic link with the home she was leaving behind.

Collins's commitment, however reluctant, was lasting. She learned the Lakota language so well that the Indians began to think she was half Sioux. She befriended Sitting Bull and, as an advocate for Indians' rights, traveled back East to speak on their behalf. Although a teacher herself, she fought the government policy that placed Indian children in boarding schools to teach them a different way of life. "It is," she said, "the home after all that educates the best American citizen." She criticized the way the government permitted railway companies and cattlemen to ignore its treaties with the natives. She drew attention to the number of Indian children dying of tuberculosis and worked with various groups seeking to reform government policies.

Finally, at the age of 53, Collins was ordained and put in charge of four churches, three log meeting houses, and two chapels with a staff of eight. Poor health prevented her from doing further missionary work and forced her final retirement at 64. Even so, she continued to write and lecture on behalf of Indian causes and to support mission work among them. "I believed in people," she wrote, "and nothing...makes me so uncomfortable as to hear one speak only of the worst, even in white people as in red. I know that few are wholly unredeemable."

A reading from *How I Became a Missionary* by Mary C. Collins

[Our pastor's wife,] Mrs. Thacher felt that one of her class must be a missionary and she said, "Now, girls, I believe one of you will be a missionary, and so I think we will always pray for God to bless the one who is to be the missionary. We did, and as one after another joined their voices in prayer, we always prayed for every blessing for that one who should be a missionary, each, no doubt, feeling as I did, that the unfortunate one would need all the good things.

After a year or two, I began to feel as if I ought to be the one. I had no desire to go on a mission, not the least. I remember staying away several times from the prayer meeting, and Mr. Thacher himself coming for me. I would give no reason, I felt very unhappy and very uncomfortable. Finally, as I sat one evening on a hassock at Mrs. Thacher's feet, my favorite seat, she said, "Come, Mary, tell me all about it; something troubles you; what is it?" I replied in a half pouting and half defiant way; "I don't want to come to prayer meeting; whenever you pray for the missionary I feel that you all mean *me*, and I don't want to be a missionary." I remember how she smiled as she tried to explain that no one should force me to be a missionary against my will. I went back to the meeting, but the feeling followed me. I shall not try to tell all the ways I tried to avoid being a missionary. I was full of life, enjoyed all the sports and pleasures of the boys and girls, could ride and drive horses when I was five years old. My mother always had a great many friends visiting her, and I had three sisters and three brothers, so that I had no desire to go off alone among savages....

About this time the call was continuous. I could not drive it away. All the time I felt as if God was saying to me, "Go ye!" I tossed on my pillow many nights fighting the thought. I felt that I could not go. Every paper I read, every sermon I heard, seemed to make me feel that I was not living the life God meant me to have....

One night as I lay thinking and planning I found every plan fall to pieces, when the thought would arise, "But what about missions?" In despair I said, "I'll settle this now and forever." I arose, kneeled down by the bed and said to the Lord something like this: "I promise to go on a foreign mission if it is best, if Thou wilt put it into Miss Whipple's heart to go with me." I arose and went to bed and to sleep. The next day when Miss Whipple came I told her, and at once she said, "I'll go." From that time to this I have never felt like turning back....

I thought when I came into the Indian work that I should stay twenty years; the time has expired, but "those horrid Indians" are no longer horrid to me. I find that my heart goes out to them all, and the Lord has wonderfully blessed me in my work. Though never very strong, I have had strength given me as I have needed it. In my work among the sick He has proved Himself a hearer and answerer of prayer. He has permitted me to see the greatest advance made toward the civilization and Christianization of the Indian that has ever been made in two decades. Young men and women whose mothers I taught are now teachers, and their children are in our school. In all the way God has been my strength.

✪ *April 28*

John Lancaster Spalding

ROMAN CATHOLIC

June 2, 1840–August 25, 1916

A negative evaluation on John Lancaster Spalding might have character-ized him as "a remote intellectual" rather than a warm, outgoing pastor, but through his intellectual gifts he touched more lives than many warmer personalities, and his aphorisms are still widely quoted. Spalding was born in Kentucky, but spent most of his life in Peoria, Illinois, a place that has become the proverbial provincial American city, but in his youth he had traveled widely for six years in Europe and was educated at Louvain, Bel-gium. Upon returning to the United States, he briefly served as rector of the Cathedral in Louisville, Kentucky, then in New York, but at the age of 37, he was made Bishop of Peoria and remained there the rest of his life. Although he was offered opportunities to transfer to the archdioceses of Chicago and New York, he chose to stay in Peoria, where he exercised as wide an influence as he might have in a larger metropolitan center.

Bishop Spalding's influence on the American Church has been compared to that of Cardinal Newman on the English Church. In Spalding's case, however, he established significant institutions, as well as writing important books. St. Francis Hospital in Peoria, begun in 1877, the year of his conse-cration as bishop, and St. Mary's Cathedral were built through his efforts, along with many schools and hospitals throughout the diocese. Beyond Peo-ria, his concern for education made him the primary force in the founding of the Catholic University of America in Washington, DC.

Anything but provincial in his own thinking, Spalding advocated mod-ernizing Roman Catholic thinking so as to bring it more in line with recent developments in philosophy and literature. He promoted higher education for women and thought they should have the vote. In an era of industrial strife, he spoke in favor of just wages for workers and helped President Theodore Roosevelt settle a coal miners' strike. He believed democracy was compatible with Roman Catholicism and would help further develop the church. The great English Roman Catholic spiritual counselor Friedrich Von Hügel met Spalding in Rome and heard him argue

with astonishing eloquence the contention that history had conclusively man-ifested and established two things; the impossibility, for any society and state that would live and grow, of the Spanish, physical force, sheer authority, and blind obedience type of Catholicism; and the incapacity of pure Protestantism, e.g. the Free Churches of America, to produce the very deepest and largest saints. Hence the future seemed to him and to myself to demand the legitimate aspirations and the undoubted benefits of Protestantism should be realized and should remain, and that corresponding changes should occur from within, in the attitude and practice of Catholicism.

Spalding was paralyzed by a stroke in 1905 and resigned three years later after 31 years as Bishop of Peoria.

Some sayings of John Lancaster Spalding

Each forward step we take we leave some phantom of ourselves behind.

If I am not pleased with myself, but should wish to be other than I am, why should I think highly of the influences which have made me what I am?

The doubt of an earnest, thoughtful, patient and laborious mind is worthy of respect. In such doubt may be found indeed more faith than in half the creeds.

As memory may be a paradise from which we cannot be driven, it may also be a hell from which we cannot escape.

Do definite good; first of all to yourself, then to definite persons.

Leave each one his touch of folly; it helps to lighten life's burden which, if he could see himself as he is, might be too heavy to carry.

The highest courage is to dare to appear to be what one is.

Your faith is what you believe, not what you know.

We are more disturbed by a calamity which threatens us than by one which has befallen us.

Contradiction is the salt which keeps truth from corruption.

✖ *April 29* _____

Pauli Murray

EPISCOPALIAN

November 20, 1910–July 1, 1985

Pauli Murray saw obstacles as challenges, not barriers. Born into a world that limited what African Americans and women could do, she set out to break down those barriers, not only for herself but for others also. She was born in Baltimore, the daughter of a schoolteacher and a nurse, but her parents died when she was still a child, so she was raised by an aunt in North Carolina. The segregated schools of that state provided so poor an education that she was turned down when she applied for admission to Hunter College in New York. She spent another year of high school in New York City, applied again, and was admitted. When she applied for admission to the law school of the University of North Carolina, she was rejected because she was black and therefore studied at Howard University instead. But the rejection at North Carolina turned her into a crusader for civil rights, determined to destroy "Jim Crow." She took part in sit-ins challenging segregation in Washington drugstores and cafeterias while at Howard. In 1942, she was a delegate to the national conference of A. Philip Randolph's March on Washington movement.

In 1946, Murray moved back to New York City to establish a law practice. In 1948, she was hired by the Women's Division of Christian Service of the Methodist Church to compile information about segregation in the south. She went beyond that mandate to gather information about all legislation on race in the country and published a book, *States' Laws on Race and Color*, which became a key document in Thurgood Marshall's legal strategy in winning the Supreme Court decision on segregated education in 1954.

As the civil rights revolution moved forward in the mid-1960s, Murray became convinced that Jim Crow was closely related to "Jane Crow," that racism and antifeminism were "different phases of the fundamental and indivisible issue of human rights." In the fall of 1965, Murray met Betty Friedan, and in the following year they and others founded the National Organization for Women. As a dedicated opponent of barriers, it was inevitable that Murray should eventually turn her attention to what she called "the submerged position of women in the church." Although she was by this time a tenured member of the faculty at Brandeis University, she left that position to be accepted as a candidate for ordination in the Diocese of Massachusetts and to enter the General Theological Seminary to prepare herself for priesthood. By the time she graduated, the Episcopal Church accepted women in the diaconate and, a few months after her diaconal ordination, women were approved for the priesthood as well. Thus, when she was ordained at the Washington National Cathedral early in 1976, she became not only one of the first women priests in her denomination, but the first African American woman as well.

The last eight years of her life were spent in Washington, DC, and Baltimore parishes and serving as a faculty member at the General Theological Seminary. Eleanor Holmes Norton wrote that "she was a civil rights activist before there was activism, and a feminist when feminists could not be found. She practiced at a major law firm and earned a renowned professorship at a major university before blacks or women did either."

A reading from Pauli Murray about her ordination and the beginning of her ordained ministry

I was the last of the six to be consecrated, and was told later that just as Bishop Creighton placed his hands upon my forehead, the sun broke through the clouds outside and sent shafts of rainbow-colored light down through the stained-glass windows. The shimmering beams of light were so striking that members of the congregation gasped. When I learned about it later, I took it as the sign of God's will I had prayed for. . . .

Five weeks later, on the weekend of Abraham Lincoln's birthday, I traveled to North Carolina to celebrate my first Holy Eucharist — also the first Eucharist to be celebrated by a woman in that state — at the Chapel of the Cross in Chapel Hill. Family history and religious tradition combined with changing folkways to make it an occasion of high drama, which attracted not only the local media but also Charles Kuralt of CBS — himself a graduate of the University of North Carolina — who came down with his "On the Road" van and television crew from New York to cover the event.

On Sunday, February 13, in the little chapel where my Grandmother Cornelia had been baptized more than a century earlier as one of "Five Servant Children Belonging to Miss Mary Ruffin Smith," I read the gospel from an ornate lectern engraved with the name of that slave-owning woman who had left part of her wealth to the Episcopal Diocese of North Carolina. A thoroughly interracial congregation crowded the chapel, and many more stood outside until they could enter to kneel at the altar rail and receive Communion. There was great irony in the fact that the first woman priest to preside at the altar of the church to which Mary Ruffin Smith had given her deepest devotion should be the granddaughter of the little girl she had sent to the balcony reserved for slaves. But more than irony marked that moment. Whatever future ministry I might have as a priest, it was given to me that day to be a symbol of healing.

All the strands of my life had come together. Descendant of slave and of slave owner, I had already been called poet, lawyer, teacher, and friend. Now I was empowered to minister the sacrament of One in whom there is no north or south, no black or white, no male or female — only the spirit of love and reconciliation drawing us all toward the goal of human wholeness.

✣ April 30

Lott Cary

BAPTIST

1780–November 10, 1828

"There never has been an hour or a minute, no, not even when the balls were flying around my head, when I could wish myself again in America." So wrote Lott Cary from Liberia where he had gone to be a missionary and to encourage black emigration from the United States. Cary had been born in slavery near Richmond, Virginia. As a young man, his behavior was hardly a model for others. But at age 27 he was persuaded to change his life, made public profession of faith, and became a member of the Baptist Church. He became so valued a worker in the tobacco warehouse where he was employed that he was able to save $850. After his first wife's death, he managed to buy his own freedom and that of his two children. Although he had not been formally educated, he taught himself to read and read widely to educate himself. Before long, he was pastor of a Baptist congregation of some 800 members.

By the time he was 35, Cary's dominating passion had become emigrating to Africa. When asked why he would leave the comfortable existence he had made for himself, Cary replied: "I am an African, and in this country, however meritorious my conduct, and respectable my character, I cannot receive the credit due to either. I wish to go to a country where I shall be estimated by my merits, not by my complexion; and I feel bound to labor for my suffering race."

In his farewell sermon to the First Baptist Meeting House in Richmond, he was reported to have said,

> I am about to leave you and expect to see your faces no more. I long to preach to the poor Africans the way of life and salvation. I don't know what may befall me, whether I may find a grave in the ocean, or among the savage men, or more savage wild beasts on the Coast of Africa; nor am I anxious what may become of me. I feel it my duty to go; and I very much fear that many of those who preach the Gospel in this country, will blush when the Saviour calls them to give an account of their labors in His cause, and tells them, "I commanded you to go into all the world, and preach the Gospel to every creature"; (and with the most forcible emphasis he exclaimed,) the Saviour may ask where have you been? what have you been doing? have you endeavored to the utmost of your ability to fulfill the commands I gave you, or have you sought your own gratification and your own ease, regardless of my commands?

In 1822, Cary set sail for Liberia with a small group of immigrants. Cary's energy and willingness to serve where needed did much to sustain the little colony in the following years. He established a church and school in Monrovia and another school, primarily for tribal people, in Christopolis. Increasingly, however, demands for his nursing skills consumed his time. At first, he refused to become involved in the civil government but eventually felt his leadership was needed there as well, though such activities limited his missionary work, always his primary concern. Nonetheless, he realized these other duties were vital to the colony's survival and its ability to serve as a base of missionary operations. In 1828, the governor deputized Cary as acting governor in his absence, but an accidental explosion, as Cary and others were preparing to defend the colony in a battle between some of the tribes and the settlers, cost him his life.

A letter from Lott Cary reporting the early progress of the colony Monrovia (Africa)

Jan. 16th, 1825.

Dear brother,

I am glad that an opportunity is afforded to hand you a few lines, which leave me and mine in good health; and, I hope, may find you enjoying the blessings of a favorable Providence. I have not much (but still something, I think) worth communicating. Since I wrote you last, the Lord has in mercy visited the settlement, and I have had the happiness to baptize nine hopeful converts; besides, a number have joined the Methodists. The natives are more and more friendly; their confidence begins to awaken. They see that it is our wish to do them good, and hostilities have ceased with them. I have daily applications to receive their children, and have ventured to take three small boys; to find clothes, and pay for their attendance at the day school — two from Grand Cape Mount, and one from Little Bassa; the two former are very promising, but the other is slow to learn, yet a fine boy. Two of them, I was obliged to send home, ten days ago, in consequence of sores, which they had; but they will return as soon as they are cured; and, in order to establish my confidence in their returning, they refused to take their clothes with them. Our Sunday school still goes on, with some hopes that the Lord will ultimately bless it to the good of numbers of the untutored tribes. The natives attend our Lord's day worship, quite regularly. We have commenced bringing out our timbers for the building of our meeting house, and have got all the large timbers on the ground, but we shall want boards, shingles, nails, window glass, &c. of which you will please to collect what you can, and send out. Please make my respects to the board, and accept of the same for yourself and family.

I am yours, very dearly,
Lott Cary

May

William Jennings Bryan

PRESBYTERIAN

March 19, 1860–July 26, 1925

No other candidate of a major political party has been defeated three times for the presidency, but William Jennings Bryan was not a typical politician. The positions he took were based on deep convictions and grounded in a vital Christian faith. At the end of his life, in the Scopes trial, he became the spokesman for the cause of Christian fundamentalism in opposition to the teaching of evolution and is therefore often remembered as a narrow-minded conservative. In reality, he was a strong advocate of many liberal causes, including woman's suffrage, the direct election of senators, the income tax, and the Department of Labor among others. As Secretary of State in the Wilson administration, Bryan, a pacifist, made a significant contribution to international relations by creating a system to arbitrate international disputes. When Woodrow Wilson responded to the sinking of the *Lusitania* with bellicose statements, Bryan resigned on principal, yet supported the allied cause once war was declared.

Bryan's first nomination for president came when, at the age of 36, he attended the Democratic convention as champion for agrarian interests in the midwest in opposition to the gold standard, which seemed to him to represent the moneyed interests of the big eastern cities. The "Cross of Gold" speech he delivered at that convention remains one of the best known orations in American history. Bryan proclaimed that "The humblest citizen in

239

all the land, when clad in the armor of a righteous cause, is stronger than all the hosts of error." His memorable closing is still remembered: "You shall not press down upon the brow of labor this crown of thorns, you shall not crucify mankind upon a cross of gold."

A more systematic presentation of his principles was laid out in "The Prince of Peace," a speech he often gave while traveling as a speaker between campaigns.

> I recognize that the most important things in life lie outside of the realm of government and that more depends upon what the individual does for himself than upon what the government does or can do for him. Men can be miserable under the best government and they can be happy under the worst government. Government affects but a part of the life which we live here and does not deal at all with the life beyond, while religion touches the infinite circle of existence as well as the small arc of that circle which we spend on earth. No greater theme, therefore, can engage our attention. When discussing questions of government I must secure the cooperation of a majority before my ideas can be put into practise, but if, in speaking on religion, I can touch one human heart for good, I have not spoken in vain no matter how large the majority may be against me.
>
> Man is a religious being; the heart instinctively seeks for a God. Whether he prays on the banks of the Ganges, prays with his face upturned toward Mecca, or, regarding all space as a temple, communes with the Heavenly Father according to the Christian creed, man is essentially devout.

Bryan went on to lay out his reasons for opposing Darwin's theory of evolution, making some points that are still worth considering:

> Go back as far as we may, we can not escape from the creative act, and it is just as easy for me to believe that God created man *as he is* as to believe that, millions of years ago, He created a germ of life and endowed it with power to develop into all that we see today. I object to the Darwinian theory, until more conclusive proof is produced, because I fear we shall lose the consciousness of God's presence in our daily life, if we must accept the theory that through all the ages no spiritual force has touched the life of man or shaped the destiny of nations.
>
> But there is another objection. The Darwinian theory represents man as reaching his present perfection by the operation of the law of hate — the merciless law by which the strong crowd out and kill off the weak. If this is the law of our development then, if there is any logic that can bind the human mind, we shall turn backward toward the beast in proportion as we substitute the law of love. I prefer to believe that love rather than hatred is the law of development. How can hatred be the law of development when nations have advanced in proportion as they have departed from that law and adopted the law of love?
>
> But, I repeat, while I do not accept the Darwinian theory I shall not quarrel with you about it; I only refer to it to remind you that it does not solve the mystery of life or explain human progress.

These views, perhaps inevitably, led Bryan to become involved with the trial of John T. Scopes, a schoolteacher in Tennessee who had taught evolution. The famous lawyer, Clarence Darrow, defended Scopes and the journalist, H. L. Mencken, poured scorn on Bryan. The verdict went against Scopes, but Bryan, worn down by the trial, died five days later.

✪ *May 2* ⎯⎯⎯⎯⎯⎯⎯⎯⎯⎯⎯⎯⎯⎯⎯⎯⎯⎯⎯⎯⎯⎯⎯⎯⎯

Félix Varela

ROMAN CATHOLIC

November 20, 1788–February 25, 1853

In the checkered history of relations between the United States and Cuba, Félix Varela has been called "one of the bridges of light," connecting the people of those two countries. As a Roman Catholic refugee from tyranny in Cuba, he worked to establish the Roman Catholic church in New York and to create democratic government in Cuba.

Although Varela was largely self-educated, he was named professor of philosophy at the Seminary of San Carlos and San Ambrosio in Havana even before his ordination in 1811. Authorized by the bishop to bring a new broom to his work, he began to teach in Spanish rather than Latin and to introduce the ideas of new philosophers like Locke, Descartes, and Condillac. A lover of music, he also helped organize the first Philharmonic Society in Cuba. Ten years later, Varela was elected to represent his country in the Spanish Cortes. This was the period when most of the nations of Latin America won their liberty from Spain. As a representative of one of two remaining Spanish colonies in the New World, Varela moved to grant wide powers to Cuba and Puerto Rico, and to abolish slavery in both. When the Cortes was dissolved and absolute rule restored, Varela was condemned to death and fled to the United States.

Irish immigrants were pouring into New York when Varela arrived. Though a new arrival himself, he vigorously threw himself into the church's ministry to them. He helped found nurseries and orphanages for children of poor widows and also established a school that gave equal opportunity to girls as well as boys. When a cholera epidemic broke out in 1832, Varela turned his attention to caring for the sick and dying, working in the hospitals and even sleeping there while the epidemic ran its course. Out of concern for the poor, Varela is said to have given away his only winter coat and his table silver.

In the midst of his ministry to the poor and the newly arrived, Varela never forgot the people of his homeland. He started a newspaper, *El Habanero,* to expound his ideas about Cuban independence, and the paper was smuggled into his homeland, where it was eagerly read. José Martí, known as the liberator of Cuba, said that Varela "taught us how to think."

Roman Catholic leaders like Archbishop Hughes of New York were uneasy with the individualism fostered by liberal democracy, but to Varela faith and freedom belonged together. His *Letters to Elpido* is a systematic exposition of the relationship between the two. In 1988, Cardinal John O'Connor of New York visited Cuba and said of Varela that "all that he did was founded in his identity as a Christian and a Catholic."

A reading from *Letters to Elpido* by Félix Varela

Several times I have thought, Elpido, about the analogy between the Catholic Church and free societies, and I have always concluded that Christianity and liberty are inseparable; and that when the latter sees itself persecuted, it finds refuge only in Christian temples.... A celestial council, in which saintly liberty reigns united to a just obedience, forms in the saintly temple, and people learn equality without losing their individuality, since the rich and the poor, the wise and the ignorant, the powerful and the weak, and even the princes themselves, along with their subjects, form a family, all considering themselves subjects of the same law and free from oppression and injustice. The August mother of this unanimous family says goodbye to her children with the blessings of heaven, recommending peace and benevolence to them, mutual charity, which, more vigorous than the law, makes up for their defects and keeps the nations in perfect harmony. She implants social obligations and advises them never to lack mutual love; that far from persecuting each other they should help each other, as sons of the Celestial Father, who loves everyone, sustains everyone and protects everyone. She tells them, in summary, to preserve outside the saintly place the Christian sentiments they have nurtured inside it, and upon going back to the world not to forget that they have lived in heaven. Yes in heaven, because of the spiritual union with the God of heaven, because of the sublime idea and celestial virtues they have received as a free gift in that august house and before the throne of the Eternal One.

With such sentiments true Christians leave the saintly temples, and if they retained them, do you think, my friend, they could be despots? Do you think that they would tread on the laws, infringe upon rights, destroy peace and spark war? It is evident, therefore, that Christianity is irreconcilable with tyranny and that any true Christian society is truly free. A Christian nation forms an immense temple, whose extension does not diminish its order but rather increases the sacred fire of love, increasing the number of virtuous persons. Liberty fears nothing when virtue is assured; and power is used with approval, and without obstacles, when justice and not perversity guides those who command.... There is no perfect society without perfect love, and an irreligious society can never be perfect. The perfection of love depends upon the object loved and the constancy and way of the one who loves; and there is only one perfect being, and that is

God; only one constant way and that is the unalterable light of religion; and there is only one just way of loving, and that is by referring all to the Supreme being.

✪ *May 3*

Emily Gardiner Neal

EPISCOPALIAN

October 22, 1910–September 23, 1989

The child of atheists, she had set her heart on a career as a professional violinist, but God saw unsuspected gifts in Emily Gardiner Neal, and to her complete surprise she became a leader in the church's healing ministry. Emily Gardiner was born in New York City and gave up her dreams of life as a violinist when she married and gave birth to two children. She then decided to be an author, and wrote numerous articles for leading magazines. When a national magazine assigned her to do an exposé of healing ministries, she decided it would be an excellent subject for a book. Attending healing services for research, however, she saw things she could not explain away. She did try; miracles after all were not admissible in a scientific world. Surely these illnesses imaginary? But the vast majority turned out to be very real. A man made blind after being pierced by a splinter of molten steel was not imagining his blindness of 20 year's standing. Perhaps the doctors had made a wrong diagnosis? But how could so many highly trained doctors be so wrong? She could not believe that doctors in general were "criminally incompetent, nor the procedures they use entirely untrustworthy." Perhaps it was a yet unexplained scientific phenomenon? But then she noticed that people had experienced not only a physical healing, but a transformation in their lives that she began to believe could only be explained by an inward and spiritual grace. So finally, after careful, skeptical investigation of over 100 cases, Neal began writing a different book than the one she had intended. Titled *A Reporter Finds God through Spiritual Healing*, it told the story of what she had seen and how lives had been changed — including her own.

Neal became a leading advocate of healing ministry and served on an Episcopal commission that presented the case for spiritual healing to the church's General Convention. A number of other books about healing followed and Neal herself found that she had a gift for that ministry. She disliked the term "healer" as a description of her ministry. She was, as she explained it, "an instrument used for *God's* healing." After 20 years of lay ministry, she was ordained a deacon and after her husband's death, she lived with a religious order as an associate member and conducted a weekly healing service.

A reading from Emily Gardiner Neal

For some, faith comes easily. In my ignorance, I had thought that those who could obey the command "Follow thou me" without question, were unthinking, rather stupid people. I know now that they are the inestimably blessed. For others, like myself, the acquisition of real faith is a difficult and often acutely painful process: a war between mind and heart. But if years ago I had managed to rationalize myself out of belief, I was, through my interest in spiritual healing, to reason myself into faith.

I was neither healed of any physical disability nor was I, in the usual sense, converted. But in seeking an explanation for the phenomenon of nonmedical healings, I was forced into an analysis of Christianity....

They say that faith is more a matter of the heart than of the mind, and this is essentially true. But there is a vast difference between belief and faith, even though the one almost invariably follows the other. Belief is the mind's acceptance, and faith is the heart's receiving. My heart was to remain locked until my mind could accept Christ.

My faith came, not as a sudden and dramatic conversion, but by means of a rather torturously-arrived-at intellectual conviction — a conviction predicated on the fact that, to me, Christianity made good sense, but to derive the sense from it, I must believe what Christ taught in its entirety, or I must believe none of it. Christianity is not a myth. It is an historical and clearly definitive religion; there are no halfway measures. I feel that neither I, a lay woman, or any theologian, however learned, can choose at random and select without authority what is convenient for the one to believe and interesting for the other to teach. If we take it upon ourselves to do so, we are degrading Christianity into a fabricated code of half-truths, and the step from a half-truth to a lie is notoriously short.

In my opinion, if we casually overlook, interpret away, or attempt to make more palatable the difficult teachings of our Lord, we are degrading Christianity into a chaotic and untrustworthy cult. To me, either the whole thing is true, or the whole thing is false. You make your choice. I made mine on the basis of the results of true Christian faith as I saw them first, in spiritual healing of the body, and as I have recognized them since, in spiritual healing of the soul. My mind's acceptance proved the key that was to open my heart to full faith.

I repudiated my background, which for so long had conditioned me against literal Christianity. I reversed my former beliefs and corrected my former misapprehensions, such as my belief that religion was for the weak. I knew now that our strength can be computed by the degree to which we depend on God, while our courage can be determined by the extent to which we dare to claim Christ's promises.

I was ready at last to confess a living God and his only begotten son, Jesus Christ, who was sent to redeem the world.

✪ *May 4*

Nathan Bangs

METHODIST

May 2, 1778–May 3, 1862

It is easy to dismiss the work of an historian as being of minor importance and to see the individual as a mere witness and scribe. That would be an unfortunate result of the activism that too often dominates the American mentality. One might dismiss the four evangelists on the same grounds. But a church based on the historical events through which God has been made known. Therefore, it must always value those who record the events of their own time, for they enable us to see how people much like ourselves have borne witness through the ages. In the case of Nathan Bangs, we see someone who both recorded the history of his church and also played a significant part in it.

Despite his limited education, Nathan Bangs became a schoolteacher and spent three years in Canada, teaching school and surveying land. While there, he joined the Methodists and served as an itinerant preacher in the Canadian provinces for six years. Upon his return to New York State in 1820, he was placed in charge of the Methodist publishing house. He soon paid off its debt and expanded the business. His authorial gifts were put to good use in the *Methodist Magazine,* which he also edited. Not content to limit himself to publishing, he helped found the Methodist missionary society and served as its secretary until, in 1841, he was appointed president of Wesleyan University at Middletown, Connecticut. A year later, he returned to pastoral work, continuing in parish ministry until he retired at the age of 74. Bangs devoted the remainder of his life to the writing for which he is best known.

His works included histories of the Methodist Church and its missions, lives of Arminius and Freeborn Garettson, essays on emancipation, sanctification, and episcopacy, and letters of advice to a young preacher. His writing is valuable not only for its preservation of history but for its focus on the importance of those events for the transformation of human lives. His biographer said, "He was, withal, a man of profound piety, of universal charity, and much admirable individuality."

A reading from the *History of the Methodist Episcopal Church* by Nathan Bangs

The whole Church organization, including the entire machinery of class-meetings, love-feasts, sacraments, missions, and education, would have been ineffective had it not been cemented together by the uniting love of God, and moved forward by his irresistible hand. To reach this result, these men of God fixed their eye upon the "mark of the prize of their high calling of God" — holiness of heart was pressed upon the people as a subject of experimental knowledge. This was a theme upon which they dwelt with peculiar delight and marked emphasis. Whatever doctrine they preached — whether repentance, faith in the atoning merits of Christ, or justification; whether they exhibited the judgment-day, the character of God, or death and eternity — they made it subservient to the attainment of this object of their ministry, namely, *holiness of heart and life.* By making this the alpha and omega of all their preaching and praying, their watching and fasting, God blessed their labours abundantly, sinners were awakened, and converted, believers were sanctified, and the Church was enlarged on every hand. This it was that gave life and animation to the whole machinery, and made it move on with a rapid success.

Take away this doctrine from Methodism, and you strip it of one of its most vital principles. Like the blood that flows through the physical system, giving life and animation to its material functions, so this principle of holiness, running through the spiritual body, gives activity to all its members, and makes them move in harmony one with the other, producing an energy of action which effects the desired result. Hence the great Head of the Church was with them. His Holy Spirit gave life and strength, infused a vigorous impulse into the heart and soul, by which those men of God were propelled forward in their holy calling, and were enabled to achieve the victories which they have won. By this means Methodism has spread from Maine to Georgia, from the Atlantic to the Pacific, to Africa, to China, and is still extending its influence in every direction. Its banner has been unfurled among the savages of our wildernesses, among the slaves of the south, as well as among the white population of the civilized communities. And this not in name only, — it has aimed its truths directly at the heart, and effected a reformation of the most radical character, converting the drunkard to a sober man, the profane swearer to a man of prayer, and the proud Pharisee to a meek and humble follower of the Lord Jesus.

See what has been accomplished in fifty years! This body of Christians has increased, as has already been said from 72,874 to more than 1,200,000. May we not therefore say, in the language of the text, "a little one has become a thousand?" And have we not abundant cause of thanksgiving to God for thus hastening the work in the way and manner he has?

✸ *May 5*

Mary Dyer

QUAKER

?–June 1, 1660

Mary Dyer came to Massachusetts with her husband in 1635 to escape religious restrictions in England. The Dyers were Puritans and joined Boston's First Church. There Mary became a friend of Ann Hutchinson,* who was soon to be tried, excommunicated, and banished to Rhode Island. The Dyers followed her, then traveled with Roger Williams to England to obtain a charter for the colony. In England, Mary Dyer became a follower of George Fox and a member of his Society of Friends or Quakers.

Quakers were not welcome in Massachusetts, so Mary planned merely to pass through Boston on her way back to Rhode Island. Nevertheless, she was arrested, and her husband won her release only by promising she would leave the colony forever, speaking to no one on her way to Rhode Island.

Mary, however, had not promised never to return, and before long she attempted to visit some Quakers in the Boston jail. She was arrested again and sentenced with three others to be hanged. Pleas from her husband and son prevailed at the last minute, but she told the court she would never agree to be silenced. After spending the winter in Long Island, Mary Dyer went back to Boston to preach. Inevitably she was arrested, and this time the sentence to be hanged was carried out. Mary Dyer was one of a very small number of Quaker martyrs, and her death contributed to the easing of anti-Quaker statutes. In 1959, the Massachusetts General Court, which had condemned her nearly 300 years before, erected a statue in her memory on the grounds of the State House in Boston. The words she wrote from her cell in the Boston jail are engraved on the base:

> *My Life not Availeth Me*
> *In Comparison to the*
> *Liberty of the Truth*

A reading from Mary Dyer's second letter written from prison, 1659, after the hanging of Marmaduke and Stephenson

Once more the General Court, Assembled in Boston, speaks Mary Dyar, even as before: My life is not accepted, neither availeth me, in Comparison of the Lives and Liberty of the Truth and Servants of the Living God, for which in the Bowels of Love and Meekness I sought you; yet nevertheless, with wicked Hands have you put two of them to Death, which makes me to feel, that the Mercies of the Wicked is Cruelty. I rather chuse to die than to live, as from you, as Guilty of their innocent Blood. Therefore, seeing my Request is hindered, I leave you to the Righteous Judge and Searcher of all Hearts, who, with the pure measure of Light he hath given to every Man to profit withal, will in his due time let you see whose Servants you are, and of whom you have taken Counsel, which desire you to search into: But all his counsel hath been slighted, and, you would none of his reproofs. Read your Portion, Prov. 1:24 to 32. "For verily the Night cometh on you apace, wherein no Man can Work, in which you shall assuredly fall to your own Master, in Obedience to the Lord, whom I serve with my Spirit, and to pity to your Souls, which you neither know nor pity: I can do no less than once more to warn you, to put away the Evil of your Doings, and Kiss the Son, the Light in you before his wrath be kindled in you; for where it is, nothing without you can help or deliver you out of his hand at all; and if these things be not so, then say, There hath been no prophet from the Lord sent amongst you: yet it is his Pleasure, by Things that are not, to bring to naught Things that are."

When I heard your last Order read, it was a disturbance unto me, that was so freely Offering up my life to him that give it me, and sent me hither to do, which Obedience being his own Work, he gloriously accompanied with his Presence, and Peace, and Love in me, in which I rested from my labour, till by your Order, and the People, I was so far disturbed, that I could not retain anymore of the words thereof, than that I should return to Prison, and there remain Forty and Eight hours; to which I submitted, finding nothing from the Lord to the contrary, that I may know what his Pleasure and Counsel is concerning me, on whom I wait therefore, for he is my Life, and the length of my Days, and as I said before, I came at his command, and go at His command.

✪ *May 6*

Fidelia Fiske

CONGREGATIONAL

May 1, 1816–July 26, 1864

"As I am permitted to see more and more of the poor degraded females of this nation, if I know my heart, I do feel a deeper interest in them, and a stronger desire to spend and be spent for them." Fidelia Fiske wrote this in 1843, after arriving in Iran as a missionary. Her story epitomizes the 19th-century missionary venture: the fervent zeal resulting from the waves of revival, the romantic sense of adventure in a world whose "farthest coasts" were more accessible than ever, the confident sense of western superiority resulting from the industrial revolution, and, at the same time, the changing role of women pressing for a larger and more equal role in society.

Fidelia Fiske graduated from the district schools in Shelbourne, Massachusetts, and became a schoolteacher. but when Mary Lyon* opened Mt. Holyoke Female Seminary in 1837, Fiske quickly seized this opportunity for higher education. Mary Lyon wanted women not only to get an education but to use that education to serve. Fidelia Fiske absorbed those principals and offered herself for service in Persia.

Persia had been the center of one of the first great civilizations, but by the 19th century Americans could see it only as backward and in need of help. Fiske was appalled at the conditions she found there in 1843. Homes were filthy, husbands beat their wives, children had no schooling, and the sick were left to die alone. As a teacher, Fidelia set to work learning the language so she could create a school. For the next 15 years, she fought to get permission from parents so that their daughters could be educated. She used her nursing skills to convince Persians of her concern for their welfare, and patiently, lovingly told anyone who would listen about God's love for them. "I felt deeply for my poor sisters before going to them," she wrote, "but there was a deeper feeling, even anguish, when I realized, from mingling with them, how very low they were. I really knew at first very little of the pit into which I was descending. I did not wish to leave them, but I did often ask, 'Can the Saviour's image ever be reflected from such hearts?' "

She had gone to Persia not expecting she would ever leave, but after 15 years, her health failed and she was persuaded to go back to America. Fiske spent the last five years of her life teaching at Mt. Holyoke, dying at the age of 48. On her deathbed, she heard a hymn about "eternal rest" and commented that the idea of heaven as a place of "rest" was not pleasant to her. She preferred to think of the saints still active and engaged, as far as possible, in those employments they most enjoyed on earth. One of her admirers said, "She seemed to me the nearest approach I ever saw, in man or woman, to my ideal of our blessed Saviour, as he appeared on the earth."

A reading from a letter by Fidelia Fiske, giving her first impressions of Persia

Seir, August 9, 1843.

My Dear Brother and Sister

I have written you in regard to my pleasant situation. I feel that my cup overflows with blessings. Seir is a small village, the people mostly Nestorians. I love to go out to their mud huts, as attempting to speak with them helps me to speak. When they see me coming, they run to bring a mat or something of the kind for me to sit on. I take my seat, as sister A. will remember I used to love to sit in childhood. Really, sister, this once considered sad defect of mine comes now well in use. When I enter a house, in scriptural style, and, in accordance with the usage of this people, I say, 'Sialama lahone' (Peace be to you), their reply is 'Shldama mashana' (Be it returned to you a hundred-fold). Then follow many expressions like these: 'I am your servant.' 'My children are your servants,' etc. Then they will cluster about me and seem exceedingly pleased with conversation. You would be amused to see me surrounded by fifteen or twenty Nestorian women and children, dressed in the manner described in Mr. Perkins' book, seeking to improve my conversational powers. I do exceedingly long to have the time come when my tongue shall be loosed, and I shall be able to speak freely with them on religious subjects. It will be pleasant to gather a little band of these poor females together, and unite with them in prayer and praise. I hope you may long think of Fidelia as going from house to house, or in the school-room surrounded by these poor degraded little girls. Yes, if it is my Father's will, I hope long to live and labor for Persia's daughters. And will not you rejoice that this privilege is mine? Oh, could you see these poor females, as they are, you would be thankful that you have a sister to spare to them! None of them read, and few of them have any correct ideas of eternity, or the God to whom they are accountable. Their days are spent in those labors, which, in our country, are performed by the other sex alone. To the fields they carry their little ones, as they engage in their work. I have seen the little child of a few months sitting in the field by its mother, while she was harvesting grain. At night they return to their homes, milk their cows, prepare supper for their husbands, and then eat alone. To eat with their husbands is the height of indelicacy in their view. They marry very young; often at the age of eighteen they are the mothers of two or three children. To be the mother of sons is considered a great blessing, but of daughters a great misfortune. Very many of the children die in infancy and childhood, owing, doubtless, to the climate. It is confidently believed by the missionaries that not one fourth part of those born survive the years of childhood.

✪ *May 7* _____

James Augustine Healy

ROMAN CATHOLIC

April 6, 1830–August 5, 1900

Terrence Powderly* was angry. He had come to Maine to organize and advocate for working men, and he had come to see the Roman Catholic bishop, hoping for an understanding reception and support for his work. Instead he had encountered a proud and imperious man who rejected his overtures brusquely and sent him back out the door.

Terrence Powderly and James Augustine Healy were both deeply devoted to their church and to the needs of those around them, but they could never have understood each other. Each had come from humble circumstances and achieved a leadership role. But perhaps because of the obstacles they had dealt with along the way, neither had the security to deal generously with opposition.

James A. Healy's father was an Irish immigrant who had won 1,300 acres of land in Georgia in a lottery. He fell in love with a mulatto slave and, since Georgia law prohibited interracial marriage, he entered into a common-law relationship that produced ten children, of whom James Augustine was one. Since the children were considered slaves and illegitimate under Georgia law, there was no schooling available to them in that state, so James Healy was sent north to be educated in a Quaker school on Long Island. Even there, he felt the sting of discrimination, not just as a black but also because of his Irish heritage. In addition, the Quakers were uncomfortable with the fact that Healy's father owned slaves. Healy, therefore, moved on to the grammar school, secondary school, and college of the newly founded Holy Cross College in Worcester, Massachusetts, where he was valedictorian of the first graduating class. When he sought ordination, however, not even the Roman Catholic Church in the United States could accommodate a black student, so he had to travel to Montreal to attend seminary. He also studied at the Sulpician Seminary in Paris and was ordained in the Cathedral of Notre Dame before returning to the Diocese of Boston to begin his ministry. He is believed to have been the first African American to be ordained a Roman Catholic priest.

Serving first as an assistant pastor, then as secretary and chancellor to the bishop, Healy was commended for his ministry during outbreaks of cholera, typhoid, and tuberculosis. He was appointed pastor of St. James Church, Boston's largest parish, where he continued to play a leading role in social ministry and worked to establish the Home for Destitute Catholic Children, the House of the Good Shepherd and St. Ann's Foundling Home. Children were always a focal point of Healy's ministry, perhaps because they are color-blind to racial differences. With them, he had no need to be on his guard.

Healy's talent as an orator was widely recognized, and he was often asked to speak at the dedication of churches. He succeeded in defending the church's tax-exempt status by pointing out to the state legislature the tremendous amount of money saved because of the church's social welfare work. In 1875, he was appointed Bishop of Portland, a diocese that included the states of Maine and New Hampshire. Over the next 25 years, he oversaw the creation of 60 new churches, 68 missions, 18 convents, and 18 schools, as well as a large number of welfare institutions while the Roman Catholic population doubled to nearly 100,000. Roman Catholics in Maine had not been thrilled by the idea of a black bishop, but he won his way with the significant French-speaking population, thanks to his fluency in their language and impressed others with his concern for the poor. He refused to live in the bishop's mansion. No wonder Terrence Powderly expected a warm reception from such a man. But in an age of harsh anti-labor laws, Powderly's Knights of Labor were a secret organization, and the Vatican prohibited membership in the Masonic Order or any other clandestine society. Torn between a natural sympathy for the needs of the working people and obedience to the church that had given him so much, it is not so surprising that Healy could only rely on the episcopal imperium to send Powderly on his way.

Children were another matter. Healy was known as "the children's Bishop" because of his efforts on behalf of Civil War widows and orphans, his opposition to child labor abuses, and because of the orphanages he had constructed. His relationship with children was more than an institutional one. The bishop loved to let children hitch their sleds to his sleigh so he could give them rides in the winter. There was always a supply of candy and cookies in his pockets for them as well. He bought one-half of an island near Portland, Maine, as a summer vacation spot for orphans and would visit them often.

Minority groups, not surprisingly, were another special interest of Healy's. He was a member of the Council of Bishop's commission for Negro and Indian missions and served as a consultant to the U.S. Bureau of Indian Affairs. He did not, however, see himself as a member of a minority group. He refused to participate in specifically African American organizations or to speak even at conventions of black Roman Catholics. "We," he said, "are of that Church where there is neither Gentile nor Jew, circumcision nor uncircumcision, barbarian nor Scythian, slave nor freeman, but Christ is all and in all."

✪ *May 8* _____

Bessie Lee Efner Rehwinkel

LUTHERAN

March 28, 1873–May 26, 1962

Of the many facets of the movement to free women to use their gifts without barriers, one was the right of women to enter fields of labor that had once been reserved only for men. As the 19th century was coming to a close, and the 20th promised to bring new opportunities in many ways, the idea of a woman physician was still very difficult for many people to imagine. Bessie Efner was undaunted by conventions that seemed outmoded to her, and determined to become a medical doctor. In this decision, she was following in a family tradition that had produced three generations of physicians.

The family was originally from Iowa, and it was here that Efner opened her first two practices despite the predictable resistance and opposition that a female doctor could expect to receive in those days. Her work was generally going well, until a series of economic calamities brought on by the financial panic of 1907 stripped her of savings, leaving her homeless, with only some clothes and some medical equipment. She also had three orphaned nieces, dependent upon her for support. It would be easy to imagine giving up under such conditions, or seeking a more secure setting, but Efner had no such intention. Having lost almost everything, she had nothing more to lose, so she turned her attention westward, where the need for her skills was more urgent than in Iowa.

In that period of economic stress, Efner decided to practice in the Territory of Wyoming, still very wild and dangerous at the time. Her practice extended 30 miles in each direction. There were no drug stores, clinics, or hospitals besides her own office anywhere in the area. She had no access to nurses to supplement her care. A horse-drawn wagon was her only transportation. It was not just advanced medical expertise that was missing; even the most rudimentary services one might find in a more urban setting were unavailable there. But Efner settled in. She was not looking for comfort or ease, but a place to help those who had no other place to turn for help.

Late one evening, a badly hurt patient was brought to her door. She took him in and cared for him in her own home. His name was Alfred Rehwinkel, a young preacher who later became her husband. They married in 1912, and, along with the nieces, moved to Pincher Creek, in Alberta, Canada, where he had been called as pastor to a collection of preaching stations. Bessie Rehwinkel was not allowed to function as a physician in Canada, but was able to offer her healing services in other capacities. In 1914, the couple moved on to Edmunton to Alfred's second call. While there, Rehwinkel continued her own education at the University of Alberta. But again, the needs of those around her captured her attention. Rehwinkel's connections to the Alberta British Columbia District of the Lutheran Church–Missouri Synod put her in position to help place German women immigrants looking for work in homes where their labors as housekeepers and nannies could be useful. She also became the unofficial nurse at Concordia College, where diphtheria, smallpox, and scarlet fever were all threats. Though recognized as a physician, Rewinckel offered as much of her training as she was allowed on behalf of her neighbors.

Bessie Rehwinkel's own health did not agree with the harsh Canadian climate. She was advised by her doctor to seek a more temperate home. Though the Rehwinkels loved Canada, the family decided to move to St. Louis, where Alfred was able to secure a position on the faculty of Concordia Seminary to support his family.

In reflecting on the faith of earlier generations, it is important to recall how many obstacles needed to be overcome. In addition to the absence of many things we now consider necessities, long-held assumptions and pre-suppositions about gender roles, appropriate behavior, and social norms hampered the aspirations of countless people who felt called to serve. Both dedication and persistence were required to enter professions still considered unsuitable to one's gender or race. The frontier demanded a rigorous existence. Income was minimal, and security nonexistent. Yet Bessie Rehwinkel and her husband did not shirk these hardships. Later, they sacrificed their own preferences for the health and career of the other.

The level of faith and commitment required to pursue a life like Bessie Rewinckel's remains a rare quality. Her pioneering spirit remains a remarkable example of faith active in love. Her willingness to alter her work to meet the needs of those around her demonstrates her deep compassion for her neighbors. Rewinckel's willingness to mother her orphaned nieces provided them with security and advantages they would otherwise have missed. At every step, Rehwinkel sought ways to give, to serve, and to support her neighbors' needs. Her disrupted career, her financial struggles, her health problems, and her need to abandon homes, first in Iowa, then Wyoming, then Canada never affected her determination to answer whatever call came to her. Losses and hard times only opened her heart wider to those whose lives needed help or healing. Her imitation of Christ bears recalling as we reflect upon our own choices and vocations.

❊ *May 9*

Roger Williams

BAPTIST

1603–died sometime between January 27 and March 15, 1683

Founder of the first Baptist Church in America, apostle of religious liberty, and creator of the state of Rhode Island, Roger Williams deserves to be numbered with Benjamin Franklin and Thomas Jefferson as one of the creators of the American pattern of civil and religious freedom. Williams was born in poverty in Wales, but attracted the attention of Sir Edward Coke, who enabled him to study at Oxford. He married in 1629, at the age of 26, and emigrated to New England the following year. Almost at once, he made himself unpopular with authorities by suggesting that a charter from the crown did not entitle settlers to take land that, for centuries, had been inhabited by Native Americans. He also disapproved of the colonists' requirement of church membership as a prerequisite for participating in civil government, arguing that they had betrayed their own principles of separatism. "I affirm," he wrote, "that that church estate, that religion and worship which is commanded, or permitted to be but one in a country, nation, or province, is not in the nature of the particular churches of Christ, but in the nature of a national or state church."

Accurate though this judgment may have been, it led to his banishment banished from the colony. Massachusetts planned to deport him back to England, but Williams evaded this by trekking into the wilderness in midwinter and establishing a new colony to the south, on Narragansett Bay, buying land from the Indians, then securing a charter from the English Parliament. This charter made them independent of the Massachusetts settlements and authorized self-rule by whatever form of government they preferred. They incorporated liberty of conscience into their first articles, freeing settlers to worship in any way they pleased so long as they did not disturb the rights of others. Another colonist baptized Williams, who then baptized 11 others, so founding the first Baptist Church in America.

A reading from *The Bloudy Tenent of Persecution for Cause of Conscience Discussed*

While I plead the cause of truth and innocency against the bloody doctrine of persecution for cause of conscience, I judge it not unfit to give alarm to myself, and to [all] men, to prepare to be persecuted or hunted for cause of conscience.

Whether thou standest charged with ten or but two talents, if thou huntest any for cause of conscience, how canst thou say thou followest the Lamb of God, who so abhorred that practice? If Paul, if Jesus Christ, were present here at London, and the question were proposed, what religion would they approve of — the papists, prelatists, Presbyterians, Independents, &c., would each say. Of mine. Of mine?

But put the second question: if one of the several sorts should by major vote attain the sword of steel, what weapons doth Christ Jesus authorize them to fight with in his cause? Do not all men hate the persecutor, and every conscience, true or false, complain of cruelty, tyranny, &c.?

Two mountains of crying guilt lie heavy upon the backs of all men that name the name of Christ, in the eyes of Jews, Turks, and Pagans.

First. The blasphemies of their idolatrous inventions, superstitions, and most unchristian conversations.

Secondly. The bloody, irreligious, and inhuman oppressions and destructions under the mask or veil of the name of Christ, &c.

Oh! how likely is the jealous Jehovah, the consuming fire, to end these present slaughters of the holy witnesses in a greater slaughter!

Six years preaching of so much truth of Christ as that time afforded in K. Edward's days, kindles the flames of Q. Mary's bloody persecutions.

Who can now but expect that after so many scores of years preaching and professing of more truth, and amongst so many great contentions amongst the very best of protestants, a fiery furnace should be heat, and who sees not now the fires kindling?

I confess I have little hopes, till those flames are over, that this discourse against the doctrine of persecution for cause of conscience should pass current, I say not amongst the wolves, and lions, but even amongst the sheep of Christ themselves. Yet, *liberavi animam meam*, I have not hid within my breast my soul's belief. And, although sleeping on the bed either of the pleasures or profits of sin, thinkest thou thy conscience bound to smite at him that dares to waken thee? Yet in the midst of all these civil and spiritual wars, I hope we shall agree in these particulars,

First. However the proud (upon the advantage of a higher earth or ground) overlook the poor, and cry out schismatics, heretics, &c, shall blasphemers and seducers escape unpunished? Yet there is a sorer punishment in the gospel for despising of Christ than Moses, even when the despiser of Moses was put to death without mercy. Heb. x. 28, 29. *He that believeth shall not be damned.* Mark xvi. 16.

Secondly. Whatever worship, ministry, ministration, the best and purest, are practised without faith and true persuasion that they are the true institutions of God, they are sin, sinful worships, ministries, &c. And however in civil things we may be servants unto men, yet in divine and spiritual things the poorest peasant must disdain the service of the highest prince. *Be ye not the servants of men*, 1 Cor. vii. [23].

Thirdly. Without search and trial no man attains this faith and right persuasion. 1 Thes. v. [21], *Try all things.*

In vain have English parliaments permitted English bibles in the poorest English houses, and the simplest man or woman to search the scriptures, if yet against their souls persuasion from the scripture, they should be forced, as if they lived in Spain or Rome itself without the sight of a bible, to believe as the church believes.

Fourthly. Having tried, we must hold fast, 1 Thes. v. [21], upon the loss of a crown, Rev. iii. [11]; we must not let go for all the fleabitings of the present afflictions, &c. Having bought truth dear, we must not sell it cheap, not the least grain of it for the whole world; no, not for the saving of souls, though our own most precious; least of all for the bitter sweetening of a little vanishing pleasure: — For a little puff of credit and reputation from the changeable breath of uncertain sons of men: for the broken bags of riches on eagles' wings: for a dream of these — any or all of these, which on our death-bed vanish and leave tormenting stings behind them. Oh! how much better is it from the love of truth, from the love of the Father of lights from whence it comes, from the love of the Son of God, who is the way and the truth, to say as he, John xviii. 37 *For this end was I born, and for this end came I into the world, that I might bear witness to the truth.*

✪ *May 10*

Gideon Blackburn

PRESBYTERIAN

August 27, 1772–August 23, 1838

It is said that Gideon Blackburn once held an audience of 1,500 enthralled for two hours in the rain. Certainly he was a man of unusual energy and commitment. Orphaned at the age of 11, he had to work in a sawmill at night to earn the money for his daily schooling. To pay for college, he became a surveyor, then sold his wages — 14 horses — to cover his bills. Licensed to preach at the age of 20, he became pastor for several congregations in eastern Tennessee and often accompanied soldiers in expeditions against the Indians.

This contact with Native Americans led to a change of heart and a concern for their "savage and wretched state." Blackburn tried to find support for a mission and, in 1803, persuaded the Presbyterian General Assembly to grant him $200 to begin work among the Cherokees. He won the approval of President John Adams and, later, funding from President Jefferson. The Cherokees remained his major focus until 1810. He started schools and

within five years is reputed to have taught four or five hundred Cherokee youths to read the Bible. Devoting part of each year to the Cherokee
work, Blackburn used the rest of his time to plant new churches in Kentucky
and Tennessee. Fundraising was one of his gifts. On a trip to Massachusetts, 3,000 people thronged to hear him. Those who remembered George
Whitefield said that Blackburn was very nearly his equal.

By 1810, however, the hardships of frontier life led him to move to an
academy in Franklin, Kentucky. In 1814, after raising troops for the War
of 1812 in which he was a chaplain, he organized a Presbyterian parish in
Nashville. In 1818, he organized the first Presbyterian Church in Alabama,
and in 1823 he moved again, to Louisville, Kentucky. Thanks to his talent for
fundraising, in 1827, he was elected president of Centre College in Danville,
Kentucky. The school was in serious financial straits, but Blackburn's fame
as a preacher helped put it on a sounder footing.

Blackburn returned to preaching in 1830, serving also as an agent for the
Kentucky State Temperance Society, but three years later he was asked to
come to Illinois and raise funds for Illinois College. Later still, he helped to
raise an endowment for a school at Carlinville, Illinois, but died before the
school could be built. That institution, not opened until 1857, then began as
a primary school, but ultimately became Blackburn Theological Seminary,
and exists today as Blackburn College.

A reading from a letter by Gideon Blackburn to an unknown recipient

Mayville December 12, 1809

Revd & very dear friend

On the 10th instant I returned from a tour of 12 weeks partly through
the Cherokee nation and partly through the frontiers of the white settlements in which time I laid 4 weeks extremely low with a billious fever the
effects of which are yet sensibly felt, but have reason to be thankfull that for
the last 4 weeks I was able to preach usually twice in the week besides the
Sabbath — The first part of my tour laid through the nation in which I was
called to examine a species of Cherokee improvement before unknown. The
laying out and extending a waggon road through part of their nation for
the distance of 60 miles without the assistance of a white man and crossing
two considerable mountains with incredible labor. While in the examination of the road I was accompanied by two gentleman of information and
respectabillity and on passing of the mountains one mile and three quarters
across, it was asked how much this part of the road could have been undertaken for supposing it had laid in a white settlements were provisions and
hands were plenty. It was agreed that from 2000 to 2500 dolls would have
been as low as possible to have executed as well as they had done. The task

would have been Herculean even amongst the whites. Part of the mountain was litterally *dug* down and rocks from 10 to 50 tons removed, they not understanding the art of blowing, all this was done by the national ardor to increase the wealth of the Nation by travellers from the State of Georgia to West Tennessee and gives an opportunity for them to erect stand on the way for the accommodation of the Passengers —

The desire for wealth — the enlargement of Design, the Knowledge and paitence of labor are clearly evinced from their circumstance. From the surplus of their cattle in the year they have sold market upwards of 700 beeves and of their hogs greatly advanced of a thousand. Their well cultivated farms are numerous. Their corn abundant and other vegetables sufficient for family use, they have several good grist mills.

Yet my dear friend notwithstanding all this improvement the government will still be proposing purchases of lands and they paralyzing every effort which can be used: Instead of this they ought to take them in their arms, give individual deeds for their lands and thus open upon them the blessings of citizenship, and eventually religious instruction.

But Sir I am discouraged not for want of success but of means. I have husbanded to the best advantage but they are nearly exhausted — owing to the constant request for their land, I cannot ask an appropriation of land which otherwise might be had sufficient to meet the expenses. The treasures of the benevolent are locked up by the iron grip of *embargos* and *non intercourse,* the minds and finances of the Genl. Govt. are employed about great national concerns — and my own domestic necessities and declining constitution conspire to say *withdraw from the scene* — Thus within grasp of my wishes I shall be obliged to yield the pursuit. I have done what ages cannot undo but like seed sown in the furrow a harvest will be produced. When I retreat from the scene I intend to look out for some favorable spot where I may finish my days in leading the minds of the congregation not only to Jesus but through the paths of Christian service. Where I shall find this place is uncertain.

In the new settlements where I spent part of my tour, I found many minds favorably disposed towards religion from forest and cane breaks I frequently drew 2 or 3 hundred souls to hear the gospel and it was delightfull to see the deep impression of truth — under the shady beach I frequently seen the tears of penitence moisten the earth and the youthful mind moulding into the immage of Jesus Christ. errors and delusions which had been *propagated* obtained currency fled like shadows before the truth.

The books you sent came to hand in my abscence thank you for your care and attention.

I am in Christian love, yours in the gospel of Christ

Gid Blackburn

✪ *May 11* _____

Rose Hawthorne Lathrop

ROMAN CATHOLIC

May 20, 1851–July 9, 1926

The factors leading to religious conversion are often mysterious. Not uncommonly, they are accompanied by a new sense of purpose in life, or a new passion for service. This was true for Rose Hawthorne Lathrop, known later as Sister Alphonsa. Her father was Nathaniel Hawthorne, the author. She grew up a 19th-century Calvinist protestant New Englander, a culture usually suspicious of Roman Catholic teaching and worship — indeed, opposed to it. Yet in its own way, Puritan tradition was a rich source of religious devotion, seeking God's will, and believing that society should be remade to reflect the divine purpose.

Rose left no writings about her conversion. She seems to have followed her husband, George, when he became a Roman Catholic. But once the shift was made, she demonstrated a striking zeal for her new faith. She had already established herself as a poet and a writer, so her joining the Catholic Church attracted more notice than it might otherwise have done. She was one of the featured speakers at the Catholic Congress held in conjunction with the World's Columbian Exposition in Chicago in 1893. There, out of step with many in her new faith community, she called for a reevaluation of the role of women in the church and in society. Rose challenged her church to celebrate and affirm the role of women and not continue to treat them as inferior members. Despite her sometimes radical positions, however, she found that her passion for social justice, along with a vocation for contemplative prayer, fit in well with the Roman tradition as it existed in America at the end of the 19th century.

Lathrop's social conscience became increasingly moved by the desperate plight of the poor, so she gave up writing to become a nurse. After her husband's death in 1897, she went even further by joining the Third Order of St. Dominic. Out of this grew a new order, founded by her: the Servants of Relief. Rose became known as Sister Alphonsa. From that point on, she concentrated on building up a community that could effectively serve the poor while maintaining its own devotional life. They cared for the poor in their own home, free of charge. They took in patients who had been pronounced incurable, taking no money from them or their families, neither receiving funds from either the government or the church. Donations all came from charitable givers. None of the money given was invested or saved, but used strictly for the care of those they tended. All the work was done by the sisters, with no hired help. Sister Alphonsa's purpose in this was three-fold: to assist the outcast and helpless, both physically and spiritually; to create opportunities for a new kind of generosity among contributors, challenging

them to give of themselves, not merely offer a token to charity; and to reform a society grown accustomed to a caste like structure of extreme wealth
supported by underpaid labor, and an underclass of the desperately poor,
neglected, and often chronically ill.

Sister Alphonsa disapproved of the ingrained stratifications of society and
the blinding self-righteousness she believed infected most charitable activities
of the well to do. She was equally critical of state-run charities, which she
considered a self-serving way for society to push the poor out of sight. Her
aim was to increase public awareness of their plight, making the needy more
visible so that the culture would grow more compassionate. She wrote,

> The first step in social reform must be to attend to the worst, most evident
> disorder. This is the physical sickness of poverty. Then, and not till then, comes
> the second step of the care of the moral sickness of poverty. I do not mean that
> we are to stand on one foot for a long time after taking the first step. Care
> of the mind and soul may easily accompany care of the wretched sufferer;
> but when we postpone the latter duty, we are re-arranging the order of our
> Lord. Not that the body is of value in comparison to the soul, but that other
> people's bodies have a peculiar value for our soul. The body was put outside
> of the soul for some reason, and when we ignore it, we assume that we have
> a more reliable judgment than the Creator's. He says that we are to take care
> of people physically, when they are afflicted physically, and this is because we
> cannot help aiding the soul at the same time. The body which we are at liberty
> to ignore is the one we do not — our own. Many activities, then, can proceed
> from, and flourish alongside of, this nursing of the poor; but it is a blunder
> to suppose that it is not itself the preliminary of fraternal comradeship, since
> Christ said it was. It is the vantage ground from which to elaborate our tactics.

Lathrop might be considered a failure since, in the early part of the 21st
century, many of the conditions she sought to amend remain with us. But
the lives she touched and the witness she bore remain both a gift and a
challenge to all who can hear.

✪ *May 12* _____

William White

EPISCOPALIAN

April 4, 1748–July 17, 1836

In the aftermath of the Revolutionary War, many believed that the Church
of England was doomed to become extinct in the New World. Before independence, it was the established church in the southern states, but that
ended with the creation of state governments, free from the crown. In New
England and the middle colonies, Anglicanism had been supported by English mission societies. That assistance also ended after the revolution. Many

Church of England clergy, sworn to pray for the English crown in their ordination vows, fled to Canada, and many of their churches were destroyed or used as stables.

William White, rector of Christ Church, Philadelphia, was one of the few who believed that the pattern of Christian life established in the Book of Common Prayer could have a place in the new nation. In 1787, he went to England and was consecrated a Bishop for Pennsylvania by English bishops. He set to work with Bishop Seabury of Connecticut and others to establish an Anglican Church in the United States. That a united Episcopal Church did indeed emerge out of the conflict is due in no small part to White's judicious wisdom and perseverance.

White was not by temperament an evangelist. He protested against the notion that a bishop should spend time to travel on the grounds that it was "inconsistent with the expectation of a learned episcopate" and "oppressive on a bishop advanced in years." Furthermore he noted, "a bishop will generally have a family, to whom a reasonable portion of his time will be as much due, as are any of his services to the church."

But perhaps such a cool and dispassionate approach was exactly what the Episcopal Church needed in those early days. If the Connecticut clergy thought laity should be excluded from the government of the church while Virginians were inclined to place church government in the hands of the laity, White could reason with both and find a way to settle the differences.

He served as Bishop of Pennsylvania for over forty years and as Presiding Bishop of the Episcopal Church from 1789 to 1835. He disliked excitement and novelty but provided a calm and steady hand at the tiller when the Episcopal Church most needed it.

A reading from an address by William White to the General Convention of the Episcopal Church on the subject of the Book of Common Prayer

On this subject of the book of Common Prayer, he (White) is desirous of impressing on the mind of his reverend brethren the guarding against even the appearance of a fault, with which some of our ministry have been untruly charged — the elevating of the book to a level with the holy Bible, by making the acceptance of the former a condition for the bestowing of the latter. The charge has been publicly made and publicly denied, and has been continued without proof; contrary, in some instances, to better knowledge. For the avoiding of the appearance of so great a fault, the best experiment will be, that each of us, within his sphere of action, and in the line the most agreeable to his judgment, should give his aid to the zeal which has been brought into action for a general dissemination of the Word of Truth: accordance with which is the greatest glory of that other book which we are accused of holding in extravagant esteem.

Let not our esteem for it be lessened by a charge so injuriously made. Besides its usefulness as a form of public worship, we have abundant evidence of its being blessed to the exciting of devotion in families and in individuals. When, during the revolutionary war, very many districts of our country had become deprived of the means of grace; in some of them, devotion was kept alive in domestic circles, by their possession of books of Common Prayer; so that when, after the lapse of many years, a Christian ministry became restored to them, the intervening privation had not obliterated the instruction of preceding times. Neither ought we to be regardless of the fact, that in many a case of a life spent in utter forgetfulness of God, and perhaps in gross sin, the recollection of the devotions of the book in question, has been the means of repentance and reformation.

For these reasons the book of Common Prayer ought to be considered as an important adjunct in our missionary efforts, both foreign and domestic. By its incitements to devotion, and by its helps in it, the cause may be aided in places in which the itineracy of the missionary will not permit him to remain. Even in the cases of a reasonable proportion of settled pastors, their flocks are generally so extended in their several places of residence, as that it is difficult to command personal aid at the times of unexpected sickness, or of the happening of any extraordinary calamity, when there would be peculiar propriety in the application for religious counsel. Far from the present intention be the dispensing with ministerial aid, in the extent to which it can be carried by the zeal and by the active labours of the minister. But there being physical limits, beyond which his agency cannot be extended, it is no small relief of the wants to which he should be ever ready to contribute his succour, that they may at least in some degree be met by the compilation, which comprehends counsels suited to all states of mind, and devotions expressive of any desires, of which present circumstances ought to be the mean of excitement.

✪ May 13 ────────────────────────────────

Mary McLeod Bethune

METHODIST

July 10, 1875–May 18, 1955

Though her parents had been slaves, Mary McLeod Bethune was asked to serve her country by at least five presidents. She was the 15th of 17 children, but the first to be born free. Several of her older siblings had been sold as slaves. Having to work on the farm, Mary had no formal education until she was 11. A scholarship enabled her to attend the Moody Bible Institute in Chicago, and when the Presbyterian Church rejected her application to serve as a missionary because she was black, she became a teacher. She worked in city jails and served lunch to the homeless. She taught school in South Carolina and Georgia before arriving in Florida. Her goal was always the same: to help educate black children. Eventually, she started her own school. "I had no furniture," she recalled. "I begged dry goods boxes and made benches and stools; begged a basin and other things I needed and in 1904, five little girls here started school. They used charcoal for pencils and crushed elderberries for ink. Tuition was 50 cents a week, but no child was refused whose parents could not afford the payment." To help expand the school, Bethune and her pupils baked pies and made ice cream to sell to nearby construction workers. By 1912, however, she had found a sponsor in James M. Gamble of the Proctor and Gamble Company and was beginning to make a name for herself on a national level. Gradually the little school was expanded to include a high school, then a junior college, then a collegiate institute, and finally, as the result of a merger, Bethune-Cookman College. Mary McLeod Bethune was its president until she retired in 1942.

Presidents Coolidge, Hoover, and Theodore Roosevelt asked her to work on such issues as child welfare, employment, housing, and education. In June of 1936, President Franklin D. Roosevelt appointed her director of African American affairs in the National Youth Administration and a special adviser on minority affairs. She was the first black woman to serve as head of a federal agency. She traveled across the country, calling for equal education and treatment for blacks. Serving in that capacity for eight years, she helped expand employment opportunities and recreational facilities for African American youth throughout the United States. She was also a special assistant to the secretary of war during World War II. Eventually she served on a committee for President Truman as well. Bethune was the first black woman to be honored with a statue in a Washington, DC, park.

A reading from an unpublished interview with Mary McLeod Bethune, in which she recalls her childhood

I could see little white boys and girls going to school every day, learning to read and write; living in comfortable homes with all types of opportunities for growth and service and to be surrounded as I was with no opportunity for school life, no chance to grow — I found myself very often yearning all along for the things that were being provided for the white children with whom I had to chop cotton every day, or pick corn, or whatever my task happened to be....

Very often I was taken along after I was old enough, and on one of these occasions I remember my mother went over to do some special work for this family of Wilsons, and I was with her. I went out into what they called their play house in the yard where they did their studying. They had pencils, slates, magazines and books.

I picked up one of the books ... and one of the girls said to me — "You can't read that — put that down. I will show you some pictures over here," and when she said to me "You can't read that — put that down" it just did something to my pride and to my heart that made me feel that some day I would read just as she was reading.

One day we were out in the field picking cotton and the mission teacher came from Maysville, five miles away, and told mother and father that the Presbyterian church had established a mission where the Negro children could go and that the children would be allowed to go.

That first morning on my way to school I kept the thought uppermost "Put that down — you can't read," and I felt that I was on my way to read and it was one of the incentives that fired me in my determination to read. And I think that because of that I grasped my lessons and my words better than the average child and it was not long before I was able to read and write. ...

My mother said when I was born I was entirely different from the rest — I was the most homely child, I was just different. In the ordinary things the children engaged in I wouldn't. I had the type of leadership like my mother. She said I was just different from the others. ... My older sisters wanted to get married early. I had no inclinations that way. I had more of a missionary spirit — the spirit of doing things for others.

Anyone sick in the community, I would tantalize my mother to make them some soup. If any child had no shoes, I always wanted to share my shoes. She had to watch me to keep me from giving away things that were mine.

Sunday afternoon I would take the farm children for miles around — I would give them whatever I had learned during the week. Poetry, reading, songs, etc. I would give to them as often as I got. As I got I gave.

At about fifteen or sixteen years of age, after completing my work in Maysville, I returned to the cotton fields. I had gotten what I could at the Mission school and did all I could in the community to keep alive the interest in education, keeping up intercession for opportunity to train myself that I might be of service to others.

On one October day, our same teacher who had been joined by Mr. Simmons, a Negro man who had done so much for the Negro people, came to the farm field and said to mother and father that they had been sending out literature about the work done at Maysville mission. And a piece of the literature had gotten into the hands of a white woman in Denver, Colorado, Miss Mary Chrisman — a rural schoolteacher who would often do dressmaking after school hours — who became interested in what had been done for the Negro children in South Carolina. And (she) wrote to the teachers asking if they could find a little girl who would make good if given a chance, and that out of the money she was earning, she would give for that little girl's education.

They had come to the farm field to tell mother and father I was the little girl they had selected to go to Scotia. It was a thrilling day for me, when I was called from the field by my father and teacher said, "Mary Jane, would you like to go to Scotia?"

I pulled my cotton sack off, got down on my knees, clasped my hands, and turned my eyes upward and thanked God for the chance that had come.

✪ May 14

Edward Hicks

QUAKER

April 4, 1780–August 23, 1849

No study of early American art can fail to include one of the many paintings done by Edward Hicks on the theme of the Peaceable Kingdom. At least 60 of these paintings were made and perhaps as many as a hundred. The Quakers generally viewed painting as a worldly vanity but as a failed farmer, Hicks found no other way to make a living. He began his painting career decorating carriages and making signs. These signs ranged from views of Washington crossing the Delaware to pictures of the moon shining through storm clouds or a jumble of hats for a hatter's shop. Paintings of the Peaceable Kingdom, a biblical theme, were less offensive to Quakers than secular paintings, so as Hicks developed his skill, he poured his faith into them. Quakers spoke of the "inner light," so Hicks's paintings glow with an inner light. It has been said that, for him, the world was all light. When he painted a farm, half the painting was a luminous sky. The people and even the animals are aglow with light.

Hicks was, however, more than a painter. His mother died in his infancy, so he was raised by one of her friends, a woman who often read to him from the Bible. Yet he had no formal religious instruction and when, at the age of 21, he received a "visitation of heavenly love," he sought guidance from several Christian groups before settling with the Society of Friends. About the age of 30, he began to preach and his ability grew with experience. He traveled widely to preach but always supported himself by working as a sign-maker and painter.

At the time of the second Great Awakening, some Quakers began to follow the example of the evangelical revival preachers, but Elias Hicks, a cousin of Edward's, led a conservative break-away group who sought to maintain the quietist pattern of the Quaker tradition. As tension between the two sects increased, Edward's paintings of the Peaceable Kingdom seemed to become less irenic. A tree split by lightening became a standard feature, while the animals assumed more aggressive stances. Yet the paintings remained suffused with light, as if Hicks were still determined to uphold the vision of a world in which the Inner Light of the Spirit would at last transform the hostilities of the natural world and the human race.

A reading from the *Memoirs* of Edward Hicks

I am, this day, sixty-three years of age, and I have thought right to attempt, at least, to write a short narrative of my life, by way of testimony to the mercy and goodness of a gracious God, through Jesus Christ, my blessed Lord and Saviour. And here it would be proper to try to explain what I mean by the term Saviour, for I shall make a free use thereof. I have been charged by some of my friends, with ambiguity of expression, and I think treated rather rudely, both publicly and privately, for use of this sublime and appropriate word, Saviour.

I have been, more especially during the last years of my life, renewedly concerned to be establish in a unity of belief with the primitive saints and the primitive Quakers. First with the beloved disciple John, where he says . . . "In him was life, and the life was the light of men." This light, that lighteneth every rational soul that cometh into the world, shineth in darkness, but the darkness comprehendeth it not, for men love darkness rather than light, because their deeds are evil; nevertheless, this is the true light, that can only give true light to the rational soul, and it is only this true light, that can give a true sense of the soul's sorrowful state; and it is only this that gives a right sorrow, and this sorrow a true repentance, not to be repented of, and such repentance gives us an admittance within the inclosure of the glorious attributes of mercy, which pardons guilty man. . . .

I have scarcely a doubt in my mind at this time, that Friends departed from the peaceable spirit of Jesus, when they descended to a level with their enemies, in litigation and religious controversy, in the late unhappy revolution. How much better it would have been for us to have suffered in silence, and like our divine Master, when the prince of this world, or the prince of the power of the air, that rules in the hearts of the children of disobedience, came, he could have found nothing of his own likeness in us: but alas! this prince of darkness and confusion found us prepared to talk too much, write too much, and preach too much; and hence he has continued too much with us.

✪ *May 15* ———————————————————————

Jane Addams

PRESBYTERIAN

September 6, 1860–May 21, 1935

"Women have not altogether fulfilled the hopes we have placed in them," said the member of the 1931 Nobel Prize Committee who presented the

Peace Prize to Jane Addams. "They have allowed too much scope to the old morality of men, the morality of war. In practical politics we have seen too little of that love, that warm maternal feeling which renders murder and war so hateful to every woman." Jane Addams had a different perspective. "I am not one of those," she said, "who believe — broadly speaking — that women are better than men. We have not wrecked railroads, nor corrupted legislatures, nor done many unholy things that men have done; but then we must remember that we have not had the chance."

But Jane Addams found plenty of ways to influence the world she lived in. At 29, she founded Hull-House, an institution that became world-famous as a model for helping the urban poor change their circumstances. Hull-House was surrounded by a crowded neighborhood of immigrant Italians, Russian and Polish Jews, Irish, Germans, Greeks, and Bohemians. Jane Addams and the other residents of the settlement house provided kindergarten and day-care facilities for children of working mothers, an employment bureau, an art gallery, libraries, and music and art classes for the area. Eventually they added a cooperative residence for working women, the first Little Theater in America, a Labor Museum, and a meeting place for trade unions. By 1903, pressure from Jane Addams and her supporters persuaded the state of Illinois to pass a strong child labor law. By 1916, Congress had followed suit.

Addams's writing drew national and international attention to her concerns. She served on the boards of the National Association for the Advancement of Colored People, the American Civil Liberties Union, the Consumers League, the General Federation of Women's Clubs, the Camp-fire Girls, the National Child Labor Committee, among many others. At the outbreak of World War I, she participated in the International Congress of Women at the Hague in 1915. She maintained her pacifist convictions even after the United States entered the war in 1917, for which the Daughters of the American Revolution expelled her. However, her work for the Women's Peace Party — later the Women's International League for Peace and Freedom of which she was the first president — led to her being awarded the Nobel Peace Prize. "To an American," said the Nobel committee's spokesperson, "an ideal is not just a beautiful mirage but a practical reality the implementation of which is every man's (sic!) duty." It was through the practical implementation of her ideals that Jane Addams made such an impact on American life.

A reading from *Twenty Years at Hull-House with Autobiographical Notes* by Jane Addams

In northern Illinois, one Sunday morning, I received the rite of baptism and became a member of the Presbyterian church in the village. At this time there was certainly no outside pressure pushing me towards such a decision, and at twenty-five one does not ordinarily take such a step from a mere desire to conform. While I was not conscious of any emotional "conversion," I took upon myself the outward expressions of the religious life with all humility and sincerity. It was doubtless true that I was

> Weary of myself and sick of asking
> What I am and what I ought to be,

and that various cherished safeguards and claims to self-dependence had been broken into by many piteous failures. But certainly I had been brought to the conclusion that "sincerely to give up one's conceit or hope of being good in one's own right is the only door to the Universe's deeper reaches." Perhaps the young clergyman recognized this as the test of the Christian temper, at any rate he required little assent to dogma or miracle, and assured me that while both the ministry and the officers of his church were obliged to subscribe to doctrines of well-known severity, the faith required to the laity was almost early Christian in its simplicity. I was conscious of no change from my childish acceptance of the teachings of the Gospels, but at this moment something persuasive within made me long for an outward symbol of fellowship, some bond of peace, some blessed spot where unity of spirit might claim right of way over all differences. There was also growing within me an almost passionate devotion to the ideals of democracy, and when in all history had these ideals been so thrillingly expressed as when the faith of the fisherman and the slave had been boldly opposed to the accepted moral belief that the well-being of a privileged few might justly be built upon the ignorance and sacrifice of the many? Who was I, with my dreams of universal fellowship, that I did not identify myself with the institutional statement of this belief, as it stood in the little village in which I was born, and without which testimony in each remote hamlet of Christendom it would be so easy for the world to slip back into the doctrines of selection and aristocracy?...

In one of the intervening summers between these European journeys I visited a western state where I had formerly invested a sum of money in mortgages. I was much horrified by the wretched conditions among the farmers, which had resulted from a long period of drought, and one forlorn picture was fairly burned into my mind. A number of starved hogs — collateral for a promissory note — were huddled into an open pen. Their backs were humped in a curious, camel-like fashion, and they were devouring one of their own number, the latest victim of absolute starvation or possibly merely the one least able to defend himself against their voracious hunger. The farmer's wife looked on indifferently, a picture of despair as she stood in the door of the bare, crude house, and the two children behind her, whom she vainly tried to keep out of sight, continually thrust forward their faces almost covered by masses of coarse, sunburned hair, and their little bare feet so black, so hard, the great cracks so filled with dust that they looked like flattened hoofs. The children could not be compared to anything so joyous as satyrs, although they appeared but half-human. It seemed to me quite impossible to receive interest from mortgages placed upon farms which might at any season be reduced to such conditions, and with great inconvenience to my agent and doubtless with hardship to the farmers, as speedily as possible I withdrew all my investment. But something had to be done with the money, and in my reaction against unseen horrors I bought a farm near my native village and also a flock of innocent-looking sheep. My partner in the enterprise had not chosen the shepherd's lot as a permanent occupation, but hoped to speedily finish his college course upon half the proceeds of our venture. This pastoral enterprise still seems to me to have been essentially sound, both economically and morally, but perhaps one partner depended too much upon the impeccability of her motives and the other found himself too preoccupied with study to know that it is not a real kindness to bed a sheepfold with straw, for certainly the venture ended in a spectacle scarcely less harrowing than the memory it was designed to obliterate. At least the sight of two hundred sheep with four rotting hoofs each, was not reassuring to one whose conscience craved economic peace. A fortunate series of sales of mutton, wool, and farm enabled the partners to end the enterprise without loss, and they passed on, one to college and the other to Europe, if not wiser, certainly sadder for the experience.

✸ *May 16*

James Guadalupe Carney

ROMAN CATHOLIC

October 29, 1924–July 1983

Americans often refer to Central American countries as "Banana Republics," a loose term conveying places where corruption is endemic, politics is a revolving door dominated by military strong men, and the people live in poverty. American businesses have exploited their resources, while American administrations have concerned themselves primarily with promoting stability for the benefit of the businesses. For centuries, the Roman Catholic Church cooperated in these arrangements while non–Roman Catholic missionaries avoided the area, believing Hispanic Christians were committed to their historic church.

By the middle of the 20th century, this arrangement was beginning to be challenged. The Peace Corps imported Americans with a different agenda, non–Roman Catholic missionaries discovered that many Central Americans were ripe for evangelical or Pentecostal conversion, and a new generation of Roman Catholic missionaries from the United States came to work not with governments but with the peasants.

James Carney was one of this new generation. He had grown up in the midwest, started college on a football scholarship, then fought in World

War II. Already critical of privilege, he refused opportunities to be trained as an officer and was censured for fraternizing with prisoners of war. Afterward, he went back to college and worked in an auto factory in a work-study program. He thought of becoming an engineer and of getting married, but the priesthood seemed to offer opportunities to deal with the issues that troubled him. He became a Jesuit, was ordained and sent to Honduras in 1961. Writing home to his sister, he described some of the local festivals, then went on to say:

> I spend a lot of time now in the social apostolate besides giving the sacraments in the 80 villages I have. I've helped 9 villages start small coops to try to solve the number one problem in Hond. which is land for the poor campesinos. We hope to make them agricultural coops, buying land together and working it together in brotherhood. This is a fine way to get across the basic Christian doctrine of living like brothers in one Family of God. I desperately need help with these coops and other community development projects we have. Not money, but missionaries, clerical or lay, with money to support them. We have the Peace Corps around here but so far they have done me more harm than good with their gringo ideas.

Increasingly, Carney identified himself with the people of the land, and in 1974 he took Honduran citizenship. As a further evidence of his identification with the people, he took the name "Padre Guadalupe." He organized labor unions and supported some peasants who tried to occupy land that belonged to a subsidiary of the United Fruit Company. "Little by little the Spirit of Jesus was showing me that these campesino brothers and sisters of mine needed more than the Word of God," wrote Carney. "I had to put into practice the Word of God, which clearly explains that love of neighbor means to give food to the hungry, clothes to the naked." Carney's attitudes made the government nervous. In 1979, with no legal process, he was exiled to Nicaragua, then controlled by the revolutionary movement known as the Sandinistas.

"The gospel of Christ, instead of being a motive for getting involved in the political struggle to change this world, is interpreted in the 'bourgeois theology'...as dealing with the 'supernatural,'" wrote Carney. "This whole trend of false spirituality says that to change the unjust structures of society you have to first change people. If individuals are just and loving, society will be just. The...great fact of reality (is) that a selfish, unjust society inevitably produces and forms selfish, exploiting, violent men and women. We must change at the same time the person and the society."

But to "change at the same time the person and then society" is not easy, especially when powerful interests are opposed to such change. Many Central Americans ultimately came to believe that armed revolution was their only alternative. Although Carney had originally been influenced by Mahatma Ghandi, constant frustrations led him to begin to see things in a different light: "During 1975, with its violent repression, my ideas on the Christian use of arms became clearer. I was gradually and finally acknowledging to myself the truth that love sometimes demands fighting back." He also said, "To be Christian is to be a revolutionary. If you are not a revolutionary, you are not a Christian."

In 1981, Carney was given the opportunity to accompany a band of insurgents moving into Honduras from Nicaragua. He was their chaplain and unarmed. What happened next may never be known. The Honduran government claimed that he died in the jungle of starvation, but other reports tell of his being arrested with some of the insurgents, being tortured, then executed. Some reports say that he was thrown alive from a helicopter.

Graham Greene's novel *The Comedians* is set amid the violence and suffering of "Papa Doc" Duvalier's Haiti, about the same time Carney served in Central America. At one point, a priest preaches at a requiem Mass for a group of rebels who have been killed, saying "though Christ condemned the disciple who struck off the ear of the high priest's servant, our hearts go out in sympathy to all who are moved to violence by the suffering of others. The Church condemns violence, but it condemns indifference more harshly. Violence can be the expression of love, indifference never." James Guadalupe Carney might well have preached that sermon.

✪ *May 17* _____

Eric Norelius

LUTHERAN

October 26, 1833–March 15, 1916

By the mid-19th century, the area we know as the upper midwest was teeming with new residents. Settlers from the eastern seaboard and a flood of new immigrants from Europe were moving to this fertile territory. Land and resources were easy to find and exploit, and opportunities for a new life abounded. Among the groups that sought to make a new home there were large numbers of Scandinavians and Germans. Their religious heritage was often Lutheran, but diverse languages and customs, as well as vast distances between congregations, made cooperation difficult. The situation required a steady hand to pull together the scattered energies and goals of the faithful and bring order and identity out of the chaos.

Eric Norelius was the man for this task. He had come from Sweden in 1850 simply as a young man searching for economic opportunity. Educated at Capital University in Columbus, Ohio, he decided to enter the ministry. He had been influenced by revivals in Sweden that did not replace classic Lutheran teachings or structures, but asserted that religious conviction needed to move beyond theological systems to touch the inner life if it was to be a vehicle for the Holy Spirit.

Many American denominations were marked by similar movements. But Norelius's cultural and Lutheran roots were sufficiently distinct from English-speaking churches or free church traditions like Methodists or Baptists, that he felt it important to develop a specifically Swedish and Lutheran body to serve the growing population from Scandinavia.

Norelius was a formative influence in establishing the Lutheran Minnesota Conference in 1858 and the Augustana Lutheran Synod in 1860. While he insisted that religious experience must be a vital reality for each individual and each congregation, he never believed that individuals or congregations could be fully faithful in isolation from each other. His sense of a need for an organized church body shaped his ministry and allowed him to be an effective leader in a time of uncertainty and flux.

Norelius was privileged to serve a number of years as the new synod's president. He was a pioneer in many kinds of ministry still with us today: informal Bible study and prayer meetings called conventicles, home visits with catechetical studies, formation of lay-led Sunday Schools and parochial schools, and a women's missionary society to tap the energy and faith of females in support of the church's ministries, especially educational programs.

Even in the midst of those hardships that are part of frontier life, Norelius held to a traditional view of the pastor and of worship. He wrote:

> My own way of procedure may be considered too churchly by some, since I very carefully follow the ritual of our church, and I cannot deny that in outward appearance, garb, etc., I like to be somewhat ministerial, as far as I can understand it. I also become more and more convinced that form, though it is not and never can be essential, still is of no little importance for religion.

An Indian massacre in Meeker County, Minnesota, in 1862 called forth Norelius's pastoral and organizational skills. Hundreds of settlers were killed or captured by the Sioux, whole towns wiped out, buildings burned, animals taken, crops destroyed, and lives disrupted. Norelius headed a special relief committee to funnel aid from all over to the now destitute farmers. His passion to serve was shown again in 1865 when he established the first Lutheran Children's Home in Minnesota. The Augustana Synod founded a similar home in Illinois, partly in response to Norelius's work. Following the lead of W. A. Passavant's* similar work, he was able to adopt a successful model to meet the needs of orphans and youth in his part of the world.

Education had been one of the primary motives for Norelius to come to America, so it is not surprising that he founded a school. From humble beginnings, the institution flourished and is now known as Gustavus Adolphus College, in St. Peter, Minnesota. Norelius knew the importance of preserving the history of his times. In 1869, he was elected the official historian of the church. His most important written work is a two-volume history of Swedish Lutheranism in America.

A reading from Norelius's journal

The outlook was surely dark, and it is a wonder that we did not immediately lose courage and return to the place whence we had come. But the Lord strengthened us. In the first place, we could not get a house. There were not enough houses for the people in the town, and the houses they had were small and in poor condition. After trying for some time to find a room somewhere, John Nilsson said to us: "I don't know of anything else for you to do than to move into my hog house for awhile." He had just built a shed which he intended to use for a hog house but which had not yet been used for that purpose. We would likely have had to live in that hog house if a carpenter, Carl Anderson, had not permitted us to move into a very small bedroom in his little cottage for a few weeks.

On the following Sunday, which is Trinity Sunday, I preached my initial sermon in a partly finished store building. To conduct worship services standing by a counter in chips and shavings certainly was not inspiring, but when circumstances are compelling it is easy to disregard external surroundings. If there is real evidence of a genuine hunger and thirst for the Word of God, all the elements for a holy festivity are present.

✪ *May 18* _____

Clarence Jordan

SOUTHERN BAPTIST

July 29, 1912–October 29, 1969

By the late 1930s, racial tensions in Louisville, Kentucky, reached such a pitch that a group of angry blacks decided to strike back. "Just like the whites kill a Negro," said one man swinging an iron pipe, "I'm going to kill a white man." Only one white man was present. He responded, "If a white man must die for this . . . let it be me. Do it now."

As a Baptist minister, Clarence Jordan took his faith seriously. A graduate of Georgia's School of Agriculture and with a doctorate from Southern Baptist Theological Seminary's graduate program in the Greek New Testament, he was well prepared to create a community in the agricultural south based solidly on New Testament principles with all the risk and danger that would involve. Years later he published a translation of Paul's letters as *The Cotton Patch Gospel* and rendered a passage from Romans as "We who live for Jesus always flirt with death."

In 1942, he and his wife, along with a few others, settled in Sumter County, Georgia, and established Koinonia Farm as a place to live out the teachings of Jesus in the midst of the poverty and racism of the rural South. They envisioned a community in which blacks and whites could work side by side, committed to four basic principles:

1. *Treat all human beings with dignity and justice*

2. *Choose love over violence.*

3. *Share all possessions and live simply.*

4. *Be stewards of the land and its natural resources.*

Reactions from the surrounding communities were not cordial. Over the next 20 years, Koinonia survived firebombs, bullets, KKK rallies, death threats, property damage, and economic boycotts. Yet visitors came from all over the world to support the enterprise through some of the worst days of local hostility.

In the 1960s, Koinonia began to build affordable housing with the help of the future owners. Millard Fuller, a businessman who had been interested in Jordan's ideas, expanded them into the well-known, worldwide program — Habitat for Humanity.

A reading from the Introduction to
The Cotton Patch Gospel by Clarence Jordan

The Church, in a very real sense, gives birth to sons of God. She is the womb in which they are conceived. In my own case this was true. The little Baptist church in which I grew up nurtured me. In its womb I learned the Scriptures. I suckled at its breasts. And the little church thought that it not only was my mother, but also my father. And when I began to go about my Father's business, the Church said, "No, son, you're piercing our hearts. We don't want to give you up." And when I finally persisted in going about my Father's business, my mother, the Church, renounced me.

It's hard for a mother whose womb conceives a child of God to quit being a mother and let that son get about his Father's business. I think this is the real tension between preachers and their congregations today. Preachers are nourished in the Church. They're educated by it. They love it. It has been the umbilical cord to life for them. And yet when they get on about their Father's business, maybe getting in jail, getting in demonstrations, spending themselves to do the will of the Father, the Church says, "No, son; come be my son. Stop being so much like your Father." the preacher has to say, "No, mother. I must be about my Father's business."

I think this is the trouble of our youth today. We have been too successful with our religious education. We have finally gotten our children to catch the point! And so they get the idea that God is to be obeyed. He is to be followed. And when these kids get out with visions in their heads and dreams in their hearts and start following the very God we have fathered and nurtured within them, then we say, "No, son; be my son. Don't be so much like your Father."

At long last, though, Mary learned to be the mother of Jesus by giving him to mankind to do his Father's business. And I hope and pray that before I pass on to glory, the little church that expelled me from its fellowship will realize that I really am its son, that I really do love it and that it will gather with me, perhaps even after the crucifixion, along with the rest of the brethren and realize that you can only be the true mother of a child of God when you relinquish your motherhood and give him to all mankind. For God did not give his son to the Church. He did not give his son to Mary. She was the mere instrument through which he came. God gave his son to the world. And when our sons and daughters give themselves with an abandon to following their Father in the lowly paths of the world, let not the Church hold back and say, "Come, children; be your mother's children." Let us grasp their hands, seeing in them the image of their Father, and say to them, "Son, though it leads you to a cross, be a good son of your daddy."

✪ *May 19*

Timothy Dwight

CONGREGATIONAL

May 14, 1752–January 11, 1817

The grandson of Jonathan Edwards lived in a different era than his illustrious ancestor, and encountered different problems. Yet Timothy Dwight possessed some of his grandfather's zeal to revive and renew the Christian church for his own day. Dwight graduated from Yale at the age of 17 and became headmaster of Hopkins Grammar School to finance his continuing education. Two years later he returned to Yale as a tutor. Three years after that, while recuperating from a serious illness, he committed himself to Christ and joined the church. He entered the ministry at 25, and shortly became a chaplain in the American revolutionary army. The year that he spent in the army introduced him to the miseries of war and gave him experiences he could never have gained from books. The needs of his family led Dwight to resign his chaplaincy so that he could work on the family farm while teaching school and preaching on weekends. After the war ended, he put the farm in other hands and became pastor of the church in Greenfield, Connecticut. There, he founded a school that provided women with the same education available to men, a radical step at the time.

When the presidency of Yale became vacant in 1795, Dwight accepted election, but found his alma mater drastically altered by the impact of the French Revolution and the growing popularity of rationalism. The entering freshman class that fall contained only one professing Christian; the upper classes had only a few more. Dwight faced the challenge head on, debating the students and tearing their arguments apart. He made Christian faith

intellectually respectable once more, so that, by 1802, a revival was under-
way, carefully nurtured by Dwight. A third of the student body had become
Christian, with many going from Yale into the ministry.

Beyond the college, Dwight involved himself in community affairs. He
campaigned for prison reform and relief for the poor, while condemning
the institution of slavery. The Dwight home had an African American cook
who was retarded, but he took time to instruct her carefully and patiently,
believing in the value of every human being. An early member of the Connecticut Society for the Abolition of Slavery, he helped establish a school in
New Haven to teach black children to read.

Dwight is the author of the hymn, still widely used that proclaims:

> I love Thy kingdom, Lord,
> The house of Thine abode,
> The church our blest Redeemer saved
> With His own precious blood.

A reading from a sermon of Timothy Dwight entitled "Each Man's Life a Plan of God"

We are born with varying characters and gifts, and are assigned to different
works for God in the world, so we may believe that there is a plan for every
one, formed, and watched over, and carried to its completion by the Divine
Friend who calls us into His service. How often we find, in our individual experience, that we never escape the besetment of peculiar difficulties or trials,
which other men around us either do not have, or grow out of as the years
move onward. We hope to escape them — we wonder that we do not, it may
be — but we find them always with us. Is it not the Lord's appointment —
not as an arbitrary or outward thing, but as a part and outgrowth of our
peculiar nature? Is not the true way of looking at it this: that we — in our
individuality of nature — were made for the accomplishment of a special Divine purpose; for the showing forth of a Divinely-formed character and life
in one particular light; and that all allotments of experience are wisely fitted
to realise the end? The work of Peter as a disciple of Jesus was intended to
be different from that of John. He was to show the development of true life
in a different way. The career followed the line of the native endowments.
The trials and successes, the defeats and victories, as they were seen in the
progress of his living and foreseen by the Master, were in accordance with
what was foreshadowed in that manifestation of the Divine purpose which
was seen in the making of the man.

We do not penetrate the heavenly wisdom, indeed, and we cannot say that
this is a full account of what we call the Providential dealing with us. But
may we not say that it is a partial one? And if it is so, surely it takes up all
our living, and every part of our experience, into God's plan and purpose —

and brings us the lesson of trust and confidence that the natural movement of our life, as we call it, is under a supernatural guidance, and that, in our allotment of every sort, and in the dying at the end, we are guarded and guided by a Father's love.

In the second place, we may notice what Jesus says to Peter in answer to his inquiry respecting the appointed destiny of his friend and associate. The manner of his own dying had been foretold to him; and now, as he sees this friend approaching, his mind naturally turns to the thought of *his* future. What of this man — what shall be his experience? The Lord answers, If I will that he tarry till I come, what is that to thee? There is in this answer nothing of definiteness — at the most, only a suggestion that John's life would be longer and quieter than that of Peter himself. But the main word for the latter disciple is the pointed question, What is that to thee? with the bidding, Follow thou me.

✹ *May 20*

Martha Gallison Moore Avery

ROMAN CATHOLIC

April 6, 1851–August 8, 1929

On Sunday morning, July 1, 1917, a strange vehicle drove into the grounds of Holy Cross Cathedral in Boston. It was painted in the papal colors with mottoes in cardinal red emblazoned in block letters on both sides. One side were the words of a Roman Catholic hymn:

> *Fierce is the fight*
> *For God and the right*
> *Sweet name of Jesus*
> *In Thee is our might.*

The other side held a quotation from George Washington's farewell address:

> *Reason and experience*
> *Forbid us to believe that*
> *National morality can prevail*
> *Where religious principles are excluded.*

When the carriage was drawn up beside a lecture platform, the top could be raised to form a sounding board decorated with a crucifix and lit by an electric light. From the hood flew a small American flag. Underneath was a Ford motor car, but surely Henry Ford never imagined such a use for one of his products.

The car had been designed by two colleagues whose lives had followed unusual paths. Martha Avery and David Goldstein were once Socialist Labor Party leaders, co-founders of the Karl Marx Class. Avery had been as the

Socialist candidate for Massachusetts state treasurer. But by the end of the 19th century, both felt disillusioned with socialism and had become converts to Roman Catholicism. What could be more logical, they reasoned, than to bring the techniques of a socialist rally to the cause of the church? They approached the Cardinal-Archbishop of Boston with their idea and he gave his slightly puzzled approval: "It's striking; it's thoroughly American; I don't know but that it is all right."

With that, their campaign began. Avery and Goldstein took their "perambulating rostrum" to Boston Common and onward to Medford, Marblehead, Salem, Plymouth, Concord, and eventually out to California where the Ford was upgraded to a Cadillac. Audiences were respectful and hecklers were treated with tolerance. "The very boldness of the venture won the courteous attention" of those who differed. Books and pamphlets were distributed along the way. Martha Avery continued to use her skills as a propagandist to argue against socialism and for the church. She was a co-founder of the Catholic Truth Guild and the Catholic lay apostolate.

A reading from *Campaigning for Christ* by Martha Avery and David Goldstein

With a growing appreciation of the part taken by the Church in erecting the civil society of the west came a growing ambition to spread the light of faith with which we were blessed, and which was growing brighter day by day.

What did it matter if there were opposition to things Catholic? Had there not been opposition to teaching Socialism in the streets? Had we not both suffered the indignity of arrest in testing our right to free speech and free assembly in the streets? Socialism we knew to be a false doctrine, but its cause made progress. Year in and year out crowds listen on Sunday to Atheism and Socialism in the streets of every large city in America. Should there not be even one voice crying in the wilderness: — make way for our Blessed Lord?

Why should not Catholics who believe they alone have the truth, go out and proclaim it from the housetops. Mayhap, God will give them the grace to save souls? There are millions of our countrymen who have never heard a layman tell the reasons for his adherence to the Church, and there are many more who have never entered a Catholic Church. Should Catholics flatter the vulgar notion that they are indeed a people apart — alien to America? Should Catholics agree that the others alone are at home in the home of their fathers, and that it is no concern of ours if our street pulpits are filled by those who flout God to His face and flaunt the red flag? Shall these millions, more sinned against than sinning, who have for generation after generation been led to believe that it is accident of birth, mere superstition, priest-craft, that holds Catholics to their faith, not have the facts in the case told to them? . . .

If ever in her divine majesty and universal holiness the Catholic Church is presented to those millions of our countrymen there will surely come converts who will love her with all their hearts. Thus we presented to ourselves over and over again the need of carrying the Catholic message to the multitude. We were too well versed in open air campaigning to fear defeat in-so-far as the ability to gather, to hold, and to keep control of an audience was concerned. That had become a commonplace in our experience.

So it seemed certain that two of the necessary conditions were fulfilled. That is to say, the field was white to the harvest and at least two reapers were eager to get to work....

The opening years of the 20th Century were beyond all dreams materially prosperous. Mechanical genius had multiplied hand labor a thousand fold and the nations of the earth were presumed to have reached so high a stage of evolution that no war cloud as big as a man's hand could be seen upon the globe. New England's most eminent educator after a swing around the earth had reported: "All's well." No doubt the super-man was on the threshold and on the other side of the door human nature as it had been known for four thousand years would be no more. Great was Diana!

All save those who held fast to Christ and Him crucified were being swept into the headlong current of that psychology where God was ignored and man supreme.

In 1914 the death knell of peace was struck and European nations were at war with one another.... This was the opportune time for Religion to get a hearing in America — the time to begin campaigning for Christ.

✪ *May 21*

Henry Knox Sherrill

EPISCOPALIAN

November 8, 1890–May 11, 1980

"As I read the New Testament," wrote Henry Knox Sherrill, "I am moved by the teaching of Jesus. Some of the sayings attributed to Him I do not wholly understand but here is presented a way which if even approximated would revolutionize every segment of our society." Understanding the gospel in this way, Henry Knox Sherrill was not afraid to undertake radical change in the Christian world. While studying at Yale, he felt called to the church's ministry and went straight from college to seminary, then served as an assistant at Trinity Church, Boston, in the pulpit made famous by Phillips Brooks. After duty as an army chaplain in France during World War I and as rector in Brookline, he was called back to Trinity Church, this time as rector. In 1930, Sherrill was elected Bishop of Massachusetts, and in 1946 he was chosen to serve as the first full-time Presiding Bishop of the Episcopal Church.

As Presiding Bishop, he moved on to a national and world stage, providing leadership for the ecumenical movement and serving as the first president of the National Council of Churches and one of the founders and a president of the World Council of Churches. Within the Episcopal Church, he established the Episcopal Church Foundation to fund church development, as well as the Presiding Bishop's Fund for World Relief (now known as "Episcopal Relief and Development"). Sherrill committed the Episcopal Church also to the civil rights movement. When the 1954 General Convention was scheduled for Houston, Texas, Sherrill realized that minority delegates would have difficulty finding housing and decided to move the convention to Honolulu, despite the criticism of white southerners, because he felt it was so important to make an unequivocal statement of support for racial integration.

It was, nevertheless, the ecumenical movement to which Sherrill was most deeply committed. It was his belief that the changes needed in the world could not take place without the leadership of a unified Christianity. In his autobiography, he wrote:

A reading from the autobiography of Henry Knox Sherrill

I cannot believe that the present conditions represent the mind of God. There are diversities of gifts, of course, but the purpose of Christ cannot embrace contradictory, even competing, ideas and aims. Truth may have many manifestations, but essentially truth is one. There is a unity in the mind of God. Our present unity, such as it is, stands only as a symbol of what can and should be....

Of one thing we may be certain, there is no magic formula evolved by conferences of church leaders and of theologians which will give us a complete solution of this problem. As has been stated, there is so much more involved, age-long loyalties and convictions, and of course human limitations and failures. There must be, also, a deep searching of mind and of heart not only on the part of the few, but of the entire constituency of our churches. I venture to suggest some of the considerations we must keep in mind.

First, there must be a sterner and more exacting devotion to truth. In a mistaken loyalty to our own tradition most of us are apt to claim too much and to take a party line for which the Apostolic Church is always the proof of our opinions, no matter how diverse they may be. Again and again I hear sweeping claims given as if they were unquestioned proven historic fact and I ask myself, "Are they true?" In the advocacy of our own causes there must be the complete honesty which prevents us from confusing propaganda and truth, for if is only the truth which is of God. Only upon such a foundation can we build a Catholic Church as willed by God.

Second, there must be deep humility. Words which occur to me often are: "For we know in part, and we prophesy in part.... For now we see through a glass, darkly...." There is mystery in the Gospel. We are all limited in this world of space and of time, and we can never properly lose the consciousness of limitation. No one of us, no group of us, no matter what may be claimed, has the wholeness of God's truth....

Finally, there will be evidenced in every relationship the quality of Christian love which is not sentimentality and weakness but strength. Ecclesiastical wrangling and bitterness cut at the very heart of the Gospel. However, given even these qualities, Christian unity will only come as the act of God. It is essential that we confer and work together, but no man-made unity is possible or will suffice. Too often unity conferences look only to the past — what happened in some other day and age. But we worship not a dead but a living God who has promised to lead us into all truth as we face the problems and the opportunities of the present and the future.

❂ *May 22* —————————————————————

Garfield Bromley Oxnam

METHODIST

August 14, 1891–March 12, 1963

Slavery, more than any other issue, created the liberal tradition in American Christianity. Many American Christians found it impossible to consider it as a merely political issue. Rather, every resource of church and state needed to be mobilized against its evil. After the Civil War, those same energies came to be focused on labor issues, urban problems, and women's suffrage. After World War II, divisions over social issues were intensified by the world-wide clash between western democracies and Communist powers to the east. Conservatives learned to accuse liberals of being not simply disturbers of the peace but communist sympathizers who endangered American freedom.

G. Bromley Oxnam was one inheritor of the liberal tradition who was unwilling to hold his peace in this controversy. When the McCarthy Committee accused liberals of being communist sympathizers, Oxnam let them know what he thought:

> A new breed of self-appointed un-American vigilantes threatens our freedom. Profaning our American traditions and desecrating our flag, masquerading as defenders of our country against the infiltration of communism and the aggression of Russia, they play the red game of setting American against American, of creating distrust and division, and of turning us from the problems that must be solved in order to become impregnable. These vigilantes produce hysteria, prepare sucker lists, and live upon the generous contributions of the fearful. They exploit the uninformed patriot. They profiteer in patriotism. These vigilantes do not carry the noosed rope, but they lynch by libel. They prepare their lying spider-web charts. They threaten educators and ministers, actors and broadcasters. Unthinking boards and commissions bow to their tyranny,

forgetting that to appease these forerunners of Hitler, of Mussolini, and of Stalin is to jeopardize freedom, and to prepare the wrists for the shackles and the mouth for the gag. In the name of law, vigilantes break the law.

Christian conservatives were outraged by the Methodist bishop's theology as well as his politics. When the Southern Baptist Convention withdrew from the World Baptist Alliance, they cited Oxnam as an example of the liberal thinking that made light of essentials of the Christian faith. They found it unacceptable that he should question a substitutionary doctrine of the atonement, when he said,

> Is God a Being who must have the accounts squared by some death, the sacrifice of a Son even, that the individual's account may be ruled off in two red lines, the balance in sin paid by a being who died long since and left a great control account from which the Deity may draw forever? Frankly, such doctrines do not help me.

But Oxnam was very clear about what he did believe: "If I were called upon to choose one word to describe Christianity, it would be love. I believe God is love. I believe nothing can separate me from the love of God. I believe God was in Christ, reconciling the world unto himself. I believe God sent Jesus Christ because 'he loved the world.'" Oxnam was impatient with believers who required assent to long lists of doctrines. "I know so little," he said, "about God, but what I know I have seen in the face of Jesus, and that is enough for the journey. When at last I know as I am known, I believe that knowledge will validate my conviction that God is love."

A Californian by birth, Oxnam studied at the University of Southern California and Boston University, then taught at both schools before being made president of DePauw University, in 1928. He became a bishop in 1936 and served in Omaha, Boston, and New York before being assigned to the Washington area in 1952. A staunch advocate of ecumenical endeavors, Oxnam was a president of the Federal Council of Churches, helped organize the National Council of Churches and the World Council of Churches, then served as president of both. *Time* magazine said, "No U.S. Protestant leader of his time preached more ardently about the causes he cared for; few churchmen were his equal at the homely, slighted arts of governing a district or chairing a conference."

A reading from *Testament of Faith* by Garfield Bromley Oxnam

I speak of Jesus Christ as Savior. I believe man can be saved from his sins. This is a negative way of putting it. I believe man can be summoned to move out in terms of truth, goodness, and beauty. He is called to love God and brother. "If ye love Me, ye will keep my commandments," said Jesus. I believe man can both love Christ and keep his commandments. I believe he will. He needs power. He cannot do this alone. The power is available. "Ye shall receive power," Jesus declared. Man is capable of absolute commitment to Christ. In that commitment, power is found. This is a power that does not curtail freedom. It creates freedom. It is a power held in trust. It finds life by giving life.

I can hear certain comment. Is he unaware of the hyena in man? No, I have seen the hyena. In fact, I know the tiger is present. I know that sincere and studious men hold that beneath the skin of civilization is the red blood of the jungle beast. But I have also seen great souls. I know what man can do, what he can be. Gandhi lived in our own generation, and Schweitzer continues to heal broken bodies in black Africa and seeks through persuasion to heal disordered minds in white America. I have seen children at play — and great men at creative tasks. I believe in man.

I know that my Redeemer liveth. God is a living being. Man has access to the divine. Jesus said, "I am the door." I believe that door is opened to every man who knocks. I see mankind passing through that door. We shall know as we are known. Mysteries will be penetrated. We shall learn that faith, hope, and love are the abiding forces, but the greatest of these is love.

✪ *May 23* _____

Joseph and Michael Hofer

HUTTERIAN BRETHREN

Joseph: ?–November 28, 1918
Michael: ?–December 2, 1918

Although the great majority of Americans are and have always been Christians, there have often been Christian groups that found it difficult to find a secure place to follow out their understanding of the gospel. The Quakers are probably the best known of such groups; the Hutterites, more obscure, are one branch of the Anabaptist movement, dating back to the 16th Century. They live simply, hold their property in common, and do not fight in wars. They follow the teaching of Jakob Hutter, their founder, who said: "Before we would strike our greatest enemy with the hand, to say nothing of with the gun or sword ... we would rather die, and let our own lives be taken."

Today, there are procedures for dealing with religious conscientious objection to military service, but in 1918 there were none. Hutterite ministers met with Federal authorities as America prepared to enter World War I, hoping to avoid unnecessary problems. They had been assured that any draftees from their colonies only needed to be involved as far as their beliefs allowed. But official assurances do not always reflect the realities faced by nonconformists.

The Hofer brothers were conscripted as part of the U.S. preparation for war. They told authorities they were willing to go to the Army base and to do nonmilitary work, but were not willing to sign military papers or wear a uniform. In spite of official promises, they found little tolerance for their position. Even on the train ride from their home in Rockport, a Hutterian settlement in South Dakota, to the military base at Fort Lewis in Washington State, they were harassed by other conscripts because of their simple homemade clothes and full beards. Upon their arrival, the Army displayed only disdain for the brothers and their deeply held beliefs.

They arrived at Fort Lewis in May of 1918 and were both dead by early December of that same year. From the first, they refused to sign their enlistment forms, put on their uniforms, or join the marching drills in the field. For this, they were locked in the Fort Lewis guardhouse. In June, Michael and Joseph, along with another brother and a brother-in-law, were tried for disobeying orders. They were all convicted and sentenced to twenty years of incarceration. From Washington, they were sent to Alcatraz in San Francisco Bay, a prison traditionally reserved for America's most dangerous criminals. Their treatment there was nothing short of barbaric. Michael and Joseph were chained at the wrists and suspended for hours at a time at a height that just barely allowed them to keep the pressure off their wrists by standing on tiptoe. Still they refused to put on a uniform, but the prison guards would not allow any other outer clothing so they were left in their underwear. Their cell was in the lower section of the prison, at sea level, so the seeping water and stone walls and floor left the men perpetually cold and damp. They were given one glass of water a day. Beatings were administered, sometimes hard enough to lead to unconsciousness. This went on for 36 hours.

The experience of the brothers was memorialized in a film called *Matewan* by John Sayles, in which one of the characters says:

> They were handcuffed to the bars of a cellhouse, eight hours a day for two full weeks. They were put with their arms up like this, so's they had to stand on their toes or those cuffs would cut into their wrists. Can't nobody stay on their toes eight hours. Pretty soon their fingers would start to swell up, they'd turn blue and then they'd crack open and the blood would run down their arms — eight hours a day, day after day, an' still they wouldn't work....
>
> Now I don't claim a thing for myself — but them fellas, never lifted a gun in their lives, you couldn't find any braver in my book.

The Hofers were finally released from their suspended posture, but still chained to the bars in the same dank cell for another three days. No food or blankets were given them; just the hard, damp floor as a place to rest. When they were moved to other cells, five days after arriving at Alcatraz, they both had scurvy and were covered with boils and insect bites. Their limbs were swollen, and they could barely walk. Other prisoners wept to see their appearance. They were kept in their cells 24 hours a day, getting only a bit of exercise on Sundays.

From June to November, Michael and Joseph remained in Alcatraz and then they were transferred to Leavenworth in Kansas, another prison for the worst convicts. Arriving exhausted and ill, they were made to stand outside in the cold air in their underwear until the middle of the night. Awakened at 5 a.m., they were again sent out to stand in the cold. Both had come down with pneumonia; unable to fight off the fatigue and weakness, both brothers fell to the ground.

Finally, on the twenty-eighth of November, their wives arrived from South Dakota. They, too, were harassed by the staff, whose members delayed their visit as long as they could. When the women were able to see their husbands, they were shocked at their condition. Joseph died later that night, and when Maria was allowed to view her husband's body, she found that the guards had dressed it in the uniform he had so bravely refused to wear in life.

Mary was joined by her father-in-law, and when Michael died only four days later, his father was able to keep the staff from putting the body in uniform. The two men left devastated wives and children, but had not allowed themselves to be bullied or threatened into violating their consciences or their Christian convictions. Simple and dignified in death as in life, the Hofers' unswerving loyalty to Christ's call as they understood it, along with their unbending resistance to violence, challenges all whose lives too easily conform to the demands of the world and its ways.

✪ *May 24*

David Brainerd

CONGREGATIONAL

April 20, 1718–October 9, 1747

His father died when he was nine, his mother when he was 14. At the age of 19, he began studying with his pastor, living in the clergyman's house, but within a year the pastor was dead as well. Perhaps, then, it is not surprising that David Brainerd's life had a special intensity about it. He contracted tuberculosis in college and his health was less than perfect for most of his short life. Yet he dedicated his life to the conversion of Native American tribes untouched by gospel. He would ride for miles through the wilderness to find and preach to them even when he had to sit down to do so because he could no longer stand.

Brainerd was 21, older than the average student, when he decided to go to college and his education was twice interrupted by serious illness. When he returned to his studies after his second illness, the college had been visited by George Whitfield and was taken up with the Great Awakening. Brainerd became part of the "New Light" faction, while the faculty remained staunchly "Old Light." Unfortunately, he was overheard making a critical comment about a faculty member and was expelled.

Casting about for direction in his life, Brainerd was licensed to preach by the New Lights but lacked a ministry until an invitation came to serve the Indians at the Forks of the Delaware River. Because conditions were too dangerous at that time, he served an internship of sorts, ministering to the Indians between Stockbridge, Massachusetts, and Albany, New York. He was then offered a pastoral position on Long Island, but was too committed to Native American ministry. He was given clearance to go to the Delaware on May 1, 1744.

Ordained as a Presbyterian, Brainerd met early discouragement that taught him to rely solely on God for success and to ground his ministry in prayer. By the end of the first year, he had gathered a congregation of well over a hundred. Now, however, Brainerd's bouts of illness became more frequent. He persisted through another winter, before retiring to Jonathan Edward's home in Massachusetts, where he died on October 9, 1747.

So brief a ministry would rarely have much lasting impact, except for the journal Brainerd kept. It was published by Edwards, who had been deeply moved by it, and John Wesley commended it to all his preachers. Brainerd's journal continues to make moving reading, and he is described as one of the most important missionaries in the history of the Christian church.

A reading from David Brainerd's journal

Lord's Day, December 29th

Preached from John 3:1–5. A number of white people were present as is usual on the Sabbath. The discourse was accompanied with power, and there were some tears among white people, as well as the Indians. But the impressions made on their hearts appeared chiefly by the extraordinary earnestness of their attention, and their heavy sighs. After public worship was over, I went to my house, intending to preach again after a short intermission: but they soon came in, one after another, with tears in their eyes, inquiring, what they should do to be saved? What I spoke was set home in such a manner that the house was soon filled with cries and groans. Upon this they all flocked together, and the most careless were almost universally seized with concern for their souls.

It was an amazing season of power, as if God had bowed the heavens and come down. So astonishingly prevalent was the operations upon old as well as young, that it seemed as if none would be left in a secure and natural state, but that God was now about to convert all the world. Tis impossible to give a just a description of the appearance of things, such as to convey an adequate idea of the effect of this influence. Some were rejoicing to see so many striving to enter in at the straight gate, and wanted to push them forward, as some expressed it. Others, both old and young, of both sexes were in tears, and in anguish of spirit, with down-cast looks like condemned malefactors, so that there seemed to be a lively emblem of the solemn day of accounts, or a mixture of heaven and hell. Their concern and religious affection were such that I could only discourse to one and another, and sometimes address them all together, and at last concluded with prayer. Such were their circumstances, that I could scarce get half an hour's intermission for speaking from half an hour before 12 till past seven at night.

December 30th

Was visited by four or five young persons under concern for their souls, most of whom were very lately awakened. The next day visited my people from house to house, and scarce left the house without some of its inhabitants in tears. They are now gathered together from all quarters, and have built them little cottages, so that more than twenty families live within a quarter of a mile of me. The next day visited them again, and found scarce one who was not under serious impressions. Strangers are almost continually dropping in, so that I have occasion repeatedly to open and inculcate the first principles of Christianity

January 4th

Prosecuted my catechetical method of instructing, found my people able to answer questions with propriety, and divers were much affected and refreshed.

Lord's Day, January 5th

Near night I intended to have proceeded in my usual method of catechizing, but while we were engaged in the first prayer, the power of God seemed to descend upon the assembly in such remarkable manner, that I thought it more expedient to insist upon the plentiful provision of the gospel, and press them to a speedy acceptance of the great salvation, then to ask them questions about doctrinal points, while numbers appeared so solicitous to obtain an interest in the great Redeemer.

✪ *May 25* ⎯⎯⎯⎯⎯⎯⎯⎯⎯⎯⎯⎯⎯⎯⎯⎯⎯⎯⎯⎯

Mary Madeleva Wolff

ROMAN CATHOLIC

May 24, 1877–July 25, 1964

In a world constantly astonished by the invention of new techniques for communication, it is worth remembering Henry Thoreau's comment when a telegraph line was first laid from Texas to Massachusetts: "What if Texas and Massachusetts have nothing to say to each other?" Sister Madeleva drew attention to a similar problem when she noted that most college graduates "have had years of organized training in the arts and sciences of the intellectual life, the physical life, the social life ... [but] ... have had not an hour of training in the arts and sciences of the spiritual life." It was her life's work to deal with that issue.

Mary Evaline Wolff was born in Wisconsin to German immigrant parents. She studied at the University of Wisconsin and earned her first degree from St. Mary's College, Notre Dame, Indiana, her master's degree at the University of Notre Dame, and her doctorate at the University of California. She taught at St. Mary's College, for seven years and then became the principal of schools in Utah and California and finally president of a college there, before returning to St. Mary's College where she was president from 1934 to 1961. The student body at St. Mary's College tripled in size during her tenure, and Mother Madeleva, as she was now called, established the first graduate school in theology explicitly for Roman Catholic laity and women religious. She became a recognized authority on higher education for women and published a book, *The Education of Sister Lucy,* that was influential in creating a systematic program for the higher education in of women in religious orders.

Traveling widely and lecturing throughout the United States, Mother Madeleva also found time to serve a term as Indiana director of the National Conference of Christians and Jews, and as president of the Poetry Society of America. In the midst of her administrative duties, she published essays and books on Chaucer and medieval literature, wrote poetry, and contributed essays to newspapers and magazines including the *New Republic,* the *Saturday Review,* and the *New York Times.*

A reading from *Addressed to Youth* by Mary Madeleva Wolff

History teaches us the fact of the Resurrection of Christ. The Apostles' Creed teaches us the fact of the resurrection of the body. This is one of the most neglected of all the articles of that Creed. Yet it is for us the most exciting and personal. It should fascinate us beyond all the thrills of radio and aviation. For it is an experience as inevitable as death, that will come to everyone. It is an experience about which we never think, the resurrection of the body; that is, my body will be restored to me after death with qualities of immortality: with lucidity, agility, impassibility. This means that with my risen body I shall be able to go from place to place with the immediacy of thought; that I shall experience no physical imperfection, sickness or death; that I can pass through a mountain range as easily as through a sunbeam; that I myself shall provide the necessary light for any possible darkness in my environment. It means that I am and possess the super-airways, the super-airsystems not only of the world but of the universe. It is not unsignificant that our most influential inventions in an age of materialism have been bent on recapturing through matter and force the attributes of our glorified bodies. They stand as eloquent intimations of the resurrection of the body. It is not unsignificant that more than one boy under military training today has described our air force as a poor parody of the Ascension.

This world of the air which we now possess can lead us into a supernatural land. It can reveal the world of brotherhood, a Christian country, an earthly paradise. It can uplift us to the discovery of the universe. Ours is the world of the air. Ours also is its apostolate, an apostolate of good works. The devils have our faith but they have neither hope nor love. Saint James says, "The devils also believe, and tremble." And they work the superhuman works of hate. Consider their tireless enterprise in the fields of the press, the moving picture, the radio, of beauty and wealth and power, in the mighty realms of the air. Our conflict is not with flesh and blood but with powers and principalities. The frontiers of the air are not palpable forests and wildernesses. Subtler barriers await us. We know them in part. We guess them in part. Are we supernaturally prepared?

Franz Werfel chides us, "Your pedestrian minds are unaware of the universe." Antoine de Saint-Exupéry asks us to listen to the laughter of the stars. Dante lifts us beyond them to the Beatific Vision. Chaucer looks down with celestial laughter on this little spot of earth. Dame Juliana sees it saved by the love of God. Vergil promises it a Prince of Peace. They are all spokesmen for times troubled and cataclysmic as our own. They are great challenges to our conquest of the air and our shaping of an air-bound peace. They reveal to us a universe without which we can never come to peace.

✪ May 26

Paul Chauncey Empie

LUTHERAN

February 10, 1909–September 1, 1979

As a founder of Lutheran World Relief and Lutheran Film Associates, Paul Chauncey Empie put his passion for a faith active in service of others to good use. In addition to what ecumenists call "Life and Work" concerns, he also engaged in the "Faith and Order" aspect of ecumenical efforts. He was active in the bilateral dialogue with the Roman Catholics and edited several of the reports issued from those talks. He was also an alternate delegate to the first Assembly of the World Council of Churches. Empie's pastoral heart and activist spirit motivated him to direct a home for orphans, establish a new congregation, work for Christian unity, help produce a classic film on Martin Luther, and campaign for more just immigration laws.

Paul Empie's wide range of interests, together with his dedication to work on behalf of so many kinds of people, well exemplify Jesus' saying about the hundred-fold harvest. Words he spoke in 1956 as head of the National Lutheran Council, ring as true today:

> Life would be simpler if the outstretched hands of our refugee brothers and sisters were not within our reach. But they are! We might at moments wish that God has arranged it otherwise, but He hasn't. As long as He has placed us in the position to be the rescuing sponsors instead of the refugees, how can we ask to be excused?

Empie did not settle for merely writing a check, or even for resettling a family. He made care of refugees a part of the consciousness of Lutherans, a calling they continue to this day. He understood the power of media to communicate a compelling story, as well as the need for Christian cooperation, whether for the sake of the church or the world.

Empie's ministry spanned years of transition for Lutherans in America. The 1950s saw serious efforts made to bring together the varied strands of Lutherans — strands whose languages, cultures, and forms of worship reflected their lands of origin. Finns, Swedes, Norwegians, Germans, Latvians, Danes, and others made up a patchwork of Lutheran traditions in the United States. Most now used English as the primary language of worship and teaching, and this change drew many of them to realize the advantages of a more unified American Lutheranism than seemed possible 100 years earlier. By the early 1960s, two national church bodies emerged: the American Lutheran Church, and the Lutheran Church in America. The former had headquarters in the midwest, the latter in the east. During times of institutional upheaval, ministries to the world can fall between the cracks as personnel and funds are shifted away to build the new denomination. Empie prevented this from occurring, so that the institutional commitment to international relief programs and projects that bears his stamp, survived the merger in 1988 that brought most American Lutherans together as the Evangelical Lutheran Church in America. Lutheran World Relief has touched countless lives with development aid, medical care, schools, disaster assistance, and refugee resettlement.

It would be wrong to consider Empie a mere bureaucrat, or a church politician. A dedicated Christian servant in a position within an organization, he influenced important ministries that affected the lives of ordinary people. Empie understood that compassion can be effectively translated through large, structured church bodies to effective work to address the needs of the world.

A reading from an address given in 1970 by Paul Chauncey Empie

Dr. Michelfelder, first executive of the Lutheran World Federation, who has a very blunt way of saying things, replied, when persons were telling him at the end of the war 'Let the government feed the starving people of Europe and let the Church get the Gospel going again." You don't walk up to a starving man and offer him a Bible to eat — or you don't go out to a river where a man is drowning, with only one hand showing, and stick a Bible in his hand and go away and let somebody else pull him out. Christ himself fed the 5,000 and then he taught them.

The two questions [of justice and of salvation] are just as inseparable as they can be. These are heretical polarizations — putting the bulk of our resources in social action or reserving most of our time for preaching the Gospel — as though the two should be competitive! Just this week, I read a very fascinating statement on the question of being conservative in religion. The author's thesis is that the Church, even though it is regarded by many as having a mission which is radical, is a sort of transformer in two senses. Of course, it must shake the people out of their complacency, get them dissatisfied with their satisfaction with the status quo. In that sense it is radical. Yet the Church's primary job is to conserve what has come down from Christ and the Apostles — to cherish that which transforms a man to be what God wants him to be; to preserve all the implications of the Gospel which can change a man from a highly sophisticated animal to a child of God.

And if you are going to preserve all these things, you are conservative — even though you must use radical methods at times! He believes that most of us are not conservative enough in the right sense. Instead of treasuring what came from Christ and the Apostles, we cling to the baggage accumulated around the church in the last couple of hundred years; affluence, comfort, security. Linked to this is the widespread assumption that the middle-class way of life, after all, is what God wants for us. . . .

So what's the answer? We have simply got to face the fact that we in the developed countries of Europe and America have got to practice austerity — we've got to lower our standard of living in order to help them — not to become affluent, for that's impossible, but to eliminate misery.

May 27

Nannie Helen Burroughs

BAPTIST

May 2, 1879–May 20, 1961

A descendant of plantation slaves in Virginia, Nannie Burroughs was taken as an infant to Washington, where she finished primary and secondary education and obtained a degree from a business college. Initially, she planned to be a schoolteacher, but after she was turned down by the Washington school system, she found an opening with the National Baptist Convention as a secretary and bookkeeper. For a time, she settled in Louisville, Kentucky, where she organized an Association of Colored Women and became a leader with the Women's Auxiliary of the church. In 1900, she delivered a speech at the National Baptist Convention entitled "How the Sisters Are Hindered from Helping," that won her national attention.

In 1908 Burroughs returned to Washington and funded the National Training School for Women and Girls. She called it "the school of the three B's — the Bible, the Bath, and the Broom" — emblems of clean lives, clean bodies, and clean homes. She agreed with Booker T. Washington that emphasis should be placed on developing economic skills so that young African Americans could find useful roles in white society. She was not willing, however, to compromise on racial equality or a woman's right to vote. A powerful orator, Burroughs denounced lynching, segregation, and discrimination in employment. When she went so far as to criticize President Woodrow Wilson for his silence on the subject of lynchings, she was placed for a time under government surveillance. A proponent of unity, she created multi-racial boards of directors and welcomed support from other churches for her projects in an era when interdenominational and interracial work was unusual.

In an article in *The Southern Workman* in 1927, Nannie Burroughs took a stand on the role of African-Americans that was well ahead of her time:

A reading from an article in *The Southern Workman* (1927) by Nannie Burroughs

Where is the Negro going and what is he going to do when he gets there? That's the question.

Despite the fact that the race is traveling at high speed materially, it cannot get within hailing distance of the race that has a thousand years lead of him in material things.... In fact, America will destroy herself and revert to barbarism if she continues to cultivate the things of the flesh and neglect the higher virtues. The Negro must not, therefore, contribute to her doom, but must ransom her. Furthermore, it will profit the Negro nothing to enter into ungodly competition for material possessions when he has gifts of greater value. The most valuable contribution which he can make to American civilization must be made out of his spiritual endowment.... The Negro has helped save America physically several times. He must make a larger contribution for her spiritual salvation....

The tragedy in this problem-solving enterprise is that the Negro is not being taught the tremendous achieving power of his virtues. He is not being taught to glorify what he is....

When the Negro learns what manner of man he is spiritually, he will wake up all over. He will stop playing white even on the stage. He will rise in the majesty of his own soul. He will glorify the beauty of his own brown skin. He will stop thinking white and go to thinking straight and living right. He will realize that wrong-reaching, wrong-bleaching and wrong-mixing have "most nigh ruin't him" and he will redeem his body and rescue his soul from the bondage of that death.... I believe it is the Negro's sacred duty to spiritualize American life and popularize his color instead of worshipping the color (or lack of color) of another race.... No race is richer in soul quality and color than the Negro. Someday he will realize and glorify them, he will popularize black.

Preachers, teachers, leaders, welfare workers are to address themselves to the supreme task of teaching the entire race to glorify what it has — its face (its color); its place (its homes and communities); its grace (its spiritual endowment). If the Negro does it there is no earthly force that can stay him.

✪ May 28

Sheldon Jackson

PRESBYTERIAN

May 18, 1834–May 2, 1909

Initially rejected for missionary work because he was barely five feet tall, Sheldon Jackson nonetheless, found a way to fulfill his call. In the estimation of some, he became "the greatest missionary since St. Paul." Certainly he covered as vast a territory as St. Paul and may well have established as many churches. Jackson began teaching in a school for Native Americans in Oklahoma but moved on to Minnesota before resigning to do "general work in the Church of the West." In the course of that "general work," he planted over 100 Presbyterian Churches in ten states or territories — Colorado, Idaho, Iowa, Minnesota, Montana, Nebraska, Nevada, Utah, Wisconsin, and Wyoming and founded schools in Arizona and New Mexico as well.

Alaska, however, was the territory on which Jackson made the greatest impact by far. Traveling across that immense area, Jackson sent back brutally honest reports on the conditions he found. The inhabitants were generally described as "a naturally noble people," and he urged that "I know of no other place where... such valuable results could be achieved by the same amount of effort in so short a time." But he did not romanticize conditions. He described one village whose inhabitants, perhaps as a result of the influence of newcomers, had become "the most degraded, poverty-stricken, brutal people we visited. Many of them were half drunk. In several of their camps we found stills at work making rum." Yet he also wrote:

> I never before saw a people so hungry for the word of God. They filled the house of the chief, where we spoke, to suffocation, and some who could not

get in climbed upon the roof and listened through the aperture for the escape of
the smoke, enduring the cold two at a time rather than miss any of our words.

Reconciling the interests of new settlers with those of the native population was an issue throughout western North America in those days.
A consensus had been reached among many people of European ancestry that Native Americans could be converted to the western civilization
in one generation, so that they would learn English and build western-style
houses, blending in with their neighbors. Jackson began with similar assumptions but found himself reluctant to wipe away customs already in
place. Where others thought children should be taken from their villages to
special schools, Jackson argued that they should remain with their families
and villages. His efforts to collect and preserve aspects of the indigenous
culture led to the creation of important museums.

In its concern for western expansion, the government ignored the shib-
boleth of "separation of church and state," asking churches to supplement
inadequate state funds for certain projects. Jackson was appointed to head
the effort and made the United States Commissioner of Education for
Alaska. Congress appropriated a mere $25,000 for the 1885–86 school year,
out of which Jackson had to pay teacher salaries (from $540 to $1,200 per
year, depending on qualifications and location of school), traveling expenses,
costs of equipment and supplies, and construction of new school buildings.
Clearly that was not enough, but churches could help — and were much
more ready to create schools if they could look to government funds to sub-
sidize their efforts. And so, with full legal authority, Sheldon contracted with
missions to do the work. There was a stipulation, however, that missionaries
must not evangelize in class.

When a fellow Presbyterian missionary became governor of the territory,
some suggested that Alaska was becoming a Presbyterian state. Yet Jackson
realized that no one church could meet the needs of the area. He portioned
the territory out to the various denominations: Canadian Anglicans were
given the Yukon River and the Arctic Coast, Methodists were given the
Aleutian Islands, Moravians the Kuskokwim region, Congregationalists the
work at Prince of Wales, Quakers the Kotzebue area, Lutherans and the
Covenant Church the area around Nome, while Presbyterians kept southeast
Alaska where they first began their work.

Jackson meanwhile spent a large part of his time in Washington, DC, as
chief lobbyist for the natives of the territory. Always, however, he remained
a missionary at heart, happily reporting the progress of efforts to evangelize "hundreds of immortal souls, who have never so much as heard that
there was a Savior." Convinced of the importance of this opportunity, he
constantly sought for others to share in the work. When he defeated former
President Benjamin Harrison for the office of moderator of the Presbyterian

Church in 1897, he charged those present to dedicate themselves fully to the task:

> Many talents are hid in napkins and buried, many stewardships are unrecognized, and many Christians are robbing God, by withholding a portion of the offerings that are his due. The Church, through her Boards, is in a debt, and the cry of the missionaries suffering from deferred payments and reduced salaries ascends before the Most High God. The cries of Church members, scattered as sheep without a shepherd — the cries of your children going down to destruction, are heard all over the land. They reach to Heaven; they are as solemn as eternity.
>
> To your knees, O Church of the Living God! The great and overwhelming need of the hour — the great, and overwhelming need of our country and Church — the great and overwhelming need of our own souls, is the fresh and immediate baptism of the Holy Spirit — a baptism which shall set every heart on fire of God to possess this land for Christ. At the close of this century we face a future of great unrest; of reconstruction; of marvelous and rapid changes. And the Church must lead and control these changes, or be overwhelmed by them.
>
> We are living in one of the greatest crises of the world's history. The age demands consecrated men and women, consecrated time, consecrated energies, and consecrated wealth. Shall it have them? "Bring ye all the tithes into the storehouse, that there may be meat in my house, and prove me now herewith, saith the Lord of Hosts, if I will not open you the windows of heaven, and pour out a blessing, that there shall not be room enough to receive it."

✪ *May 29*

Noah Seattle

ROMAN CATHOLIC

1786–1866

As Christian evangelists found receptive hearts among the native peoples of the continent the converts sometimes became teachers with the Europeans as their students. Applying concepts and customs from their tribal traditions to their newfound faith in Christ, wise leaders addressed issues in ways that white settlers had not imagined. Chief Seattle was one such leader. His mother, Scholitza, was the daughter of a Duwamish chief and his father, Schweabe, a chief of the Suquamish tribe near the Puget Sound. Seattle had already been named chief in his early 20s. His courage and leadership had been proved in battles between various tribes. Though he cherished his own tradition, he was also fascinated by some of the pioneering whites who moved into the area. A number of Indians, including Seattle, were converted to Christianity in the 1830s by French Roman Catholic missionaries. Seattle was named Noah at baptism, and he committed himself to work for peace between his people and the newcomers. Some tribes, however, continued to resist the new settlers and battles continued to erupt between them.

When the governor of the Washington Territory proposed a new treaty in 1855 that would grant a reservation to the native peoples, Seattle accepted the offer as a peaceful solution to the clash of cultures. Although he realized his people might not prosper under the new arrangement, he felt that bloodshed would not advance their cause either. He had hoped dialogue might bring about genuine coexistence between Indians and the settlers. In the end, the treaty ensured that the Suquamish and Duwamish tribes would survive temporarily, but in limited conditions. Seattle knew that a vast cultural gulf separated his tribes and their perception of the land from the dominant white understanding. Even those settlers who gained their livelihood from the land seemed not to hold it in the same reverence as the native populations did.

In about 1854, Seattle delivered a speech transcribed by Dr. Henry Smith, who was in the audience. It was not published for many years, and there remains some uncertainty about its accuracy. However, its overall sentiment — a call for the growing nation to reconsider its treatment both of its land and of the native peoples who originally occupied it — is undoubtedly Seattle's message. Conscious that white settlements were driving out his people, he nevertheless resisted becoming vengeful, bitter, or fearful. His charity under the circumstances is almost beyond imagination and his resignation about the fate of his own people remains painful to hear.

> The great, and I presume also good, white chief sends us word that he wants to buy our lands but is willing to allow us to reserve enough to live on comfortably. This indeed appears generous, for the red man no longer has rights that he need respect, and the offer may be wise, also, for we are no longer in need of a great country. There was a time when our people covered the whole land as the waves of a wind-ruffled sea cover its floor. But that time has long since passed away with the greatness of tribes almost forgotten. I will not mourn over our untimely decay, nor reproach my paleface brothers with hastening it, for we, too, may have been somewhat to blame....
>
> But let us hope that hostilities between the red man and his pale-faced brothers may never return. We would have everything to lose, and nothing to gain.

In 1855, Seattle signed the Port Elliott Treaty, creating a reservation in the northwest and ceding most Indian lands to the Federal government. He nonetheless took this opportunity to address a letter to President Franklin Pierce:

> We know the White Man does not understand our ways. One portion of the land is the same to him as the next, for he is a stranger who comes in the night and takes from the land whatever he needs. The earth is not his brother, but his enemy, and when he has conquered it, he moves on.
>
> One thing we know, which the White Man may one day discover — Our God is the same God. You may think now that you own Him as you wish to

own our land; but you cannot. He is the God of humanity, and his compassion is equal for the red man and the white. The earth is precious to him, and to harm the earth is to heap contempt on its Creator.... Even the white man cannot be exempt from the common destiny. We may be brothers after all. We shall see.

Even today, many people reject Seattle's belief that humanity needs to be intimately connected to the land. Some do not even accept the desirability that we should see all people as brothers and sisters. His conviction that prolonged exposure to a sterile or toxic environment will dull our senses to our surroundings is reflected in this brief statement:

> There is no quiet place in the white man's cities, no place to hear the leaves of spring or the rustle of insects' wings. Perhaps it is because I am a savage and do not understand, but the clatter only seems to insult the ears.

Today, many Christians feel the divine call to a renewed relationship with the whole of creation. The life of Chief Seattle is imbued with this spirit. As we learn to honor and recover the heritage of Native Americans, Seattle's wisdom and compassion remains a legacy to be treasured.

✛ *May 30*

Anne Ayres

EPISCOPALIAN

January 3, 1816–February 9, 1896

By the middle of the 19th century, women were taking a more prominent role in public life. They became vocal champions of abolition, women's suffrage, and prison reform, and took leading roles in improving health care and education. Anne Ayres pioneered in a somewhat different direction. She founded the first non–Roman Catholic religious order for women in the United States.

Born in England, Ayres came to New York with her family when she was 20 and found work, as many young educated women did, as a tutor for young girls of wealthy families. One of her pupils was the niece of William Augustus Muhlenberg, one of the most creative clergy of his day. Inspired by one of his sermons, Ayres decided to devote her life to the church, and in November, 1845, she formally dedicated herself to Christian service in a private ceremony conducted by Muhlenberg. Seven years later Muhlenberg and Ayres created the Sisterhood of the Holy Communion with Anne Ayres as the "First Sister."

Because they hesitated to stir up needless trouble by seeming to model their new order on traditional monasticism, each member took renewable three-year vows, pledging not to marry during that time, rather than the more familiar vow of lifetime chastity. They wore a prescribed style of dress but not the traditional habits. Their ministry was primarily nursing at a small infirmary, established at Muhlenberg's Church of the Holy Communion and, later, at St. Luke's Hospital in Manhattan and St. Johnland on Long Island. The latter was a "Christian industrial community" Muhlenberg founded to provide a full range of social services to the poor. The Sisterhood of the Holy Communion never became very large and ceased to exist in 1940, but it provided the inspiration for a revival of religious life in the Episcopal Church and the creation of a variety of new orders for both men and women throughout the waning years of the 19th century and afterward.

A reading from *Practical Thoughts on Sisterhood* by Anne Ayres

My Dear Friend — A brief absence from my usual duties affords the opportunity I have so long desired for answering, at some length, the various thoughts and questions contained in your letter, on the organization of the voluntary labors of Christian women.

 You say that you have thrown out these questions "in the hope that they will elicit from me some hints which may guide those who are groping after light, how best to systematize and employ the services of such of our sex as desire to give a larger portion of their time to the Lord who bought them." I do not know how well qualified I am to be of use in this way, but your special interest in the subject makes it very agreeable to me to sit down for a talk with you of things which might be, if the unmarried female communicants of our Church were ready, in any number, to give themselves to the service of charity as a vocation.

 Would that the companying together of Christian women, in the way we are thinking of, and for the purpose of carrying on the different charitable institutions among us, were not still so much in the future. Look at your own experience in this regard. You are making your initiation in a field of unquestioned usefulness and excellence, one which pre-eminently demands the sisterly co-operation and devotion of refined and intelligent women. Now how many of such women have come to your assistance during the year that has passed? I do not mean as transient helpers and sympathizers, doing just so much as is easy, convenient, or agreeable; but how many, giving their time and energies unreservedly and ungrudgingly, can you count upon to share your toils and your cares? Perhaps, scarce one. And why? Is it not because our Christianity is of so low an order, because we are so entangled with the world, so uninstructed, not only in the spirit of sacrifice, but in the spirit of gospel brotherhood, so used to loving our neighbors a little, and ourselves, very much, and so content with just getting to Heaven, not perceiving that "there are many gains and many losses in Christ, over and above that unappreciable one of the soul? ... "

 I cannot help wishing that our bishops and pastors would speak more directly to us women, on these points than they do. It is customary to urge men to the work of the ministry, missions, etc., and should not holy arguments be sometimes addressed to us, also, to stir us up to something in the Christian life more distinct and impressive than that now common to us? Yet when do we hear a word from the pulpit to this effect? We women have a little faith, we have warm affections and pure impulses, we have heads and hands; why not show us that we are not living up to our vocation, not turning to good account the powers we are indued with, that communicants though we be, we are frittering away our lives, "spending our money for that which is not bread and our labor for that which satisfieth not;" or, at the best, allowing ourselves to be dwarfed and cramped into the niches of custom and worldly conformity, when we might be developing, by healthful exercise in pure Christian air, toward perfect stature in Christ?

Our reverend teachers must forgive me if I seem to speak undutifully. I do not mean to be presumptuous, but I feel that, if they would set these things forth, as they know how to do, and if all would pray earnestly for the outpouring of larger grace upon us, there would be some hope of an answer to that almost audible groan of yours, when, after relating to me your rescue of the unhappy child from its wretched, drunken mother, you cry out, "What can we women do?" It is not without strong reason that I attach importance to preaching of this kind; for it was a sermon, delivered now nearly twenty years ago, which gave the first impulse to the formation of the community to which I belong. The faithful words entered "as a nail in a sure place," and from them sprang, in due time, the first Protestant Sisterhood in this country.

✠ *May 31*

Jacob Albright

UNITED METHODIST

May 1, 1759–May 18, 1808

German pietism inspired John Wesley's conversion and shaped his ministry. In turn, English Methodism inspired Jacob Albright's conversion, molding his future path. Yet although he had been born in Pennsylvania and lived in America his whole life, he never spoke English fluently and founded, in effect, a German Methodist Church.

Jacob Albright began life as a farmer and was baptized in the Lutheran Church of his parents. Although he left no written record of his ministry, one of his disciples wrote down what Albright had often told him in a kind of "second-hand autobiography." Describing his early years, Albright remembered:

> I wandered carelessly on the path of life, was joyful with those who were joyful and thought little of the purpose of human existence. I did not heed the duties

of a human being, much less of a Christian. I lived as if this brief time would last forever and committed many sins for which God has promised a severe punishment.

However, when several of his children died during an epidemic, his spiritual crisis moved him to seek help from a Methodist pastor. With this guidance, Albright began searching for a deeper experience of God's love. Describing this period, he said:

> I thought, Oh if only I had my life to live again and had it to do over again, how entirely differently would I organize my behavior! I recognized not only my sins and felt their magnitude, but from this recognition followed a lively remorse, and immediately therefrom the resolution in future to desist from all sin and to so order my life that I could at least put my conscience at rest, even if I at the same time had no hope for the forgiveness of the offenses against my Creator and Redeemer of which I had been guilty. Just as my heart experienced this lively feeling of remorse, and this firm resolution for betterment emerged in my soul, so I also felt the need of prayer in order to pour out my heart before the Lord. I felt the power to pray deeply, heartily and with submission. I fell upon my knees; bitter tears of remorse flowed down my cheeks and a long, warm and fervent prayer for grace and pardon for my sins rose to the throne of the Most High. This incessant and warm supplication at last brought me nearer and nearer to my enlightenment. I felt the power to consecrate myself to the good and surrender my will entirely to God's will

Albright became a member of a Methodist group and began to feel called to ministry:

> By nature I had no gift for speaking at all and must freely confess that I was less suited for it than anyone else who might have stood up. But when I felt myself transported by the Spirit of God, when prayer had brought my soul closer to my Redeemer, when I was on fire with abhorrence toward sin, when the righteousness of a severely testing Judge stood before my eyes and I at the same time also felt His overwhelming love toward His fallen creatures, then I was grasped by an inspiration that unlatched my mouth so that eloquence streamed from my lips and God's grace worked through my words to the conversion of fallen and unconverted Christians and to the edification of the faithful.

The Methodists, however, were unwilling to license Albright as an evangelist since he could not minister to English-language congregations, nor did they want to enable a German-language ministry for fear of creating a parallel ethnic church. Eventually, he concluded that he must minister to his German-speaking neighbors on his own, and set out to prepare himself:

> I immediately readied myself to travel and prepared myself in such a way as I regarded appropriate. Qualification to proclaim the Gospel I sought only from the Lord, in incessant prayer and in searching in His revealed Word. I also sought to consecrate my body entirely to the service of the Lord, and so to

prepare it that no passion, desire, nor love of comfort might limit or hinder my career. For God clearly showed me what a miserable and unfortunate condition it is to preach the practice of virtue to others and be reprehensible oneself (I Cor. 9:26–27). Therefore I fasted, at the beginning, whole weeks long, so that my body often was so fevered and inflamed that I had to bathe myself in cold water in order to cool down the inflammation of my members. And overall, I did everything within my power in order to stun my sensuality, so that my own flesh could not rule, but the Spirit of Christ within (Rom. 8:5–13). And God so powerfully blessed my efforts that my heart was almost constantly lifted up to Him and attained the capacity to preserve me temperate in all things; to love God alone above all else and my neighbor as myself (Matt. 22:37–39). For God and Christ with His Spirit so enlivened my soul that I lived not to myself but to the honor of my God (Rom. 14:7–9) and the welfare of my fellow humans and neighbors. In possession of such grace, which was a gift of the Lord, equipped with the power of His righteousness and holiness, sealed with His Spirit (Eph. 1:13–14), in love, faith and hope (I Cor. 13:13), I set out on the itinerant ministry in the year 1796, in the month of October, in order to obey the call of God in the revelation of His holy will through the Gospel.

Over the next 12 years, Albright made some 300 converts, before his labors wore him out and he died. Many predicted that his little band of converts would die out. But the little band of leaders he had trained continued to spread the word until, by the end of the 19th century, their followers numbered 150,000. After Albright's death, the group called themselves the Evangelical Association and then the Evangelical Church. This church merged with the United Brethren as the Evangelical United Brethren. In 1968, that church merged, at last, with the Methodists, who once refused Jacob Albright's ministry. They are now the United Methodist Church.

June

⊗ June 1

Philip William Otterbein

UNITED BRETHREN

June 4, 1726–November 17, 1813

When Phillip William Otterbein died, the great Methodist leader Francis Asbury,* exclaimed, "Is Father Otterbein dead? Great and good man of God! An honor to his church and country. One of the greatest scholars and divines that ever came to American, or born in it."

Otterbein came from the German Reformed tradition and had been invited to America by a Dutch Reformed Church in need of pastors. His perspective was broad, extending across denominational lines. In Europe, Mennonites had been slaughtered both by Roman Catholics and Protestants. Yet when Otterbein heard a Mennonite preach, he greeted him, saying, "We are brethren." He believed that sharing communion would help unify churches. When his congregation formulated a book of discipline, he had them put in the following statement: "It becomes our duty, according to the gospel, to commune with and admit to the Lord's table, professors, to whatever order or sort of the Christian church they belong." When Francis Asbury became a superintendent for the Methodists, Otterbein took part in the ordination.

Over nearly 40 years of friendship, Asbury and Otterbein discussed unity and the value of Methodist practices. Otterbein himself instituted many of them in the congregations he served: prayer groups, group meetings, and the raising up of lay preachers. He feared, however, that formal adoption of

Methodist discipline would deepen divisions between his own followers and other Christians. Reluctantly, he agreed to the ordination of a bishop for his newly organized Church of the United Brethren in Christ. Reluctantly he accepted ordination as a bishop himself. He believed that denominational affiliation should never stand in the way of participation in the larger church. He always tried to reach out to the church beyond his own denomination, seeking the greater reality of Christianity surpassing any human boundaries.

Otterbein's ecumenical perspective was firmly grounded in his evangelical outlook, which focused on the experience of Christ-in-us. "If there is no Christ in us," he said, "there is no Christ for us." It was "as members of Christ" that every Christian should "use his gifts readily and cheerfully for the advantage and welfare of other members" whatever their denominational affiliation. In an age which both American culture and Christian churches were trying to define their identities, Otterbein was a man ahead of his time — concerned to be one in Christ alone.

Otterbein had a rare ability to speak plainly about matters of the faith, as in this response to a questioner:

> You ask what sanctification is, and what is accomplished thereby. Here the best thing for us to do would be that we both pray for the spirit of sanctification, since before we do this we cannot by any means comprehend it. The word of God speaks, however, plainly enough, making a difference between justification and sanctification. And this difference accords also with reason; for, is it not one thing when Pharaoh takes Joseph from prison, and another when he enrobes him in kingly apparel and sets him a prince over the whole land of Egypt?
>
> You ask what faith is, how we live by it, and how, through it, we live continually free from sin. That you descend so low as to ask what faith is astonishes me, especially as you otherwise are so high-minded. But what it is to live by faith, let your children, who perform the duties the mother enjoins, and who live meantime without caring for bread, tell you. He that denies the possibility of living without sin, denies God, and deserves no other answer than the one the Savior gave the Sadducees — "Ye do err, not knowing the Scriptures, nor the power of God." (Matthew xxii. 29).

But he could display passionate concern when writing to a friend:

> Friend Hoeflich: — Although writing causes me much trouble, I feel bound in my conscience to write to you these few lines. I had not thought to receive from time to time such unpleasant news from you. You are, since you left Baltimore, above all measure in the habit of using strong drink. Some of your friends had a suspicion of your drinking while you were yet in Baltimore; but as we were not sure about it we hoped you were wronged in this, because we thought much better of you than the facts warranted.
>
> Oh, this pains us very much. We must hear all around, "Hoeflich is a great drunkard." Is it possible? A man that knows the truth and confesses it, fallen

so awfully! This we had not expected. We hoped that you would be salt in your neighborhood — a light and leader. Alas! it is to the contrary.

My friend, you bring yourself into great calamity. You bring sorrow upon your family. Your children will despise, scorn you. But that is the least consideration. For a man to profess God with his mouth and to deny him with his works — that is awful. O Hoeflich, you will be lost. But that is not all. You hurt the cause of Christ; and besides strengthening the wicked in their ways, you entice others and become a partaker of their sins, and make yourself guilty of their blood, whereby you bring upon yourself an awful judgment. Tremble, and turn! You must either decide to go to hell or give up drinking; There is no other way; and this you know and believe. Hoeflich, O Hoeflich, turn quickly. Leave off; it is time. Give up drinking; Otherwise God will give you up, and then, oh, woe!

You ask, "Is there any help for me?" There can be; there must be; there is. Your strength is too feeble; but the power of the Almighty is sufficient. But you must give up strong drink. You must give it up entirely. And dare you hesitate? Is it not much better to suffer thirst in this world than to thirst in hell through eternity? Oh, resolve to quit drinking!

✪ June 2

Lemuel Haynes

CONGREGATIONAL

July 18, 1753–September 28, 1883

The child of a black father he never knew and a white mother who refused to acknowledge him, Lemuel Haynes managed to make a place for himself as a black man in white society long before such a thing was even imagined in most of American society. Brought up as an indentured servant in a white family where he was treated as one of the children, Haynes learned to be a farmer, but he spent his evenings by the fireside, reading borrowed books. When the Revolutionary War broke out, Haynes enlisted in the Continental Army and fought at Roxbury outside Boston and at Fort Ticonderoga. Wars have a way of drawing soldiers out of their familiar life and enabling them to imagine changes they would otherwise never have considered. Haynes's experience of fighting for his nation's independence led him to think about those who were still in bondage. He composed an essay on the subject, "Liberty Further Extended."

The abolition movement was still far in the future, so, as an educated man of mixed-race, Haynes needed to make a place for himself in the world as it was. He studied Latin and Greek with local clergy, and was ordained by the Congregationalists in Litchfield County, Connecticut — the first black man to become a pastor in any American mainstream church. He became a gifted and eloquent preacher whose rebuttal of Universalist claims was reprinted throughout the northeast in over 70 editions and remained in print 30 years after his death. In 1804, he was awarded an honorary M.A., the first African American to receive such an honor.

His ability to turn a phrase could be used to devastating effect as when a neighboring minister lost all his sermons in a fire and Haynes commented, "Well, don't you think they gave more light than they had ever done before?" The same rapier wit skewered his own Rutland congregation when they voted him out after 30 years service. "They were so sagacious," he remarked, "that at the end of that time they found out that he was *a nigger,* and so turned him away." In 1822, he became pastor of a congregation in Granville, New York, and remained in that position until his death.

A reading from "Liberty Further Extended" by Lemuel Haynes

Shall a mans Couler Be the Decisive Criterion whereby to Judg of his natural right? or Becaus a man is not of the same couler with his Neighbour, shall he Be Deprived of those things that Distuingsheth [Distinguisheth] him from the Beasts of the field?

I would ask, whence is it that an Englishman is so far Distinguished from an Affrican in point of Natural privilege? Did he recieve it in his origenal constitution? or By Some Subsequent grant? Or Does he Bost of some hygher Descent that gives him this pre-heminance? for my part I can find no such revelation. It is a Lamantable consequence of the fall, that mankind, have an insatiable thurst after Superorety one over another: So that however common or prevalent the practise may be, it Does not amount, Even to a Surcomstance, that the practise is warrentable.

God has been pleas'd to distiungs [distinguish] some men from others, as to natural abilitys. But not as to natural *right,* as they came out of his hands.

But sometimes men by their flagitious practise forfeit their Liberty into the hands of men. By Becomeing unfit for society; But have the *affricans* Ever as a Nation, forfited their Liberty in this manner? What Ever individuals have done; yet, I Believe, no such Chaleng can be made upon them, as a Body. As there should be Some rule whereby to govern the conduct of men; so it is the Deuty, and intrest of a community, to form a system of *Law,* that is calculated to promote the commercial intrest of Each other: and so Long as it produses so Blessed an Effect, it should be maintained. But when, instead of contributing to the well Being of the community, it proves banefull to its subjects over whome it Extends, then it is hygh time to call it in question. Should any ask, where shall we find any system of Law whereby to regulate our moral Conduct? I think their is none so Explicit and indeffinite, as that which was given By the Blessed Saviour of the world. *As you would that men should do unto you, do you Even so to them.* One would think, that the mention of the precept, would strike conviction to the heart of these Slavetraders; unless an aviricious Disposision, governs the Laws of humanity....

But I Cannot persuade myself to make a period to this Small *Treatise*, without humbly addressing myself, more perticularly, unto all such as are Concearn'd in the practise of *Slave-keeping*.

Sirs, Should I persue the Dictates of nature, resulting from a sense of my own inability, I should be far from attempting to form this address:

Nevertheless, I think that a mere Superficial reflection upon the merits of the Cause, may Serve as an ample apology, for this humble attempt. Therefore hopeing you will take it well at my hands, I persume, (tho' with the greatest Submission) to Crave your attention, while I offer you a few words.

Perhaps you will think the proceeding pages unworthy of Speculation: well. Let that be as it will; I would Sollicit you Seriously to reflect on your conduct, wheather you are not gilty of unjust Oppression. Can you wash your hands, and say, I am Clean from this Sin? Perhaps you will Dare to Say it Before men; But Dare you Say it Before the tremendous tribunal of that God Before Whom we must all, in a few precarious moments appear? then whatever fair glosses we may have put upon our Conduct, that god whose Eyes pervade the utmost Extent of human tho't, and Surveys with one intuitive view, the affairs of men; he will Examin into the matter himself, and will set Every thing upon its own Basis; and impartiallity Shall Be Seen nourishing throughout that Sollemn assembly. Alas! Shall men hazard their precious Souls for a little of the transetory things of time. O *Sirs!* Let that pity, and compassion, which is peculiar to mankind. Especially to Englishmen, no Longer Lie Dormant in your Breast: Let it run free thro' Disinterested Benevolence, then how would these iron yoaks Spontaneously fall from the gauled Necks of the oppress'd! And that Disparity, in point of Natural previlege, which is the Bane of Society, would Be Cast upon the utmost coasts of Oblivion.

✪ June 3

Peter the Aleut

ORTHODOX

died 1815

A routine trading journey ended in martyrdom when Peter the Aleut, a simple hunter, found his adopted faith put to the ultimate test. Peter's tribal name was Cungagnaq (pronounced Choong-UGH-noq) and he was born on Kodiak Island sometime before 1800. Russian Orthodox missionaries of St. Herman's monastery had been spreading the faith in that area for some time. Many of the inhabitants were converted, among them Cungagnaq. At his baptism, he was given the Christian name, Peter.

At that period, The Russian-American Company's business ran along the southern coast of Alaska. Because of the climate, various staples had to be imported from more temperate locations, so the Russians established an outpost farther down the coast, about 50 miles north of the present city of San Francisco. The site was called Fort Ross, from the word for Russia — Rossiia. Over 300 men worked the land there, supplying the Russians to their north with vital provisions. However, this meant that the colony lay in close proximity to Spanish colonies and missions, scattered throughout present-day California. The Spanish claims included "Alta" — or upper — California, including the area around Fort Ross. They did not want the Russians in "their" territory, nor did Roman Catholic missionaries harbor tolerant attitudes toward other varieties of Christianity. The government of Spain demanded that Russian authorities close Fort Ross. Foreign trade within California was forbidden by Spain, and all Russian ships were banned from entering, or even coming near the Spanish trading centers. In 1815, a new Spanish governor, Lieutenant Pablo Vincente de Sola, outlawed Russian trapping and trading and ordered the arrest of close to 100 Russians and Aleuts who had disregarded earlier orders to leave. These men were enslaved, beaten, and mistreated. Some were exchanged for supplies that had been bound for Alaska.

Against this background, a Russian named Tarasov led a small party of 14 Aleut seal and otter hunters from the Russian-American Company to hunt offshore around California in 1815. Peter was one of the group. The journey should not have been an especially dangerous one, but unfortunately, the Spaniards captured and vandalized the ship, took the crew prisoner, and brought them to San Francisco for trial. Peter was confronted with the kind of savagery faced by the earliest Christian martyrs. As part of the proceedings, the Spanish clergy insisted that the captives embrace Roman Catholicism. Peter and his companions showed them their baptismal crosses and said "We are Christians; we have been baptized," but their captors would not recognize the validity of the Orthodox faith. The Aleuts were accused of being heretics and schismatics and threatened with torture if they did not recant. They were given time to think it over, but when the Spaniards returned, the captives still showed no sign of willingness to renounce their faith. Peter was seized and one toe cut off each foot. According to an eyewitness to the events, he simply said: "I am a Christian; I will not betray my faith." Joint by joint, his fingers were all cut off, then his hands, and finally he was disemboweled and died. Before the next victim could be harmed, the captors received orders to cease the torture. Steadfast to the end, Peter's death bears witness to his faith and trust in the gospel.

The First Epistle of Peter in the New Testament (I Peter 4:12ff) reminds us that we are not to be surprised if fiery trials come upon us. It is hard to imagine, however, that the author envisioned baptized Christians torturing other baptized Christians to death. Nationalism, colonialism, fear, suspicion, and religious zeal come together to make a deadly combination. The Spaniards could not accept that the Aleuts were bound to them in Christ, and thus destroyed a brother in the Lord. The joyful gift of new life brought by one Christian missionary was counted as worthless by another missionary in the name of the same Christ.

Should we forget that ecumenical progress made in the latter part of the 20th century is a mighty work of God, we need to remember the bloody, hate-filled relationships between rival Christian bodies in earlier eras. That traditions once motivated by such animosity toward one another could begin to see each other as fellow servants of Christ, even in some cases, trusted friends, is a miracle unfolding before our eyes. In 1980, St. Peter the Aleut was recognized by the Orthodox Church as the "Martyr of San Francisco." His feast day is September 24th. He was the third Orthodox Christian to be martyred in North America, and the first in California. As frightening as it is to realize that at any time we may be called upon to defend our faith with our lives, it is heartening to realize that in such times, we are surrounded by a "great cloud of witnesses" (Hebrews 12:1ff). Peter's faith was apparently unremarkable for most of his life, but his courage and unrelenting loyalty to Christ during his final day is a proclamation of faith we need to keep before us.

✪ *June 4*

Harriet Beecher Stowe

EPISCOPALIAN

June 14, 1811–July 1, 1896

Although she was a daughter, a sister, and the mother of prominent Con-gregational clergy, Harriet Beecher Stowe joined the Episcopal Church in Connecticut, she wrote several devotional books, and worked with the Bishop of Florida to build an Episcopal Church near her winter home. For 18 years, she had lived in Cincinnati, Ohio, directly across the river from a slave-holding community and it was there that she became familiar with the difficulties of fugitive slaves. From friends and her own travels, she learned more about slavery and began to write Uncle Tom's Cabin when her hus-band took a position at Bowdoin College in Maine. A play based on the novel was widely performed and played before large audiences. The story of black hardship and indifferent or cruel slave-owners affected many read-ers profoundly. There is a legend that when Stowe met Abraham Lincoln, he greeted her as "the little lady that started this big war."

A reading from *Footsteps of the Master* by Harriet Beecher Stowe

Intimately connected with the forty days of solitude and fasting is the mysterious story of the Temptation.

We are told in the Epistle to the Hebrews that our Lord was exposed to a peculiar severity of trial in order that he might understand the sufferings and wants of us feeble human beings. "For in that...who are tempted" [Heb. 2:18]. We are to understand, then, that however divine was our Lord's nature in his pre-existent state, he chose to assume our weakness and our limitations, and to meet and overcome the temptations of Satan by just such means as are left to us—by faith and prayer and the study of God's Word.

There are many theories respecting thus remarkable history of the temptation. Some suppose the Evil Spirit to have assumed a visible form, and to have been appreciably present. But if we accept the statement we have quoted from the Epistle to the Hebrews, that our Lord was tempted in all respects as we are, it must have been an invisible and spiritual presence with which he contended. The temptations must have presented themselves to him, as to us, by thoughts injected into his mind.

It seems probable that, of many forms of temptation which he passed through, the three of which we are told are selected as specimens, and if we notice we shall see that they represent certain radical sources of trial to the whole human race.

We are told that the temptation of Christ was so real that he *suffered*, being tempted. He knew that he must disappoint the expectations of all his friends who had set their hearts on the temporal kingdom, that he was leading them on to a season of unutterable darkness of sorrow. The cross was bitter to him, in prospect as in reality, but never for a moment did he allow himself to swerve from it. As the time drew near, he said, "Now is my soul troubled, and what shall I say? *Father, glorify thy name!*"

Is not this life-long temptation which Christ overcame one that meets us all every day and hour? To live an unworldly life; never to seek place or power or wealth by making the least sacrifice of conscience or principle; is it easy? Is it common? Yet he who chose rather to die on the cross than to yield in the slightest degree his high spiritual mission can feel for our temptations and succor us even here.

The apostle speaks of life as a *race* set before us, which we are to win by laying aside every impediment and looking steadfastly to Jesus who "for the sake of the joy that was set before him endured the cross." Our victories over self are to be gained not so much by self-reproaches and self-conflicts as by the enthusiasm of looking away from ourselves to him who has overcome for us. Our Christ is not dead, but alive for evermore! A living presence, ever near to the soul that seeks salvation from sin. And to the struggling and the tempted he says, "Look to me, and be saved."

✷ *June 5*

Adoniram Judson

BAPTIST

August 9, 1788–April 12, 1850

In a day when deism and atheism were fashionable, Adoniram Judson abandoned the faith of his father, a Congregational minister, to join with other college students on what seemed to them all to be a more intelligent path. Judson was a brilliant student who had learned to read at three, studied theology as a child, and befriended the brightest and best of his fellow students at Providence College (later Brown University). After graduation, he decided to see the country and found himself one night in an inn where only one room was left. The innkeeper apologized for the fact that a man lay critically ill, perhaps dying, in the next room, but Judson assured him that it would not matter; he might feel a certain sympathy for the poor fellow but not be disturbed. However, groans from the next room kept him awake and the next morning he learned not only that the sick person had died, but that it had been his best friend in college and, in fact, the one who converted him to deism.

Deeply troubled, Judson returned home and resolved to give his life to Christ. He studied at Andover seminary and, feeling called to serve in the mission field, he had to establish the first Congregational Board of Foreign Missions to provide support for his efforts. Traveling to India, he was turned away by the East India Company and so journeyed on to Burma, a country of over 10 million people, without a single Christian. To complicate matters, he had decided that only a mature baptism by immersion was biblically warranted, and so refused further support from the Congregational Church. This meant he had no funds until he could find a Baptist board to support him.

It took six years to make the first convert. During a 14-year period, Judson suffered one calamity after another: he was imprisoned for nearly two years on the suspicion that he was a British spy, threatened with execution, and lost his wife and children. Yet one by one, new converts came and his translation of the Bible into Burmese progressed steadily to its completion. He had prayed to see 100 converts, but by the time of his death at 62, there were 100 native pastors and over 7,000 Burmese and Karen Christians.

A reading from "Advice to Missionary Candidates" by Adoniram Judson

To the Foreign Missionary Association of the Hamilton Literary and Theological Institution, N.Y.

DEAR BRETHREN: Yours of November last, from the pen of your Corresponding Secretary, Mr. William Dean, is before me. It is one of the few letters that I feel called upon to answer, for you ask my advice on several important points. There is, also, in the sentiments you express, something so congenial to my own, that I feel my heart knit to the members of your association, and instead of commonplace reply, am desirous of setting down a few items which may be profitable to you in your future course. Brief items they must be, for want of time forbids my expatiating.

In commencing my remarks, I take you as you are. You are contemplating a missionary life.

First, then, let it be a missionary life; that is, come out for life, and not for a limited term. Do not fancy that you have a true missionary spirit, while you are intending all along to leave the heathen soon after acquiring their language. Leave them! for what? To spend the rest of your days in enjoying the ease and plenty of your native land?

Secondly. In choosing a companion for life, have particular regard to a good constitution, and not wantonly, or without good cause, bring a burden on yourselves and the mission.

Thirdly. Be not ravenous to do good on board ship. Missionaries have frequently done more hurt than good, by injudicious zeal, during their passage out.

Fourthly. Take care that the attention you receive at home, the unfavorable circumstances in which you will be placed on board ship, and the missionary examples you may possibly meet with at some missionary stations, do not transform you from living missionaries to mere skeletons before you reach the place of your destination. It may be profitable to bear in mind, that a large proportion of those who come out on a mission to the East die within five years after leaving their native land. Walk softly, therefore; death is narrowly watching your steps....

Eighthly. Never lay up money for yourselves or your families. Trust in God from day to day, and verily you shall be fed....

Ninthly. Beware of that indolence which leads to a neglect of bodily exercise. The poor health and premature death of most Europeans in the East must be eminently ascribed to the most wanton neglect of bodily exercise.

Tenthly. Beware of genteel living. Maintain as little intercourse as possible with fashionable European society. The mode of living adopted by many missionaries in the East is quite inconsistent with that familiar intercourse with the natives which is essential to a missionary.

There are many points of self-denial that I should like to touch upon; but a consciousness of my own deficiency constrains me to be silent. I have also left untouched several topics of vital importance, it having been my aim to select such only as appear to me to have been not much noticed or enforced. I hope you will excuse the monitorial style that I have accidentally adopted. I assure you, I mean no harm.

In regard to your inquiries concerning studies, qualifications, etc., nothing occurs that I think would be particularly useful, except the simple remark, that I fear too much stress begins to be laid on what is termed a thorough classical education.

Praying that you may be guided in all your deliberations, and that I may yet have the pleasure of welcoming some of you to these heathen shores, I remain

> Your affectionate brother,
> A. JUDSON
> Maulmain, June 25, 1832

✪ *June 6*

Elias Boudinot

PRESBYTERIAN

May 2, 1740–October 24, 1821

We usually think of George Washington as "First President of the United States," but Elias Boudinot has a claim to the title as well. When the Continental Congress assembled in 1782 to chart the future course of the independent colonies, Elias Boudinot was chosen to serve as President of the United States in Congress Assembled. In that capacity he signed the Treaty of Paris that brought the Revolutionary War to an end. Afterward, he served as a member of the House of Representatives in the first three Congresses and then for 10 more years as the director of the United States Mint.

When Boudinot retired from public life, he turned his attention to a number of causes that interested him. He wrote a biography of William Tennent, a Presbyterian pastor, a rebuttal to Thomas Paine's "Age of Reason" called "Age of Revelation," and a study of the second coming of Christ. Boudinot was president of the General Assembly of the Presbyterian Church, worked to establish a seminary at Princeton, then served as a trustee of the university, where, in 1805, he established the natural history department. His fascination with Native Americans prompted him to study their languages and customs, hoping to demonstrate that they were the lost tribes of Israel. Thanks to this interest, he worked to enable some Native Americans to get a better education. Three of them attended the foreign mission school in Cornwall, Connecticut. Boudinot allowed one of them — later an important Cherokee leader — to take his name.

Boudinot was strongly opposed to slavery, demanding of his fellow citizens,

> How will you answer, in the great day of inquisition for blood, for the share you have had in that horrid traffic in the souls of men, called the Guinea trade? How will you account for the contradiction between your national declarations in the day of distress and humiliation, and your political conduct, under the smiles of divine Providence, since your deliverance has been effected?

But Boudinot's most lasting contribution to the future of his country was probably his work for the creation of the American Bible Society. Reports had come back from the frontier of the lack of churches, clergy, and Bibles in the west, and Boudinot came to the conclusion that there was a need for a national Bible society. However, over 100 state and local Bible societies saw Boudinot's initiative as a threat to their existence and worked to defeat it. When a convention came together, his health did not permit him to attend, so he wrote instructions to the presiding officer arguing that if the proposal was defeated, the minority should proceed to create a national society anyway. This proposal was adopted and Boudinot, who was chosen to serve as first president of the society, contributed $10,000 toward its work.

Boudinot's will left, among many other bequests, a grant of 13,000 acres to the mayor and corporation of Philadelphia to provide the poor with wood at low prices, as well as $200 to buy spectacles to help those with bad eyesight read the Bible.

A reading from an Independence Day address by Elias Boudinot

We are all the workmanship of the same Divine hand. With our Creator, abstractly considered, there are neither kings nor subjects, masters nor servants, otherwise than as stewards of his appointment, to serve each other according to our different opportunities and abilities, and of course accountable for the manner in which we perform our duty. He is no respecter of persons.

He beholds all with an equal eye, and although "order is Heaven's first law," and He has made it essential to good government and necessary for the welfare of every community, that there should be distinctions among members of the same society, yet this difference is originally designed for the service, benefit and best good of the whole and not for their oppression or destruction.

It is our duty then, as a people acting on principles of universal application, to convince mankind of the truth and practicability of them, by carrying them into actual exercise, for the happiness of our fellow-men, without suffering them to be perverted to oppression or licentiousness.

The eyes of the nations of the earth are fast opening, and the inhabitants of this globe, not-withstanding it is 1700 years since the promulgation of that invaluable precept, "Thou shalt love thy neighbor as thyself," are but just beginning to discover their brotherhood to each other, and that all men, however different with regard to nation or color, have an essential interest in each other's welfare.

Let it then be our peculiar constant care, and vigilant attention, to inculcate this sacred principle, and to hand it down to posterity, improved by every generous and liberal practice, that while we are rejoicing in our own political and religious privileges, we may with pleasure contemplate the happy period, when all the nations of the earth shall join in the triumph of this day, and the universal anthem of praise shall arise to the Universal Creator, in return for the general joy.

Another essential ingredient in the happiness we enjoy as a nation, and which arises from the principles of our revolution, is the right that every people have to govern themselves in such a manner as they judge best calculated for the common benefit.

It is a principle interwoven with our Constitution, and not one of the least blessings purchased by that glorious struggle, to the commemoration of which this day is specially devoted, that every man has a natural right to be governed by laws of his own making, either in person or by his representative; and that no authority ought justly to be exercised over him that is not derived from the people, of whom he is one.

This, fellow-citizens is a most important practicable principle, first carried into complete execution by the United States of America. To you, ye citizens of America! do the inhabitants of the earth look with eager attention for the success of a measure on which their happiness and prosperity so manifestly depend.

✪ *June 7* ───────────────────────────────────

Catherine FitzGibbon

ROMAN CATHOLIC

May 12, 1823–August 14, 1896

When nine-year-old Catherine FitzGibbon's parents brought her to America from her home in London in 1832, she entered a world she would someday change for the better. Her family settled in Brooklyn, and in 1850, when she was 23, FitzGibbon entered the Sisters of Charity in Mount St. Vincent, New York, and took the name, Sister Mary Irene. During her novitiate, FitzGibbon taught at a parish school, St. Peter's Academy. In 1858, she became the superior of St. Peter's convent, but ultimately her contribution would extend far beyond any parochial classroom or community of the sisters.

During those years, the United States underwent a serious upheaval. The regional tensions that would erupt into the Civil War and the social changes brought about by the Industrial Revolution impacted many households. Social bonds and structures that once provided families with the resources to raise their children within strong, extended networks deteriorated. Urbanization brought households to cities where the old village and farm community connections did not function. In large cities like New York, children were abandoned in ever larger numbers, and there were nowhere near enough institutions to receive and care for them. Many youngsters were sent to city-run charity homes where other poor citizens offered whatever care they could. Worst of all, provisions for infants' care were woefully inadequate. If the government had a reputation for neglect, Christians had a reputation for offering hospitality and compassion for the lost and destitute. It was not uncommon for nuns to find infants left on the doorsteps of convents or church buildings, but the practice of abandoning infants had become so frequent it had to be dealt with in a more organized manner.

FitzGibbon was one who saw this need and suggested that Roman Catholics ought to establish a facility for the care of these children. It simply would not do to ignore their plight, or deal with them on a case-to-case basis. Establishments that could provide that kind of care were well-known in Europe; FitzGibbon felt they could be effectively utilized in America. Archbishop McCloskey agreed, gave his blessing to the establishment of a "Foundling Asylum," and in 1869, he appointed FitzGibbon to make it happen. She lost no time tackling her new duties, first visiting several cities to assess the dimensions of the problem. She found Mrs. Paul Thebaud to direct the new home and established an organization of women to raise funds. A building on 12th Street was rented and, on October 11, 1869, opened its doors to the first resident. It was staffed by four sisters under FitzGibbon's supervision. Within a month its population swelled to 44. At the end of the first year, a larger home had to be found. The need was so great, and FitzGibbon's work so effective, that in 1870 New York donated an entire block and $100,000 as seed money for a new building. Private donations and fund-raising matched the initial grant. Located between Third and Lexington Avenues and 68th and 69th Streets, the new home opened in October of 1873. The building housed between 600 and 700 youth at various times. In 1909, New York City was paying $1,000 each day to operate the shelter. In addition, the church donated $40,000 each year.

The city continued of course to grow, and so did its needs. With the support of her church, FitzGibbon continued to address the problems, finding ways to provide compassionate care to ever-larger circles of the populace. She offered support to about 500 homeless or poor mothers every year, organizing St. Ann's Maternity Hospital in 1880 for their care. A year later, two other hospitals opened: St. John for Children and Nazareth Hospital on the Hudson. She also established Seton Hospital for tubercular patients, raising the required $350,000 herself.

Her close contact with all these groups of needy mothers and children led her to creative solutions for their circumstances. She did not want simply to offer care, but to look for more permanent solutions, and, if possible, help her young people experience family life. Whenever practical, FitzGibbon preferred placing abandoned children in foster homes, with adoption following where feasible. Poor women were housed and offered support to keep them together with their children.

FitzGibbon died in the city whose most vulnerable she had cared for with such consistency and compassion all her adult life. Her vision and creativity augmented her compassionate heart to provide hope for thousands who would otherwise have been left with none.

✪ *June 8*

Elizabeth Fedde

LUTHERAN

1850–February 25, 1921

The life of a deaconess in the late 1800s was rigorous, but the Lutheran deaconess movement offered deeply committed women an opportunity to serve the church in an official church capacity long before the ordained ministry became an option. Elizabeth Fedde was a Norwegian who had entered the movement, as many did, to use her nursing skills for the sake of the sick. Her brother, who had preceded her to the United States, saw the growing needs of Norwegian sailors and their families in New York City. In 1882, he wrote his sister a birthday letter, inviting her to join him in ministering to this community. She accepted, and within nine days of her arrival, organized the Norwegian Relief Society, with the help of a local pastor. In the first two years, she ran a boarding house for sailors, opened a school for deaconesses in Brooklyn, and established a hospital with nine beds.

Before a decade had passed, Fedde had created the Norwegian Lutheran Deaconesses' Home and Hospital in Brooklyn which, by the mid-1950s, had over 200 beds and merged operations with the Lutheran Hospital of Manhattan. Renamed Lutheran Medical Center, it included in its services community clinics, a nursing school, an internship and residency program, and a disaster plan. Later, it added mental health services, a medical records library school, and a chaplaincy training program.

Fedde was able to start so many ministries despite a lack of financial support. Her deaconess house in Norway could not support her, nor could the struggling deaconess community in Pittsburgh. No Lutheran synod took responsibility for sponsoring her work. Yet Sister Elizabeth, as she was known, managed to persuade local pastors and Lutheran congregations to fund her ministry. But money only solves some kinds of problems. Fedde also needed more deaconesses, and neither Norway nor Pittsburgh could supply her. So she worked with her board of directors to establish a deaconess-training program. Her society's mission was "to help poor and suffering countrymen in their spiritual and bodily needs." It became the first Norwegian-American deaconess mother house.

In 1888, Fedde traveled to Minneapolis to open a new deaconess-training center and hospital there and to assist in planning a hospital for Chicago. Though she eventually returned to Norway, her ministry in the United States continued to bear fruit. Her many administrative and organizational accomplishments are undoubtedly impressive, but it was Fedde's pastoral heart which made her work so authentically Christian. Excerpts from her diary give us a clear picture of her faith and compassion:

A reading from the excerpts from the diary of Elizabeth Fedde

July 4: During a troubled watch night on Smith Street surrounded by flies, bedbugs, lamp smoke, unpleasant odors of all kinds, and very, very warm, I cared for two sick; home; then went to the Emigrant Hospital, where I spent the day with six Scandinavians, mostly with a Stavanger man who likely hasn't a long time left. His face brightened when he saw me, and immediately he told me that his mother had been with him; I said he probably had dreamed that, but he was certain that she had been close to him today. He wanted so much to be saved and had always loved Jesus, but he could not believe that he would receive the forgiveness of sin. Although he said he could not recall a single Scripture passage, when I read, "For God so loved the world, that He gave His only begotten Son," he interrupted me with "that whosoever believeth in Him shall not perish but have everlasting life." And I taught him a couple of Bible verses besides. I recited them for him and he repeated. Then after a while we parted, and he asked me to come again soon.

August 10: Today have visited many unfamiliar places; called on two Episcopal Sisters to get some data on children's homes and other rescue institutions; then to Castle Garden; from there to the Emigrant Hospital, where we met ten Scandinavians. A young man from Trondhjem, very downcast and yet brave, discouraged because earthly fortune evades him and brave because he is a freethinker. Poor man, only Christ's love can melt the ice in his cold heart. He had, like most of [the immigrants], come without money and so, to earn money, hired out to sea even though he is an office worker; the first day he jumped on a plank and got a nail in his foot. There was nothing to do but go to the hospital for care; now he is not strong and has no money; when he has some clothes, he goes to the pawnbrokers to exchange them for money. We stood and talked long together. He stood his ground, but when I said that I prayed God every day that He would send me to those He wanted me to see and that I was sure that God had arranged the meeting with him, tears ran down his cheeks, and they said more than words. When I gave him my address and told him that he must always come to me, no matter what his need, and I would help, great tears ran down that man's cheeks and the handclasp and look he gave me said more than a thousand words.

Fedde's tireless energy, her great compassion, her willingness to take on a large challenge, and her steadfast faith all make her life a cause for celebration.

✪ *June 9*

George Washington Carver
METHODIST
1864?–January 5, 1943

The connection between faith and peanuts may not be immediately obvious to most of us, but for George Washington Carver it was a living reality. Peanuts were far from being George Washington Carver's sole interest in life, but they made him famous. He had sought to discover an alternative crop for southern farmers who were depleting the soil by growing nothing but cotton. Long before it was fashionable, Carter preached the gospel of sustainable agriculture. In his eyes, exploitation of the soil was sinful for the same reason that exploiting other human beings was sinful — kindness and justice were as important to the earth as to other people. Carver recommended and worked to develop little-known crops, like sweet potatoes, black-eyed peas, alfalfa, and soybeans. But when he developed ways to turn the lowly peanut into candy, ink, ice cream flavorings, mayonnaise, cheese, shampoo, instant coffee, flour, soap, rubber, face powder, plastics, adhesives, axle grease, and pickles, that caught people's attention.

Carver was born into slavery sometime during the Civil War. His father died in an accident and he and his mother were carried off by bandits, but someone found the infant and brought him back to the plantation in return for a horse valued at $300. No schooling was available in the area for him, but he enrolled elsewhere and was able to board with a black family and help with chores to pay his way. Later, he hitched a ride to Kansas and pursued an education while working at odd jobs — cook, launderer, and grocery clerk — to pay his way. Turned down by a Presbyterian college because of his race, he found a Methodist school that would accept him. When his art teacher noticed his skill with plants, he persuaded Carver to transfer to the Iowa State Agricultural College. Iowa State was so impressed with the young student's abilities that they kept him on as a graduate student and then as a member of the faculty. His fame spread, and Booker T. Washington, the best known black educator in the country, offered him the opportunity to establish an agricultural school and experiment station at Tuskegee Institute in Alabama. Carver had never lived in the deep south, but he had made it his goal "to be of the greatest good to the greatest number of my people possible," so he accepted the position, feeling that he held a key that could unlock the door of opportunity for many others.

The newly established institute published bulletins reporting on new research in language a farmer could understand. A Movable School in the form of a wagon traveled to local farms with exhibits and demonstrations. Eventually even white farmers asked Carver to lecture about his work, and the Ways and Means Committee of the House of Representatives called him to Washington to report on his work. Thomas Edison and Henry Ford became supporters, and Presidents Coolidge and Roosevelt made time to meet with him.

Throughout his life, faith was a central aspect of Carver's work. He rose regularly at 4 a.m. and began his day with meditation. After he retired from other teaching, he still continued to teach Sunday evening Bible class at his church. Frequently, he cited intuition and divine revelation as the twin sources of his discoveries. When a Senator asked him where he learned all these things, he told him it was from the Bible because "it tells about the God who made the peanut. I asked Him to show me what to do with the peanut, and He did."

A reading from an essay by George Washington Carver

The study of nature is not only entertaining, but instructive and the only true method that leads up to the development of a creative mind and a clear understanding of the great natural principle which surrounds every branch of business in which we may engage. Aside from this it encourages investigation, stimulates and develops originality in a way that helps the student to find himself more quickly and accurately than any plan yet worked out.

The singing birds, the buzzing bees, the opening flower, and the budding trees, along with other forms of animate and inanimate matter, all have their marvelous creation story to tell each searcher for truth....

Even the ancient Greeks with their imperfect knowledge of insects recognized this truth, when they gave the same Greek name psyche to the Soul, or the spirit of life, and alike to the butterfly.

They sculptured over the effigy of their dead the figure of a butterfly floating away as it were in his breath. Poets to this day follow the simile.

More and more as we come closer and closer in touch with nature and its teachings are we able to see the Divine and are therefore fitted to interpret correctly the various languages spoken by all forms of nature about from the frail little mushroom, which seems to spring up in a night and perish ere the morning sun sinks to rest in the western horizon, to the giant red woods of the Pacific slope that have stood the storms for centuries and vie with the snow-capped peaks of the loftiest mountains, in their magnificence and grandeur.

First, to me ... are the little windows through which God permits me to commune with Him, and to see much of His glory, majesty, and power by simply lifting the curtain and looking in.

Second, I love to think of nature as unlimited broadcasting stations, through which God speaks to us every day, every hour and every moment of our lives, if we will only tune in and remain so.

Third, I am more and more convinced, as I search for truth that no ardent student of nature, can "Behold the lilies of the field"; or "Look unto the hills," or study even the microscopic wonders of a stagnant pool of water, and honestly declare himself to be an Infidel.

To those who already love nature, I need only to say, pursue its truths with a new zest, and give to the world the value of the answers to the many questions you have asked the greatest of all teachers — Mother Nature.

To those who have as yet not learned the secret of true happiness, which is the joy of coming into the closest relationship with the Maker and Preserver of all things: begin now to study the little things in your own door yard, going from the known to the nearest related unknown for indeed each new truth brings one nearer to God.

✪ *June 10*

Elizabeth Leslie Rous Comstock

QUAKER

October 30, 1815–August 3, 1891

Elizabeth Comstock, a Quaker from birth, was born and married in England. When her husband died three years after their marriage, she kept a shop for a time, but then emigrated to Canada. She brought with her the influence of Elizabeth Fry, an English Quaker who carried on an extensive prison ministry and worked for reforms in that area. Comstock stayed in Canada for a short time, then remarried and moved to Michigan, where she became active in Quaker societies and began a prison ministry. "It is a blessed mission," she wrote, "to visit the poor prisoners, and to know 'That mercy to the bondman shown. It is mercy unto Him.'" Her visitations covered a wide area:

> Most of the State prisons, penitentiaries, and many of the county gaols, and city prisons in our Northern States (except New England) I have seen, and many a tale of woe have I listened to, and endeavoured, as way has opened before me, and as strength has been vouchsafed, to comfort the afflicted and warn the careless.

In the years before the Civil War, Comstock became involved in abolition work and the Underground Railroad and tells many a tale of how the Friends outwitted those who came in pursuit of the escaping slaves. When the war began, she traveled to visit the battlefields and military hospitals. When the war was over, she extended her ministry to freed slaves in Kansas and the Native Americans in the upper midwest while continuing her prison ministry. Through all this activity she wrote vivid letters to friends in England and elsewhere describing the conditions she found and the efforts she made to provide a ministry in these various situations.

Readings from the letters of Elizabeth Comstock

Prison visiting

Laport, Indiana, fifteen miles south of Lake Michigan, [March], 1862.

We have stood upon the southern shore of Lake Michigan, and we have visited the State's Prison for the northern division of Indiana in the City of Michigan. It was an affecting sight. The chaplain of the prison escorted us, and introduced us there, and gained permission for me to have an audience of the prisoners, near three hundred in number. The sight of their misery and wretchedness almost overpowered me. It was well that I had an hour to recover my composure, after first seeing them in their cells, before they were assembled for our meeting.... I urged upon them the importance of cherishing every right feeling, and fostering every good impression and resolution, as these beginnings of a better life, though small at first, would grow if encouraged — that the commencement of both good and evil in our hearts is small at first, yet may largely increase, and illustrated my meaning by tracing the growth of evil and sin in their hearts since they first began to wander from the paths of rectitude. When I had finished, cousin P. B. Hathaway, my companion, offered a very appropriate prayer. When our meeting ended we mingled with them, and entered into conversation, many of them pressed round us eager to shake hands, and asked us to come again. A company of fifteen or twenty was introduced to me by their chaplain, with the announcement "Mrs. Comstock, these men have resolved to lead different lives." I shook hands with the little group, and spoke a few words of encouragement to them to persevere in their resolution. They urgently requested me to stay and attend their prayer meeting, which they have got up amongst themselves. I would willingly have done so, but we had to hasten to a meeting we had appointed for the citizens in the Methodist Church.

The extent of her ministry

During the past year, I have traveled 5,750 miles, have visited and [had] meetings with 52,850 sick and wounded soldiers, 17,100 prisoners, 16,060 inmates of almshouses, 520 blind, 1,125 widows, 3,250 insane, 5,450 orphans, 5,850 children in refuges and asylums, 1,987 poor fallen women, 6,900 coloured people; I have had twelve meetings with Hicksite Friends, twenty-six with citizens in large cities, two with young men, one with mothers, two with Christian ladies. With children altogether, from the little ones in infant schools to the young aspirants for collegiate honours, I have visited or had meetings with 26,500, many of them in Sabbath schools and mission schools.

Military hospitals

I went into a hospital in Virginia one day. A youth of about nineteen seemed to be dying. The soldier who was waiting upon him said, "It's of no use for you to speak to him — he don't know nothing." Had been badly wounded in the battle of Fredericksburg — lay thirty-six hours on the battlefield before he was picked up, and brought to the hospital, and during the two or three days he had been there, had not been able to answer any questions, or give any information; had only spoken in incoherent ramblings, or in the ravings of delirium. I enquired his name, but they could not tell it; said the nurse and doctor had both been trying in vain to find out; I asked for his knapsack, thinking that by searching it I might find some paper, book, name or initials, by which he might be identified. In vain, for knapsack, coat, cap and belt had all been lost on the battle-field. I stood looking upon the youthful face, and remembering that there is one Name that will sometimes reach the dying ear, and touch a chord of memory when all others were forgotten, I said, — "Jesus can make a dying bed Feel soft as downy pillows are, While on His breast I lean my head, And breathe my life out sweetly there." He opened his eyes, and, with an earnest appealing look at me, tried to speak. There was sufficient of memory and of reason left for him to remember his mother, and of sight to see that a woman stood beside him; and, mistaking me for his far-distant mother, he said. "Mother, I knew you would come." I longed to know that another name, besides that of mother, was precious in that solemn hour, and I spoke of Him who said, "As one whom his mother comforteth, so will I comfort you." I spoke of Him whom God hath highly exalted, and hath given Him a name that is above every name, that "at the name of Jesus every knee should bow, and every tongue confess that Jesus Christ is Lord, to the glory of God the Father." Again the large blue eyes opened, and rested upon me with an appealing look, and he spoke once more. Listening attentively, I caught the words, uttered with feeble, faltering accents, "Mother, I am going to Jesus." They were the last he spoke. I tried vainly to get the mother's name; the interval had passed away, or the power of speech gone. I stood beside him until his voice was silenced by the hand of death, and closed his eyes.

✪ June 11 _____

Asahel Nettleton

CONGREGATIONAL

April 21, 1783–May 16, 1844

The first half of the 19th century was a time of enormous change and tension in American life. The Revolution was over, and a new nation was being created, but some felt that the principles that brought the first settlers were being forgotten in the process. Asahel Nettleton was born just before the decisive battles of war for Independence. He was raised in a pious home and taught the Westminster Shorter Catechism. Its truths remained fundamental to him for the rest of his life.

At age of 17, Nettleton became convinced that his life was essentially frivolous. This first made him dislike the God of Scripture and hope he didn't exist. In spiritual distress, the young man anguished for nearly a year until he found himself changed and began to delight in those matters that had so distressed him before. Now the God of the Scriptures appeared to him as lovely and the Savior "exceedingly precious." He understood this conversion was not his own doing but the work of God's sovereign will.

Financial limitations largely determined Nettleton's subsequent course. He managed to find the money to begin a course of study at Yale in 1805, hoping to become a missionary. But the debts he accumulated attending college conspired with other factors to prevent that. Nettleton contracted typhus, but, more positively, he proved to be such an effective preacher in Connecticut that the Congregational church urged him to stay there.

In 1812, at the invitation of Connecticut clergy, Nettleton began an itinerant ministry based on several firm principles. He would do nothing to undermine congregations with pastors, and he would only preach where there was evidence that the Spirit had preceded him. Furthermore, he would labor to root out any spirit of "enthusiasm." Nettleton continued his revival ministry for 11 years until another bout of typhus weakened him further. He used the time of his illness to compose a widely used hymnal, then returned to preaching. Despite his impaired health, his work sometimes took him as far away as Virginia and the Carolinas, even to England.

During these years, he became involved in a public dispute with Charles Finney and his followers who took a more pragmatic approach to revival. Unlike Nettleton, they believed that logic and persuasion could be used to save those who would not respond otherwise. A conference between the two left neither side persuaded. Nettleton was one of the founders of the Theological Institute of Connecticut, which promulgated his position. He spent his last years lecturing on evangelism and preaching as his strength allowed.

A reading from a sermon by Asahel Nettleton

Every effort has been made by the ingenuity of man, by palpably erroneous schemes, and by plausible ones, to wrest the glory of this work from the hands of the divine Spirit, and claim the operation for ourselves; at least to share in the honor of it. After all, its origin can be traced only to the free and sovereign grace and Almighty power of God. The work is all his; and the glory must and will forever belong exclusively to him.

It is a doctrine supported by the great light of the Reformation and by the pillars of the evangelical churches ever since: that regeneration is a physical work. And by this they mean there is an actual new creation, as absolutely so as when the world was created; that a new spiritual taste or discernment, and principle is implanted by a sovereign creative operation, and not simply a new direction given to the old faculties.

Such a work being proved, the whole system of evangelical truth; the doctrines of grace; of divine sovereignty; of election; of redemption only by Christ; of human depravity and others connected with them, all flow from it. There is one grand, harmonious, and perfect system: and God is the sum — the substance and the glory of all.

My friends, I am fully aware of the difficulties incident to the doctrines here laid down. I know full well how ready the natural heart is both to oppose, and misconstrue them. But if the Bible supports them, it is enough. Here our carnal reason must bow. Here our proud hearts must submit. Charge them with mystery — with inconsistency — with unprofitableness, O sinner, and you assail not man, but God. Look on his word and read. There it stands; and it is written in characters of light, "which were born not of blood, nor of the will of the flesh, nor of the will of man, but of God."

This is the only birth which can fit us for heaven, "Except a man be born again, he cannot see the kingdom of God." We may please our fancies, and gratify our self-righteousness, by adopting loose Pelagian sentiments on this subject; we may remonstrate against such absolute dependence on the grace of God as has now been advocated, but a new heart, and a right spirit will after all be found of such absolute necessity, that without them we must perish forever.

✪ *June 12*

James E. Walsh

ROMAN CATHOLIC

April 30, 1891–July 28, 1981

James Walsh spent 22 years imprisoned in China — ten years under house arrest, two years in detention prison, ten years serving out his sentence as a "spy" — so that, when he was released at last, he was so emaciated he could not stand without help. But when asked how he now felt about the Chinese people, he responded, "The Chinese are wonderful people. They are people that I've given my life to, and I want to use my talents to raise them up.... They all have something in them that makes you love them."

James E. Walsh was one of the original Maryknoll missioners when the conversion of China was the first great objective of that society. Among the first six men to join the order, he went out to China in 1918. He was surprised from the beginning by the remarkable goodness of the Chinese people. It rather scandalized him, in those days, to discover that "pagan people... could be so good without the grace and aid and inspiration of the Christian religion." Soon, Walsh came to understand that God did not abandon a people merely because they were not Christian and that Divine Providence was at work preparing them for the gospel. He learned the Chinese proverb, "Within the four seas all men are brothers." No part of his prison experience shook that attitude.

In 1927, Walsh was made a bishop to serve the Kongmoon diocese. In 1936, he was called back to Maryknoll to serve as Superior General of the order, but when his term ended in 1946, he returned to China. Two years later he was placed under house arrest. Walsh could easily have left China before this happened. It seems that the Communist authorities rather hoped he would. But once he made a commitment, he would not abandon it. "I think it is the plain duty of all Catholic missionaries," he wrote, "to remain where they are until prevented from doing so by physical force. If internment should intervene in the case of some, or even death, it should simply be regarded as a normal risk that is inherent in our state of life...and as a small price to pay for carrying out our duty."

One could always pray. When Walsh found himself in imprisoned, he said to himself, "This is what I've dreamed of — time to say all the prayers I couldn't say when I was working."

A reading from "Description of a Missioner" by James E. Walsh

It is better to be a saint than a good missioner; but is it harder?

A saint is a man of logic, or, in other words, one who lives what he believes....The good missioner, in his role of being all things to all men, would qualify rather as a man of psychology. The saint luxuriates in the strong beauty of a divinely exigent religion to the extent of converting himself; whereas the good missioner, while he does not necessarily go to such a length, at least approximates it in a measure by trying to mirror that same divine appeal in all manner of multifold ways in order to convert others. To accomplish this he need not be a saint, but he must come close to passing for one. And in order to achieve this hoax he must be so many things that a saint is, and he must do so many things that a saint does, that it becomes for him a serious question if the easiest way to the goal is not simply to be a saint in the first place and be done with it. In short, is it easier to imitate a saint, or to be one?...

The task of a missioner is to go to the place where he is not wanted to sell a pearl whose value, although of great price, is not recognized, to people who are determined not to accept it, even as a gift....

He sallies out to convert the world, but the world does not convert. He meets disappointments. They multiply to make discouragement. Meanwhile he is a stranger in a strange land. All his overtures require just a little extra effort; meet just a little extra ridicule, fancied or real; remain just a little against the grain.... He begins to pray long prayers and to do voluminous spiritual reading. He becomes an expert in mystical theology; he is an authority on prayer; he reads many lives of the saints, maybe even writes a few. All good in its place and in its measure; but not missionary work.

Not a substitute for climbing mountains and riding horses and floundering in rice fields and visiting villages and entertaining mandarins and jollying shopkeepers and encouraging students and curing sick people and tending lepers and teaching children and harboring abandoned babies, not to mention the thousand and one other active works that make up the real vocation of the man who was sent to be all things to all men. Not a substitute, and not even an excuse.... And so, instead of trying to imitate the saint, it would be better for him to concentrate, on the less complex process of being one. For him it is at once the easiest and the only way. And, incidentally, it is doubtless the reason why missioners abound, while the good missioner is almost as rare as the saint whose vocation his own so closely resembles.

✪ *June 13*

Thomas Gallaudet

EPISCOPALIAN

June 3, 1822–August 27, 1890

Early in the 19th century, a Congregational minister named Thomas Hopkins Gallaudet learned the French system of sign language for the deaf. Returning to America, he founded a school in Hartford, Connecticut, to teach it. His wife was deaf, so their son, Thomas Gallaudet, learned sign language at home to communicate with his mother and with playmates in the deaf school. The younger Gallaudet was ordained in the Episcopal Church in 1851 and soon came to believe that he had a special call to minister to the hearing-impaired. He felt that the formal liturgy of the Episcopal Church would be especially suitable for deaf people and easy for them to follow. In 1852, he founded St. Ann's Church, New York, as the first parish for the deaf. In 1859, the congregation purchased a church building as a center for deaf ministry. Gallaudet remained in charge of St. Ann's for the rest of his life, but also traveled to start up similar congregations in Baltimore, Philadelphia, Boston, Washington, and Albany.

At a time when American missionaries were traveling across the globe to proclaim the gospel to those who had not heard it, Gallaudet crossed another less visible boundary to preach the gospel visually so that it could be "heard" in an otherwise silent world.

A reading from the sermon preached at the first service held at St. Ann's Church for Deaf-Mutes by Thomas Gallaudet

Mysteries in spiritual matters surround us at every step of our pilgrimage, and it is utterly vain for self-complacent philosophers to attempt to fathom them. Must we not, in our littleness, exclaim, "We know not how," as we behold the amazing work which has gone on since the Church of Christ was sent out from the feeble beginning of a grain of mustard seed, on her purifying, elevating mission, leading multitudes from their tendencies towards sin and eternal ruin, into that path of life and peace which shineth brighter and brighter unto the perfect day? Yes, for the sake of Jesus Christ, none the less the Son of God because he was the son of man, the Church of the living God — the pillar and the ground of the truth — has gone on, from the upper room in Jerusalem, where the number of the believing company was about one hundred and twenty — a small grain of mustard seed to plant in this world of sin and misery — has gone on, through successive generations, with its ministry, its preaching, its sacraments, its inspired Record of God's dealings with mankind, and its principles of his covenants of mercy — all its holy institutions and godly discipline. It has gone on, through clouds and sunshine, through good report and evil report — withstanding the attacks of myriads issuing from the gates of hell — surviving the onsets of worldlings without and the treachery of hypocrites within. It has grown to be the goodly tree, extending its branches from the river even unto the ends of the earth, proving the instrument of eternal salvation to countless multitudes of Adam's descendants — repenting, believing, obeying — and yet we know not how.

The growth of the spiritual kingdom, as a divinely appointed organization, is a mystery; and the growth of spiritual life in the hearts of each individual member of the spiritual kingdom is a mystery. We behold indications, from time to time, marking the gradual progress of these two kinds of growth: we believe in them, as realities coming to pass, in consequence of Christ's redemption, and yet we know not how. "The wind blows where it chooses, and you hear the sound of it, but you do not know where it comes from or where it goes. So it is with everyone who is born of the Spirit." (John 3:8)

Oh! let those to whom the gospel announcements have come, be not faithless, but believing. Beholding the wonderful work which God, through Christ, has wrought for mankind by the mysterious instrumentalities of his infinitely wise appointment, let all become genuine, devout communicants of the organization which has existed, though they know not how, for upward of eighteen hundred years, as the grand regeneration of the human race; and in due time, they shall be the possessors of the peace of God, which passing understanding, is the earnest of the good things to come in the future life, of which it hath not entered into the heart of man to conceive. Oh! let us have entire faith in the Divine arrangements for the growth of spiritual life, although they are to us, in our present condition, unfathomable mysteries.

✪ *June 14*

Francis Wayland

BAPTIST

March 11, 1796–September 30, 1865

"I am of no sect," Francis Wayland told the students at Brown. "Never ...have I uttered a word with the conscious intention of proselytizing you to the denomination of which I am a member.... You have all your own religious preferences, as you are connected with the different persuasions of Protestant Christianity. We would have you enjoy these preferences to the uttermost; and in this institution you have from the beginning, enjoyed them to the uttermost, not as a favor, but as an inalienable right."

Brown was a Baptist college, and Wayland, as its president, was a Baptist pastor, but Rhode Island had been founded by Roger Williams and other refugees from the Massachusetts Bay Colony's theocracy to be a place of religious freedom, and Wayland was imbued with that same spirit. So there was room for freedom, but Wayland was also a man of deep faith, committed to communicating that faith to others. He had been a tutor at Union College for four years and pastor of a church in Boston for five years before going to Brown, and he continued to be both a teacher and pastor. He gave lectures on psychology, political economy, and ethics, then preached weekly to the students in the chapel. He also attended their prayer meetings and brought them together for instruction in the Bible.

Before Wayland became its president, Brown had suffered a breakdown of discipline. He moved immediately to restore order. Professors and instructors were to spend the day and evening in campus apartments and were to visit student rooms at least twice every 24 hours. Alcohol was banned from the college rooms and the barrel of ale that had been kept in the cellar was removed. On the other hand, Wayland wished students to have some choice in the courses they took, so he introduced a revolutionary elective system. The curriculum was revised to introduce more up-to-date materials and subjects.

Eventually Wayland's reforms proved to be more than the trustees could accept. He had suggested that the college be open to students who wanted to take selected courses even if they could not enroll full time, as a way for Brown to extend its influence into the community. He also argued this would increase revenues at a time when the colleges finances were shaky. But that was too progressive for the trustees and Wayland was forced to resign. He spent the last ten years of his life engaged in charitable works, with a particular concern for prison reform. It is said that the inmates of the Rhode Island state prison wept when they heard of his death.

Although Francis Wayland wrote a number of important books, one of the most significant contains his correspondence with a leading southern clergyman, Richard Fuller, on the subject of slavery. This lengthy exchange was published in 1847, an era when people on both sides still found it possible to listen respectfully to one another and respond charitably.

A reading from a letter to Richard Fuller by Francis Wayland

If now we look back over the course of these remarks, I think we may easily discover the manner in which, commencing so widely asunder, we have come at last so nearly to coincide. In the first place, excluding from your definition of slavery all right to interfere with the intellectual, moral, social, and domestic condition of man, and admitting that for such interference slavery furnishes neither excuse nor palliation, you limit the institution which you defend to the mere right to oblige another to labor for us without his contract or consent. In the second place, ... you defend a condition which may be voluntary, limited by contract, and one which the laborer would not consent to relinquish. In the third place, you affirm that this condition, even thus modified, could not properly be perpetuated. In how much soever then we may differ in our course of reasoning, the practical conclusions to which we arrive are singularly coincident. ...

All history informs us that absolute liberty is too violent a stimulant to be safely administered to a race which have long been bred in slavery. They must be taught and become accustomed to the responsibilities which it involves before they can use it aright. All this requires caution, boldness, philanthropy, and humble but earnest trust in God. "Prayers and pains," said Elliott, "with the blessing of God can do any thing." I do not pretend to dictate as to the *manner* in which this is to be done. This I leave to you, who are so much better able to judge. All I ask is, that the views which you entertain, so far as I understand them, be carried out into practice; and, in doing this, I here promise to give you my poor aid to any extent that I am able to render it. ...

This is the first time in my life — and I hope it may be the last — in which it has fallen to my lot to engage in controversy. Be assured, my dear brother, that it has given me pain whenever I have been obliged to differ from one for whom I cherish so affectionate a regard. For that Christian urbanity with which you treated whatever I have written, from my heart I thank you. If I have in any manner been able to avoid the errors into which many have fallen who have treated on this subject, I ascribe it mainly to the influence of your example, and to the unfeigned esteem which I entertain for your character, as a gentleman and a scholar, a clergyman and a Christian. Or rather, if we have been enabled without bitterness to express our views on a subject which is so liable to arouse the worst passions of our fallen nature, let us ascribe it all to that love of God shed abroad in our hearts, which teaches us to treat as a brother every disciple of our common Lord, though he may embrace opinions in many ways different from our own. God grant that we may both meet in that world where neither of us shall any more see through a glass darkly, but where we shall see as we are seen, and know as we are known.

I am, dear brother, yours with every sentiment of affection,

The Author of the Moral Science

✪ *June 15*

Joseph Badger

PRESBYTERIAN

February 28, 1757–April 5, 1846

Until the end of the Revolutionary War, the regions beyond the Allegheny Mountains were largely the preserve of the fur traders and Native Americans. The end of the war brought a wave of new settlers, many of them former soldiers looking for new land to settle. With them also came missionaries of the same background, sharing the hardships of pioneer life.

Among these pioneer-missionaries was Joseph Badger. He had fought in the Revolution and then entered Yale to study for the ministry. Having no money to pay for an education, he spent three months building a planetarium for the college and was paid $100 for his efforts. For a while, he served parishes in Connecticut, but, in 1800, he accepted a commission from the Connecticut Missionary Society to labor as a missionary in the Western Reserve of Ohio, or New Connecticut, as it was then called.

Traveling alone, leading his horse for almost 200 miles where the path was too narrow for riding, and swimming the Mahoning River, Badger made his way to Ohio and spent the next year visiting settlers in their isolated cabins and exploring the possibility of ministry to the Indians in northern Ohio and Michigan. At the end of the year, he reported back to the mission society, then headed west again, this time with his wife, six children, and their household goods in a four-horse wagon. After two months, they reached Austenburg, Ohio, where he built a log cabin without floor, door, furniture, or even chinking between the logs. Leaving his family there to plant a garden, Badger set off on a missionary journey that kept him away for three months. For the next three years, he occupied himself with such missionary journeys, then for four more years as a missionary to the Indians in the area of Sandusky. Over the next 16 years, Badger carried on a ministry to the settlers and Indians, supported in part by the people he served and in part by the Massachusetts Missionary Society. He received no regular support, however, until, at the age of 70, he was given a pension by the War Department for his service in the Revolution and settled into a small parish in Gustavus in Trumbull County, Ohio. Finally, at the age of 79 and in declining health, he asked to be allowed to retire. He is remembered still as the great pioneer of the Western Reserve.

A reading from *A Memoir of Joseph Badger*

There are false teachers now, who hold and preach a doctrine of falling from grace; for a final apostacy, after the renewing of the Holy Spirit; and perish in their sins. There are many who profess to be christians, who fall away from their profession, but not from grace. But to return to the subject. Let anyone read with an honest unprejudiced mind the 7th chapter of Romans from the 9th verse to the end; he will see that St. Paul did not teach the doctrine of perfectionism. There must be a great deal of twisting and perverting from the most obvious meaning of words and phrases to make scriptures referred to above, speak subversive of their true meaning. President Edwards, was one of the most able writers; none have gone before him; he wrote extensively on subjects of christian theology and searched them to the bottom. He did not pass over in silence perfectionism; but reprobates the doctrine in a few words. If there had been a denomination forming in his day, in order to establish that doctrine, and make themselves a great name, Mr. Edwards would not have passed it over, until he had made it appear that it was not a Bible doctrine. I have not seen Mahan's, nor Dr. Woods' books you refer to: my decayed strength and decline of life renders it impossible for me to attend to the controversies of the present day. The Bible satisfies me. You mentioned the difficulty laboring in your mind, about going to the communion table, with some in the church who walked disorderly. The object of the Lord's Supper is to bring into remembrance the dying love of Jesus Christ, for the salvation of a dying world. The intrusion of false brethren does not alter the nature and design of the ordinance; neither ought it to alter the views and feelings of others; each one will be responsible for his own exercises, and not for others. In such cases, it is not advisable for any member to leave the church on account of disorderly members. By such a step, they put themselves out of the way of assisting the church in her difficulties, and also expose themselves to censure. No one can be justified in leaving the church and her communion, until she becomes reputedly anti-christian. I know it is common for individual members, when there are offended by the irregular walk of one or more members of the church, to absent themselves from communion, but in so doing they violate covenant vows, and discourage others. The better way would be to resort to prayer more fervently, and to greater diligence in reproving, with christian meekness and love. Often set before the offender the character of a christian, drawn from the Bible; and the danger and ruin of the contrary — make the conscience uneasy if possible, but with plain truth and pleasant words. The Bible is the sword of the Spirit, it is the best weapon to contend with against error and immorality; but it requires much reading and prayer to use it skillfully. I pray earnestly the Lord will direct you in the way he has revealed in the Holy Oracles.

✪ June 16 _____

Stephen Theodore Badin

ROMAN CATHOLIC

July 17, 1768–April 21, 1853

"I was an American in feeling and conviction," said Stephen Badin toward the end of his life, "long before I became a naturalized citizen of this Republic. I would now die with a devotion next to that which I owe my God for the country of my choice." Badin gave freely of his life and labor to his adopted country. As a young man, he escaped to America as a refugee from the Terror in France. He had begun studying for the priesthood there until his seminary was closed by the revolutionary government. Many of the faculty immigrated to America. Badin came with them and helped to establish the first Roman Catholic seminary there. After another year and half of study, he became the first priest ordained in the United States.

When Bishop Carroll* assigned him to the new state of Kentucky, Badin demurred, suggesting that he was too young and still unfamiliar with the language. The bishop suggested they each keep a novena and pray about it. Nine days later neither man's mind had changed, but the bishop nonetheless sent Badin off to the wilderness. It took two months for him and an older priest to walk from Baltimore to Pittsburgh and several more weeks to float down the Ohio River to Maysville. They walked the last 60 or 70 miles to Lexington. There, on November 30, 1793, Stephen Badin said his first Mass in the state of Kentucky. The older priest who had accompanied him moved on the next spring to New Orleans, and for the next 14 years, Badin was left alone to provide for the spiritual needs of the scattered settlements that covered an area of more than 120 miles. He built new congregations and churches, and it was said that he never missed an appointment. Baden rode more an estimated 100,000 miles or more during his ministry in Kentucky. A second priest joined him in 1806, and in 1811 Benedict Joseph Flaget was appointed at Badin's suggestion as the first Bishop of Bardstown.

With the coming of more priests, tensions and misunderstandings arose. Badin had had his own way for a long time, so the adjustment to collegiality did not come easily. After 25 years, he returned to France and spent 10 years working in a parish there, but keeping the Kentucky mission always in his prayers and supporting it with money and various supplies. The frontier, however, was now in his blood, so in 1828, he returned to America to serve briefly in Michigan, then for seven years in a mission to the Pottawatamie Indians. Baden bought 524 acres of land in Indiana for the Indian mission but sold it to the bishop when the Indians moved. He stipulated that it be used for charitable or educational purposes hoping it might be used for an orphanage. Instead, it became the campus of Notre Dame University.

One biographer described Stephen Badin as a "cantankerous hurricane of vehemence and energy [who] gave himself to his evangelical work without stint or measure." Baden wrote two books about Roman Catholic principles, as well as an account of his mission work in Kentucky but his spirit is best reflected in a prayer he wrote when he was 80. It was printed in *The Advocate* on November 11, 1848, with a note saying that it was lately composed by Fr. Badin.

A reading from "Supplication to the Divine Attributes" by Stephen Badin

O Infinite Sanctity of God, purify and sanctify me!

O profound Wisdom of God, enlighten me!

O incomprehensible Immensity of God, possess me and make me ever attentive to Thy presence!

O wonderful Providence of God, protect and conduct me! O almighty Power of God, sustain me!

O Longanimity and Patience of God, bear with me!

O tender Mercy of God, have compassion on me!

O ineffable Goodness of God, attach me to Thee forever!

O Beauty of God, always ancient and always new, attract me!

O dreadful Justice of God, spare me!

O amiable Clemency of God, be propitious to me, a sinner!

O Lord God of Sciences, make me wise unto salvation!

O infallible Veracity of God, strengthen my faith!

O consoling Fidelity of God, increase my trust and hope in Thee!

O immense and eternal Charity of God, grant me grace to love Thee always, and above all created things, which are as nothing compared to Thee!

O admirable Immutability and Liberty of God, make me constant and faithful to my vows and good resolutions!

O Lord God of Virtues, fortify me!

O God, terrible in Thy Judgments, favor me with a perpetual fear of sin and of Thy wrath!

O God, Judge of the living and the dead, Whose piercing eye scrutinizes the reins and hearts of men, make me sensible of the errors of my life!

O God, Whose eternal Vengeance is unavoidable except through
  repentance, make me a true and sincere penitent!
O God, Whose name is Holy and Awful, grant that I may always
  pronounce it with reverence!
O God, Whose Will is righteous and supreme, make me resigned to it!
O stupendous Majesty of God, I offer Thee all homage, humbly
  prostrate at the foot of Thy imperial throne!
O sovereign Grandeur of God, make me humble and little in my own
  eyes!
O sublime Glory of God, be at all times exalted by men on earth, as
  Thou art by angels in heaven!
O blessed Eternity of God, prepare me, call me, receive me!
O benevolent Munificence of God, give me this day, and at the hour
  of death, the Heavenly Bread that gives life everlasting!
O God, Infinite in all Thy perfections, be all in all, be all in me, now
  and forever! Amen.

✸ *June 17*

Joshua Kocherthal

LUTHERAN

c. 1650–1719

Europe at the beginning of the 18th century was in chaos. Though the Thirty
Years War had officially ended, unofficial violence continued. Louis XIV authorized French troops to raid and plunder the Palatinate, an area along the
Rhine. Roman Catholic France continued to harass the Protestant Rhineland, hoping to reduce the entire region to a wasteland and drive out any
who survived the attacks. Because of this, many residents chose to emigrate to the New World. One such group was led by their pastor, Joshua
Kocherthal. The trip did not go smoothly. The party of 41 — 10 women, 10
men, and 21 children — sailed down the Rhine toward England. They were
very poor, since most of their possessions had been destroyed in raids. They
had no store of money, food, or other necessities. They could not get permits
to emigrate from the local authorities who were afraid such a move could
weaken leadership in the Palatine. But they persevered until they arrived in
England.

Once there, they asked to become naturalized British citizens or "denizens
of the kingdom" as the status was called. They explained that they were
willing workers who could aid the English in their colonization of the New
World. They needed help, but their loyalty and industriousness would soon
benefit their British sponsors. Kocherthal summarized their situation: "We
humbly take leave to represent that they are very necessitous and in the utmost want, not having at present anything to subsist themselves; that they

have been rendered to this by the ravages committed by the French in the Lower Palatinate, where they lost all they had." Lengthy negotiations followed, outlining the work they would do in the colonies and the best place to send them. Antigua and Jamaica were considered, as was New York. At length, a decision was made to send them up the Hudson to an unsettled area near the present city of Newburgh, New York. Kocherthal comforted and guided his flock throughout the difficult journey. They were at sea for nine weeks during the late fall of 1708. Two children were born on the ship, and the passengers suffered predictable diseases. Kocherthal preached and administered the sacraments regularly and baptized the babies. The party arrived in New York in December and spent the winter in the city.

As spring came on, they moved upriver to their new homes. Each member was granted 50 acres of land. Kocherthal was given 500 acres to build and support a church, and 250 for his family. But the beginning of a new community needed constant support from more established towns. Before the party left England, the authorities had appointed a governor, Francis Lovelace, but sadly, he had become ill aboard ship and died in May of 1709. Without his connections, the Palatinates could not get the provisions they needed. They sought help from the City Council of New York, who agreed to assist for the first year. There were constant shortages of needed supplies. Kocherthal finally decided to go back to see the Queen, who had granted them her assistance when they first came to England. He could not trust the New Yorkers to stand by the newcomers to the full extent necessary.

Kocherthal's plan was not simply to request more money or increased rations, but to create a new business venture that he felt sure would rival the cane and tobacco trade. The Rhineland was good country for vineyards, and the area in New York where his people settled had the right weather and soil for cultivating grapes. He had thought the matter through and listed items needed to begin the new enterprise. In England, the Board of Trade heard his request. This same organization had met with the Palatines when they first arrived in England. Unfortunately, they were unimpressed by Kocherthal's latest scheme. In the original agreement, the Germans were to be employed in the production of naval provisions like tar, pitch, and masts. The new colonies had these raw materials in abundance. But somehow, the settlers never got into this work.

Their colony could not hold together, and soon the Germans spread out across the Schoharie and Mohawk valleys. Kocherthal continued to minister to them. He became a traveling pastor, moving from settlement to settlement, preaching, marrying, baptizing, teaching doctrine, and dispensing advice as it was needed. He was sometimes accompanied by the Dutch Reformed pastor whose territory overlapped Kocherthal's. If one was unable to attend to a need, his colleague would make the visits and keep the records. Pious, studious, wise, and visionary, Kocherthal helped develop what we now call upstate New York. He was a leader to help his beleaguered fellow

Germans escape the cruelties they had borne in the Old World. In him, too, they found an eager advocate, a committed churchman, a knowledgeable diplomat, and a constant care-giver. Though his ministry in America life was not long, Joshua Kocherthal left his mark on the growing American nation, spreading the Lutheran presence on the new continent.

✪ *June 18*

Harriet Tubman

AFRICAN METHODIST

c. 1821–March 10, 1913

Harriet Tubman learned endurance from the hardships she suffered as a slave. Forced to work long hours and carry heavy burdens, beaten with a whip until she had lifelong scars, she acquired the stamina she would need as the most famous conductor on the Underground Railroad. She gave the Lord the credit, telling others that "Thanks to Him, on my underground railroad, I never run my train off the track and I never lost a single passenger."

When Tubman was 13, an overseer flung a two-pound weight at her and cracked her skull. Although she nearly died, her mother nursed her back to health and she began to pray for her master, "Oh, dear Lord, change that man's heart and make him a Christian." But she heard that he planned to send her south on a chain gang and she changed her prayer to say, "Lord, if you ain't never going to change that man's heart, kill him, Lord, so he won't do no more mischief." The master died suddenly, unreformed, and Harriet was devastated. "Oh, then it 'peared like I would give the world full of silver and gold, if I had it," she said, "to bring that poor soul back, I would give myself; I would give everything! But he was gone, I couldn't pray for him no more."

Unwilling to endure further torment, Tubman talked her two brothers into attempting to escape to the north. They turned back, fearing what would happen if they were captured, but Harriet pressed on. Finding herself free but lonely, she went back for her family and many others. Nineteen times she made the journey, leading over 300 slaves to freedom. They called her "the Moses of her people" and $40,000 was offered as a reward for her capture, "dead or alive."

Ten years before she died, Tubman gave her home and 25 acres of land to the African Methodist Episcopal Zion Church of Auburn, New York, where she was living, so that a home for the sick, the poor, and the homeless might be established. It irritated her that the black citizens of Auburn charged $100 for admission: "What's the good of a Home," she asked, "if a person who wants to get in has to have money?"

In her later years, she became a famous storyteller. Although she never learned to read, she had memorized many verses of the Bible and her deep voice was charged with the rhythms of the King James Version. She told how it had felt to reach the land of freedom:

> I looked at my hands, to see if I was the same person now I was free. There was such a glory over everything, the sun came like gold through the trees, and over the fields, and I felt like I was in heaven....
>
> I had crossed the line of which I had so long been dreaming. I was free; but there was no one to welcome me to the land of freedom, I was a stranger in a strange land, and my home after all was down in the old cabin quarter, with the old folks, and my brothers and sisters. But to this solemn resolution I came; I was free, and they should be free also; I would make a home for them in the North, and the Lord helping me, I would bring them all there. Oh, how I prayed then, lying all alone on the cold, damp ground; "Oh, dear Lord," I said, "I ain't got no friend but you. Come to my help, Lord, for I'm in trouble!"

She told what it had been like to care for wounded soldiers during the Civil War:

> I'd go to the hospital, I would, early every morning. I'd get a big chunk of ice, I would, and put it in a basin, and fill it with water; then I'd take a sponge and begin. First man I'd come to, I'd thrash away the flies, and they'd rise, they would, like bees round a hive. Then I'd begin to bathe the wounds, and by the time I'd bathed off three or four, the fire and heat would have melted the ice and made the water warm, and it would be as red as clear blood. Then I'd go and get more ice. I would, and by the time I got to the next ones, the flies would be round the first ones black and thick as ever.

She told what it had been like to accompany Union soldiers on the Combahee River raid, June 2, 1863, in which she helped Union forces carry over 700 slaves to freedom:

> I never saw such a sight; we laughed, and laughed, and laughed. Here you'd see a woman with a pail on her head, rice a-smoking in it just as she'd taken it from the fire, young one hanging on behind, one hand round her forehead to hold on, the other hand digging into the rice-pot, eating with all its might; hold of her dress two or three more; down her back a bag with a pig in it. One woman brought two pigs, a white one and a black one; we took them all on board; named the white pig Beauregard, and the black pig Jeff Davis. Sometimes the women would come with twins hanging around their necks; appears like I never saw so many twins in my life; bags on their shoulders, baskets on their heads, and young ones tagging behind, all loaded; pigs squealing, chickens screaming, young ones squalling.

Harriet Tubman said, "There was one of two things I had a right to: liberty, or death; if I could not have one, I would have the other; for no man should take me alive; I should fight for my liberty as long as my strength lasted, and when the time came for me to go, the Lord would let them take me."

✪ *June 19* ——————————————————————

Anthony Benezet

QUAKER

January 31, 1713–May 3, 1784

Anthony Benezet and John Woolman* were pioneers of the abolitionist movement. At first, they needed to persuade the Quakers of the importance of the issue. While Woolam's influence was felt most among fellow believers in America, Benezet's influence extended to England as well. Working together, Woolman and Benezet persuaded the Philadelphia Yearly Meeting of the Society of Friends to take an official position against the practice of buying and selling slaves, and, eventually, to disown Quakers who would not comply

Born in France, the child of French Huguenots, Anthony Benezet and his family emigrated to England when he was three, then to Philadelphia when he was 17. In his new home, Benezet set out to follow the family tradition as a merchant but, failing in that, turned to teaching. At the famous Friends' English School of Philadelphia (now the William Penn Charter School), he became an excellent teacher, though he disliked the disciplinary measures that were common in those days. In 1750, he began to instruct the children of slaves and free blacks in his home. In 1754, he left the Friends' School to begin the first public school in the country exclusively for girls. Although he was often hindered by poor health, he continued to teach slave children in his home until 1770, when he was able to create the Negro School at Philadelphia.

From 1770 on, his teaching career was supplemented by an active campaign against slavery. Working almost alone at first, Benezet strove to persuade the Society of Friends that slavery was incompatible with Christian faith. He also published a series of tracts on the subject, one of which, *Some Historical Account of Guinea,* was probably more influential in England than America. He corresponded with John Wesley and others who distributed his works and wrote similar essays themselves.

At a time when few white people, even among the abolitionists, knew black people well and questioned their ability to equal white people in education, Benezet could write from firsthand experience that he, as "teacher of a school...for many years, had opportunity of knowing the temper and genius of the Africans," and could "with truth and sincerity declare amongst them as great a variety of talents, equally capable of improvement, as amongst a like number of whites."

He died in 1781, greatly honored by the black community in Philadelphia and noted as "the single most prolific antislavery writer and the most influential advocate of the Negro's rights on either side of the Atlantic."

A reading from the introduction to *Some Historical Account of Guinea* by Anthony Benezet

The slavery of the Negroes having, of late, drawn the attention of many serious minded people; several tracts have been published setting forth its inconsistency with every christian and moral virtue, which it is hoped will have weight with the judicious; especially at a time when the liberties of mankind are become so much the subject of general attention. For the satisfaction of the serious enquirer who may not have the opportunity of seeing those tracts, and such others who are sincerely desirous that the iniquity of this practice may become effectually apparent, to those in whose power, it may be to put a stop to any farther progress therein; it is proposed, hereby, to republish the most material parts of said tracts; and in order to enable the reader to form a true judgment of this matter, which, tho' so very important, is generally disregarded, or so artfully misrepresented by those whose interest leads them to vindicate it, as to bias the opinions of people otherwise upright; some account will be here given of the different parts of Africa, from which the Negroes are brought to America; with an impartial relation from what motives the Europeans were first induced to undertake, and have since continued this iniquitous traffic. And here it will not be improper to premise, that tho' wars, arising from the common depravity of human nature, have happened, as well among the Negroes as other nations, and the weak sometimes been made captives to the strong; yet nothing appears, in the various relations of the intercourse and trade for a long time carried on by the Europeans on that coast, which would induce us to believe, that there is any real foundation for that argument, so commonly advanced in vindication of that trade, viz. "That the slavery of the Negroes took its rise from a desire, in the purchasers, to save the lives of such of them as were taken captives in war, who would otherwise have been sacrificed to the implacable revenge of their conquerors." A plea which when compared with the history of those times, will appear to be destitute of Truth; and to have been advanced, and urged, principally by such as were concerned in reaping the gain of this infamous traffic, as a palliation of that, against which their own reason and conscience must have raised fearful objections.

✸ *June 20* _____

Anne Bradstreet

CONGREGATIONAL

1612?–September 16, 1672

Poetry and Puritanism might seem an unlikely combination, but the stony New England soil produced a number of significant poets who expressed their faith and, indeed, their doubts — in rhyme and meter. The first Puritan poets, Anne Bradstreet and Edward Taylor, wrote privately, and their work was not widely published until the 20th century. Bradstreet's verse first appeared in England, printed by her brother without her consent.

Now Anne Bradstreet is generally recognized as the first American poet. She was born in England in comfortable circumstances but in a Puritan family and married at the age of 16. Two years later, tensions between the established church and dissenters were increasing, so the Bradstreets emigrated to Massachusetts. They sailed with Governor Winthrop and heard his shipboard sermon expounding his vision of "a city set on a hill" as the society the colonists were to create. Anne herself was filled with doubts both about her faith and her move to New England. Poetry provided a means to sort out her thoughts, even as she raised eight children and performed the onerous duties of a 17th-century housewife.

Although Bradstreet's early poems are often imitative of others, her later work shows more depth and a greater maturity of style. She wrote about the familiar experiences of life: her sickness, her husband's absence on business, the changing seasons, deaths of children and grandchildren, the fire in which her home, along with her writing, were destroyed, and the contrast between Old England and New. The "Contemplations" reveal her deepening understanding of God's love and are considered her strongest work. They . Although preoccupied with the tasks on which their survival depended, Puritans were nonetheless trained to see this world's passing events in the light of eternity. Such a perspective served Bradstreet in good stead as the fire consumed her home:

> And when I could no longer look,
> I blest his Name that gave and took...
>
> It was his own; it was not mine;
> Far be it that I should repine.

A similar perspective fills the "Contemplations":

> Art thou so full of glory, that no Eye
> Hath strength, they shining Rayes thus to behold?
> And is thy splendid Throne erect so high?
> As to approach it, can no earthly mould.
> How full of glory then must thy Creator be?
> Who gave this bright light luster unto thee:
> Admir'd, ador'd. for ever, be that Majesty.

A reading from Anne Bradstreet's meditations

Meditations When My Soul Hath Been Refreshed
with the Consolations Which the World Knowes Not

Lord, why should I doubt any more when thou hast given me such assured Pledges of thy Love? First, thou art my Creator, I thy creature; thou my master, I thy servant. But hence arises not my comfort: Thou art my Father, I thy child. Yee shall [be] my Sons and Daughters, saith the Lord Almighty. Christ is my Brother; I ascend unto my Father and your Father, unto my God and your God. But least this should not bee enough, thy maker is thy husband. Nay, more, I am a member of his Body; he, my head. Such Priviledges, had not the Word of Truth made them known, who or where is the man that durst in his heart have presumed to have thought it? So wonderfull are these thoughts that my spirit failes in me at the consideration thereof; and I am confounded to think that God, who hath done so much for me, should have so little from me. But this is my comfort, when I come into Heaven, I shall understand perfectly what he hath done for me, and then shall I bee able to praise him as I ought. Lord, haveing this hope, let me purefie myself as thou art Pure, and let me bee no more affraid of death, but even desire to bee dissolved, and bee with thee, which is best of All.

July 8th. 1656.

I had a sore fitt of fainting, which lasted 2 or 3 dayes, but not in that extremity which at first it took me, and so much the sorer it was to me because my dear husband was from home (who is my chiefest comforter on Earth); but my God, who never failed me, was not absent, but helped me, and gratiously manifested his Love to me, which I dare not passe by without Remembrance, that it may bee a support to me when I shall have occasion to read this hereafter, and to others that shall read it when I shall possesse that I now hope for, that so they may bee encouragd to trust in him who is the only Portion of his Servants. O Lord, let me never forgett thy Goodnes, nor question thy faithfullnes to me, for thou art my God: Thou hast said, and shall not I believe it?

Thou hast given me a pledge of that Inheritance thou hast promised to bestow upon me. O, never let Satan prevail against me, but strengthen my faith in Thee, 'till I shall attain the end of my hopes, even the Salvation of my Soul. Come, Lord Jesus; come quickly.

✪ *June 21*

Edward Joseph Flanagan

ROMAN CATHOLIC

July 13, 1886–May 15, 1948

To have a movie based on one's life starring Spencer Tracy may well have been the highest accolade America could bestow in the mid-20th century. *Father Flanagan of Boys Town* told a story already familiar to millions, because Edward Joseph Flanagan had a way of getting people's attention for the causes in which he believed. First among those causes was the plight of boys who had gotten into some sort of trouble, who were homeless or simply needed a friend. "There are no bad boys," said Flanagan. "There is only bad environment, bad training, bad example, bad thinking." Boys Town was created to prove it.

Edward Flanagan was born in Ireland and followed two older siblings to America at the age of 18. His path to the priesthood was circuitous. First he was sent to a college in Maryland, and then to Dunwoodie Seminary in New York. His career at Dunwoodie was cut short by tuberculosis, so he traveled west to regain his health, staying with a brother who was already a priest in Nebraska. When he applied to the Bishop in Nebraska for ordination, he was sent to study in Rome but again his health failed and he was sent back to Nebraska, where he could only find work as a bookkeeper in a meat-packing plant. Two years there restored his health sufficiently to think about ordination again. This time, Switzerland was recommended because its climate would be good for his lungs. In 1912, he was ordained at Innsbruck.

Back in Omaha and assigned to a parish, Edward Flanagan noticed the troubles of migrant workers who, because of drought, could find no crops to pick. They needed a place to stay, he decided, and with a dollar here and five dollars there, he bought a dilapidated hotel and created a refuge for homeless men. The young ones especially got his attention — boys with no home needed a place perhaps more than the men. He said, "I know what happens to youth if God is not a part of daily life." Somehow, in 1917, he found $90 to rent a large house in Omaha and take the first step toward creating Boys Town.

The institution Edward Flanagan created on that farm outside Omaha drew boys from all over the United States, of every race and faith. Although some had been arrested and imprisoned for serious crimes, there were no walls or gates. Instead, there were classrooms and sports fields and a swimming pool. Here, they could get the guidance and support they needed to start over and build new lives. At his death Fr. Flanagan was hailed as "the most beloved priest in the United States."

A reading from Father Flanagan's radio comments in the 1930s

I read in the paper the other day the story of a fifteen-year old boy under arrest for murder — killing a man during a holdup, the boy is being charged with first-degree murder. The controversy over the charge is waxing warm.

Some people insist that the boy should not be tried as a hardened, adult criminal. Others say the boy deserves the full penalty of the law.

Now, I am for a trial in this case — but I say — the right defendant is not being put on trial.... That boy did not come into the world predisposed to crime, not by any manner of means. When that boy was a babe, he was as much a potential good citizen, a leader, as any babe who ever grew up to be a good citizen and leader.

When, then, did he go wrong — where did the bad influence turn him to crime and to murder and to the prospect of facing the chair or life imprisonment at an age when most kids are still going to school or playing games? If we can answer that question perhaps we can decide who should be on trial.

Did the boy's parents give him that out of life which he should have — not merely some sort of existence, a little food, a few rags, a place to throw himself to sleep? Did they do anything about building up his ideals, about instilling self-respect, love or decency, friendship for his fellow man, belief in God?

And his teachers, did they pause in their duties to do more than set up an arithmetic assignment for him to do and to punish him and label him as incorrigible when he committed some minor wrong? Did they try to understand him and have time for sympathetic, human relationship?

Did the policeman walking his beat in the poor neighborhood in which little Johnny lived, make a friend of Johnny, teach him to respect the law, let him know that the police were his friends, or did he run the little boy off the streets and predict a bad end for him?

Was there proper, organized recreation provided for his neighborhood? Or did the street gangs run his end of town?

And what part did society play in making the boy feel he was part of a "good, healthy" society, that he and his fellows had a place in making a better world, that he was growing into a self-respecting, society-respecting man?

We must answer these questions before we put this youngster on trial — and I think I have the answers: The parents just didn't care much how the boy grew up; the teachers were too swamped with work and hundreds of other children to even think of helping this one boy; the cop on the beat thought his job was to keep the kids in fear of him; society went its willful unregarding way — holding to the theory that the threat of punishment should keep people good.

Now, who should be on trial? Certainly not this misguided youngster who can't differentiate between right and wrong."

✪ *June 22*

Paul Jones

EPISCOPALIAN

November 25, 1880–September 4, 1941

Paul Jones was the Bishop of Utah when the United States entered World War I. The people of Utah, which was a newly admitted state, were eager to show their patriotism and embarrassed by the fact that the local Episcopal bishop was an avowed pacifist who declared war un-Christian. When the Episcopal House of Bishops took up the question, they first supported Jones, but then backed away, requesting his resignation. Jones resigned as requested and spent the next ten years of his life as executive director of the Fellowship of Reconciliation, speaking and writing on behalf of peace. He spent his final years as college chaplain in Ohio but also ran for governor on the Socialist ticket. "Where I serve the church," he said when he resigned as Bishop of Utah, "is of small importance, so long as I can make my life count in the cause of Christ."

A statement made by Bishop Jones to the House of Bishops concerning his pacifist convictions

In the first place, let me say that I, as a loyal citizen, am whole-heartedly for this country of ours in which all my hopes and ideals and interests are bound up. I believe most sincerely that German brutality and aggression must be stopped, and I am willing, if need be, to give my life and what I possess, to bring that about. I want to see the extension of real democracy in the world, and am ready to help that cause to the utmost; and finally, I want to see a sound and lasting peace brought to the world as a close to the terrible convulsion in which the nations are involved.

But the question is that of method. It is not enough to say that the majority have decided on war as the only means of attaining those things and therefore we must all co-operate. I believe that it is not as easy as that, for the problem goes deeper.

If we are to reconcile men to God, to build up the brotherhood of the kingdom, preach love, forbearance and forgiveness, teach the ideals that are worth more than all else, rebuke evil, and stand for the good even unto death, then I do not see how it can be the duty of the church or its representatives to aid or encourage the way of war, which so obviously breaks down brotherhood, replaces love and forbearance by bitterness and wrath, sacrifices ideals to expediency, and takes the way of fear instead of that of faith. I believe that it is always the Church's duty to hold up before men the way of the cross; the one way our Lord has given us for overcoming the world....

Prayer is, I believe, the best test of the whole matter. If it is right and our honest duty to fight the war to a finish, then we should use the Church's great weapon of prayer to that end; but the most ardent Christian supporter of the war, though he may use general terms, revolts against praying that our every bullet may find its mark, or that our embargoes may bring starvation to every German home. We know that those things would bring the war to a speedy, triumphant close, but the Church cannot pray that way. And a purpose that you cannot pray for is a poor one for Christians to be engaged in....

I would appeal to my own Church on the larger ground of our claims to Catholicity. How can we ever say again that we are the Church for men of all nations and ages, if we so abandon the world ideal and become the willing instrument of a national government? We must stand for the whole truth of God for the winning of men and society to His allegiance, and it savors too much of Mohammedanism with its policy of carrying religion by the sword for me to try to twist a justification for this war and a sanctification of its prosecution out of the apparent righteousness of the purpose for which it was begun. If the method is wrong, I believe that the Church should have nothing to do with it; for back of the things that may possibly be achieved by the war, stands the terrible indictment that will be made that the Church abandoned the way of the cross that she was teaching....

As I believe, then, that the adoption of the way of Christ would be the best thing possible for this land we love and through it for all the world, I must, with all the wisdom God has given me, and with all the earnestness which I possess, try to reach men with that message in the terms which I can express it. If you believe that the church and the nation are better off without my message, I am quite ready to accede to your judgment, but as long as I represent the Church as I do now, it seems to me that I would be apostate to my high commission did I take any other course. And if I have misinterpreted the meaning of the Gospel, I shall be glad to be set right.

✪ *June 23*

Jacob Bower

BAPTIST

September 26, 1786–?

Born in Pennsylvania to German Baptist parents, Jacob Bower moved with his family to Kentucky, where he came under the influence of Universalist preachers. At 25, however, the fear of judgment was awakened in him by several events: a promise to his father, meeting people on their way to the execution of a murderer, and a series of earthquakes in the midwest. After long months of wrestling with his conscience, he came to believe that Christ died on the cross for him personally and he could, therefore, be forgiven.

As a result, he was flooded with peace and joy and two years later began a long career as a Baptist preacher.

In his long, hardworking life, Bower rode over 40,000 miles, bringing the gospel to others, organizing churches, and ordaining new ministers. About 1826, he moved to Illinois rather than continue to live in a slave state, and in 1836 he accepted appointment as a missionary of the Home Mission Society. Over the next sixteen years, Bower estimated that he traveled over 40,000 miles and preached nearly 3,000 sermons. In the same period of time he organized 14 churches and ordained 12 ministers.

Bower's autobiography, completed in 1857 at the request of the Illinois Baptist Pastoral Union, has been called "representative of the average frontier Baptist preacher." It reveals a man who was poorly educated but deeply devoted to his work At times he was unable to preach because of illness or injury. On one occasion, he had to borrow money at 20 percent to buy "bred & meat, and other articles of living." A collection was taken to help him pay his debts, but he writes that he was resolved to go on as he had always done: "preach all I could pay, or no pay."

A reading from the autobiography of Jacob Bower

This year 1841. Rode 2361 miles, preached 189 times. constituted 1 church 1842. Fryday January 28th Elder Moses Lemon & myself commenced a protracted meeting at Mt. Gilead church. Green co. In eight days 76 persons professed a hope in Christ and we baptized them. At this meeting I relinquished my pastoral labours with them, haveing served them as pastor for near ten years. And Eld. Moses Lemon accepted a call, and supplied them. I know not how long.

February 21st. I went to St. Louis and preached seven sermons for the African Baptist church. The church was much stired up — settled all their difficulties and disputes, and invited me to return and preach for them again. I went home — made arrangements — and returned again in March 24.

And preached about 30 sermons for them, and about 80 professed a hope in the Saviour, and Eld. J. B. Mechum Baptized them. This was a most interestin meeting. I enjoyed as much of the divine presence at this meeting as I have done at any time since I left Kentucky. On one occasion while I was preaching, with a most powerful fealing in my whole soul, and a state of deep fealing in the congregation. The old collerd pastor was siting in the pulpit behind me; frequently saying, hai-hai-hai. At length he sprung to his feet and exclaimed with a thundering voice. "I will not hold my peace when truth comes with such power, hai." And soon nearly all the professing part of the congregation were on their feet too, hollowing, Glory to God. Hallalujah. Hallalujah. Glory Hallalujah. Bless the Lord. praise the Lord. Hallalujah. AMEN. AMEN. &c. I think I may safely say, that I never saw a congregation of professing people enjoy themselves so well no where. They appeared to be a happy people indeed. At the close of this meeting, when I was about to lieve them [and to their praise I would say it] the collected more for me, than I have ever received from any congregation for the same time of service. The sewed bountifully — they also rept bountifully. After this large accession to their numbers, they pulled down their old house, and built a splendid Meeting House on the same lot of ground; and soon had it paid for.

The month of June I spent with the churches in S. Louis c.o. preaching almost every day. Then I took a tour in Ballard & McCracken counties in Kentucky, and returned home, July 21st, in this tour I travelled about 700 miles, and preached 63 sermons, and delivered one or two Temperance lectures.

The last of July & first of August, I attended a protracted meet at Ramneys creek M.H. pike county M-o. and preached 24 sermons, with their pastor Eld. A. D. Landrum there were between 30 & 40 professed a good hope in the saviour and were Baptized.

The 4th Lords day in August, I attended the Blue River Association, and was appointed by that body to corrispond with the Missouri Association held at Salem M.H. on Cold water in St. Louis county 2nd Saturday in september. The Board of that Association employed me to preach for the churches in that Association for three months. I spent a part of September and october November and a part of December, I preached almost every day — was wonderfully favoured with the divine presence — have sweet liberty in preaching all the time, and Baptized 21 happy converts — heard of the hopeful conversion of 210 persons. This was a year in which I enjoyed much help from the Lord. and I trust that much good was done. To God be all the Glory.

✪ *June 24*

Francis James Grimké

PRESBYTERIAN

November 4, 1850–October 11, 1937

The complicated interrelationships between black and white in the ante-bellum south are well illustrated in the story of Francis Grimké. Although his father was a slave-owner, his mother was a slave. Grimké's father died when he was five, and although he left instructions that the boy should be freed, his older half-brother attempted twice to return him to slavery. Grimké sought to avoid this fate by serving as a valet to a Confederate officer, but when the regiment returned to Charleston, the half-brother had him arrested and placed in a workhouse. When he became dangerously ill, he was rescued by his mother's family, but his half-brother again intervened and sold him to a Confederate officer. Later Angelina Grimké,* who had left the south to become an abolitionist leader, saw his name in a newspaper account and wrote to him. She discovered that he was her nephew and became a supporter of his work.

At the end of the war, a teacher who knew Francis Grimké sent him north to receive an education, and he graduated from Lincoln University, studied law briefly, and then went to Princeton Seminary to be educated for the Presbyterian ministry. After graduation, he was called to the Fifteenth Street Presbyterian Church in Washington, where he served, except for four years in Florida, until his death in 1937.

With ever stronger insistence over the years, Grimké advocated racial justice and equality. Where Booker T. Washington and others advocated a gradual approach, he was uncompromising in his condemnation of white racism, challenging white Americans from the president down to work more consistently for an end to injustice. Grimké was a leader in the formation of the National Association for the Advancement of Colored People and issued an annual report on the progress being made toward full equality. He worked to abolish lynching, establish equality of education, provide better health resources, and encourage blacks to exercise their right to vote. A trustee of Howard University, he nonetheless turned down its presidency on the grounds that he was a minister of the gospel, not an administrator. Again and again, Grimké called attention to what he called the "hydra-headed monster" of racism. "Why should there be churches made up of white Christians, and churches made up of colored Christians in the same community," he asked, "if they are all Christians . . . and if the same Holy Spirit dwells in their hearts?" "He knew no compromise," says Carter G. Woodson who edited his sermons, "and did not listen to any excuses." Sometimes alone in his positions, Grimké used his pulpit to remind the nation of ideals unfulfilled and the task yet to be done.

A passage from a sermon on prayer by Francis Grimké

There is nothing clearer in the Word of God than the fact that there is power in prayer, that, through it, effects may be produced, that definite results may be accomplished. This power may be made to play an important part in the great struggle through which we are passing in this country. It played a most important part, I believe, in the struggle out of bondage into freedom. We speak of the labors of Garrison and Sumner and Phillips, and the whole host of anti-slavery agitators; we speak of the Emancipation Proclamation, and of the clash of arms, as agents in bringing about the final result: and they were most important agents, — too much cannot be said in praise of all that was done, of the magnificent fight that was made by our soldiers in the face of rebel bullets, and by the reformers on the bloodless fields of thought and sentiment, — of the moral heroism and physical courage that were displayed. But the poor slave himself, I believe, had a part in that struggle second to none; it was the part which he played on his knees. In the rude cabins of the South, in lonely places, in the seclusion of the forest, in the darkness of the night the voice of the slave was heard in piteous appeals to heaven. When they were hoeing in the cotton field, when the crack of the overseer's whip was sounding in their ears, when their backs were smarting under the lash of the hard taskmaster, when they stood upon the auction block, when families were broken up, — the father going in one direction, the mother in another, and the children in still another, — there went up from their bleeding hearts the cry to heaven, "How long, O Lord, how long?" Every day, every night, almost every hour in the day, the cry of their bleeding hearts was poured into the ear of heaven. And I believe, as mighty as were the other influences, there was none more potential than this. Prayer was their only weapon at that time, and how mightily did they wield it. And we know with what result. The answer came at last, and they went out from under the yoke of bondage, free men and free women; went out, after wrestling earnestly in prayer with God for deliverance. The God, who said to Moses, "I have seen the affliction of My people in Egypt, and have heard their cry, and am come down to deliver them," came down in answer to the prayers that went up from the rude cabins of the South, from the cane-brakes and the rice fields, and the cotton patches, and brought deliverance. And this same power is available today. Lawless ruffians may keep the Negro away from the polls by shotguns; and by unrighteous laws and intimidation may shut him out of first-class cars, but there is no power by which all the combined forces of evil in the South can keep him from approaching the throne of grace. Here is one thing, thank God, that this Negro-hating spirit cannot do, — it cannot prevent him from praying.

✠ *June 25* _____

Demetrius A. Gallitzin

ROMAN CATHOLIC

December 22, 1770–May 6, 1840

A Russian Orthodox prince is not the kind of person you would expect to be a Roman Catholic missionary in the Allegheny Mountains of Pennsylvania, but Demetrius Augustin Gallitzin was called by the Holy Spirit to serve there. For many years, his father was a Russian ambassador to European courts. The envoy came to know Voltaire, Diderot, and other Enlightenment figures, and became alienated from the church of his childhood. Demetrius was brought up with no religious training until his mother rediscovered her faith and pleaded with her son to become a Christian. After studying various churches, he decided to become a Roman Catholic.

His father's advice directed him to the New World. Demetrius had belonged to the Austrian army when political changes left him without a career. The elder Gallitzin thought he might become an engineer in America. Demetrius arrived in Baltimore in 1792 and was so struck by the needs of the church there that he resolved to devote his life and fortune to its service. He was accepted as one of the first students in Bishop Carroll's new seminary and became the first priest to be trained and ordained in the United States.

After serving in the scattered parishes of the Baltimore area and eastern Pennsylvania, Gallitzin received a call to visit a dying woman in the Allegheny Mountains who wished to be received into the Church of Rome. Father Gallitzin ministered to her and conceived the idea of creating a Roman Catholic community there on the frontier. With the permission of Bishop Carroll, Gallitzin bought 400 acres of land with his own money, built a log church 44 feet long, and began serving the people within a radius of 100 miles. For many years, he was the only priest between the Susquehanna and Potomac rivers in the east and Lake Erie in the west, an area that now covers the better part of three dioceses. Using his own resources, he helped the settlers create sawmills, gristmills, tanneries, and other industries. It is estimated that he spent over $150,000 of his own money, and would have spent more had parts of it not been squandered by his sister's husband and confiscated by the Russian government. Never accepting a salary, Demetrius supported himself by starting a farm to meet his own needs and the cost of the various enterprises he established. It also provided help for those in need in his congregations.

Gallitzin's reputation for holiness was such that he was nominated twice for bishoprics, but declined them both, preferring to continue the work that he had begun.

A reading from a defense of the Roman Catholic Church written by Demetrius Gallitzin in response to an attack by a Protestant minister

We believe that, although created to the image of God, we may defile in ourselves that image, and thus remove ourselves from our original destination. We believe that we shall only then attain the object of our destination, if we try to keep up in ourselves that image undefiled; or in other words, if we try to be, and to become more and more similar to our Creator. . . . In short, sir, we believe that, in order to become saints in heaven, we must lead a holy life upon earth; and that all the external acts of religion which we practice, can never afford a substitute for a holy and virtuous life. We believe and teach from all the catholic pulpits in the world, that confidence in external acts of religion, unsupported and unaccompanied by the practice of virtue, is a most abominable presumption and real superstition.

To convince you, sir, that such is the real belief of catholics, I refer you to all the catholic catechisms, prayer-books, meditations, sermons; in short, to all the spiritual books of any kind that ever were published in any part of the catholic world. Being provided with books of that kind from almost every catholic country in Europe, I readily offer them to the inspection of any person curious to ascertain the doctrines of catholics on so important a subject, on which misrepresentation has created so many prejudices. What more common, indeed, than to bear it said that a catholic, or if you choose a papist, puts so much confidence in his priest, that it matters little to him whether he commits sin or not; for after having broken all the commandments of God, he thinks he has nothing to do but to confess his sins to the priest, and behold, from the gulph of perdition he leaps at once into paradise!

Catholics, then, among whom there are thousands and thousands of men eminent for their genius and learning, men of the most transcendent talents, celebrated in all the different branches of literature; and, what is much better, famed for the most genuine, the most heroic virtue: Catholics then, I say, are believed, or at least represented, to be most brutally stupid! But let us proceed....

Hush into silence your prejudices; listen and adore; humble yourself with St. Paul into the very dust; pray for light, and you shall see it brighter than the dazzling rays of the mid-day sun. Ask for grace to overcome human respect, and all carnal considerations, (those obstacles which Satan raises to prevent the conversion of millions) and that grace will be imparted to you. Seek the kingdom of Heaven, (by which, in scripture-language, is often meant the church of Christ — the catholic church as yet in a state of suffering, persecuted, ridiculed, tried like gold in the furnace; as yet, wandering through the dreary and frightful desert, but on its way to the land of promise) you will find — and with it you will enter the mansions of eternal peace. That you and all your hearers may obtain that blessing of blessings, is the sincere desire, and shall be the constant prayer, of

> Your humble and obedient servant,
> DEMETRIUS A. GALLITZIN

✪ *June 26*

Johan Campanious

LUTHERAN

August 15, 1601–September 17, 1683

Early Lutheran settlements around what is now Philadelphia, Pennsylvania, Trenton, New Jersey, and Wilmington, Delaware, provided many interactions between incoming Europeans and the native populations. Some whites saw these as opportunities for trade, others found indigenous tribes a kind of curiosity, still others regarded them as a threat. Sometimes, evangelization has had a sorry connection to cultural imperialism. Yet, often, it has affirmed the universal grace of God and proclaimed human equality. Johan Campanious was the latter kind of missionary. A native of Stockholm, he was educated at the University of Uppsala and ordained in 1633. He arrived in North America in February of 1643, where a small group of Swedes had gathered along the Delaware River around the area then known as Tinicum, an island. Campanious succeeded Reorus Torkillus, the previous minister to the colony. Governor Printz had established the civil administration on Tinicum, near the current site of Philadelphia. Campanious dedicated a Swedish church there in September of 1646.

But Campanious did not want to limit his evangelizing to European settlers. He therefore learned the Lenni-Lenape language of the local native tribes, and began a translation of Luther's Small Catechism, which he completed after his return to Sweden. Published in Stockholm in 1696, it was accompanied by two Indian-Swedish vocabularies, also compiled by him. These were the foundation for the books brought later by Jonas Auren, Eric Bjork, and Andrew Rodman, when they came to serve fledgling congregations in this area a few years later. Campanious's work among Indians anticipated John Eliot's ministry in New England.

At one point, in the mid-1600s, ten of the Indian Chiefs of the area were invited by the secular authorities to a conference at Tinicum. They were welcomed in the name of the Swedish Queen and given assurances of her favor. Prior agreements were reaffirmed and a request for continued peace and partnership were made. The governor provided both gifts and entertainment for his Indian guests who seemed to appreciate the welcome and were receptive to his offers of ongoing friendship. From Campanious we have an account of part of the gathering. According to him, one of their chiefs, named Naaman, gave an address in which "he rebuked the rest for having spoken evil of the Swedes, and done them an injury, hoping they would do so no more, for that the Swedes were very good people." The chief went on to note that "the Swedes and the Indians had been as one body and one heart, and that thenceforward they should be as one head, at the same time making a motion as if he were tying a strong knot; and then made this comparison, that as the calabash was round without any crack, so they should be a compact body without any fissure."

Faithfulness does not always ensure success. Campanious's efforts failed to build a Christian congregation among the Indians. They were apparently willing to hear of the Christian God and to appreciate the divine majesty and mercy Campanious preached. This initial openness induced him to learn their language and begin his translations, and, thanks to him, the Swedes can take the credit for the first missionary outreach to Indians in Pennsylvania.

It is also probable that the very first work translated into an Indian language in North America was Campanious's version of Luther's Catechism.

Here, in colonial Philadelphia, we see the continuation of a holy instinct at work. The Septuagint allowed Greek-speaking Jews to read their Scriptures without first learning Hebrew and Aramaic. Paul spoke to the Athenians as one of their own, making the gospel comprehensible to their philosophically attuned minds. Jerome's translation of the entire Bible, both Old and New Testaments, from their ancient tongues to the Latin vernacular of the Roman Empire, opened their glory to the western world. Luther's and Wycliffe's German and English translations put the stories of God's people into the hands and hearts of all the literate laity in their respective countries.

When Campanious preached the Good News to Native Americans in a language they could understand, he was standing in a long line of evangelists, preachers and prophets. Such work is rarely a one-way effort. Was the Swedish typesetter affected by producing books in Lenni Lenape? Were new images of the wideness of God's mercy imprinted upon the minds of Scandinavians as they heard about a project to translate one of their most cherished theological works into a vocabulary vastly unlike any they had ever heard? What seeds of peace were sown between colonialists and aboriginal peoples when one of the newcomers engaged in the difficult task of deciphering the speech of the host people, never previously learned or studied outside the community? And what new insights into our own well-known Scripture are revealed as ancient idioms are teased to fit a new syntax and grammar?

Campanious may not have been aware of all these issues as he worked. Yet in his willingness to reach beyond the familiar for the sake of bringing God's grace to a new culture, he embodied the spirit of Jesus in Matthew 28: "Go therefore, and teach all nations, baptizing them in the name of the Father, and of the Son, and of the Holy Spirit, teaching them to observe all that I have commanded you."

✪ *June 27*

Julia A. J. Foote

AFRICAN METHODIST EPISCOPAL ZION

1823–November 22, 1900

Even in upstate New York in the first part of the 19th century, former slaves faced prejudice and discrimination. Julia A. J. Foote's parents had won their freedom, but their daughter was barred from school in the city of Schenectady. By placing her as servant with a family in the countryside, they enabled her to gain two years of education, but then she had to come home and help raise the smaller children. When Julia was 15, her family moved to Albany and she joined an African Methodist Episcopal Church. She won "the sweet peace of sanctification" a year and a half later. When she married George

Foote two years later and moved to Boston, she joined the African Methodist Episcopal Zion Church, alienating her husband by holding meetings in her home. Some church members thought she should have access to the pulpit, but the pastor insisted it would be inappropriate. When Foote continued to hold home meetings, he barred her from the congregation. Appeals to higher church authorities were ignored or rejected.

Since she could not preach in her home town, Foote began traveling through upstate New York and found herself accepted in many Methodist pulpits. When her father died in 1849, she expanded her ministry, preaching in Ohio, Michigan, and even Canada. Throat problems forced her to stop public speaking for a number of years, but when a wave of revival swept the midwest in the early 1870s, she began preaching again. In 1894, Julia Foote became the first woman ordained a deacon in the AME Zion Church and, before she died, she became the second woman to be ordained an elder.

A reading from a sermon by Julia A. J. Foote

As we look at the professing Christians of today, the question arises. Are they not all conformed to the maxims and fashions of this world, even many of those who profess to have been sanctified? But they say the transforming and renewing here spoken of means, as it says, the mind, not the clothing. But, if the mind be renewed, it must affect the clothing. It is by the Word of God we are to be judged, not by our opinion of the Word; hence, to the law and the testimony. In a like manner the Word also says: "That women adorn themselves in modest apparel, with shamefacedness and sobriety, not with broidered hair, or gold, or pearls, or costly array, but which becometh a woman professing godliness, with good works" (1 Tim. 2:9, 10; 1 Pet. 3:3–5). I might quote many passages to the same effect, if I had time or room. Will you not hunt them up, and read carefully and prayerfully for yourselves?

Dear Christians, is not the low state of pure religion among all the churches the result of this worldly-mindedness? There is much outward show; and doth not this outward show portend the sore judgments of God to be executed upon the ministers and members? Malachi 2:7, says: "The priest's lips should keep knowledge," etc. But it is a lamentable fact that too many priests' lips speak vanity. Many profess to teach, but few are able to feed the lambs, while the sheep are dying for lack of nourishment and the true knowledge of salvation.

The priests' office being to stand between God and the people, they ought to know the mind of God toward his people — what the acceptable and perfect will of God is. Under the law, it was required that the priests should be without blemish — having the whole of the inward and outward man as complete, uniform and consistent as it was possible to be under that dispensation; thereby showing the great purity that is required by God in all those who approach near unto him. "Speak unto Aaron and his sons that they separate themselves" (Lev. 22:2), etc. The Lord here gives a charge to the priests, under a severe penalty, that in all their approaches they shall sanctify themselves. Thus God would teach his ministers and people that he is a holy God, and will be worshiped in the beauty of holiness by all those who come into his presence.

Many may fill his office in the church outwardly, and God may in much mercy draw nigh to the people when devoutly assembled to worship him; but, if the minister has not had previous recourse to the fountain which is opened for sin and uncleanness, and felt the sanctifying and renewing influences of the Holy Ghost, he will feel himself shut out from these divine communications. Oh, that God may baptize the ministry and church with the Holy Ghost and with fire.

By the baptism of fire the church must be purged from its dead forms and notions respecting the inbeing of sin in all believers till death. The Master said: "Now ye are clean through the word which I have spoken unto you; abide in me," etc. (John 15:3–4). Oh! blessed union. Christian, God wants to establish your heart unblamable in holiness. (1 Thess. 1:13; 4:7; Heb. 12:14; Rom. 6:19). Will you let him do it, by putting away all filthiness of the flesh as well as of the spirit? "Know ye not that ye are the temple of God?" etc. (1 Cor. 3:16, 17; 2 Cor. 6:16, 17). Thus we will continue to search and find what the will of God is concerning his children. 1 Thess. 4:3, 4. Bless God! we may all have that inward, instantaneous sanctification, whereby the root the inbeing of sin, is destroyed.

✪ *June 28*

Susan B. Anthony

QUAKER

February 15, 1820–March 13, 1906

The movement to gain equal rights for women possessed formidable champions. One of the most memorable was Susan B. Anthony. From her Quaker roots, she gained the resolve and perseverance to stay the course in a fight often painfully lacking in concrete signs of success. As for many Quakers, a life of service and activism for justice was, for her, an act of faith. Starting out as a teacher, Anthony became involved in the Temperance movement, which attempted to rescue families from the devastating toll of alcoholism. Originally seeking to protect women and children from abusive or neglectful husbands, it became a forerunner of other woman's rights movements. Anthony was one of the founders of the Woman's State Temperance Society of New York and gave her first speech for the organization in 1849. This experience, along with her friendship with Elizabeth Cady Stanton* and Amelia Bloomer,* whom she had met at an antislavery meeting in 1851, brought her into the cause of Women's Rights. Writing, speaking, traveling, and organizing for a change in laws regarding women's rights, especially suffrage, became her life's work. Never married, she dedicated herself wholeheartedly to the cause of women. In 1900, her influence opened the doors of the University of Rochester to female students.

Though respected now, during her lifetime Anthony was the subject of much scorn and attack. While she was an inspiration to her allies (relatively few in number in the 19th century), she was regarded with disdain by countless men and women of her day. Her image was caricatured in unflattering newspaper cartoons and commentary. Unswerving in her dedication to the movement for women's equality, Anthony raised the hackles of those people unable to see beyond the status quo of a world dominated by white men. Despite her image as an unswerving and formidable adversary, she had a softer side as well. Stanton said of her: "She has a broad and generous nature, and a depth of tenderness that few women possess."

In November of 1872, Anthony was arrested for trying to vote in the presidential election. The judge directed the jury to find Anthony guilty. She was convicted in January of 1874 and later submitted a two-page petition to the United States Congress requesting a remittance of her conviction. She, Stanton, and Matilda Joslyn Gage published the *History of Woman Suffrage* in four volumes between 1881 and 1902. She died before her work bore its fruit in the 19th Amendment.

A reading from Susan B. Anthony's "Constitutional Argument" of 1872

Friends and Fellow-Citizens: I stand before you under indictment for the alleged crime of having voted at the last presidential election, without having the lawful right to vote. It shall be my work this evening to prove to you that in so doing, I not only committed no crime, but instead simply exercised my citizen's right, guaranteed to me and all United States citizens by the National Constitution beyond the power of any State to deny.

Our democratic-republican government is based on the idea of the natural right of every individual member thereof to a voice and a vote in making and executing the laws. We assert the providence of government to be to secure the people in the enjoyment of their inalienable rights. We throw to the winds the old dogma that government can give rights. No one denies that before governments were organized each individual possessed the right to protect his own life, liberty and property. When 100 or 1,000,000 people enter into a free government, they do not barter away their natural rights; they simply pledge themselves to protect each other in the enjoyment of them through prescribed judicial and legislative tribunals. They agree to abandon the methods of brute force in the adjustment of their differences, and adopt those of civilization.

Nor can you find a word in any of the grand documents left us by the fathers that assumes for government the power to create or to confer rights. The Declaration of Independence, the United States Constitution, the constitutions of the several states and the organic laws of the territories, all alike propose to protect the people in the exercise of their God-given rights. Not one of them pretends to bestow rights.

"All men are created equal, and endowed by their Creator with certain inalienable rights. Among these are life, liberty, and the pursuit of happiness. That to secure these, governments are instituted among men, deriving their just powers from the consent of the governed."

Here is no shadow of government authority over rights, nor any exclusion of any from their full and equal enjoyment. Here is pronounced the right of all men, and "consequently," as the Quaker preacher said, "of all women," to a voice in the government.

✪ *June 29*

John Eliot

CONGREGATIONAL

July 31, 1604–May 21, 1690

The seal of the Commonwealth of Massachusetts shows a Native American and the words of St. Paul's vision of a man of Macedonia saying, "Come over and help us." Evangelizing the Indians was a stated purpose of all the early settlements in the western hemisphere, but the difficulty of establishing colonies in a harsh climate and the settlers' concern for their own welfare usually impeded this objective. John Eliot was among the few who took it seriously. He spent his life ministering to the native population of Massachusetts, and by the time of his death, there were thousands of "praying Indians."

Eliot was born in England. He seems to have graduated from Cambridge and been ordained in the established church. He came under Puritan influence and immigrated to the New World in 1631. Although offered opportunities within existing congregations, he seems from the first to have centered his attention on the native population. He spent three or four days at a time among them, working to learn the Algonquin language, but it was not until 1646 that he began to preach to them, first in English, then a year later, in their own language and began to make converts. By 1654, he produced a catechism in Algonquin, and, in 1659, the first Bible. English supporters sent over a trained printer, a printing press, and paper to enable Eliot to publish his New Testament in 1661 and a complete Bible in 1663.

It was the first Bible to be printed in the new world, a feat not to be repeated for another century. Eliot wrote and translated several other works
as well for the benefit of the converts and also contributed to an early book
of psalms for the use of the colonists.

To help the Indians preserve their culture, Eliot persuaded the Commonwealth to set aside land for their use. He established one town for them in
1651, another several years later, and eventually 14 such villages. Many,
however, were destroyed in King Phillip's War, a native chief's attempt to
drive out the European settlers. Eliot continued to preach to the Indians
until he could no longer travel and after that taught both Indian and African
American children who came to his house for lessons until his death in 1690.

A reading from John Eliot's *Brief Narrative of the Progress of the Gospel among the Indians of New England*

In as much as now we have ordained *Indian Officers* unto the Ministry
of the Gospel, it is needful to add a word or two of Apology: I find it
hopeless to expect *English* Officers in our *Indian* Churches; the work is full
of hardship, hard labor, and chargeable also, and the *Indians* not yet capable
to give considerable support and maintenance; and Men have bodies, and
must live of the Gospel: And what comes from England is liable to hazard
and uncertainties. On such grounds as these partly, but especially from the
secret wise governance of Jesus Christ, the Lord of the Harvest; there is no
appearance of hope for their souls feeding in that way: they must be trained
up to be able to live of themselves in the ways of the Gospel of Christ; and
through the riches of God's Grace and Love, so many of themselves who
are expert in the Scriptures, are able to teach each other: An *English* young
man raw in that language, coming to teach among our *Christian-Indians*,
would be much to their loss; there be of themselves such as be more able,
especially being advantaged that he speaketh his own language, and knoweth
their manners. Such *English* as shall hereafter teach them, must begin with a
People that begin to pray unto God, (and such opportunities we have many)
and then as they grow in knowledge, he will grow (if he be diligent) in ability
of speech to communicate the knowledge of Christ unto them. And seeing
they must have Teachers amongst themselves, they must also be taught to be
Teachers: for which cause I have begun to teach them the Art of Teaching,
and I find some of them very capable. And while I live, my purpose is, (by
the Grace of Christ assisting) to make it one of my chief cares and labors
to teach them some of the Liberal Arts and Sciences, and the way how to
analyze, and lay out into particulars both the Works and Word of God; and
how to communicate knowledge to others methodically and skillfully, and
especially the method of Divinity. There be sundry Ministers who live in an
opportunity of beginning with a People, and for time to come I shall cease

my importuning of others, and only work to persuade such unto the ministry of Jesus Christ, it being one part of our ministerial charge to preach to the world in the Name of Jesus, and from amongst them to gather subjects to his holy kingdom. The Bible, and the catechism drawn out of the Bible, are general helps to all parts and places about us and are the groundwork of community amongst all our Indian churches and Christians.

✪ *June 30*

Thomas Merton

ROMAN CATHOLIC

January 31, 1915–December 10, 1968

One of the best known spiritual writers in 20th-century America, Thomas Merton was born in France, traveled in Europe with his artist parents, and studied briefly at Cambridge University in England before coming to the United States and earning a master's degree from Columbia University. An agnostic as a young man, Merton was drawn gradually into the Christian faith and ultimately became a Roman Catholic. After teaching English and working in a Harlem settlement house, he entered the Trappist order in 1941. Although he had taken the Trappist vows of silence and solitude, Merton rocketed to fame with his best-selling autobiography, *The Seven Storey Mountain* (1948). His reputation grew as he published poetry, meditations, and social criticism.

Exploring more widely in the realm of spiritual experience, Merton became interested in oriental mysticism and its parallels with Western Christian tradition. He journeyed to Bangkok, Thailand, in 1968, to attend an interfaith conference of Buddhist and Christian monks. It was while he was attending that meeting, that Merton was accidentally electrocuted.

A reading from *The Asian Journal of Thomas Merton*

The discoveries of Freud and others in modern times have, of course, alerted us to the fact that there are certain imperatives of culture and of conscience which appear pure on the surface and are in fact bestial in their roots. The greatest inhumanities have been perpetrated in the name of "humanity," "civilization," "progress," "freedom," "my country," and of course "God." This reminds us that in the cultivation of an inner spiritual consciousness there is a perpetual danger of self-deception, narcissism, self-righteous evasion of truth. In other words, the standard temptation of religious and spiritually minded people is to cultivate an inner sense of rightness or of peace, and make this subjective feeling the final test of everything. As long as this feeling of rightness remains with them, they will do anything under the sun. But this inner feeling (as Auschwitz and the Eichmann case have shown) can coexist with the ultimate in human corruption.

The hazard of the spiritual quest is of course that its genuineness cannot be left to our own isolated subjective judgment alone. The fact that I am turned on doesn't prove anything whatever. (Nor does the fact that I am turned off.) We do not simply create our own lives on our own terms. Any attempt to do so is ultimately an affirmation of our individual self as ultimate and supreme. This is a self-idolatry which is diametrically opposed to Krishna consciousness or to any other authentic form of religious or metaphysical consciousness.

The *Gita* sees that the basic problem of man is his endemic refusal to live by a will other than his own. For in striving to live entirely by his own individual will, instead of becoming free, man is enslaved by forces even more exterior and more delusory than his own transient fancies. He projects himself out of the present into the future. He tries to make for himself a future that accords with his own fantasy, and thereby escape from a present reality which he does not fully accept. And yet, when he moves into the future he wanted to create for himself, it becomes a present that is once again repugnant to him. And yet this is what he had "made" for himself — it is his karma. In accepting the present in all its reality as something to be dealt with precisely as it is, man comes to grips at once with his karma and with a providential will which, ultimately, is more his own than what he currently experiences, on a superficial level, as "his own will." It is in surrendering a false and illusory liberty on the superficial level that man unites himself with the inner ground of reality and freedom in himself which is the will of God, of Krishna, of Providence, of Tao. These concepts do not all exactly coincide, but they have much in common. It is by remaining open to an infinite number of unexpected possibilities which transcend his own imagination and capacity to plan that man really fulfills his own need tor freedom. The Gita, like the Gospels, teaches us to live in awareness of an inner truth that exceeds the grasp of our thought and cannot be subject to our own control. In following mere appetite for power we are slaves of appetite. In obedience to that truth we are at last free.

Frances Perkins

EPISCOPALIAN

April 10, 1882–May 14, 1965

"I came to Washington," said Frances Perkins, "to work for God, FDR, and the millions of forgotten, plain common workingmen." It is a common thing for politicians to make generic references to God, but sometimes difficult to determine if they are sincere. It is rarer still to discover that they make regular retreats in a convent. During her time as Secretary of Labor in Franklin Roosevelt's administration, Perkins often visited the All Saints Convent in nearby Catonsville, Maryland. "I have discovered," she said, "the rule of silence is one of the many beautiful things of life." As the first woman to serve in a presidential cabinet and as one of Roosevelt's most important advisors in the effort to radically reform American labor practices, Perkins had need of a strong and clear faith. After leaving office, she gave a lecture at St. Thomas Church, New York, in which she gave an account of her belief which centered on the

> great and mighty principle which is presented to us in the Incarnation...the overwhelming principle of God and man made one; of God and man reconciled to each other, and through that, of course, of man's possibility to be reconciled to himself; that is, to comprehend himself, and to go on living with this Divine aid which comes to him through the Incarnation.

It is the reason for man's effort, it is the cause of man's effort to build a Christian society. This knowledge of the Incarnation, this fact of the Incarnation, gives to man the capacity with God to love his fellow creatures, and to work, and to cooperate with God for the establishment of a Christian order of society. A kind of holy society which we conceive to be the will of God who made man, and taking upon himself our nature, made possible for us to understand what are the almost limitless possibilities for the development of the nature of man.

Frances Perkins began her professional life as a teacher and student of economics and sociology. Frequently involved in service organizations, she became increasingly aware of the hardships of working people, immigrants, and especially of working women. In 1911, she was a witness to the Triangle Shirtwaist Factory Fire, watching the trapped young women pray, then leap off the window ledges into the streets below. Governor Al Smith of New York brought her into his administration and Franklin Roosevelt continued to give her important state positions. Against Smith's advice ("I have always thought that, as a rule, men will take advice from a woman, but it is hard for them to take orders from a woman") Roosevelt brought her into his cabinet, and she served the whole twelve years of his administration. She had seen firsthand:

the specter of unemployment — of starvation, of hunger, of the wandering boys, of the broken homes, of the families separated while somebody went out to look for work — (that) stalked everywhere. The unpaid rent, the eviction notices, the furniture and bedding on the sidewalk, the old lady weeping over it, the children crying, the father out looking for a truck to move their belongings himself to his sister's flat or some relative's already overcrowded tenement, or just sitting there bewilderedly waiting for some charity officer to come and move him somewhere. I saw goods stay on the sidewalk in front of the same house with the same children weeping on top of the blankets for 3 days before anybody came to relieve the situation!

Perkins understood that new laws were desperately needed and set out to persuade Roosevelt. At first, he thought of Social Security as "the dole" and opposed it. "Oh, we don't want the dole; not the dole!" Perkins said, "I had a great time to get him to quiet down and stop talking about the dole; to try to think about the realities."

Before I was appointed, I had a little conversation with Roosevelt in which I said perhaps he didn't want me to be the Secretary of Labor because if I were, I should want to do this, and this, and this. Among the things I wanted to do was find a way of getting unemployment insurance, old-age insurance, and health insurance. I remember he looked so startled, and he said, "Well, do you think it can be done?"

I said, "I don't know." He said, "Well, there are constitutional problems, aren't there?" "Yes, very severe constitutional problems," I said. "But what have we been elected for except to solve the constitutional problems? Lots of other problems have been solved by the people of the United States, and there is no reason why this one shouldn't be solved."

"Well," he said, "do you think you can do it?" "I don't know," I said, but I wanted to try. "I want to know if I have your authorization. I won't ask you to promise anything." He looked at me and nodded wisely. "All right," he said, "I will authorize you to try, and if you succeed, that's fine."

Perkins was the primary force behind the adoption of the Social Security system and considered it her most lasting and significant achievement. Historian Arthur Schlesinger, Jr., described her as: "Brisk and articulate . . . and intent on beating sense into the heads of those foolish people who resisted progress. She had pungency of character, a dry wit, an inner gaiety, an instinct for practicality, a profound vein of religious feeling, and a compulsion to instruct." Perkins asserted that there was a natural connection between religion and politics. It was, she said, "[the] duty of Christian people to take part in politics. I feel that more sincerely than I can possibly say. The withdrawal of Christian people of high purpose and nobility of mind and heart, the withdrawal of people like that from political life, has been a terrible loss not only to the world, but particularly to our form and organization of government and society."

✪ *July 2* _____

Barton W. Stone
CHRISTIAN CHURCH, DISCIPLES OF CHRIST
December 24, 1772–November 9, 1844

Most Christians who came to America came from countries where the church was united because it was the religion of the country, and dissent was not tolerated. Several of the early colonies began by establishing one denomination or another, but then the United States Constitution explicitly forbade this. Christians would need to discover their own unity — or not. Some of the founding fathers thought that the United States would invent a purified — and probably simplified — version of Christianity. But the first determined effort to find a way toward unity was launched by Barton Stone. The Bible and baptism would be the sole requirements of his followers. They would be simply "Disciples of Christ" or the "Christian Church."

Stone had joined the Presbyterians as a young man and been ordained but soon decided that there were too many discrepancies between the Westminster Confession and the Bible. When he enunciated his new faith at the Cane Ridge Revival of 1801, he was accused of Arminianism and severed from his presbytery. He formed his own presbytery hoping to be joined by other Presbyterians, but this did not happen to the degree he had hoped. Nonetheless, Stone's movement grew over the next 20 years until they began to come in contact in Kentucky with disciples of Alexander Campbell,* who had begun a similar movement in 1809 in Pennsylvania. Meetings at Christmas and New Year in 1831–1832 resulted in a formal merger between the two bodies.

There were, naturally, differences between them. Campbell's background was Baptist, and he had adopted a weekly observance of the Lord's Supper. Stone was nervous of the Campbellite's emphasis on the Holy Spirit. The Campbellites, on the other hand, were suspicious of Stone's views on the Trinity. Stone's followers thought the Campbellites were too emotional, and the Campbellites thought the Stoneites were too cerebral. Still, both were enough concerned unity among Christ's followers that they were willing to overlook the others' differences. Stone drew up the formal statement that there is but one thing necessary as far as faith is concerned and that is believing that Jesus is the Son of God, and there is but one act required for entrance into the Christian fellowship, and that is baptism by immersion. Although Campbell was younger than Stone and had begun his movement more recently, Stone was willing for the sake of unity to let Campbell have the preeminence. Their movement has remained a significant presence on the American scene — although, despite the hopes of its founders, it became only one more denomination among many divided churches.

A reading from *An Address to the Christian Churches in Kentucky, Tennessee, Ohio on Several Important Doctrines of Religion* by Barton Stone

The doctrines of the Bible, we believe, have never divided christians; but human opinions of those doctrines without charity, have always done the mischief. Man, poor, ignorant man, would dictate to the consciences of his fellows; and if they do not receive his *dogmas* or opinions, they are branded with the odious names of *heretic, infidel, &c*, and their name and sentiments are trumpeted abroad, distorted, misrepresented and blackened — for what purpose? Professedly to promote the interests of religion — but intentionally, I fear, with many, just to excite the popular clamor and indignation against them, and to raise themselves on their ruins. — Poor, weak man wishes the world to believe him infallible. If not, why so tenacious of untenable principles? Why not abandon them when proved to have no foundation in truth? Why not relinquish them when refuted with the clearest evidence? It must be, because he cannot brook the idea of being accounted a fallible man. Yet all, but the Pope of Rome, and a few of his degenerate sons in our day, disclaim infallibility, at least in words.

Believing mankind to be fallible creatures, we therefore feel a spirit of toleration and union for all those christians, who maintain the divinity of the Bible, and walk humbly in all the commandments and ordinances of the

Lord Jesus Christ, and who live by faith in his name, though they may hold opinions contrary to ours. We wish others to exercise the same spirit toward us, that we might be mutually edified — that the interests of our Redeemer's kingdom might be advanced — and that foul blot upon christianity, *the division of christians*, might be wiped away, and thus a powerful weapon against revelation be wrested from the hand of infidelity. We ardently desire to see this spirit universally prevail throughout the churches of the various denominations.

✪ *July 3*

John Quincy Adams
CONGREGATIONAL
July 11, 1767–February 23, 1848

One of the least well remembered of American Presidents, John Quincy Adams made a career in the foreign service before his election to the presidency, served one term, then somewhat to his surprise was sent back to Washington as a member of the House of Representatives, where he served for the rest of his life. He thought it would be an honor for an ex-president even to serve as a town selectman "if elevated thereto by the people."

As president, Adams had a bold vision and accomplished much. His first message to the Congress proposed a national program to unite the country through a network of highways and canals. And, anticipating Theodore Roosevelt by almost a century, he suggested conservation of the public domain, using funds from the sale of public lands. Before leaving office, Adams broke ground for the 185-mile C & O Canal. He urged also the establishment of a national university, the financing of scientific expeditions, and the erection of an observatory.

Yet his primary mark was made in his later years, as a member of Congress and as an advocate of civil rights. It had been customary to table without debate resolutions opposed to slavery. Adams opposed this "gag rule" and finally achieved its defeat. He presented petitions against slavery to the House and opposed admitting the Union of Texas as a slave state. The fact that a petition on this subject was signed by several women led one member of Congress to suggest that they should stick to their domestic duties. Adams, who, it should be noted, read his Bible daily, responded:

> Are women to have no opinions or actions on subjects relating to the general welfare? Where did the gentleman get this principle? Did he find it in the sacred history [the Bible] — in the language of Miriam the prophetess, in one of the noblest and most sublime songs of triumph that ever met the human eye or ear? Did the gentleman never hear of Deborah, to whom the children of Israel came up for judgment? Has he forgotten the deed of Jael, who slew the

dreaded enemy of her country? Has he forgotten Esther, who by her petition saved her people and her country?

One of Adams's final acts of service to his country was to defend the slaves who had rebelled and taken over the ship *Amistad*. They landed in Connecticut, where they were imprisoned and brought to trial. At 74, Adams argued the case before the Supreme Court. He told the justices that the idea that free men should be returned to slavery was "monstrous." The court agreed and returned the men to Africa.

A reading from a letter of John Quincy Adams to his son

ST. PETERSBURG, Sept., 1811.

My Dear Son:

In your letter of the 18th January to your mother, you mentioned that you read to your aunt a chapter in the Bible or a section of Doddridge's Annotations every evening. This information gave me real pleasure; for so great is my veneration for the Bible, and so strong my belief, that when duly read and meditated on, it is of all books in the world, that which contributes most to make men good, wise, and happy — that the earlier my children begin to read it, the more steadily they pursue the practice of reading it throughout their lives, the more lively and confident will be my hopes that they will prove useful citizens to their country, respectable members of society, and a real blessing to their parents. But I hope you have now arrived at an age to understand that reading, even in the Bible, is a thing in itself, neither good nor bad, but that all the good which can be drawn from it, is by the use and improvement of what you have read, with the help of your own reflection. Young people sometimes boast of how many books, and how much they have read; when, instead of boasting, they ought to be ashamed of having wasted so much time, to so little profit....

Let us, then, search the Scriptures; and, in order to pursue our inquiries with methodical order, let us consider the various sources of information, that we may draw from this study. The Bible contains the revelation of the will of God. It contains the history of the creation of the world, and of mankind; and afterward the history of one peculiar nation, certainly the most extraordinary nation that has ever appeared upon the earth. It contains a system of religion, and of morality, which we may examine upon its own merits, independent of the sanction it receives from being the Word of God; and it contains a numerous collection of books, written at different ages of the world, by different authors, which we may survey as curious monuments of antiquity, and as literary compositions. In what light so ever we regard it, whether with reference to revelation, to literature, to history, or to morality — it is an invaluable and inexhaustible mine of knowledge and virtue.

I shall number separately those letters that I mean to write you upon the subject of the Bible, and as, after they are finished, I shall perhaps ask you to read them all together, or to look over them again myself, you must keep them on separate file. I wish that hereafter they may be useful to your brothers and sisters, as well as to you. As you will receive them as a token of affection for you, during my absence, I pray that they may be worthy to read by them all with benefit to themselves, if it please God, that they should live to be able to understand them.

From your affectionate Father,
JOHN QUINCY ADAMS

✪ *July 4*

Rosa Parks

AFRICAN METHODIST EPISCOPAL

February 4, 1913–October 24, 2005

The story of how Rosa Parks refused to give up her seat one day on a bus in Montgomery, Alabama, has become one of the most emblematic moments in the history of modern American life. She herself has often said that she did it because she was "just tired." But she was not too exhausted to act on her quiet, dignified principles. Her resistance that day had been shaped by a lifetime of values inculcated from church, school, family, and friends.

As a young girl getting ready to go to church, Rosa Louise McCauley could not have imagined how the lessons she was learning and her developing strength would help turn a culture upside down. Yet the Word of God found a willing heart in the youthful McCauley — later known to the world as Rosa Parks. In her autobiography, appropriately titled *Quiet Strength,* she wrote, "Every day before supper and before we went to services on Sundays, my grandmother would read the Bible to me, and my grandfather would pray. We even had devotions before going to pick cotton in the fields. Prayer and the Bible became a part of my everyday thoughts and beliefs. I learned to put my trust in God and to seek Him as my strength." In the same book she said: "I'd like for [readers] to know that I had a very spiritual background and that I believe in church and my faith and that has helped to give me the strength and courage to live as I did."

Both her sense of justice and her hopefulness were gleaned from her spiritual grounding and gave Parks a reason to seek the best for herself, for her neighbors, and for her nation. Her wise mother, Leona, told her daughter to "take advantage of the opportunities, no matter how few they were." So when, at 11, Rosa had an opportunity to get a better education at the Montgomery Industrial School for Girls, she took it. This private school had been established by northerners to give African American girls in the South a boost toward success. The school constantly stressed the intrinsic value of each student. In addition to her faith, Rosa was strengthened by the guidance of her teachers and mentors. Nevertheless, positive influences lived side-by-side with the fear that she felt hearing the Ku Klux Klan ride past her home at night. The biblical vision of a God who loved all people was juxtaposed with a society in which there were daily humiliations and dangers. All these factors shaped her for a momentous role in United States racial history.

After she married, Parks and her husband became members of the local National Association for the Advancement of Colored People (NAACP) in Montgomery. There she experienced a community united in the struggle for racial equality. She spent part of her time working at Maxwell Air Force Base, where segregation was not allowed. She had ridden unsegregated buses on the base, which increased her frustration with the public buses of her town. Certain court rulings had begun to erode racist policies, but they only struck down limited laws, such as those applying to interstate transportation. Local buses remained exempt from change.

On December 1, 1955, Parks boarded a public bus after a day's work, moved automatically to the "colored" section in the back and took her seat. Soon the "white" section filled up. At the next stop, some more white passengers climbed aboard. Though in such cases it was not uncommon for them to stand, on this day the driver ordered that they be given seats in the "colored" section. Three black passengers rose to move further back, but Parks was tired. Later, she claimed her real motivation was that she was tired of being mistreated. She refused to stand. When the driver threatened her with arrest, she simply told him to go ahead. Her faith and self-confidence, her sense of support among her antisegregationist friends, along with her knowledge of other similar cases led her to stand — no, to sit — firm and let history take its course.

Rosa Parks was arrested, but the forces which intended to demean her were themselves brought low. She was well known in her community, held in high esteem, and her supporters were not about to let her case simply fall through the cracks. A young preacher, Martin Luther King, Jr.,* came to her aid and so did her NAACP associates. A boycott was organized against the public buses of Montgomery that lasted 382 days. This time, the Supreme Court delivered not some narrowly interpreted local ruling, but declared segregated buses unconstitutional and, indeed, the whole range of "Jim Crow" regulations that kept segregation in place. "Separate but equal" had been a euphemism for blatant white privilege and brutal racial injustice. Once questioned, it could not continue.

By her willingness to take on the worst that the legal system and cultural powers could mete out, Parks struck a lethal blow to a long tradition of racist mistreatment of people of color in America. Though she never had the satisfaction of seeing full equality and bonds of mutual affection and respect between people of all ethnic backgrounds become a reality, she remained a staunch defender of that vision, and a faithful servant of the God of all people.

Though she became famous, Rosa Parks remained humble. She always recognized her debt to those who taught her, stood by her, and supported her through the worst and best of times. When she was awarded the Presidential Medal of Freedom in 1996 and the Congressional Gold Medal in 1999, she said that the courage of countless others who struggled to end segregation had finally been recognized officially. On her death, Rosa Parks became the first woman to lie in state in our nation's capital. From simple Sunday School student to national, even international heroine, Rosa Parks's life remains a sign of hope.

✪ *July 5*

Boniface Wimmer

ROMAN CATHOLIC

June 14, 1809–December 8, 1887

The thriving state of Christian churches in the United States is often attributed to the variety of denominations competing for members. Evangelistic efforts directed at particular ethnic traditions have added a rich variety of influences to the smorgasbord of American Christianity, so that efforts designed for one group end by providing resources for unintended beneficiaries. Boniface Wimmer, for example, established Benedictine life in the United States because of a particular concern for German immigrants although his work eventually expanded to include other groups. Born in Bavaria, Wimmer became a priest at the age 21 and entered the Benedictine order, only recently restored in that country. Hearing stories from returning missionaries about the needs of the German settlers in the New World, he became determined to plant a Benedictine community for their benefit. In 1846, he embarked with a group of 20 students and candidates for the order, explaining to those who went with him that life in their new home would be filled with difficulties and sacrifices, and they should not come unless they were willing to carry the cross of absolute self-sacrifice and make the will and the glory of God their sole motive in the undertaking.

Wimmer was given some land about 40 miles east of Pittsburgh, so his group settled there to establish St. Vincent's Abbey. It still stands in that location, along with a college and seminary. The Benedictine order has traditionally sought rural areas for its monasteries so the monks could support themselves with some kind of labor while providing a center of prayer and education for the neighborhood. Among those who had come with him from Germany were a tailor, a shoemaker, a brewer, and a blacksmith, trades that helped provide for the monks and useful to the farmers among whom they lived. American bishops sent out appeals for German-speaking priests to take charge of parishes in German communities and Wimmer was often able to respond with members of his community. Over the next 40 years, monks from St. Vincent's established abbeys in Kansas, North Carolina, Alabama, Colorado, Illinois, and Minnesota, always preferring rural locations where traditional Benedictine life could thrive. Smaller missions and parishes grew up in 25 states, so that by 1885, the work Wimmer established ministered to 100,000 people.

Wimmer has been described as a man of "attractive manner, fine business ability . . . large scholarship" and "generous to a fault." As such people often are, he was also strong-willed and did not easily yield to authority. His relationship with the first Benedictine nuns was thorny; he diverted funds intended for them to other projects and replaced an abbess who had a mind of her own. He did, nonetheless, establish work that has endured, and he has been called the preeminent Roman Catholic missionary in 19th-century America.

A reading from Boniface Wimmer's 1845 proposal to establish the Benedictine order in America

When we consider North America as it is today, we can see at a glance that there is no other country in the world which offers greater opportunities for the establishment and spread of the Benedictine Order, no country that is so much like our old Europe was. There are found immense forests, large uncultivated tracts of land in the interior, most fertile lands which command but a nominal price; often for miles and miles no village is to be seen, not to speak of cities. In country districts no schools, no churches are to be found. The German colonists are scattered, uncultured, ignorant, hundreds of miles away from the nearest German-speaking priest, for, practically, they can make their homes where they please. There are no good books, no Catholic papers, no holy pictures. The destitute and unfortunate have no one to offer them a hospitable roof, the orphans naturally become the victims of vice and irreligion — in a word, the conditions in America today are like those of Europe 1000 years ago, when the Benedictine Order attained its fullest development and effectiveness by its wonderful adaptability and stability. . . .

It is said that the young American is not inclined to devote himself to the sacred ministry because it is so easy for him to secure a wife and home; that the American has nothing in view but to heap up the riches of this world; that fathers need their sons on the farms or in the workshops and, therefore, do not care to see them study. But, let me ask, is it not the same here in Europe? Are the rich always pleased when their sons study for the priesthood? Are all Germans in America well-to-do or rich? Are they not as a rule the very poorest and to a certain extent the menials of the rest? Moreover, is the first thought of a boy directed to matrimony? Is it any wonder that he should show no inclination for the priesthood when he sees a priest scarcely once a year; when divine services are held in churches which resemble hovels rather than churches, without pomp and ceremony, when the priest has to divest himself of his priestly dignity, often travels on horseback, in disguise, looking more like a drummer than a priest, when the boy sees nothing in the life of a priest but sacrifice, labor and fatigue?

But all this would become quite different if boys could come in daily contact with priests, if they received instructions from them, if the priest could appear to advantage, better dressed and better housed than the ordinary settler, if young men could learn from observation to realize and appreciate the advantages of a community life, if they could learn to understand that while the life of a priest requires self-denial and sacrifice, his hopes of a great reward are also well grounded. Yes, I do not doubt but that hundreds, especially of the lower classes, would prefer to spend their lives in well regulated monasteries in suitable and reasonable occupations, than to gain a meager livelihood by incessant hard labor in forest regions.

✸ *July 6*

Francis Scott Key

EPISCOPALIAN

August 1, 1779–January 11, 1843

Even if he had not written the "Star Spangled Banner," Francis Scott Key's name would deserve to be known. Key was a successful lawyer who argued cases before the Supreme Court, and a man of deep faith and strong principle. He believed that anyone who had been accused was entitled to a good lawyer to defend him. When former vice president Aaron Burr was charged with treason because some suspected he was trying to create a new nation in the west, many lawyers refused to get involved, but Key took the case — and won. He put his knowledge of the law to work for slaves attempting to gain their freedom, offering them pro bono advice because he felt that poverty should be no bar to legal services.

Key came from a wealthy family and owned slaves. He believed the institution of slavery was wrong, but he thought the solution would be to establish colonies in Africa for them. He served on a committee working toward that goal and did what he could to arouse support for the cause. A man of faith, he seriously considered ordination and served the church in various lay capacities. He often spoke of the importance of faith for individuals and for society.

During the War of 1812, Key became involved in the matter that was to make him famous. A doctor had been taken prisoner by the British, and his friends approached Key as a lawyer who might be able to negotiate his release. With another man experienced in such negotiations, Key went out in a small boat to meet the British Navy. The officers were cordial and agreed to release the doctor — but not until they had shelled Fort McHenry in the Baltimore harbor. Since Key and his companion had overheard some of the plans, the British held them overnight as well. Through the dark, Key watched the British rockets light up the night sky and caught an occasional glimpse of the flag still flying over the fort. At last the shelling ceased, but in the darkness it was impossible to tell whether the fort had surrendered. Daylight revealed the flag still flying. On the return journey with his colleague and the doctor, Key began to write the words that have become so familiar to us. Almost immediately, the poem was printed and distributed on a handbill. Key called it "The Defence of Fort McHenry," but everyone else called it "The Star-Spangled Banner."

A reading from a speech by Francis Scott Key delivered at Bristol College, July 23, 1834, before the Philologian Society

The influence of religion upon mankind has been seen and felt in all ages, and the nature of man and his situation in this life show that it can never cease to be one of the most powerful agents in the formation of human character and in the regulation of human conduct. The Almighty has placed his intelligent creatures in intimate and necessary association and dependence upon each other. They thus acquire, as it was intended they should, often insensibly, most of these principles, habits, and feelings which govern them through life. The intercourse producing these great results is mental. The impressions are communicated through the understanding and the affections. Upon this great mass of feeling and thinking beings it is plain that ignorance can produce little effect, and that the influence of men upon each other will be, in a greater measure, proportioned to their mental improvement. No man perhaps is so weak as not to be placed in circumstances which enable him to operate upon a few within his reach; but high literary attainments claim and receive the attention of all. Men thus fitted to human intercourse have a ready passport into every social community and into every habitation of civilized man. They propose and discuss every subject connected with the interest of human beings; and they speak upon these subjects to their fellow men of their own age and to the remotest generations. The effects thus produced are impossible to estimate. How often has the perusal of a single book awakened the attention of its reader, roused his energies to new action, turned his thoughts into a new channel, changed the whole course and habits of his life, and enabled him in his turn to bring the force of intellectual power to bear upon the world, and communicate to hundreds of thousands like himself, the impulses he has thus received. The good and the evil that men do live after them. There are, perhaps, few persons now present, who have not received deep and abiding impressions, forming prominent points in their character and daily influencing their conduct, from the works of men who have been for years and even centuries in their graves. And this great operation of mind upon mind will go on from generation to generation. Some of its great results we see in the wonderful improvements around us, of which the world a few years since was ignorant and incredulous. What they are to be, is known only to Him who has given this power to His creatures to be improved for his glory. Is such a power as this to be denied to the Christian? May he not avail himself of such an aid in the course he is to run? Is it inconsistent with his character to wield such a weapon in his warfare? A mistaken opinion upon this subject certainly once prevailed in the world. Some well-meaning Christians may even yet doubt the advantages of a literary education and we have reason to fear that there are many who, though they may not object to it, are yet indifferent to the reception of such an ally to the Christian cause. It may be useful therefore to examine this question, and determine whether the friends of religion shall avail themselves of one of the most powerful means of influencing the world, or leave it to its adversaries.

✷ *July 7*

Sarah Grimké

QUAKER

November 26, 1792–December 23, 1873

A South Carolina plantation seems an unlikely setting for the childhood of a woman considered one of the most dangerous abolitionists in the country. Sarah Grimké was raised in luxury with slaves attending to her needs. When she was five years old and saw a slave being whipped, she tried to board a steamboat to travel to a place where such things didn't happen. As a teenager she waited till after dark, then taught her maid to read by firelight. When her parents learned that she meant to go to college and become a judge like her father, she was forbidden to use her brother's books.

When Sarah was 26, she was finally able to travel north, accompanying her father who sought medical care in Philadelphia. There she made contact with the Society of Friends and became a Quaker. Three years after her father's death, she moved to Philadelphia, returning to Charleston only to convert her sister, Angelina, to the Quaker faith and bring her north also. The slaves who were their portion of the estate were set free.

Yet even the Quakers could not contain Sarah Grimké's free spirit. When the great abolitionist, William Lloyd Garrison,* published a letter Angelina had written him (without her permission), they rebuked her. Given a choice between maintaining good standing in the Quaker community or affirming the letter and working actively against slavery, Sarah and Angelina chose the latter course. Since Quaker opposition was based on the notion that women should not speak in public, the confrontation prompted both Grimké sisters to take up the cause of women's rights as well. In spite of their falling out with the Quakers, both sisters based their opposition to slavery and their support for women's rights on firm scriptural basis. Sarah grounded her writing on a knowledge of the Hebrew Scriptures as well as the English. Her analysis of the Hebrew led her to believe that God's "curse" on Eve was in fact a prophecy.

When Sarah was nearly 80, she and her sister attempted to vote to test the scope of the 15th amendment to the constitution which many feminists believed applied to themselves as well as former slaves. Although she lived to see former slaves exercising the franchise, she was still unable to exercise it herself.

A reading from a letter of Sarah Grimké

God designed woman to be a help meet for man in every good and perfect work. She was part of himself, as if Jehovah designed to make the oneness and identity of man and woman perfect and complete; and when the glorious work of their creation was finished, "the morning stars sang together, and all the sons of God shouted for joy.

This blissful condition was not long enjoyed by our first parents. Eve, it would seem from history, was wandering alone amid the bowers of Paradise, when the serpent met with her. From her reply to Satan, it is evident that the command not to eat "of the tree that is in the midst of the garden," was given to both, although the term man was used when the prohibition was issued by God. "And the woman said unto the serpent, we may eat of the fruit of the trees of the garden, but of the fruit of the tree which is in the midst of the garden, God hath said, Ye shall not eat of it, neither shall Ye touch it, lest Ye die." Here the woman was exposed to temptation from a being with whom she was unacquainted. She had been accustomed to associate with her beloved partner, and to hold communion with God and with angels; but of satanic intelligence, she was in all probability entirely ignorant. Through the subtlety of the serpent, she was beguiled. And "when she saw that the tree was good for food, and that it was pleasant to the eyes, and a tree to be desired to make one wise, she took of the fruit thereof and did eat."

We next find Adam involved in the same sin, not through the instrumentality of a super-natural agent, but through that of his equal, a being whom he must have known was liable to transgress the divine command, because he must have felt that he was himself a free agent, and that he was restrained from disobedience only by the exercise of faith and love towards his Creator. Had Adam tenderly reproved his wife, and endeavored to lead her to repentance instead of sharing in her guilt, I should be much more ready to accord to man that superiority which he claims; but as the facts stand disclosed by the sacred historian, it appears to men that to say the least, there was as much weakness exhibited by Adam as by Eve. They both fell from innocence, and consequently from happiness, but not from equality.

Let us next examine the conduct of this fallen pair, when Jehovah interrogated them respecting their fault. They both frankly confessed their guilt. "The man said, the woman who thou gavest to be with me, she gave me of the tree and I did eat. And the woman said, the serpent beguiled me and I did eat." And the Lord God said unto the woman, "Thou wilt be subject unto thy husband, and he will rule over thee." That this did not allude to the subjection of woman to man is manifest, because the same mode of expression is used in speaking to Cain of Abel. The truth is that the curse, as it is termed, which was pronounced by Jehovah upon woman, is a simple prophecy. The Hebrew, like the French language, uses the same word to express shall and will. Our translators having been accustomed to exercise their lordship over their wives, and seeing only through the medium of a perverted judgment, very naturally, though I think not very learnedly or very kindly, translated it shall instead of will, and thus converted a prediction to Eve into a command to Adam; for observe, it is addressed to the woman and not to the man. the consequence of the fall was an immediate struggle for dominion, and Jehovah foretold which would gain the ascendancy; but as he created them in his image, as that image manifestly was not lost by the fall, because it is urged in Gen 9:6, as an argument why the life of man should not be taken by his fellow man, there is no reason to suppose that sin produced any distinction between them as moral, intellectual, and responsible beings. Man might just as well have endeavored by hard labor to fulfill the prophecy, thorns and thistles will the earth bring forth to thee, as to pretend to accomplish the other, "he will rule over thee," by asserting dominion over his wife.

Here then I plant myself. God created us equal; — he created us free agents; — he is our Lawgiver, our King, and our Judge, and to him alone is woman bound to be in subjection, and to him alone is she accountable for the use of those talents with which Her Heavenly Father has entrusted her. One is her Master even Christ.

✪ *July 8* _____

John Black

PRESBYTERIAN

October 2, 1768–October 25, 1849

Many characteristic divisions among churches in America were imported from Europe and have persisted in spite of reformers holding up visions of unity. How can common ground be established when so many issues divide us? Few theologians have explored this subject more carefully or charitably than John Black. A native of Ireland who was educated at the University of Glasgow, he fled his native country "as an exile for liberty" at the time of the Irish insurrection in 1797. Licensed to serve the Reformed Presbyterian Church, he was assigned to a ministry in western Pennsylvania and gathered a congregation that eventually included all the societies of Covenanters west of the Allegheny Mountains. When this congregation was divided in 1806, Black became pastor of a parish in the Pittsburgh area. In 1820, he was elected professor of Latin and Greek in the Western University of Pennsylvania, but he resigned that position in 1832 and later served briefly as president of Duquesne College. It was said of him that "His power as a pulpit orator won him fame all over the country.... As a man of learning he had few equals in his day, and his facile and graceful pen gained him a large circle of admirers." Black wrote a book entitled *The Bible against Slavery*, but his most interesting work is his thoughtful study of the nature and grounds for Christian unity.

Black began from the premise that human beings were made for unity:

> It is peculiar to man to be a social being. Irrational creatures assemble together, by a blind instinctive propensity of their nature. Society is predicated upon rationality, and is the property only of intelligence. It proceeds upon a moral principle, and not on the ground, either of instinct, or mere necessity. Society, thus constitutional to man, has God himself for its author, and can no more be said to be a creature of human fabrication, than intelligence or rationality. It was God who declared that it was not good that man should be alone; because he had created him with a social nature.

Thus, it would also be natural for Christians to come together:

> Social worship does not originate in any positive institution of a visible church, but in the constitution of man, as a rational and social being. There is no sense, in which, it is good for the man to be alone. All men are bound by the constitution of human nature, to worship God in their social, as well as in their individual capacity.

And, as Christians, love will cast out all tendency to division:

> All real Christians love one another. They all love Christ, and cannot but love all who bear his image. And this is the characteristic mark of all who love him — they have his Father's name written in their foreheads. All such will delight to mingle their voices, their hearts and affections, in religious exercises. They will speak of Christ — of the wonders of his love, and the wonders of his grace, with pleasure and delight. They will join in his praises. They will talk together in recommending him more and more. The theme is inexhaustible. They will unite in addressing him, for they love prayer, and they have one heart. One spirit actuates them.

What a wonderful possibility. Unfortunately, there is a need for doctrinal agreement:

But that communion which is strictly ecclesiastical, is to be extended only to such as agree in the same terms of church communion. Can two walk together except they be agreed. Undoubtedly they cannot. They would fall out by the way. If brethren dwell together, it must be in unity, or their character will be extremely unbecoming.

But what of communion? Black poses the obvious objection:

All Christians are agreed, or nearly so, in their views of the Sacrament of the Lord's Supper; why then, may they not take this family meal together? All Christians, whatever may be their creed, have a common interest in the provision which Christ has appointed, for the nutriment, growth and consolation of his body, and all have a right to shew forth his death till he come.

Black's response is spelled out in a series of points. There is room here for only one of them:

This communion is self-contradictory. The parties are of different communions. They have previously pledged themselves to different public creeds. Yet at the sacramental table they declare that they are one — One bread, and drinking into one spirit. At that moment their hearts belie their public profession. They arise from the communion table, and immediately take up, each his own creed, and declare their union a farce. Or else they mutually recognize each other's creed — the same from which they differ! Can any thing be more contradictory?

Black does not see how unity is possible at present without contradiction of principles, but he knows it is God's will for the church and he presents it with eloquence:

This subject calls upon us to bewail the divisions, that prevent the children of God from taking sweet counsel together, and going to the house of God in company. Alas! for our sins, "the great Shepherd hath cut asunder his staff, even bands, that he might break the brotherhood between Judah and Israel." Let us grieve for the afflictions of Joseph, and for the divisions of Reuben, let there be great searchings of heart. Let us earnestly pray that the Lord would heal all our breaches. — Let us also use all lawful endeavours, that they may be speedily and effectually healed. While we lament that the attempts that are generally made, are only to heal the wound of the daughter of Zion slightly, and to say peace, peace, when there is no peace.

Yet, let us be encouraged. The time is not far distant, when Zion shall arise, and put on her beautiful garments, and glorious things shall once more be spoken of the city of the LORD. The time is fixed. Jesus hath declared the decree. In due time it shall bring forth. The LORD hath spoken, and himself will bring it to pass. "He will yet turn to his people a pure language, that they may all call upon the name of the LORD, and serve him with one consent."

✪ *July 9*

Flannery O'Conner

ROMAN CATHOLIC

March 25, 1925–August 2, 1964

Readers familiar with Flannery O'Conner's work may think it strange to find her in these pages. Her characters are tragic, sometimes horrifying. The situations she depicts are dark, filled with anger, fear, violence, or apathy. These hardly seem themes of faith. Yet the Bible itself is not a light-hearted fairy tale, nor do its main characters or events emit a soft, pastel glow. Consider, for example, the story from St. Matthew's gospel about King Herod's slaughter of the children of Bethlehem, and we begin to catch the similarity with O'Conner's perspective. A pompous minor monarch is overwhelmed with petty jealousy over the prospect that a newborn child might someday have a claim on his (or his son's) throne. When deceit fails to locate the boy, he lashes out by butchering all the baby boys of the town. Matthew quotes Jeremiah at this point:

> *A voice was heard in Ramah,*
> *wailing and loud lamentation,*
> *Rachel weeping for her children;*
> *she refused to be consoled,*
> *because they were no more.*

If Scripture can puncture our Christmas gaiety with such brutality, perhaps we can appreciate O'Conner's writing as a similar kind of commentary on lives devoid of faith or hope.

Though she did not live long, Flannery O'Conner knew much about suffering. She was diagnosed with lupus, which seriously constrained her activities and shortened her days. But, as a devout Roman Catholic, she also knew a lot about grace. She writes in her essay "The Fiction Writer and His Country":

> When I look at stories I have written I find that they are, for the most part, about people who are poor, who are afflicted in both mind and body, who have little — or at best a distorted — sense of spiritual purpose, and whose actions do not apparently give the reader a great assurance of the joy of life.
>
> Yet how is this? For I am no disbeliever in spiritual purposes and no vague believer. I see from the standpoint of Christian orthodoxy. This means that for me the meaning of life is centered in our Redemption by Christ and what I see in the world I see in relation to that....
>
> The novelist with Christian concerns will find in modern life distortions which are repugnant to him, and his problem will be to make these appear as distortions to an audience which is used to seeing them as natural; and he

may well be forced to take ever more violent means to get his vision across to this hostile audience. When you can assume that your audience holds the same beliefs you do, you can relax a little and use more normal means of talking to it; when you have to assume that it does not, then you have to make your vision apparent by shock — to the hard of hearing you shout, and for the almost-blind you draw large and startling figures.

In *Mystery and Manners* O'Conner says:

> For the last few centuries we have lived in a world which has been increasingly convinced that the reaches of reality are very close to the surface, that there is no ultimate divine source, that the things of the world do not pour forth from God.... For nearly two centuries the popular spirit of each succeeding generation had tended more and more to the view that the mysteries of life will eventually fall before modern man.... In twentieth century fiction it increasingly happens that the meaningless, absurd world impinges upon the sacred consciousness of author and character; author and character seldom now go out to explore and penetrate a world in which the sacred is reflected.

Fiction provided O'Conner with a medium to show how the shadow of human sin and our capacity for harm darkens our eyes. Like the mystic St. John of the Cross, O'Conner does not use her faith as a means to leapfrog over the stark condition of humanity and the soul's blindness into a sweet, misty paradise. Rather, faith gives her the courage to speak hard and fearsome truths in such a way as to allow the reader to understand God's promises as a remarkable contrast to evil and death. Salvation is not a tidying up of a few minor troubles, nor a slight adjustment in a not-quite-perfect world. It is God's drastic re-creation of humanity torn, bound, and bent on self-destruction. Those who believe in a God whose love will not let the universe careen into its own darkness and oblivion need not be confused by O'Conner's tales. In them we see who we are, and what we would be doomed to be were it not for the "new heaven and new earth" promised through Christ.

We learn from Jesus that fiction can be a powerful means for expressing the truth. His carefully crafted parables open our eyes to the truth about ourselves, our God, and our world. In a similar way, O'Conner's imagination is a forceful lever that pries open our dark closets and hidden fears. With consummate skill and startling effectiveness, she challenges us to question our comfortable assumptions, reach beyond our façades, and seek with eager hearts for a redemption we do not regulate or produce. Her fictional world may renew our courage to face a world whose only hope is, as it ever was, in God.

✸ *July 10*

Absalom Jones

EPISCOPALIAN

February 13, 1746–1818

Absalom Jones was born a house slave in 1746, but he taught himself to read out of the New Testament and other books. At 16, he was sold to a store owner in Philadelphia, where he attended a night school for blacks. In 1770, he married Mary, another slave, and made an agreement with his master to buy her freedom so that his children would be born free. Borrowing some of the money required, Jones worked, often until after midnight, to pay the debt, then to purchase his own freedom in 1784.

Meanwhile he became involved in the life of a Methodist Church where he served as a lay minister with his friend, Richard Allen.* Alarmed by the increasing black membership, the white church leaders decided to require blacks to sit only in the balcony, but they failed to notify them. When ushers attempted to remove blacks during opening prayers the next Sunday, Jones and Allen asked to be allowed to wait until the prayer was over. When the ushers refused to wait, the blacks walked out in a body.

Jones, whose former owner was an Episcopalian, conferred with William White,* the Episcopal Bishop of Philadelphia, who agreed to accept the group as an Episcopal parish with control over their own affairs. The bishop allowed Jones to serve as lay reader until, upon completion of his studies, he could be ordained and serve as rector. Jones wrote a statement explaining that the purpose for their action in founding the church was "to arise out of the dust and shake ourselves, and throw off that servile fear, that the habit of oppression and bondage trained us up in."

In October of 1794, the congregation was admitted to the diocese as St. Thomas African Episcopal Church. Bishop White ordained Jones as deacon in 1795, and as priest seven years later. In the year before St. Thomas Church was admitted to the diocese, Philadelphia endured a yellow fever epidemic. The greatest the country had ever known, it claimed the lives of nearly 4,000 people. In late summer, as the number of deaths began to climb, 20,000 citizens, including George Washington, Thomas Jefferson, and other members of the federal government (then based in Philadelphia) fled to the countryside. When an appeal was made for help in burying the dead, Jones and Allen, who had formed a self-help society of African Americans, came forward to serve as nurses, cart drivers, and grave diggers in order to prevent a complete breakdown of civil life. Though it was thought at first that blacks could not contract the disease, well over 200 of them died also.

A reading from a sermon preached by Absalom Jones on January 1, 1808, celebrating the abolition of the slave trade by the Congress of the United States

The history of the world shows us, that the deliverance of the children of Israel from their bondage, is not the only instance, in which it has pleased God to appear in behalf of oppressed and distressed nations, as the deliverer of the innocent, and of those who call upon his name. He is as unchangeable in his nature and character, as he is in his wisdom and power. The great and blessed event, which we have this day met to celebrate, is a striking proof, that the God of heaven and earth is the same, yesterday, and today, and for ever. Yes, my brethren, the nations from which most of us have descended, and the country in which some of us were born, have been visited by the tender mercy of the Common Father of the human race. He has seen the affliction of our countrymen, with an eye of pity. He has seen ships fitted out from different, ports in Europe and America, and freighted with trinkets to be exchanged for the bodies and souls of men. He has seen the anguish which has taken place, when parents have been torn from their children. and children from their parents, and conveyed, with their hands and feet bound in fetters, on board of ships prepared to receive them. He has seen them thrust in crowds into the holds of those ships, where many of them have perished from the want of air. He has seen such of them as have escaped from that noxious place of confinement, leap into the ocean; with a faint hope of swimming back to their native shore, or a determination to seek an early retreat from their impending misery, in a watery grave. He has seen them exposed for sale, like horses and cattle, upon the wharves; or, like bales of goods, in warehouses of West India and American sea ports. He has seen the pangs of separation between members of the same family. He has seen them driven into the sugar, the rice, and the tobacco fields, and compelled to work in spite of the habits of ease which they derived from the natural fertility of their own country in the open air, beneath a burning sun, with scarcely as much clothing upon them as modesty required. He has seen them faint beneath the pressure of their labours. He has seen them return to their smoky huts in the evening, with nothing to satisfy their hunger but a scanty allowance of roots; and these, cultivated for themselves, on that day only, which God ordained as a day of rest for man and beast. He has seen the neglect with which their masters have treated their immortal souls; not only in withholding religious instruction from them, but, in some instances, depriving them of access to the means of obtaining it. He has seen all the different modes of torture, by means of the ship, the screw, the pincers, and the red hot iron, which have been exercised upon their bodies by inhuman overseers, overseers, did I say? Yes, but not by these only. Our God has seen

masters and mistresses, educated in fashionable life, sometimes take the instruments of torture into their own hands, and, deaf to the cries and shrieks
of their agonizing slaves, exceed even their overseers in cruelty. Inhuman
wretches! though You have been deaf to their cries and shrieks, they have
been heard in Heaven. The ears of Jehovah have been constantly open to
them. He has heard the prayers that have ascended from the hearts of his
people; and, he has, as in the case of his ancient and chosen people the
Jews, *come down to deliver* our suffering countrymen from the hands of
their oppressors.

He *came down* into the United States, when they declared, in the constitution which they framed in 1788, that the trade in our African fellow-men,
should cease in the year 1808: He *came down* into the British Parliament.
when they passed a law to put an end to the same iniquitous trade in May
1807: He *came down* into the Congress of the United States, the last winter,
when they passed, a similar law, the operation of which commences on this
happy day. Dear land of our ancestors! thou shalt no more be stained with
the blood of thy children, shed by British and American hands: the ocean
shall no more afford a refuge to their bodies, from impending slavery: nor
shall the shores of the British West India island, and of the United States,
any more witness the anguish of families, parted for ever by a public sale.
For this signal interposition of the God of mercies, in behalf of our brethren,
it becomes us this day to offer up our united thanks. Let the song of angels,
which was first heard in the air at the birth of our Saviour, be heard this day
in our assembly. *Glory* to *God in the highest,* for these first fruits of *peace
upon earth, and good-will to man.* O let us *give thanks unto the Lord:* let
us *call upon his name,* and *make known his deeds among the people.* Let us
sing psalms unto him and talk of all his wondrous works.

✸ *July 11*

Daniel A. Payne

AFRICAN METHODIST EPISCOPAL

February 24, 1811–November 2, 1893

In 1865, Daniel A. Payne led a delegation of clergy and teachers to the
newly liberated state of South Carolina to organize the first southern Annual
Conference of the African Methodist Episcopal Church. Ironically, Payne
had left the same state 30 years earlier after a law was passed forbidding
anyone to teach slaves or free persons of color. Now he was back to put
in place an organization of, by, and for "free persons of color" that would
eventually include 11 such conferences.

Payne himself was born of free parents in South Carolina. Trained as
a carpenter, his insatiable curiosity led him to teach himself any subject
on which materials could be found — Greek, botany, and geography were

among the disciplines he mastered. At 18, he opened a school to teach others, but moved north when such schools became illegal.

Payne discovered his faith at the age of 18 in the Methodist Church, studied theology in the Lutheran Seminary in Gettysburg, Pennsylvania, and served first as pastor of a Presbyterian Church in Troy, New York. It became evident, however, that blacks were given little opportunity in white-dominated churches, and therefore Payne joined the African Methodist Episcopal Church in 1841. Elected to serve as a bishop in 1852, he traveled widely even though he was not always welcome. In 1855, he was briefly arrested for "violating the laws of the State by coming into St. Louis to preach the gospel." His interest in education persisted. In 1863, he purchased land for Wilberforce University in Ohio for $10,000. Payne served as president of Wilberforce — the first black president of an American university — for 16 years.

A reading from *Recollections of Seventy Years* by Daniel A. Payne

As an educator thou didst lead me from Charleston, S.C., to Philadelphia, Pa.; from Philadelphia to Washington, D.C.; from Washington to Baltimore, and from Baltimore to Wilberforce, O. Over Northern lands, over Southern States, over foreign countries, back to my native State, through storm and calm, through dangers seen and unseen — in the sweltering South, back to the freezing North. Where next, O thou Giver of life, thou Author of all its possibilities — where next? "O the depth of the riches both of the wisdom and knowledge of God! How unsearchable are his judgments, and thy ways past finding out!"

And now I feel my years of labor coming to a close. I consecrate, O thou Most High and Holy One, the remainder of my days to thy divine service. Let the past sins and errors of my life be all forgiven; let all my guilt be washed away in the blood of the Lamb; and give, give unto me the mind that was in Him who went about doing good, and was obedient unto death, even the death of the cross! All the work of salvation and of education committed to my oversight, vouchsafe to bless, to build up, and to establish for the benefit of all the generations and to all the races. Let the translation of the Bible and the diffusion of its life-giving truths, by the living missionaries, go on without faltering. Let the victories of thy conquering cross be ever increasing! Let its living trophies in the heathen world be as innumerable as the stars in the skies, and as countless as the sands upon the ocean shores! To all these glorious ends, O Lord Jesus, make thy aged and feeble servant helpful! Let my science bow down before thee and become consecrated by thee. Let my philosophy kiss thy feet, as Mary kissed the feet of Jesus, and be enlightened by thine unerring, thine immortal truth.

But what will be the use of these recollections of men and things; what of these reflections on them if they will not awaken some slumbering boy; if they fail to excite the latent faculties of a sportive lad; if they be not effective in stimulating the energies of some youth, who, having strong, pure, good blood flowing from a large, broad heart through his entire body, is by nature fitted to accomplish good work for God in heaven and good tidings for man on earth? O youthful reader, hear me! The spirit of Rev. John Brown, of Haddington, Scotland, aroused my soul to a life of usefulness. Shall not my soul start thee on a career of study and usefulness that shall be pleasing to thy Creator, and that will bring blessings to mankind?

> *For a useful life by holy wisdom crowned,*
> *Is all I ask, let weal or woe abound.*

✪ *July 12*

Nathaniel W. Taylor

CONGREGATIONAL

June 23, 1786–1858

Pilgrims and Puritans came to New England with clear ideas about sin and salvation, but what seemed evident to the first generation seemed less so to the second and third. Less than 40 years after the first settlements, a conference of Connecticut and Massachusetts clergy approved a "half-way Covenant" that recognized the baptized as church members whether or not they had had a personal experience of grace. American life remained a challenge to Christians as they struggled to discern whether a changing world required a church that must change so it could speak to new realities, or whether the world must somehow be changed by the proclamation of an unchanging gospel.

By the 19th century, American democracy and the expansion of the western frontier offered freedoms and opportunities early settlers could not have imagined. Calvinist emphasis on human sinfulness and predestination clashed with seemingly boundless possibilities. Nathaniel Taylor attempted to address the problem. For him, "original sin" was a universal tendency, not a birth stain; human beings were free and rational, condemned only by their own actions. The love of God was stressed more than the judgment of God. But Taylor's theology is never simply a logical system; it is always a theology in the service of evangelism and deeply concerned to encourage human beings to respond to the free grace of a loving God.

As pastor of New Haven's First Church (from 1811 to 1822) and professor of theology at Yale Divinity School from its foundation in 1822 until his death in 1858, Taylor was considered the most important American theologian of his generation. His challenge still speaks with power.

A reading from a sermon by Nathaniel Taylor

Consider now what the Lord can do, and what he will do, for you. There is a Being in whose favor is life, and whose loving-kindness is better than life. True it is, in his service many things grateful to your corrupt appetites must be abandoned; much self-denial must be practiced; many conflicts must be sustained. We would not deceive you with unreal representations. After all, who will say that the good things of this life are not ordinarily distributed as bountifully to the righteous as to the wicked? Be this as it may, there is one who will give you as much of these things as infinite wisdom sees best for you. Who would wish for more? If a friend of infinite wisdom and kindness will choose for you, who would wish to choose for himself? There is one who can and will be your refuge in every time of trouble. How delightful amid all the strange and disastrous changes and calamities, to lift an eye of joy and confidence upward to an almighty omnipresent friend, to cast away all solicitude, and to lean safely on his everlasting arm? There is an infinite Being who will impart peace to your soul, give you the privileges of the children of the highest, and hold frequent and delightful communion with you in this world. He will give an interest in those promises whose length and breadth and height and depth have no limit but his own boundless goodness, and accompany that interest with a humble hope that these promises are yours. He will deliver you from the vexation and the defilement of sinful passions, create within you the moral image of his own unspotted purity, unite you in heart, in principle, in conduct, in employments, and, of course, in bliss, with himself and with the holy universe. He will lift upon you the light of his countenance as a foretaste of heaven, cleanse you from guilt in that blood which satisfies every claim of eternal justice; he will, as the eternal Spirit, dwell in you to enlighten, guide, sanctify, strengthen, and comfort you. He will impart to you that submission, and confidence, and gratitude, and love, which are the elements of the Christian character — holy and heavenly elements that shall survive the lapse of ages and flourish in eternal beauty. He will erect and finish a kingdom that will show what infinite power, directed by infinite wisdom and goodness can do, to bless his creatures and make you a partaker in its joys — joys as pure as heaven and lasting as his throne. In a word, there is one who is the fountain and source of all good — who made the heavens and the earth — the giver of all that ministers to the good of man, whose presence diffuses joy and rapture through all the hosts of heaven — who is full of glory, bliss and goodness, and who gives them to all who love him. Who, then, can halt between two opinions any longer; what ground can there be for a moment's hesitation! Who does not say, the Lord, he is God — the Lord, he is God?

✪ July 13

Georges Florovsky

ORTHODOX

August 28, 1893–August 11, 1979

As the tide of immigration to America broadened to include people from southern and eastern Europe, Christian traditions that had been separated as much by geography as by theology suddenly found themselves living side by side. The Orthodox from eastern Europe had long been divided from western Christianity. Ancient suspicions and hostilities made it difficult for them talk with Christians of other traditions without being accused of forsaking their own. These tensions were clearly illustrated in the life of Georges Florovsky. His participation in ecumenical dialogue and his efforts to orient St. Vladimir's Seminary in suburban New York toward the realities of American culture created such tensions that he resigned after five years as its dean. Yet its library was subsequently named in his honor. He customarily wore a jaunty blue beret with his black cassock. One critic thought it emblematic of a man whose body was "clothed in the Church," while "his head was constantly under the force of fashionable thought and academic reason." However controversial he was, few would question his status as the most influential Orthodox theologian of the 20th century.

Born in Russia, Florovsky was educated in law and social sciences. After the Communist Revolution, he first moved to Prague, where he married, then on to Paris, where he joined the faculty of St. Sergius Institute and was ordained to the priesthood. While at St. Sergius, Florovsky produced his two most influential theological writings: one on the 4th-, 5th-, and 6th-century theologians, and the second, a study of Russian theology. He was one of 14 Christian leaders called on to form the World Council of Churches in 1934. He continued to play a central part in the work of the Council's Faith and Order Commission until his death.

Frustrated by the lack of ecumenical interest at St. Sergius, Florovsky moved to New York in 1948 to teach at St. Vladimir. Two years later, he became its dean. Attempting to bring the seminary into the mainstream of American culture, Florovsky insisted that instruction be in English, but his attempts at further change met such fierce resistance that he moved on to teach at Boston University, Holy Cross Greek Orthodox School of Theology, Harvard Divinity School, and finally, for the last 15 years of his life, at Princeton University. Convinced that the early fathers had vital insights for the contemporary church, and that the Orthodox Church had major contributions to make to the western church, Florovsky forged bonds of deep affection with Roman Catholics, Anglicans, and Protestants. His books and articles continue to inspire lay people as well as scholars.

Readings from the writings of Georges Florovsky

On the role of Christ

Christ conquered the world. This victory consists in His having created His own Church. In the midst of the vanity and poverty, of the weakness and suffering of human history, He laid the foundations of a "new being." The Church is Christ's work on earth; it is the image and abode of His blessed Presence in the world. And on the day of Pentecost the Holy Spirit descended on the Church, which was then represented by the twelve Apostles and those who were with them. He entered into the world in order to abide with us and act more fully than He had ever acted before; "for the Spirit was not yet given, because Jesus was not yet glorified" (John 7:39). The Holy Spirit descended once and for always. This is a tremendous and unfathomable mystery. He lives and abides ceaselessly in the church. In the Church we receive the Spirit of adoption (Rom. 8:15). Through reaching towards and accepting the Holy Ghost we become eternally God's. In the Church our salvation is perfected; the sanctification and transfiguration, the thesis of the human race is accomplished.

On the church

The catholicity of the Church is not a quantitative or a geographical conception. It does not at all depend on the world-wide dispersion of the faithful. The universality of the Church is the consequence or the manifestation, but not the cause or the foundation of its catholicity. The world-wide extension or the universality of the Church is only an outward sign, one that is not absolutely necessary. The Church was catholic even when Christian communities were but solitary rare islands in a sea of unbelief and paganism. And the Church will remain catholic even unto the end of time when the mystery of the "falling away" will be revealed, when the Church once more will dwindle to a "small flock." "When the Son of Man cometh, shall He find faith on the earth?" (Luke 18:8)

On the Scriptures

We cannot assert that Scripture is self-sufficient; and this not because it is incomplete, or inexact, or has any defects, but because Scripture in its very essence does not lay claim to self-sufficiency. We can say that Scripture is a God-inspired scheme or image (*eikón*) of truth, but not truth itself. Strange to say, we often limit the freedom of the Church as a whole, for the sake of furthering the freedom of individual Christians. In the name of individual freedom the Catholic, ecumenical freedom of the Church is denied and limited. The liberty of the Church is shackled by an abstract biblical standard for the sake of setting free individual consciousness from the spiritual demands enforced by the experience of the Church. This is a denial of catholicity, a destruction of catholic consciousness; this is the sin of the Reformation.

On theology

Theology must be carried out not merely to satisfy our intellectual curiosity, but in order to live, to have life abundantly in the Truth of God, which is not a system of ideas, but a Person — Jesus Christ. In this task the Fathers of the Church can be the only sure and safe guides.

✪ *July 14* _____

Emma Francis

LUTHERAN

December 7, 1875–April 8, 1945

At her confirmation, Emma Francis had pledged to "give my whole life to God." Most confirmation students make some similar promise or declaration, but few take the words as seriously as she did. The massive social problems, both in the Virgin Islands and in New York, were, to her mind, essentially spiritual in nature. Homes devoid of sound scriptural foundation and lives, lived disconnected to the community of the church, fostered instability and trouble for the younger generation. Francis believed that a simple personal piety, developed within the context of the Bible and the church, would defend against the sins of the world. Her own piety of prayer, morning and evening devotions along with regular corporate worship, was her own source of strength and a model for the youth whose burdens she hoped to alleviate

Emma Francis was the first African American deaconess in the Lutheran Church. Her work focused on youth in a ministry that began and ended on St. Croix in the Virgin Islands, with a six-year interval in Harlem. Born on St. Kitts to the Rev. Joseph and Mary H. Francis, Emma started out as a teacher and parish-and youth-worker in St. Croix at the Ebenezer Home for Girls. In 1921, she moved to New York, where she was consecrated as a deaconess. She also helped found the Lutheran Church of the Transfiguration and served with the West Indies Mission Board. After assisting in the formation of the parish, she returned to the Virgin Islands and to her work at the Ebenezer Home.

It cannot be known how many people derived hope and direction from her work. At least one young woman, Edith Prince, went on to become a deaconess herself and worked with Francis both in Harlem and in the Virgin Islands. Some of Francis's concerns might sound quaint to us. In a letter to a pastor in the 1930s, for example, she writes "Our Lutheran Church has now an opportunity to bring a special evangelical message again to the community that has become great in Sabbath breaking and movies, dance & music not suited to the Lord's Day." But her objection was to the growing dominance of a kind of culture of entertainment that did not just coexist with piety, but competed with it. Francis could see that as a very traditional society become enamored of the newest fads, it could lose its soul. The youngest generation would suffer the most profound effects of a diminished or discarded faith. Emma Francis could have acquiesced and joined the ranks of the spell-bound culture. She could have opted out, choosing a life of solitude and prayer. She could have chosen a finger-pointing stance and blamed prominent leaders. But instead, she chose to put herself in the midst of the problem, where needs were greatest, and do her best to be a Christian, loving presence to children who needed just such a compassionate and steadfast mentor.

A Scripture text exemplifying Francis's outlook is commonly referenced by Lutheran deaconesses. It is II Corinthians 5:14 "For the love of Christ controls us, because we are convinced that one has died for all; therefore all have died." For Francis, the "love of Christ" was not theory, or a theological buzzword, much less a platitude to be tossed off. Christ's love for us "controls us," directs us, calls us, challenges us, and equips us for a life of service to the neighbor. A life of piety, for Francis, was a life of service. It would be hollow indeed to praise God without acting compassionately on behalf of young people whom, today, we would call "youth at risk." Drawing on the resources of her own religious tradition, with its emphasis on the Bible, the free gift of Grace, and the responsibility of Christians to be about God's work in the world while not being conformed to it, Francis put her energies to God's purposes as she perceived them in her time and place. In a letter to another Sister in 1931, Francis said "One should never seek a work for . . . ease and comfort or the praise and honor of the world, but rather for the glory of God." In her life, these words became a public proclamation of God's love for all humanity.

At a time when it was still unusual, Francis's work had a multiracial focus. She ministered to Germans, Cubans, and African Americans, learning German and Spanish to communicate more freely with people whose primary language was not English. Her work did not always run smoothly. Like all Christian servants, Francis experienced her own obstacles and burdens. In one letter she wrote, "God is God. He alone is All-wise. On Him we must trust for the future although it appears dark to us." Trust in Him she did, and her legacy bears a good testimony. Being the first African American deaconess is noteworthy, but, more importantly, the hearts and minds she touched eloquently declare the effect one faithful life can have in the world.

✪ *July 15*

Benjamin Titus Roberts

FREE METHODIST

July 25, 1823–February 27, 1893

The local Presbyterian minister knew Ben Titus well enough to be sure that he didn't smoke or drink, that he stood at the top of his class, worked hard on the farm, and had memorized whole chapters of Scripture. He offered to pay for Roberts's education as an ideal candidate for ordination. But "I cannot accept your offer," the young man told the minister; "I have not been converted." The offer was made again after a while, but was again rejected. Ben Roberts not only knew that he was not converted, he dreamed of becoming a successful lawyer. At the age of 16, he became a schoolteacher, then entered a law office in Little Falls, New York, to pursue his ambition. But a stammering witness made by a member of an otherwise lifeless church made the first dent in Roberts's resistance. For three weeks he resisted what the Spirit was telling him, seeking to remain in control of his life. But he failed, and yielded an unconditional surrender. He was 20 years old and the change filled him with joy.

To prepare himself for his new vocation, Roberts attended Wesleyan University, graduated, and was accepted for the ministry of the Methodist Church in upstate New York. He ministered to churches in that area for 14 years. But he became increasingly distressed by contradictions between Methodist faith and practice, and finally felt compelled to speak out.

Some pastors, he noted, had joined secret societies like the Masons and Odd Fellows. Churches charged pew rents. Slavery was tolerated. Worst of all, self-sacrifice was substituted for faith in Christ as the means of salvation. Roberts's charges were more than the authorities could tolerate. He was censured, then expelled. But his opinions were shared by others, so in 1860, they formed the Free Methodist Church. It did not charge pew rents, opposed slavery, and provided equal representation for lay and clergy members in its governing body. Its object was to restore the quest for holiness that had been such a part of the original vision of John and Charles Wesley. An early publication of the new denomination proclaimed, "Their mission is twofold — to maintain the Bible standard of Christianity, and to preach the Gospel to the poor."

Roberts founded a college, edited a magazine, and wrote a number of books explaining the concept of holiness. 17 years after his death, the Methodist Church acknowledged that it had erred in expelling him.

A reading from an essay by Benjamin T. Roberts entitled "Holiness Not Understood"

In our day we see that which we deem essential to holiness purposely omitted in instructions upon this subject. Popular sins, are, to say the least, silently tolerated. During the War of the rebellion, in a popular meeting for the promotion of holiness in the city of New York, brother and deputy Newton thanked the Lord for President Lincoln's Emancipation Proclamation. He was at once called to order for introducing a topic calculated to disturb the harmony of the meeting. There are many works on the subject of holiness, written in the days of slave-holding to circulate among slave-holders, and not a word to be found in them condemning the practice. The same spirit which led to silence respecting slave-holding in the days when all the popular churches welcomed the slave-holders to their communion, today utterly ignore the existence of sins which God's word plainly condemns, but which the leading churches openly tolerate. That which encourages what God forbids is not wholeness. The name of a thing does not give it its nature....

The persecution to which the saints of God have always been subjected shows that holiness is not recognized when seen. The word declares, "Yea, and all that live godly in Christ Jesus shall suffer persecution" (2 Tim. 3:12). This persecution varies in its form with the prevailing spirit of the age. But whatever shape it assumes, persecution never assigns as its reason the godliness of its victims. Their obstinacy, or contumacy, or disloyalty, or heresy is assigned as the cause of their sufferings. Christ was put to death as an imposter. Luther was excommunicated as a heretic, and Wesley and Whitefield were hunted as fanatics. Their persecutors were the professed children of God, and they believed it to be a zeal for holiness which instigated their opposition to those who furnished bright examples of holiness in their lives.

On the other hand, there are those who make holiness comprise attributes which are entirely beyond the reach of a human being in our present condition. They give a meaning to the term which the scriptures do not warrant. According to their standard, a holy person cannot make a mistake in judgment, either through ignorance or misapprehension. He must not only do right, as he understands it, but do right as they understand it, under all circumstances. They measure others by their own infallibility. They make no allowances for lack of judgment or for imperfect training. He who professes holiness must be, according to their views, beyond the reach of unfriendly criticism. In addition to all this, he must never fall. Should he ever afterward manifest any disposition contrary to his profession, it is then assumed that all along he was either deceived or hypocritical. If he lost holiness, the conclusion is not only that he never had holiness, but that no one ever did or ever will. In short, holiness is pronounced unattainable because some who appeared once to have attained it did not persevere to the end.

Thus a false standard of holiness is raised, and then holiness is declared to be an impossibility, because no one is found to come up to this imaginary standard. We are told to aim our arrow at the sun, and then are ridiculed because we fall short of the mark. The moral perfections of God are presented as our standard, and then we are gravely told that we cannot attain it.

✪ *July 16*

Sarah Mapps Douglass

QUAKER

September 9, 1806–September 18, 1882

Born of free and prosperous parents who hired a private tutor for her as a child, Sarah M. Douglass was a member of the Society of Friends who were leaders in the fight against slavery. At first she avoided involving herself in this struggle, withdrawing into "a little world of my own" and determining she would "not move beyond its precincts." But when a bill was introduced into the Pennsylvania legislature that would have required all blacks to carry passes, her complacency was shaken. "I beheld the oppressor lurking on the border of my own peaceful home! I saw his iron hand stretched forth to seize me as his prey, and the cause of the slave became my own." Sarah Douglass became a founding member of the Philadelphia Female Antislavery Society, served as a member of its Board of Directors, contributed articles to *The Liberator,* and worked with the Grimké sisters* and others to advance the black cause.

Douglass made her primary impact as an educator. "Religion and education," she once said, "would raise us to equality with the fairest in the land." In 1828, she opened a private school for black children, and from 1853 until her death taught at the Institute for Colored Youth — the forerunner of Cheyney University of Pennsylvania. When an opportunity to take a medical course at the Ladies' Institute of the Pennsylvania Medical University presented itself, Douglass became the first African American to attend. Afterward, she introduced courses on physiology into the curriculum of the institute and lectured on health and physiology to black groups in New York and Philadelphia.

The "iron hand" of the oppressor remained an ever present reality, however, even among the Friends. While she was teaching in New York for a while, she went to the Friends meeting there and was asked by a member, "Does thee go out ahouse cleaning." She wrote to a friend,

> I looked at her with astonishment, my eyes filled with tears & I answered no.... Judge what were my feelings, a stranger in a strange land, think of the time, the place & this the first salutation I received in a house consecrated to

Him. I wept during the whole of that meeting & for many succeeding sabbaths & I believe they were not the tears of wounded pride alone.

A reading from a letter by Sarah Douglass to William Bassett, a Quaker living in Massachusetts

The questions you ask me, make me feel my weakness, and in view of the great responsibility that rests upon me in answering them, my flesh trembles; yet will I cast my burden on Him, who is strength in weakness and resolve to do my duty; to tell the truth and leave the consequences to God. . . . And as you request to know particularly about Arch Street Meeting, I may say that the experience of years has made me wise in this fact, that there is a bench set apart at that meeting for our people, whether officially appointed or not I cannot say; but this I am free to say that my mother and myself were told to sit there, and that a friend sat at each end of the bench to prevent white persons from sitting there. And even when a child my soul was made sad with hearing five or six times during the course of one meeting this language of remonstrance addressed to those who were willing to sit by us. "This bench is for the black people." "This bench is for the people of color," And oftentimes I wept, at other times I felt indignant and queried in my own mind are these people Christians. Now it seems clear to me that had not this bench been set apart for oppressed Americans there would have been no necessity for the oft repeated and galling remonstrance, galling indeed, because I *believe they despise us for our color*. I have not been in Arch Street Meeting for four years; but my mother goes once a week and frequently she has a *whole long bench* to herself. The assertion that our people who attend their meetings prefer sitting by themselves, is not true. A very dear friend of ours, that fears God and who has been a constant attender of Friends meeting from his childhood, says . . . several years ago a friend came to me and told me that "Friends" had appointed a back bench for us. I told him with some warmth that I had just as lief sit on the floor as sit there. I do not care about it. Friends do not do the thing that is right. Judge now, I pray you, whether this man preferred sitting by himself. Two sons of the person I have just mentioned, have left attending Friends meetings within the last few months because they could no longer endure the "scorning of those that are at ease, and the contempt of the proud." Conversing with one of them today, I asked, why did you leave Friends. "Because they do not know how to treat me, I do not like to sit on a back bench and be treated with contempt, so I go where I am better treated." . . . In reply to your question "whether there appears to be a diminution of prejudice towards you among Friends," I unhesitatingly answer, no. I have heard it frequently remarked and have observed it myself, that in proportion as we become intellectual and respectable, so in proportion does their disgust and prejudice increase.

Yet while I speak this of Friends as a body, I am happy to say that there is in this city a "noble few" who have cleansed their garments from the foul stain of prejudice, and are doing all their hands find to do in promoting the moral and mental elevation of oppressed Americans. Some of these are members of Anti-Slavery Societies and others belong to the old abolition School....

Did all the members of Friends society feel for us, as the sisters Grimké do, how soon, how very soon would the fetters be stricken from the captive and cruel prejudice be driven from the bosoms of the professed followers of Christ.

✪ July 17 _____

Robert Elliott Speer

PRESBYTERIAN

September 10, 1867–November 23, 1947

In every generation new challenges to the Christian faith arise, and in every age new voices speak in its defense. In the 19th and 20th centuries, Christian Scriptures were scrutinized by scholars according to the same techniques accorded other historical documents, and this perusal, along with scientific advances, raised new and important questions. For some minds, this new academic dissection resulted in a heightened skepticism about religion in general, and Christianity in particular. In the early years of the 20th century, Robert Speer began to address the doubts and questions of his age with a straightforward clarity.

Speer, a layman, was a dedicated missionary and ecumenist. Convinced that Christianity was superior to other religions, he might seem narrow-minded by some standards today. But in the context of his time he was opposed by the staunchest conservative voices of the fundamentalist movement and criticized for allowing liberals into the mission field. Nonetheless, he won the backing of his church and was elected moderator of the Presbyterian General Assembly in 1927. Speer also served as president of the Federal Council of Churches in 1920. Orthodox in his faith, Speer was progressive on social issues and an advocate for justice and equality in relation to racial issues and women's rights. He was also a prolific writer, whose books included biographies of important Christians, studies of Christian mission, and personal testimonies of the meaning and value of Christian faith.

A reading from *The Meaning of Christ to Me* by Robert Elliott Speer

Christianity is the only one of the great religions of the world which calls itself by the name of its founder. Other great religions are named after their founders by us. They were not so named by their own adherents. This is not a mere accident; it is a fact of the deepest significance. To be sure, the name Christian was given originally by enemies, but it was given by them because, from without, they had already discerned the essential and distinguishing character of the new religion, and had been impressed by the inseparable connection which, they saw, existed between it and its founder Jesus Christ. The disciples of the new religion presently accepted the name as the most appropriate name possible for them and their faith. They themselves were aware that the relationship in which they stood to Jesus Christ was the central and fundamental thing in their religion. So long as He had been on earth their religion had consisted in personally following Him, in finding their fellowship in His company, in drawing their nourishment from His words, in coming to understand His Person and His Mission, and in resting their hearts on the peace and quiet which they found with Him. And after He was gone they perceived that their religion consisted in a relationship to Him of a far more vital and wonderful kind than they had understood while He was here. For now they realized that it did not consist only in the mere memory of a good man who was gone, in the effort to recall the things which He had said, and to comfort their hearts with recollections of joyful hours of His flesh. They realized that it consisted in a living relationship to Him, as still a living person with them, while their faith was not a recollection of what Jesus had taught, or the mere memory of a lovely human character, but a unique relationship to an abiding, supernatural Person who had died for them and was their God and Saviour. . . .

The main problem of Christianity is this of Jesus Christ: Who was He, and what are we to think of Him? We cannot do any thinking about Christianity at all that is direct or adequate without coming at once to think of the problem of the Person of Jesus Christ, who stands at the heart of His religion, without whom the Christian religion is not the religion of Christ. Nay, far more than this is to be said. Christ is Christianity. Christianity is Christ. In the truest sense it is not a religion at all. Religion is the quest of man for God. Christianity is the quest of God for man. . . . It is not a human speculation about God. It is a divine revelation delivering them from its power. This work which we see Christ doing today in the lives of men is no human work. Today, as of old, Christ is transforming character and nature, doing the work of God on the life of man.

And now, last of all, why is it that if we have grounds for belief in the deity of Christ such as these there are so many men and women who do not believe that Christ is the Son of God? Well, in the first place; some of them have never done any thinking about it, They have listened to what other people have said, and what the other people have said was only what they heard somebody else say. They themselves have never done any real, conscientious, consecutive reflection on the problem of Christ at all. Some of our want of faith in Christ simply springs from shallowness, superficiality, or intellectual neglect.

In the second place, a great many have no adequate conception of the person of Christ simply because they have never studied the original documents. If you will saturate your mind and heart with the four Gospels for twelve months, if you will read them through, all four every week, and not only read them but dwell upon the character of Christ as it comes out in them, letting your imagination play with the freedom of the Spirit of life upon that life of Christ, that word of Christ, that personality of Christ, you will come back twelve months from now with your faith in the deity of Christ as the Son of God established unassailably.

✪ July 18 _____

Agnes Repplier

ROMAN CATHOLIC

April 1, 1855–December 15, 1950

If you log on to the Internet and type the name Agnes Repplier into your web browser, you will find your screen filled with references to her and almost all of them will be selected quotations. Look at the quotations and you will encounter a polished writer with a sophisticated wit:

> *It is not depravity that afflicts the human race so much as a general lack of intelligence.*

> *It is not easy to find happiness in ourselves, and it is not possible to find it elsewhere.*

> *Democracy forever teases us with the contrast between its ideals and its realities, between its heroic possibilities and its sorry achievements.*

> *Too much rigidity on the part of teachers should be followed by a brisk spirit of insubordination on the part of the taught.*

You would not be surprised to discover that an author who could turn such phrases wrote for the *Atlantic Monthly* and published several collections of essays "esteemed for their scholarship and wit." You might be surprised, however, to learn that this writer was a practicing Christian whose first book, *In Our Convent Days,* recalled her time in a Roman Catholic girls school and who also wrote biographies of early missionaries including Jacques Marquette and Junípero Serra.

The last quotation above should also be noted for its reflection of hard experience. Agnes Repplier's mother attempted to teach her daughter to read but failed. Eventually, Repplier taught herself to read at the age of ten. She was then dispatched to a convent school but after two years was asked not to return because of her "willfulness and independent spirit." A "Seminary for Young Ladies" took up the challenge next but after three terms she was dismissed "for rebelling against the headmistress's authority."

Faced with such a "brisk spirit of insubordination," her mother gave up the struggle and left her daughter to her own devices. Agnes proceeded to use the tools she had been given to teach herself and found a place for her writing in *Catholic World* and *Young Catholic*. Before she was 30, her work was appearing in the *Atlantic Monthly*. Even in this secular context, her faith shone through, though with a difference. In a day when women most often wrote stories about family life and Roman Catholics wrote most often about their piety, Repplier took the world for her subject, seeing no need to weigh in on specifically familial or religious issues. She was who she was and she wrote to show others the world as she saw it. By the time she died, it no longer seemed remarkable for a Roman Catholic woman to find her place in the broad stream of American life. Agnes Repplier helped make this possible.

A reading from an essay by Agnes Repplier

Our days are made up of moments and our years of days, and every swift realization of a lawful joy is a distinct and lasting gain in our onward flight to eternity.

It seems to me strangely cruel that this philosophy of pleasure should be so ruthlessly at variance with the ethical criticism of our day. If it has come down to us as a gracious gift from the most cheerful and not the least wholesome of heathens, it has been broadened and brightened into fresh comeliness by the spirit of Christianity, which is, above all things, a spirit of lawful and recognized joy. Nothing is more plain to us in the teaching of the early Church than that asceticism is for the chosen few, and enjoyment, diffused, genial, temperate, and pure enjoyment, is for the many. "Put on, therefore, gladness that hath always favor with God, and is acceptable unto him, and delight thyself in it; for every man that is glad doeth the things that are good, and thinketh good thoughts, despising grief"(Shepherd of Hermas). Through all the centuries, rational Christianity has still taught us bravely to endure what we must, and gratefully to enjoy what we can. There is a very charming and sensible letter on this point, written by the Abbé Duval to Madame de Rémusat, who was disposed to reproach herself a little for her own happiness, and to think that she had no right to be so comfortable and so well content.

"You say that you are happy," writes this gentlest and wisest of confessors; "why then distress yourself? Your happiness is a proof of God's love toward you; and if in your heart you truly love Him, can you refuse to respond to the divine benevolence? ... Engrave upon your conscience this fundamental truth: that religion demands order above all things; and that, since the institutions of society have been allowed and consecrated, there is encouragement for those duties by which they are maintained.... But especially banish from your mind the error that our pains alone are acceptable to God. A general willingness to bear trials is enough. Never fear but life and time will bring it. Dispose yourself beforehand to resignation, and meanwhile thank God incessantly for the peace which pervades your lot."

This is something very different from Ruskin's ethics, — from the plain statement that we have no right to be happy while our brother suffers, no right to put feathers in our own child's hat, while somebody else's child goes featherless and ragged. But there is a certain staying power in the older and simpler doctrine, and an admirable truth in the gentle suggestion that we need not vex ourselves too deeply with the notion of our ultimate freedom from trial. It was not given to Madame de Rémusat, any more than it is given to us, to ride in untroubled gladness over a stony world. All that she attained, all that we can hope for, are distinct and happy moments, brief intervals from pain, or from that rational *ennui* which is inseparable from the conditions of human life.

✸ *July 19*

Martha Laurens Ramsay

EPISCOPALIAN

November 3, 1759–June 10, 1811

It is easy to review the public accomplishments and speeches of Christians after they have died but much more difficult to assess their inner spiritual lives. Yet there may be more to learn from the inner struggle of an individual than from the outward expression of faith. In recent years, the keeping of spiritual diaries has come back into fashion, but in the late 18th century, they were less common. The private journal kept by Martha Laurens Ramsay between 1791 and 1808 provides a valuable insight into the effort made by a lay woman of that time to grow in her life of faithfulness.

Martha Laurens was born to a wealthy family in Charleston, South Carolina. She traveled with her father, a President of the Continental Congress and representative of the American cause in France and England. Returning to Charleston after the Revolution, she married a doctor and was a housewife and mother for 24 years, until her death at the age of 51. During the time she kept her journal, she went through a period of severe emotional depression. "I am in straits, trials, and perplexities of soul and body," she wrote. "My outward affairs can only be helped by thy providence; my spiritual troubles by thy grace."

The journal was kept secret until just before her death when she told her husband of its existence. He published it, believing it would serve as an example of the civic and spiritual virtues Americans ought to uphold.

Under the title, *Memoirs of the Life of Martha Laurens Ramsay,* the journal remained in print until 1890.

A reading from the journal of Martha Laurens Ramsay

August 23, 1794

On a review of the last week, I find that my mind has been much exercised in spiritual things; that I have been much more earnest in private prayer, and sought my God in the watches of the night, and yet I cannot perceive an increase in sanctification, according to my desire; nor that strength against sin, which my soul pants after. O my God, be pleased to give me holiness! Enable me to go on, to serve my blessed Saviour fully, and to walk with that uprightness, that uniformity, that heavenly-mindedness, which I owe to him who has bought me with so great a price, and whose mercy and love toward me is so great and so constant....

November 19, 1797

O Father, Son, and Holy Ghost, I give myself up to thee, to be, and to do, and to bear whatever thou shalt see fit for me during my journey through life! Renouncing all self-government, I desire to have my will swallowed up in thy divine will and to submit myself to thy rightful authority and the merciful disposal of and majesty of heaven, supremely desiring nothing but salvation for me and mine, and persuaded that God will order all things better for me than I could for myself. Yet, since O Lord, thou dost not only permit, but encourage us to come nigh to thy throne of grace, and to spread our wants before thee, permit a poor worm to claim this privilege, and to relieve her sorrows by pouring them out before thee, and beseeching the interference of thy mercy in her present concerns. Doth God care for the sparrows, and will he not care for his people? Thou dost care, O Lord! And my faith and hope are in thee, that now, even now, O my God, thou wilt show that, though for some months past thou hast appeared to hide thy face from me, to reject me, and cover thyself as with a thick cloud on account of my transgressions, thou wilt no longer break thy bruised reed, but that for me, even me, most unworthy, there shall be a gracious revival — a merciful and providential lifting up.

Shall not the Judge of the whole earth do right? Oh yes, he will. Shall not he, who freely gave his own Son for us, deal kindly by his redeemed ones? Oh yes, he will. Be not, therefore, cast down, O my soul, neither be thou disquieted within me, for I shall yet praise him, who is the light of my countenance and my God; yes, I will even now praise him.

February 3, 1799

So far as I know my own heart, I think I desire resignation to the divine will, more than I desire any earthly good. I have some temporal affairs pressing on my mind, and am hanging on Providence for the events of the two ensuing days. Yet I trust, that a desire to live to God, and to grow in grace, are still greater anxieties with me than any worldly concerns; yet the Lord, who knoweth our frames, and considereth of what we are made, and is well acquainted with our different temperaments and constitutions, sees that I am not wholly devoid of agitation; but I trust, he also sees that it is of the chastened kind, and in that degree not inconsistent with sincere piety, and trust in himself. Indeed, I hope I may even say that I feel holy joy in God, and a thorough conviction that he will do all things well. Hitherto he hath helped me, and he will not now forsake me. He hath cared for my soul, he will not be unmindful of my lesser concerns. He hath prepared my heart to pray, he will surely hear my cry. I am so ignorant, even of what would be good for me, that it is my glory to put my trust in his wisdom; so weak that I rejoice in his power; so blind that I am thankful to be guided by him. If he chooses to grant that which I desire, to his praise shall it be recorded. . . .

March 5, 1802

On looking into this book, I see it is near a twelvemonth since I have noted in writing, any of the Lord's dealings with me; yet surely my heart, with grateful remembrance, looks back on many trials gone through; on many mercies received. In all the perplexities of our situation, how good has God been, not only to hold our souls in life, but to give the enjoyment of vigorous health to my dear husband and family, that we have neither had the additional expenses nor the additional anxieties of sickness to our other cares, and in the midst of cares, how graciously have I been supported and assisted. In times of greatest need, God has helped!

✪ *July 20*

Benjamin Tucker Tanner

AFRICAN METHODIST

December 25, 1835–1923

The first generation of significant black leadership in the Christian church emerged at the end of the 18th century. Through the first part of the 19th century, black churches grew slowly, developing a larger body of leaders. The aftermath of the Civil War provided them with opportunities for rapid expansion among the newly freed black population of the southern states. The African Methodist Episcopal Church, founded by Richard Allen,* was the strongest of these churches and readiest to respond to the challenge.

Benjamin Tucker Tanner was one of the African Methodist leaders during this critical period. He and his wife had escaped from the south by the Underground Railroad. Tanner attended Presbyterian schools, Avery Institute and Western Theological Seminary, then briefly served a Presbyterian

Church in Washington, DC, before returning to the Baltimore conference of the African Methodist Church in April 1862.

Tanner served first as a missionary in Alexandria, where he organized the first congregation of his church in Virginia. He then went to Georgetown, DC, and then, in 1864, to Frederick, Maryland. But his special gift was writing and teaching, so in 1866 he was asked to organize a conference school in Frederick, Maryland, and take charge of the schools of the Freedmen's bureau in Frederick County. He was elected secretary of the General Conference of 1868 and was chosen editor of the *Christian Recorder* in 1872. In 1884 Tanner became the managing editor of a new church publication, the *A.M.E. Church Review.* Tanner soon realized that there was a great need to provide resources for black children, so he fought to establish a children's newspaper, the *Child's Recorder.* In editorials and articles he worked to focus attention on the importance of strong black families to the future of African American citizens as they took their places in the church and the wider society.

Tanner was made a bishop in 1888. Among his publications were *Paul versus Pius Ninth* (Baltimore, 1865); *An Apology for African Methodism* (1867); *The Negro's Origin, Is the Negro Cursed?* (Philadelphia, 1869); and *Outline of the History and Government of the A.M.E. Church* (1883).

A reading from *An Apology for African Methodism* by Benjamin T. Tanner

The giant crime committed by the Founders of the African M.E. Church, against the prejudiced white American, and the timid black — the crime which seems unpardonable, was that they dared to organize a Church of men, men to think for themselves, men to talk for themselves, men to act for themselves: A Church of men who support from their own substance, however scanty, the ministration of the Word which they receive; men who spurn to have their churches built for them, and their pastors supported from the coffers of some charitable organization; men who prefer to live by the sweat of their own brow and be free. Not that the members of this communion are filled with evil pride, for they exhibit a spirit no more haughty nor overbearing than Paul, who never neglected to remind the world that he was a man and a Roman citizen.

Slavery and prejudice, stood up like demons before (Richard) Allen and his compeers, and forbade them to use the talents which God had given.

Slavery bellowed in one ear, "You may obey but you shall not rule."

Prejudice thundered in the other, "You may hear but you shall not speak." And to utterly break their spirits, they both took up the damning refrain, "God may permit you to be Levites, but not Priests."

They listened! and more than half dismayed they asked themselves, "If we are not to think, for what purpose were reasoning faculties bestowed? if not to talk, why were our tongues created?" If there be a fitness of things in creation; 'considered they in their sober reflection,' and the intellect was given to one class, with which it was to think and reason, and the tongue for utterance, and the muscular strength for every sphere of action, surely for the same high purposes were they conferred on all. But if it be true, that our white brethren must do all the thinking and controlling, all the preaching; with the multiplied ministrations of the Gospel, then indeed is there an unfathomable mystery in the fact that we are made like them, with mind and voice and strength — we whose normal condition, they teach, is *only to work.* "Why not the horse and ox have mind and speech as well." Thus doubtless they reasoned., in substance, and never having heard that the Lord repented Him, of having bestowed rational powers upon the Negro, they concluded that they must use them at their peril, lest they be condemned like him who buried his one talent....

Allen was no advocate of Church divisions; he had read with trembling, the thundering imprecations against all who dare to rend the visible body of the Saviour; hence, when compelled to leave, let it be said to his praise, that he made no attempt to bring in a new Ministry, or to institute rites and ceremonies not authorized by the Church. He sought only to have the acknowledged Ordinances conducted by pure and impartial hands; and who is there that will dare to brand the word "Schismatic" upon the old man's brow?

✪ *July 21*

James W. C. Pennington
PRESBYTERIAN/CONGREGATIONAL
1807–October 20, 1870

When James Pennington was 20 years old, he decided he had been beaten too often by his master and the time had come to escape. Fleeing slavery, he found himself in Pennsylvania, asked where he could find work, and was directed to the home of a Quaker, William Wright. Seeing the dirty, ragged fugitive on his doorstep asking for work, Wright said, "Well, come in and take thy breakfast, and get warm, and we will talk about it; thee must be cold without any coat." For six months Pennington worked there and also began to learn reading, writing, and astronomy. Fearful of slave catchers, he moved on after six months and settled in Brooklyn, where he found a good job and continued to study with private tutors and in evening school. He began to ask himself what he could do for "that vast body of suffering brotherhood I have left behind." In 1831, just three years after escaping from slavery, Pennington was chosen as a delegate to the first full-fledged national black convention.

For a while Pennington taught school on Long Island, but he wanted to be ordained. After auditing some courses at Yale Divinity School, which would not admit him as a regular student, he finally achieved his goal in 1838 and became pastor of a Congregational Church in New Town, Long Island. Two years later, he was called to a Congregational Church in Hartford, Connecticut, later known as the Talcott Street Congregational Church. Settled in his ministry, Pennington turned his energies to educational, missionary, and antislavery activities. School attendance was not compulsory in those days. In any event, most state school districts excluded black children. Even where schools were provided, as in New Haven, the budget for teachers' salaries, classroom equipment, and books was much less than in the white schools and classes had to be held in the church because there was no other building provided. Pennington wrote a textbook on black origins to prove that all human beings have the same descent and intellect and are subject to a common law. The book included an essay on prejudice and recommended methods for dealing with it.

Within a few weeks of his arrival in Hartford, Pennington was chosen to serve on the executive committee of the newly established American and Foreign Anti-Slavery Society. He became deeply involved in efforts to prevent escaped slaves from being returned to the south. In 1843, he was chosen to go to London to attend the second world antislavery convention. He spoke there on a number of occasions that summer. On his return to Connecticut, Pennington began to condemn prejudices that infected even members of abolition societies and to point out that separate black and white churches meant that many black congregations had inferior teachers and preachers. These ideas took root and attitudes began to change. Pennington found himself invited to speak in white churches. Called to a New York congregation in 1848, he helped organize the New York Legal Rights Association, one of the earliest civil rights societies in the country. He continued to write and preach and work for civil rights until his death in 1870. The story of his years in slavery and escape to freedom, *The Fugitive Blacksmith*, remains one of the most important slave narratives.

An excerpt from a speech by James Pennington entitled "The Reasonableness of the Abolition of Slavery at the South: A Legitimate Inference from the Success of British Emancipation."

And here is an eternal truth that is destined to beat away every refuge of lies that can be brought by the ingenuity of critics, tyrants and cavilers, to support slavery. When you have made of man a slave by a seven-fold process of selling, bartering and chaining, and garnished him with that rough and bloody brush, the cart-whip, and set him to the full by blowing into the eyes of his mind cloud after cloud of moral darkness, his own immortality still remains. Subtract from him what you can, immortality still remains; and this is a weapon in the bosom of the slave which is more terrible and terrifying to the slaveholder than the thunder of triumphal artillery in the ears of a retreating army. At every stripe of the cart-whip there is a plaintive shriek which betokens the inwardly dwelling immortality of the soul.

The law of 1838 came, and the bondman received back his wife, his children, his Bible, his Sabbath, his sanctuary.

Oh, what moral sublimity is here, when the law spoke with such stern eloquence to the tyrant, in regard to the personal liberty and rights of the slave, and the mandate was, *"give them, give them back!"* and when the man of chains and stripes came forth, and reached out his hand to receive the precious trust!

How was he to act? How did he act? How has he acted since? How is he acting to-day?

Echo, songs of praise; echo, ye sacred chapels; echo, school houses; echo, ye railroads of beautiful cottages; ye villages, VICTORIA and WILBERFORCE; echo, ye colored magistrates, lawyers, merchants, members of assembly, governors and secretaries, and still the echo comes; how are they acting? Look over and see. Then let us make a bold push, for our day is hard by. We devote this day to rejoice with the West India freedman. When it has passed, we will go down again like "good Samaritans," and put our shoulder close by the American slave, and make, we say, a bold push for *his* day. With the Bible and the Declaration of Independence for our weapons, we will make a bold push for the day begins. In the course of events, it dawns. The fruitful womb of time is already pregnant with another heir, and *that* heir is ours. The last was born yonder, but the next shall be born here. They tell us that slavery is here, and that it must remain; and that it is useless to discuss it, So say the public men with private motives. They say that however desirable it may be that slavery should be abolished, it can not be done. IT IS IMPOSSIBLE. So said the British slaveholder. We lay down as a general truth, that what is desirable is possible with God, is possible unto us, with His aid. *Upon this basis, what have we to do in order to success?* Why, to concentrate our energies upon this desirable object. Let our means harmonize with the moral government of God. Let our plans harmonize with His wisdom. Let our action harmonize with the perceptible economy of Providence. And what becomes of the impossibility? It is annihilated.

✪ *July 22*

Margaret Louise Keasey

ROMAN CATHOLIC

January 9, 1885–November 22, 1931

Saints are often reluctant. Isaiah and Jeremiah were reluctant to accept their commissions; so were Peter and Paul. The Virgin Mary apparently thought the Angel Gabriel had come to the wrong address. Margaret Louise Keasey had been content to be a teacher in the public schools of Butler County, Pennsylvania, though she could imagine being called to some sort of special ministry to the poor. Indeed, when it was suggested that she go south to work with the Rev. Thomas Augustine Judge* in Opelika, Alabama, she was quite willing to go. But when Judge told her she was to be principal of his school, she accused him of joking. He had to pound on the table and talk about the virtue of obedience before she would agree to serve. When he told her that she was to be Reverend Mother of a new religious community, she thought he must be referring to someone else with the same name as hers, and looked around the room to see who it might be. When she realized he meant her, she spent the night crying. When she was asked to make speeches, she tried to avoid the obligation. When it became necessary to ask bishops for support, she tried to find someone else to do it. But Judge was right; Lou Keasey had a vocation; and step by step she grew into the role to which she was called.

Twelve years later, the order she had founded worked in Philadelphia and Puerto Rico as well as Alabama; a wealthy benefactor had presented them with a 50-bed hospital in Gadsden, Alabama. By that time, Louise Keasey was traveling constantly, conferring with bishops, and serving as chief executive of a very large organization. Raising funds was always on her agenda, but so too was choosing hats and dresses for the sisters, since the rule said they should follow "the style of the day" — which, of course, meant constant change. She wrote to a friend that she would like to find a little town with about 50 residents, all of them daily communicants, where she could have a "nice, quiet mission... with hot and cold running water (and) electric lights. Now you see by this I really want a quiet life. I have had such an exciting time for the past twelve years that I would just like to settle down and think out how it all happened." She wrote to another friend, "God help me. It is hard to please everybody." But she had the necessary perspective to write in another letter: "I do feel sorry for Father Loftus.... I do believe that he means well. But of course you know, saints differ; so it is nothing unusual for Father Loftus and Father Judge to differ. One time, not so long ago, I differed with Father Lenahan of Tuscaloosa and you know he is a saint."

Contending, as she had to, with differing saints, Keasey managed to make most of them comfortable with her decisions. A young seminarian wrote of her,

> Now Mother Boniface [her name in the order]...was so much easier because she was this-worldly; not that she was worldly in wanting the things of ths world, but she had this human warmth which was so evident....It was her capacity to embrace everybody and make everybody feel special." Another new recruit for the companion men's order said, "I think we loved her for the things she did for us and the way she listened to what we had to say. We knew she would always be on our side. Although she never had any favorites, she was always on the side of the oppressed or the crushed....She said what she thought was right before God and her conscience; that was her greatness.

At the end of a long report on the work in Puerto Rico, Keasey commented:

> Now I think I have given you a slight idea of some of the work in Aquadilla — the school, the doctrine classes out on the hills and streets, in the house itself and at the church, the work with the outer Cenacle working for an active lay apostolate and helping the poor and the sick, sending them milk, food, clothes and paying their rent, getting medical aid and sending the priests to dying and very sick people who are found in the poor little huts. You may think you have seen poverty and misery in the States, but in Puerto Rico it is indescribably worse. Some say they never knew anything better so don't miss what they never had. Ah! but they feel hunger as keenly as any in the States.

When Keasey died in a typhoid outbreak at the age of 46, the preacher at her requiem said, "Although burdened with the many perplexing cares of her high office, she never lost interest in the welfare of her charges, nor in the many and varied activities in which they were engaged. She moved among her Sisters with a kind courtesy that never failed; and, so profound was her humility that the observer would not guess she was the Superior of the Community." But, then, she had never wanted to be.

Two months after her death came word that the Missionary Servants of the Most Blessed Trinity had at last been recognized as a full-fledged community by the authorities in Rome.

✪ *July 23* _____

William L. Herzfeld

LUTHERAN

June 9, 1937–May 9, 2002

William Herzfeld envisioned a new church — new not in name only, or in organizational structure, not "staid, stoic and familiar" but instead fresh with "wide-screen vision, living color and stereophonic sound." Originally from Mobile, Alabama, Herzfeld graduated from Immanuel Lutheran College and Immanuel Lutheran Seminary in Greensboro, North Carolina and was ordained by the Lutheran Church–Missouri Synod (LCMS) in 1961. He served pastorates at Christ Church, Tuscaloosa, Alabama, and Bethlehem Church, Oakland, California, before moving into other areas of ministry. In Alabama, he helped organize the Tuscaloosa chapter of the Southern Christian Leadership Conference (SCLC) and served as its first president. He was also president of the Alabama State SCLC, where he became a close associate of the late Dr. Martin Luther King, Jr. While in Tuscaloosa, he served the LCMS Southern District in several leadership roles.

After the LCMS split, the Association of Evangelical Lutheran Churches (AELC) was formed, and Herzfeld cast his lot with the "moderates." That experience drained and demoralized many who lived through it, but Herzfeld continued with undiminished vigor in the new, young church body that had been born, becoming its Presiding Bishop. Later, he helped steer the AELC into the merger that became the Evangelical Lutheran Church in America (ELCA). Some members questioned the wisdom of this step, but thanks to Herzfeld's leadership, the smallest and youngest of the three Lutheran bodies involved provided essential leadership and passion for a unified Lutheran Church in America. Herzfeld was the first African American to head an American Lutheran church body. He brought a deep concern about racism and injustice to his position. He also believed passionately that strong ecclesial bodies were necessary to form the faith so that it might make an impact on a hurting world.

While he was AELC presiding bishop, Herzfeld also worked as a leader on the Commission for a New Lutheran Church, the formal body working out the details of the biggest Lutheran merger in North American history. "He was so supportive and understanding during those early years of the church and transition," said the Rev. Herbert W. Chilstrom, first Presiding Bishop of the ELCA from 1987 to 1995. "Not only was he a source of factual information, but he was simply a wise man. His perception was uncanny." Presiding Bishop Mark S. Hanson said of him, "Herzfeld was truly a Spirit-filled leader who heeded Christ's command to be a witness throughout the world. He was a witness to God's desire for justice as he worked tirelessly for the end of racism. He was a witness to God's desire for peace as he built bridges of reconciliation and cooperation between global churches." These testimonies indicate Herzfeld's impact, not only on his own denomination, but on the larger community of Christians worldwide. He felt that if Christ were among us today, he would likely be found "sleeping on a park bench or finding warmth on a farm that had been deserted." Chilstrom called Herzfeld "a delightful travel companion — always in good humor — and that was especially important in those early years." The two maintained that bond, and when Herzfeld died, Chilstrom said. "I've lost a good friend."

Herzfeld's leadership also affected the Lutheran World Federation, the World Council of Churches, and the National Conference of Black Churchmen. Eventually he became a vice president of the National Council of Churches in Christ in the U.S.A. and president of Church World Service and Witness, the NCC's relief arm. "Will was a valued friend and colleague of all of us in the ecumenical movement and was particularly loved and respected for the spiritual quality of the leadership he gave to Church World Service and the National Council of Churches," said the Rev. Bob Edgar, NCC general secretary. "We nicknamed him 'the Chaplain,' and always appreciated the insights and the wisdom born of deep faith that he shared with us."

Herzfeld also served as associate director of the ELCA Division for Global Mission. In this capacity, he helped place some 300 missionaries and volunteers and also visited Lutherans in Africa. Only days before his death, Herzfeld had been both to Cameroon and to the Central African Republic, which was ordaining its first female pastor. Herzfeld participated in the ceremony. Bonnie L. Jensen, then executive director of the global mission unit, said of him: "Will was a person with uncanny insight, constant respect for people, and a focus on the gospel. He conveyed the partnership, accompaniment, of a large North American church with churches in other lands in a manner that transcended economic, cultural, and political boundaries."

H. George Anderson, the ELCA's second Presiding Bishop, said, "Will helped this church become a supportive companion to younger Lutheran Churches around the world. His legacy is a stronger global church." Hertzfeld once said "I don't have any problem communicating with anybody who is suffering or who has undergone oppression." In fact, his life is a testament to that. The Bishop of the Central Diocese of the Evangelical Lutheran Church in Southern Africa, Ndanganeni Phaswana, addressed his memorial service in Chicago May 18: "To the church in Africa, Will was more than a friend. He was a brother and a father." However impressive his resume, Herzfeld's compassion, insight, and pastoral heart were even more remarkable. When he died of cerebral malaria, he was just 64 years old.

✪ *July 24* _____

Russell H. Conwell

BAPTIST

February 15, 1843–December 6, 1925

Immigrants to America have come most often with one of two visions: freedom to serve God according to their convictions and opportunity to make money. Sometimes the two visions come together in a version of the gospel that suggests both liberties may be the same thing. Recent interpretations of this idea include The *Power of Positive Thinking* by Norman Vincent Peale and *The Be Happy Attitudes* by Robert Shuler. These authors had a distinguished predecessor in Russell H. Conwell, but in Conwell's case there was also a focus on the good that money can do. The fortune he made was used in socially constructive ways.

Conwell served for two years in the Civil War before becoming a lawyer. His parents were devout Christians who operated a station on the Underground Railroad and helped Frederick Douglass, among others, escape to freedom. But Russell Conwell was an atheist until a colleague in the Civil War inspired him to rethink his views. His law practice made Conwell wealthy but did not satisfy him, so he studied theology and was ordained in the American Baptist Church. When members of a crumbling congregation came to ask his advice, he offered his help and soon created a flourishing congregation. Called to a struggling congregation in Philadelphia, he soon developed it into one of the largest congregations in the country. A young man asked help in preparing for the ministry, and Conwell offered to teach him and his friends one night a week. Ten years later, he found himself president of a college with 4200 students. Temple College, named for the Temple Baptist Church of which Conwell was pastor, grew into the well-known Temple University.

Conwell served as pastor of his congregation for 43 years and as president of Temple College for 37 years, but his greatest fame resulted from a lecture he put together hurriedly for a reunion of his army unit. He had no thought of giving it again, but by the time of his death he had delivered it over 6,000 times. The lecture was titled "Acres of Diamonds" and told stories of people who had overlooked wealth at home while they sought elsewhere for a fortune. "Money is power," he said, "and you ought to be reasonably ambitious to have it. You ought because you can do more good with it than you could do without it. Money printed your Bible, money builds your churches, money sends your missionaries, and money pays your preachers, and you would not have many of them, either, if you did not pay them.... The man who gets the largest salary can do the most good with the power that is furnished to him. Of course he can, if his spirit be right to use it for what it is given to him." He drew the biblical distinction between wealth and the love of wealth and said, "If you can honestly attain unto riches, it is your Christian and godly duty to do so."

Wealth, he taught, can do much good. At his death, it was said that he had enabled over 10,000 men to get a college education with the proceeds of his one lecture.

A reading from the lecture "Acres of Diamonds" by Russell H. Conwell

Great men, I have said, are very simple men. Just as many great men here as are to be found anywhere. The greatest error in judging great men is that we think that they always hold an office. The world knows nothing of its greatest men. Who are the great men of the world? The young man and young woman may well ask the question. It is not necessary that they should hold an office, and yet that is the popular idea. That is the idea we teach now in our high schools and common schools, that the great men of the world are those who hold some high office, and unless we change that very soon and do away with that prejudice, we are going to change to an empire. There is no question about it. We must teach that men are great only on their intrinsic value, and not on the position they may incidentally happen to occupy. And yet, don't blame the young men saying that they are going to be great when they get into some official position.

I ASK THIS AUDIENCE again who of you are going to be great? Says a young man: "I am going to be great." "When are you going to be great?" "When I am elected to some political office." Won't you learn the lesson, young man; that it is prima facie evidence of littleness to hold public office under our form of government? Think of it. This is a government of the people, and by the people, and for the people, and not for the officeholder, and if the people in this country rule as they always should rule, an office-holder is only the servant of the people, and the Bible says that "the servant cannot be greater than his master."

The Bible says that "he that is sent cannot be greater than he who sent him." In this country the people are the masters, and the officeholders can never be greater than the people; they should be honest servants of the people, but they are not our greatest men. Young man, remember that you never heard of a great man holding any political office in this country unless he took that office at an expense to himself. It is a loss to every great man to take a public office in our country. Bear this in mind, young man, that you cannot be made great by a political election. . . .

He who can give to this people better streets, better homes, better schools, better churches, more religion, more of happiness, more of God, he that can be a blessing to the community in which he lives tonight will be great anywhere, but he who cannot be a blessing where he now lives will never be great anywhere on the face of God's earth. "We live in deeds, not years, in feeling, not in figures on a dial; in thoughts, not breaths; we should count time by heart throbs, in the cause of right." Bailey says: "He most lives who thinks most."

If you forget everything I have said to you, do not forget this, because it contains more in two lines than all I have said. Baily says: "He most lives who thinks most, who feels the noblest, and who acts the best."

✪ *July 25*

Walter A. Scott

DISCIPLES OF CHRIST

October 31, 1796–April 23, 1861

Jesus prayed at the Last Supper that his disciples would be one but Christians have, from the very beginning, found that goal elusive. Paul urged unity on the quarreling Corinthians, and Constantine assembled the first ecumenical council to give Christians a common creed. When European Christians came to North America, many of them believed that the New World might allow Christians at last to become one. Instead, America has provided opportunities for further divisions.

The ancestors of the present-day Disciples of Christ or Christian Church spoke of a "Restoration Movement" that would unite Christians by going back to the most fundamental tenets of the faith. Walter Scott was among the best-loved of the early leaders of that movement. Not wanting to become a divisive figure, himself, he left so little record of his life that biographers have been frustrated. But one of them noted that he "lived so much for others that he had little thought or care for himself." Born in Scotland, Scott was educated at the University of Edinburgh. When he came to America in 1818, he found a position as a Latin tutor on Long Island. Setting off to see more of the country a year later, he went to teach at an academy in Pittsburgh whose principal, George Forrester, had decided to make the Bible his only authority and guide in matters of religion.

Scott had been raised in Presbyterian tradition, but was convinced by the logic of Forrester's arguments. It now seemed evident to him that the central tenant of the Christian faith could be stated in four words: "Jesus is the Christ." Beyond that, he developed a "five finger exercise" as the plan of salvation: "Faith to change the heart. Repentance to change the life. Baptism to change the state. Remission of sins to cleanse the guilt. The gift of the Holy Spirit to make one a participant in the Divine Nature."

At first, he had trouble finding people to share this simple faith. Then, however, he met Alexander Campbell* and the two resolved to build a church that would stand on this apostolic foundation. Campbell became the leader of the Restoration Movement (which came to be known as the Disciples of Christ or the Christian Church), but Scott was its preeminent preacher and evangelist. Over the next 35 years, he traveled nearly 90,000 miles, preached over 9,000 sermons, and personally baptized 1,207 converts. When he died in 1861, Alexander Campbell wrote:

> Next to my father, he was the most cordial and indefatigable colaborer in the origin and progress of the present Reformation.... I knew him well, I knew him long. I loved him much. By the eye of faith and hope, methinks I see him in Abraham's bosom.

A reading from Walter Scott on the gift of the Spirit

But what are the fruits of a holy spirit? Paul says they are joy, peace, long suffering, gentleness, goodness, fidelity, meekness, temperance, against such there is no (written) law.

Now how many unholy Baptists are there? how many unholy Presbyterians, how many unholy Methodists, Episcopalians, Independents, and schismatics of every name? Well may the editor say we are still in Babylon! Ah me! when shall we return, and discern between the righteous and the wicked: between him that serves God and him that serves him not? Ah apostatizing christians, grievers and quenchers of the Spirit of our God, are we not ashamed?

Now, reader, let us return to God and holiness, for without it no one shall see his face — and believe me that a disputatious mind is not a holy mind — an intemperate, unmeek, or unfaithful spirit is not a holy spirit — neither is one that does not practice goodness, and gentleness, and long suffering, and peace — neither the mind that does not love, or does not rejoice in Jesus. Ye cavillers, ye conceited few, who boast of your scriptural knowledge; but whose spirits, nevertheless, cannot move even the elements of the heavenly oracles, let me whisper to you a secret, that the kingdom of heaven is not so much in an abundant knowledge, as in an abundant spirit of righteousness, peace and holy joy.

Thus the faith, love, and hope of the gospel, with the gift of the Holy Spirit, are all proofs of our individual personal adoption.

The gift of the Spirit provides the experience of salvation:

But after all, what would it profit me to understand all that the Revelations (sic) have said of the church general, what happiness should I derive from the most perfect acquaintance with what is written of the primitive institutions, or of the twelve apostles, or even of Jesus himself, in all the scriptures generally, and in the four gospels in particular, unless at the same time I knew that I myself were individually and personally interested in the great salvation.

This brings us precisely to what is vulgarly called "experimental religion;" a phrase which, by the way, means nothing more than those personal proofs and evidences of our individual adoption into the family of God, which are to be found in the character of every genuine christian.

Experimental religion, then, (for I scorn to fight about the sound when we have agreed upon the sense) — experimental religion, I say, is one of those subjects which the Holy Spirit has shown to be of importance, inasmuch as he has condescended to discourse upon the christian graces and gifts which constitute what we call by this rotten phrase, "experimental religion." ... All christians know that they have been begotten by God by the spirit which he has given them. Thus the faith, love, and hope of the gospel, with the gift of the Holy Spirit, are all proofs of our individual personal adoption.

✪ *July 26*

Alexander McLeod

PRESBYTERIAN

June 12, 1774–February 17, 1833

The son of a noted Scottish cleric, Alexander McLeod arrived in New York in 1792. After studying at Union College, he studied theology with James McKinney and was licensed by the Reformed Presbytery at Coldenham, New York, in 1799. He was then called to a pastorate in Coldenham in 1800. Up to this point, his career is unremarkable: a studious Scot arrives in America, is educated, and wins his first job. Here, however, McLeod departed from the norm. Aware that some slave owners had signed his letter of call, he refused the appointment on that basis and told the presbytery in a letter. His petition sparked a conversation and led to a unanimous decision that "no slave-holder should be allowed the communion of the Church." Remarkably, the decision was taken so seriously that some of the slave-holding families did, in fact, end the practice and divest themselves of their slaves. To persuade a church body to act decisively on a momentous issue is noteworthy in itself; for members of that church to follow its leading is even more remarkable. This young Presbyterian minister pioneered principles that would only be generally recognized by his adopted nation after a bloody war in the distant future.

A reading from *Negro Slavery Unjustifiable: A Discourse* by Alexander McLeod

> Whosoever looketh unto the perfect law of liberty, and continueth therein; he being not a forgetful hearer, but a doer of the work; this man shall be blessed in his deed. James 1:25.

The Author of this Discourse had a call presented to him, in November, 1800, to take the pastoral charge of a congregation in the county of Orange, in the State of New-York. He perceived among the subscribers the names of some whom he knew to be holders of slaves, He doubted the consistency of enslaving the Negroes with the Christian system, and was unwilling to enter into a full ecclesiastic communion with those who continued the practice. He hesitated to accept the call; but took an early opportunity of writing to the Elders of the Church, and of intimating to the Presbytery his sentiments respecting slavery.

The Reformed Presbytery has judicially condemned the practice, and warned their connections against it. This produced an additional evidence of the force of Christian principle, It triumphed over self-interest; and, in several parts of the United States, have men sacrificed, on the altar of Religion, the property which the civil law gave them in their fellow men, There is not a slave-holder now in the communion of the Reformed Presbytery.

A sense of duty determined the author to commit this Discourse to the press. In the publication of it he has particularly in view the instruction and establishment of those inhabitants of Orange who have placed themselves under his pastoral care. Through them he addresses all into whose hands the Discourse may come.

If the Redeemer shall be pleased to bless it, and render it the means of ameliorating the bondage, or of procuring the liberty of any miserable African, the author shall receive more than a recompense.

Exodus 21:16. *He that stealeth a man, and selleth him, or if he be found in his hand, he shall surely be put to death.*

God is omnipotent. His omnipotence is necessary, and independent of every other being. He is the source from which all power flows. Whatever physical force can be exerted by man, is derived from his Maker. In the exercise of natural power man is under a law to God. He is indeed a free agent; but the divine law circumscribes his sphere of action, and marks out boundaries which he cannot pass with impunity. To exert his natural powers under the direction of law is right: to exercise any powers derived from God, contrary to his declared will, is wrong. Whatever is included in the grant God has made to the human family, is one of the *rights of man;* and beyond this grant, contrary to God's law, man cannot claim a right, until he shakes off his dependency, and elevates his own authority until it become paramount to that which is exercised by Jehovah. Whosoever attempts to deprive any of the human family of the former, or put him in possession of the latter, is guilty of treason against Heaven, unless he is expressly commissioned, in this particular instance, to contradict the general principles of law, by the same great authority from which the law derives its binding force. He who, without this authority, breaks over the barriers of law, and, with physical force, deprives his neighbour of liberty or property, is an enemy to God and to man; much more so he who commences an unprovoked attack on any of his fellow men, and, with lawless power, steals him from his connections, barters him for some other commodity, or forces him to labour for the benefit of another, and that other an *enemy,* who has committed, or countenanced the *commission* of the theft.

The divine law declares this a crime, and prescribes the punishment. *He who stealeth a man, and selleth him, or if he be found in his hand, he shall surely be put to death.*

This law was given to the Hebrews as a body politic; but it proceeds on a moral ground, and is, consequently, obligatory still on every subject of moral government.

From the text, I consider myself authorised to lay before you the following proposition:

The practice of buying, holding, or selling our unoffending fellow creatures as slaves is immoral.

The text will certainly support this proposition, According to the common principles of law, the receiver of stolen goods, if he know them to be such, is esteemed guilty as well as the thief. The slave holder never had a right to force a man into his service, or to retain him, without an equivalent. To sell him, therefore, is to tempt another to sin, and to dispose of that, for money, to which he never had a right.

✪ *July 27*

Austin Carroll
ROMAN CATHOLIC
February 23, 1835–November 29, 1909

In the early years of the Christian church, a certain Mathetes wrote a letter to Diognetus that characterized Christians in the following way: "Every foreign land is their fatherland and yet for them every fatherland is a foreign land. . . . They busy themselves on earth, but their citizenship is in heaven."

The description remains valid for many Christians today but seems especially fitting for Margaret Anne Carroll. Born in Ireland, she took the name Sister Austin Carroll at 18, when she joined a rather new religious order, the Sisters of Mercy. She had barely taken her final vows when, at 21, she was chosen to respond to an appeal for help in the United States. Arriving in Providence, Rhode Island, she went on to work in Hartford, Buffalo, Rochester, Omaha, St. Louis, and New Orleans. Her love for Ireland endured through all these moves, yet whether in the unaccustomed chill of New England or the equally unaccustomed warmth of Louisiana, Austin Carroll made herself at home, serving God by meeting the needs of those around her.

Those needs usually included the creation and staffing of schools along with assistance for the sick and the poor. The Civil War was raging during Austin Carroll's early years in America, so there were hospitals to visit, injured soldiers in need of assistance, and war-torn families to be helped. In St. Louis 25,000 soldiers in an improvised field hospital were visited daily by the sisters. Both there and in New Orleans, Carroll visited prisoners. She and her sisters also nursed victims of the frequent yellow fever epidemics in New Orleans.

Somehow, in the midst of this varied ministry, Austin Carroll found time to write. Her bibliography includes 20 books of her own composition with nearly as many translated or edited by her as well as many articles in journals, magazines, and newspapers. The income from the writing helped finance the schools and other ministries of the sisters.

Increasingly over the years, administrative duties were added to her work. As Superior of the New Orleans Province, it was her responsibility to develop new schools and convents. Financing the schools was always a challenge, since the sisters were especially eager to educate children of limited means and to include black students as well as whites in their ministry. Often their schools were the only ones open to black children. Carroll took particular pride in the accomplishments of the young women in her schools and was convinced they could succeed in any walk of life. "When occasion requires," she wrote, "they have a patient endurance, a noble bravery, and an invincible energy which go far to prove that the term 'weaker sex' has nothing to do with the soul." She had hoped to create a woman's college and saw her inability to do so as one of her greatest failures. Nonetheless, many schools and convents, libraries and other charitable institutions across the south bore witness to her success in living out the ideals of her order.

A reading from an essay by Austin Carroll from *Catholic World* concerning the true purpose of education

Nowadays, certainly, your prime rascals have been educated rascals. Yes, to live by one's wits; to regard duties as optional; to have an unwholesome fear of the pickaxe and the shovel, the broom and the wash-board, the ironing-table and the cook-stove; to find idleness, gambling, cheating, forgery more to one's taste than honest labor, is a state of things not entirely unknown in the romantic region which La Salle called by the sweet-sounding name, Louisiana. And inside the prison-walls, as the writer knows from personal experience gained by visiting prisons and conversing with their unfortunate inmates, it is not the booby or the dunce that predominates, but the keen-witted knave, whose intellect has been polished at the expense of heart and conscience, and whose chief regret is that his nefarious plans and projects have come to naught.

It is pleasant to take mild views, but it is misleading to look at things through the prism of self-conceit. The first step towards righting a wrong is to see and admit that it is a wrong, for there is a wonderful remedial power in truth. Let us, then, frankly own that education, apart from the theory and practice of the laws of God, has done little or nothing to eliminate crime in Louisiana or elsewhere. As to religion, the editor of the New York Methodist calls the public schools "hot-beds of infidelity;" as to morality, M. W. Hazen tells us in the Boston Journal of Education, March 17, 1881, that they are "dangerous to the family, the state, and the nation." It would be impossible that such a system could eradicate crime. But could a just method be reduced to practice for educating not merely the intellect or the physique, but the whole man, on the basis of accountability to the Deity, then indeed would true culture flourish, vice be diminished, and solid progress replace glittering rhetoric.

Hence let virtue be the foundation of popular education, and the results will be worthy of the zeal with which earnest men and women labor in the great cause. Then will the wolf dwell with the lamb, and the leopard lie down with the kid; the fierce and sanguinary and the gentle and good mingle in lowly adoration of Him "by whom kings reign and lawgivers decree just things...." "Popular education," says Guizot, "to be truly good and socially useful, must be fundamentally religious." And a greater than Guizot, O'Connell, the only Catholic quoted in this lengthy article, was wont to say: "Education without religion is worse than ignorance." If, then, you ask once more why education has been not only less successful in preventing crime than its advocates might have expected, but positively unsuccessful, I reply in strong old Saxon, on part of scholars ignorant of their obligations and their accountability to an all-seeing Judge: "They cunnen not the Ten Commandments." Or, if they do know them, it is only by rote and without any practical application.

✪ *July 28*

Enmegabowh

EPISCOPALIAN

?–June 12, 1902

Early North American settlements claimed that one of their primary objectives was "conversion of the Natives." Yet amidst the stress of establishing viable communities in a hostile environment, most settlers were so concerned with their own security that they spent little time evangelizing. Although missionaries were dispatched to proselytize Indians, their efforts were often hampered by their own unfamiliarity with the culture, and by the growing instability of native communities pushed off their traditional lands by white western expansion. The rare Native American with qualifications for ministry also found himself all too often called on to serve as a mediator and not fully trusted by either side.

The story of Enmegabowh, the first Native American ordained to the priesthood of the Episcopal Church, vividly illustrates the conflicts such men faced. Enmegabowh described his own upbringing in the traditions of his people:

> I will give you a little of my first being and wanderings here and elsewhere. Of course I was born in a heathen country. My parents were heathen; worshipped to wood and stone. I was brought up in and trained in the Grand Medicine worship when quite young. But still I can remember all the teachings which

have been taught me. Bye-and-bye I was initiated into the lodge and was fully considered a worthy member in the lodge.

Methodist missionaries were present, however, and commended themselves to the Ojibwa leadership as a resource against the alcoholism and hopelessness that was slowly destroying the Native American culture. Enmegabowh enlisted in this cause and was trained as a teacher and evangelist. In that capacity he came into Minnesota in 1841, serving various mission stations over the next ten years. He also married and his wife was baptized. Gradually, however, he became discouraged by the failure of white missionaries to stay with the work. At least once, he tried to return to Canada. But the storms that disrupted his voyage reminded him of Jonah's story, so he decided to persevere in his ministry in Minnesota.

In 1851, he was given a copy of the Episcopal Prayer Book and felt that it provided the solid framework he had been looking for. Soon afterward, he converted several leading Ojibwas to the faith and wrote proudly, "Here...is another big Indian witness for the love of Jesus." He thought the story should be told to those "Palefaces...who have their doubts of an Indian becoming truly Christian, that Indian [sic] can love Jesus with all his heart and can be happy as well as your Palefaces who love Jesus." In 1859, Enmegabowh was ordained a deacon in the Episcopal Church and in that same year Henry Benjamin Whipple* was consecrated as Bishop of Minnesota. The bishop became a staunch supporter and colleague in the years that followed.

Growing tensions between settlers and Native Americans persuaded some young Ojibwa that the time had come for them to go on the warpath. They approached Enmegabowh, who replied: "I am glad to hear you think me worthy to make known to me your object in visiting Crow Wing. My friends, I presume you all understand what it will bring about. If you kill the white man, you will cause a general warfare and the whites will drive us away from our country and perhaps will eventually sweep us away from the face of the earth." Enmegabowh offered to serve as intermediary and secured promises from American authorities that satisfied the Native Americans for a time. But later that same year, the Sioux came up with a similar plan and also told Enmegabowh their intentions. He responded:

> My friends, you all know me. For years I have stood before you and tried to save you from your present condition and the consequences of your sin's doing. If you knew as much as I know of the greatness and power of the whites against whom you are expected to fight, you would not entertain the idea to thus strike against heavy rocks. You may kill a few in the beginning, but in the end you will all be swept away from the face of the earth, and annihilated forever. I love you all. I see and know just exactly how the war will terminate. As a friend who loves you, I would ask you all as wise men to think and well consider whether your present plan is to your salvation or death. Consider well.

Removing his own family out of harm's way, Enmegabowh warned the local army post of the danger. For many years, he lost the trust of his own people. Sometimes, his life was threatened. Yet he persevered in his ministry and in 1867 Bishop Whipple ordained him to the priesthood, a first among Episcopalians.

As white settlements increased, Enmegabowh and Bishop Whipple saw no alternative to moving the Ojibwas away from areas now taken over by farmers and loggers. It was clear to Enmegabowh what was happening to his people as he observed to one of his correspondents: "Look, look! You have taken away the hunting ground from them; having deprived them of everything from which they had derived daily support. When they were depending alone on their own exertions for support they never begged nor disturbed you by begging."

On the new White Earth reservation, Emegabowh was at last able to carry on a peaceful ministry:

> A little comfortable log house had been provided for my dwelling house. Sunday came, and to my great astonishment, chiefs and headmen, women and children, of all grades, came to listen to my teachings. I was moved with compassion to see them seek shelter and strong stockade for shelter, the most impregnable fortress of Christian religion, the only hope of salvation for my unfortunate race.... During the winter we used the largest wigwam or log house, and during the summer I held my public services under the shade of the trees. In the second year I had nearly all the chiefs and the leading men and women and many children under my teachings.

An advocate for his people and a mediator between whites and Native Americans, Enmegabowh died in 1902 after 44 years of ministry to his church and people.

✠ July 29

Catherine Livingston Garrettson

METHODIST

1752–1849

Though born into a prominent and historic Hudson River family, Catherine Livingston did not fit into the life she inherited. She was "converted" while reading the Book of Common Prayer, an odd religious experience for her upbringing, but at least it came from the proper book for a wealthy Episcopal family. When her mother's housekeeper gave her some of John Wesley's books and she became a Methodist, her parents were horrified. Methodism was for poor people. But Catherine found little satisfaction in the social life of her neighbors. She attended balls and parties, but then pondered, with a close friend, the emptiness of it all. She then had the bad taste to fall in love with a Methodist circuit rider, Freeborn Garrettson. For five years her mother opposed the match, but finally, Catherine's brothers and sisters persuaded her that a 39-year-old woman was running out of options and so the marriage took place.

Freeborn Garrettson was one of the notable early Methodist preachers. Like his wife, he had come to a profoundly life-changing conversion. He, too, had abandoned the pleasant life he had inherited, freed his slaves, given them his land, and set off to reach the gospel. He served for a while in Nova Scotia and began evangelizing in eastern New York and western New England. After his marriage to Catherine in 1793, he settled in New York but continued to preach across most of the eastern states. In 1799, the Garrettsons built a substantial home on the banks of the Hudson, using money Catherine inherited. There, she cared for her daughter and husband and developed a ministry of hospitality. Bishop Asbury named the house "Traveler's Rest," and many an exhausted Methodist preacher without a home of his own found it a place of refreshment.

Some six weeks after her conversion, Catherine started a diary which eventually comprised 15 volumes. It is a remarkable journal of mystical experiences, with the traditional elements of purgation, illumination, dark night of the soul, and mystical union. After her marriage, the entries became briefer. She was more likely to pen letters to friends and family. Her life became bound up with others, so there was far less time for introspection and solitary prayer. This journal, however, along with her letters and papers, provides invaluable insight into the spiritual life of an American woman in the early years of the republic.

A reading from the journal of Catherine Livingston

Monday March 10. Still my ingratitude hung with weight upon my mind. Ah! Why did I so soon fall from the sweet communion I have so lately had with the pure Father of Lights and my beloved Jesus — but still he is my friend, for he is the Sinners Friend, and I am his tho' every way unworthy to be called his Child. Deeply humbled under a sense of my fault and my knowledge, that unless the Lord took from the fear of man, I was liable to fall into the same error continually — I looked up to my Saviour for every thing I needed, and I was again under reading his word, brought out of bondage into the Glorious Liberty of the Children of God. A way was opened I was received, and encircled in the Arms of divine love. Glory to a Sin pardoning God! — My mouth was opened to sing his praises, Who is my God and my all. The presence of God was continually with me throughout the remainder of the day. — But at Night in my approaches to a throne of Grace and Mercy. How shall I discribe or who will believe the report of what the Lord God gracious and merciful, Condescended to reveal to the Eyes of the weakest and least of his creatures — In prayer Jesus was present with me operating on my heart by his holy Spirit.

I was filled sweetly with ye love of God shed abroad in my heart and leaving me with nothing to ask for. All was bliss and holy Joy. When gradually this gave way to a solemn waiting before God. The Father answered a request I had made a few nights before that he would show me his Glory. — In wonder and astonishment I gazed — I am not sensible how long. I fell back my hands were raised. It seemed to be rising — I raised with it my hands and my face elivated, still on my knees, but as it passed on, my face still turned involuntarily towards it, and my whole body was obedient. I was struck down upon my back, lost to solemn awe and wonder. I lay and felt what a poor Insignificant Creature he is whose breath is in his nostrils. I prayed fervently to the Lord Jesus in whom alone I have strength, that he would be pleased to save me from all delusion: and guide me ever by his holy Spirit. My mind was deeply exercised — I knew it was Impossible to see God and live. I knew that out of Christ he is a consuming fire. With my bodily Eye I saw nothing all was presented to my mind, and what I then saw, no pen or tongue can ever discribe. I felt as did Daniel a faintness and trembling come over me: I arose as soon as I had power, and again threw myself on my knees. With fervent prayer and vehement desire. I cried to my Beloved and my Friend, to come and stand between the Aweful Holy God and his poor Catherine. I found the veiws of the purity and Glory of ye divinity which I had lately seen were sufficient if given in a greater degree to have crumbled me Into my native dust and had not His Lord Jesus put Strength in to me, and prepared my Soul for this wonderful display of the Divine perfection: I must have perished under the great views which I had.

✪ *July 30*

Charles G. Finney

PRESBYTERIAN/CONGREGATIONAL

August 29, 1792–August 16, 1875

Brought up outside organized religion and trained as a lawyer, Charles G. Finney's conversion grew out of his own reading of the Bible. As a lawyer, his duty was to persuade skeptics on a jury. As a preacher, he brought the same technique to the pulpit. In simple and repetitive language, he would urge his hearers to come forward and be converted — and they came. Finney was 29 years old and working as a lawyer in Jefferson County, New York, when he was converted. He immediately left his practice of the law and began to preach at revivals in the community. He was ordained by the presbytery the next year after studying with the pastor of the church in Adams. Gradually his preaching carried him to other nearby churches, then to Utica and Schenectady, then to Philadelphia, Buffalo, and Boston.

Although he called for lives transformed by Christ, and brought hundreds, then thousands to conversion, Finney never manipulated feelings, and discouraged any display of emotion in his hearers. Contrary to the custom of the times, he never read his sermons. He said a lawyer could never persuade a jury by reading them an essay. His impact on his audiences was powerful. One account said, "When he opened his mouth he was aiming a gun. When he spoke bombardment began." Yet he appealed to reason. His arguments were often organized under 40 or 50 headings. Each might be very brief, but the thought progressed logically.

In 1832, Finney took charge of a congregation in New York City, moving in 1836 to the Broadway Tabernacle, which was built for him according to his own specifications so that in a gathering of 2,500, no one would be more than 80 feet from the speaker. Not content to limit himself to one ministry, however, Finney also accepted a position as professor of theology at the newly created Oberlin College on Ohio's western frontier. Thereafter, he divided his time in various ways between Oberlin and New York — though still participating in evangelistic crusades in England and Scotland as well as various parts of the United States. He published a series of books on revival and systematic theology, some of which are still read.

A reading from Finney's *Lectures on Systematic Theology*

I am not aware that any respectable writer has laid much stress upon other passages than those I have examined, as expressly teaching, or unequivocally implying the fact of the fall and ruin of real saints. There may be such writers and such passages as those of which I speak; but if there are, I do not recollect to have seen them.

1. If the doctrine under consideration is not true, I cannot see upon what ground we can affirm, or even confidently hope, that many of our pious friends who have died have gone to heaven. Suppose they held on their way until the last hours of life. If we may not believe that the faithfulness of God prevailed to keep them through the last conflict, what reason have we to affirm that they were preserved from sin and apostasy in their last hours, and saved? If the sovereign grace of God do not protect them against the wiles and malice of Satan, in their feebleness, and in the wreck of their habitation of clay, what has become of them? I must confess that, if I did not expect the covenanted mercy and faithfulness of God to prevail, and to sustain the soul under such circumstances, I should have very little expectation that any would be saved. If I could have any confidence that Christians would stand fast while in health, aside from the truth of this doctrine, still I should expect that Satan would overcome them in the end, when they passed through the last great struggle. Who could then trust to the strength of his own purposes?

2. But I could no more hope, that myself or any one else, would persevere in holiness in our best estate, even for one day or hour, if not kept by the power of God through faith, than I could hope to fly to heaven. As I have before said, there is no hope of any one's persevering, except in so far as free grace anticipates and secures the concurrence of free will. The soul must be

called, and effectually called, and perpetually called, or it will not follow Christ for an hour. I say again, that by effectual calling, I do not mean an irresistible calling. I do not mean a calling that cannot, or that might not be resisted; but I do mean by an effectual calling, a calling that is not in fact resisted, a calling that does in fact secure the voluntary obedience of the soul. This is my only hope in respect to myself, or anybody else. This grace I regard as vouchsafed to me in the covenant of grace, or as a reward of Christ's obedience unto death. It is pledged, to secure the salvation of those whom the Father has from eternity given to the Son. The Holy Spirit is given to them to secure their salvation, and I have no expectation that any others will ever be saved. But these, every one of them, will surely be saved. There is, there can be, no hope for any others. Others are able to repent, but they will not. Others might be saved, if they would believe, and comply with the conditions of salvation, but they will not.

We have seen, that none come to Christ, except they are drawn of the Father, and that the Father draws to Christ those and those only whom he has given to Christ, and also, that it is the Father's design that of those whom he has given to Christ, he should lose none, but that he should raise them up at the last day. This is the only hope that any will be saved. Strike out this foundation, and what shall the righteous do? Strike out from the Bible the doctrine of God's covenanted faithfulness to Christ — the truth that the Father has given to him a certain number whose salvation he foresees that he could and should secure, and I despair of myself and of every body else. Where is any other ground of hope? I know not where.

✪ *July 31*

John LaFarge

ROMAN CATHOLIC

March 31, 1835–November 14, 1910

If John LaFarge had been less talented, he might be better known. His interests, however, were wide-ranging. While he produced significant works of art, his name is less well known today than Louis Comfort Tiffany, who took one aspect of LaFarge's genius and concentrated on it. LaFarge, on the other hand, was always interested in exploring new areas. After inventing the opalescent glass technique that made Tiffany famous, he traveled to Japan and became a pioneer in learning from Japanese tradition. He executed murals and still-lifes. He wrote books on art. In an era when ecumenism was in its earliest stages and Roman Catholics were still on the fringes of the mainstream of American life, Lafarge, as a Roman Catholic, produced works for Baptist, Episcopal, Presbyterian, and Congregational churches in addition to some in his own tradition.

John LaFarge was born of French parents in New York City and, at first, intended to pursue a career in law. He traveled to Europe as a young man and was struck by the stained glass in the great cathedrals. He studied with the French artist, Couture, but returned to the United States still set for a career in law. Before long, however, he was painting still-lifes and water colors and drawing illustrations for books. A mural done for Trinity Church, Boston, in 1873 made him famous. He went on to paint murals for the Vanderbilts, William Whitney, Henry Clay Frick, the United Congregational Church in Newport, Harvard University, Bowdoin College, the State Capitol in Minnesota, the Supreme Court building in Baltimore, and a great many churches on the east coast and elsewhere.

It was said of him that "though naturally a questioner, he venerated the traditions of religious art, and preserved always his childlike Catholic Faith and reverence."

A reading from John LaFarge

Most of the work done to embody the feelings of the moment according to the fashion of the moment, loses its meaning later. . . . And so it has been for an enormous mass of works of art destined for the use of religion; more properly, perhaps, for the use of the clergy, or for personal satisfaction of certain types of the religious mind, in which works of Art have been so completely the Handmaid of Religion, that to-day — a day of other wishes and requests — looks upon them as void of religious feeling, And so they are, as far as art is concerned; because art alone can carry from age to age the personal feelings of the artist, through which alone he can express religious feeling. Of course at the time many such things — I mean such points to be observed by the artist, to suit his patron — were matters of great consequence in the general world, which is a world of momentary views and necessities; not in the world of art. If the artist felt these things himself, and saw in them elements for the building and formation of this work, then, however much we may have lost the intention of the patron or of the public which the artist tried to please, there still remains the evidence of his likings; there still remain the other less transient truths which appealed to him as an artist. To-day, far removed as we are from the external agitation that troubled the theologies of the seventeenth century, we cannot be moved, as many a clergyman then was, by the figure of the crucified Christ, represented as hanging rigidly from His uplifted arms, thereby, to a person who looked upon art as merely a handmaid of religion, appearing to have died for the few and not for all; because the latter idea required outstretched arms. You will see that this special verity, if I may so call it out of respect for others, which the theologian cared for, is not the sort of verity which art can best embody. It needs explanation and support outside of the statement concerning it made by the artist.

Philip Berrigan

ROMAN CATHOLIC

October 5, 1923–December 6, 2002

During the turbulent 1960s and '70s, Christians were deeply divided about the war in Vietnam. Individuals were torn between patriotism and a desire to support the nation's military on the one hand, and a growing feeling that this struggle was futile and costing the United States young lives and money better spent on social problems at home on the other. Church bodies, too, had divisions within their membership. With a few exceptions, the Christian churches remained eerily silent about the ongoing destruction in southeast Asia.

Philip Berrigan was one of the exceptions. His consistent and courageous witness to peace won him admiration from some, scorn from others. Twice nominated for the Nobel Peace Prize, he also made the FBI's list of Ten Most Wanted for his protests against war. He was himself a veteran of World War II. His military service allowed him to witness firsthand the degrading effects of racism upon American culture, as well as war's violence and devastation. After leaving the military, he attended seminary and began to take part in demonstrations in favor of civil rights for African Americans.

Philip and his brother, Daniel, teamed up with Thomas Merton to plan more public and effective antiwar efforts. Their writing and speaking led to more dramatic protests. In October 1967, Berrigan and a few others entered the Baltimore Customs House and poured blood (including his own) on Selective Service records stored there. While awaiting arrest, the group distributed scriptures. They calmly explained their actions to the draft board employees. Berrigan is quoted as saying, "This sacrificial and constructive act is meant to protest the pitiful waste of American and Vietnamese blood in Indochina." Because of this event, Berrigan became the first Roman Catholic priest to be arrested in the United States for civil disobedience. His sentence was six years in jail.

In 1969, he was released on bail and planned a new protest to gain attention for the antiwar movement and the moral wrong of the war. He and eight others (later known as the Catonsville Nine) went into the Selective Service office in Catonsville, Maryland, and burned almost 400 draft records with homemade napalm. Everyone in the group was Roman Catholic, and they released the following statement: "We confront the Catholic Church, other Christian bodies and the synagogues of America, with their silence and cowardice in the face of our country's crimes. We are convinced that the religious bureaucracy in this country is racist, is an accomplice in this war, and is hostile to the poor." This time, Berrigan was sentenced to three and a half years and received virtually no support from his church body.

In September of 1980, Berrigan and his brother Daniel were joined by six others, calling themselves the "Plowshares Movement" and initiating a new form of protest. They entered the General Electric Nuclear Missile Re-entry Division in King of Prussia, Pennsylvania, which produced nose cones for warheads. They hammered on two nose cones, poured blood over documents, and prayed intercessions for peace. There followed nearly ten years of trials and appeals, but eventually they were released.

Berrigan's final gesture for Ploughshares took place late in 1999. This time, the target was a group of A-10 Warthog warplanes. Again convicted and sentenced, he was released near the end of 2001. Berrigan died of cancer in Jonah House, a community in which members embrace a simple lifestyle, share a life of prayer, and bear witness to the violence that flows from militarism and consumerism. It was cofounded by Berrigan and others in the early 1970s. Because of his highly publicized protests, Berrigan spent some 11 years in prison. In addition to lecturing and teaching, he was the author of six books, including his autobiography, *Fighting the Lamb's War.*

Just days before his death, he wrote: "I die with the conviction, held since 1968 and Catonsville that nuclear weapons are the scourge of the earth; to mine for them, manufacture them, deploy them, use them, is a curse against God, the human family, and the earth itself." Though he left the Jesuits and the Roman Catholic priesthood, Berrigan's faith remained the core of his understanding of historical events. His moral vision, shaped by the prophets and the gospels, energized him to be a forceful agent of God in the face of what he considered to be national crimes of idolatry. Unafraid, he accepted arrest and imprisonment as part of the cost of faithfulness to his Lord in an era so bent on death and destruction. He believed he was standing against a whole structure of greed, coercion, deception, and violence that had become a norm for many and which needed to be named and confronted, so that an alternative could be offered. Berrigan's witness is that one's life can be used to display biblical and spiritual options to a society blinded by its own need for power and control.

✪ *August 2*

Henry B. Whipple

EPISCOPALIAN

February 15, 1822–September 16, 1901

A strange accident made Henry B. Whipple the first Bishop of Minnesota. The diocese held an election in which two other candidates were deadlocked. A single vote had been cast for Henry Whipple by someone who had met him only once, but had been favorably impressed. As the deadlock persisted, votes shifted to the unknown compromise candidate so, at the age of 37, Whipple became the youngest bishop in the church.

Minnesota was then a frontier state where relations between Native Americans and newcomers were tense. Whipple made evangelizing of the Indians a priority. Seeing the difficulties they faced, he acted as their advocate with state and national authorities. The westward tide of white settlement continued to push the Native Americans out of their lands, and the Bureau of Indian Affairs in Washington did little for them. Indian Agents frequently lied to the them, misappropriating their funds. Whipple soon became known as one white man the Native Americans could trust. They called him "Straight Tongue."

Not long after Whipple's election, the Civil War broke out. As the Union armies suffered defeats, the Indians thought it might be their opportunity to regain some of what they had lost. On August 18, 1862, Sioux warriors attacked in Minnesota, and the state was soon in flames. Many settlers and soldiers were killed and, when it was over, angry whites called for the remaining Indians to be driven from the state. Whipple appealed for calm and wrote to the president of the United States to tell him what needed to be done. For the remainder of Whipple's episcopacy, Washington turned often to him for leadership, as did the Native Americans. Even in England, where Whipple attended three Lambeth Conferences, he was known as the Apostle to the Indians.

Whipple was a builder as well. The Shattuck School and St. Mary's Hall were created to provide a good education for young men and women. Seabury Seminary was founded so that men studying for ordination would not have to travel to the east. A cathedral was erected in Faribault to serve as a central gathering point for the diocese.

By the time of his death, the man who had once been the church's youngest bishop had served over 40 years, been awarded honorary degrees by five English universities, and was recognized as a leader in both the religious and secular world.

A reading from a letter to President Lincoln from Bishop Whipple

TO THE PRESIDENT OF THE UNITED STATES.

The sad condition of the Indians of this State, who are my heathen wards, compels me to address you on their behalf. I ask only justice for a wronged and neglected race. I write the more cheerfully because I believe that the intentions of the Government have always been kind; but they have been thwarted by dishonest servants, ill-conceived plans, and defective instructions.

Before their treaty with the United States, the Indians of Minnesota were as favorably situated as an uncivilized race could well be. Their lakes, forests, and prairies furnished abundant game, and their hunts supplied them with valuable furs for the purchase of all articles of traffic. The great argument to secure the sale of their lands is the promise of their civilization. . . . Remember, the parties to this contract are a great Christian Nation and a poor heathen people. From the day of the treaty a rapid deterioration takes place. The Indian has sold the hunting-grounds necessary for his comfort as a wild man; His tribal relations are weakened; his chief's power and influence circumscribed; and he will soon be left a helpless man without a government, a protector, or a friend, unless treaty is observed.

The Indian agents who are placed in trust of the honor and faith of the Government are generally selected without any reference to their fitness for the place. The Congressional delegation desires to award John Doe for party work, and John Doe desires the place because there is a tradition on the border that an Indian agent with fifteen hundred dollars a year can retire upon an ample fortune in four years. . . . They are often men without any fitness, sometimes a disgrace to a Christian nation; whiskey-sellers, barroom loungers, debauchers, selected to guide a heathen people. Then follow all the evils of bad example, of inefficiency, and of dishonesty, — the school a sham, the supplies wasted, the improvement fund curtailed by fraudulent contracts. The Indian, bewildered, conscious of wrong, but helpless, has no refuge but to sink into a depth of brutishness. . . .

The United States has virtually left the Indian without protection. . . . The sale of whiskey, the open licentiousness, the neglect and want are fast dooming this people to death, and as sure as there is a God much of the guilt lies at the Nation's door.

The first thing needed is honesty. There has been a marked deterioration in Indian affairs since the office has become one of mere political favoritism. . . .

The second step is to frame instructions so that the Indian shall be the ward of the Government. They cannot live without law. We have broken up, in part, their tribal relations, and they must have something in their place.

Whenever the Indian desires to abandon his wild life, the Government ought to aid him in building a house, in opening his farm, in providing utensils and implements of labor. . . .

The schools should be ample to receive all children who desire to attend. . . .

In all future treaties it ought to be the object of the Government to pay the Indians in kind. . . .

I have written to you freely with all the frankness with which a Christian bishop has the right to write to the Chief Ruler of a great Christian Nation. My design has not been to complain of individuals, nor to make accusations. Bad as I believe some of the appointments to be, they are the fault of a political system. When I came to Minnesota I was startled at the degradation at my door. I give these men missions; God has blessed me, and I would count every trial I have had as a way of roses if I could save this people.

May God guide you and give you grace to order all things, so that the Government shall deal righteously with the Indian nations in its charge.

Your servant for Christ's sake,
H. B. WHIPPLE,
Bishop of Minnesota.

❂ *August 3*

Lucy Whitehead McGill Peabody

BAPTIST

March 2, 1861–February 26, 1949

Lucy McGill did not envision becoming a missionary when she was growing up in Rochester, New York. When she met and fell in love with Norman Waterbury, a theological student, she thought to find happiness as the wife of a pastor in a pleasant American community. Norman, however, felt called to work in an overseas mission Lucy therefore decided to go with him. She set sail at the age of 20, a month after their marriage, for a new life in India.

Lucy had been teaching in a state school for the deaf when she met Norman. As soon as she gained some knowledge of Telugu, she set out with a native Bible woman to visit villages around Madras, make friends among the women, and share with them useful ideas for preparing food, caring for children, and preventing disease. Then she and her companion would introduce programs for children and start a Bible study group. Norman meanwhile had made such progress in the language that he was appointed to translate the Bible into Telugu. Unfortunately, only five years after arriving in India, he died of dysentery, leaving Lucy with two small children.

Six years after her marriage, Lucy found herself back in Rochester, teaching the deaf and volunteering to do whatever she could to support mission work "except speak in public." "That," she said, "I cannot do." She could do administrative work, however, and when she was asked two years later to move to Boston for a position with the Woman's Baptist Foreign Mission Society, she was glad to be able to support herself and her small family doing work to which she was now deeply committed.

Perhaps she could not speak in public, but she knew how to enlist others, knew how to organize work effectively, and knew how to provide materials that would interest and involve others. Before long she was working with Helen Montgomery* to organize mission summer schools that would bring together representatives of local churches and missionaries on home leave. Soon hundreds of women could broaden their horizons by acquiring new talents, then going home to inspire still others. It was through her work that Lucy Waterbury met Henry Peabody, a wealthy importer and exporter who had begun to support world mission after the death of his first wife. The marriage lasted only two years. Henry Peabody died of a sudden stroke, but left his widow with the means to devote herself more fully than before to the work she cared about. She organized a plan to publish children's literature, helped organize a golden jubilee celebration of American women's missionary work, and worked again with Helen Montgomery to create a Federation of Woman's Boards of Foreign Missions in 1916. The two women also established the World Day of Prayer for Mission, still observed annually in many churches.

In 1913, Lucy Peabody and Helen Montgomery set out to travel around the world and see for themselves what women were doing in foreign mission. On her return, Lucy Peabody wrote a little book called *The Meddlesome Missionary*, responding to the criticisms she had heard.

> [One] charge is, that the missionary is meddlesome. Why should he presume to insult these beautiful ancient faiths by intruding his meek, mild message? What business has he in the East at all, and being there, why does he not attend to his own affairs and cease meddling with minds, morals, manners and, above all, with religion? ...
>
> We took some pains to investigate the ... charge as we traveled through Egypt, India, Burma, China, Korea, and Japan, and we finally came to an entire agreement with the criticism, that the missionary is an inveterate meddler. Indeed, to be a missionary indicates a meddlesome nature. Most people are quite content to stay comfortably at home without concerning themselves about the sufferings or needs of those so far away. Most of us do not even care to meddle with the wretched and neglected in our own town. A missionary, then, is one who, instead of attending to his own affairs, deliberately turns his attention to the affairs of people in other countries.

David Livingston made himself somewhat notorious by meddling with the slave trade of Africa. William Carey meddled with "suttee," and incited Lord Bentinck to stop, by English law, the burning of Hindu widows. The cessation of the opium traffic in China was helped by the interference of missionaries.

Women missionaries have been especially disagreeable through their meddling with the condition of child wives and the atrocities practised on little widows. Medical missionaries are perhaps the most meddlesome of all.

But, seriously, why should these people go out of their way at great expense of time and sacrifice of life, to change conditions in Eastern countries? We must go back for the answer to the question put one day by way of argumentation in an Eastern city. A certain man, seeking to justify himself in an exclusive position, said to a great social leader "Who is *my* neighbor?" The reply came in Oriental story form — an illustration of a man who was traveling on a dangerous road and met with robbers who took all he had and left him for dead. Several distinguished citizens passed by and said calmly, "It is none of our affair." Then came one of another race, who, with some effort and loss of time, rescued the suffering man and answered for all time the question, "Who is my neighbor?"

To state the case etymologically and geographically, "neighbor" means next door. On our west, we find our next neighbors are in China and Japan, and down the world street, around the corner, is India.... Both England and India have welcomed American missionaries and their meddling has resulted in a chain of Christian schools, grading from kindergarten to college; in great medical settlements with hospitals and dispensaries; in training schools for industrial work; in Christian communities; in homes for defectives and lepers....

If those who seek to justify themselves in a selfish and narrow policy of exclusion, utterly opposed to the teaching of Jesus would go with open minds into the centres of missionary effort they would gain a new vision of world neighborliness and a new appreciation of the value of the meddlesome missionary.

One final note: in the 1920s, campaigning for Women's Christian Colleges in Asia, Lucy Peabody became what she had sworn she could never be: an effective, principled speaker traveling coast to coast to win support for another cause. Nobody in America, it was said of her, had done more to promote liberal cooperative projects than she.

✪ *August 4*

Stephen G. Cary

QUAKER

September 21, 1915–July 30, 2002

Stephen Cary had been brought up in a Quaker household and committed himself early to working for peace. World War II made him subject to the draft, but, for the first time in its history, the United States had created a program for conscientious objectors. Cary was placed in the Civilian Public Service program and spent the war years doing forestry work in various parts of the country. Though the program was poorly organized, by the end of the war Cary had demonstrated some organizational and leadership skills, so he was assigned to work with the American Friend's Service Committee in war-torn Europe. Partly due to his efforts, this work was awarded the Nobel Peace Prize in 1947. Later, Cary said of his experiences in Europe:

> I think [it was] the first time I came in contact with the face of massive evil...the appalling destruction, the terrible breakdown of community, but most of all the suffering of multitudes of men, women, and children — the bereaved, the homeless, the cold and hungry, the sick — millions existing with their lives in ruin.

He would never forget the sight of the death camp at Auschwitz. Later, he would see the killing fields of Cambodia and the provincial hospitals in Vietnam, where children burned by napalm and shattered by shells fired by American battleships, lay three to a bed, staring at the ceiling. "That, too," he wrote, "was the face of evil."

Cary worked for two years in post-war Europe, traveling the continent from Italy to Finland to see what was needed and look for ways to provide everything from blankets and warm clothes to community centers and re-built homes. On his return, he served in a variety of roles with the American Friends Service Committee. The AFSC had been created in 1917 to serve victims of war and as a way for Quakers to serve in a nonmilitary role. He was drawn to it as a way to do "what I could to strengthen peace and broaden justice in a nation where wealth and power made it at once the world's greatest threat and its greatest source of hope."

Over the next fifty years, Cary continued to work, directly or indirectly, with the AFSC. He was committed to the proposition that "faith does not depend on relevance (but) minority views *are* relevant in a democratic society." He recalled a week in 1962 when the AFSC was simultaneously attacked in Indiana for being pro-Communist and in Leningrad for being Fascist lackeys. "In both," Cary wrote, "we were pursuing our standard course, refusing to make devils out of enemies, and exploring approaches to conflict that neither surrendered in the face of evil nor compelled us to do evil in the name of doing good."

In pursuit of that objective, Cary marched in Selma, Alabama, with Martin Luther King, Jr.,* where a friend was mortally wounded. He fasted outside the White House for a week in protest against the Vietnam War. He visited Pinochet's Chile and Ortega's Nicaragua and was arrested for participating in a Poor People's March in Washington, then again for attempting to prevent the loading of bombs on a warship bound for Vietnam. He barely avoided being attacked by 20 naked women at a Doukhobor settlement in Canada. His central witness was always in the cause of peace.

"It seems to me," he said, "that in our (American) support of militarism we crucify Christ afresh every day."

In the midst of these tumultuous events, Cary accepted appointment as vice president for development at Haverford College. He had come to believe that education was critical to the future of the world community and that the Quaker values associated with Friends' schools were more important than ever. But those were tumultuous years on American campuses and Cary found himself involved in student protests, issues of racism, more visits to Washington, and tough decisions about accepting or rejecting funds from government sources linked to military programs or Middle Eastern sources of dubious integrity. Brief service as interim president of the college led to a final 12 years as chairman of the National Board of the American Friends Service Committee.

In Cary's autobiography, *Intrepid Quaker,* published after his death, he summed up the meaning of his faith:

> As a Quaker, I believe that there is a Light that dwells within each human being on earth, and gives to each of us the capacity to know directly the will of God. It follows for us that the presence of this Light endows each life with a sacred dimension, so that it must not be debased or exploited or destroyed for any reason or under any circumstance. Though God alone knows how far I could find strength to sustain this witness should I be tested, I still hold it as an article of faith. Evil must be resisted — one cannot be neutral between justice and injustice — but the resistance must be by means that reflect the spirit of Christ. . . .
>
> Many times in this service I have seen our workers fail. They have helped to feed and clothe and serve a community, but they could not reach to the hatred, the despair, the selfishness, or the anger that paralyzed and consumed it. But I have also seen miracles where hatred has been exorcized, the estranged reconciled, the depraved reborn, and the violent made peaceable — sometimes in the most difficult and unlikely places.

When asked what such a spirit might be able to accomplish, Cary answered, "I do not know, for Jesus has not given us a success ethic; he assures us only that love endures — forever."

✪ August 5

Mary Hannah Fulton

PRESBYTERIAN

May 31, 1854–January 7, 1927

Mary Fulton grew up during a period of intense interest in foreign missions. Opportunities for medical training were opening for women as well, so she decided to become a medical missionary. Her older brother had already established a post in China and begun a mission there. As soon as she graduated from Woman's Medical College in Pennsylvania in 1884, the Presbyterian Board of Foreign Missions sponsored her to go to Canton. Anti-western sentiments were increasing in many parts of China, making mission work dangerous and unpredictable, but nothing deterred Fulton's commitment.

Fulton's attention to the details of the lives of her Chinese neighbors led her to offer hospitality, healing, hope, and love. Her perseverance in the face of danger and turmoil demonstrates the power of God in the compassion of Christians.

A reading from Mary Fulton's memoirs, *Inasmuch*

In the midst of this [the ongoing missionary work of Fulton and her colleagues], a black cloud seemed about to burst over China, and we were not permitted to go back to Canton. All the missionaries were ordered in from the interior. The serious trouble began in the north by the so-called Boxers killing native Christians and foreigners, looting and burning their buildings. The imperial troops turned in and helped in burning the legations at Peking and killing the German Minister. All consuls have warned foreigners to go to places where they can be protected. Nearly all the Canton missionaries are here in Hong Kong or in Macao.

We heard that all foreigners in Peking had been massacred; that they had fled to the British legation building. With little food and ammunition, they had held out for ten days. That was all we heard for weeks. Later, a report came that they were still holding out.

No troops had been able to get to Peking. Over ninety Protestant missionaries, beside Roman Catholics, and hundreds of native Christians have been massacred; most of them in a brutal and horrible manner. The Empress Dowager and Emperor have both escaped and there is practically no government at Peking. Everything is in an unsettled and chaotic condition.

At Lung Kong, to the south of Canton, a large number of Christians' homes were looted. Some were abducted and some killed.

At Shek Lung the chapel was looted. Thirty-two of our converts escaped with nothing save the clothes they had on. In a few days the Tung Kun hospital, church, and the doctor's house were burned. The Wesleyan chapel at Sun Vi had been looted. About ten of my brother's chapels in the interior have been looted.

The trouble seems to be growing stronger in the south. One night they tried to blow up the Viceroy's yamen. Several persons were killed. Troops from different nations finally reached Peking and liberated the besieged foreigners.

Slowly we are resuming our work in Canton and things seem to be getting back to normal.

After a flood, when a number of the country people were made homeless, a mother brought her three-weeks old daughter to Canton to sell her, as she had absolutely nothing wherewith to support her. The father had taken the two sons and gone north hoping to find work. After walking the streets of Canton all day and offering the little girl whenever she had opportunity, for twenty-five cents, she finally decided to lay it down somewhere and leave it. Before doing so she asked every passerby if there was any place where she could dispose of the child and they told her of our hospital.

Just at dusk she came in and told her story. We invited her to stay; put her in a clean room and kept her for months until she could wean the baby. At the end of that time, having become well and having heard the Gospel, she desired to return to her husband and children, while we were willing to adopt the little girl. Dr. Loh took her into her own home and brought her up as her daughter.

A patient whose husband had cast her out because she had paralysis was brought to the hospital, where for a year she was unable to lift her hand to feed herself. One of Dr. Niles' blind girls, who is acting as a Bible woman in the hospital, led the woman to Christ. At the end of two years she was able to walk and had learned to read the New Testament. We made her a Bible woman and most faithfully did she preach the Gospel to in-patients and out-patients.

One day she came in distress, saying that her two little nieces had been held as ransom and were about to be sold. It is a common custom, when a man goes into debt, to send one of his women to the home of the creditor to be held there until payment is made. If no payment is made, the women are sold. I sent for the father to bring up the two children, who were six years of age, twins, and asked him the amount of the debt. It was one hundred twenty-five dollars. This I gave to him with the understanding that I was not buying the girls in any way and that he was to take them back home but he was never to dispose of them without consulting me. Soon we had them in a Christian school, where for years they gave promise of being fine students.

✸ *August 6* ─────────────────────────────

Marianne Cope
(Barbara Koob, Mother Marianne of Molokai)

ROMAN CATHOLIC

January 23, 1838–August 9, 1918

Marianne Cope was 45-years-old when she received a letter that changed her life for the third and final time. The first time was when, at nearly two years old, she was brought from Germany to Utica, New York, by her parents.

They had hoped to make a better life for themselves, but the reality proved disappointing, so Barbara (Marianne's name at baptism) had to leave school after eighth grade to work in a factory to help support the family. The second major change in her life came when, at 24, she entered the Order of St. Francis to dedicate herself to God as a teacher and nurse. She took the name "Marianne," and thrived in her new life, becoming superior of the convent, a member of the council of the community, and finally provincial superior of the whole community with its various convents, schools, and hospitals. When the sisters opened the first hospital in Syracuse, Marianne was soon put in charge. Over the next eight years, she paid off its debt, expanded the hospital, and, unusually for that period, opened it to all in need, regardless of race, creed, or color. But then a letter came which changed everything once again.

A Roman Catholic priest in Hawaii wrote asking for help with their schools and hospitals. Fifty communities were invited, but only Marianne Cope responded to the call.

> I am hungry for the work and I wish with all my heart to be one of the chosen ones, whose privilege it will be, to sacrifice themselves for the salvation of the souls of the poor Islanders. . . . I am not afraid of any disease. Waking and sleeping I am on the Islands. Do not laugh at me, for being so wholly absorbed in that one wish, one thought, to be a worker in that large field.

With six other sisters as companions, Cope found herself in charge of a hospital that served as receiving center for patients with leprosy from all the Hawaiian islands. It is uncertain how leprosy arrived in that part of the world, but it had become an epidemic in a population with no natural resistance to this or many other new diseases. At the hospital, patients were examined, with the worst cases moved on to an isolated location on the island of Molokai where Damien de Veuster, a Belgian priest, had dedicated his life to the residents. The sisters were appalled at the "filth, swarms of flies, the stench of open, untreated sores" but set to work with buckets and brooms to establish cleanliness and order.

The greatest need, however, lay elsewhere. The peninsula on Molokai was a natural prison, surrounded on three sides by the Pacific Ocean and on the fourth by steep cliffs. Exiled and hopeless, the patients there established a kind of jungle law, drinking, fighting, abusing women and children, and abandoning the weakest to die without care. When a benefactor provided money for a home for leprous women and girls, Marianne took charge. After Damien died, a committee asked Marianne "in whom we have much confidence" to take on that work as well. "It would be my greatest delight," she wrote, "even to minister to the abandoned 'lepers.' . . . We will cheerfully accept the work. . . . For us, it is happiness to be able to comfort, in a measure, the poor exiles, and we rejoice that we are the unworthy agents of our heavenly Father through whom He deigns to show His great love and mercy to the sufferers."

The work was far from easy and there were times when the burden seemed overwhelming. One of the sisters, in a moment of discouragement, once asked, "How long, Oh Lord must I see only those that are sick and covered with leprosy?" Fortunately, Marianne Cope possessed the qualities needed to strengthen her companions: never-failing optimism, serenity, a caring nature, and the rare gift of cheerfulness.

When the sisters were first asked about moving to Molokai, she had written, "With regard to the Sisters, now here, the largest number including myself, are cheerfully willing to undertake the work, and I am confident that other Sisters of our Order will cheerfully volunteer to come and join us...." "Cheerfully" was a word she used often; the same spirit that had made hospitals homelike in upstate New York, would work to make even Molokai a place of life.

And so Marianne Cope took over the settlement homes and carried on that ministry with loving devotion for the remaining 35 years of her life. Her priority remained those women and girls so frequently abused by the male patients. The task as she saw it was not simply medical but social and cultural as well. Her patients were taught to sew and do needlework and gardening. The sisters made dresses for the girls in the latest styles and helped them decorate their rooms. Mother Marianne of Molokai (as she was now known) had gone to Hawaii to establish the order before returning to Syracuse. Her home community kept sending heartfelt pleas for her to come back and apply her administrative skills there once more. Yet who else could have brought cheerfulness to Molokai? "Life was to be lived," wrote Marianne Cope, "even in the face of death."

✸ August 7

Joseph Sittler

LUTHERAN

September 26, 1904–December 28, 1987

The beginning of public concern over environmental issues is often credited to the 1962 publication of Rachel Carson's book *Silent Spring*, but Joseph Sittler was raising it at least a dozen years earlier. From the first, he felt a concern for the relationship between human beings and the created world. His first published work, in 1937, was a four-part series of articles entitled "The Parable of the Soils." His last, *Gravity & Grace* (1986), opens with a chapter on "Nature and Grace."

Joseph Sittler was born in Ohio, the son of a Lutheran pastor, and graduated from Ohio's Wittenberg University before going on to study at Hamma Divinity School, Oberlin College, Case Western Reserve, the University of

Chicago, and the University of Heidelberg, Germany. He was ordained in 1930 and served as a pastor in Ohio for 13 years before going to teach at Chicago Lutheran Theological Seminary (1943–1957) and the University of Chicago Divinity School (1957–1973). For many years, he served on the Faith and Order Commission of the World Council of Churches. A speech he gave in 1961 at the New Delhi assembly of the World Council of Churches established him as an international Christian expert on the environmental crisis.

Sittler proclaimed that our "increasing distance from the natural world ...has almost stripped us of the possibility to talk of ourselves in relation to God's creation." Stewardship is commonly cited as the primary focus of Christian's ecological concern. However, he saw it as a larger and richer matter of grace: "The focal region of God's grace is not less than that of the whole creation." He spoke of grace as the "energy of love" that becomes known within the whole fabric of daily human existence. His writings on the need for a Christian commitment to our planet continue to raise the consciousness of those who read them.

A reading from a sermon entitled "The Care of the Earth" by Joseph Sittler

If the creation, including our fellow creatures, is impiously used apart from a gracious primeval joy in it the very richness of the creation becomes a judgment. This has a cleansing and orderly meaning for everything in the world of nature, from the sewage we dump into our streams to the cosmic sewage we dump into the fallout.

Abuse is use without grace; it is always a failure in the counterpoint of use and enjoyment. When things are not used in ways determined by joy in the things themselves, this violated potentiality of joy (timid as all things holy, but relentless and blunt in its reprisals) withdraws and leaves us, not perhaps with immediate positive damnations but with something much worse — the wan, ghastly, negative damnations of use without joy, stuff without grace, a busy, fabricating world with the shine gone off, personal relations for the nature of which we have invented the eloquent term, contact, staring without beholding, even fornication without finding.

God is useful. But not if he is sought for use. Ivan, in The Brothers Kara-mazov, saw that, and Dostoevski meant it as a witness to the holy and joy-begetting God whom he saw turned into an ecclesiastical club to frighten impoverished peasants with, when he had his character say, "I deny God for God's sake!"

All of this has, I think, something to say to us as teachers and students to whom this university is ever freshly available for enjoyment and use. For consider this: the basis of discovery is curiosity, and what is curiosity but the peculiar joy of the mind in its own given nature? Sheer curiosity, without immediate anticipation of ends and uses, has done most to envision new ends and fresh uses. But curiosity does this in virtue of a strange counterpoint of use and enjoyment. Bacon declared that "studies are for delight," the secular counterpart of "glorify God and enjoy him forever." The Creator who is the fountain of joy, and the creation which is the material of university study, are here brought together in an ultimate way. It is significant that the university, the institutional solidification of the fact that studies are for delight, is an idea and a creation of a culture that once affirmed that men should glorify God and enjoy him forever.

Use is blessed when enjoyment is honored. Piety is deepest practicality, for it properly relates use and enjoyment. And a world sacramentally received in joy is a world sanely used. There is an economics of use only; it moves toward the destruction of both use and joy. And there is an economics of joy; it moves toward the intelligence of use and the enhancement of joy. That this vision involves a radical new understanding of the clean and fruitful earth is certainly so. But this vision, deeply religious in its genesis, is not so very absurd now that natural damnation is in orbit, and man's befouling of his ancient home has spread his death and dirt among the stars.

✪ August 8

Jesse Lee

METHODIST

March 12, 1758–March 12, 1816

Just before the American Revolution, the first Methodist preachers arrived in Virginia. The 15-year-old Jesse Lee was converted along with his parents. By 1775, a circuit had been organized with three Methodist circuit riders and soon afterward a great revival began. "I had never seen anything like it," Jesse Lee wrote in his journal. "Some would be seized with a trembling and in a few moments drop on the floor, as if they were dead; while others were embracing each other with streaming eyes, and all lost in wonder, love, and praise." As the revival continued, Lee wrote, "I felt a sweet distress in my soul for holiness of heart and life. I sensibly felt, while I was seeking purity of heart, that I grew in grace and in the knowledge of God. This concern of soul lasted some time, till at length I could say, I have nothing but the love of Christ in my heart."

When Lee was drafted into the South Carolina militia to repel British forces in 1780, he refused to fight, so he was made a chaplain. At the end of the war, he was appointed to a local circuit and later accompanied Bishop Asbury* in organizing circuits in North Carolina, Virginia, Maryland, and New Jersey. By 1789, Jesse Lee had been sent to introduce the Methodist way to New England, and his success was such that he was nicknamed "The

Apostle of Methodism." Within five years, he and a helper were riding 17 circuits in the New England states. Jesse had grown to such a size that he had to take two horses with him so that when one was worn out he could ride the other.

Before he died, Jesse Lee wrote *A Short History of the Methodists* and served for six terms as chaplain to Congress.

A reading from a sermon preached by Jesse Lee

We cannot tell how long a person may be seeking the Lord before he finds him. Some men are awakened, convicted, repent of their sins, and are born again on the same day; while others are seeking the Lord for many months before they are converted. All that I can say with regard to the time when a man shall find the Lord is this, "Ye shall seek me, and find me, when ye shall search for me with all your heart." Many persons seek the Lord as if they expected to be justified by the law; they reason thus with themselves: I have been such a sinner I cannot expect to be converted yet; I must pray more, and mourn longer before my sins can be forgiven. If this is the case with any of you, it is a sufficient proof that you are seeking justification by the works of the law; and you may seek it thus, and mourn for your sins all the days of your life, and mourn for them after you are dead, and still mourn in vain. But if you expect to be justified by faith, then you may look for the blessing every moment, look for it now, look for it where you are sitting, look for it while I am speaking, for "All things are possible to him that believeth." This need not be put off any longer, the Lord is willing to do this great work for you now. O for faith to believe in, and to lay hold on Christ.

In order to die in the Lord, we must be previously acquainted with the Lord. This includes experimental religion. I have already considered how a person becomes acquainted with the Lord, that is, to know the Lord in the forgiveness of his sins. But to be acquainted with the Lord, includes this much, to know his fear and to know his love.

To know his love signifies a knowledge of the love of God in our hearts, and an inward evidence that we love the Lord. A man that loves the Lord sincerely, loves him better than his wife, or his children, or his property, or his own life. In a word, he loves the Lord better than he loves all that he has in the world; and would sooner choose to die now and go to heaven, then to renounce his interest in Christ forever, and live long in this world, and go to hell at last.

When a person first feels the love of God in his soul, he has such pleasing sensations as he never before witnessed, and he cannot keep it to himself: he will wish to make it known to his friends; and at that time, he feels love for all mankind, and a fervent desire that all the world may be brought to know the Lord from the least to the greatest. This inward acquaintance with the

Lord which every Christian feels is to him worth more than all the treasures of Egypt.

"What hath the world to equal this?"

"This solid joy, this constant bliss?"

Words cannot describe the happiness which is felt by the Christian; it is something better felt than expressed. I would say with the apostle, "Eye hath not seen, nor ear heard, neither have entered into the heart of man, the things which God hath prepared for them that love him." (I Cor. 2:9)

✪ *August 9*

Donaldina Cameron

PRESBYTERIAN

July 26, 1869–January 4, 1968

As an immigrant herself, Donaldina Cameron dedicated her life to serving other, less fortunate immigrants. She was born in New Zealand in 1869, but her family moved to California when she was two. Her mother died when she was five and her father's ranch eventually failed, so he spent the rest of his life working for others. When Cameron was 27, a family friend suggested that she spend a year working in the Presbyterian Mission House in San Francisco's Chinatown. It became her life's work.

The Presbyterian Mission House was chartered for the purpose of rescuing Chinese girls and women from abusive circumstances created by congressional acts that prevented Asian workers both from sending for Chinese wives or marrying non-Chinese wives. The small ratio of Chinese women to men encouraged prostitution, and to stock the brothels girls and young women, mostly from Canton, were bought, kidnapped, or coerced into coming to the United States. The life of the average Chinese prostitute was brutal and short. Most died of harsh treatment within five years.

Untrained and naive at first, Cameron soon learned the art of rescuing girls. These expeditions often took the form of secret nighttime raids conducted with axe-and sledgehammer-wielding policemen. She became expert at finding children hidden under trap doors and behind false walls. The owners did not take the loss of their property lightly, since many of their prostitutes were worth thousands of dollars. The Mission Home and its inhabitants were under constant legal and physical assault from the brothel owners.

By 1900, Cameron had become superintendent of the Home. Later, she was instrumental in establishing the Ming Quong Home for Chinese girls and the Chung Mei Home for Chinese boys. When the great San Francisco earthquake and fire of 1906 forced Cameron and her girls out of the Mission Home, she braved the oncoming fire and military police to retrieve the records that gave her guardianship rights. The records were saved, but the

Mission Home itself was destroyed, one of many buildings dynamited to try to stop the spreading fire.

Cameron continued to fight for the freedom of Chinese girls and women in the courts, at the podium, and to perform rescues in towns across the country until her retirement in 1934. While she was by no means a lone force, Donaldina Cameron is credited with breaking the back of the Chinese slave trade in the U.S., and the rescue and education of nearly 3,000 girls. In 1942, the old Mission Home, rebuilt in 1908, was renamed "Donaldina Cameron House" in her honor.

A reading from Donaldina Cameron on the 1906 San Francisco earthquake and fire

We only aim to leave a few words of testimony to bear witness in coming years to the kind care of a loving heavenly Father, and also to the unselfish courage displayed by our Chinese girls throughout the terrifying and distressing experiences of the days in which our city and the Home we loved were wiped out of existence.

The terrible earthquake shock that in one instant roused a sleeping city, spared not in its rude awakening the peacefully sleeping house at 920 Sacramento Street. During the never-to-be-forgotten moments the solid earth took on the motions of an angry ocean while chimneys crashed on to our roof, while plaster and ornaments strewed the floors.

There was terror and consternation among the fifty Chinese and Japanese girls and children in the Home, but not one symptom of panic, or of cowardice. Older girls forgot their own fears in anxiety to care for and soothe the little ones. Not one attempted to seek safety alone....

The first great shock over, we thanked God for having spared our lives, and looked forth to see how others had fared. Already columns of smoke were rising like signals of alarm, but so great was the relief of present deliverance no dread of another form of danger troubled us at that early hour.

To calm the frightened children and see that they were dressed, to reduce in some measure the chaos of our Home again to a semblance of order, were our first cares. Then the problem of breakfast for so large a family in a chimneyless house had to be faced. This last perplexity was promptly solved by our efficient matron, Miss [Minnie L.] Ferree, who almost before the bricks stopped falling had managed to secure from a nearby bakery a large basket of bread.

This, with some apples and a kettle of tea sent in by our neighbor, Mrs. Ng Poon Chew, was the last meal eaten in the hospitable dining-room of "920." Our girls gathered round the little white tables, sang as usual the morning hymn, then repeated the Twenty-third Psalm with more feeling and a deeper realization of its unfailing promises than ever before.

The simple meal was not finished when another severe shock startled all from their places. We hurried to the upper floor. Opening an eastern window and looking across the city, our anxiety became a certainty of approaching danger. The small wreaths of smoke had rapidly changed into dark ominous clouds, hiding in places the bright waters of the bay....

One plan after another was suggested. At length the First Presbyterian Church at the corner of Van Ness Avenue and Sacramento Street was decided upon as a safe place, as it had stood the earthquake well and was far removed at that time from the burning districts....

To have our Chinese girls on the streets among these crowds after nightfall was a danger too great to risk. As hastily, therefore, as we could work amidst the confusion and excitement, we gathered some bedding, a little food, and a few garments together and the last of the girls left the Mission Home....

At break of day the little band were hurriedly preparing for another march, the shelter of the night being no longer secure. Fire menaced from three directions. What, tragedy, what pathos, and what comedy too, were crowded into our lives these two days?...

But to all things there is an end, and so the long walk to the Ferry at the foot of Market Street ended. A boat was about to cross the bay to Sausalito. Our desired haven was the Seminary at San Anselmo. We lost no time going on board. It was a thankful though a completely exhausted company that sank down... and bundles and babies on the lower deck of the steamer, too weary to walk to the salon. But tired and homeless, knowing not where that night we were to lay our heads, our only feeling was one of gratitude for deliverance as we looked over the group of more than sixty young faces and realized how God had cared for His children.

✠ *August 10*

Michael Williams

ROMAN CATHOLIC

February 5, 1877–October 12, 1950

The years after World War I were a stimulating time to be a Roman Catholic in America. The immigrant church was growing up, elbowing its way into the main stream of American life. Nothing gave stronger evidence of this than the foundation of a new magazine, *The Commonweal.* Its goal was to provide a forum for Roman Catholic laity "to discuss public affairs." In addition, it reviewed important publications of the day, and published original fiction, essays, and poetry." Its pages were

> open to writers holding different forms of Christian belief, and in some cases to authors who do not profess any form of Christian faith. Where the opinion of its editors, contributors and readers differs on subjects yet unsettled

by competent authority, it will be an open forum for the discussion of such differences in a spirit of good temper.

Michael Williams, the editor, arrived at this position by a circuitous route. He had been born and educated in Canada, but after his father died, he left college and the church, eventually moving to Boston to try to make a living by writing poetry and fiction. He became a reporter for the *Boston Post* and then for the *New York World* and *Evening Telegram,* moved to San Francisco to edit the *Examiner,* then came east again to work with Upton Sinclair on *Good Health.* Still not satisfied that he had found his place in life, he moved again to California where he had a conversion experience that led him back to the Roman Catholic Church. He published an account of his experience in *The Book of High Romance,* which brought him into contact with leading Roman Catholic intellectuals and convinced him of the need for a magazine in which they could publish their work.

Those were the days when H. L. Mencken used the pages of the *American Mercury* to denounce everyone who struck him as less intelligent than he. Williams took offense at Mencken's derogatory comments about the intellectual attainments of the bishops of the Roman Catholic Church and countered by defining the role of a bishop in an article titled "Bishops and Brains":

> There are great and marvelous intellectual luminaries in the calendar of saints — names like St. Paul, St. Jerome, St. Augustine, St. Thomas of Aquin, and scores of others are typical examples. But they were not named saints simply because of their intellect. Thousands of other names are on that glorious list, of persons who were totally undistinguished for intellectual gifts. But the obscure beggars, and tramps, ex-thieves, humble parish priests, cloistered nuns, former sailors and soldiers, even a lawyer or two, whose names appear side by side with those of the great lamps of the illuminated intellect, shared in common the one thing needful — heroic goodness.
>
> The bishops of the Catholic Church are not always either saints or marvelous lights of intellectual eminence, sometimes perhaps they would with difficulty qualify for even the lower degrees of goodness. But human goodness is always what they seek; it is goodness more than intellect which they know to be the one thing above all others desirable. As bishops, each and every one of them today, as through all the centuries since the beginning of the Church, and as it will be until the end of the world, are first of all the shepherds of souls.

Williams edited his new journal for 13 years, from 1924 to 1937, providing a Roman Catholic perspective on such issues of the day as evolution and the New Deal. His support for Generalissimo Franco in the Spanish Civil War created a rift on the editorial staff, and Williams resigned as editor, though he continued to contribute to the magazine. A new generation of Roman Catholic intellectuals nurtured by him, took over. Their mere existence witnessed to the importance of his work.

A reading from Michael Williams in *The Commonweal*

We believe that The Commonweal will be so fundamentally different to our contemporaries that in place of competition in an over-crowded field we shall occupy a position that hitherto has been left vacant. For the difference between The Commonweal and other weekly literary reviews designed for general circulation is that The Commonweal will be definitely Christian in its presentation of orthodox religious principles and their application to the subjects that fall within its purview: principles which until now have not, we believe, been expressed in American journalism except through the medium of the official organs of the Catholic Church and of the various denominations. As a sure background The Commonweal will have the continuous unbroken tradition and teachings of the historic Mother church. But it will be in no sense — nor could it possibly assert itself to be — an authoritative or authorized mouthpiece of the Catholic Church. It will be the independent, personal product of its editors and contributors, who, for the most part, will be laymen. . . .

As opposed to the present confused, confusing, and conflicting complex of private opinions, and personal impressionism, mirrored in so many influential journals, the editors of The Commonweal believe that nothing can do so much for the betterment, the happiness, and the peace of the American people as the influence of the enduring and tested principles of Catholic Christianity. To that high task The Commonweal is dedicated.

✪ *August 11* _____

Amelia Bloomer

EPISCOPALIAN

May 27, 1818–December 30, 1894

Unfortunately, her name is forever associated with a type of woman's undergarment, but Amelia Bloomer was actually a distinguished writer, publisher, and social reformer and a pioneer in the woman's suffrage movement. She was also devoted to her church. When she moved to Cedar Bluffs, Iowa, she helped organize an Episcopal congregation in the community and entertained visiting missionaries in her home. She took it for granted that God was at work in the causes she espoused, writing, "The same power that brought the slave out of bondage will, in His own good time and way, bring about the emancipation of women, and make her the equal in power and dominion that she was in the beginning."

Perhaps that same sense of a leading power arose from the way her own life developed. The initiatives often came from others. She married a man who believed in women's rights, and they agreed to omit the word "obey" in the woman's marriage promise. Although Bloomer had only two years of formal education, her spouse wanted her to write articles on temperance, abolition, and women's issues for his local paper in upstate New York. Before long, she started *Lily* — the first magazine exclusively for women. Its theme was the temperance movement, a feminist issue, since so many women suffered abuse from alcoholic husbands. When she encountered Susan B. Anthony* and Elizabeth Cady Stanton* at the Woman's Rights Convention in 1848, they were not impressed by her. "She has not the spirit of the reformer," wrote Stanton to Anthony. "At the first woman's rights convention, but four years ago, she stood aloof and laughed at us. It was only with great effort and patience that she has been brought up to her present position."

Yet Bloomer became an articulate speaker for women's rights. Using her magazine as a vehicle, she wrote that women ought to be admitted to institutions of higher learning, that they should own property and receive paychecks in their own name, and that the law should do more to protect victims of abuse. She even produced a woman's Bible to challenge patriarchal views

And, yes, she did advocate less restrictive clothing. The whalebone, tight-laced corsets, and voluminous skirts then fashionable restricted movement and injured health. Dressing like this made women, in Bloomer's words, "unpaid street sweepers." She didn't invent the garment that was given her name, but Bloomer did popularize it. She gave up wearing bloomers herself after eight years, though, because she felt they detracted attention from issues that mattered more.

A reading from the *Life and Writings of Amelia Bloomer,* compiled by Dexter C. Bloomer, her husband

How any unprejudiced and unbiased mind can read the original account of the Creation and Fall and gather therefrom that the woman committed the greater sin, I cannot understand. When Eve was first asked to eat of the forbidden fruit she refused, and it was only after her scruples were overcome by promises of great knowledge that she gave way to sin. But how was it with Adam who was with her? He took and ate what she offered him without any scruples of conscience, or promises on her part of great things to follow — certainly showing no superiority of goodness, or intellect, or strength of character fitting him for the headship. The command not to eat of the Tree of Life was given to him before her creation, and he was doubly bound to keep it; yet he not only permitted her to partake of the tree without remonstrating with her against it and warning her of the wrong, but ate it himself without objection or hesitation. And then, when inquired of by God concerning what he had done, instead of standing up like an honorable man and confessing the wrong, he weakly tried to shield himself by throwing the blame on the woman. As the account stands, he showed the greater feebleness of resistance and evinced a pliancy of character and a readiness "to yield to temptation" that cannot be justly charged to the woman. As the account stands, man has much more to blush for than to boast of.

While we are willing to accept this original account of the Creation and Fall, we are not willing that man should add tenfold to woman's share of sin and put a construction on the whole matter that we believe was never intended by the Creator. Eve had no more to do with bringing sin into the world than had Adam, nor did the Creator charge any more upon her. The punishment inflicted upon them for their transgression, was as heavy upon him as upon her. Her sorrows were to be multiplied; and so, too, was he to eat his bread in sorrow and earn it with the sweat of his face amid thorns and thistles. To her, no injunction to labor was given; upon her no toil was imposed, no ground cursed for her sake.

The Bible is brought forward to prove the subordination of woman and to show that, because St. Paul told the ignorant women of his time to keep silent in the churches, the educated, intelligent women of these times must not only occupy the same position in the church and the family but must not aspire to the rights of citizenship.

✪ *August 12*

Peter Cartwright

METHODIST

1785–September 25, 1872

Few more colorful figures than Peter Cartwright are to be found in American history, and his autobiography, in print to this day, provides essential reading for those who wish to gain a clearer understanding of frontier life and religion. Cartwright was converted at a camp meeting when he was 16, and two years later, he began to ride circuit and preach. It wasn't an easy life, but he was not easily discouraged. He faced floods, thieves, hunger, and disease as he persevered with his ministry. Once, when bullies tried to break up camp meetings, Cartwright met them head on: sweeping one off his horse, and scaring the others off by calling to nonexistent colleagues to surround them in the dark woods. He chased after his saddlebags when they were swept away in a flooded river and went days at a time without food on more than one occasion. Cartwright even told the future president, General Andrew Jackson, that he would go to hell if he didn't repent.

Cartwright powerfully evoked the spirit of the camp meetings he attended:

> Raising my voice, [I] gave them as warm an exhortation as I could command. Suddenly an awful power fell on the congregation, and they instantly fell right and left, and cried aloud for mercy. I suppose there were not less than thirty

> persons smitten down; the young, the old, and middle-aged indiscriminately, were operated on in this way. My voice at this time was strong and clear; and I could sing, exhort, pray, and preach almost all the time, day and night. I went through the assembly, singing, exhorting, praying, and directing poor sinners to Christ.

Often he would preach for hours at a stretch, and the camp meetings sometimes went on for days.

Cartwright opposed slavery and counted it as a benefit of Methodist preaching that where they had labored there was "a stop put to trading in slaves." He moved his own family from Kentucky to Illinois for fear one of his daughters might marry a slave-owner. Methodist preachers were often illiterate, but Cartwright valued education and helped establish Methodist schools and colleges. Wherever he went, he left behind books and tracts to strengthen his converts in their new commitment. Cartwright served several terms in the Illinois legislature, defeating future president Abraham Lincoln in one campaign. Later, however, when he ran for Congress Lincoln defeated him.

A reading from the closing paragraphs of Peter Cartwright's autobiography

Thus you have a very small view of the progress and prosperity of the Methodist Episcopal Church in twenty years of her history. In these estimates we make no account of the thousands that were awakened and converted by her instrumentalities, and had joined other branches of the Church of Christ, nor of the thousands that had died in the triumphs of faith and gone home to heaven.

When we consider that these United States had just emerged from colonial dependence, and had passed a bloody revolution of seven years continuance, and were yet surrounded by hundreds of thousands of bloody savages, hostile to the last degree, and that we were without credit abroad and without means or money at home, we may well join with the venerable founder of Methodism, Mr. John Wesley, and say that "God had strangely set us free as a nation." And, on the other hand, in reference to the Methodist Episcopal Church, when we consider that her ministers were illiterate, and not only opposed and denounced by the Catholics, but by all Protestant Churches; that we were everywhere spoken against, caricatured, and misrepresented; without colleges und seminaries, without religious books or periodicals, without missionary funds, and almost all other religious means; and our ministers did not for many years, on average, receive over fifty dollars for a support annually, and a Methodist preacher's library almost entirely consisted of a Bible, Hymn Book, and a Discipline, may we not, without boasting, say with one of old, "What hath God wrought?"

A Methodist preacher in those days, when he felt that God had called him to preach, instead of hunting up a college or biblical institute, hunted up a hardy pony or a horse, and some traveling apparatus, and with his library always at hand, namely, Bible, Hymn Book, and Discipline, he started, and with a text that never wore out nor grew stale, he cried, "Behold the Lamb of God that taketh away the sin of the world." In this way he went through storms of wind, hail, snow, and rain; climbed hills and mountains, traversed valleys, plunged through swamps, swam swollen streams, lay out all night, wet, weary, and hungry, held his horse by the bridle all night, or tied him to a limb, slept with his saddle blanket for a bed, his saddle or saddle bags his pillow, and his old big coat or blanket, if he had any, for a covering. Often he slept in dirty cabins, on earthen floors, before the fire; ate roasting ears for bread, drank butter-milk for coffee, or sage tea for imperial; took, with a hearty zest, deer or bear meat, or wild turkey, for breakfast, dinner, and supper, if he could get it. His text was always ready, "Behold the Lamb of God," &c. This was old-fashioned Methodist preacher fare and fortune. Under such circumstances, who among us would now say, "Here am I, Lord, send me?"

✪ *August 13* ───────────────────────────────

Jean Kenyon Mackenzie

PRESBYTERIAN

January 6, 1874–September 2, 1936

Jean Mackenzkie discovered her faith within her family circle. Her father, Robert, was a professor and president of San Francisco Theological Seminary. After a period of study, Mackenzie became active in the Presbyterian Board of Foreign Missions and traveled to Cameroon, then a German colony, under their auspices. She spent ten years of evangelistic and educational work in the smaller villages of the country before returning to America in 1914 to recover from an accident. At that point, the French took control of Cameroon and threatened to close the Presbyterian mission that had sponsored her work. The Foreign Mission Board called upon Mackenzie to return to Africa to try to keep the mission open. Her efforts were successful, and the mission was able to continue its work. Mackenzie then returned to the United States, where her writings about Africa and the Christian missionary task there were praised for their literary merit as well as her thoughtful appraisal of the role of missions in the developing world. She wrote:

> When we talk of the education of the peoples of Africa, do we mean something that involves a break with their own past or something which is the fulfillment of that past? The danger is great that what is most truly and deeply

the African's own, because it is the expression of his native aptitudes and capacities, may be submerged and lost. In that case, the Africans will become what the French call *deracinés* — people without roots. The individual will be like a plant torn from its natural surroundings, with the result that its power of growth is arrested and impeded. He will lack all those deeper formative influences which are supplied not by direct instruction but by the unconscious absorption of the spirit of a society which is permeated with the rich traditions of the past.

It is part of the great task of education in Africa to build a bridge between the African's heritage from the past and the new world in which he is called to live. He must be helped by a wise education to understand, appreciate and respect both what is good and capable of development in his own past — his tribal customs and traditions, his folk-lore, art and music, and at the same time the new forces and influences that are invading his life. . . . But he will be able to assimilate the new knowledge only if he has his roots securely fixed in the natural soil of an enveloping and supporting social tradition.

Mackenzie's perspective on the value of indigenous social structure and outlook reflect a position not always shared by other missionaries. Many sought to impose European or American dress, language, culture, politics, art, music, and norms as part of their efforts to spread the Christian faith, so it is refreshing to read of Mackenzie's desire to preserve and build upon the tribal heritage of the people with whom she ministered. She was well aware of the insidious nature of feelings of racial superiority and their effects. In her writings, she illustrated the capacity for leadership among the local population and discussed the missionary's proper place in equipping it. She believed that the gospel is more than words about a distant heaven or personal rebirth. It speaks of transforming compassion and the commitment Christ's followers must have to all people, in all their real needs:

There is a medical outpost in a forest neighborhood and the man in charge of it is a leader. His name is Mbula Mfum. He has a hospital of 178 beds. He had an idea that industry was good for his patients, and there they are at work under his care — blacksmiths making knives, axes, hoes, and other tools; woodcarvers producing bowls, spoons, little stools; basket makers busy, potters busy, and Mbula Mfum busy. For he has a school as well as a workshop and a hospital — "that patients might learn to read the good news and take it back to their people."

Mbula is too wise a leader not to have an assistant in his school. Ten year old Abesola, who has brought her enlarged spleen to that hospital, is his assistant. There are the makings of a leader in that child, as any wise head will tell you. All she needs is training. . . . There is our opportunity, and the thing that is expected of us — that we shall train them. Do not make a mistake; it is an enormous task — and it is the least we can do. We have come to the Kingdom of God in Africa for such a time as this.

Mackenzie was never narrowly denominational in her perspective. She did not labor to promote the cause of Presbyterianism, nor see it as the only answer to the needs of the Africans. Her appreciation of her comrades in the cause, especially the Africans working at the task, is evident as her story continues:

> Whoever you are and of whatever household of the family of God — how can you not be knowing of your African brother and sister — their service and noble constancy — the lives they live — yes the deaths they die?... how can you not be knowing of Edna Mgoneli, who lost her first baby and who was told before the birth of her second child that she must be very quiet till it should be born, but who could not refuse to nurse her people during the epidemic of influenza when in 1918 so many Africans died.... When her child was born, both child and mother were too tired to live. In a few days they died of the influenza. These are not things to be forgetting. They are things that are true, that are lovely, that are of good report — in thinking of these things and in publishing them we are perhaps overcoming in our own heart and in our family and in the small place that is ours in the world — that most terrible and evil thing — race prejudice.

Jean Mackenzie's dedication, sensitivity, and ability to draw us into the world of emergent African Christianity are gifts that enrich the whole church.

✪ *August 14*

Gustave Weigel

ROMAN CATHOLIC

January 15, 1906–January 3, 1964

In the long span of Christian history, ecumenism is a new development, and we are still learning our way. The first seeds were sown in the late 19th century with, for example, the framing of the Lambeth Quadrilateral. The 1910 World Missionary Conference in Edinburgh and the first Faith and Order Conference in 1927 demonstrated its sturdy growth. None of these involved the Roman Catholic Church. Only toward the middle of the 20th century did Roman Catholic and non–Roman Catholic ecumenists began to talk to each other with any seriousness. A leader in this dialogue was Gustave Weigel.

Weigel grew up in Buffalo, New York, and was admitted to the Jesuit novitiate on graduating from high school at the age of 16. Making his way through a series of Jesuit schools, he earned a doctorate in philosophy, and two years after that was ordained to the priesthood. Following his ordination, he went to Rome to study, acquiring a doctorate in theology in 1937. From Rome he went to Chile to teach for 11 years. He became dean of the School of Theology in Santiago. He was 42-years-old when he returned to his native country with a different perspective from any he might have acquired had he remained within the Jesuit system in the United States.

In 1948, the United States was still recovering from World War II. No one suspected the revolution that Pope John XXIII would unleash on the church ten years later through the Second Vatican Council. Nevertheless, Weigel immersed himself in the study of ecumenism, urging Roman Catholics to pay attention to what was happening among non-Roman Christians and traveling widely to lecture at universities from the institutions of the Ivy League through the midwest and on the west coast. As Roman Catholics were learning about the non-Roman churches, those churches were beginning to realize that the Roman Catholic Church was now a significant presence in America. Weigel coauthored *An American Dialogue* with Professor Robert McAfee Brown of the Union Theological Seminary of New York and wrote a review of Tillich's *Systematic Theology* that was widely read and appreciated.

Ecumenism, in Weigel's opinion was unavoidable. "Whether we like it or not," he wrote, "Protestants and Catholics are inevitably related to each other by the concept of opposition, and the opposition is stronger the nearer we approach the moment of the split of one from the other. Today we are all striving manfully to overcome the sense of opposition, but we are descendants of the past and history works in all of us."

Gustave Weigel worked to turn history in the direction of Christ's vision for the church: "That they all may be one." In two typical passages, he sets out first to allow Roman Catholics and non–Roman Catholics to see through one another's eyes, then to remind his readers of the need for patience and a faithful reliance on God:

Readings from Gustave Weigel

The Protestant is deeply convinced that the shoe is on the other foot. He finds that his own position is humble and reasonable, for he is willing to make concessions and he expects the Catholics to do the same. He knows that there are serious differences between the Catholic and Protestant faiths, and he is handsomely willing to come with an open mind to the analysis of these differences, and if need be he is ready to split the differences in a gentlemanly fashion. But he sees that the Catholics, have no such intention. They demand that he give up everything which is peculiar and essential to his specifically Protestant position. This he finds un-charitable, unreasonable and intransigent, with the result that he is filled with irritation and impatience.

Yet without realizing it the Protestant spontaneously and in good faith demands that the Catholic, with whom he wishes to discuss, give up his Catholicism while he, the Protestant, can go on being Protestant. It is true that the Catholic in his turn asks the Protestant to cease being Protestant as the price of reunion, but the Catholic knows and admits that this is his demand. The Protestant is not even aware that his position is identical and just as intransigent.

The ecumenical movement is both an idea and an historical fact. The idea in its abstract purity is simple enough; it is an invitation to the churches professing faith in Jesus Christ to come together in the hope that in some future day they will all be one. The coming together is the immediate goal of the idea. The final union is a desired consequence. It is very important to keep these two facets distinct. As so many voices within the historical movement have declared, the final union of the churches must be God's work, exercised in His good time. The coming together is man's work, not indeed without God's grace, yet always with a human appeal two man's action founded on divine trust.

Keeping these distinct elements in mind, ecumenists will not lose courage if their efforts do not quickly achieve the consequence for which they hope. If they can bring the churches together to hold dialogue, their purpose has been achieved and they need not be disheartened. The rest lies in the hands of God, whose will the ecumenist will accept with faith and obedience.

✠ *August 15*

Jonathan Myrick Daniels

EPISCOPALIAN

March 20, 1939–August 14, 1965

"Every foreign land is to them a fatherland and every fatherland a foreign land.... They spend their existence upon earth, but their citizenship is in heaven." These words of a second-century writer described the strange way in which Christians seemed to be both a part of their society and yet somehow apart from it at the same time. For many American Christians in the Civil Rights era of 1960s, those ancient words suddenly became very real. Old assumptions about the comfortable relationship between Christian faith and American society were called into question and found to be not valid. On all sides of the struggle, that which had been long been taken for granted was found, in fact, to be false.

Jonathan Daniels, an Episcopal seminarian, responded to the call to go south in the "freedom summer" of 1965 to help register African American voters and challenge a pattern of life that had been in place for nearly a hundred years. The south he discovered was part of a different country from the one he had known before. He wrote about it in a report for his seminary newspaper:

> Reality is kaleidoscopic in the black belt. Now you see it; now you don't. The view is never the same. Climate is an affair of the soul as well as the body: today the sun sears the earth, and a man goes limp in its scorching. Tomorrow and yesterday sullen rains chill bones.... Fire and ice ... the advantages of both may be obtained with ease in the black belt. Light, dark, white, black: a way of life blurs, and the focus shifts. Black, white, black.... A rhythm ripples in

the sun, pounds in steaming. stinking shacks, dances in the blood. Reality is kaleidoscopic in the black belt. Sometimes vision changes with it.

Seminarians grow accustomed to being met with smiles by senior citizens and puzzled looks by their peers, but rarely encounter hostility. Yet Daniels was entering a church in Selma on Palm Sunday when a fellow worshiper greeted him as "You god-damned scum." Vestry members, judges, and leading citizens focused their wrath on anyone disturbing the established order, assuming the church was a comfortable part of that. They had heard but not understood Mary's song about "putting down the mighty from their seats and raising up the humble."

Where does the vision come from that questions what the rest of society accepts? Where do we find the courage to follow a different way, to face the hostility even of other Christians? How different can Christians be without doing more harm than good? Such questions came vividly alive for Jonathan Daniels and his companions. The young seminarian understood that the choices being made were not simple: love and hatred were mixed up in people on both sides of the race issue in America.

> Sometimes we confront the posse, and sometimes we hold a child. Sometimes we stand with men who have learned to hate, and sometimes we must stand a little apart from them. Our life in Selma is filled with ambiguity, and in that we share with men everywhere.

Like the early Christian witness, Daniels could write, "We are beginning to see as we never saw before that we are truly in the world and yet ultimately not of it." He was sickened by signs saying "White Only," but uncomfortable as well with making too "smart" an answer to a segregationist. He wrote: "We are beginning to believe deeply in original sin" — theirs and ours."

In the midst of this ambiguity, the reality of hatred remained, along with the possibility of death. Shortly after writing his report, Daniels was struck down by a white supremacist's bullet. An instinctive reaction led Daniels to throw himself in front of a young black woman when a white man aimed a rifle at her. Yet instincts are the product of prayer and a commitment to justice made long before the event. Daniels seems to have understood that his commitment might require the highest price. He also knew that the way of life can conquer the powers of death. He had written not long before:

> A crooked man climbed a crooked tree on a crooked hill. Somewhere, in the mists of the past, a tenor sang of valleys lifted up and hills made low. Death at the heart of life, and life in the midst of death. The tree of life is indeed a Cross.

✪ *August 16*

Joanna P. Moore

BAPTIST

September 26, 1832–April 15, 1916

"During the last fourteen years," Joanna Moore wrote, "I have been asked to write the story of my life, but I have said; 'No, no, I am too busy living my life to stop to write it. If lives are ever written on earth it should be when that life has begun in eternity;' or I said, 'There are too many books now, if read there will be no time left to read God's blessed book, the Bible, and why write a book that no one has time to read?' " But when they told her that such a book might be helpful to "the dear colored people of the United States" to whom she had devoted her life, she reconsidered. "Whatever will help them," she said, "I stand ready to do, if first of all, it will glorify God."

Joanna was a teacher first and foremost. She was offered a chance to attend a boarding school when she was 14, and the following summer, a neighbor with 14 children asked her to run a summer school for them and some other neighbors nearby. Joanna was thrilled. Her father wondered whether she could maintain discipline, but she never found it a problem.

> I only used the rod three times that I can remember in all my fifteen years of teaching, and then it did no good. They said I did not know how to administer such punishment, and perhaps they were right. My schools were never very quiet; there was freedom, but not real disorder.

Moore was 31 by the time of the Civil War. She heard that 1,000 women and children were being guarded by a regiment of colored troops on an island in the Mississippi. That was the real beginning of her ministry. After the war, she moved south to teach freed slaves how to read in Arkansas, Tennessee, Louisiana, and Mississippi. Despite opposition from some white churches, she wanted to teach blacks how to build independent lives. Before 1877, missionary work had not been open to women in the Baptist Church, but that year the new Women's Baptist Home Mission Society was founded, and Joanna Moore was chosen to be its first commissioned missionary. Before long she was supervising 3,000 "Fireside Schools," created to help families learn their duties to one to another. Fireside Schools also supplied people with reading material, especially the Bible, and worked to "inculcate temperance, industry, neighborly helpfulness, and greater attention to the work of the church." By the time Moore died, she had become so identified with the black people among whom she worked that she requested to be buried in a black cemetery.

A reading from Joanna Moore's description of the work of the Women's Baptist Home Mission Society

Its great object is to reach the neglected citizens of the United States. This is done by its missionaries, of whom I am one, going from house to house with Jesus by our side, the Bible in our hands and the old story of Jesus and his love on our lips, telling it over and over again, till darkness and sin are gone. We do not wait for sinners to come to our churches, but go into all the homes we have time and strength to reach, for we know that among the rubbish of sin are some of the precious jewels that will shine in the Savior's diadem, and with God's help we will find them.

Besides these visits we have sewing schools and children's meetings. Our first lesson is Jesus, and that dear name is the power that reforms and makes beautiful the children we find in our visits. We teach them to keep their clothes, their homes, and their persons neat and clean, and to be kind and helpful to their parents.

This is a great work and the laborers are few. One of our great duties as missionaries is to set others at work. I know two of the excuses you will make: 1, "I have no time," and 2, "I do not know how."

As to time, you have twenty-four hours every day. Do not spend it in idle gossip. Suppose we ask you to give thirty minutes each day to a quiet earnest Bible lesson with your neighbors, or some poor lost sinner. Remember, it should be quiet. I heard a sister, the other day, call across the street these words: "You wicked sinner, you better go and pray," etc. That was not right. This is a sacred subject, and you should strive to speak of it when your friend is alone and you can kneel beside her and ask the Holy Spirit to give power to your words.

Somewhere along the streets going or coming from work, you can take a little neglected child by the hand and coax its mother to let it come to Sabbath school; or you can call on some careless member of the church. Sisters, if you will ask God, He will give you every day a little piece of work to do for him. . . .

Now about the second excuse, "I do not know how." Well, let me see what you do know. You know how to be a good faithful wife and mother, sending or rather bringing your own children to church and Sunday school. If so, your example will help your neighbor. Do you know God's love and peace in your own soul? If so, the Holy Spirit will teach you how to tell others. Remember you do not know how to do this work unless you do it for God's honor and glory and not to get a big name for yourself. Self coming up for praise is likely to be what will spoil your Christian work more than anything else. . . . Sisters, we are working for Christ; we can afford to wait for our pay till Jesus takes us by the hand and introduces us to the glories of heaven with the blessed words, "Well done, good and faithful servant."

✪ *August 17*

Elias Hicks

QUAKER

March 19, 1748–February 27, 1830

The Quaker ideal of a society of friends guided entirely by the inner working of the Holy Spirit requires an intensity of devotion if unity is to be maintained. A society without constituted authorities or a decision-making system is vulnerable when strongly differing opinions arise. So it was that early 19th-century Quakers divided over the impact of the Great Awakening, which led some of them away from their roots and toward evangelical preaching and an insistence on traditional statements of faith.

Elias Hicks was a leader among those who refused to be coerced into the new teaching. This resulted in a split between his followers, known as "Hicksites," and the evangelical wing, often referred to as "Orthodox," although their orthodoxy belonged to the evangelical churches, not the Quaker tradition.

Hicks was born into a Quaker family, but his mother died when he was 11, so he was raised by an elder brother and his wife. Elias fell away from Quaker behavior for a while, but during the Revolutionary War, he became concerned about the state of his soul and returned to a strict, old-fashioned kind of Quaker life. He became a farmer and, though he had little formal education, he read widely and meditated deeply on his faith. Before long, he was traveling to other Quaker meetings in New England, the Middle Atlantic states, and even into the south, bearing his witness to the centrality of the Inward Light and testifying also against slavery.

But Hicks's commitment to the nondoctrinal quietism of the Quaker tradition conflicted with the outlook of some English Quakers visiting America. They advocated a more evangelically orthodox Christianity and their views influenced American Quakers caught up in the thriving trade and manufacturing of cities. This growing division came to a head in 1827 when irreconcilable positions led to a separation between the two factions, a separation accompanied by anger and, in some areas, lawsuits and even violence.

Elias Hicks died shortly after the separation, but just before his death he wrote to his followers, bidding them "Be of good cheer, for no new thing has happened to us; for it has ever been the lot of the righteous to pass through many trials and tribulations." The passions separating Quaker factions have softened over the years and all the Yearly Meetings with which local societies are affiliated cooperate today in the American Friends Service Committee, which works in areas of human need.

Readings from sermons delivered by Elias Hicks in 1825 and 1826

On the Christian life

We read of a state in which man becomes a new creature; "he that is in Christ is a new creature." What is it to be in Christ? It is to come up into that righteousness which he came up into. He had to war with temptations as we have. One temptation after another assailed him; and as he overcame one, the divine light took place of it: just so it must be with us, if we are ever made fit for the kingdom of heaven....

Here we see how the blessed Jesus went on, and how he began. He said he did not come to do his own will, but the will of the Father, that sent him. Just so with us, my friends; this is the end of our coming into the world, not to do our own will, but the will of him that has blessed us with this state of being, and endowed us with these passions, which bring about our probationary state. We feel that we are placed in a state of probation; and we feel and know that it is done by our Creator; and, therefore, we must conclude that it is the best situation in which infinite wisdom and perfect justice could have placed us. There could have been nothing more excellent; for if there could have been, our gracious Creator would have placed his creature man in the best situation — in the best possible state to effect the great end of his creation. Therefore, this probationary state, is the best state that infinite wisdom could have selected, to effect the great design.

Oh! my friends, how glorious the view, I say, how glorious the view, when we are brought to witness and to see how divine wisdom intended we should rise from a state of mere innocency, into a state of glorification, by a conquest over all its enemies, over every thing which could obtrude itself upon the soul, or divert it from its proper duty.

We must not expect that the grace of God will save us, without faith in its sufficiency. There is but one way that I ever found, and that is, to be obedient to its teachings, and attentive to its operation upon the mind. As we attend to it, it will open our understandings; we shall learn to know its excellency; and in proportion as we are attentive to it, we shall love it for its excellency and goodness. "For by grace are ye saved, through faith; and that not of yourselves: it is the gift of God."

On slavery

We know, to the utmost certainty what slavery is, and not any thing in Heaven can make it plainer, than it is. If we know it to be unjust, will we still wait for the Lord to tell us it is so? He will never do it; for he has already done it, by the means which he appointed for that purpose. But being unjust to man in our common way of life — being, too many of us, in the way of darkness, we can have fellowship with the works of darkness; although we are called out of it all.

I know not how to leave this subject, for my soul is in it. Oh! may it be our desire and our resolution, my friends, willingly to take up the cross and despise the shame; — although individuals may point the finger of scorn at us, and say it is a little thing — don't let us regard these things. We are not accountable to man, but to our Creator, who is doing every thing to make the way plain and intelligibly clear to us.

✪ *August 18* _____

Jacob Abbott

CONGREGATIONAL

November 14, 1803–October 31, 1879

Children's literature has become a major branch of the publishing industry. Today, there are books of every description for children of every age. It was not always so. In the early 19th century, children often learned to read from the Bible. No concessions were made to beginners. It was Jacob Abbott who changed all that. He was trained for the ministry but first worked as professor of mathematics and natural philosophy at Amherst College. He then founded the Mount Vernon School for Young Ladies in Boston. Abbot briefly served as pastor of Eliot Congregational Church, which he founded in Roxbury, Massachusetts. With his brothers, he established the Mount Vernon School for Boys in New York City. His concern for the education of the young inspired him to write books children might find interesting. For boys there was a series about "Rollo" beginning with *Rollo Learning to Talk* and *Rollo Learning to Read*. Abbott encouraged parents to become teachers of their children:

> Parents find it very difficult to employ little children. "Mother, what shall I do?" and sometimes even, "Mother, what shall I do after I have done this?" are heard so often that they sometimes exhaust even maternal patience. These little volumes will, we hope, in some cases, provide an answer to the questions. The writer has endeavored to make them such that children would take an interest in reading them to themselves, and to their younger brothers and sisters, and in repeating them to one another.

The Rollo books were designed to be read first with children so that children then might learn to read for themselves. For example:

> Should you like to know how Rollo learned to read? I will tell you. It is very hard work to learn to read, and it takes a great while to do it. I will tell you how Rollo did it.
>
> One evening Rollo was sitting on the floor by the side of the fire, play-ing with his blocks. He was trying to build a meeting-house. He could make the meeting-house very well, all except the steeple, but the steeple would tumble down.

Presently, his father said, "Rollo, you may put your blocks into the basket, and put the basket in its place, in the closet, and then come to me."

Rollo obeyed.

Then Rollo's father took him up into his lap, and took a little book out of his pocket. Rollo was glad. He thought he was going to look at some pictures. But he was disappointed.

He was disappointed, — that is he found there were no pictures in the book, and was sorry.

His father said, "I suppose you thought there were pictures in this book."

"Yes sir," said Rollo.

"There are none," said his father; "I have not got this book to amuse you. I am going to have you learn to read out of it, and learning to read is hard work."

But once the initial hard work was done, the child could follow Rollo on a series of adventures, including a prolonged tour of Europe in ten volumes. For girls there were books about Cousin Lucy. For parents there were books of advice and some of it seems a bit stern:

The parental authority must, therefore, be established — by gentle means, if possible — but it must by all means be established, and be firmly maintained. If you can not govern your child without corporal punishment, it is better to resort to it than not to govern him at all.

But Abbott also wanted parents to understand that a child's ability to understand develops gradually and cannot be rushed:

Now the qualities and characteristics of the soul...come to maturity at different periods of life; so that the mother, in feeling dejected and sad because she can not awaken in the mind of her child the gratitude and the consideration for her comfort and happiness which she desires, is simply looking for a certain kind of fruit at the wrong time.

The mother may sometimes derive from certain religious considerations the idea that she is bound to look upon the moral delinquencies and dangers which she observes in her children, under an aspect more stern and severe than seems to be here recommended. But a little reflection must convince us that the way to true repentance of, and turning from sin, is not necessarily through the suffering of terror and distress. The Gospel is not an instrumentality for producing terror and distress, even as means to an end. It is an instrumentality for saving us from these ills; and the Divine Spirit, in the hidden and mysterious influence which it exercises in forming, or transforming, the human soul into the image of God, must be as ready, it would seem, to sanction and bless efforts made by a mother to allure her child away from its sins by loving and gentle invitations and encouragements, as any attempts to drive her from them by the agency of terror or pain. It would seem that no one who remembers the way in which Jesus Christ dealt with the children that were brought to him could possibly have any doubt of this.

That books for children should differ from those written for adults, that spiritual development should be nurtured, that there are developmental stages in children's growth, that kindness and gentleness are essential — all this is now taken for granted by nearly everyone. Jacob Abbott deserves a great deal of the credit.

✹ *August 19* _____

Ileana Hapsburg (Mother Alexandra)

ORTHODOX

January 5, 1909–January 21, 1991

Often, a deeply committed lay Christian can make a stronger impact than the professional clergy. If that lay person is also a princess, Americans, for all their commitment to democracy, are even more impressed. Princess Ileana was the daughter of King Ferdinand and Queen Marie of Romania. She grew up in Bucharest as a member of the Orthodox Church. Her mother devoted herself to works of charity and the princess followed her example. She married an Austrian Archduke and had six children but moved her family back to Romania to escape the Nazis during World War II. There, she built a hospital in honor of her mother and, serving as a member of the Romanian Red Cross, personally cared for the wounded during the war years. When the Communists succeeded the Nazis, forcing the abdication of her nephew, King Michael, she fled the country with her family, moving first to Switzerland, then to Argentina, and finally to the United States. She brought with her the tiara her mother had worn on an American tour in 1926, wrapped in her nightgown. Its sale provided funds to enable the family to begin a new life.

To support her family, Ileana turned to writing and public speaking, but when the children were grown she went to France to become a nun. She was sent back to the United States in 1968 to establish a convent. The Orthodox Monastery of the Transfiguration was established in Ellwood City, Pennsylvania, and Princess Ileana, now Mother Alexandra, served as abbess until her death in 1991. Throughout this final stage of her life, she continued to speak and write, using her gifts to draw attention to the Christian faith and the Orthodox Church. She wrote a book called *I Live Again* to tell the story of her life, and composed others on the Nicene Creed, about angels, and about the Orthodox Church and also wrote a story for children.

A reading on the Jesus Prayer by Ileana Hapsburg

The Jesus Prayer, or the Prayer of the Heart, centers on the Holy Name itself. It may be said in its entirety: "Lord Jesus Christ, Son of God, have mercy upon me, a sinner"; it may be changed to "us sinners" or to other persons named, or it may be shortened. The power lies in the name of Jesus; thus "Jesus," alone, may fulfill the whole need of the one who prays.

The Jesus Prayer can be used for worship and petition; as intercession, invocation, adoration, and as thanksgiving. It is a means by which we lay all that is in our hearts, both for God and man, at the feet of Jesus. It is a means of communion with God and with all those who pray. The fact that we can train our hearts to go on praying even when we sleep, keeps us uninterruptedly within the community of prayer. This is no fanciful statement; many have experienced this life-giving fact. We cannot, of course, attain this continuity of prayer all at once, but it is achievable; for all that is worthwhile we must " . . . run with patience the race that is set before us . . . " (Hebrews 12:1).

I had a most striking proof of uninterrupted communion with all those who pray when I lately underwent surgery. I lay long under anesthesia. "Jesus" had been my last conscious thought, and the first word on my lips as I awoke. It was marvelous beyond words to find that although I knew nothing of what was happening to my body I never lost cognizance of being prayed for and of praying myself. After such an experience one no longer wonders that there are great souls who devote their lives exclusively to prayer.

Prayer has always been of very real importance to me, and the habit formed in early childhood of morning and evening prayer has never left me; but in the practice of the Jesus Prayer I am but a beginner. I would, nonetheless, like to awaken interest in this prayer because, even if I have only touched the hem of a heavenly garment, I have touched it — and the joy is so great I would share it with others. It is not every man's way of prayer; you may not find in it the same joy that I find, for your way may be quite a different one — yet equally bountiful.

In fear and joy, in loneliness and companionship, it is ever with me. Not only in the silence of daily devotions, but at all times and in all places. It transforms, for me, frowns into smiles; it beautifies, as if a film had been washed off an old picture so that the colors appear clear and bright, like nature on a warm spring day after a shower. Even despair has become attenuated and repentance has achieved its purpose.

When I arise in the morning, it starts me joyfully upon a new day. When I travel by air, land, or sea, it sings within my breast. When I stand upon a platform and face my listeners, it beats encouragement. When I gather my children around me, it murmurs a blessing. And at the end of a weary day, when I lay me down to rest, I give my heart over to Jesus: "(Lord) into thy hands I commend my spirit." I sleep — but my heart as it beats prays on: "JESUS."

✪ *August 20*

Franklin Clark Fry

LUTHERAN

August 30, 1900–June 6, 1968

Franklin Clark Fry did for Lutherans in the 20th century what Muhlenberg had done for them in the 18th. He brought a vision and an organization to the Lutheran Church in America where before, there had been division and distrust among different sects. Not only did Fry pull together several strands of Lutherans in America; he was also a moving force in the ecumenical and international involvement of Lutherans after World War II and until his death.

Fry came from a dynasty of Lutheran clergy. When, at 44, he was elected to preside in the United Lutheran Church in America (ULCA), he joked that some of the voters thought they were voting for his father and some his grandfather, which accounted for his high vote totals. His own credentials were solid, and his personal presence made him an effective leader. He stood over six feet tall, had a boyish sense of humor, a razor-sharp intellect, a love for the minutiae of constitutional and organizational work, an immense store of energy, and an ability to remember details about both people and events that astounded his peers.

Fry's vision for American Lutheranism has shaped the understanding of most Lutherans in this country today. He saw the church solidly founded on its own confessional tradition, but active in conversation and joint activity with Christians of other backgrounds, both in America and around the world. In his first President's Report to the ULCA after visiting war-torn Europe in 1945, Fry had this to say:

> As Christians we must look and only as Christians can we look without flinching.... The mists are thick over the future and, peer anxiously as we may, we cannot pierce through them.... In the face of every portent, faith is no longer optional. It never was! The leading of God is not a pious platitude, a vaporous sentiment. It is the indispensable, our single rational reliance, humanity's one chance to live.... Almost everything else has cracked. The Gospel has not. Christ's and His Church's goals are unscathed.... The metronome of religion must be speeded up to match the startlingly fast metronome of the world.... Our pace is still tragically too slow. The giant in modern Christianity, and specifically in the United Lutheran Church in America, has barely stirred. He must rise! This is the day! Opportunity condemns itself unless it is seized.... Fathers and Brethren, what makes us so sure that our time, the years of our lives and our civilization, will not run out? How can we dawdle along?

Fry did not dawdle. He met the demands of the presidency of the ULCA until its merger into the Lutheran Church in America (LCA) in 1962, then continued as president of that body until his death in 1968. He served with equal vigor and influence as president of Lutheran World Relief and the Lutheran World Federation (LWF). He became the first treasurer of LWF, the first vice-chairman of the World Council of Churches Central Committee and later its chairman. Nationally, he served on the executive committee of the National Lutheran Council, was vice chairman of American Relief for Korea, and chaired the National Council of Churches Policy and Strategy Committee. These were not honorary posts, or figurehead positions. Fry used them to effect real change for both church and world. Through these connections, he was called upon to negotiate with the Communist leaders of Hungary for the release of Bishop Lajos Ordass, who had been confined to house arrest, and won his freedom.

Fry's understanding of every aspect of church organization, from congregation to synod, to international federation, was typically Lutheran: we passively receive God's gifts but are then called to respond actively.

> A congregation ought to be exactly nothing, ideally, except a fellowship of those who hear the Word and receive the Sacraments and obey the Lord. The church of Jesus Christ as we think of it is usually thought of in the active voice. We do it. We create the fellowship. We are the church. The truth is . . . the church of Jesus Christ is in the form and body of the passive verb. We are acted upon — we are addressed — we are grasped — we are thrust out into the world — we are no longer our own — we are bought with a price. We are used as His instrument.

Under Fry's leadership, the ULCA added almost 500 congregations, and 1,000 pastors between 1944 and 1958. The Foreign Mission Board's budget swelled from less than one half million dollars to over two million. Total giving to all causes within the ULCA shot up from about $24 million to over $100 million in his first 15 years as President. To other Christians, it may seem a simple matter for Lutherans to find common ground. But the situation in Europe after World War II was not just one of physical damage and massive loss of human life; it was also the source of extreme enmity between German and Nordic Christians. A *Time* magazine article in 1958 quoted Fry's recollection of what he had seen in his work with Lutheran World Relief:

> It wasn't just a question of relief. Danish and Norwegian Lutherans hated German Lutherans; they felt contempt for Swedish Lutherans. No one would talk to anyone else. At first we got nowhere. But at the 1947 convention of the Lutheran World Federation we surrounded every anti with several pros so he would have to talk to them. And it worked. Now the federation is the most cohesive body of its kind. We've begun to think together more than ever.

In the ecumenical sphere, Fry's gifts were just as effective. W. A. Visser 't Hooft, who served with him on the World Council of Churches, recalled his comments to an early session of the Central Committee:

The World Council's aim is not the dilution of faith into a solution; not the reduction of confessions into a shapeless amalgam. The World Council's method is for churches to meet around the Word of God. Its hope for achieving unity does not rest upon the discovery of how to compromise but upon the discovery of what the Scriptures teach.

✸ *August 21*

Frances Willard

METHODIST

September 28, 1839–February 18, 1898

Her voice was compared by a young admirer to "a silver trumpet sounding the note of human right." Frances Willard spent her life trying to make that voice heard, although not always successfully. Like many campaigners for women's rights, she came to the movement circuitously. Working for temperance, she found herself handicapped as a woman. To achieve her first goal, she would need to take on the second cause as well.

She had begun her career as a teacher and became dean of women at Northwestern University. She abandoned education, however, in favor of the temperance movement. She was among the organizers of the Chicago Woman's Christian Temperance Union in 1874, became president of the National Woman's Christian Temperance Union in 1879, and was elected president of the World's Woman's Christian Temperance Union in 1891. She was also among the founders of the Prohibition Party. For many years she accepted no payment for her work in these positions, supporting herself by the fees she was given for speaking engagements.

The goal of the temperance movement was the prohibition of alcoholic beverages, and that required legal action. Since women could not yet vote, they had no direct influence on legislation. Willard was not slow to realize that her goal would not be achieved so long as women were disenfranchised. As it happened, more than 20 years after Frances Willard's death, women were granted that right, and prohibition — the "noble experiment" — soon followed. But women's suffrage, the secondary goal, was her lasting achievement.

Toward the goal of organizing women and giving them all a voice like hers, Willard served as the president of the National Council of Women, the International Council of Women, and the vice president of the Universal Peace Union in order to help mobilize the female population. She was also an organizer of the General Federation of Women's Clubs. She endeavored with equal fervor to obtain a voice for women in the councils of her church. Although the Rock River Conference elected her to serve as a lay delegate to the General Conference of the Methodist Church in 1888, she was denied her seat when she arrived. That struggle, too, was successful only after her death.

A reading from the journal of Frances E. Willard

How near God comes to us, and we know it not! How blind we are to His infinite, unceasing, all-encompassing goodness! Filling the whole universe — finding its simile only in light that floats richly & joyfully & abundantly over every thing — God's goodness; God's pity! Themes for an angel to dwell on, but for mortals to *feel* and *know* every moment of their lives....

I have united with the Methodist Church because I like its views of the Doctrines taught in the Bible, better than those of any other branch of God's militant church, because I have been reared in it, & for me to attach myself to any other would cause great sorrow & dissatisfaction in quarters where I should most desire to avoid such consequences, — other things being equal. In my life, I have seen a great deal of narrowmindedness & bigotry — down right bigotry manifested by church members — those who profess to be followers of Him who said in his great, all-encompassing wisdom and kindness "There is neither male nor female, bond or free, but ye are *one* in *Christ.* Before I ever declared myself determined to live, — being helped by God — a Christian life, I resolved to educate in myself an antisectarian spirit — to live against it, write against it, talk against it, always. And I honestly believe that I regard all the churches — the branches, rather, of the *One* Church — with feelings of *equal kindness* & fellowship. For myself under existing circumstances I prefer the one to which I belong, but that a person belonged to *that* church & was a true Christian, would be to me no more of a recommendation than that he was a true Christian & belonged to any other. The churches are all good & fighting nobly & zealously to make the world better and happier. O, I earnestly pray that as I grow older the kindly, all-loving, catholic spirit may more deeply seat itself in my heart!

I intend to observe all the customs & usages of the church. I have resolved never to be absent from Sabbath services, Communion, Sunday School, Class Meeting or prayer meeting, save when it is *unavoidable.* I will talk to any one upon the only Great Subject in the world, whenever &c wherever, &c however, my best, prayer-guided judgment teaches me that it will be appropriate — that it will not be so ill-timed that it will so jar upon the individual's prejudices & modes of thinking as to be the means of ill to him rather than of good.

✹ *August 22* _____

John Witherspoon

PRESBYTERIAN

February 5, 1723–November 15,1794

Princeton University had been unlucky in its choices of president. The first five men to hold the position lasted a total of less than 20 years; two died within months of assuming office. Increasingly, the Trustees looked enviously across the sea, wondering how they could entice John Witherspoon to take up the post. Witherspoon was a respected and successful clergyman in Scotland when, in 1766, the directors of Princeton College elected him president. He had been educated at Edinburgh, had received an honorary doctorate from St. Andrews, and was a well-known leader of the "Popular Party" of the Church of Scotland. Upon hearing of his election, he declined. But Princeton would not take "no" for an answer. Through friends (and perhaps more importantly, his wife), they pressed him to reconsider and finally, after much reflection, Witherspoon agreed. The Princeton Trustees then had to elect him again, which they did, and he was sworn in as the sixth president in 1768.

Witherspoon's arrival inspired much fanfare. Lamps in windows illuminated his way to the college as he approached from Philadelphia. He found an institution in need of much tending. Preparation for entering students was not uniform, faculty members were few, graduating classes were shrinking, and the finances were so weak, the board had to borrow money to pay him.

Witherspoon turned out to have been a wise choice. Well educated himself, he placed a high value on formal education. He had learned to read by age four and was well versed in Hebrew, Greek, and Latin by the age of 13. He was also a gifted speaker who, without notes, could give inspiring and eloquent homilies and addresses in a manner refreshingly distinct from the too-common practice in America of reading sermons. He recognized the need to reaffirm the original purpose of Princeton's founding: to make it a source of pastoral leadership in the churches. Inner conversion of the potential parsons was important, of course, but Witherspoon was convinced that the quality of intellect was also vital. He believed that a solid grounding in academic disciplines was a necessary element for church leadership.

Witherspoon set to work traveling widely to increase the student body and the general support for the school throughout the colonies. His itinerary included Boston, New York, Williamsburg, and other centers of population and power. He hired new professors to handle courses in which his own expertise was inadequate. He added buildings and generally built up the reputation of the school. He bolstered Princeton's connection to primary schools and strengthened the quality of the course work there. Though Witherspoon recruited a teacher for mathematics and astronomy in 1771, he himself was responsible for teaching moral philosophy, divinity, rhetoric, and history. He embraced and fostered a strict Calvinist doctrine in the chapel services and the school in general. Not content to be a teacher and administrator, Witherspoon continued to preach, usually speaking twice on Sundays. Described as "solemn and graceful" in the pulpit with a "melodious" voice, his preaching was said to be "loaded with good sense and adorned (with) elegance and beauty." His oratory was not dependent upon extraneous words or gestures. When a visitor saw how well tended his vegetable garden was, he said: "Doctor, I see no flowers in your garden." Whitherspoon simply said: "No, nor in my discourses either."

Witherspoon had a finely tuned understanding of freedom, based on British concepts of liberty and John Locke's political philosophy. As tensions between England and the colonies increased, it seemed to Witherspoon that England's policies in North America conflicted with that liberty, which turned him into a strong supporter of the colonial cause. He was no stranger to political conflict, having led militiamen in support of the Royalists during the Jacobite rebellion. For a time he had been a captive of "the Pretender's" men and imprisoned. In North America, the rebellion of the colonists appeared to Witherspoon to be a legitimate cause and one to which he gave his full support.

Without forsaking his work at Princeton, Witherspoon began engaging in politics as a delegate to the Constitutional Convention. He also served two terms in the New Jersey legislature and was the only clergyman to sign the Declaration of Independence. A man of common sense, he thought through his ideas with care and found practical applications for them. He also had a well-developed sense of humor. An insomniac, Witherspoon had trouble staying alert by mid-afternoon. At one session of the New Jersey legislature, he made a motion to conclude all business by dinner. The motion failed, and Witherspoon said, "There are two kinds of speaking that are very interesting... perfect sense and perfect nonsense. When there is speaking in either of these ways I shall engage to be all attention. But when there is speaking, as there often is, halfway between sense and nonsense, you must bear with me if I fall asleep."

Witherspoon's efforts on behalf of Princeton proved fruitful. Enrollment increased, as did income. Moreover, the original vision of those who started the college, to produce men who would be "ornaments of the State as well as the Church, became more focused and better realized. Witherspoon's pupils included a future president and vice-president of the United States, nine cabinet officers, 21 senators, 39 congressmen, three justices of the Supreme Court, and 12 state governors. Five of the nine Princeton graduates among the 55 members of the Constitutional Convention of 1787 were students of Witherspoon's.

In the course of his efforts to make Princeton the premier Presbyterian college in America, Witherspoon also managed to build bridges between some of the bitterly divided Presbyterian factions in the colonies, setting the stage for a fully unified Presbyterian Church. Described as a man of "presence," it has been said that except for George Washington, no man in America commanded more respect than Witherspoon. Perhaps equally gratifying to the Trustees of the University, he outlasted the first five presidents combined by a good six years.

✪ August 23

Ellen Gates Starr

ROMAN CATHOLIC

March 19, 1859–February 10, 1940

After the Civil War ended, Americans were able to turn their energies toward the Industrial Revolution. Christians who had fought against slavery began to realize that a growing number of factory workers had also become enslaved to a system that limited their opportunities and destroyed their health. In attempting to come to grips with this new evil, Christians chose various remedies. Perhaps the most systematic efforts came from Socialists who had been converted by Marx's analysis of the evils of industrialization.

In England and other European countries, many thoughtful people found Socialism and Christianity so compatible that they came to believe all Christians ought to be Socialists. Among Americans, less conscious of a feudal past and more assured they could change society within the system, Socialism never had the same appeal. Yet some who were attracted to it played a significant role in effecting change. Through their writing, their political efforts, and their creation of new institutions, they helped transform American society by placing limits on the exploitation of workers and providing institutions like Hull House in Chicago that worked with individuals to enrich their lives in various practical ways.

Ellen Gates Starr cofounded Hull House with Jane Addams,* but was strikingly different in her orientation and concerns. Both women had been deeply influenced by the English Fabian Socialists, but where Addams was a practical "do-gooder" with a vaguely defined Protestant ethic, Starr's activity became increasingly based on a growing religious commitment that finally led her to become a Roman Catholic and a member of a religious order.

Like Addams, Starr was born in Illinois and attended Rockford College where she and Addams met. A Unitarian by upbringing, Starr became an Episcopalian at the age of 25. She taught school for ten years and then, after traveling to Europe and seeing the work of the English Fabian Socialists, she joined with Addams to establish Hull House as a center of outreach in a poor neighborhood of Chicago. Unlike Addams, Starr also participated in labor union activities, especially for women. She was arrested for protesting and for trying to incite others to protest. One of the most succinct expressions of her evolving viewpoint is the following undated essay.

A reading from "Why I am a Socialist" by Ellen Gates Starr

I became a Socialist because I was a Christian. The Christian religion teaches that all men are to be regarded as brothers, that no one should wish to profit by the loss or disadvantage of others; as all winners must do under a competitive system; that none should enjoy "two coats" while others are coatless; that, in effect, "none should have cake till all have bread." "Civilized" life is in grotesque contrast to all this. And the individual, acting individualistically, is helpless to modify it very much.... "Society" or "the state" must see to it that strangers are entertained; that the hungry are fed and the destitute provided for. Does it? "Christendom" is a sorry spectacle of "unbrotherliness." Nothing resembling Christianity — nothing resembling the old Hebrew law. If I had space to quote the Prophets I could show you that they had some very good social standards. They were radicals — the prophets. "Very extreme." Isaiah and Jeremiah would not be permitted to talk as they did to or of the master class in public places nowadays. What to do? One's eye scanned the horizon for any political system which even proposed doing anything to abolish privilege, to stem the tide of concentrating wealth and power, steadily increasing and intensifying in the hands of a smaller and more terribly oppressive minority while the majority increased in ratio and in suffering.

Many Christians who would otherwise be Socialists are frightened because many Socialists are materialists. Socialism does not make a materialist of me; nor does even the capitalistic system; but I can easily understand how the latter drives many to it. I should expect fewer materialists under a Socialist regime.

Socialism only, so far as I could find out, offered any effective method to put down the mighty from their seats and to exalt the humble and meek; to fill the hungry with good things and to send the rich if not quite "empty away," at least relieved of some of their unnecessary and arrogant fullness. Nothing at all in sight to cure it; nothing in the programs of the Republican or Democratic parties hinging at any such procedure. The Socialist Party proposed, without violence, quite lawfully, by the ballot, to tax away the preposterous aggregations of money and power. It proposed that all necessary things should be made for the use of all, not for concentrating power over their fellow men in the hands of those few who control manufacturing and distribution. It proposed to house and feed and clothe and educate everybody decently, it proposed to allow all who were able the opportunity to do these things for themselves. And those who were unable, through youth or age or feebleness, it proposed to care for in comfort and with respect. The methods were modern, practical, scientific, and peaceable. The object was such a society as Christian precepts could be practiced in; even Christians admit that it is impossible under present conditions to carry out the teachings of Christ. Well, then, if that be true, what is wrong? The teachings of Christ or present conditions?

Let us face that alternative. I faced it and I became a Socialist. When I cast a vote, I cast it for no "good man" who "has a chance of winning" and might make things a trifle better for his term of office. I cast it, uncompromisingly, for an ideal; for a total and lasting change in our whole unchristian system of life.

✪ *August 24*

Alexander Crummell

EPISCOPALIAN

March 3, 1819–September 10, 1898

Alexander Crummell, like James Theodore Holly,* was born free. Along with many other members of that generation of black leaders who came to maturity just before the Civil War, he came to believe that the future of African Americans lay in Africa. In words that seem precursors to the rhetoric of the black power movement in the late 20th century, Crummell and his fellows appealed to black pride and even spoke of black power. Indeed, Crummell went so far as to speak of "The Destined Superiority of the Negro." At a time when white people still considered negroes inferior to whites, such statements may have provided a needed balance.

Crummell grew up in New York City. He was educated in the parish school of St. Philip's Church, a black Episcopal congregation, then at a boarding school in New Hampshire organized by abolitionists, and at the Oneida Institute. He was accepted as a candidate for ordination at the General Theological Seminary, but only on the condition that he would not reside at the school, eat in its refectory, or sit in its lecture halls. Rather than submit to such restrictions, Crummell studied privately and was ordained to the priesthood in 1844. After working for a while in small black congregations in the north, he went to England and earned a degree at Cambridge University before going to Liberia to serve there as a mission priest for 20 years.

Discouraged by the slow pace of his efforts in Liberia and lack of financial support, Crummell returned to the United States in 1872, where he served for 25 years as rector of St. Luke's Church, Washington, DC. He was one of the founders of the American Negro Academy, an exclusive body of 40, dedicated to supporting the work of the black intelligentsia in science, economics, education, religion, and the arts. His emphasis on black pride had a major influence on the ideas of many African American leaders, including W. E. B. Du Bois and Marcus Garvey.

A reading from "The Destined Superiority of the Negro" by Alexander Crummell

We have seen today, the great truth, that when God does not destroy a people, but, on the contrary, trains and disciplines it, it is an indication that

He intends to make something of them, and to do something for them. It signifies that He is graciously interested in such a people. In a sense, not equal, indeed, to the case of the Jews, but parallel, in a lower degree, such a people are a "chosen people" of the Lord. There is, so to speak, a *covenant* relation which God has established between Himself and them; dim and partial, at first, in its manifestations; but which is sure to come to the sight of men and angels, clear, distinct, and luminous. You may take it as a sure and undoubted fact that God presides, with sovereign care, over such a people; and will surely preserve, educate, and build them up.

The discussion of this morning teaches us that the Negro race, of which we are a part, and which, as yet, in great simplicity and with vast difficulties, is struggling for place and position in this land, discovers, most exactly, in its history, the principle I have stated. And we have in this fact the assurance that the Almighty is interested in all the great problems of civilization and of grace carrying on among us. All this is God's work. He has brought this race through a wilderness of disasters; and at last put them in the large, open place of liberty; but not, you may be assured, for eventual decline and final ruin. You need not entertain the shadow of a doubt that the work which God has begun and is now carrying on, is for the elevation and success of the Negro. This is the significance and worth of all effort and all achievement, of every signal providence, in this cause; or, otherwise, all the labors of men and all the mightiness of God is vanity! Nothing, believe me, on earth; nothing brought from perdition, can keep back this destined advance of the Negro race. No conspiracies of men or devils! The slave trade could not crush them out. Slavery, dread, direful, and malignant, could only stay it for a time. But now it is coming, coming, I grant, through dark and trying events, but surely coming. The Negro — black curly headed, despised, repulsed, sneered at — is, nevertheless, a vital being, and irrepressible. Everywhere on earth has been given him, by the Almighty, assurance, self-assertion, and influence. The rise of two Negro states within a century, feeble though they be, has a bearing upon this subject. The numerous emancipations, which now leave not more than a chain or two to be unfastened, have, likewise, a deep, moral significance. Thus, too, the rise in the world of illustrious Negroes, as Toussaint L'Ouverture, Henry Christophe, Benjamin Eustace the Philanthropist, Stephen Allan Benson, and Bishop Crowther.

With all these providential indications in our favor, let us bless God and take courage. Casting aside everything trifling and frivolous, let us lay hold of every element of power, in the brain; in literature, art, and science; in industrial pursuits; in the soil; in cooperative association; in mechanical ingenuity; and above all, in the religion of our God; and so march on in the pathway of progress to that superiority and eminence which is our rightful heritage, and which is evidently the promise of our God!

✪ *August 25*

Annie Armstrong
BAPTIST
July 11, 1850–December 20, 1938

Just as a parish secretary is often the center around whom the life of a parish revolves, so the secretary at the desk of denominational headquarters can influence the life and mission of a national church. Annie Armstrong helped organize the Women's Mission Union of the Southern Baptist Convention, then served as its first corresponding secretary from 1888 to 1906. The foreword to a collection of her letters calls her "one of the most influential women in American Church History" and notes that a constant theme of her letters is her opinion of "how things ought to be." Adjectives used to describe her include, "combative, kindhearted, tenacious," and "conscientious."

The thousands of letters that went out from "Miss Annie" to churches and church officials and missionaries provide an intimate view of her life. One letter descries her day in terms that any denominational official would recognize:

> Meetings, meetings, meetings are the order of the day. I knew that I had to attend one today, but I find it will be necessary for me this morning to go to the Annual Meeting of the Women's Christian Temperance Union and make an appeal for workers for the Bayview (our City poorhouse) Mission. I did not know that I had to do this until on my way to the Mission Rooms this morning, so I shall have to go before that *august* body, trusting to make a very eloquent appeal without any preparation whatever. It has been my theory that no one had a right to make a public address without thorough preparation; but, of late, I have been forced to frequently trust to the inspiration of the moment, when making appeals, for I often have not time enough to arrange my ideas.

She goes on to describe how, at the last minute, she had been asked to preside at a meeting when the woman who was supposed to had to stay home with a sick child, and concludes, "There is excitement in this sort of life, but it certainly is not conducive to health to work under such high pressure. No one would think, though, from the way I have been rambling on, that I must try, if possible, to reply to two days' mail this morning."

Although she questioned whether her life might be "conducive to health," she never spared herself and was seldom sick. She was at her desk an hour and a half before breakfast, at the office by 9 a.m., home for lunch between 1:00 and 2:00 in the afternoon, then back at the Mission Rooms until 6:00. After dinner, she would "usually rest for a few moments" before returning to her work until 10:30 or 11:00 at night. She wrote:

> I thoroughly believe if God gives us a work to do He will supply physical as well as spiritual strength...I do though realize at times that he lays us aside in order that we may be better fitted to do His work.

Details mattered to her, as did doing things "the right way." After discussing what return address and postmark would be on a particular mailing, she concludes, "I do not suppose one person out of a thousand will notice this. This I consider the best way, and it is the only way in which the Secretary of the Women's Mission Union is willing to do this work."

For many years, Armstrong accepted no salary on the grounds that it would be inconsistent with her principle that women should offer themselves for work without remuneration. Although her views about the position of women in the church would no longer find wide acceptance, she took them so seriously that she eventually resigned rather than compromise. Her refusal to accept payment was one issue. The other concerned the establishment of a training school for women missionaries and their inclusion in classes at the adjacent Southern Baptist Theological Seminary in Louisville, Kentucky. She considered it went against the Bible for women to be preachers. Until she turned 80, Armstrong spent the next 20 years managing homes in Baltimore for aged men and women and serving her local church in many capacities. Just months before she died, she sent the following message to the WMU on its 50th anniversary:

> My message for the Union in its fiftieth year is that I hope it may grow every year stronger and better. I would link with this thought the Scripture verse: "Speak unto the children of Israel that they go forward."
>
> For the young women in Y.W.A. my wish is that they "grow in grace and in the Knowledge of our Lord and Savior Jesus Christ."
>
> Do the Girls' Auxiliary members know the two verses most often read and committed to memory? — "For God so loved the world that he gave His only begotten Son that Whosoever believeth on Him should not perish but have eternal life.... The Lord is my Shepherd."
>
> Tell the Royal Ambassadors to "be strong in the Lord and in the power of His might." I can say with emphasis that I have found this verse to be true.
>
> My message for the Sunbeams is the Shepherd Psalm. To encourage you in your special offerings for missions I would say: "Blessed are ye that sow beside the waters." Water suggests expansion and growth. After study of God's Word comes study of the fields. Then People pray. Then they give.

✸ *August 26*

John Ettwein

MORAVIAN

June 29, 1721–1802

John Ettwein "was an unusually pious boy" by his own account and responded readily to the teaching of two "awakened" students who came to serve his community in Bavaria's Black Forest. Overcoming opposition from his father, he attended services regularly and was made an assistant teacher.

Continuing to work with the Moravian leaders, Ettwein married, was made a deacon, and moved to London for three years after, which, at the age of 33, he emigrated to America with a group of more than 50 other Moravians. Ettwein often journeyed into the forest to find Indians so he could bring the gospel to them. His evangelistic journeys took him up and down the east coast from Georgia to Massachusetts, where he preached to settlers and Native Americans alike. One journey spanned 2,000 miles; on another, he claimed to have lost a quarter of his weight; once he was not under a roof for eight weeks, while on still another he recorded that he was "three times in mortal danger."

Ettwein was ordained a presbyter in 1764. Two decades later, he became a bishop in the Moravian Church. During the Revolutionary War, he represented the Moravians before the Continental Congress when they refused to bear arms or participate in the military. At the same time, he represented Native Americans who requested that land be set aside for those who had become Christians. He obtained grants of 5,000 acres from the state of Pennsylvania and 12,000 acres from Congress.

A reading from the journal of John Ettwein

I see now with longing the end of my pilgrimage. If He has taken my journeys to heart, if my doings have somewhat pleased him, then all the honor goes to Him alone. The shortcomings and mistakes in it have not remained hidden to me.

I have had the honor of preaching publicly in churches or courthouses, in barns or other gathering places, in twelve of the United States of North America, and to praise my crucified Savior and the reconciliation through his blood to [people of] all kinds of religious convictions. I even had the occasion to tell many Indians of such varied nations as the Wampanos, Mahikans, Delawares, Munseys, and from the six united Nations, who released them from the devil and from their sins through His blood, and paid so high a price for them as his possessions; I also baptized two adults. I was in the towns of the Catawbas, saw 150 Cherokee warriors in Bethabara, and spoke with their chief through their interpreter. Moreover, I have seen Chickasaws, Nanitkoks, Shawanoes, and Tuscaroras, and felt thereby what it might feel like to be a Heathen-messenger. When the main hospital was in Bethlehem during the Revolutionary War, I was Comforter of the Sick and Hospital-Preacher, and twice a week held a talk for around six hundred sick soldiers. The feeling that I did not work for naught was a great payment to me. I had neither disgust nor horror, and the infectious air did not do any damage to me, although many Brethren were infected with the sickness, and the same was the occasion for the deaths of seven Single Brethren, among whom was my twenty-year-old son Johannes. The experience of the care of my dear Father in Heaven, and the protection of his Holy Angel on my many journeys over water and over land, I cannot count. More than twenty times I was dangerously thrown from a horse without sustaining any injury, and I was rescued from water several times when I was near drowning. I can praise my dear Lord with thanks and submission, that He was with me wherever I found myself. That I was honored to be His servant in the Brüdergemeine, and was far and wide a witness to His Death, often laid me weeping at His feet with the words: How did I come to this? He loved me ever and ever, and even brought me to him! I can do nothing other than rejoice humbly over my state of bliss, because it is pure mercy! I pray to Him in the dust for everything that He did for me and to me. His mercy will preserve me until I see Him. I am devoted to him like a child; He does with me as it pleases Him! He never comes to me too soon. I wait for Him from one morning's waking until the next.

✪ August 27 _____

Mark Hopkins

CONGREGATIONAL

February 4, 1802–June 17, 1887

President James A. Garfield once said something to the effect that his idea of a higher education was a student on one end of a log and Mark Hopkins on the other. Garfield had been a student of Hopkins at Williams College where Hopkins was tutor, professor, and finally president for 36 years. Hopkins was a teacher in the broadest sense of the word: widely read and familiar with the work of the great minds of western culture, his concern was to impart those ideas to his students in a way that would enable the students to put them to use as they developed their own characters for whatever roles they would play in their communities. His focus on putting ideas into action is also reflected in his interest in foreign missions and his service for 30 years as president of the American Board of Commissioners for Foreign Missions (the American Congregational Mission Board).

During Hopkins's life, American Christianity wrestled with such issues as abolition, woman's suffrage, and the industrial revolution, but the issue that most engaged Hopkins was the church's response to Darwin's theory of evolution. His own work anticipated Darwin, giving him the tools with which to respond. In 1833, Hopkins had published an essay "On the Argument from Nature for the Divine Existence," over 20 years before the appearance of Darwin's 1859 book, *On the Evolution of Species*. Here and in subsequent work, Hopkins combined ideas from Jonathan Edwards and his Congregational inheritance with the Aristotelian concept of a great chain of being in which each lower member is the condition of a higher. Hopkins believed that each stage was lifted to the next higher stage by the addition of some external force. Morality, purpose, and freedom, he argued, could not come from a mechanistic process but must be supplied by a Deity. Hopkins grouped together all notions of evolution that found a driving force within nature itself. Necessity, law, immanence, and a tendency to pantheism were contrasted with a chain of being rising into personality which, in turn, allowed freedom of choice and self-determination, along with an intuition of supernatural man, and transcendent Deity. For him, faith was ultimately a relationship between the human person and a personal God. These issues, a continuing theme in Hopkins's writing, remain relevant in our own time.

A reading from *The Law of Love* by Mark Hopkins

A devotional spirit may be cultivated —

1. By the exercise of devotion.

This is on the principle that all our active powers are strengthened by exercise. There is no active power that does not gain facility and scope by repeated acts under the direction of will.

2. A devotional spirit may be cultivated by a right use of Nature.

The physical universe is but a visible expression of the power and the thought of God. This power and thought are seen in the very constitution of matter. It was not any matter, but such matter, and in such proportions, that was needed for the forms that we see, and for vital processes. The varieties and affinities and relative quantities of matter as much show that it was created, and for a purpose, as its forms and movements show that it is used for a purpose. It is therefore the voice of Science as well as of Revelation that He "hath measured the waters in the hollow of his hand, and meted out heaven" — that is the extent of the atmosphere — "with the span, and comprehended the dust of the earth in a measure, and weighed the mountains in scales, and the hills in a balance...."

But all this may be regarded with two habits of mind utterly different.

Through the element of uniformity in nature it is possible to regard it as having no relation to a personal God. Through that element God so hides himself behind his works that very many are practically, and some theoretically, pantheistic or atheistic. They see nothing in Nature but impersonal forces and fixed relations.

A devotional spirit is the opposite of this. Through Nature it sees God. It sees, and cultivates the habit of seeing Him in everything. To such a spirit the earth and the heavens are a temple, the only temple worthy of God.... This is the spirit which it is the duty and happiness of man to cultivate. The highest use of Nature is not the support of man, but to lead him up to God.

3. A devotional spirit may also be cultivated by observing the Providence of God as it respects Nations, individuals, and particularly ourselves.

The warp of our earthly life is those uniformities, called laws, without which there could be no education of the race, and no rational conduct. But these laws intersect and modify each other. They are so related to the results of human will, and the results of different wills apparently unrelated so combine and converge to unexpected ends, as to have produced an impression almost universal that the filling in of those seeming contingencies which go to make up the completed pattern of our lives is controlled by wise design. In this is Providence....

4. But the main nutriment of a devotional spirit must be found in the Scriptures.

In the Scriptures we have an unequivocal revelation of God as personal, and so of his attributes as moral. It is only in view of personality and moral attributes that devotion can spring up. Sentiment and sentimentalism there may be in view of force regarded as impersonal, but not devotion, not worship. These require a Father in Heaven, an infinite God, universal in his government and perfect in his moral character.... The attributes and character of God as made known in the Scriptures hold the same relation to devotion that the infinity of space, and the awful force that sustains and moves in it the array of suns and planets, holds to the emotion of sublimity; and as nothing can supersede infinite space in that relation, so nothing can supersede the God of the Bible as the ground and stimulus of the highest possible devotion.

✪ *August 28* ————————————————————————————————————

Thomas Wyatt Turner

ROMAN CATHOLIC

March 16, 1877–April 21, 1978

His parents had been slaves and his father was a sharecropper, but by the time Thomas Wyatt Turner died, the Supreme Court had ruled that segregation was illegal and the Civil Rights revolution had made overt discrimination unacceptable. Turner played an important part in these changes during his long lifetime, leading the fight from within the Roman Catholic Church.

As a boy growing up in Maryland, Turner attended Episcopal schools because Roman Catholic academies refused to accept him. When he wanted to study for a doctorate, he went to Cornell because Catholic University (which later gave him an honorary degree) would not admit him. Nonetheless, Turner remained faithful to his church and organized the Federated Colored Catholics (FCC) in 1925 to work for change from within. He served as president of the FCC until 1934, although the organization became less effective after it was forced to become part of the Catholic Interracial Council in 1933. Outside the church, Turner also played a leading part in working for interracial progress. He was a founding member of the NAACP in 1909 and provided leadership in both the Washington and Baltimore branches.

Although his work for interracial progress now seems to overshadow his scientific work, Turner actually compiled a significant record in his chosen field of botany. As early as 1918 the United States Department of Agriculture sent him to Maine to examine potato fields and he continued to be called on by the government throughout his life. His doctoral dissertation, entitled "Studies of the Mechanism of the Physiological Effects of certain Mineral Salts in Altering the Ratio of Top Growth to Root Growth in Seed Plants," was published in the *American Journal of Botany*. He served as professor of botany at both Howard University and Hampton Institute at different times, organized the Virginia Conference of College Science Teachers in 1931, and was a member of the American Association for the Advancement of Science and of the American Society of Horticultural Science.

At the 1934 convention of the Federated Colored Catholics, Thomas Wyatt Turner presented the president's report, highlighting problems facing African Americans within the church.

A reading from the president's report by Thomas Wyatt Turner

It is needless to say here that neither is the significance of the movement fully appreciated: nor have serious efforts at assimilation gone very far among our groups up to the present time: this one may easily see from the numerous complaints of members who feel that we are forgetting the essential matters which brought the organization into existence. Our programs should be both informational and constructive, the bright as well as the dark side of the picture should be presented, but the thing uppermost in the minds of thinking Negroes should have largest place.

I have made some canvass of the opinions of our people as to what things give them most concern for their spiritual and temporal futures. The answers are practically unanimous. They are the blind alleys in which our boys generally get lost on the way to Holy Orders; the hesitation of many local clergy to select Negro boys to present as Novitiates to their respective Bishops. The hesitation of Bishops to sponsor Negro boys for the Diocesan Seminary or any other Seminary for that matter: the color bar set up in so many of the Catholic schools, elementary, secondary and collegiate: the ugly segregations practiced in so many of the churches running the whole gamut from side door entrance and refusal to hear confessions to passing over colored communicants at the altar if they dared to come forward before the whites had all left. These conditions are not pleasant to contemplate but they will be uppermost in the mind and will not down until they are seriously taken under consideration by a sympathetic hierarchy. There is no Negro community North or South which is not confronted with some or all of them, and it is for this reason that our programs must give more and more attention to an intelligent presentation of existing facts both for the sake of information and as the basis of securing the aid necessary to eradicate them.

From year to year I have been impressed with the need of reemphasizing the paramount aims of the organization and the purpose of these annual gatherings with the expenditure of so much effort, so much time and a not-to-be-despised amount of money. The need of this re-emphasis is no less impelling today in my judgment, than it was eight years ago. For us the improvement of conditions as mentioned in the above paragraph take precedence over all others. Economic and social problems of the Negro Catholic merge imperceptibly among the universal struggles of the whole group, but the problems which he meets with in the Church cannot be so generalized.

We are groping today more or less blindly to find some means of gaining active assistance of the majority group. The intolerance directed toward our group finds too much approval or silent acquiescence from many of those to whom we must look for advice, which is to be attributed to a basic impediment in fully appreciating what our or any other group must have in order to live and grow. The dissemination of information of the right sort will in the long run help such an attitude.

✪ August 29 _____

Cordelia Cox

LUTHERAN

March 30, 1901–March 5, 1997

In an age of sound bites and multimedia presentations, it may be hard to imagine that attending a lecture might be a life-changing experience. But when Cordelia Cox went to a presentation in Richmond, Virginia, to hear about Lutheran efforts to resettle refugees after World War II, her life was changed. She felt moved to learn more about a problem affecting so much of her world: not merely to feel sorry for people whose lives had been devastated by war, not only to add them to her prayer list or send her check to a relief agency, but to change her way of life and the focus of her career. In the end, the lives of all those helped by her efforts took new direction. She did not simply become one of the many who worked in the field of refugee settlement, but became the director of Lutheran Resettlement Services, then known as the Lutheran Council in America's Division of Welfare.

Cox was the first woman to head a major U.S. Lutheran agency. She directed post–World War II refugee resettlement as director of Lutheran Immigration from 1948 to 1957, a period of intense struggle. There was much economic restructuring as America returned to a peace-time economy. Then the Cold War fed fear and suspicion in the United States about foreign immigrants. American families, too, were coping with war-time losses and relocations. All these factors intensified Cox's struggle to work for refugees from what some have called "the last good war."

A social work educator, Cox used her training to coordinate the efforts of a cadre of college students in Europe with the many offers of help from individuals willing to supply housing or work. In addition to the office work, Cox personally met ships bringing immigrants, involving herself in the lives of those receiving her agency's assistance. She oversaw the U.S. resettlement of more than 57,000 refugees from the Baltic States and Eastern Europe. She saw these refugees as "people of strength, integrity and real ability." Cox helped develop a previously undefined church-state relationship for resettling refugees. She once said, "I think we strengthened both our church and our country immensely."

After leaving the Lutheran Immigration and Refugee Service, Cox served as executive secretary of the Lutheran Welfare Council of Metropolitan New York, a position that only ended with her retirement in 1961 at age 73. Even then, she continued to offer her skills as a consultant for the cutting-edge Council on Social Work Education from 1961 to 1966, as well as doing consultations in undergraduate education for the U.S. Department of Health, Education, and Welfare from 1966 to 1971. Cox also consulted in the training of foreign students in social work.

Still, at age 73, her energy to try new ventures was inexhaustible. At an age when many of us are golfing, fishing, knitting, or sitting on our porches watching the sun set, she joined the Peace Corps and traveled to Western Samoa to teach a social science curriculum she had prepared. She died at 95, just after returning to Richmond from that call.

It is often not the type of deeds done, but the circumstances of doing them that make a life seem inspirational. To be drawn into refugee service because of a lecture, then, after a long career in a difficult field, to embark on another equally demanding course calls all of us to reexamine our own sense of purpose and imagination. How is it that some need to pull back and care for their own most immediate needs after a great conflict, while others are all the more motivated to care for others? Cox was drawn into a position of responsibility by a sense of compassion from which she could not back away. If she ever felt like making excuses as to why she could not do more, she resisted the temptation. Martin Luther taught that our moral responsibility is to do whatever we can to assist the needs of our neighbors. Christ forced us to rethink who we call our neighbors, to broaden the definition to include strangers, even former enemies. Cox took these teachings to heart, making them the framework for her own ethics and vocational commitments. This moral focus, combined with her administrative skill and personal energy, created an agency whose value cannot be measured. The humanitarian disaster that would have occurred if people like Cox had not come to the refugees' aid would have multiplied the human cost of World War II in ways difficult to imagine or to measure. The benefits for so many, brought about by successful integration of the resettled refugees cannot ever be fully assessed.

But the issue here is not simply the vast numbers of people affected. Courageously saving one life can have more moral value than a dispassionate act that helps many. What may be of more significance in Cox's life is the way in which a situation of such magnitude did not evoke timidity or hopelessness, but determination and commitment. "What can one person do?" is the question so often asked in the face of overwhelming devastation. Cordelia Cox answered that question, rising to the challenge of her time.

✪ *August 30*

James Osgood Andrews

METHODIST

May 5, 1794–May 1, 1871

The deepening division between North and South that led at last to the Civil War was present also in the churches, perhaps most of all in the Methodist Church, which was strongly represented in both sections. Tensions came to a head in 1844, when northern Methodists, committed to abolition, forced an issue that resulted in the church dividing. James Osgood Andrews unwillingly found himself at the center of the controversy.

A native of Georgia, Andrews began preaching at 18. He went on to serve congregations in Georgia and South Carolina and, in 1832, was elected bishop at the General Conference in Philadelphia. When his first wife died, he married a widow who had inherited slaves from her first husband. Though Georgia made it illegal to free slaves, Andrews immediately executed legal papers renouncing personal property rights in their ownership and control. The Methodist Church, sometimes more concerned with personal holiness than social reform, had tried to avoid divisive slavery issues but, as a minimum concession to the abolition party, agreed that bishops could not be slave owners. Although Andrews was technically in compliance with this standard, northern delegates were nonetheless determined to force the issue. They brought a resolution to the General Conference requiring him to renounce his office until he severed connections with anyone owning slaves. After several days of debate, this resolution was adopted. From the beginning of the controversy, Andrews offered to resign as bishop rather than create division, but the southern delegates insisted that he should remain, and proceeded to separate themselves from the northern church.

Unable to sell the slaves and dissuaded from resigning his office, Andrews continued as a bishop until his death. The charge he gave those presenting themselves to serve as Methodist preachers reflects a high view of the calling and an insistence on holiness of life in those who would ride the Methodist circuits.

A reading from Bishop James Osgood Andrews's charge to Methodist preachers

We ask, have you faith in God? We mean not that faith which is merely general — which simply recognizes the truth of the scriptures, and receives the orthodox interpretation of them, and lets the heart and the conscience remain untouched; — which leaves the soul in all its actual guilt, unchanged by the mighty renovating influence of the Holy Ghost. The faith of which we inquire, is that by which a man is justified from all his guilt through the blood of the atoning Lamb; and which is followed by a sense of God's pardoning mercy; — the witness of the Holy Ghost to the fact of your adoption into God's family. This precious truth you are to preach, and you must first have felt its power, to do this efficiently. We mean by this question, First — have you experienced a thorough change of heart? have you been converted to God? Secondly, we ask whether your faith lives in healthful vigor? is it to-day abiding as a vital principle in your heart? Can you trust God? Have you in your heart a realizing sense of the presence of him who is invisible? You will find this essential to your proper and successful ministration of the word of life. Without it your heart will fail in the cloudy and dark day, when the storm is loud and the waves are running high. Nothing can sustain a man in the work of the ministry but a divine persuasion of the presence of the ever living God. Without this, our ministrations may be teeming with wisdom and beautiful oratory, but they will be powerless. The light which we show forth may be brilliant, but it will be the cold moonbeam playing among the crags of the towering iceberg. There will be no heat: no thawing power will go forth with it. My beloved brethren, look well to yourselves on this point. See that you are right here. An error here will be of fatal tendency in all your future course. We have a high regard for genius, and talent, and mental cultivation up to the highest point; but so far as the ministry is concerned, we deem it specially necessary to keep our hearts fully and always imbued with the conviction that any or all of these are worse than worthless in substitution for thorough personal piety. In these days of innovation and novelty, we have need to guard this point with great strictness.

But the man who is to teach others the way to heaven, must have contended on the field of temptation. He must have felt deeply the plague of inbred corruption, and sought earnestly for deliverance. He has fairly entered the arena of Christian conflict, and gained important victories: but he is still a soldier, harnessed and girded for battle: his mortal enemy, sin, is to be destroyed. The struggle may be severe, but success is sure. Our conquering leader hath pledged our success; his blood, his word, his spirit insure it.

✪ *August 31*

Archibald Alexander

PRESBYTERIAN

April 17, 1772–October 22, 1851

The Great Awakening was the first great wave of revival to sweep across the American colonies. It left, in its wake, deep divisions between those who considered agreement in theology to be of first importance and those who believed that the experience of new life was the critical factor. Princeton University traces its origins to the need felt by the New Light faction for a school to train its clergy.

By the 19th century, the expansion of human knowledge had become so great that specialized types of education became necessary, and churches could no longer expect that a standard college education, including a wider variety of subjects, would provide an adequate theological foundation. The New Light Presbyterians therefore began to feel the need of a seminary as well as a college.

Archibald Alexander, the founding father of the Princeton Seminary, was born in a log cabin in western Virginia. He learned the catechism at the age of seven but thought of religion as a purely intellectual matter until, at the age of 17, he was employed to read sermons to an elderly lady. Overwhelmed by the image of Christ's patience with sinners, he read further and came to an experience of God's love that led him to profess a living faith.

Alexander was educated at the future Washington and Lee College and ordained before he was 20. After several years of itinerant ministry on the Virginia frontier, he was called, at the age of 25, to become president of Hampden-Sydney College and train others for ministry. A decade later, he was called to serve a congregation in Philadelphia. There he helped create the Philadelphia Bible Society and worked to promote evangelism among the poor. But the need for a further training for the ministry remained, and in 1812, the Presbyterian General Assembly elected Alexander as the first professor of the church's new seminary in Princeton, New Jersey, now known as Princeton Theological Seminary. It began with three students who studied Greek, Hebrew, and the Old and New Testament in the professor's home. Although Alexander insisted that his students experience the living Christ, he was also a scholar who wrote a number of books. His *Brief Outline of the Evidences of the Christian Religion* (1825) passed through several editions and was translated into various languages.

A reading from *Practical Directions How to Grow in Grace and Make Progress in Piety* by Archibald Alexander

An entire and confident reliance on the promises and providence of God, however dark may be your horizon, or however many difficulties environ you, is a sign that you have learned to live by faith; and humble contentment with your condition, though it be one of poverty and obscurity, shows that you have profited by sitting at the feet of Jesus.

Diligence in the duties of our calling, with a view to the glory of God, is an evidence not to be despised.

Indeed there is no surer standard of spiritual growth than a habit of aiming at the glory of God in everything. That mind which is steady to the main end gives as good evidence of being touched by divine grace as the tendency of the needle to the pole proves that it has been touched by the magnet.

Increasing love to the brethren is a sure sign of growth; for as brotherly love is a proof of the existence of grace, so is the exercise of such love a proof of vigor in the divine life. This love, when pure, is not confined within those limits which party spirit circumscribes, but overleaping all the barriers of sects and denominations, it embraces the disciples of Christ wherever it finds them.

A healthy state of piety is always a growing state; that child which grows not at all must be sickly. If we would enjoy spiritual comfort, we must be in a thriving condition. None enjoy the pleasures of bodily health, but they who are in health. If we would be useful to the Church and the world we must be growing Christians. If we would live in daily preparation for our change, we must endeavor to grow in grace daily.

The aged saint, laden with the fruits of righteousness, is like a shock of corn fully ripe, which is ready for the garner; or like a mature fruit which gradually loosens its hold of the tree until at last it gently falls off. Thus the aged, mature Christian departs in peace.

As growth in grace is gradual, and the progress from day to day imperceptible, we should aim to do something in this work every day. We should die daily unto sin and live unto righteousness. Sometimes the children of God grow faster when in the fiery furnace than elsewhere. As metals are purified by being cast into the fire, so saints have their dross consumed and their evidences brightened, by being cast into the furnace of affliction. "Beloved, think it not strange concerning the fiery trial which shall try you, as though some strange thing happened unto you," but rejoice, because "the trial of your faith, being much more precious than of gold that perishes, though it be tried with fire, shall be found unto praise, and honor, and glory.

✪ September 1

Thomas Baldwin

BAPTIST

December 23, 1753–August 29, 1825

Thomas Baldwin is chiefly remembered for his support for both foreign and domestic mission and for his articulate defense of Baptist principles. Born in Connecticut, he began his public career as a member of the New Hampshire legislature. At the age 27, he became a Baptist and was ordained as an evangelist three years later. For seven years, Baldwin conducted an itinerant ministry among the scattered New Hampshire settlements and was then installed as pastor of the Second Baptist Church of Boston where he served until his death 35 years later. There he became one of the organizers of the Massachusetts Baptist Missionary Society and began publishing the *Massachusetts Baptist Missionary Magazine,* later called the *American Baptist Missionary Magazine,* which he edited for the rest of his life. He also wrote books defending and explaining Baptist principles, including *Open Communion Examined,* and *Series of Friendly Letters in which the Distinguishing Sentiments of the Baptists are Explained and Vindicated,* as well as numerous sermons.

Baldwin was a strong supporter of missionary work, in particular of Adoniram Judson* in Burma, but he also remained deeply involved in the development of state and federal institutions of government. He was frequently elected chaplain to the General Court of Massachusetts, served in 1821 as a member of the Constitutional Convention for the Commonwealth of Massachusetts, and preached the election-day sermon in 1802. Though not a college graduate, he greatly valued education and served for many years as a trustee and fellow of Brown University, of Waterville College, and also of Columbian College. Baldwin helped found the first Baptist seminary in America in Newton, Massachusetts.

A reading from an Election Day sermon by Thomas Baldwin

Permit me briefly to observe on two or three particular spirits of the right of private judgment, as what is commonly called Liberty of conscience is one of our dearest privileges. This right is unalienable in its nature. For the enjoyment of this, our forefathers left their friends and country, and sought asylum in this that was then a howling wilderness. But precious as this privilege is, it is liable to abuse. Its very malicious design may be concealed under the cloak of religious liberty. It is to be feared that many, under this pretense, are in reality opposing and endeavoring to destroy all religion, some by denying, others by corrupting its important doctrines and institutions. This is an abuse for which there is no legal remedy. It seems to be beyond the jurisdiction of the civil magistrate. According to our context, his power extends only to the punishment of evildoers, and not erroneous or heretical opinions. He that undertakes to decide on another's sincerity, wants certainly to know his heart; otherwise, in attempting to root out these tares, you'll be in danger of destroying the wheat. I know of nothing but light that will remove darkness; nor any antidote to error but truth. If men will abuse their Christian Liberty, they must answer it to God.

Another important privilege is the right of electing our own civil rulers. This is the distinguishing criterion of a free government. But we are in great danger of abusing the privilege; and especially at such a season as the present, when party spirit is wrought up to its highest pitch. When we suffer our prejudices and passions to influence our choice; when our judgment and conscience are sacrificed at the Shrine of party feeling; when we pass over tried merit, and prefer the candidate because he is of a particular party; do we not then abuse our liberty? If our elections are biased and corrupted, our Government will be corrupt, and consequently, our liberty will be endangered.

I plead once more the right to investigate the official conduct of all public agencies, and in a respectful decent manner to publish our opinions of them, is one of the privileges of free peoples. But, when under a pretense, we calumniate and asperge the characters of our rulers, and endeavor to expose them to public contempt, this is a very malicious and dangerous abuse of our liberty. It is not easy to calculate the extent of this mischief, for by traducing their characters, and misrepresenting their motives and measures, we destroy public confidence, and prepare the minds of the less informed part of the community for complete opposition and revolt. This abuse has also another bad effect: It tends to alienate one citizen from another and kindle flames of discord throughout the nation.

To guard against this, we need only to reflect that our national safety and prosperity to date depended chiefly upon our union. So long as we continue virtuous and united we have little to fear. But should patient heaven, offended by our aggravated provocations, give us up to a spirit of national distraction and discord, our ruin would be speedy and inevitable

Is it not then the duty of every friend to his country to discountenance every attempt to alienate one part of our citizens from another? Whoever endeavors to induce the belief that the interests of one state, are incompatible with those of another, or with the interests of all, ought to be considered, at least, as a very doubtful friend.

✪ September 2

Charles Henry Brent

EPISCOPALIAN

April 9, 1862–March 27, 1929

Few Americans if any were involved in as many of the great issues of the 20th century or provided leadership in so many critical areas as Charles Henry Brent. Ordained to the priesthood of the Anglican Church in Canada in 1887, he began his ministry in Buffalo, New York, but soon moved on to an inner city parish in Boston where he served for ten years. In 1901, he was chosen to be the Episcopal Church's first missionary bishop in the Philippines. After seeing firsthand the devastation caused by opiates in oriental societies, Brent organized the first international conference on the drug trade. He also took part in the first World Mission Conference in Edinburgh in 1910 and resigned his position in the Philippines to serve as a chaplain to the American Expeditionary Forces in Europe during World War I. After the armistice, he was elected Bishop of Western New York and turned his energy toward the Faith and Order movement. His efforts culminated in the first International Conference on Faith and Order in Lausanne, Switzerland, in 1927, at which he presided. It was said of him that he "prayed the conference into existence." Prayer was always central to his life and his collected prayers are a valuable treasury of Christian devotion.

A reading from *Things That Matter: The Best of the Writings of Charles Henry Brent*

There are but two great realities in the vast universe — the heart of God and the heart of man, and each is ever seeking the other. It is this that makes adventure for God not an experiment, but a certainty. The appeal issuing from man's abysmal need is met by the amplitude of the divine supply.

The thought of God's keeping tryst with us is a winsome thought. When we go to pray, God has already come to the meeting-place. We are never there first. The great thing to remember is that God, being Who He is, is more ready to hear than we to pray, more eager to give than we to receive, more active to find us than we to find Him. God is ever seeking man: His ear is more sensitive to the words, His heart to the desires of men, than the aspen leaf to the summer breeze, than the compass needle to the call of the poles.

Fellowship with the Divine is as normal as fellowship with man.

Active or dormant, the instinct of prayer abides, a faithful tenant, in every soul. The instinct to pray may be undeveloped, or paralyzed by violence, or it may lie bed-ridden in the soul through long neglect; but even so, no benumbed faculty is more readily roused to life and nerved to action than that of prayer. The faculty is there; no one is without it. Whether it expands, and how, is only a question of the will of the person concerned.

Prayer is man's side of converse with God; it is speech Godward, and worship is man's whole life of friendship with God, the flowing out, as it were, of all that tide of emotion and service which is love's best speech.

The essence of prayer is desire, forming itself into hope and aspiration, and mounting up into effort, in the direction of the unattained. Prayer is the address made by human personality to that with which it is desired to establish affiliations. It is a movement of the whole being which reaches after the heart's desire.

Humankind cannot be fairly divided into those who pray and those who do not pray, for everybody prays. Prayer is the universal practice of human nature. There is no commoner form of activity.

Prayer is the committal of our way unto the Lord, just as a deed of trust is the committal of our possessions to those who can handle them better than we. By living one day with God, preparation is made for living all days with God.

One may say that the real end of prayer is not so much to get this or that single desire granted, as to put human life into full and joyful conformity with the will of God.

Prayer is love melted into worship.

✪ September 3

James B. Finley

METHODIST

July 1, 1781–September 6, 1857

Don't run; I shall not be long-winded. Just hold on a moment, as I have but few words to say. I always did despise long introductions to sermons, and scarcely ever listen to one with any degree of patience. I have an equal dislike to a long introduction to a book, and, hence, *verbum sat.*

The following pages contain a brief, unvarnished narrative of the incidents of my life; and as, in the providence of God, I was permitted to grow up with the west it may not be uninteresting to the people of the west, to be made more fully acquainted with my somewhat eventful history.

For upward of forty years I have been constantly engaged in preaching the Gospel of Jesus Christ, in the woods, cities, and villages of the west; and nearly all that time, with few exceptions, such as I have noted, my name has been on the effective list of traveling preachers.

My time, with what talents I had, has all been consecrated to the Church of my choice, and now, after the lapse of almost half a century in the service of the Church, I would not recall what I have done and suffered for Christ's sake. The only regret that I have is, that I did not accomplish more.

With this proclamation, James B. Finley began his autobiography. Fortunately his "few words" proved to be a full-length report not only on his own life but on the early 19th-century revivals and even of the work begun among the Wyandotte Indians. Finley grew up on the frontier, and though he was the son of a Methodist preacher, he enjoyed a rather secular life as a young man. Even his "conversion" at the famous Cane Ridge Camp Meeting of 1801 didn't last long, but he was truly converted in 1808. A year later, he became a missionary, assigned to the Muskingum district. Determined to organize his district properly, Finley met with the leaders wherever he went.

At every meeting I set myself to work to find out the exact state of religion among the officiary; and, to enable me more fully to do so, I took a list of all the names, and went into a regular class meeting examination. This was a novel procedure, but it was made a great blessing to every official member, and before I had passed around my district twice, it was all on fire. O, what blessed times! The fire was soon carried out by preachers, exhorters, leaders, and stewards, and by spring the whole Church throughout the vast field of my labor was in a blaze.

For the next eight years, Finley became a circuit rider. He stood up to the challenges of backwoods critics, sometimes using his fists to bring them under control. In 1816 he was made a presiding elder, responsible for a territory as large as some states. When Finley attended his second General Conference in 1821, he was appointed a missionary to the Wyandotte Indians, where he strove to improve their social conditions and establish schools. Working with them turned him into a critic of the federal government's Indian policies.

In 1844, Finley was a catalyst in the schism between the northern and southern branches of the Methodist Church when he introduced a resolution critical of James Osgood Andrews,* a southern bishop who owned slaves. Still later, Finley served as chaplain to the Ohio Penitentiary. He wrote a number of books, and his pictures of the frontier revivals are remarkably vivid.

A reading from James B. Finley

But few can look upon a camp meeting scene and not be moved. Such a scene as is presented by an encampment at night, to one who has never witnessed any thing like it before, must be impressive. To look upon the long ranges of tents surrounding a large area, in each corner of which bright fires are lighted up, and then from tent and tree to see innumerable lamps hung out, casting their lights among the branches and illuminating all the ground, would remind one of the descriptions given of an oriental wedding scene, when, at midnight, the cry is heard, "Behold, the bridegroom cometh. Go ye forth to meet him." Then the sound of the trumpet, and the gathering together of thousands, who pass to and fro with lights and torches, all has a tendency to awaken the most solemn reflections. And when the holy song rises from a thousand voices, and floats out upon the stillness of the night air, the listener must feel that surely such a place is holy ground. These camp meetings were seasons of special mercy to thousands, and many who came to curse remained to pray for salvation and seek an interest in the blessed Savior.

These meetings exhibited nothing to the spectator unacquainted with them but a scene of confusion, such as scarcely could be put into human language. They were generally opened with a sermon or exhortation, at the close of which there would be a universal cry for mercy, some bursting forth in loud ejaculations of prayer of thanksgiving for the truth; some breaking forth in strong and powerful exhortations, others flying to their careless friends with tears of compassion, entreating them to fly to Christ for mercy; some, struck with terror and conviction, hastening through the crowd to escape, or pulling away from their relations, others trembling, weeping, crying for mercy; some falling and swooning away, till every appearance of life was gone and the extremities of the body assumed the coldness of death. These were surrounded with a company of the pious, singing melodious songs adapted to the time, and praying for their conversion. But there were others collected in circles round this variegated scene, contending for and against the work.

✪ *September 4* ─────────────────────────────

Bayard Rustin

QUAKER

March 17, 1912–August 24, 1987

In the Christian lexicon, the word "contemplative" has a noble and pious sound. Yet for many Christians, piety is more faithfully evident in activism. Bayard Rustin was a man who embodied activism. From his beginnings with the American Friends Service Committee, where he served as Race Relations Secretary, he moved on to work with A. Philip Randolph (president of the Brotherhood of Sleeping Car Porters, an important black trade union).

Rustin also worked simultaneously with the Fellowship of Reconciliation (FOR) and became the first field secretary of the Congress of Racial Equality (CORE). In the early 1940s he traveled to California for FOR and the American Friends Service Committee, trying to safeguard the property of Japanese-Americans incarcerated in internment facilities.

With other committed pacifist Quakers, Rustin refused to register for the draft, a very unpopular step during a war that had great national support. Rustin went even further in his protest by refusing to perform civilian service, for which he served three years in prison.

As early as 1947, in association with the FOR and CORE, Rustin took part in the first freedom ride in the southern United States. A precursor to later protests led by Dr. Martin Luther King, Jr., this action challenged many segregationist policies that were technically illegal, but still in effect in many areas. The protesters were subject to beatings, arrests, and fines. Rustin was sentenced to a chain gang for a brief period. His writing about that experience in the *New York Post* led to the abolition of chain gangs in North Carolina. In the late 1940s, Mr. Rustin helped bring about President Truman's decision to dismantle segregation within the American military.

Rustin's international concerns extended to efforts to bring an end to colonial rule and to establish democracies in India, Ghana, Nigeria, and South Africa. His commitment required courage and faith but especially so for him because by putting himself in the forefront for the sake of justice and freedom, he drew attention to his sexuality. He was gay, which only compounded the discrimination he experienced as a man of color and encouraged his opponents' efforts to restrain him. In 1953, he was arrested on a morals charge. The FOR let him go, but the War Resisters League, another antiwar organization, brought him on board.

In 1956, Rustin joined forces with Dr. Martin Luther King, Jr. His mastery of theory, strategies, and tactics of nonviolence shaped the civil rights movement as it evolved under Dr. King. As deputy director, Rustin was chief organizer of the 1963 March on Washington for Jobs and Freedom, the setting for Dr. King's memorable "I Have a Dream" speech. Voter registration, labor rights, international human rights battles, and refugee issues all combined in Rustin's life of activist faith.

Toward the end of his life, Rustin talked openly about his experience of antigay prejudice, addressed gay and lesbian groups, and spoke in favor of New York City's gay rights bill.

Bayard Rustin exemplifies two of Jesus' teachings: "Do unto others as you would have them do unto you" and "As you do for the least of these, you did unto me." The myriad injustices and stubborn prejudices of our world are not meant to remain unchallenged or unchanged by those whose faith is rooted in Christ. Through his persistent involvement and courageous convictions, we see what can be done by one whose unwillingness to accommodate to suffering or wickedness led to a life of service and action for a broken world.

✪ *September 5* _____

Francis Makemie

PRESBYTERIAN

1657/58–1708

Certain American colonies were founded to provide particular religious groups opportunity to live out their faith in freedom with support, rather than interference, from the government. A few of these colonies tolerated other religious groups, as well, but most did not. Francis Makemie, a Presbyterian missionary, came to Maryland in 1683 from the north of Ireland at the invitation of a member of Lord Baltimore's Council. His reputation as a preacher went ahead of him, and crowds quickly gathered to hear him proclaim the gospel. In 1690, Makemie married the daughter of a wealthy planter and seemed to have established himself well in the area.

But the law was changed shortly after his marriage. In 1689, the English Parliament had passed the Toleration Act, providing a degree of religious liberty, but in 1692 the Church of England became the established church in Maryland. Now, dissenters like Makemie needed to obtain special permits and were required to pay a special tax to support the clergy of the Church of England. In 1699, the missionary was arrested for preaching without a government license and brought before the Council at Williamsburg where he defended himself so vigorously that he was granted the unprecedented right to preach anywhere in the colony. The House of Burgesses subsequently made it clear that the Act of Toleration was in force in the colony.

In the spring of 1706, a meeting of Presbyterians in the Philadelphia area chose Makemie as elected moderator. This was the first established presbytery in the area. As a result, Makemie is often called the "Father of American Presbyterianism."

Eight years later, Makemie again found himself testing the degree of liberty available in the colonies. On a journey to Boston, he was asked to speak at a house gathering and did so, unaware that the governor (with whom Makemie was staying) had denied him permission to speak. He was imprisoned for two months, but a trial declared him innocent of any offense. The governor tried to make him pay court costs, but this too failed and the governor was subsequently recalled. The sermon for which Makemie was arrested was subsequently printed and was the first Presbyterian sermon published in America.

Makemie died the following year at the age of 50, worn down by these events, but the trials in which he was involved mark important milestones on the road to religious freedom in America.

A reading from Francis Makemie's report on his trial in New York

(Makemie refers to himself in the third person)

Ingenuous Reader,

You have here a Specimen of the Cloggs & Fetters with which the Liberty of Dissenters are intangled at New-York and Jersey-Government beyond any places in Her Majesties Dominions; And when the Conditions, and Impositions required, are as heavy, and uneasy to be bore; and as great a Scruple of Conscience as the grounds of their Separation and Dissent, it is next to no Liberty at all.

And what the Consequences of such practices, if persisted in, will prove to such a Place, where Dissenters are above twenty to one, for one Church-man, and where men and money are so much wanting, for the defence of New-York, both by Sea and Land, which not many years, (by demands of men and money from the Neighbouring Colonies on the Continent) was represented, as their only Barrier and Frontier, I leave to thinking men, and considering Politicians to answer; besides the difficulties and discouragements laid in the way of such as would Import themselves, and the ready and shortest way to promote Deserters from those Provinces.

I cannot omit a true, and strange Story, I lately heard of, that during the Imprisonment of these two Gentlemen, either to find out a Crime, none being specified in the Mittimus, or to aggravate their imaginary fault: An Order was given to Major Sandford of East-Jersey, to put sundry persons upon Examination, and their Oaths, to discover what Discourse they had with sundry of their friends, at the House of Mr. Jasper Crane in New-York-Town in East Jersey, where Mr. Samuel Metyen, Mr. Crane, and another, gave their Depositions before Major Sandford, but found nothing to their purpose: Tho the practice is not to be outdone, yea, scarce paralleled by Spanish Inquisition; for no men are safe in their most private Conversations, if most intimate Friends can be compelled upon Oath, to betray one anothers Secrets. If this is agreeable to English Constitution and Priviledges, I confess, we have been hitherto in the Dark.

Preaching in a Private House was a Crime, and Preaching since, after being declared Not Guilty by a Legal Tryal, in a Publick church, allowed by Law to the French, is since resented as a greater, by that Unchristian Clamour, made soon after, by some High-flown Spark's pretended Sons of the Church, who with a great deal of unbounded fury declared. If such things were allowed, their Church was ruined: which is a language of the same nature of those High-Flyers in England, who were declared by a Vote of the House of Lords, Enemies to the QUEEN and Government, for suggesting, the Church of England was in danger, from the Liberty, or Toleration of Dissenters.

Tho' Preaching a Sermon, and Printing it as the cause of Imprisonment, be reputed a Libel, to justifie opening of Letters, and seizing Books, without restoration or satisfaction, I hope it will be no crime, for Losers to speak, in telling the World, what we have suffered on sundry accounts; not only by Imprisonment, and the exorbitant expensive prosecution; and besides great loss of time, many diminutive reproaches upon our Reputations, by a Set of men, who could reach by their Short Horns to no higher degree of Persecution: And all this for Preaching one Sermon, without obtaining a Licence, which they could not, *in terminis* submit to, neither can nor dare in Conscience do to this day.

And even for such as have this new moulded Licence, it is a Crime to Preach in another place then is expressed in said Licence, or for any to Preach in the Pulpits: if a People wants a Minister, they must have a Licence to call one, whither from New-England or Europe, a Licence to admit Ministers to attend any Ordination, and limited for number, and tyed up from exercising their Ministry without Licence, tho' in a transient manner; which has drove some out of the Government, and deterred others from coming thereunto; which informs all, what Liberty of Conscience Dissenters do enjoy.

Mr. Makemie since the Tryal, narrowly escaped a second Prosecution, for Preaching another Sermon: as some say, with a new Charge of being the Author of the Jersey Paper called, FORGET and FORGIVE; which is so groundless a Charge, in which his accusers cannot believe themselves, while the Authors smile at the mistake, and other men are suffering Imprisonment on account of said Paper, and will appear to have been composed before Mr. Makemie came into these Parts.

✪ *September 6* _____

Stanley Rother

ROMAN CATHOLIC

March 27, 1935–July 28, 1981

Stanley Rother was one of those missionaries caught up in the violence that swept through Central America in the latter part of the 20th century. Some lost their lives because they had taken sides in the political battles being waged, but Rother seems to have cared only to carry on his ministry and avoid trouble. Trouble, however, surrounded him. The government forces trying to control rebellions breaking out against dictatorship and oppression of the poor were indiscriminate in their brutality. Foreign clergy were notorious for their sympathy with the peasants and Rother was an American priest. Apparently this was enough to put him at risk. Rother knew he was in danger and did leave for a while. But having committed himself to the T'zutuhil-Mayan Indians of Guatemala, he returned to continue that work. "The shepherd," he wrote, "cannot run at the first sign of danger."

He was 46 years old when he was shot in his rectory in the parish of Santiago Atitlán. Two bishops and 35 priests came together to celebrate his funeral Mass, while so many attended the service that the pews had to be taken out of the church to accommodate the crowd. His family insisted on taking his body back to Oklahoma for burial, but allowed his heart to be removed and buried beneath the floor of the church. The shrine erected above the spot is now a center for pilgrimage and prayer.

Rother was a farm boy from Oklahoma, often kidded for not being especially bright. But he worked hard, was ordained at the age of 28, and went to Guatemala to the parish of Santiago Atitlán. There he remained, except for a brief retreat, for the remaining 18 years of his life. He loved the people of the area and they loved him. If he could have avoided the political wars, he would have done so. But to remain completely uninvolved would have been impossible. From 1966 to 1998, Guatemala was torn by civil war. The people of Santiago suffered from 30 years of violence. In October of 1980, a battalion of soldiers arrived to garrison Santiago Atitlán. Just after midnight on October 24, the manager of a small local radio station, La Voz de Atitlán, was abducted from his home by a group of masked men. A few days later his tortured body was found along a roadside. Later, the soldiers raided the station, destroying the studio equipment and files. Over the next several weeks, nine other people working in the radio station, health services, and other social agencies were similarly killed. On January 6, 1980, ten men from the village were killed by Guatemalan military forces at Chacaya, about three miles from Santiago Atitlán. They had been working their fields when the surprise attack occurred. Death threats, disappearances, and assassinations became commonplace in the area. The church served as a refuge for many families who spent each night sleeping in the sanctuary it offered.

For a time, the violence subsided and on January 5, 1981, Rother wrote home to a friend:

> Things have been pretty quiet here the past couple of weeks until just last Saturday night. Probably the most sought after catechist has been staying here in the rectory off and on, and almost constantly of late. He had been eating and sleeping here, and usually visiting his wife and two kids in late afternoon. He had a key to the house and was approaching Saturday night about 7:45, when he was intercepted by a group of four kidnappers. Three apparently tried to grab him at the far side of the church. He got to within fifteen feet of the door and was holding on to the bannister and yelling for help. . . . I was listening to music but also heard the noise, and by the time I realized what was happening, grabbed a jacket and got outside, they had taken him down the front steps of the church and were putting him in a waiting car. In the process they had broken the bannister where the rectory porch joins the church, and I just stood there wanting to jump down to help, but knowing that I would be killed or taken along also. The car sped off with him yelling for help but no one was able to do so.

Then I realized that I had just witnessed a kidnapping of someone that we had gotten to know and love and was unable to do anything about it. They had his mouth covered, but I can still hear his muffled screams for help.... He was 30 years old, left a wife and two boys, ages 3 and 1. May he rest in peace!

The violence was not all on one side. Not long afterward, guerillas attacked an army convoy in the area and in retaliation 17 townspeople were randomly picked up and killed. At that point, Rother learned that he was also targeted for death and left the country. He returned on April 11, but on July 28, nuns discovered his bullet-filled body in the rectory. He was the ninth priest killed in Guatemala that year. The shrine in the church bears the inscription, "Unless a grain of wheat falls and dies, it bears no fruit. But if it dies, it bears much fruit."

✹ September 7

Timothy Lull

LUTHERAN

April 8, 1943–May 20, 2003

Frequently, new American churches have been formed to promote greater unity among Christians. All too often those hopes have been frustrated, with the end result being one more separate church. The formation of the Evangelical Lutheran Church in America seems to chart a different path. At its inception, it united three separate Lutheran groups, and over the next few years, the ELCA pioneered full communion agreements with the Reformed Churches, the Episcopal Church, the Presbyterian Church, and the Moravians. In all this, Timothy Lull was a significant leader, a theologian with the concerns of a pastor.

From the beginning, the ELCA needed and wanted its own "ethos," distinct from its parent bodies. Relationships among theologians, bishops, elected lay leaders, and appointed administrators were left to evolve. The church held no predetermined positions on social issues. Throughout this process of growth and maturing, Lull played an active and positive role.

Briefly a parish pastor in Massachusetts, Lull had been invited to apply for a position at the Lutheran Theological Seminary in Philadelphia. He accepted the call and began a life of academic leadership first at the Philadelphia seminary as a professor, then, later, at Pacific Lutheran Theological Seminary as a professor and dean, and finally as president.

Lull's specialty was the life and theology of Martin Luther, and he was a popular speaker around the church. Among his writings are: *Called to Confess Christ* and *My Conversations with Martin Luther*. He edited *A Common Calling* and *Martin Luther's Basic Theological Writings*.

Along with his teaching, writing, and speaking, Lull made major contributions to the developing ELCA vision of ecclesiology, ecumenism, ethics, and a missional theology for the church. His support for and interpretation of the ELCA's ecumenical agreements contributed to their fruitful reception.

Lull consistently strove for a church and theology that addressed both Christians and the world they inhabit, and one that would be understandable and accessible for both clergy and laity.

While the ELCA was finding its voice, Lull forcefully called for a church engaged with the culture and able to bring the healing gospel message to the myriad social problems besetting humanity. Lull died at 60 from cancer, but his influence on the ELCA and wider church will continue to shape the future.

A reading from Timothy Lull's address to the 2003 graduating class of Philadelphia Theological Seminary

You are completing seminary at a time of renewed excitement about the global mission of the church. You are about to take up ministries and vocations of various sorts, but all of them occasions for witnessing to Jesus Christ and the power of the gospel. As you have come from many places to this school, so we pray that Christ will go with you wherever you may be called — even to the ends of the earth.

You have had moments of wonderful community here. Most of you have made friendships in this place that will last the rest of your life. You have also known moments of isolation, discouragement, and loneliness. You understand the longing for community that fills our world. We pray that you will build on what you have learned here about how such community can be fostered, and also forgive those times when this institution has not served you well.

As the church grew and its mission became more complex, the disciples said, "It is not right that we should neglect the word of God in order to wait on tables" (Acts 6:2).

The work of God in the world gets carried out by a variety of ministries. The different degrees and certificates that you receive today reflect that diversity. We pray that you have seen here a sense of mutual respect for different callings that will help you avoid the tendency that has haunted the church to set some above others, demeaning or marginalizing those set aside for service. Not so! You have heard in this place that the free Christian lord of all is also the willing servant of all.

You have studied theology in a vibrant and diverse metropolitan area. You have learned here at PLTS, in the Graduate Theological Union, and in the churches of this region about God's great vision of showing no partiality. May you go forth to heal the broken places of our world and to help take down the walls that still divide us from each other.

You go into a church and a society full of conflict, with men and women who hold quite different visions about what God's will is for us on many burning issues. We pray that you have courage and wisdom in discerning what we are to do, and boldness and mutuality in bringing divided people together to promote the unity of the spirit in the bond of peace.

When God gave out the talents, you received your full share and more. Talents are to be used and not hoarded. Many of you are already heading cheerfully to places that you could not have imagined when you entered this school. Others are starting down more predictable paths. Others do not yet know what awaits them after this day. But we pray that you will continue to be open to surprises and adventures, as befits alums of this seminary, and that you will not suppress those visions that cry out for the help that you can give.

They shed tears as they parted in Ephesus, for that congregation sensed that they would never see Paul again. There will be more laughter than tears today, and we anticipate many happy reunions. Yet this group will never again be assembled in quite this form. So you deserve to go forth with the best and only blessing that we can really offer — our commendation to you of our good and loving God and of this message of grace that sustains us in all comings and goings. So we pass on to you what we also received: "Now (we) commend you to God and to the message of God's grace."

✪ *September 8* _____

Isabel Alice Hartley Crawford

BAPTIST

May 26, 1865–November 18, 1961

The final years of the 19th century and the beginning of the 20th saw the cessation of wars between Native Americans and the white settlers. The former now found themselves confined to reserved areas, at the mercy of a largely indifferent government in Washington. At this juncture, missionaries like Isabel Crawford most often became their advocates.

Crawford was the daughter of a Baptist pastor who had served in the Canadian northwest and the Dakotas. Isabel shared her father's sense of commitment. As a student missionary in Chicago, she was assigned to the red light district where she learned the reality of life in a ghetto and developed compassion for the unfortunate. She planned to serve her church overseas, but the principal of the Baptist Mission Training School instead asked her to go to a newly organized station among the Kiowa Indians in Oklahoma. Here, she realized that the Kiowas were hemmed in by pioneer settlers on their land who were hunting their game and using up their natural resources, while the government did little to interfere. In spite of her out-spokenness on this and other issues, Crawford was reappointed to a larger Indian community at Saddle Mountain.

Here, she broke with her sponsoring church when she assisted a lay inter-preter to administer the Lord's Supper. She believed that the Indians' need for communion overrode the church's restrictions. She was almost certainly the first woman to administer communion in the Baptist Church, but it led to her resignation. Crawford continued, however, to travel widely as a lecturer and an advocate both for Indian rights and for Baptist missionary work. In later years, she served the Allegany Indian Reservation in western New York State and once again became embroiled in controversy when she protested the transfer of the Red House Church to the Presbyterians. This time Craw-ford won her point. She was buried on the Saddle Mountain Reservation among the people she had adopted as her own.

Readings from Isabel Crawford's diary of her first days among the Kiowas

April 12th, Sunday

It rained all night and all day.

Fortunately there was a little two-roomed house on the hill and men, women, children, dogs and missionary all crowded into it.

A roaring fire was made in the cook-stove and steam rose and fell like wreaths of smoke from an engine.

A few who had heard the news came in haste through the storm, and squeezing themselves into the mass of living, moving, damp humanity stood before me with hands raised to their mouths.

When they had recovered sufficiently from their surprise these were some of the things they signed:

"We like this. You, one woman all alone among Indians and no skeered."

"No White Jesus man ever sat down with us. One Jesus woman all alone and no skeered. This is good."

"We like you for coming this way. You trust us."

"We have no one to tell us about Jesus over here. The Great Father has brought you to us."

"We thank you for coming, but the thank you to Jesus is away ahead."

All day long a simple service continued and when darkness closed in I was glad to drop to sleep on any kind of a bed, in any kind of a corner.

April 26th, Sunday

In the afternoon in the bottom of a wagon we drove seven miles to Sugar Creek, where a number of Indians, in holiday attire, sat under an arbor made of branches of trees. We talked to them about Jesus and at the close four men, wrapped from their heads to their feet in white sheets, emerged from a big white tepee close to the arbor. One behind the other they came towards me and in turn took my hand and prayed with eyes very shut.

> Oh, Great Spirit of Jesus, come to our hearts to-day. White people think we pray to another god but we do not. We heard the talk of this white woman. While we sat worshipping in our council tepee, and we have come out to pray for her.
>
> Who made the sun? Who made these mountains? Who made this creek? Who made these trees and who brought the "leetle woman" over here?
>
> The Great God, our Father, that He may teach us more. She is your child. We are your children. We will call her no more white woman but sister.
>
> How can we show that we believe you sent her?
>
> By saying thank you, thank you, thank you to Jesus! We have spoken.

The prayers ended, the leader took me by the hand and followed by the other white robed figures, led me into the Ghost-Dance tepee and to the chief's seat.

Christmas 1902

It is not the actual gospel work that uses the missionaries up, but combinations of unlooked-for experiences and aggravations. Our swill pail is kept in a space between the house and the shed, the tenant emptying it every evening. In the midst of the rush a pig escaped from his pen and upset it right across our path. We removed it to the shed, putting it on the top of an old stove and next day a dog found it and brought its whole contents down over the Christmas things. Something else upset the ash pail and something else tore open a sack of corn-meal. We had no time to clean up messes, eat, sleep, mend tears or rub on liniment. We got like hornets. The devil beat us all right but we kept right on with the work.

✪ *September 9* ⎯⎯⎯⎯⎯⎯⎯⎯⎯⎯⎯⎯⎯⎯⎯⎯⎯⎯⎯⎯⎯⎯

Charles Sheldon

CONGREGATIONAL

February 26, 1857–February 24, 1946

Charles Sheldon thought he understood why people weren't coming to the Sunday evening service: it wasn't very interesting. And he knew why it wasn't: he didn't have enough ideas for two sermons every Sunday. So he decided to try some changes. One thing he had always loved and been good at was telling stories. He had begun writing stories, personality sketches, and light verse before he started college at Brown and seminary at Andover Newton and kept it up, though without much success. Sometimes he would write a story a day for weeks at a time. So, if people were bored with his sermons, he would tell them a story, and each week's story would be left incomplete so people would have to come back to hear how it all came out.

That's how it started. It worked. Soon the church was packed. And it remained packed until Sheldon retired 30 years later. But the climax came in the seventh year of the series when Pastor Sheldon was inspired to tell the story of a town where a stranger taught them to ask, "What would Jesus do?" That series was published under the title *In His Steps* and sold like hot cakes. Unfortunately Sheldon's publisher didn't write good contracts, so within a year 16 different publishers were turning out copies. But Sheldon hadn't written to get rich but to change lives. It did do that, and it still does.

The local newspaper had a new publisher who wondered what would happen if Charles Sheldon were to edit the paper according to his principles. For a week, Sheldon edited the paper, choosing or refusing stories on one principle: What would Jesus do? The widely publicized experiment sold a lot of papers, but results were pretty dull, so the experiment was quickly called off.

It's unfortunate that most people don't know more about Charles Sheldon, who was more than a successful storyteller. His first congregation was in Waterbury, Vermont, in 1886. The town had a chronic problem with typhoid, and Sheldon thought it might be caused by the water supply because the wells the town used were near some pig pens. He got them to change the water supply, and people stopped getting sick.

Sheldon was part of "an emerging Christocentric liberalism" that was changing the churches at the beginning of the 19th century. When he was called to Topeka, Kansas, he worked to obtain social services for the black community. Not even World War II convinced him to abandon his pacifist principles. War, it seemed to him, was not something that Jesus would do, and that was all that mattered.

A reading from *In His Steps* by Charles Sheldon

The sermon had come to a close. Mr. Maxwell had just turned the half of the big Bible over upon his manuscript and was about to sit down as the quartet prepared to arise to sing the closing selection ... when the entire congregation was startled by the sound of a man's voice. It came from the rear of the church, from one of the seats under the gallery. The next moment the figure of a man came out of the shadow there and walked down the middle aisle. Before the startled congregation fairly realized what was going on the man had reached the open space in front of the pulpit and had turned about facing the people.

"I've been wondering since I came in here" — they were the words he used under the gallery, and he repeated them — "if it would be just the thing to say a word at the close of the service. I'm not drunk and I'm not crazy, and I am perfectly harmless, but if I die, as there is every likelihood I shall in a few days, I want the satisfaction of thinking that I said my say in a place like this, and before this sort of a crowd.... "

"I heard some people singing at a church prayer meeting the other night,

All for Jesus, all for Jesus,
All my being's ransomed powers,
All my thoughts, and all my doings,
All my days, and all my hours.

and I kept wondering as I sat on the steps outside just what they meant by it. It seems to me there's an awful lot of trouble in the world that somehow wouldn't exist if all the people who sing such songs went and lived them out. I suppose I don't understand. But what would Jesus do? Is that what you mean by following His steps? It seems to me sometimes as if the people in the big churches had good clothes and nice houses to live in, and money to spend for luxuries, and could go away on summer vacations and all that, while the people outside the churches, thousands of them, I mean, die in tenements, and walk the streets for jobs, and never have a piano or a picture in the house, and grow up in misery and drunkenness and sin."

The man suddenly gave a queer lurch over in the direction of the communion table and laid one grimy hand on it. His hat fell upon the carpet at his feet. A stir went through the congregation. Dr. West half rose from his pew, but as yet the silence was unbroken by any voice or movement worth mentioning in the audience. The man passed his other hand across his eyes, and then, without any warning, fell heavily forward on his face, full length up the aisle.

✪ *September 10* _____

Mary Elizabeth Lange

ROMAN CATHOLIC

1784?–February 3, 1882

The Baltimore of 1828 was not prepared for Elizabeth Lange. Like so many others, she had fled the bloodshed in Haiti and found herself in Maryland. All around the city, she saw children of other Haitian refugees for whom no education was available. An educated woman herself, with some small funds left to her by her father, she gathered children in her home where, for ten years, she operated an informal school. As a devout member of the Roman Catholic Church, she joined three confraternities, but sensed a call to do more, telling her priest, Monsieur Moranville, the pastor of

St. Patrick's Church in Fells Point, of her desire to consecrate her life to God as a religious. On July 2, 1828, she knelt with three other black women in a Baltimore rowhouse to take simple vows and create a new order.

There was more than enough work for them to do, with children of Haitian immigrants to educate, widows and elderly women to be cared for, and cholera epidemics that required nurses brave enough to tend the sick and dying. The Oblate Sisters of Providence responded to all these needs, and those members of the Haitian community in a position to do so gave them what support they could. Lange was not willing to settle for less than the best. She consulted with the president of St. Mary's College in shaping the curriculum for her school. Music, the classics, and fine arts were included. School records show that the students were involved in choirs, concerts, and recitals.

It is hard to imagine obstacles greater than those the sisters faced. They were black in a slave-holding state, women in a male-dominated society, Roman Catholics in a Protestant nation, and French-speaking aliens in an English city. Even in Baltimore, with its Roman Catholic heritage, citizens were not prepared to show respect for black women simply because they were habited as nuns. The first house they occupied was made unavailable within a year, and other houses nearby were similarly "unavailable" or too expensive. They endured verbal insults and even threats of violence. Archbishop Whitfield, however, was on the side of the sisters, saying more than once, "I gave my permission and approval with full knowledge of what some people would say." In 1831, word came that the Pope had approved the new community and that the Oblates of Providence would be linked with the Oblates of St. Francis and so with other sisterhoods of the Roman Catholic Church throughout the world.

But none of this could change the reality of pre–Civil War Baltimore. The next archbishop, Samuel Eccleston, saw no particular reason to support an order of black sisters. "Cui est bono?," he asked. ("What good is it?") Sulpician priests in the city, themselves French refugees, had been staunch supporters of the sisters, but their French headquarters demanded that they concentrate on their primary objective of creating a seminary. Now the sisters had no Mass and no confessor, no adequate funds even for food and clothing. They were often cold and hungry. The diocesan authorities suggested that they give up their unrealistic dream and dissolve their community. By 1845, the number of students had dwindled to 20 of whom ten were orphans. The sisters took in washing, ironing, and mending to support themselves; two of the sisters earned a meager income by working in the seminary kitchen.

Help came most unexpectedly from a newly ordained Bavarian immigrant, Thaddeus Anwander, who, after meeting the sisters, resolved to support them. Going to the archbishop on his knees, he begged to be appointed their director. "What's the use?" asked the archbishop, but Anwander persisted and his humility touched his superior. Permission was given, and Anwander began to go from house to house, begging for money and asking black parents to enroll their children in the school. Now the order's fortunes revived. There were 60 boarding students and 100 day students; the number of sisters doubled. The archbishop himself became friendly, and the Jesuits were persuaded to take responsibility for guidance of the Oblates. By this time, the Civil War was in progress and the sisters became aware of the growing number of orphans of black soldiers for whom there were still no schools in Baltimore. Mary Lange, still an optimist, opened a new school for girls. The Jesuits provided money for an additional building — on condition that the sisters do the washing and mending for Loyola College. After the war, opportunities abounded. The sisters were asked to open schools in New Orleans and Philadelphia as well as in the Baltimore area. They were eager to respond and opened new schools as requested, but within a few years they had to be closed for lack of funds. In 1872, the sisters were forced to go begging on the streets of Washington.

Centuries earlier, Julian of Norwich, had written, "God did not say, 'You shall not be tempested, you shall not be travailed, you shall not be dis-eased;' but he said, 'You shall not be overcome.'" Mary Lange was not overcome. She saw the 50th anniversary of her taking of vows with her order still doing the work no one else would take on.

✖ *September 11* _____

Samuel Isaac Joseph Schereschewsky

EPISCOPALIAN

May 6, 1831–October 15, 1906

Samuel Isaac Joseph Schereschewsky was born in Lithuania to Jewish parents. He intended to become a rabbi, but while studying in Germany, he was converted to Christianity, influenced by missionaries he encountered as well as his own study of a Hebrew translation of the New Testament. Schereschewsky traveled to the United States and entered a Presbyterian seminary in Pittsburgh, but he was unable to accept the Calvinist doctrine of predestination and moved on to New York where he entered the General Theological Seminary. Shortly after his ordination in the Episcopal Church, he responded to an appeal for missionaries to serve in China. A fine linguist, he learned Chinese characters on the voyage out so that, on arrival, he could begin translating the Bible and Book of Common Prayer for the people he served. From the first, he insisted on the importance of knowing the language. He wrote,

There have, indeed, been missionaries, who almost immediately after their arrival, having picked up a few broken phrases, commenced, as they supposed, to preach the Gospel to the heathen, but which preaching most likely consisted in nothing more than uttering some sounds wholly unintelligible to the hearers. It can fairly be asserted that preaching the Gospel in such a manner is exhibiting a zeal without much knowledge.

When the Bishop of Shanghai died, Schereschewsky was nominated as his successor. Despite his objections, he became the third bishop of that diocese. He established the school that became St. John's University, now one of the leading institutions of higher education in China, but a stroke forced Schereschewsky's resignation after only six years. Almost completely paralyzed, he retired to Tokyo, Japan, and spent the remainder of his life translating the Bible into two versions of Chinese, literary and spoken, although he was only capable of using the middle finger of his crippled right hand to press the typewriter keys. Shortly before his death, he remarked to a visitor, "I have sat in this chair for over twenty years. It seemed very hard at first. But God knew best. He kept me for the work for which I was best fitted."

A reading from an appeal by Bishop Schereschewsky for funds to establish a college in China

From the earliest days of the Church, education has been an important agent in the propagation of Christianity. During the Middle Ages education was one of the chief instrumentalities by which Christianity was introduced among European nations.... And if education has been an element of such importance in establishing Christianity in the West, have we any reason to believe that it will be a less powerful agent in establishing Christianity in the East? Not only so, but it seems to me that our endeavor to propagate the Christian religion *among* such a people as the Chinese (without it), would be most identified with the national life. It is only necessary as a proof of this to refer to the vastness of their literature, and the profound respect that has been accorded to the pursuit of learning and literary men. A "literary degree" is the "open sesame" to all avenues of distinction in China, and in that land above all others the influence of such an institution as the one proposed could hardly fail to produce results exceeding perhaps our most sanguine expectations.

Again, the better one is acquainted with the state of things in China, and the more one studies the Chinese people with an heartfelt desire for their speedy conversion to Christianity, the more strongly one is convinced that the most effective agency that can be employed in carrying on the great work of evangelizing that nation, must be thoroughly trained native Ministers, who shall go forth to proclaim the Gospel with a might and power which only a native Ministry can possess. A college such as the one proposed would be undoubtedly the most efficient means of attracting Chinese young men from all parts of the Empire, and bringing them under the influences of our Christian religion and Christian civilization.

And from these young men, with God's Blessing, we might look for constant accessions to the ranks of a native Ministry, and for hearty and efficient co-workers in carrying on the work of the Church in China.

Having thus briefly stated the pressing need of a Missionary College in China, and having indicated the importance of such an institution in carrying out our missionary work there, it remains to be considered whether the establishment of such a college as the one proposed is a practicable undertaking. Certainly so if the Church can only be aroused to the importance of the enterprise, and provide the means to carry it out. China, long hermetically sealed from intercourse with Christian nations, is now thrown open to Missionary enterprise, and there is nothing to hinder the establishment of such a college in any part of China where Missionaries have found free scope for carrying on their work.

To begin this institution, I have appealed to the Church for a sum of money not less than one hundred thousand dollars. In the city of Philadelphia and elsewhere I have obtained promises for an amount equal to about one-third of that sum, and I pray that God may put it into the hearts of our Church people to complete the desired amount wherewith to commence the proposed institution, the need and value of which I have very imperfectly placed before them.

That our Church may be willing to give to China a Missionary College as an enduring testimony of our love to our Lord and Master is my earnest prayer.

✪ September 12 _____

William Leroy Stidger

METHODIST

March 16, 1885–August 7, 1949

Stirred by a conversion experience at a revival in 1899 when he was 14 years old, Bill Stidger began a ministry that was to touch the lives of countless people, but more than that, he was to become one of the most effective and visionary users of public media for the spread of the gospel. He published over 24 books between 1911 and 1948, including biographies, poetry, sermon texts, and stories. However, it was his flair for advertising, radio, and publicity that opened new options for spreading the Christian message.

Stidger attended Allegheny College in Pennsylvania, where he delighted in sports and other extracurricular activities. While he was a student, a gathering of Methodist bishops on campus presented a series of addresses to the students. It was during these meetings that Stidger's earlier conversion began to focus on ordination and becoming a preacher. In 1909, he went on to study at the School of Theology at Boston University, an institution that taught the modernist approach to biblical interpretation. This took new scientific worldviews growing out of Darwin's work into account. The school had set itself on a very different course from the fundamentalist impulse gripping much popular Christianity of the time. Stidger had come out of a "fire and brimstone" kind of background and had not been previously exposed to the kind of openness he found at BU. But he was fascinated, especially by the lectures of his beloved professor, Borden Parker Bowne. Bowne died suddenly during class, leaving the school and Stidger in a state of shock.

Stidger left the school, but not his calling. He moved to Rhode Island and took a job as vice president of East Greenwich Academy, a Methodist prep school just south of Providence. While there, he was also called by a local Baptist congregation to fill its pulpit because they were having difficulty finding a suitable Baptist replacement. There Stidger began to try out some new ideas about spreading the gospel through carefully crafted events.

Ordained by the Methodist Episcopal Church in 1913, Stidger was sent to serve a new congregation in San Francisco that same year. He immediately focused on increasing attendance at the small church. At first, he called at homes, distributed pamphlets, asked members to bring friends, and similar tried-and-true methods of church growth. But these initial efforts gained only a few new members and as his first year came toward a close, he decided that he had failed to raise his congregation's profile in the community. At this point, he conceived the idea of installing a revolving, electrically lighted cross on the top of the building. Plans were made, though they involved financial risk. Stidger made sure there was significant publicity for the dedication of the new cross, which, because of the location of the building, could be seen from most of the city.

On the day appointed, a large crowd gathered for an uplifting service in the church. Then the cross was illuminated and began to rotate just as planned. This kind of public event, coordinated with excellent music, innovative preaching, and follow-up led to noteworthy increases in attendance.

In 1916, Stidger began to develop a progressive social voice. He sided with restaurant workers who were fighting for an eight-hour day. Many clergy were convinced by the Chamber of Commerce that the union was being unreasonable, but Stidger opted to stand with the workers. Although the Methodist Church had endorsed better labor conditions, not all clergy were prepared to take sides in contentious labor struggles. Stidger did, and was received with great enthusiasm as a speaker at union meetings.

In 1934, Stidger began his radio ministry. The program was called Goodwill Radio Chapel, part of the ministry of Morgan Memorial Church, where he was on the staff. He had found a new medium through which to deliver the gospel of Christ. Over time, radio broadcasts increased. By the late

1930s, he was hosting *Getting the Most out of Life* five days a week, year round, discussing the practical benefits of Christian values with the widest audience available.

Stidger was widely criticized for his innovations and involvement in social issues. Many saw him as a publicist, rather than a man of faith. Yet his focus on mission rings out in this response to a question put to him at an open forum: "Just what are your goals in preaching; what are you getting at; and what do you want to accomplish?"

Stidger's reply is set out in his book *Personal Power:*

> First, my goal in preaching is to be educational... Jesus looked upon himself as a teacher, first of all.
>
> Second, my goal is inspirational. I must take tired men and rest them. I must take men who have been beaten about in the competitive world and relax them. I must take weary women and bring them quiet and repose. In a word, I must take men out of time and make them feel eternal. I must make them know that they are made but a little lower than the angels and crowned with life everlasting.
>
> Third, I must make men realize the best that is in them, and I must do that in every sermon....
>
> Fourth, I must bring a sense of peace to their souls, peace with their own warring natures, peace with their neighbors, peace with God.
>
> Fifth, I must bring to them in every way I know how that Jesus said that He came to give the abundant life.
>
> Sixth, I must aim to bring them to God and to bring God to them through Jesus our Savior.

Stidger's innovations for building up Christ's church have become commonplace in an age of parish websites and church growth workshops. Yet his pioneering spirit, which encountered much misunderstanding and opposition in his own day, set the stage for a church more attuned to a culture's fascination with technology and willing to employ it to address the world's spiritual hunger.

✪ *September 13*

Albert Benjamin Simpson

CHRISTIAN AND MISSIONARY ALLIANCE

December 15, 1843–October 29, 1919

Brought up on a barren frontier farm in western Ontario, Canada, A. B. Simpson had to earn his own way through college. He had long been convinced that he was called to ministry, so he worked as a teacher to earn money, graduated with honors, and was called at the age of 22 to a large Presbyterian Church in Hamilton, Ontario. There, he started a mid-week service, paid off the parish mortgage, and created a variety of new programs. At that period, pastors usually served a congregation for life but eight years later Simpson was called to a congregation in Louisville, Kentucky. This church also grew under his leadership, but when they outgrew the building they were using, Simpson wanted it replaced with something plain and functional, while the elders wanted something more elaborate. The elders won, but Simpson left before the debt incurred was paid off to accept a call to New York City.

The move to New York provided an opportunity to work with immigrants from Europe. Evangelism became a more prominent priority for Simpson. Seeking and receiving a "baptism in the Holy Spirit," he felt spiritually transformed. "Never," he wrote, "has my heart known . . . such a thrill of joy." When he decided that he could no longer accept infant baptism, he resigned his pastorate to begin a new ministry focused more completely on evangelism. A training program for workers led to the creation of the Nyack College, while a gathering in Maine in the summer of 1887 led to the formation of the Christian Alliance and the Evangelical Missionary Alliance. The two organizations eventually merged to became the Christian and Missionary Alliance. Simpson wanted a simple and flexible organization. He was convinced that the Lord would provide, but his efforts often fell short for lack of preparation. Four of the first five missionaries the Alliance sent to Africa died or returned almost at once. Language training seemed unnecessary to Simpson, since the first Christians had received a gift of tongues. But gradually, the need for better training prevailed, and by 1895, there were 300 missionaries in the field. Attempts at a greater definition of what the Christian and Missionary Alliance stood for resulted in a document that defined the organization as a nonecclesiastical body that taught the necessity of a conversion experience followed by progressive sanctification and affirmed the doctrine of healing, in the atonement, and the pre-millennial return of Christ. On other points, the conference advised freedom.

It was said of Simpson that

> He sought to provide a fellowship only, and looked with suspicion upon anything like rigid organization. He wanted the Alliance to be a spiritual association of believers who hungered to know the fullness of the blessing of the Gospel of Christ, working concertedly for the speedy evangelization of the world.

He was haunted by a sense of urgency, believing that the time was short and that souls needed to be saved quickly. His preaching and writing, centered on the conversion experience, impatient of structure, organization, and creedal definition, had much in common with the modern Pentecostal movement, which began shortly before Simpson's death and drew many of his churches into its orbit.

A reading from *The Holy Spirit: Power from on High* by A. B. Simpson

The wonderful events of our time are the beginning of those overturnings which are to bring in the kingdom of Christ and His Millennial reign. The Ancient of Days is already working among the nations, and through the power of the Spirit of God is breaking down the barriers and opening up the highway for Christ's return. The same Holy Ghost that of old touched the hearts of heathen kings and made them God's instruments in accomplishing His purpose, is calling out to-day the various providential agencies which are but part of God's plan for the approaching end of the age. Surely, the extraordinary events that are so rapidly happening around us in every quarter of the globe are full of portentous meaning.

The wonderful progress of knowledge; the running to and fro of men, with their commercial activities and their methods of transportation and communication by land and sea; wars and rumors of wars disturbing the whole political realm; revolutions and upheavals of society and political institutions; all these are full of meaning and. promise, and through them all moves the steadfast purpose of the Holy Ghost, whose "eyes run to and fro throughout the whole earth," and whose hand is moving men to the fulfillment of His higher will. . . .

Beloved, if we are truly filled with the Holy Ghost and longing for the coming of Christ, we shall be active witnesses and workers in preparing for Him. We shall be found faithful to our trust wherever God has placed us. We will be soul winners at home, and if we cannot go abroad we will help others go and give the gospel quickly to all the world.

How much of our religious life is comfortable sentimentalism, taking the pleasant part, enjoying the selfish luxury, doing as much Christian work as is agreeable, and yet knowing little or nothing of the ceaseless self-sacrificing, and intense devotion of the Lord Jesus Christ to finish His work and bring this revolted world back to His Father.

Oh beloved, are we wholly in earnest? Have we too "a baptism to be baptised with, and are we straitened until it be accomplished?" Are we going forth "as much as lieth in us" to give the Gospel of the Kingdom to all nations that the end may speedily come?

Perhaps, dear brother, as you read these lines God may be calling you to go forth and call home the lost disciple who shall complete the number of the Bride and then bring back our adorable Redeemer.

Nay perhaps, dear sinner, as you read these lines, you may be the soul for whom Christ is waiting to complete His glorious Bride, as He calls you, "Whosoever will let him take the water of life freely."

✪ *September 14* _____

Lucy Craft Laney

PRESBYTERIAN

April 14, 1854–October 23, 1933

Although she was born in Georgia before the Civil War, Lucy Craft Laney was born free. Her father, a carpenter and ordained elder of the Old School Presbyterian Church, had saved enough money to buy his freedom, then that of his wife before he married her. Lucy attended a high school in Macon established by the American Missionary Society and was a member of the first graduating class of Atlanta University.

For ten years, Laney taught in the public schools of Georgia, but she was discontented with the limited curricula available for Negro students. Finally, in 1883, she began a school of her own with six students, using a room in the basement of Christ Presbyterian Church in Augusta. Instead of the vocational training offered by many schools for blacks in the reconstruction era, she taught a full liberal arts curriculum, urging her graduates to aspire to the best colleges in the country. Laney's school was named the Haines Normal and Industrial Institute in honor of Mrs. Francine E. H. Haines, president of the Woman's Department of the Presbyterian Church, U.S.A., who had been so impressed by a presentation Laney gave at a Presbyterian General Assembly that she raised $10,000 to put the institute on a secure financial basis. Mary McLeod Bethune* was one of the first teachers in the school and early graduates included a future physician and a college president. Eventually Laney was able to create an academy with 27 teachers and over 700 students in the elementary and high school divisions. She also developed the first kindergarten in Atlanta, along with a program to train nurses. The Institute suffered financially during the Depression and finally closed in 1949, but the Lucy C. Laney High School still stands on the same site. It witnesses to the impact made by Laney's commitment to providing the best possible education for African Americans.

A reading from Lucy Craft Laney at a 1899 conference in Hampton, Virginia

If the educated colored woman has a burden, — and we believe she has — what is that burden? How can it be lightened, how may it be lifted? What it is can be readily seen perhaps better than told, for it constantly annoys to irritation; it bulges out as did the load of Bunyan's Christian — ignorance — with its inseparable companions, shame and crime and prejudice.

That our position may be more readily understood, let us refer to the past.... During the days of training in our first mission school — slavery — that which is the foundation of right training and good government, the basic rock of all true culture — the home, with its fire-side training, mother's moulding, woman's care, was not only neglected but utterly disregarded. There was no time in the institution for such teaching. We know that there were, even in the first days of that school, isolated cases of men and women of high moral character and great intellectual worth, as Phillis Wheatley, Sojourner Truth,* and John Chavers, whose work and lives should have taught, or at least suggested to their instructors, the capabilities and possibilities of their dusky slave pupils. The progress and the struggles of these for noble things should have led their instructors to see how the souls and minds of this people then yearned for light — the real life. But alas! these dull teachers, like many modern pedagogues and school-keepers, failed to know their pupils — to find out their real needs, and hence had no cause to study methods of better and best development of the boys and girls under their care. What other result could come from such training or want of training than a conditioned race such as we now have? For two hundred years they married or were given in marriage. Oft times marriage ceremonies were performed for them by the learned minister of the master's church; more often there was simply a consorting by the master's consent, but it was always understood that these unions for cause, or without cause, might be more easily broken, than a divorce can be obtained in Indiana or Dakota. Without going so long a distance as from New York to Connecticut, the separated could take other companions for life, for a long or short time; for during those two hundred and fifty years there was not a single marriage legalized in a single southern state, where dwelt the mass of this people. There was something of the philosopher in the plantation preacher, who, at the close of the marriage ceremony, had the dusky couple join their right hands, and then called upon the assembled congregation to sing, as he lined it out, "Plunged in a gulf Of dark despair," for well he knew the sequel of many such unions. If it so happened that a husband and wife were parted by those who owned them, such owners often consoled those thus parted with the fact that he could get another wife; she, another husband. Such was the sanctity of the marriage vow that was taught and held for over two hundred and fifty years. Habit is indeed second nature. This is the race inheritance. I thank God not of all, for we know, each of us, of instances, of holding most sacred the plighted love and keeping faithfully and sacredly the marriage vows. We know of pure homes and of growing old together. Blessed heritage! If we only had the gold there might be many "Golden Weddings." Despair not; the crushing burden of immorality which has its root in the disregard of the marriage vow can be lightened. It must be, and the educated colored woman can and will do her part in lifting this burden.

✺ *September 15* _____

Godfrey Diekmann

ROMAN CATHOLIC

April 7, 1908–February 22, 2002

Whether hunting for mushrooms to enrich his monastery's diet, marching in Selma with Martin Luther King, Jr.,* or serving as a consultant at the Second Vatican Council, Godfrey Diekmann brought a unique and surprising zest to every aspect of his life for over 90 years. Born a few miles from the place where he died, and a member of the Benedictine order from the age of 18, it would not have been surprising to find him to be a man with narrow horizons and limited vision. But he was nothing like that. Diekmann discovered St. Paul's vision of the church as the Body of Christ when he was 18. It radically changed his understanding of the faith. He looked back on it as a conversion experience. Equally central to his understanding was the patristic saying: "He became human that we might become divine." Diekmann once wrote,

> All of us, every member of Christ, has been called, has been set aside by God for His purposes. From all eternity God has, as it were, laid His hand on the head of each one of us, and in baptism has *consecrated* us to do His work and to bear His fruit. We are not our own. We cannot use our time and talents merely as we ourselves please. We belong to God — who has actually deigned to make the redemption of the world dependent upon our collaboration!

Diekmann's particular calling was as a liturgical scholar. An expert on the history of the liturgy, he made it his business to work for the renewal of liturgy, making it fresh by calling into question eucharistic patterns left over from the Middle Ages. An ardent supporter of inclusive language in the liturgy, women's ordination, and married clergy, he realized that such transformations would not happen overnight. "The momentum of 1,600 years cannot be reversed in a mere generation," Diekmann cautioned. "The doctrinal foundations have been firmly placed by Vatican II, and contrary to increasingly pessimistic evaluations, the substructures of renewal are being placed, often by trial and error if not by official initiative."

"Official initiative," Diekmann knew well was not likely to move the church forward. A story tells how at the end of a service in the papal chapel, Diekmann had been seen kneeling in prayer but was staring intensely at the pope (Paul VI) in a way that seemed almost rude. Questioned about it later by his friends, he said, "You all know that I am not happy with much of that man's leadership of the Church. For that, I don't like him. But I was not STARING at the pope. What I was doing was WILLING MYSELF TO LOVE HIM" (original emphasis).

Diekmann's concerns were far broader than those of the Vatican. He was a member of the National Lutheran-Catholic Dialogue, a founder and member of the Interdenominational International Consultation on English Texts in the Liturgy, and cofounder with the Quaker leader, Douglas Steere (1901–1995), of the Ecumenical Institute of Spirituality.

His own church hardly knew what to make of him. The Catholic University in Washington once banned him from teaching in its summer program, yet later awarded him an honorary degree. Diekmann had an explanation for everything in a mantra he was fond of repeating: "I believe in the Holy Spirit."

A reading from *Come, Let Us Worship* by Godfrey Diekmann

Permit me, now, to become quite personal. I have been a priest twenty-four years, and I believe that rarely has there been a day in that span of time when in some way or other I haven't been made conscious of the fact of this *vocation*. I have been a teacher in a boys' college for more than twenty years, and never has a year passed that I did not have a moral certainty in my own mind that many a boy sitting in front of me in my class would have made a much better priest than I, *if* God had chosen him. That is not false humility; that is ordinary common sense. The reason God chose me, consecrated me, can only be the reason of God's mercy, of God's predilection. Certainly it was no merit on my part. And if there is one motivation that should urge me to lead at least a minimum good, holy, priestly life, it is this awareness that God has chosen me. The laity too, expect their priests to try to lead a holy life, and rightly so, for they know that priests have been *called* and *consecrated* by God to carry on His all-important work.

Have we not, however, limited this powerful motivation to holiness too exclusively to priests? When St. Paul speaks of vocation, when he exults in the fact of being elect, of being called, of being chosen, he is not speaking about his priestly dignity. He is speaking about the basic vocation of being called to be members of Christ. And actually, there is less difference (though the difference, obviously, is great) between one in holy orders and a lay member of Christ, than there is between such a member of Christ and those who have not been given this grace. In other words, the idea of *vocation* and of *consecration* is something we priests have no right to keep to ourselves. It is a rightful heritage of each member of the Body of Christ: a motivation which could and should be a powerful incentive to holiness. . . .

✪ *September 16* —————————————————————————

Terence Vincent Powderly

ROMAN CATHOLIC

January 22, 1849–June 24, 1924

Those European churches whose members emigrated to the United States brought with them Old World traditions of strongly hierarchical authority.

In the New World, however, their members were often poor people struggling against exploitive conditions in mines and factories, trying to obtain
fair standards of pay and decent working conditions. Thus those who set
out to organize the workers sometimes found little support, even opposition, from church leadership. Terence Powderly was a Roman Catholic labor
leader who believed that Christian tradition spoke for the poor in ways not
always reflected in the hierarchy of his own church.

The son of Irish immigrants, Powderly dropped out of school at the age
of 13 and went to work first on the railroad and then as a machinist. At the
age of 22, he joined a union and at the age of 25 was sworn into the Knights
of Labor, a union that operated as a secret society and became a major force
in American industrial relations for a time. Powderly thought labor issues
could be resolved by establishing a society with a proper relationship with
God. He wrote:

> Here we are of all races, we come from everywhere to make a family that
> has no family tree, a family with no common ancestor, and yet a family that
> may be traced back to the greatest of all common ancestors — God the Father.
> We are all children of Him who gave us birth and everything following it
> to make us happy, contented, prosperous, if we but use His gifts wisely and
> intelligently. It is because we allowed some to monopolize all the gifts, that
> there is dissatisfaction, distrust and want in the land. We affect reverence for
> and belief in God, yet sneer at him who tells us that God gave this earth to all
> His children, to be used for the benefit of all.

As a labor leader and powerful orator, Powderly was feared and reviled
by employers and the press. Yet he managed to convince Cardinal Gibbons
of the justice of his cause and persuaded him to present it in a favorable light
in Rome. Other leaders of the church were less supportive. Powderly's autobiography relates an encounter with the Roman Catholic bishop of Maine
that illustrates graphically the independent spirit nourished among American
Christians:

> In 1884 I delivered a course of sermons on the labor question in Maine.
> On reaching Portland, on my way home, I received a summons from Bishop
> Healy* of the Portland diocese to call upon him. It was on Saturday. I reached
> the city at one o'clock, received his message on my arrival at my hotel, and
> without waiting for dinner went to the bishop's residence. I sent up my name,
> and with it, the information that I was very tired (the truth is I was not only
> tired but sick) and that if he could see me soon it would be agreeable. I sat in his
> reception room an hour and three-quarters before he came in and then he told
> me he had been resting. He received me very coldly and his first question was:
>   "Are you a Catholic?"
>   I answered in the affirmative, and he continued:
>   "Then what right have you to speak in my state without permission?"
>   Thinking that I might have misunderstood him I asked what he meant by
> "his state," and received this reply;

"I mean my state, the state of Maine. You are, so I am informed, lecturing in it, and I want to know why you do so without first obtaining my permission."

I replied that I did not understand why I should obtain permission.

"Aren't you a Catholic?" he asked.

"Yes, I am a Catholic but what has that to do with it?" I answered.

"It has everything to do with it. You are in duty bound to consult your superiors in such matters. The talks you are giving have a bearing on faith and morals, and I first want to know what you intend speaking on before granting permission to allow you traipse through this diocese."

I arose and taking my hat said:

"I speak only on the labor question, I do not meddle with religion, I do not interfere with the faith or morals of any man, I am a freeborn American, and do not acknowledge your right, or the right of any other man no matter what his religion or position in society may be, to question me for doing that which I have a right to do under the laws of my country. If that is what you wanted me for and you have nothing else to say to me I shall retire."

As I walked toward the door he raised his hand and said:

"Stop, I have a word or two to say to you. You have done wrong as a Catholic. You should have consulted with me before speaking in this state, and I shall bring the matter to the attention of your bishop. Do not speak in my state again until I give consent."

Up to that time I listened to him patiently but, when he repeated his use of the term "my state," I became indignant, lost my temper, and told him that there were a few people in the state of Maine who did not belong to him, that human slavery had been abolished, and that it was a piece of presumption on his part to assume that Maine was all his. Perhaps I should not have said that, it did not better the matter any, but I feel that the provocation was sufficient to call out what I said, and have no apology to offer for it. I continued my lecture tour through Maine.

✪ *September 17*

Daniel Coker

AFRICAN METHODIST

1780–1846

When Richard Allen* called a conference of black Methodist congregations in 1816 to organize a new denomination and choose a leader, the conference secretary, Daniel Coker, was elected. Perhaps because of his light complexion, a controversial issue, Coker declined the election, and Richard Allen was then chosen as the new denomination's first head.

At birth, Daniel Coker's name was Isaac Wright. He was the son of a white indentured servant, Susan Coker, and Edward Wright, an African slave. Assigned to accompanying his white half-brothers to school as their servant, Coker took advantage of the opportunity and learned to read and write. He freed himself from slavery by escaping to New York, where he changed his name to Daniel Coker to avoid discovery as a fugitive. He met the Methodist pioneer, Bishop Francis Asbury,* in New York and was ordained as a Methodist minister. Coker taught and preached and began to advocate independence for the black Methodists. In 1810, he wrote *A Dialogue between a Virginian and an African Minister* — an important anti-slavery pamphlet. It consists of an imaginary dialogue between a Virginia gentleman and an African minister, who persuades the Virginian that slavery is not sanctioned by Scripture.

In 1820, Coker went to Liberia and Sierra Leone as a missionary, but the white-run American Colonization Society never trusted him with a position of responsibility. He succeeded in founding a church in Freetown, where he died in 1846.

Readings from Daniel Coker's diary

At Sea, Feb. 19, Saturday.

We have been two days busily engaged in laying out the plan of a city and organizing our societies. Love prevails. While writing these lines I sit at the cabin window. Our ship Elizabeth lashes the foaming brine, and while I look back on the closing track, the words of the prophet occur: Isa. ch. 18. — Oh! my soul, what is God about to do for Africa? Surely something great."

When the coast came in view, he wrote:

Thank the Lord I have seen Africa.

The reality of Africa surprised him:

Sierra Leone, Friday, March 10.

This morning I went on shore. In passing through the market, I saw strange things. There were many of the natives, both male and female, with their produce of various kinds. They were all nearly naked, both men and women. (Isaiah, 20th ch.) I saw sheep, pork, fowls, fish in abundance; oysters, sweet potatoes, and all kinds of tropical produce. I was led to say, surely, nature is prodigal of her bounties. I was stopped in the street by some of the American friends who, recognizing me, said, the last Sacrament that I received in America, I received from your hands, (at Philadelphia, when I was there on a visit.) They invited me into their houses and treated me with great kindness.

A letter to friends in America spoke of his hopes for the work he had come to do:

To *all my dear African Brethren in America, I send these few lines —* greeting:

Dear brethren! — To all you who love the Lord Jesus Christ and his kingdom, — I would with pleasure inform you that I, with about 90 of our

American coloured brethren, have arrived safe in Africa. We find the land to be good, and the natives kind, only those, who, from intercourse with the slave-traders, become otherwise. There is a great work here to do. Thousands, and thousands of souls here, to be converted from Paganism and Mahometanism to the religion of Jesus. Oh! brethren, who will come over to the help of the Lord? If you come as baptists, come to establish an African baptist church, and not to encourage division. If you come as presbyterians, come to support an African presbyterian church, and not to make divisions. If you come as protestants, come to support an African protestant church, and not to make divisions. If you come as methodists, come to support an African methodist church. We wish to know nothing of *Bethel* and of *Sharp-street* in Africa — leave all these divisions in America. Before these heathens, all should be sweetly united; and if darkness is driven from this land, it must be by a united effort among Christians. The Sharp-street brethren will be to me as the Bethel brethren; all will be alike. I wish to forget all such names and distinctions. Those who will come in love, to do good, and spread the gospel — come, in the name of God, come! Otherwise, they had better stay away; for nothing but love and union will do good among these heathens. God grant that many such may come over to help with this great work.

> I am yours, in the bonds of a pure gospel,
> Daniel Coker.
> March 29, 1820

✪ *September 18*

Robert Lewis Dabney

PRESBYTERIAN

March 5, 1820–January 3, 1898

Farmer, architect, inventor, theologian, economist, soldier, poet, preacher — Robert Lewis Dabney possessed a wide range of abilities and was able to make use of all of them. His father died when he was 13, so Dabney's education was interrupted more than once by the need to return to the farm and care for his mother. He began his education at Hampton-Sydney College, returned to the farm for two years, then completed his college education at the University of Virginia. Two more years were spent in farming and schoolteaching before Dabney felt free to move on to the Union Theological Seminary to complete his education. Eight years of pastoral work followed during which he also built a home and operated a farm before he was called back to the seminary to teach theology — the work that would occupy the largest amount of his time for the remainder of his life.

But not even a professor of theology could avoid involvement in the convulsions leading up to the Civil War. Dabney believed in the Union but, like Robert E. Lee and many others, he considered the state to be his true

country, so followed it into secession when division came. He had been of-
fered the opportunity to serve the Fifth Avenue Presbyterian Church in New
York, the largest Presbyterian Church in the country, just before the war, and
also to teach at Princeton Seminary, the leading seminary of his church. But
Dabney turned both down to stay in his native Virginia. He tried to avoid
the next call that came, a request that he serve as Chief of Staff to General
Stonewall Jackson, but Jackson would not take "No" as an answer and
Dabney reluctantly accepted. Although he served well in his new role, his
constitution was not equal to the challenge of military life. After six months,
he had to return home and resume his preaching and teaching. A year later,
when Stonewall Jackson died, he was called on by Jackson's widow to write
his biography and spent the next year and half in that endeavor.

The end of the war brought chaos to the south instead of peace, yet
Dabney found the energy to concentrate on his theological work. In 1870
he published *Sacred Rhetoric,* in 1871 his *Systematic Theology,* and in 1875
The Sensualistic Philosophy of the 19th Century. In his day, he was often
considered to be the premier philosopher in the country, sometimes ranked
even above Jonathan Edwards in the minds of his contemporaries.

Dabney accepted the chair of mental and moral philosophy in the University of Texas of Austin in 1883 and continued his teaching until his death
in 1898, even though he had lost his sight to glaucoma some eight years
earlier.

A reading from a sermon on dying preached to
Stonewall Jackson and his men in August of 1861
in the woods of Virginia

I believe that heaven is as truly a place as was that paradise of the primeval
world where the holy Adam dwelt. When we first arrive there we shall be
disembodied spirits. But finite spirits have their locality. But where is this
place? In what charter of this vast universe? In what sphere do the Man
Jesus and his ransomed ones now dwell? When death batters down the
walls of the earthly tabernacle, whither shall the dispossessed soul set out?
To what direction shall it turn in beginning its mysterious journey? It knows
not; it needs a skillful, powerful and friendly guide. . . .

It is a delightful belief, to which the gospel seems to give most solid
support, that our Redeemer is accustomed to employ in this mission his
holy angels. What Christian has failed to derive sublime satisfaction as he
has read the allegorical description in the Pilgrim's Progress of Christian and
Hopeful crossing the river of death, and ascending with a rejoicing company
of angels to the gate of the celestial city. It is, indeed, but an allegory, which
likens death to a river. But it is no allegory — it is a literal and blessed truth —
that angels receive and assist the departing souls which Christ redeems. "Are

they not all ministering spirits, sent forth to minister to them who shall be heirs of salvation?"...

Oh! blessed resting place! "In thy presence is fulness of joy; at thy right hand are pleasures for evermore." Let us, brethren, live and die like believing Stephen, and our spirits will be received to the place where the God-man holds his regal court, to go out thence no more forever. We shall see him on his throne, so gloriously earned; we shall see the same face which beamed love upon the sisters of Bethany and upon the beloved disciple, and which wept at the grave of his friend; not, as then, marred with our griefs and pensive with the burden of our sorrows, but shining as the sun. Yet that splendor will not sear our vision; it will be the light of love. We shall see the very hands which were pierced for us; not then bleeding, but reaching forth to us the scepter of universal dominion to guide and protect us....

But, alas! all whom I address have not the faith and holiness of Stephen. They live in wilful impenitence, and call not on the name of Christ. Yet they too must pass through this iron gate of death! On whom will you call, you who have neglected your Savior, when you pass down into this valley of great darkness; when the inexorable veil begins to descend, shutting out human help and sympathy from your despairing eyes; when death thrusts out your wretched soul from its abused tenement; when you launch forth into the void immense, a naked, shivering ghost; when you stand before the great white throne? Can you face these horrors alone? How will you endure a beggared, undone eternity?...

Call on Christ, then, today, in repentance and faith, in order that you may be entitled to call upon him in the hour of your extremity. Own him now as your Lord, that he may confess you then as his people.

✪ *September 19*

Katherine Drexel

ROMAN CATHOLIC

November 26, 1858–March 3, 1955

Katherine Drexel was a methodical young woman. She had made her debut in Philadelphia society, but when she began to think that she might have a call to be a nun, she sat down to list the arguments for and against. For it was the fact that "Jesus Christ has given His life for me. It is but just that I should give Him mine." But on the other side was "How could I bear separation from my family? I have never been away from home for more than two weeks?" and also "I hate community life. I should think it maddening to come in constant contact with many different *old maidish* dispositions. I hate never to be alone."

Since she did not feel she had reached a definite answer, for two years she corresponded with a trusted advisor and bishop who argued strongly that she could serve the church better in secular life. But this finally convinced her that she did indeed have a vocation. Faced with her decision, her advisor switched course and set out to persuade her that she should found an order to carry on a ministry to Native Americans and freed slaves. Drexel was interested in such work and had traveled west to visit churches on the reservations. She had contributed generously from the millions her father had left her. Nonetheless, she felt called to a contemplative life and wondered why existing orders might not carry out such a mission. Her advisor was now all the more convinced that she should found an order, so at last she relented, served a novitiate in an existing order, and on February 12, 1891, Drexel founded the Sisters of the Blessed Sacrament for Indians and Colored People.

Her long-resisted vocation met a very real need, and new schools for Indian children were built in Arizona and New Mexico and for blacks in such southern cities as Richmond and Nashville. Drexel lived in poverty, applying her substantial resources fully to the needs of others. By the time she died, the order had over 500 members living in 51 convents and serving more than 60 schools, as well as Xavier University in New Orleans, the first American Roman Catholic institution of higher education for blacks. A newspaper editorial called her "one of the most remarkable women in America" and noted that she had given her life to "the poor and forgotten people."

A reading from a 1903 letter of Katherine Drexel to the sisters at St. Michael's School in Arizona

I wish I had some more days to spend with you, I much feared I failed to express the real consolation my visit was to me. Do you know it seemed like the realization of years, yes, longings of the last fifteen years? When I looked at you, the virgin mothers of the poor Navajos, my heart was full of gratitude to God because He had beyond all expectation, fulfilled the desires He Himself had given me, to do something for these poor pagans. You know God gave me this desire one or two years before I entered religion or ever dreamed that God would permit me to be a sister.

And so, on this visit I looked up in wonder at God's wonderful ways and thought how little we imagine what may be the result of listening and acting on a desire He puts into the heart. If He puts it into the heart. He will bless it, if we try to act upon it, and great will be the effect before God. It will be success before God, even if it be not so to our weak understanding. For God means that which He breathes into the soul should bring forth fruit to eternal life. God in His great condescension to my weakness has let me see with my own eyes the good results of this desire of fifteen years ago. When one is strong in the spiritual life He does not always permit this. He makes us adore without understanding.

How fifteen years ago, could I have believed that eleven of my own spiritual daughters would be amongst the Navajos and that each one of them would have a mother's heart for them. That, God has given to you, along with big earnest desires for the salvation of your spiritual children, the Navajos. These are the desires God has placed in your hearts and great will be the effect if you continue as you do, to nourish these desires and act upon them. He will fulfill your desires with good things far beyond your expectations, especially as you have so cheerfully endured the sacrifices of the foundation of this Convent.... With God's help you were able to get through last winter's privations. Years ago you would not have believed you would have had the strength. Who gave you the strength? God! He will give you more strength this year.

✪ *September 20*

Jackson Kemper

EPISCOPALIAN

December 24, 1789–May 24, 1870

At the end of the American Revolution, many people doubted that the Church of England, even when it was renamed the "Episcopal Church," could continue to exist in an independent country and expected to see it cease to exist within their lifetimes. Instead, a new generation of leaders appeared who were persuaded that Anglicanism could become as truly a national church for America as ever it was for England. In 1835, the Episcopal Church's General Convention resolved to make the whole church a mission society and to choose bishops to lead the effort to establish the church in the west.

Jackson Kemper was the first of the new missionary bishops chosen. He was assigned jurisdiction over a territory that would eventually become the states of Indiana, Iowa, Kansas, Minnesota, Missouri, Nebraska, and Wisconsin. Like early missionaries of other churches with similar charges, he was sometimes called affectionately the "bishop of all out-doors" and also "the apostle of the Northwest." On horseback and foot, through blinding snowstorms, sleeping on one-room cabin floors, and sharing a single spoon with his companions, Kemper traveled some 300,000 miles over the next 35 years. In less than 20 years, the Episcopal Church in Wisconsin was able to form a diocese and elect Kemper as its bishop. Five years later, he resigned from his larger jurisdiction. During the 35 years he served as a bishop, he created a college and a seminary, consecrated 100 churches, ordained 200 men to the priesthood, and confirmed 10,000 people.

A man of limitless vision, he asked the Board of Missions of the Episcopal Church, "May it not be our duty to convert the world — may not this high, this inestimable privilege be offered to *us!* And are we prepared — are we doing at the present moment *even one tenth* part of what we are capable? ... With the talents we possess ... and the privileges we enjoy, cannot our faith, our liberality, and our self-denial *greatly* increase?"

A reading from a sermon on mission preached by Jackson Kemper in St. Paul's Chapel, New York, on October 7, 1841

There are many yet living who have witnessed the rise and growth of the sacred cause of missions within the boundaries of the American Church. It was very feeble at its commencement, and had but few friends to sustain it. They watched its progress with deep and anxious solicitude. Sometimes it was deemed inexpedient, if not wrong — sometimes it was contemned or treated with cold indifference — again every measure was thoroughly canvassed — and every false or unsuccessful effort was ridiculed. The ordeal was severe, but highly salutary; for, in the process of time, the doubting were satisfied, and objections, once formidable, were removed. At last, we acknowledged it to be the work of the Lord — we ranked ourselves as a Missionary Church — we openly confessed that the Field was the World. ...

Brethren of the Society on whose concerns we are now assembled! Sustain, I beseech you, our missions, and increase the laborers. Put forth every effort, so that at last the Valley of the Mississippi, the country on our south-western Atlantic coast, and likewise that on the borders of the Upper Lakes, may blossom as the rose. A trust, a sacred trust is committed to us — let us not be *unfaithful*. There is that scattereth and yet increaseth. You are aware of the promises of God. Your hearts have often glowed when meditating upon the declarations of prophecy. Can we not hasten the time when the Saviour's kingdom shall come — when peace and good will shall reign triumphant? Remember the early labors of the primitive Church, and her wonderful success. We are now co-workers with the Most High — co-workers in his great and glorious designs. If much good can be accomplished — if a strict economy in all things, and an increased interest in the work will enable us to command more time and more money — withhold not your exertions, lest haply ye be found fighting against God. Be entreated by the love of Christ — more sacrifices can yet be made — more, more, many more fields can yet be possessed in our day. Let us up and be doing, for the Lord is with us. Send forth missionary bishops to Africa and Texas. Let the leaven spread — the grain of mustard grow — the net be cast into the deepest waters. *God will give the increase.* It is for us to plant and water.

Constrained by the undying love of Christ to love the immortal souls of our fellow beings — let us be ready for the privilege, if it is ever conferred, to scatter the precious seed on every field — to erect the banner of the cross on every mountain. Let us at least hasten the time — by our prayers, our exertions, and our sacrifices — when the joyous sound shall burst from every heart, "How beautiful are the feet of them that preach the Gospel of peace, and bring glad tidings of good things."

✪ *September 21*

Sojourner Truth (Isabella Baumfree)

BAPTIST

1797–1883

Born black and female at the end of the 18th century, Isabella Baumfree had two strikes against her — but only two. To balance the account, she stood six feet tall and had a commanding voice and personality. She used these assets to preach the gospel and for other causes as well.

She told her own story this way:

> I was boun' a slave in the State of Noo Yo'k, Ulster County, 'mong de low Dutch. W'en I was ten years old, I couldn't speak a word of English, an' hab no eddicati'n at all. Dere's wonder what dey has done fur me. As I tole you w'en I was soile, my master died, an' we was goin' to hab an auction. We was all brought up to be sole. My mother, my fader was very ole, my brudder younger 'en myself, an' my mother took my han'. Dey opened a canoby ob hebben, an' she sat down an' I an' my brudder sat down by her, en she says, "Look up to de moon an' stars dat shine upon you father an' upon you mother when you sole far away, an' upon you brudders an' sisters, dat is sole far away," for dere was a great number ob us, an' was all sole away befor' my membrance. I asked her who had made de moon an' de stars, an' she says, "God," an' says I, Where is God? "Oh!"; says she, "chile, he sits in de sky, an' he hears you w'en you ax him w'en you are away from us to make your marster an' misteress good, an' he will do it."

So Isabella prayed, but her new master paired her with another slave against her will, when she was just 13. She bore him five children. Her master promised to set her free during the period before New York State put an end to slavery, but he reneged on his promise so Isabella ran away with her youngest child. She settled for a while in New York City and worked as a domestic, but a religious experience changed her life and set her traveling on a mission.

> When I left the house of bondage, I left everything behind. I wa'n't goin' to keep nothin' of Egypt on me, an' so I went to the Lord an' asked him to give me a new name. And the Lord gave me Sojourner, because I was to travel up an' down the land, showin' the people their sins, an' bein' a sign unto them. Afterward I told the Lord I wanted another name, 'cause everybody else had two names; and the Lord gave me Truth, because I was to declare the truth to the people.
>
> Ye see some ladies have given me a white banner, "Proclaim liberty throughout the land unto all the inhabitants thereof." Well, I journeys round to

camp-meetin's, an' wherever folk is, an' I sets up my baner, an then I sings, an' then folks always comes up round me, an' then I preaches to 'em. I tells 'em about Jesus, an' I tells them about the sins of this people. A great many always comes to hear me; an' they're right good to me, too, an' say they want to hear me again.

She preached "God's truth and plan for salvation" in Long Island and Connecticut and arrived in Northampton, Massachusetts, where she met and worked with such abolitionists as William Lloyd Garrison, Frederick Douglass, and Olive Gilbert. Later she went to Washington, met President Lincoln, and spoke before the Congress. She spoke about abolition and woman's suffrage as well as her own experience of slavery. She is best remembered for a speech she gave at a women's rights conference when she noticed that no one was addressing the rights of black women.

Dat man ober dar say dat womin needs to be helped over carriages, and lifted ober ditches and to have the best place everywhere. Nobody eber helps me into carriages, or ober muddpuddles, or bigs me any best place. And ain't I a woman? Look at me Looka at me arm. I have ploughes and planted and gathered into barns, and no man could head me! And ain't I a woman.

The words "And ain't I a woman," remains the phrase most associated with her memory but her testimony to her faith needs to be heard as well:

I know what it is to be taken in the barn an' tied up an' de blood drawed out ob yere bare back, an' I tell you it would make you think 'bout God. Yes, an' den I felt, O God, ef I was you an' you felt like I do, an' asked me for help I would help you — now why won't you help me? Trooly I done know but God has helped me. But I got no good marster ontil de las' time I was sole, an' den I found one an' his name was Jesus. Oh, I tell ye, didn't I fine a good marster when I use to feel so bad, when I use to say, O God, how ken I libe? I'm sorely prest both widin and widout. W'en God gi' me dat marster he healed all de wounds up. My soul rejoiced. I used to hate de w'ite pepul so, an' I tell ye w'en de lobe come in me I had so much lobe I didn't know what to lobe. Den de w'ite pepul come, an' I thought dat lobe was too good fur dem. Den I said, Yea, God, I'll lobe ev'ybuddy an' de w'ite pepul too. Ever since dat, dat lobe has continued an' kep' me 'mong de w'ite pepul.... On'y think ob it! Ain't it wonderful dat God gives lobe enough to de Ethiopians to lobe you?"

✸ *September 22* _____

Samuel Eli Cornish

PRESBYTERIAN

1795–November 6, 1858

Looking back from the privileged security of the 21st century, a campaign to end slavery would seem a cause around which most people of good will could unite. In reality, people of good will in the early 19th century found themselves deeply, often angrily, divided over the direction such a campaign should take. Should it, for example, cooperate closely with women's suffrage? Should it accept women in leadership positions? Should it support a campaign to colonize Africa with freed slaves? And should it make use of demonstrations and force to resist the fugitive slave laws?

Samuel Eli Cornish was a leader among northern blacks campaigning to end slavery. Sometimes the choices he made look radical, at other times, conservative. He had come to Philadelphia as a young man and had been deeply impressed by the ministry of John Gloucester, the first black Presbyterian minister. Gloucester trained Cornish with a committee of white ministers. Already in failing health, he soon began to use the younger man to assist him and even to fill in for him. Licensed to preach, Cornish then served as a missionary in Maryland before moving to New York City in 1821, where he organized the New Demeter Street Presbyterian Church, the first African American Presbyterian congregation in that city. He was ordained in 1822.

Moved by the abject poverty of the black populations of Philadelphia and New York, Cornish became convinced that it was essential to persuade both races that living conditions and educational opportunities must be improved, since otherwise, abolishing slavery would do little to change the circumstances of African Americans. Toward that end, Cornish founded the country's first black newspaper, *Freedom's Journal,* in 1827. As a recognized spokesman of that community, Cornish joined in 1833 with Arthur Tappan, Lewis Tappan,* William Lloyd Garrison,* and Theodore Weld* to form the Anti-Slavery Society. When women were elected to the board, however, the Tappans,* James Birney, and Gerrit Smith, along with Cornish, left to establish a rival organization, the American and Foreign Anti-Slavery Society. Refusing to support the woman's rights movement, it concentrated exclusively on the subject of slavery.

Freedom's Journal survived about two years. However, in 1837, Cornish started the *Colored American,* subsidized by noted white abolitionist Arthur Tappan. His editorial position also lasted only a short time because, more conservative than many of his younger contemporaries, Cornish found himself in the minority about the use of demonstrations and force to resist the fugitive slave laws. In the last decades before the Civil War, as society became increasingly polarized, his emphasis on education and social improvement seemed too cautious to many. Cornish retired to the northern part of the city, where he formed a new congregation, Emmanuel Church. Nonetheless, he continued to sit on the boards of two mission societies, and on the executive committee of the American and Foreign Anti-Slavery Society. Till his death in 1858, he spoke out against the Fugitive Slave Law and in opposition to colonization schemes in Africa.

A reading from an open letter from Samuel Eli Cornish to the Hon. Theodore Frelinghuysen and the Hon. Benjamin F. Butler, New York, on the subject of African colonization, April 1, 1840

Failing in their appeal to the colored people where it ought, in fairness, to have ended, the Shareholders next had recourse to the *whites*, with whom they knew it could be made more effectively. To this end, a new school was instituted, whose teachers first discovered and taught the dogma, that there is in the white man an inherent prejudice against his colored brother, so fixed, that its removal, whilst the latter remains *in this country*, is not only beyond all human power, but beyond Christianity itself, "the power of God"; but that it might surely be mitigated at least, if not extinguished, provided the Atlantic Ocean could be made to roll between them.

PREJUDICE! What is it? Lexicographers tell us, it is a decision of the mind formed without due examination of the facts or arguments which are necessary to a just and impartial determination. And *prejudice against* COLOR! What does this mean. You are both sensible — nay, learned men. Pray instruct us in this mystery of slave-holding philosophy — scarcely spoken of in Britain, wholly unknown and unfelt among the learned, the wise and refined of France and the nations of Europe. Can prejudice exist against that which has in it nothing of the moral or the intellectual? Is it a down right absurdity to say of men that they are prejudiced against *sound* or *sight* — against the *earth*, or the *sea*, or the *air*, or *light*? And is it less one to say, that they are prejudiced against *color*? If not, how is it, gentlemen, that you can connect your names and give your influence to a great National movement, (one which it pleased you to say, we were more indebted to for the integrity of the Union than to any other cause since its commencement) resting for support on a *philosophical absurdity?* Or how, is it a scheme of benevolence which can be carried on, only by keeping up a prejudice against your poor brother, when you would not venture alone into your closets before our Common Father, and praying, say —

We thank thee, O God, for the success which has thus far attended the efforts which have been made to raise up and increase prejudice against the work of thy hand in the person of our colored brethren; — carry it on to a full consummation; but if this cannot be granted, change, thou, then, their color; and in all things pertaining to their form and visage let thy work of Infinite Wisdom be so modified as to adapt itself to the prejudices of us, a happier and more favored portion of the race — that we may thus, be persuaded to love them as brethren belonging to the great family thou hast made.

✱ September 23

Francis Clement Kelley

ROMAN CATHOLIC

November 24, 1870–February 1, 1948

Why would a Roman Catholic priest born on Prince Edward Island in Canada, who had spent most of his ministry in Detroit and Chicago, be appointed Bishop of Oklahoma? Some said it was because he had been a champion of rural mission and was being given an opportunity to put words into practice. Others said it was because the new Archbishop of Chicago thought there was not room enough in his city for himself and a man often described as the best known Roman Catholic priest in America. Whatever the reason, it did not prevent Francis Clement Kelley from continuing to be a major figure in the church. He had already played a role in the post–World War I peace conference in Paris, negotiated with the British Foreign Office over the expulsion of German priests from India, and visited the White House and State Department in Washington to negotiate with President Woodrow Wilson and Secretary of State William Jennings Bryan about American policy in Mexico.

How did a Roman Catholic priest in Chicago become involved in all that? Serving as a chaplain in the National Guard during the Spanish-American War may have given him a taste of life outside his parish. More importantly, his efforts to raise money for his urban congregation in Detroit took him to rural sections of America, alerting him to the church's needs outside cities where the majority of Roman Catholics were then concentrated. When he suggested an organization to provide such support, he was encouraged to found it himself, and the result was the Catholic Church Extension Society, with a central office in Chicago and a staff of 200. Raising funds and responding to pleas for help made Kelley a national figure.

When religious refugees from the Mexican Revolution flooded into Texas, the Church Extension Society came to their help. Neither American nor Vatican diplomats in 1910 were particularly sensitive to the issue. A member of the Vatican press corps told Kelley that Mexicans were simply "ungovernable" while an American vice-counsel reported that the church was the worst thing in Mexico "next to prostitution." A special advisor sent there by President Wilson told him that what the country needed was Protestantism. Kelley, on the other hand, saw a church in danger of being extinguished, with clergy fleeing for their lives. His efforts to provide funds and sanctuary made him the chosen spokesperson for the Mexican hierarchy who called him "the guardian angel" of their church.

For some 25 years, the church in Mexico continued to look to Kelley for help and he provided it, crossing swords with Wilson more than once. Yet he had time for a wide range of other activities. His friends included such unlikely companions as the cynical journalist, H. L. Mencken, and the free-thinking oilman, Frank Phillips. He sponsored the building of the first radically new church building in America, negotiated Roman Catholic involvement in the Boy Scouts of America, rescued the National Catholic Welfare Conference from bankruptcy, gave the invocation at two national political conventions, and used the new medium of radio to broadcast his sermons. Somehow, he also found time to write 18 widely distributed books. Two of these brought the trials of the Mexican church to a wide audience, while another included a train wreck, a veiled woman, diplomats, and secret agents. He regretted only that his administrative duties permitted him to make few converts and that his writing had not produced the "perfect book of apologetics."

Readings from the writings of Francis Clement Kelley

Will it do for you to carry on as your predecessors did, to be the quiet head of a diocese full of parishes and pastors who, Sunday after Sunday, go on acting as if they had no care or duty but to see that Masses are said on time, sacraments administered, children catechized, sick attended, interest on the debt paid, and five minute *ferverinos* preached? Your predecessors saw to these things. They gave little or no thought to the "other sheep" who do not seem to want their ministration. . . . Nevertheless, there were the few shepherds who did go out to the "other sheep" in spite of the fact that the effort had to be crowded in between insistent duties within the fold. We know who these men were and we hold their memory sacred. Why not, now that we have the clergy we need, and now that the bleating from outside is sounding nearer and clearer, why *not*, I say, imitate that few?

A vain man can declaim, but he cannot preach. He can split the ears, but he cannot reach the heart. He can send a congregation out saying, "How lovely!" but he cannot get them to say, "O Lord, forgive me."

The stern theologian with his measuring rod and his scissors will always be with us. We cannot make him either laugh or make him weep. He just won't descend to eloquence. He walks among us as straight as a ramrod with his eyes to the firmament. He won't pick the flowers by the roadside to color his wisdom. . . . We couldn't do without the theologian but most of us wouldn't want to be like him. We have to play. We have to sing. The path would be tiresome without laughter to brighten it. Not all writers can ignore the weather and take sun, shade and storm, as indifferently as does the theologian. Indeed not many readers either. The truth can be reasoned, declaimed, or chanted. It often smiles.

Remember always that it is not yourself for whom you are writing but your readers. There would be no value in writing what only you would understand. Write to convince others or you waste your time. It is a sin to waste time.... Find the highest and noblest objective and try to serve it. Mine was and still is the keeping and spreading of the faith.

✪ *September 24*

Clara Louise Maass

LUTHERAN

June 28, 1876–August 24, 1901

Clara Maass entered the relatively new field of nursing when she was just 17 years old as a way to give expression to her faith in practical acts of caring for others. Her exceptional skill and dedication earned her the title of head nurse at Newark German Hospital by the age of 21. Most people would have found her position challenging enough, but Clara felt called to use her nurse's training in the United States Army. She served in Florida, Cuba, and the Philippines during the Spanish-American War. Peacetime might have prompted another person to return to a safer civilian medical career, but not Clara Maass. In 1900, Major William Gorgas, a sanitation officer, requested her assistance in Cuba. He wanted her to investigate the cause of yellow fever, a devastating disease whose origin was as yet unknown.

One theory of the time was that the malady was spread by personal contact, but a Cuban doctor, Carlos Juan Finlay, suspected that it might be transmitted by mosquito bites. A crude but effective test was proposed — find human subjects to be bitten by infected mosquitoes and see if they became ill. Clara Maass was the only American woman to volunteer. She did in fact become ill, but recovered. In August of 1901 she again offered herself to be bitten. This time, she succumbed to the fever in ten days. Her sacrifice permitted researchers finally to establish the cause and therefore create a means to prevent yellow fever.

Jesus tells us, "Greater love has no one than this, that he lay down his life for his friends" (John 15:13). A fitting epitaph for Clara Maass might be: "Greater love has no one than this, that she lay down her life for generations of complete strangers." We might find it foolish for a skilled and compassionate nurse to risk death when she might have allowed less "valuable" people to be the guinea pigs. Prudence is a virtue. Yet the wisdom of Christ can be foolishness to the world. In the face of an ongoing epidemic, with the prospect of certain death for generations to come, rash courage can become holy obedience.

Martyrdom is not suicide. Risking death to serve others has always been part of Christian faith. It is based not on hopelessness or despair, but the confidence that faith, courage, and compassion can be the fabric from which God will weave a tapestry of blessing. The loss of Clara Maass deprived American medicine of a fine practitioner. Nevertheless, her willingness to help control yellow fever gained the lives of untold numbers who would otherwise have been its victims.

When Jesus calls us to "take up your cross," this can mean many things. For most people, it probably involves a steady, practical course of daily service. But for some, it can mean sacrifice of one's very life for others. It is surely no shame that Clara's classmates and colleagues labored all their lives as nurses in clean hospitals, safe at home. Their dedication, too, saved lives. But Clara's willingness to give up her life in the quest for advances in medical knowledge must be seen as a faithful response to Christ's call to "follow me."

✪ *September 25*

Melville B. Cox

METHODIST

November 9, 1799–July 21, 1833

Melville Cox may well have had one of the shortest missionary careers. He sailed for Liberia in November of 1832, arrived in Monrovia four months later, and died after only four months in Africa. Yet in those four months he had held a camp meeting, started regular services, established a Sunday School, and put a mission strategy in place. In fact, he had done all that in a few weeks. Thereafter, he was too sick to accomplish much more. He had been seriously ill with tuberculosis for several years before leaving the United States and contracted malaria soon after arriving in Africa. But Cox was a man with nothing to lose. He had lost his wife and child not long before and knew his own death could not be far away. This simply increased his determination to make sure that whatever time he had left would count for something.

A student told Cox he would die if he went to Africa. Cox responded, "If I die in Africa, you must come and write my epitaph." When the student asked what that epitaph should be, Cox replied in words that became a watchword for Methodists interested in mission: "Let a thousand die before Africa be given up!"

Born in Maine, raised on a farm, and educated only in the local school, Cox learned to love books and worked for a while in a bookstore. His parents had been among the first Methodist converts in Maine and Cox agonized over his salvation until at 19, "God, for Christ's sake, forgave my sins, and imparted, to my soul 'peace and joy in the Holy Ghost,' while, almost from the depths of despair, I was pleading for mercy alone in the woods." Two years later, he delivered his first sermon and a few months later was licensed as a local preacher. But tuberculosis hampered his activities, so he moved south, hoping that a warmer climate might restore his health. He preached for a while in Virginia but again tuberculosis prevented him from working as he would have liked.

The Methodist Church had established a mission society in 1819 and raised funds to support a missionary but had not found anyone to send. In 1831, Cox volunteered to serve in South America, but the bishop to whom he spoke persuaded him that the need in Africa was greater. So Cox became the first missionary sent to Africa by American Methodists. Though his time proved short, his witness inspired so many others that when he died, five missionaries were sent out to replace him.

A reading from the diary of Melville Cox

Half past three: — *I have seen Liberia, and live.* It rises up, as yet, but like a cloud of heaven.

Saturday, 9. — Rev. Brother Williams, the acting governor of the colony, has very kindly given me up his own room, until I can obtain a house. The governor bids me board with him.

Sunday, 10. — I can scarcely realize that I have attended church in Liberia, and heard the gospel where, twelve years since, were heard only the shouts of the pagan, or perhaps the infidel prayers of the mussulman. But why wonder? God's light and truth have long since received that divine impetus which will stop only with the conversion of a world.

Tuesday, 12. — I love Liberia more than ever. It is humble in its appearance, compared with Bathurst and Free Town; its buildings are smaller, and have less neatness, less taste, and less comfort about them. But, after all, I doubt if this be a real fault. The emigrants were mostly poor on their arrival, and necessity, in the true spirit of the pilgrims of New England, as the mother of virtue, compelled them to be economical. Time and industry will remedy the evil, if evil it be. The great question is — Is there a good foundation? are there *resources* in Liberia for a great and growing republic. I have no doubt of it. There is, however, much yet to be done. We need missions — missions by white men here. We need, too, schools and *white* teachers in them. Should, a gracious God spare my life, I propose —

1. To establish a mission at Grand Bassa, to connect with it a school, and to give the care of both into the hands of a local preacher who has just arrived from Virginia.

2. To establish the "New York Mission" at Sego, on the Niger. Our brother, to get there, must go by the way of the Gambia river. He can ascend this river within ten days' walk of the Tanen. At Tenda, Mr. Grant, a merchant at Bathurst, on the Gambia, and a great friend of the Methodists, has a factory; and by the time our missionary can get there, he will have another at Sego.

3. I want to establish a school here, which will connect with it agriculture and art. I propose the Maine Wesleyan Seminary as a model, as near as may be. There should be a large farm. This, in a few years, would support the whole school. There must also be shoemakers, tanners, blacksmiths, carpenters, &c. The native children must be taken and boarded, kept entirely clear from their parents or associates, and bound to the school until they are eighteen or twenty-one.
4. I have another mission on my mind, either for the interior or at Cape Mount. I am not yet satisfied, which is the better place.

I have purchased a mission house at Monrovia for which I shall draw on the Society for five hundred dollars. It has connected with it considerable land, left by the devoted Ashman for missionary purposes. I consider the purchase as particularly providential, and worth, at least, to the mission, a thousand dollars.

✪ *September 26*

Abby Kelly Foster

QUAKER

January 15, 1811–January 14, 1887

In common with many young women in the middle of the 19th century, Abby Kelly Foster was raised on a farm, provided with a good education, and became a teacher. But as a Quaker, Foster had been exposed to a tradition of dissent. When William Lloyd Garrison's *Liberator* came to her attention, her passions were aroused by descriptions of slavery's evils. She became the secretary of the Lynn Anti-Slavery Society, and, in 1838, founded the New England Anti-Resistant Society (an extreme pacifist group).

Renowned for her charm, grace, intellect, and dignity, Foster did not shy away from difficult issues then usually considered outside the proper realm of feminine concerns. She lectured before mixed audiences of men and women — gatherings known in some circles as "promiscuous audiences." Within a couple of years, in 1839, Foster's interests expanded to include women's rights. Her lectures are credited with the conversion of many women to both feminist and abolitionist causes.

In 1840, Foster's appointment to the Board of the American Anti-Slavery Society caused a schism in that body, where many felt women should not be placed in positions of authority. Foster relocated to Ohio to carry on her work there. She preferred traveling and lecturing with African American orators, whose testimonies carried more moral weight than those of white speakers at white gatherings. She became an eyewitness to racial prejudice, watching the kind of treatment her colleagues received. Frederick Douglass and Sojourner Truth* were among her speaking companions. Douglass called Foster "perhaps the most successful of us. Her youth and simple

Quaker beauty, combined with her wonderful earnestness, her large knowledge and great logical power bore down all opposition wherever she spoke, though she was pelted with foul eggs and no less foul words from the noisy mobs which attended us."

Foster's husband, Stephen, was equally committed both to abolition and women's suffrage. The pair began to attend worship uninvited to raise the issue of slavery. Ignoring orders to stop their disruptions, they were sometimes arrested or simply dragged outside. Foster learned to let her body go limp on such occasions, requiring her opponents to haul her out of meetings.

For Foster, slavery was an ethical issue. She believed that if slaves were freed simply as a tactic to preserve the Union, or for other political motives, racism would contaminate the entire nation and its future. From our vantage point, her concern seems well-founded. In 1845, the Fosters moved to the Western Reserve, where she established the Western Antislavery Society. In short order, she also helped start a noteworthy publication, *The Antislavery Bugle.*

Suffragettes and abolitionists often gathered at conventions to encourage and challenge one another. The mainstream press held such meetings in derision, as the following report on the women's rights convention in Worcester Massachusetts (where Foster was one of the speakers) demonstrates:

> THE NEW YORK HERALD, Friday, October 25, 1850, WOMAN'S RIGHTS CONVENTION. AWFUL COMBINATION OF SOCIALISM, ABOLITIONISM, AND INFIDELITY.
>
> *The Pantalettes Striking for the Pantaloons, Bible and Constitution Repudiated.*

At that meeting Foster was quoted as saying:

> I do not talk of woman's rights, but of human rights, the rights of human beings. I do not come to ask [for] them, but to demand them; not to get down on my knees and beg for them, but to claim them. "Sauce for the goose is sauce for the gander." We have our rights, and the right to revolt, as did our fathers against King George the Third — the right to rise up and cut the tyrants' throats. On this subject I scorn to talk like a woman. We must give them the truth, and not twaddle. We must not be mealy mouthed with our tyrants in broadcloth and tight clothes.

The paper went on to comment:

> In short, in the harangue of Abby, she simply demanded that men and women should be treated as human beings all alike — that the sexes should be forgotten in society — that property and votes and offices, civil, religious and military, even to the right of cutting throats, should belong to woman as well as to man. She urged that the work should be commenced by educating both sexes together, and that all distinction in society between man and woman should be abolished, and that a woman was just as well qualified to be President as a man.

Combining suffrage for women with freedom for blacks struck many as a tactical mistake because it offended a large segment of the white male population that might otherwise be inclined to consider women's suffrage. Some people, then as now, considered gender equality and race to be entirely separate matters. Even women who understood that justice for slaves was morally right feared that combining it with women's rights hampered the progress of both causes. Of course, some white women did not accept that blacks should have the same freedoms they wanted for themselves. Abolitionists, likewise, feared their cause might be tainted by the struggle for women's rights. A few, Foster prominent among them, believed that justice did not have clear gender or racial boundaries. As the civil rights movement would affirm more than a century later, no one is fully free when injustice is tolerated for any group or person.

Foster believed God would not speak up for one group's emancipation while remaining silent about another. She cried out for full participation in society, culture, and politics for women and men of all conditions and backgrounds. Nothing less would satisfy the divine mandate for justice.

✷ *September 27*

Jonathan Dickinson

PRESBYTERIAN

April 22, 1688–October 7, 1747

The Reformed tradition flowing out of John Calvin's Geneva arrived on American shores in at least three separate but related strains: the Congregational Church established itself in New England, the Dutch Reformed Church planted itself in New York, and the Presbyterians, coming from Scotland and Ireland, established themselves in New Jersey and further south. The Great Awakening created more tensions among and within these traditions as "New Lights" and "Old Lights" debated the new type of evangelism promulgated by George Whitfield and his followers.

Jonathan Dickinson was born in Massachusetts, graduated from Yale as a Congregationalist, and was ordained in that tradition when he moved to New Jersey, in 1709, to serve a congregation in Elizabeth (then called Elizabethtown). Eight years later, however, he persuaded his congregation to become Presbyterian, arguing that this denomination offered the advantage of a structured relationship with other churches. Dickinson became a leader in the Philadelphia presbytery, and also in the larger body of which it was a member, the Synod of Philadelphia, of which he was twice elected moderator.

Dickinson was a moderate who, although preferring the Presbyterian approach, opposed the 1721 proposal that every minister in the Synod of

Philadelphia should be required "to give his hearty assent" to the West-minster Confession of Faith. While holding to those doctrines himself, he believed, on principle, that the imposition of any creed was an infringement of the individual clergyman's rights. In the same way, when the Great Awakening swept through in 1738, Dickinson defended the new movement while opposing its more violent expressions. His temperament is evident in the title of one of his best-known books, *The Reasonableness of Christianity.* Here, he writes, "No one of whatever sect or party ever did or ever will get to heaven without true and unfeigned faith; nor will any true believer, however denominated, fall short of eternal life. Faith transforms the soul into the divine nature, and God cannot be displeased with his own image, wherever it is."

A man of many parts, Dickinson served his community as pastor, lawyer, and physician, instructing young men preparing for any of these professions. Eventually, he decided that an institution was needed to provide a more structured educational system so he worked with others to create the College of New Jersey, later Princeton University. The new college met in Dickinson's manse, using his library and making his parlor serve as the classroom, his dining room as the refectory. He himself served as its first president but died less than six months after taking up the position. The parish he had served for nearly 40 years mourned him as one who had been its "glory and joy."

A reading from *The Reasonableness of Christianity, in four sermons* by Jonathan Dickinson

Concern yourselves as little as possible with matters of doubtful disputes: But where you must be of a party choose the charitable side.

There will be different sentiments among Christians, as long as we are on this side Jordan. We shall not come to an exact unity in all articles of faith, until that which is in part shall be done away; and we know even as also we are known. But can't we bear with the different thoughts, as well as different complexions of those that agree with us in the essentials of Christianity; and receive one another as Christ also received us, to the glory of God? Have we no way to prove ourselves disciples of the Prince of Peace, but by wranglings, contentions, strife and debate? This is a direct means to destroy all practical religion; and wholly root out all serious vital piety.

It's true, we can't ourselves be of two contrary persuasions. It's of necessity, that we part ways with those, in some disputed points, with whom we may agree in the main foundations of our faith and hope; and with whom we hope to join in eternal anthems of praise. But how shall plain and weak Christians act in this case? How shall they know with what party to join? It's impossible that I should now descend to particular directions in this case; I must therefore content myself with commending that general rule of the apostle, 2 Timothy 2:22: *follow righteousness, faith, charity, peace, with them that call on the Lord out of a pure heart.* Never herd yourselves with those that are for cutting off all the Protestant churches, but themselves, from the fold of Christ; nor expect it to be saved by damming everybody but yourselves

Finally, constantly and fervently committ your souls to the keeping and conduct of our Lord Jesus Christ.

We are liable to a thousand mistakes; but we have a safe and sure pilot, upon whom we may boldly depend. *If we commit our way to him, he will bring it pass.* If he leaves us to lesser mistakes, he will save us from damning errors, unless our own sins and sloth put us out of his protection. We must therefore not only carefully and diligently try ourselves; but with greatest earnestness and constancy implore the directions of his holy spirit; and wrestle with him by earnest prayer, that he will *search us and try us, and see if there be any wicked way in us, and lead us in the way everlasting:* that he will *guide us by his counsel, and afterward bring us to glory.* And in that way, we may with courage conclude with the apostle, 2 Timothy 1:12. *I know whom I have trusted; and am persuaded, that he is able to keep that which I have committed to him, against that day.*

✪ September 28 ───────────────────────────────

Richard McSorley

ROMAN CATHOLIC

October 2, 1914–October 17, 2002

The imminence of one's execution, Samuel Johnson remarked, wonderfully concentrates the mind. Richard McSorley learned this early in life, and though he did not die after all, his entire approach to life was transformed. McSorley was reared in a strict Roman Catholic home, where attendance at daily Mass was expected and one's elders were respected. At 18, he joined the Society of Jesus to study. Seven years later, having earned his Ph.D., he was sent to the Philippines to teach. During World War II, he was captured by Japanese forces there, imprisoned, tortured, and very nearly executed. At the end of the war, he returned to the United States and was ordained a priest.

One can only imagine how his imprisonment affected him emotionally, since he rarely referred to it. But McSorley did talk about his reactions to conditions in his native America. He had been raised to believe that God wanted his followers to strive for justice, peace, human dignity, and courage. Yet in McSorley's Maryland parish, these values seemed to be absent, and he was horrified by the overt racial discrimination he saw all around him. Both in the church community and in the wider society, the degradation of African Americans was too consistent and too obvious to avoid. Other whites might overlook it, but McSorley was unable to ignore so clear a violation of God's intentions for us. Black people received communion only after all the whites had and were forced to sit in a separate part of the nave. He was also shocked to discover racism in himself. He had fired an African American cleaning woman because he wanted volunteers to do the work. It had not occurred to him that she needed the money and that his act might affect her family. One cold day, when McSorley was having trouble lighting the fire, the only person who volunteered to help him was the husband of this same woman. The discrepancy between his callous decision and the nobility and grace of this man acted as a wake-up call.

McSorley's words and actions began to reflect his growing discomfort with racism. He threatened to publicize a local ambulance company's refusal to help a black woman, forcing them to give her aid. He called upon the Roman Catholic establishment publicly and officially to oppose segregation. The Ku Klux Klan came close to assassinating him.

McSorley was powerfully affected by the work of Martin Luther King, Jr.* It reaffirmed his dedication to the struggle for equality and the dignity of every human being. As often happens in following Jesus, an awareness of one cause leads to perceptions of others. The heart that yearns for God's kingdom is seldom satisfied with a narrow agenda. In the years of the Cold War, the arms race between the Soviet Union and the United States kept escalating. Both sides were ostensibly reluctant to use their growing stock-piles of nuclear weapons because of a strategy called "Mutually Assured Destruction" (MAD). The theory was that if both sides knew a nuclear war was unwinnable, neither side would dare start one, but opponents of this thinking worried that a technological error or human mistake might unleash the awful power of the bombs and missiles.

McSorley began to question the justification for building nuclear weapons at all, much less threatening to use them. He believed that the church needed to pay more attention to Jesus's teaching: love your enemies and do good to those who hurt you. But in that era, the Roman Catholic Church subscribed to the "Just War Theory," which holds that Christians can participate in a war if it meets certain conditions: it must be declared by an official leader; it must be a last resort to other means of settling the problem; it must protect civilians; and it must not cause more damage than whatever evil it was designed to destroy. McSorley set out to demonstrate the absurdity of a Christian "Just War" by proposing that we also teach a "Just Adultery" ethic. Since it would be unthinkable to support "Just Adultery," it would be, he suggested, even more ridiculous to support "Just War."

As an outgrowth of his passion for peace, McSorley established the Roman Catholic movement known as Pax Christi — the Peace of Christ. His resistance did not, of course, attain its goal of making the church fully committed to peace and justice in all its forms, but his witness continues to challenge each generation to confront its own impulses to violence and injustice, and to renew the gospel vision of a reconciled humanity.

A reading from Richard McSorley

The taproot of violence in our society today is our intent to use nuclear weapons. Once we have agreed to that, all other evil is minor in comparison. Until we squarely face the question of our consent to use nuclear weapons, any hope of large-scale improvement of public morality is doomed to failure. Even the possession of weapons that cannot be morally used is wrong. They are a threat to peace and might even be the cause of nuclear war. The nuclear weapons of Communists may destroy our bodies, but the intent to use nuclear weapons destroys our souls.

I see my mission in life, as God has made it known to me, to help make the Catholic church what it should be, a peace church. To be Christians means to have respect for life in all its forms and in today's nuclear age that means Christians must become active witnesses for peace and must firmly oppose all forms of war.

The trouble is that the church gives a false image of Christ. The church never says that war is good and Christ is a war-maker. They never do that. But they don't say anything. What's behind it is that the church wants to benefit from the state — tax exemption is the bribe for silence. So you have a kind of dance of death going on between the church and the state. They don't step on each other's toes. The state wants background support from the churches: "God bless your wars. God be with you." It all started with the emperor of Rome giving buildings to the church in the third century under Constantine. The church has never recovered.

✖ September 29 ─────────────────────────────

H. Baxter Liebler

EPISCOPALIAN

November 26, 1889–November 21, 1982

"Quirky" and "eccentric" were among the adjectives applied to H. Baxter Liebler. He wore his hair long and tied back in the Navajo fashion and strode the desert in a cassock and broad-brimmed hat. His vision was far ahead of his time, and he was totally committed to his ministry. Even as a child, he had been fascinated by stories about Native Americans, but he was 53 before he found a way to realize his desires. Liebler started out in business in Manhattan, then became an Episcopal priest and founded a parish he served for 25 years in Greenwich, Connecticut.

On a vacation in the southwest in 1942, he discovered what he had been looking for: a people outside the purview of both church and state. The next year, Liebler returned with a small team of committed men and women able to start a school, a clinic, and a church, striving to make God's love real to a people who had never heard the gospel.

Liebler learned the notoriously difficult Navajo language, and their culture, incorporating whatever he could into the prayers and liturgy he used. The Gloria of his eucharist was composed of Plains Indian melodies, the Sanctus was an Omaha melody, and the Agnus Dei came from the music of the Zuni. A Navajo man said of the chants in Liebler's Eucharistic celebration. "This is where the Navajo and white man's prayers meet.... They go around together sunwise, and then they reach out in all directions."

Liebler said of the Navajo he first encountered,

> They were, to outward appearance at least, a happy, picturesque and contented people, living from day to day by herding their sheep and goats, with ample leisure to gamble, attend native ceremonials or perhaps put in a whole day riding by wagon to a trading post, bargaining and trading, perhaps staying overnight (every trading post had a hogan nearby), with a colorful religion full of charming ceremonies, songs and prayers quite adequate to all their needs. Actually they were deeply suspicious, undernourished, the most illiterate of all racial groups in the continental United States, with a high incidence of tuberculosis and other lethal diseases, as well as of such afflictions as trachoma, pterygium (almost unknown elsewhere on the continent) and with a religion which, for all its beauty, has no place for self-denial or for help to the needy outside of one's own clan.
>
> These sad features were masked under genial smiles derived from a fatalistic outlook on life. One cannot fight "Washeen-doan," and one must accept things as they are: be nice to the white man, and get out of him what one can before he fleeces you.

Liebler's school and clinic were not central to his vision. When the government finally began to establish state-run facilities in the area, he was quite content to let it take over such programs. He was there to proclaim the gospel and to draw together a community of believers who understood the Christian faith. For Liebler, that meant building up a worshiping community and he would not let artificial barriers prevent the Navajo from coming. He wrote:

> The mass was open to all who wished to attend, and in countless instances fulfilled the words of Christ, "I, if I be lifted up, will draw all men unto me." The most completely uninstructed Navajo, entering our church for the first time, knew at once that he was confronted by worship. This was no gazing meeting, no debate or gabfest; it was a group intent upon the Way that draws all men to the Infinite.

Liebler's description of his first baptism shows his philosophy at work.

> As we approached the hogan there was the unmistakable sound of a medicine man at work — song and rattle.... As we entered, the medicine man stopped

his song.... There was hardly a bit of flesh left on the poor wasted body. The medicine man looked up at me with a welcoming smile, summoning his best English. "Me make prayer good. You make Jesus-talk." Holding up two fingers closed jointly together, he added, "Two good make strong good." ... Then, as best I could, I explained what baptism means — the regeneration of the soul, the pouring in of sanctifying grace, incorporation into the mystical body of Christ.... But I could see they were grasping at any straw. So I told the medicine man that I would make Jesus talk which would make the body's soul holy and ready to meet our Creator. If God willed to restore health despite the neglect the child suffered, we should be thankful; if in his wisdom this little one's soul should be the first of the northern Navajos to enter into the very presence of God and to offer his continuous prayers for the redemption of the Navajo people, that would be reason for even deeper gratitude.

All of the traditional ceremonies were used — salt, oils, white cloth, candle — in addition, of course, to the essential water and form of words. The flickering light of the fire was reflected in the silver coins and buttons on the mother's velveteen blouse and in the eyes of the other children, the medicine man and the parents. It was a sight never to be forgotten — the first baptism. And the mode seemed prophetic of our whole approach to this people: the cooperating medicine man, the simplicity of surroundings, together with a scrupulous observance of traditional details of ceremonial.

Eventually, hundreds were baptized and thousands influenced by his work. When he began his ministry, the prevailing philosophy had been that the Navajo should become "Americanized" and learn to fit into the prevailing culture. Liebler saw it differently. "Deepest respect for Navajo ways and traditions" were to be encouraged, "excepting only such elements as are opposed to sound hygiene or Christian morals."

By the time Liebler retired in 1962, his outlook had become widely accepted. The Episcopal Church organized a Navajoland Area Mission in 1979 with the first Navajo priest, Steven Tsosie Plummer, who later became its first bishop. Meanwhile, Liebler moved deeper still into the Navajo area and created a retreat center and a new mission, where he worked until his death at the age of 92

✪ September 30

Helen Barrett Montgomery

BAPTIST

July 31, 1861–October 19, 1934

There are so many translations and paraphrases of the Bible in existence today that we might suppose — wrongly — that it was ever so. In fact, throughout the late 19th and early 20th centuries there were few alternatives to the King James Version. Thus, when Helen Barrett Montgomery was teaching a class of underprivileged boys and found it difficult to get them interested in the Bible, she decided she would have to make her own translation. It was remarkable that anyone should make that effort, much less a woman, but still more remarkable that Montgomery's translation proved so innovative in a number of ways still followed today.

In her work, Montgomery's aim was "to consider young people, busy Sunday-School teachers, and foreigners, and to try to make [the Bible] plain." She wanted an edition that would be "easy to be carried in the pocket or in a hand-bag, to stimulate the daily reading of the Gospels." Her New Testament was arranged in paragraphs, with verse numbers relegated to the margins. Old Testament quotations are in italics and poetry is indented to distinguish it from prose. Speech is indicated with quotation marks and footnotes are provided to explain matters that may puzzle readers. Sometimes square brackets are used also to clarify terms or provide information that may be needed for understanding.

Montgomery was also ahead of her time in her translation and interpretation of passages that had been used to justify a subordinate place for women. So, when Paul writes to the Corinthians "let the women keep silence in the churches," Montgomery interprets the material as a quotation from the Corinthians' letter to Paul with which he disagrees. Some of these ideas have become generally accepted by biblical scholars, but they were highly controversial at the time. Although Montgomery was the first woman to translate the New Testament from Greek to English, she would be noteworthy quite apart from that. She was a friend of Susan B. Anthony* and active in the woman's suffrage movement. She became the first woman elected to public office in Rochester, New York, and the first woman pastor in her denomination. She also served as president of her denomination and for ten years as president of the Woman's American Baptist Foreign Mission Society. She wrote a number of books on mission and prayer. She organized the first World Day of Prayer, still an annual event in many American churches. For all her scholarly and political achievements, prayer remained central to her life.

A reading from *Prayer and Missions* by Helen Barrett Montgomery

The Bible is itself the world's supreme book of prayer. Prayer conditions it, accompanies it, is interwoven throughout its texture, permeates it like air or sunshine. Without the Bible our very technique of prayer was wanting; without it our supreme examples of victorious prayer would fail us; without it the whole argument and encouragement for praying men would be lacking. When compared with the whole experience of the race in prayer, the Bible seems like a sunlit garden set in the midst of a desert. It over-tops the prayer heights of other sacred books as the Himalayas soar above the foothills. The world turns to the Bible to find its deepest expression of the prayer-life.

When one studies the phenomenon of the Bible's supremacy in the matter of prayer, many questions rise. How came it that this weak nation, living in this tiny land, came to write the prayer history of the race? How came it that hymns and prayers and temple ritual written for this little people came to be adopted by the race as its best expression of worship and petition? How came it that the example of patriarch and prophet and priest and apostle came to be searched by all who would discover the laws of prayer? The simplest, most sufficient answer is contained in the Bible itself: "Holy men of old spoke as they were moved by the Spirit of God."

The inspiration of the Bible is implicit in the facts. The record was "God-breathed," and so is profitable to all mankind.

Now the Bible, which is the vehicle of the gospel, brings to light an inner message of prayer which is dynamic. The Bible may bring the knowledge of Christ to a nation or an individual, but if there is no appropriation of prayer-power there is no life, no movement. It is important that men should know the gospel, it is more important that they should pray the gospel. If they pray, the gospel proceeds; if they do not pray the gospel halts. Its victories are wholly wrought by prayer; its defeats proceed from prayerlessness.

The church needs to "recapture its first fine, careless rapture" of prayer. Many things have led to the neglect of prayer; the swift and only half-digested progress of scientific knowledge, the sudden accumulation of material gains, the failure to maintain habits of church-going and Bible reading; the decay of family religion. But its neglect, if continued, is fatal. Our only power, now or ever, is of God, and any study which will bring professing Christians fact to face with the facts will bring us to our knees.

October

✸ *October 1*

Albert Barnes

PRESBYTERIAN

December 1, 1798–December 24, 1870

Few denominations have been as concerned with doctrinal purity as the Presbyterian Church. Division and reunion have marked its history. Albert Barnes lived through some of the bitterest controversies, and was, in fact, often at the center of them, since he was a widely published author, a seminary professor, and finally moderator of the General Assembly. Nonetheless, through his personal humility (he allowed no academic titles to be used with his name) and his combination of fairness and firmness, he managed to gain respect, even admiration from all who knew him.

Barnes came from upstate New York. He was a skeptic in his early years, but while he was in college, the Second Great Awakening swept the country and he experienced a deep change. This transformation caused him to abandon his plan to enter the law and dedicate himself to preparation for ordained ministry. Graduating from Hamilton College, he went on to Princeton Seminary. After five years as pastor of the Presbyterian Church in Morristown, New Jersey, he was called to the First Presbyterian Church of Philadelphia and remained connected with that church for the rest of his life. While serving in Morristown, he began work on a series of commentaries on the Bible that eventually sold more than half a million copies in the United States, even more in Great Britain, and was translated into the languages of France, China, and India.

Barnes wrote that

> the existence of different opinions on the doctrines of religion in the Christian
> Church has always been referred to, by certain persons, as a reproach against
> Christianity; but with little reason. If such a difference is a reproach at all,
> it should not be regarded as such against the Christian religion, but against
> the human mind; but it is against neither. It is better that mind should be
> independent and free, though it does work differently; it is better that grace
> should be free, though it develops itself in different forms and manifestations,
> than that there should be dead, and lifeless, and cold uniformity.

"Bigotry, and selfishness, and pride, and the love of power are always
present," he observed, but even apart from these, difference and division
are inevitable.

> The attempt to make all men see those profound and mysterious doctrines
> alike, whether by argument, or by force, has thus far always failed, and in
> the present condition of things must always extensively fail. Men have dif-
> ferent kinds of mental structure; they possess different temperaments; they
> receive a different education; they see objects from different points of view;
> they estimate the value of things by different measures.

Though Barnes could be tolerant of theological difference, in regard to slavery he was unyielding. "The present," he wrote four years before the Civil
War broke out, "is eminently a time when the views of every man on the subject of slavery should be uttered in unambiguous tones.... There has never
been a time ... when so much guilt would be incurred by silence." Slavery
was "evil in its origin, evil in its bearing on the morals of men, evil in its
relation to religion, evil in its influence on the master and on the slave — on
the body and the soul — on the North and the South, evil in its relation to
time and its relations to eternity."

After the war, however, Barnes found religion dramatically changed: "The
collision now between Christianity and the world is substantially a new
form of collision; the attack is from a new quarter, and with new weapons;
the questions involved are deeper than those with which the church has
heretofore grappled; the results of the conflict, so far as we can see, are to
be final."

Whereas many reacted with anger, however, Barnes understood that
human beings could misunderstand both their own faith and the questions
at issue. Called to deliver a series of lectures in 1870 on the "Evidences of
Christianity in the Nineteenth Century," he took care to point out that it
is "always a fair question, when there is an apparent collision between the
Bible and science, whether the collision is, in fact, between the scientific truth
and the *Bible*, or between that truth and the prevailing and received *interpretation* of the Bible. The one is by no means to be assumed as synonymous
with the other."

This careful approach to controversy not only won Barnes widespread respect but served the Christian cause by enabling church people to grasp a deeper level of their faith and bring it to bear more intelligently on the issues of the world around them.

✪ *October 2*

John Joseph Hughes

ROMAN CATHOLIC

June 24, 1797–January 3, 1864

"I wanted to come to a country," said John Joseph Hughes, "in which no stigma of inferiority would be impressed on my brow, simply because I professed one creed or another." The United States was not like that, unfortunately, but it was less prejudiced than Hughes's native Ireland. Hughes was 20 years old when he came to Maryland with his family. He found work as a stone mason and gardener at St. Mary's Seminary. Hoping to study for the priesthood, he applied for admission but was turned down. Not far from the seminary was a rock where Mother Elizabeth Seton, the first American canonized by the Roman Church as a saint, often spent time in prayer and meditation. She met the young immigrant one day, was impressed by his character, and spoke to the seminary officials on his behalf.

Admitted to the seminary in 1820 and ordained in 1826, Hughes was assigned to a parish in Philadelphia. The City of Brotherly Love was hardly a place where everyone could expect to be treated equally, but the young priest knew that it was possible to protest against inequality and appeal to the ideals that had animated the founders of the new republic. His public debate with a leading Protestant clergyman gained attention from the Vatican, as well as the former Dean of his seminary, now Bishop of New York. In 1838, at the age of 41, John Hughes became New York's assisting bishop. Four years later, he was made the fourth bishop of the diocese.

New York City was in the throes of enormous change. A flood of immigrants from Ireland faced a countering tide of nativist prejudice. Rioters in Philadelphia had burned down two Irish Catholic churches and were threatening to move northward. Hughes notified the mayor that he had stationed armed guards around each of his churches and would meet fire with fire. The mayor made sure there was no need for the bishop to make good on the threat.

Hughes felt that the public schools functioned largely for the Protestant establishment. He pressured the government to fund Roman Catholic schools as well. His efforts were defeated, but the legislature went so far as to outlaw all religious instruction in the public schools. It hadn't been what Hughes hoped for, so he redoubled his efforts to establish a parochial school system.

But that was only one area of growth. By the time of his death, Hughes's see had grown so much it was divided into five dioceses. He stayed in New York City, which, though it covered much less area than when he first began, now had 85 priests instead of the 40 he started with. Throughout much of his episcopacy, it was said that he dedicated a new church on the average of one every ten weeks. When he arrived in the city, it had only one religious order; by the time of his death, there were ten. Hughes founded St. Joseph's Seminary as well as the college that became Fordham University. During the Civil War, President Lincoln sent him to England, France, and Spain as a special emissary to keep those countries from intervening on behalf of the Confederacy.

In 1850, the Pope made New York an Archdiocese, and Hughes became the first American Archbishop. His efforts on behalf of Roman Catholics in America were balanced by his attempts to communicate to the Vatican the unique nature of American democracy. By the time of his death, the uneducated young gardener from County Mayo had transformed the church in the largest city of the country and made his mark on the country as a whole. Understandably, his achievements are not indications of a peaceful personality. One of his priests said he was "a tyrant, but with feeling." A biographer called him "the best known, if not exactly the best loved Catholic bishop in the country."

A reading from a report by Archbishop Hughes to the Vatican on the state of the Roman Catholic Church in America

We come now to the Revolutions in Europe. During the period last under consideration [immediately above Hughes had been deploring the excessive immigration of the previous twenty years] their rebound on New York was most perilous to the faith and morals of the people committed to my charge. I cannot help regarding it as a singular protection of Almighty God, and a singular evidence of the interposition of the Blessed Virgin Mary, under whose patronage this Diocese had been especially placed from its origin, under the title of the "Assumption," now, under that of the "Immaculate Conception," that we have escaped the ordeal with so little injury to the principles of our Religion. In this Country, "Liberty" is the watch word, the boast, the pride of all men. The general tone of the Country would seem to require that every man should touch his hat whenever the word "Liberty" is pronounced in his presence. This, you can easily imagine, applies especially to all aspirants for public office, and to the very numerous and ubiquitous class of professional politicians. Sensible men though imbued in heart with the same feeling, yet oftentimes ridicule this extravagant display of it among the classes to which I have referred.

Liberty, in this Country, has a very clear and specific meaning. It is not understood in Europe, as it is here. Here, it means the vindication of personal rights; the fair support of public laws; the maintenance, at all hazards, of public order, according to those laws; the right to change them when they are found to be absurd or oppressive. Such, in brief, is the meaning of the word liberty, as understood by the people of the United States. Of course, you will think of the excesses that have been committed from time to time by mobs, "lynch laws" &c, as marring the correctness of the foregoing statement. But I can assure you that these excesses are regarded, here, as outrages and violations of liberty, the same as they would be in Europe.

✪ October 3

Cynthia Clark Wedel

EPISCOPALIAN

August 26, 1908–August 24, 1986

Throughout the 19th century, women's roles in the church underwent gradual change. Methodist women began to preach, while women of a number of denominations became leaders of the abolitionist and temperance movements. Some organized mission societies and served as missionaries, both at home and abroad. Women's societies in the churches provided opportunities to acquire leadership skills and prepare for more prominent ecclesiastical and secular roles. By the middle of the 20th century, the time had come for women to be treated as equals in the life of the church. "Women's work," argued Cynthia Wedel, should no longer be segregated:

> As the skills of lay people are seen as a great untapped resource for the Church in all its activities, artificial lines between the work of men and women becomes obviously ridiculous. As far as we know, from the earliest days of Christianity, men and women have received precisely the same baptism.

Cynthia Wedel started out in a rather traditional female leadership position: she was director of the Christian education program at her home parish in Evanston, Illinois. Later, however, she eventually moved to New York to work at the Episcopal Church's national offices. There she married an Episcopal priest, Theodore Wedel, and moved with him to Washington when he was made warden of the College of Preachers. Her career blossomed, and she earned a Ph.D. in psychology from George Washington University, taught religion at the National Cathedral School for Girls, became heavily involved as a volunteer in the Girls Scouts and American Red Cross, and a member of the national executive board of the Episcopal Woman's Auxiliary. Her leadership role in the Episcopal Church led to ecumenical involvement. She served as national president of the United Church Women, president of the National Council of Churches (the first woman to do so), a delegate to assemblies of the World Council of Churches, and was an official observer at Vatican Council II.

When arguments about women's ordination became bitter among Episcopalians, Wedel suggested that the church's understanding of ministry would be deepened and enlarged by the presence of both genders in the priesthood. But she insisted that the debate should not overshadow the importance of lay ministry in the church. True to her background in Christian education, she sought ways to bring people together. When Alvin Toffler's best-selling *Future Shock* captured American discomfort with the contemporary world, Cynthia Wedel responded by producing a study guide for parishes entitled *Faith or Fear and Future Shock*.

A reading from *Faith or Fear and Future Shock* by Cynthia Clark Wedel

Human analogies about God are always dangerous, but there is an analogy in the love of good parents for a child. A baby has done nothing himself to earn his parents' love. Their love is poured out freely upon him in care, protection, guidance. He may not be able to express gratitude until he is much older, but he does learn that he can trust his parents, and that he is usually wise when he obeys them. In a sense, all real love between human beings is like this. It is always a free gift. Did you ever earn the love of a friend?

And when we know that someone loves us, we trust such a person.

So, because we are sure of God's love for us we can trust his guiding hand in the new developments of the present and the future. Even though, at the moment, some things which are happening in our world look very bad to us, we can remember that God is in charge and that if we will try to discern his will in the events of our time, we may be able to work with him to accomplish it. Even in the midst of future shock, we are called on to love God with all our heart and soul and mind and strength and to love our neighbors as ourselves.

In our relationships with other people, the Covenant of God has created a community of acceptance, support/concern for justice, love of others, and a sense of mission. The church, the people of God, is a community which can take people frightened and bruised by future shock and help them find a new sense of purpose and strength to cope with the world as it is. In the midst of all the novelty, we can be a community who remembers God's standards of justice, and who shows concern for the integrity and the needs of all his children. We have a deep sense of mission which calls on us to develop new patterns of social life which may overcome some of the unfairness and injustices of the past.

Finally, the fact that we belong to a covenant people can give each of us a deep sense of personal identity. Because I am reconciled to God, and loved and accepted by his people, I know who I am, where I belong, and where I am going in life. I do not have to run after every new fad that comes along in order to try to find myself. And because we can have this inner security and serenity, we will not be afraid as individuals or as the church to speak and act boldly for what we know to be right.

✪ *October 4*

Howard Thurman

BAPTIST

November 18, 1899–April 10, 1981

If Martin Luther King, Jr.,* was the voice of the civil rights movement, Howard Thurman might be considered its theologian. Deeply influenced by the Quaker Rufus Jones* and Mahatma Gandhi, Thurman incorporated their teachings on pacifism and nonviolence into the American Social Gospel movement in such books as *Jesus and the Disinherited* (1949) that suggested ways of combating oppressive forces in society and profoundly affected King and other leaders of the American civil rights movement.

Born in Florida, Thurman was educated at Morehouse College, Rochester Theological Seminary, and Haverford College, where he studied under Rufus Jones. Ordained as a Baptist, Thurman served as pastor of a Baptist parish in Oberlin, Ohio, before becoming professor of religion and director of religious life at Morehouse and Spelman colleges in Atlanta. In 1932, he was made professor of theology and dean of Rankin Chapel at Howard University in Washington. He left that prestigious position to cofound the Church for the Fellowship of All Peoples in San Francisco, a congregation dedicated to breaking down walls that separate human beings on any basis of race, color, creed, or national origin so they could worship together and work for peace. "Do not be silent," Thurman told them; "there is no limit to the power that may be released through you."

In 1953, Thurman moved to Boston University, where he served until his retirement in 1965 as professor of spiritual resources and dean of Marsh Chapel — the first black dean at a traditionally white university. *Life* magazine named him one of the 12 great preachers of the 20th century.

A reading from *Mysticism and the Experience of Love* by Howard Thurman

There is a steady anxiety that surrounds man's experience of love. Sometimes the radiance of love is so soft and gentle that the individual sees himself with all harsh lines wiped away and all limitations blended with his strength in so happy a combination that strength seems to be everywhere and weakness is nowhere to be found. This is a part of the magic, the spell of love. Sometimes the radiance of love kindles old fires that have long since grown cold from the neglect of despair, or new fires are kindled by a hope born full blown without beginning and without ending. Sometimes the radiance of love blesses a life with a vision of its possibilities never dreamed of and never sought, which vision stimulates to new endeavor and summons all latent powers to energize the life at its innermost core.

But there are other ways by which love works its perfect work. It may stab the spirit by calling forth a bitter, scathing self-judgment. The heights to which it calls may seem so high that all incentive is lost and the individual is stricken with an utter hopelessness and despair. It may throw in relief old and forgotten weaknesses which one had accepted, but now they stir in their place to offer themselves as testimony of one's unworthiness and to challenge the love with their embarrassing authenticity. It is at such times that one expects the love to be dimmed under the mistaken notion that love is at long last based upon merit and worth.

Behold the miracle! Love has no awareness of merit or de-merit — it has no scale by which its portion may be weighed or measured. It does not seek to balance giving and receiving. Love loves; that is its nature. But this does not mean that love is blind, naive or pretentious. It does mean that love holds its object securely in its grasp calling all that it sees by its true name but surrounding all with a wisdom born both of its passion and its understanding. Here is no traffic in sentimentality, no catering to weakness or to strength. Instead there is robust vitality that quickens the roots of personality creating an unfolding of the self that redefines, reshapes and makes all things new. Thus the experience is so fundamental in quality that the individual knows that what is happening to him can outlast all things without itself being dissipated or lost.

Whence comes this power which seems to be the point of referral for all experience and the essence of all meaning? No created thing, no single unit of life can be the source of such fullness and completeness. For in the experience itself a man is caught and held by something so much more than he can ever think or be that there is but one word by which its meaning can be encompassed — God. Hence the Psalmist says that as long as the Love of God shines on us undimmed, not only may no darkness obscure but also may we find our way to other hearts at a point in them beyond all weakness and all strength, beyond all that is good and beyond all that is evil. There is no thing outside ourselves, no circumstance, no condition, no vicissitude, that can ultimately separate us from the love of God and from the love of each other. And we pour out our gratitude to God that this is so!

✪ October 5

Eugene Carson Blake

PRESBYTERIAN

November 7, 1906–July 31, 1985

As stated clerk of the Presbyterian Church from 1951 to 1954, president of the National Council of Churches from 1954 to 1966, and secretary of the World Council of Churches from 1966 to 1972, Eugene Carson Blake occupied positions from which he could speak forcefully to American society. But others have held those positions without making nearly the impact that Blake did during those critical years. He became the stated clerk at the time when Senator Joseph McCarthy's influence had reached its peak. Political and religious leaders attempted to avoid coming under his fire, but not Blake, who denounced his malicious influence on the country. In addition, he joined with other Christian leaders to make an early witness against segregation and was arrested for attempting to desegregate an amusement park in Maryland.

When Blake moved on to become president of the National Council of Churches, he used that position also to wage war against racism in American life and to raise questions about the growing American involvement in the war in Vietnam. In 1960, he preached the sermon for which he is best known, calling on four major American denominations — Episcopal, United Presbyterian, United Methodist, and United Church of Christ — to come together to form a body that would be both truly "Catholic" and truly "Reformed." This invitation, issued jointly with Episcopal Bishop James Pike of California, led to the formation of the Consultation on Church Union (COCU) and. much later, to a larger consultation, Churches Uniting in Christ (CUIC). After his retirement in 1972, Blake became active in Bread for the World, a Christian agency seeking to help people in the developing countries. Throughout his ministry, he called on Christians to work with others against injustice and oppression and for greater opportunity for those in need.

A reading from an article entitled "God, Morality, and Politics" by Eugene Carson Blake

Do not misunderstand what I am saying. I am neither a Marxist nor a communist, although I have been charged from time to time with being both. What I am saying is that since World War II, the beginning which we made with the Marshall Plan and the forming of the U.N. has been largely spoiled by the cold war psychology that has been so popular in our democracy. The result is that our government, both the State Department and the Pentagon, has found it easier to win support by appealing to American fear than to American morality — or even to American intelligence or common sense.

Boasting about our heritage of freedom, we allied ourselves with some of the worst dictators all over the world, as long as they were, in our judgment, anti-communist. We have justified all sorts of immoral political acts either because we thought that they would weaken communism or (even a more immoral excuse) that since the communists were doing them, so must we. Witness the invasion of Cuba, the attempted assassination of Castro, the war in Vietnam, including the bombing of the defenseless villages, the Christmas bombing of Hanoi, the secret bombing of Cambodia, and the support of a military revolution against the democratically elected government of Allende in Chile.

These, and other such actions, have been occasioned far more by fear of communism than by concern for justice. This pathological fear at its worst was so bad that one of our greatest generals, George Marshall, was charged with being a communist, a disloyal American.

In many parts of our nation, among many Christians, the World Council of Churches is generally distrusted. Some Americans have believed that since there are eastern European churches represented at the highest levels of the World Council, the Council is therefore communist-dominated. But the churches in eastern Europe are not communist bodies; they are Christian bodies. Although the governments of their nations do influence them, who can say that the Christian churches in the United States are entirely free of government influence?

But God is greater than a nation, any nation. God is greater than an ideology. The embarrassing thing to be noted today is that the social ethics related to Marxism is more generally admired by more people than the social ethics practiced by the people of the United States through our government.

Despite our increasing military strength, we are less confident of peace, more fearful of war, while the gap continues to grow between the rich and the poor amongst the nations of the world and within them.... Peace at home or in the world cannot be secured by force or by armaments. The realists are those who have God's vision and commit themselves to it with faith and courage.

This is where the importance of the church must be seen. Will we, as Christians, go on blessing what we know is wrong?...

Those who make that choice can find hope for today, along with their faith, and so can live by the prophets' vision of a day when all shall "beat their swords into plowshares and their spears into pruning hooks; nation shall not lift up sword against nation, neither shall they learn war any more."

✪ October 6 _____

Noah Webster

CONGREGATIONAL

October 16, 1758–May 28, 1843

Noah Webster's three passions were education, American democracy, and the Christian faith. He came of age during a period of major political and religious upheaval. Both the Second Great Awakening and the American Revolution, in which he fought, affected him profoundly. Webster had been molded by his Congregational background, which always saw connections between the community of faith and the wider civil society. His religious background was Congregationalism, which always saw connections between the community of faith and the wider civil society. His own faith was not just intellectual or a habit formed in youth; it was a deep and heartfelt experience. His recounting of his conversion contains these words: "I closed my books, yielded to the influence which could not be resisted or mistaken and was led by a spontaneous impulse to repentance, prayer and entire submission of myself to my maker and redeemer."

Originally from Connecticut, Webster looked outward toward the new nation, seeking to bring his passion and gifts to the new Republic in every way he could. He did not see education as a path to achieving success or prosperity for the individual, but rather as society's means for producing wise and faithful leaders and citizens. His own love of learning and words was unquenchable.

The Websters had been farmers in West Hartford, Connecticut. For colonial families in such circumstances, college was difficult to manage. Webster had two brothers and two sisters, and all the children were needed for farm work. Nonetheless, his fascination with knowledge prompted his parents to send him to Yale, the one college in Connecticut at the time. He then went on to study law, and graduated from the country's first law school in Litchfield, Connecticut.

Webster found many shortcomings in the education available to his generation, especially the reliance on textbooks imported from England. Convinced that a new nation needed the cohesiveness only a common language can provide, and feeling that America possessed a distinctive linguistic heritage of its own, he began creating a dictionary when he was 43. This volume standardized American spelling, added new words not found in imported dictionaries (like skunk and squash), and brought some consistency to pronunciation. It took him 27 years to finish it, but in the end, Webster's dictionary contained 70,000 words. In addition to this great work, he wrote a textbook, *A Grammatical Institute of the English Language* (1783). It became the most popular American book of the day. Benjamin Franklin used it to instruct his granddaughter, and it continued in use for nearly a century. Both dictionary and grammar addressed a vital cultural need. Without their influence, Americans might have continued to speak a jumble of regional dialects. These books provided a linguistic foundation for the political structures rising from the Revolution.

Webster imagined the new country would produce an informed citizenry, wise enough to elect the best possible leaders. They would be literate not only through knowing the definitions of words, but in understanding God's purpose in their own history. To this end, Webster also produced an American Bible. "Education is of no use without the Bible," he said.

> The religion which has introduced civil liberty is the religion of Christ and His apostles, which enjoins humility, piety, and benevolence; which acknowledges in every person a brother, or a sister, and a citizen with equal rights. This is genuine Christianity, and to this we owe our free Constitutions of Government.

In addition to these accomplishments, Webster advocated strongly for a national constitution and began one of the first daily newspapers in America, *The American Minerva,* which he used to support his hero, George Washington. With this paper, Webster helped establish the press as a means for American political discourse. Webster was an editor, a student of epidemics, a climatologist, an advocate of copyright laws, and a founder of Amherst College in Massachusetts. In his *History of the United States,* Webster wrote:

> When you become entitled to exercise the right of voting for public officers, let it be impressed on your mind that God commands you to choose for rulers, "just men who will rule in the fear of God." The preservation of [our] government depends on the faithful discharge of this Duty; if the citizens neglect their Duty and place unprincipled men in office, the government will soon be corrupted; laws will be made, not for the public good so much as for selfish or local purposes; corrupt or incompetent men will be appointed to execute the Laws; the public revenues will be squandered on unworthy men; and the rights of the citizen will be violated or disregarded. If [our] government fails to secure public prosperity and happiness, it must be because the citizens neglect the Divine Commands, and elect bad men to make and administer the Laws.

Webster's unswerving commitment to Christ and his great vision for his new country combined to help produce institutions and resources that shaped generations of leaders and citizens.

✠ *October 7*

Catherine Louisa Marthens

LUTHERAN

July 17, 1828–January 12, 1899

Louisa Marthens is one of many significant figures whose ministries were influenced by W. A. Passavant.* She had been instructed and motivated by

Passavant in her faith and had become interested in the revived Deaconess movement in Germany under Pastor Fliedner. As her mentor made plans to establish a similar community in America, Marthens eagerly volunteered to join its ranks. Both Passavant's hospitals and orphanages needed her skills as nurse and administrator. The duties of a Deaconess were not light. Passavant's account of his trip to Germany reports that he saw Fliedner's work in person:

> The principle he laid down was, that the deaconesses must be willing to be servants of Christ alone, to devote their time and faculties entirely and exclusively to Him, and not to look to pecuniary emoluments or any other comfort the world can give, but to do the work of charity and self-denial out of gratitude to Him who came down to serve them, before they knew Him, even to death.

At home in America, Marthens established a series of "General Principles":

> The association of Christian females is purely voluntary. The members unite without persuasion, remain without vows, and retire without restraint.
>
> It is not an order, but the restoration of an office, that of "Servant" or Deaconess in the primitive church.
>
> Its members heartily confess the faith, engage in the worship and observe the discipline of the Evangelical Lutheran Church.
>
> Its object is habitually to engage in works of mercy among the sick and poor, the ignorant and fatherless, and other suffering members of our Lord's body. In the better attainment of this object, the association is incorporated and fully empowered to establish and conduct the necessary charitable institutions.
>
> Not earthly reward and honor but the desire for an opportunity to manifest their gratitude to Jesus Christ in the way revealed in His word, has influenced the members to associate themselves as servants of Christ and His church.

Regulations

> The members of the Institution shall consist of the deaconess proper and the probationers, both of whom shall be received into the association in the manner hereinafter provided.
>
> They shall alike be subject to the Director and the Directing Sister in regard to the designation of their field of labor and manner of performance and shall conscientiously observe both the letter and the spirit of its principles and regulations.
>
> They shall reside in the Parent House, unless appointed to labor elsewhere by the Board of Managers, in which case they shall still retain their connection with the parent association, continuing subject to its rules, reporting statedly to its Director and Directing Sister, and holding themselves in readiness to be recalled or to be transferred elsewhere whenever deemed necessary or proper by those in authority.

The internal government and regulation of the association shall be vested in the Director and the Directing Sister, both of whom are elected by the joint suffrages of the Sisters and the Board of Directors according to the mode described in the charter. The relation of the Directing Sister towards the other members is, as far as possible, that of a mother or an elder sister, while that of Director is, as far as possible, that of the Head of the Family and the spiritual guide.

The sisters shall wear a plain, economical habit, as much as possible conforming in style, expense and color, which shall be black or gray or blue on week days as they may prefer. In regard to the other articles of dress, the counsel of the Director is first to be sought before being purchased. The wearing of a sister's habit is voluntary to the probationers during the probationary year, but all display or ornament is to be avoided.

Marthens steadfastly handled her patients' struggles with serious diseases, resistance from townspeople, needy groups of orphans, the demands of the deaconate community, and the rigors of getting new institutions up and running. Her sense of Christ's call to these arduous services strengthened her for the tasks she was given. A contemporary report of her work tells how:

> In 1850, the first American deaconess was solemnly set apart for the ministry of mercy within its [the Seventh Street Church in Pittsburgh] walls. Her name was Catherine Louisa Marthens. She had been catechized and confirmed by Mr. Passavant. From his lips she had heard the story of the blessed work of the Kaiserwerth deaconesses. She was present when the four sisters from Kaiserwerth were consecrated by Pastor Fliedner. When the hospital was opened in Allegheny and no means were at hand she heard how her pastor and student Waters had washed and nursed the first patients. Her heart, warm in its first love to the Saviour, moved her to offer her services, and she became the first regular nurse. She helped to nurse the first cholera patients. She was present when the house was mobbed and stoned as a "pest house." She stood by her post, moved with the patients to Lacyville, and became the first nurse of the Pittsburgh Infirmary. She became the first matron of the Pittsburgh Orphan Home. She took the four orphans from the Pittsburgh Home to the new orphanage in Germantown, and helped to set that institution of mercy going. She afterwards became the Matron of the Girls' Orphan Home in Rochester, Pa., and in later years was the Matron and guiding spirit of the Passavant Hospital in Jacksonville, Ill.

In the same report, we learn that she went to Germantown with the four children from Pittsburgh in March of 1859, and within eight weeks had received another seven. A small house had been purchased for children without families. Marthens found a matron for the institution before she returned to Pittsburgh. Her courage in founding a Protestant community to care for the sick, dying, and outcasts never faltered, because of her conviction that through this labor she served Christ. She remains an inspiration to this day.

✪ October 8

Benjamin Randal

FREE WILL BAPTISTS

1749–October 22, 1808

George Whitefield preached conversion throughout New England in the year Benjamin Randal turned 21, but Randal found his preaching "disgustful." He was opposed to all traveling preachers, believing they stirred up "delusion and enthusiasm." He went to hear Whitefield preach, but remained unmoved by the spectacle. When "the tears began to roll down from his eyes, it immediately raised an evil spirit within me. Ah, thought I, you are a worthless, noisy fellow; all you want is to make the people cry out; my good old minister does not do so, and he is as good a man as you, and much better."

Randal went to hear Whitefield a second time with the same result, but the following Sunday, September 30, 1770, he heard that Whitefield had dropped dead. "The first thoughts that passed through my mind were, Whitefield is now in heaven, and I am in the road to hell. I shall never hear his voice any more." He continued in this agony for two weeks, then one day some words from the Epistle to the Hebrews came into his mind, "But now once in the end of the world hath he appeared to put away sin by the sacrifice of himself." As he turned them over in his mind, he came to see that Christ had indeed died for all and that salvation was freely available.

> Now I saw that God had ever been my friend; and that he had ever been waiting to be gracious to me. My joy became unspeakable and full of glory. My soul was inflamed with love to God, as my great Creator, as my only Redeemer; and to the Holy Ghost, as my Reprover and blessed Comforter. O, what love I felt to all mankind, and wished that they all might share in that fullness, which I saw so extensive and so free for them all...O, what love I felt to all mankind, and wished that they all might share in that fullness, which I saw so extensive and so free for them all.

Randal associated himself with his local Baptist Church but argued with them over predestination, and at last they cast him out. With some others, he then formed a new association that eventually became the Free Will Baptist Church. Randal carried the gospel of grace available to all throughout New England. Disappointed with his efforts, he complained in 1807: "Having traveled only 2,593 miles, and having been so much ill, I have attended only 203 public meetings, besides weddings and funerals." When he died, he was not yet 60 years old and had spent over 31 years of his life helping build the Free Will Baptists into a national movement.

A reading from a final letter of Benjamin Randal

I am strong in the belief of the universal love of God to all men in the atonement; and in the universal appearance of the light, love and grace of God to all men; and that the salvation or damnation of mankind, turns upon their receiving or rejecting the same. I know from God that the doctrine which teacheth that it is impossible for any of those for whom Christ died to sin themselves to hell, is a doctrine of error, invented to destroy souls; and do now in my last moments, bear my testimony against it; and also against that shocking, inconsistent, Calvinistic doctrine, of eternal election and reprobation. I rejoice much to see how fast Christ is consuming it, by the breath of his mouth, and the brightness of his appearing. I am strong in the belief of the blessed ordinances of the gospel, as we find them recorded in the scriptures, and as we now practice them; and also in our order and discipline.

Now, brethren, I am going to leave the Connexion with you, and I know not on whom my mantle will fall; I will it to whom the Lord will; I hope it will fall on some one a thousand times more fit for it than ever I was. The thing I most fear, that will hinder the advancement of the cause, is "Who shall be the greatest?" I have discovered so much of it, I have, and do greatly fear. O my brethren, "Humility goeth before promotion, and a haughty spirit before a fall." Let nothing be done among you through strife or vain glory, but in holiness of mind, let each esteem others better than themselves. There is some branches, and in some members in this Connexion, I think, a great inclination to mingle with the world; and this I fear will cause a great deal of trouble. O, beware of it, I pray you; for we are called out from the world, and from every people under heaven; and our prosperity wholly depends on our following our heavenly Leader; and if we do not, God will raise him another people, and we shall sink as others have done before us. I have many things to say, but I forbear now, and hope the Lord will enable me to leave my charge to the whole Connexion. I here end, sending my love to the meeting, to all my friends, my enemies, and to all my fellow men.

From your dying servant and brother in our Lord Jesus Christ. Farewell.

B. Randal

✪ *October 9* _____

Elias Benjamin Sanford

CONGREGATIONAL

June 6, 1843–July 3, 1932

In the early days of American settlement, particular churches tended to establish themselves in separate areas: Congregationalists in New England, the Reformed tradition in the Hudson Valley, Quakers in Pennsylvania, Anglicans in Virginia, and so forth. But with new waves of immigration and western expansion, these divisions began to change, stimulating cooperative relationships among denominations. Elias Sanford had begun his work as an ordained Methodist minister in Connecticut, but he soon became a Congregational pastor, serving in Cornwall and other small towns in the northwest corner of the state. Though this area was largely rural, Sanford's summer congregation included such luminaries as the president of Yale, along with many other well-connected clergy and lay people. Sanford continued his studies at Yale, then spent the first part of 1868 traveling across Europe through France, Italy, Germany, and England. In England he listened to Gladstone and Disraeli debate the Irish Church bill.

Returning to Cornwall, he started writing articles for the *Union Advocate,* edited by a Lutheran pastor in Pittsburgh. Before long, he was asked to edit a new magazine, *Church Union,* which would suggest "plans and methods by which evangelical denominations of the United States can give best expression to their oneness in Christ." Ecumenical efforts were growing among adherents of the social gospel and among organizations devoted to social welfare like the Young Men's Christian Association (Y.M.C.A.). In 1894, the Open and Institutional Church League was established across denominational lines and Sanford directed its campaign to broaden the scope of cooperative social service work. In the next year, he was instrumental in the founding of the National Federation of Churches and Church Workers.

Searching for ever more inclusive interdenominational agencies, Sanford helped plan the Carnegie Hall Conference of 1905 at which 29 denominations were represented. This, in turn, laid the groundwork for the formation of the Federal Council of Churches in 1908, the ancestor of today's National Council of Churches. Sanford served as corresponding secretary of the FCC from 1908 to 1913 and continued as an honorary secretary of the organization until his death in 1932. He was suspicious of schemes for organic union, fearing that it "would logically and of very necessity, if accomplished, compel every other communion to bow in submission to Rome." As an evangelical, he saw such an eventuality as "an iridescent dream that is not in accord with New Testament authority and the leadership of our Lord and Saviour Jesus Christ the Head of the Church." In these early days of ecumenical effort, the focus was necessarily on attainable goals rather than possibilities that, a century later, remain to be realized.

A reading from Elias Sanford's views on Christian unity

I can see no signs that Protestantism is an effete and dying phase of Christianity. Rather I rejoice in signs that it is passing into a period when polemic and theological discussion is giving place to a united world conquering spirit in the name of Him who prayed "that they may all be one: even as thou. Father, art in me, and I in thee, that they also may be in us: that the world may believe that thou didst send me."

The bringing of Roman, Greek and Reformed Churches into one great Catholic Body appears, from my point of view, a goal that aside from the impossibility of its achievement is by no means desirable. The unity for which our Lord prayed is the unity of the spirit. It cannot be forced by legislation or secured by submission. The beautiful allegory in which Christ speaks of Himself as the Good Shepherd gives us guidance. There is indeed but *one flock*, but there is room in the pastures of Divine love and service for many folds. Not so many as to interfere with each other and by divisive strife fail to keep open the paths that at the call of the Shepherd's voice will bring them constantly together for life, shelter and protection in the common flock.

The goal of Church Federation is not an easy, sentimental expression of fraternal good will. It is a call to an unselfish cooperative working together of the followers of Christ. Deploring divisions that have broken denominational households into separated ranks, it rejoices in signs and actions that are already betokening the healing of these schisms of a past that no longer should prevail as barriers of separation. With this coming together of individual folds let us remember the law of unity in diversity that exists and controls both in the realm of nature and the structure of society and government. Let us get back to the fountain head of authority and commission. "Now there are diversities of gifts, but the same Spirit. And there are diversities of ministrations, and the same Lord. And there are diversities of workings, but the same God, who worketh all things in all." ...

We wax eloquent, and it is well, over the lack of comity and interdenominational cooperation in the planting of new churches, and the best strategic use of Protestant Christian forces, but I am confident I do not go astray in saying that the annals of all the constituent bodies of the Federal Council of Churches will disclose as flagrant and selfish violations of the spirit of comity within their fellowship as we unhappily find on a larger scale in the history of denominational missionary and church extension activities. The unity for which our Lord prayed was of the spirit. When His Spirit and purposes are enthroned in the hearts of the leaders, as well as that of the rank and file of our denominational flocks, then will His prayer be answered. These convictions and the facts and factors that must be taken into account in all decisions looking towards the goal of united action, have come to take possession more and more of my thought, as wider reading of history and contact with the problems confronting the Protestant church life of the United States have been granted to me.

✪ October 10

John Courtney Murray

ROMAN CATHOLIC

September 12, 1904–August 16, 1967

The first Christians to settle in New England came looking for freedom to order church life in a new way. They hoped to create a state that would support such a church, but this desire was impeded by political realities: all members of the colony did not share the same beliefs, and they remained subject to the British government. The resulting compromises limited the state's control of religion, permitting the church a freedom it had rarely known before.

Roman Catholics did not play a significant role in this emerging order until well into the 19th century, but those who came discovered that they liked the experience of freedom and found themselves constantly explaining and defending the American system to a suspicious Vatican. Yet the growing influence of Roman Catholics in America made them a force to be reckoned with, even in Rome. With Vatican Council II, the American Church found in John Courtney Murray a voice of such influence that his contribution was reflected in statements on religious liberty that not only acknowledged the existence of a new world but welcomed it.

John Courtney Murray joined the Jesuit order at the age of 16 and spent his life in theological study. In 1937, he earned a doctorate from the Gregorian University in Rome and became a professor of theology at the Jesuit school in Woodstock, Maryland, where he remained until his death. Professors of theology are rarely influential in the larger society, but Murray specialized in relationships between church and state. His particular concern was to demonstrate the compatibility of the American constitution and Roman Catholicism. As a representative of the American Roman Catholic bishops, Murray helped draft the 1943 "Declaration on World Peace," an interfaith statement of principles for postwar reconstruction. In 1950, he served as a consultant to the religious affairs section of the Allied High Command in Germany and recommended a close constitutional arrangement between the restored German state and churches.

In spite of his growing influence, the Vatican's distrust of such views remained strong. Throughout the 1950s, Murray's freedom to write and lecture was limited. Rome still kept an index of books and movies it forbade its people to read or see. Murray argued that participating in the public debate would be more effective than attempts at coercion. Debate would deepen the moral commitment of all Americans, while preserving the "genius" of American freedom. Gradually his views gained a larger audience and he was invited to take part in the Second Vatican Council. There, he made crucial contributions to the council's statement on religious liberty, *Dignitatis Humanae.*

A reading from an article on the Ecumenical Revolution by John Courtney Murray

It has been remarked that the modern world looks much like the medieval world turned inside out. In medieval times the world — the small and circumscribed "inhabited earth" known as the *oikoumene* was Christian. The secular world existed at the interior of this Christian world, largely in the form of the secular power. Now, however, the world, grown to vastly greater dimensions, is secular. And the religious thing, in all its forms, exists at the interior of this secular world.

This fact of contemporary life was recognized by the Vatican Council II speaking for the [Roman] Catholic Church. The fact was not merely accepted as a fact; it was also acknowledged to be in conformity with the right scheme of things. The sacred at the interior of the secular — that is the way things should be. The Christian call is to exist within a world that has "come of age," that is, come to its rightful secularity. This vocation is to be fulfilled by Christian presence in the Secular City — this we all recognize today. But the vocation has a farther reach, toward presence in the secular university.

This presence is becoming a possibility today, as it was not a few years ago. The ecumenical dialogue has caught the attention of the world of secular learning, as it has also caught the attention of the civic community. Obviously, the ecumenical movement is much more than a movement of ideas, but it is also that. Hence it is a valid object of university interest. High talk about religion, not only as a human concern but as a body of knowledge capable of validating itself in its own terms, is becoming a possibility within the Academy. Thus one might hope that the ecumenical movement could serve to give some new quality and substance to the university enterprise, at the same time that the university could serve to sustain and invigorate the ecumenical movement.

If this development were to occur, the consequences would be manifold. It might help for instance, to rescue the ecumenical movement from a *cul de sac* into which it might possibly head. I mean the trap of being simply an affair of the churches, or if you will, an affair of the church and synagogue. The ecumenical movement would be untrue to itself, if it were to fall into this trap. Certainly we Christians are not called simply to witness to one another. The call is to witness to the world — to all the worlds of human life, in the appropriate form which witness should take within each of them. There is a form appropriate to the university, namely, theological scholarship imbued with the ecumenical spirit. It has nothing to do with propaganda; it is directed to intelligence and it looks simply to create understanding. What is more, this form of scholarly theological witness cannot take place except in dialogue with the university, wherein the *genius loci* is the pursuit of truth.

I suggest that our response to the challenge of ecumenism must include a willingness to move forward into this new area of dialogue.

✵ *October 11*

William Porcher DuBose

EPISCOPALIAN

April 11, 1836–August 18, 1918

The Anglican tradition was shaped by the attempt to hold together Catholic and Protestant understandings of the Christian faith in a single, inclusive church. It is not an approach likely to produce clearly stated theological systems. Yet the effort to understand divergent positions can sometimes enable the church to hear new truths and see their relevance for age-old doctrine.

William Porcher DuBose has been called the "most creative theologian in the history of the Episcopal Church." During a time of deep divisions, he sought to learn from the new and to find ways to move beyond the controversies of the moment. In his early years, this was very necessary. He had served as an officer in the Confederate army. Wounded, captured, and held for two months as a prisoner of war, he experienced firsthand the cost of unresolved differences.

Having studied theology at the University of the South before the war, DuBose was ordained after his release, served as a chaplain for the rest of the war, and then served as rector of a South Carolina parish for five years before beginning his lifework on the faculty of the University of the South. Darwin's theory of evolution created enormous controversy during those years. DuBose believed that Christianity had much to learn from that theory. In his mind, there was a vital link between the theory of evolution and the gospel proclamation that "the Word became flesh and dwelt among us." If God created a material world, then there was no stark division between the natural and supernatural, nor any reason why a creating God could not work through an evolutionary process. In a similar way, he argued that God's particular incarnation in Christ reveals the divinity generally present in all humanity and the need for all men and women to realize their humanity in Christ.

Some years after his death, the notorious Scopes trial was held not far from the university where DuBose taught. Controversies about evolution have not been resolved for many Christians, even today. Yet it is the patient examination of issues and the synthesizing of the best of contemporary thought with Christian faith by theologians such as William Porcher DuBose that will enable the whole church to resolve such issues at last so that it can speak intelligently in ways the world can understand.

A reading from *High Priesthood and Sacrifice* by William Porcher DuBose

We have our religion through the medium of languages that have been long dead, and that present tendencies in education threaten to render more and more dead to us. Along with the languages, there is a growing disposition to relegate the ideas, the entire symbolic expression and form, of Christianity to the past. The modern world calls for modern modes of thought and modern forms of speech. We have to meet that demand and be able to answer and satisfy whatever of reason or truth there is in it....

The time will never come when the Christian Church can surrender or neglect the Hebrew and Greek sources of its inspiration and life. And the world itself will be the richer and better if it will help us not to do so; if in all the channels and courses of higher education it will multiply the facilities and help us to magnify the importance of these best means to its own highest culture. There are two tasks before us as students and teachers of Christianity. The first is to know and understand our sources. To begin with, we must know our Old Testament as we have never known it before, if we are to take part in the new interpretation of our New Testament that the times demand. For each time must have its own living interpretation, since the interpretation cannot but be, in half measure at least, relative to the time. If the divine part in it is fixed, the human is progressive and changing just in so far as it is living.

All science of life now is a science of beginnings and of growth or of evolution. The New Testament as absolutely transcends the Old as it fulfils it; but on the other hand, it is as actually the culmination and completion of the Old Testament as it transcends it. The thought, the language, the life of Christianity are from the very beginning Hebrew, transformed and as far as possible universalized by transition through Greek thought and speech. All this history has its meaning, and enters largely into the meaning and form of Christianity as we have it. But it brings with it also its embarrassments. The most immediate consequence comes to us in the manifest fact that we are attempting to address the world to-day, in the matter of its profoundest interest, in terms of the world two thousand years ago. We have first to know what those terms meant then, and to prove that all they meant then they mean now, and mean for all men in time. Are our Bible and our Creeds to be recognized by us as antiquated? Are the Hebrew phrases and terms of priesthood and sacrifice, and the Greek or Gentile application of them to the Cross of Christ, waxed old and ready to vanish away? Forever no! — but if not, then we must take measures to preserve them, and the only way to preserve them is to make them as living today, as much part of our thought and our speech and our life now, as they were two thousand years ago.

In order to do that, we must cease to treat the phraseology, the forms, definitions, and dogmas of Christianity as sacred relics, too sacred to be handled. We must take them out of their napkins, strip them of their cerements, and turn them into current coin. We must let them do business in the life that is living now, and take part in the thought and feeling and activity of the men of the world of today.

✷ October 12 ─────────────────────

Walter Rauschenbusch

BAPTIST

October 4, 1861–July 25, 1918

The 1970 publication of *Christianity and the Social Order* made its author, Walter Rauschenbusch, the recognized spokesperson for the "Social Gospel" movement in American Christianity. The son of a Lutheran pastor ministering to German immigrants, Rauschenbusch studied in Germany and the United States before his 1886 ordination in a German Baptist Church in New York City. In that year, one of the mayoral candidates, Walter George, was working on the problem of how to deal with poverty in a rapidly changing society. With two other Baptist clergy, Rauschenbusch formed the Brotherhood of the Kingdom and began publishing a monthly journal "in the interests of the working people." Although he always considered himself an evangelist, Rauschenbusch's influence came primarily from his seminary teaching and writing. He believed that bringing individuals to a new birth in Christ required also a transformation of the social order, based on Christian principles of equal rights and an equitable distribution of economic power.

A reading from *A Public Ministry* by Walter Rauschenbusch

Sin is a social force. It runs from man to man along the lines of social contact. Its impact on the individual becomes most overwhelming when sin is most completely socialized. Salvation, too, is a social force. It is exerted by groups that are charged with divine will and love. It becomes durable and complete in the measure in which the individual is built into a social organism that is ruled by justice, cleanness, and love. A full salvation demands a Christian social order which will serve as the spiritual environment of the individual. In the little catechism which Luther wrote for the common people he has a charmingly true reply to the question: "What is 'our daily bread'?" He says: "All that belongs to the nourishment and need of our body, meat and drink, clothes and shoes, house and home, field and cattle, money and property, a good wife and good children, good servants and good rulers, good government, good weather, peace, health, education, honor, good friends, trusty neighbors, and such like." Yes, especially "such like." In the same way "salvation" involves a saved environment. For a baby it means the breast and heart and love of a mother, and a father who can keep the mother in proper condition. For a workingman salvation includes a happy home, clean neighbors, a steady job, eight hours a day, a boss that treats him as a man, a labor union that is well led, the sense of doing his own best work and not being used up to give others money to burn, faith in God and in the final triumph and present power of the right, a sense of being part of a movement that is lifting his class and all mankind, "and such like." Therefore the conception of salvation which is contained in the word "the kingdom of God" is a truer and completer conception than that which is contained in the word "justification by faith," as surely as the whole is better than a part.

It must be plain to any thoughtful observer that immense numbers of men are turning away from traditional religion, not because they have lapsed into sin, but because they have become modernized in their knowledge and points of view. Religion itself is an eternal need of humanity, but any given form of religion may become antiquated and inadequate, leaving the youngest and liveliest minds unsatisfied, or even repelling where it ought to attract. The real religious leaders of this generation must face the problem how they can give to modern men the inestimable boon of experiencing God as a joy and a power, and of living in him as their fathers did. I claim that social Christianity is by all tokens the great highway by which this present generation can come to God.

For one thing, it puts an end to most of the old conflicts between religion and science. The building of the kingdom of God on earth requires surprisingly little dogma and speculative theology, and a tremendous quantity of holy will and scientific good sense. It does not set up a series of propositions which need constant modernizing and which repel the most active intellects, but it summons all to help in transforming the world into a reign of righteousness, and men of good will are not very far apart on that. That kind of religion has no quarrel with science. It needs science to interpret the universe which Christianity wants to transform. Social Christianity sets up fewer obstacles for the intellect and puts far heavier tasks on the will, and all that is sound in modern life will accept that change with profound relief.

Social Christianity would also remove one other obstacle which bars even more men out of religion than the scientific difficulties of belief. The most effective argument against religion today is that religion has been "against the people." The people are coming to their own at last. For a century and a half at least they have been on the upgrade, climbing with inexpressible toil and suffering toward freedom, equality, and brotherhood. The spirit of Christ has been their most powerful ally, but the official church, taking Christendom as a whole, has thrown the bulk of its great resources to the side of those who are in possession, and against those who were in such deadly need of its aid. This is the great scandal which will not down. Scientific doubt may alienate thousands, but the resentment against the church for going over to the enemy has alienated entire nations. Nothing would so expiate that guilt and win back the lost respect for religion, as determined cooperation on the part of the church in creating a social order in which the just aspirations of the working class will be satisfied. Those Christian men who are the outstanding and bold friends of the people's cause are today the most effective apologists of Christianity.

The Christian demand for the kingdom of God on earth responds to the passionate desire for liberty which pervades and inspires the modern world.

✪ *October 13* _____

Rufus Jones

QUAKER

January 25, 1863–June 16, 1948

Upon first learning that Rufus Jones spent 41 years of his life teaching mysticism at a traditionally Quaker college, one might imagine a man who made little impact on the world around him. But Rufus Jones believed that love could make a difference and acted on it. He thought that those who believe in nonviolence should be actively engaged wherever violence and injustice are dominating human lives.

In 1917, during the World War I, Jones cofounded and became the first president of the American Friends Service Committee, formed to enable conscientious objectors to help civilian victims of that war. After the war ended, when no country would provide assistance to the defeated and starving German people, Rufus Jones negotiated with the American government to allow the AFSC to set up child-feeding programs both in Germany and in Russia.

By 1938, Rufus Jones and other Quaker representatives were negotiating with the Gestapo in an attempt to bring relief to Jews suffering under the Nazi regime. The war began before they could put any program into action, but Quaker relief work continued so effectively that, in 1947, the American Friends Service Committee and its older British counterpart, the Friends Service Council, were awarded the Nobel Peace Prize for that work.

Rufus Jones was primarily a scholar. He is recognized as the principal author of the seven-volume standard history of the Quaker movement. Jones also wrote and lectured extensively on the history of mysticism, distinguishing between the negative and affirmative types. Negative mysticism, in his view, often led a mystic to expect his experience of God to terminate in "a mental blank, an everlasting Nay," and the loss of the idea of a personal God. Jones recognized that affirmative and negative always include elements of the other, but it was the affirmative type of mysticism that appealed to him. "The focal idea of this new type of mysticism," Jones wrote, "is the glowing faith that there is something divine in man which under right influences and responses can become the dominant feature of a person's whole life."

A reading from *Rethinking Quaker Principles* by Rufus Jones

Finally, here at the end, I shall put what might well have come first, the constant return of Friends to the springs and sources of life in worship.

We may hold it as settled that we cannot change the world from ways of war to ways of peace, nor can we rebuild the social order on right lines for future generations, without the influence and guidance and inspiration of vital religion. A world built on purely secular lines would be a world that would fester and spoil and corrupt as has always happened. We must above everything else find our way back to the springs of life and refreshment for the hearts and souls of men. Religious faith when it takes us back to the true source of power removes from the mind the peril of bewildering unsettlement. It turns water to wine. It brings prodigals home. It sets men on their feet. It raises life out of death. It turns sunsets to sunrises. It makes the impossible become possible. The master secret of life is the attainment of the power of serenity in the midst of stress and action and adventure.

One of the most significant contributions which the Quakers have made has been in the discovery of the value of silent communion and their practice of it as a source of strength and equipment. They begin all their meals in silence. They open all their meetings with a time of quiet, even their meetings for business, and they approach every practical task with a period of hush. It may, I think, be taken as a demonstrated fact that hush and silence minister to a consciousness of mutual and reciprocal communion with God. The soul in these deep moments of quiet seems to be both giving and receiving — to be breathing in a diviner life, and to be pouring out in response its own highest and noblest aspirations and expectations. Different exponents of religious faith differ widely in their emphasis on what is essential in belief and form and practice, but the representatives of all faiths, of all communions, of all systems, or of none, might find themselves moved, quickened, vitalized, refreshed, and girded for the duties and tasks of life by periods of expectant, palpitating hush with others who are fused together into one group of worshipping men and women.

✹ *October 14*

Charles H. Parkhurst

PRESBYTERIAN

April 17, 1842–September 8, 1933

"Politics" it is often said, "has no place in the pulpit." Yet, at the same time, preachers are often charged with being irrelevant to people's real lives. Charles Parkhurst was one man not afraid to bring "real life" into his preaching, even though he became deeply involved in politics by so doing. In 1880, he had been called to the pulpit of Madison Square Presbyterian Church in New York City. For 12 years, he preached solid theological sermons to the prosperous people of Manhattan. But as years passed, he grew increasingly aware of the corruption pervading the city's government and at last, decided to tell his congregation what he saw. Politicians fought back, summoning him before a grand jury where he had to admit he had no evidence. But rather than drop the charges, he went out to get the evidence. With a private detective and a friend, Parkhurst went into gambling dens and houses of prostitution, sometimes finding police who would offer directions. He returned with eyewitness accounts of malfeasance.

Tammany Hall started as a social club, but became involved in politics under the leadership of Aaron Burr. By the end of the 19th century, it made itself so indispensable to newly arrived immigrants that it could control not only city hall but the courts as well. The Tweed Ring, which controlled Tammany Hall in the 1870s, sold the city $5 park benches for $600 and brooms for $41,000. Rebuilding of City Hall Park was estimated to cost $300,000. Eventually, it totaled $13 million. Parkhurst was neither the first to attack Tammany Hall, nor the last. Its power survived well into the second half of the 20th century. Nevertheless, Parkhurst's revelations put a major crimp in its operations for years, demonstrating that the pulpit can be an effective tool for changing the whole tone of a community's life.

Christianity, Parkhurst said, is the "salt of the earth . . . and Christianity is the antiseptic that is to be rubbed into it in order to arrest the process of decay." To the charge that he was politicizing the pulpit, he responded:

> This is not bringing politics into the pulpit, politics as such. The particular political stripe of a municipal administration is no matter of our interest, and none of our business; but to strike at iniquity is a part of the business of the church, indeed, it is *the* business of the church. It is primarily what the church is for, no matter in what connection sin may find itself associated and intermixed. If it fall properly within the jurisdiction of this church to try to convert Third Avenue drunkards from their alcoholism, then certainly it is germane to the functions of this church to strike the sturdiest blows it is capable of at a municipal administration whose supreme mission it is to protect, foster, and propagate alcoholism. If it is proper for us to go around cleaning up after the devil, it is proper for us to fight the devil.

A reading from Charles Parkhurst's first sermon attacking municipal corruption

We are living in a wicked world, and we are fallen upon bad times. And the question that has been pressing upon my heart these days and weeks past has been, What can I do?

We are not thinking just now so much of the world at large as we are of the particular part of the world that it is our doubtful privilege to live in. We are not saying that the times are any worse than they have been; but the evil that is in them is giving most uncommonly distinct tokens of its presence and vitality, and it is making a good many earnest people serious. They are asking, What is to be done? What is there that I can do? In its municipal life our city is thoroughly rotten. Here is an immense city reaching out arms of evangelization to every quarter of the globe; and yet every step that we take looking to the moral betterment of this city has to be taken directly in the teeth of the damnable pack of administrative blood-hounds that are fattening themselves on the ethical flesh and blood of our citizenship.

We have a right to demand that the Mayor and those associated with him in administering the affairs of this municipality should not put obstructions in the path of our ameliorating endeavors; and they do. There is not a form under which the devil disguises himself that so perplexes us in our efforts, or so bewilders us in the devising of our schemes as the polluted harpies that, under the pretence of governing this city, are feeding day and night on its quivering vitals. They are a lying, perjured, rum-soaked, and libidinous lot. If we try to close up a house of prostitution or of assignation, we, in the guilelessness of our innocent imaginations, might have supposed that the arm of the city government that takes official cognizance of such matters, would like nothing so well as to watch day-times and sit up nights for the purpose of bringing these dirty malefactors to their deserts. On the contrary, the arm of the city government that takes official cognizance of such matters evinces but a languid interest, shows no genius in ferreting out crime, prosecutes only when it has to, and has a mind so keenly judicial that almost no amount of evidence that can be heaped up is accepted as sufficient to warrant indictment.

We do not say that the proposition to raid noted houses of assignation touches our city government at a sensitive spot. We do not say that they frequent them; nor do we say that it is money in their pockets to have them maintained. We only say (we think a good deal more, but we only say) that so far as relates to the blotting out of such houses the strength of the municipal administration is practically leagued with them rather than arrayed against them.

✪ *October 15*

Benedict Joseph Flaget

ROMAN CATHOLIC

November 7, 1763–February 11, 1850

Orphaned at the age of two, Benedict Joseph Flaget was brought up by an aunt in France and entered a Sulpician seminary at the age of 17. He was ordained seven years later and became a teacher of dogmatic theology in Nantes and then Angers. When the French Revolution closed the seminaries, Flaget volunteered for work in America, arriving in Baltimore in 1792. Bishop Carroll* sent him off to the frontier as missionary to Native Americans but brought him back two years later to teach at Georgetown College. In 1810, despite his objections, he was made Bishop of Bardstown — a territory including everything west of the Appalachians and east of the Mississippi, except Louisiana. For almost 40 years, Flaget rode across this territory establishing churches and other institutions, settling disputes, and administering the sacraments. His self-denial and holiness of life were such that his advice was sought in the appointments of most of the American bishops chosen during his time. By 1830, in failing health, he resigned his see, but objections from clergy and laity were so strong that he was forced to continue in office. Three years later he won further praise for his ministry to the people of Bardstown during a cholera epidemic. In 1843, he built a convent and hospital at his own expense and finally, in 1848, was able to leave the diocese to his coadjutor and spend the last two years of his life in retirement. By that time, there were 11 dioceses in the area he had served.

Readings from Bishop Flaget's diary

To give you a clear idea of the bishoprics of the United States, I propose to lay before you a brief statement of the condition in which I found myself, after the Holy See, on the representation of Bishop Carroll, had nominated me to the bishopric of Bardstown. I was compelled to accept the appointment, whether I would or not; I had not a cent at my disposal; the Pope and the Cardinals, who were dispersed by the revolution, were not able to make me the slightest present; and Archbishop Carroll, though he had been Bishop for more than sixteen [twenty] years, was still poorer than myself; for he had debts, and I owed nothing. Nevertheless, my consecration took place on the 4th of November, 1810; but for want of money to defray the expenses of the journey, I could not undertake it. It was only six months afterwards, that, through a subscription made by my friends in Baltimore, I was enabled to reach Bardstown, my episcopal see....

While we were there (in Louisville), the faithful of my episcopal city put themselves in motion to receive me in a manner conformable to my dignity. They dispatched for my use a fine equipage drawn by two horses; and a son of one among the principal inhabitants considered himself honored in being the driver. Horses were furnished to all those who accompanied me, and four wagons transported our baggage.

It was then, for the first time, that I saw the bright side of the episcopacy, and that I began to feel its dangers. Nevertheless, God be thanked, if some movements of vanity glided into my heart, they had not a long time to fix their abode therein. The roads were so detestable, that, in spite of my beautiful chargers and my excellent driver, I was obliged to perform part of the journey on foot; and I should have traveled the entire way, had not one of my young seminarians dismounted and presented me his horse....

The next day, the sun was not risen when we were already on our journey. The roads were much better; I entered the carriage with two of my suite. I was not the more exalted for all this; the idea that I was henceforward to speak, to write, and to act as Bishop; cast me into a profound sadness.

How many sighs did I not breathe forth while traversing the four or five remaining leagues of our journey.

At the distance of a half league (a mile and a half) from town, an ecclesiastic of my Diocese, accompanied by the principal inhabitants, came out to meet me. So soon as they had perceived us, they dismounted to receive my benediction. I gave it to them, but with how trembling a hand, and with what heaviness of heart! Mutual compliments were now exchanged, and then we all together proceeded towards the town. This *cortege*, though simple and modest in itself, is something very new and extraordinary in this country. It was the first time a Bishop was ever seen in these parts; and it was I, the very last of the last tribe, who was to have this honor!

In entering the town, I devoted myself to all the guardian angels who reside therein, and I prayed to God, with all my heart, to make me die a thousand times, should I not become an instrument of His glory in this new Diocese. O my dear brother, have compassion on me, overloaded with so heavy a burden, and pray fervently to God that he would vouchsafe to lighten it.

✪ October 16

Elizabeth Burke (Sr. Joan Margaret, SSM)

EPISCOPALIAN

August 22, 1906–December 16, 2005

Sister Joan seldom wrote about herself; but she told wonderful stories about others. She wrote, for example, about Josianne David:

> There is a child here who doesn't wave when she passes you in the corridors, rather she calls your name and purses her lips as though she were blowing a kiss. The reason is because Josianne cannot wave. She was born without arms.
>
> Josianne is thirteen now and she has been coming to St. Vincent's, first as an out-patient and later as a school girl, since she was fifteen months old. As a small child, learning to walk was difficult for her, without arms it is very hard to attain a sense of balance, but her mother and the physiotherapists worked patiently and taught her not only to walk but to do with her feet and toes the tasks that other infants learn naturally to perform with their hands.
>
> Another problem which arose as Josianne grew was a severe spinal curvature and at the age of eleven she had an operation to alleviate this condition. A second, smaller, operation was found to be necessary a year later but by God's grace we believe that now no more surgery will be needed.
>
> As a toddler Josianne was shy and nervous but over the years, with the help of her teachers and the many friends she has made at St. Vincent's, she has become a sturdy, confident young girl. Not only does she write and do all her schoolwork easily and capably with her feet, but she has also learned to crochet to a very professional standard!

It has been a prayer of ours that one day Josianne could be fitted with artificial arms. Unfortunately, because she has no scapular motion she needs pneumatically driven arms and the cost of such limbs has always been way beyond the reach of what St. Vincent's can spend on one particular child. It is so evident, seeing the matter of fact and confident manner in which Josianne deals with her disability, that Our Lord has healed her spiritually, that we have the confidence and the gumption to believe that He will provide a way, too, for Josianne to be fitted with the artificial limbs which, even now, could so enrich her life.

But Josianne's was only one of many stories Sister Joan told. There was little Georgie who came to her at two years of age, a helpless cripple and severely undernourished. "Today," she wrote, "he runs — yes, actually runs — to greet us. He throws his arms around us. He laughs all over with the joy of living. Medical science has triumphed over his physical problems. Christian love has triumphed over his personal ones!" And there was the story of Rosita who had lost her eyesight through malnutrition but who "blossomed and flourished" as she learned Braille: "a joyful, outgoing child ... some day Rosita may be a teacher of Braille at St. Vincent's School."

Sister Joan was over 40 years old when she began her life's ministry with these children and others like them. She had been a nun for 17 years before that and had done a "frontier ministry" in Canada and parish work in Utica, New York, before she was sent to Haiti. Arriving in Haiti to teach in the convent school, she came in contact with three badly handicapped children and learned that there was no help of any sort available for their problems in Haiti. So she worked with the three children, one deaf, one blind, and one physically handicapped, under a tree. Out of her efforts came the founding of St. Vincent's School for Handicapped Children. By the time she retired, there were 360 children enrolled, the majority of them as boarders. The school had its educational component but also a medical clinic, a clinic for physiotherapy, and a workshop for making braces and prostheses. "Be all you can be," Sister Joan told the children, "and don't feel sorry for yourselves."

Early in her time in Haiti, Sister Joan was told that the president's wife had held a charity fashion show and was sending a check for $1,600 dollars for her work. "You can well imagine the thanksgivings I was offering up ... so that I barely heard anything ... and I thought how little faith I had had, because things had been so hard this month. I had not even been able to meet the November salaries for the teachers. I should have had faith enough to know that our Lord would take care of the needs of His Work."

"How little faith I had," she wrote, but even a little faith can move mountains, or change lives. One of her pupils, born blind, became a world-famous violinist. Another, born without arms or legs, was fitted for artificial limbs and became an artist. A handbell choir she organized was invited to play in the United Sates and in Europe. She worked with a Baptist hospital and a Methodist hospital to eliminate polio and tuberculosis Trained as a physical therapist, Sister Joan traveled the world to attend conferences on the handicapped and she was honored twice by the Haitian government and fifteen times by international societies concerned for the disabled. She brought specialists to Haiti to help her with the work and took some children to the United States for treatment.

"Indomitable" was the word most often used to describe Sister Joan. "She was short and square and walked very quickly," said another member of the order. "She would get up at four in the morning for her private prayer time until six. Then, after the eucharist, she would be off to the school with a banana for the pet monkey and treats for the children to be there for the beginning of the school day at 8 a.m. She would work there and at the clinics until she returned to the Convent for Evening Prayer at 5 p.m." "Retiring" at 94, after nearly 50 years in Haiti, she returned to the United States. Until her death at the age of 99, she continued to work to raise funds for the ministry she had created.

�֍ *October 17* _____

Georgia Elma Harkness

METHODIST

April 21, 1891–August 2, 1974

At a period when most women, especially those living in small, rural communities, accepted the social conditions that limited their opportunities, Georgia Harkness behaved as if she were living a century later and could do anything she felt called to do. Harkness, New York, a tiny hamlet in the Adirondack Mountains, did nothing to encourage her to consider an academic career. Nor did her parents transmit a living faith. She was taught to pray by a hired girl. Despite these handicaps, Harkness graduated from Cornell University with honors and from Boston University with a Ph.D. in philosophy. She studied at Harvard and Yale, then at Union Theological Seminary, finally becoming a professor of philosophy at Mount Holyoke Woman's College in 1937. She was the first woman to hold such a position in the United States. In 1938, Harkness was ordained a local elder. Women were not accepted for any higher ordination at the Troy Annual Conference, but, in any case, she felt called to exemplify lay ministry. When she became professor of applied theology at Garrett Biblical Institute in 1939, she was recognized as the country's most visible woman theologian.

Many thought she was overstepping sacred boundaries. At the Amsterdam Conference of the World Council of Churches in 1948, Karl Barth demanded that she explain how she could justify the ordination of women. She answered, "The Old Testament states that both male and female are created in the image of God; Jesus assumed always that men and women are equal before God." Barth responded that she was totally wrong, that woman was made from Adam's rib and that in Ephesians 5, Christ is head of the church so man is head of woman. When a friend of Harkness asked Barth about her later, he responded, "Remember me not of that woman!"

She was never afraid to challenge long-held traditions in the church. On the ransom theory of the atonement, she commented, "Sin cannot be cancelled by someone else paying the bill." Even St. Paul was not beyond her criticism; his great error, she said, was "overemphasizing Christ's death to the exclusion of his ministry;" his second error was "the introduction of original sin as an inherited curse from Adam's disobedience." She pointed out that after "The Fall" in Genesis 3, the Old Testament says practically nothing about the origin of sin, but Paul takes that same chapter and makes "a doctrine of it that became fastened upon centuries of subsequent thought." Her own theology emphasized both personal salvation and the need to address the evils of society, which for her included sexism, racism, militarism, and classism. She wrote, "If in some measure God has been able to use my words to speak in plain language to common folks, the reason is not hard to find. It is simply this — that I am one myself."

A reading from *The Dark Night of the Soul* by Georgia Harkness

It is, perhaps, effrontery to suggest that there is anything new to say on the problem of evil. Has it not all been said many times, in volumes innumerable and in discussions that, like the stream of pain itself, flow through the ages? I do not claim any great new revelation. However, there is an aspect of the problem I have seldom found recognized in the books and sermons to which I have been exposed through a good many years.

Our Christian faith affirms that as workers together with God we can transform some evil situations. Those we cannot transform we must seek to transcend by God's strength. The last word in the problem of evil, whether evil be conceived as sin or as suffering, is not to be found in a theoretical explanation but in the promise repeatedly validated in Christian experience: "My grace is sufficient for thee: for my power is made perfect in weakness."

But is it? Why did the psalmist pray, "Take not thy holy Spirit from me," unless he thought that sometimes the Holy Spirit evaded his most earnest seeking? Why did Jesus in his moment of darkest agony pray, "My God, my God, why hast thou forsaken me?" Why, save that he felt cut off from the face of God at the very moment he needed most to see it? This is the deepest hell — not merely to suffer, but to suffer and seek in vain for God's sustaining presence.

When in quietness and confidence one can say, "If I make my bed in hell, behold, thou art there!" then anything is endurable. With this victorious faith, Christians through the ages have met and conquered affliction. But the depths of the mystery of the problem of evil appear at the point where the Christian does not find this possible. Believing in God, sensitive to his will, seeking earnestly for God's presence, he cries to God out of the depths. And his own words come back to mock him.....

The wise counselor and understanding Christian will put the emphasis on God's forgiveness as the counterpart of man's repentance, on surrender and trust as pre-requisite to the lifting by God of a burden that is intolerable. The Christian gospel means, after all, not that we save ourselves by our repentance, but that God saves us when we repent. This ought to be all one needs to say. Yet the fact remains that sometimes persons of deep spiritual sensitivity, earnestly desiring to trust their lives to God's keeping, find they must cry out as did our Lord, "My God, why hast thou forsaken me?" And this worst of all hells may last, not momentarily, but for days, months, years....It is then that "hope deferred maketh the heart sick...."

It is not the callous sinner who lives in this kind of hell, but the sensitive soul who is caught by the unresolved conflict of his insight and his impotence. Deprived either of spiritual promptings or of the power to follow them by any measure of free consent, one does not find himself in this situation. A person may live sanely in stolid bovine complacency or insanely in a world of psychic delusions, but he does not find himself at the same time pursued by the Hound of Heaven and cut off from God's presence. On the other hand, when one has both the spiritual promptings of the Christian gospel and normal control of his will, the problem does not appear. The way of salvation is assured, for through repentance and surrender one does find forgiveness and power. The Christian way is justified by its fruits, and our preaching is not vain.

✪ October 18

Stephen Return Riggs

PRESBYTERIAN

March 23, 1812–August 24, 1883

"To learn an unwritten language," wrote Stephen Riggs, "and to reduce it to a form that can be seen as well as heard, is confessedly a work of no small magnitude. Hitherto it has seemed to exist only in sound. But it has been, all through the past ages, worked out and up by the forges of human hearts. It has been made to express the lightest thoughts as well as the heart-throbs of men and women and children in their generations. The human mind, in its most untutored state, is God's creation. It may not stamp purity nor even goodness on its language, but it always, I think, stamps it with the deepest philosophy. So far, at, least, language is of divine origin."

The first task of a missionary in a new field is, of course, to learn the language of those to whom he or she would speak. It is all too easy to approach that task as if it were simply an obstacle to be dealt with: to learn a code so that messages can be sent. Stephen Return Riggs was one of those rare individuals who understood that it is possible to learn from the language being learned, that it is a storehouse of information about the people who use it and the way in which they have come to understand the nature and meaning of life. It is equally vital to understand that words are continuously being coined, and meanings are always shifting. Stephen Riggs knew that language is a living thing.

> The unlearned Dakota may not be able to give any definition for any single word that he has been using all his life-time, — he may say, "It means that, and can't mean any thing else" — yet, all the while, in the mental workshop of the people, unconsciously and very slowly it may be, but no less very surely, these words of air are newly coined. No angle can turn up, but by and by it will be worn off by use. No ungrammatical expression can come in that will not be rejected by the best thinkers and speakers. New words will be coined to meet the mind's wants; and new forms of expression, which at the first are bungling descriptions only, will be pared down and tucked up so as to come into harmony with the living language.

Riggs grew up in Ohio and was educated at Jefferson College and Western Theological Seminary. He began his ministry in Massachusetts in 1836, but a doctor friend recognized that Riggs's gift with languages could make him useful in the new mission work just begun on the upper Minnesota River among the Sioux. In 1837, Riggs married Mary Longley and moved there in the same year. Mission work and translation became their life. Theirs was a shared ministry and Riggs acknowledged this in his autobiography: *Mary and I: Forty Years with the Sioux.* Their work progressed slowly, but Riggs understood that was to be expected:

> When we missionaries had gathered and expressed and arranged the words of this language, what had we to put into it, and what great gifts had we for the Dakota people? What will you give me? has always been their cry. We brought to them the Word of Life, the Gospel of Salvation through faith in Jesus Christ our Lord, as contained in the Bible. Not to preach Christ to them only that they might have life, but to engraft his living words into their living thoughts, so that they might grow into his spirit more and more, was the object of our coming. The labor of writing the language was undertaken as a means to a greater end. To put God's thoughts into their speech, and to teach them to read in their own tongue the wonderful works of God, was what brought us to the land of the Dakotas. But they could not appreciate this. Ever and anon came the question, What will you give me? And so, when we would proclaim "the old, old story" to those proud Dakota men at Lac-qui-parle, we had to begin with kettles of boiled pumpkins, turnips, and potatoes. The bread that perisheth could be appreciated — the Bread of Life was still beyond their comprehension. But by and by it was to find its proper nesting-place.

A few years later, Riggs could report that progress was being made:

It pleased God to make this winter one of fruitfulness. Mr. Renville was active in persuading those under his influence to attend the religious meetings, the schoolroom was crowded on Sabbaths, and the Word, imperfectly as it was spoken, was used by the Spirit upon those dark minds. There was evidently a quickening of the church. They were interested in prayer. What is prayer? — and how shall we pray? became questions of interest with them. One woman who had received at her baptism the name of Catherine, and who still lives a believing life at the end of forty years, was then troubled to know how prayer could reach God. I told her in this we were all little children. God recognized our condition in this respect, and had told us that, as earthly fathers and mothers were willing, and desirous of giving good gifts to their children, he was more willing to give the Holy Spirit to them that ask him. Besides, he made the ear, and shall he not hear? He made, in a large sense, all language, and shall he not he able to understand Dakota words? The very word for "pray" in the Dakota language was "to cry to" — *chakiya*. Prayer was now, as through all ages it had been, the child's cry in the ear of the Great Father. So there appeared to be a working upward of many hearts.

Early in February Mr. Pond, Mr. Renville, and Mr. Huggins, Mr. Gavan and myself, after due examination and instruction, agreed to receive ten Dakotas into the church — all women. I baptized them and their children — twenty-eight in all — on one Sabbath morning. It was to us a day of cheer. To these Dakota Gentiles also God had indeed opened the door of faith. Blessed be his name for ever and ever.

The Riggs's work progressed within the larger context of the expansion of the European population as they moved from the eastern states. The Sioux were being pushed out of their ancestral lands. In 1862, there was a native uprising in which hundreds of settlers were killed. Since, with only one exception, the Indians saved all missionaries, Riggs thereafter added to his work a ministry to imprisoned Sioux people and advocacy for them in Washington. His translation work continued, producing readers, primers, and portions of the Bible along with grammars, dictionaries, and such classics of western culture as *The Pilgrim's Progress* and Guyot's *Elementary Geography*. In 1880, three years before his death, Riggs published *Dakota Wowapi Waken: The Holy Bible in the Language of the Dakotas*.

✠ *October 19* _____

Edward McGlynn

ROMAN CATHOLIC

September 27, 1837–January 7, 1900

As Roman Catholic immigrants flooded into the United States in the late 19th century, their church leaders strove to build up the institution to accommodate them. Fearing lest they be assimilated into a Protestant culture, they tried to separate church members as far as possible from what they saw as the negative influence of the public schools. Edward McGlynn saw the situation differently. It seemed to him that the church's first priority should be the relief of the poor and ought to work with all institutions that had similar concerns.

Such views were inevitably controversial. When McGlynn began to take a leading role in secular organizations, the authorities called him to account. He had been influenced by Henry George's 1880 book, *Progress and Poverty.* To McGlynn, its explanations and solutions made sense. To the Archbishop of New York, Michael Corrigan, however, thought George's ideas smacked of Socialism and seemed to call for the abolition of private property. The Archbishop first removed Fr. McGlynn from his parish, then, in 1886, excommunicated him.

Refusing to retract his ideas, McGlynn organized an Anti-Poverty League and traveled widely for the next six years to propagate his ideas. When Pope Leo XIII issued an encyclical on labor conditions, "Rerum Novarum," Henry George took the opportunity to defend his theories in a letter to the pope, who in turn reinstated Fr. McGlynn. McGlynn spent the last eight years of his ministry as pastor of St. Mary's Church in Newburgh, New York, and continued to work with clergy of other churches and to speak out for working people and the poor. He gave so generously from the funds and material goods in his possession that when he died, it was said that his clothes were too poor to give away.

At his death, the local newspaper wrote, "he was years in advance" of his own church and that "he taught not alone the doctrines of that Church in whose behalf he labored constantly, but he taught also the doctrine of humanity in its broadest sense. He believed in the Fatherhood of God and Brotherhood of Man, and his teaching reached the hearts of the masses everywhere.... Creed and denomination counted less with him than did humanity."

Readings from the writings of Edward McGlynn

I was not born to be a mere agitator or a professor of political economy. I was born to be a preacher of God's truth to men. I was born to minister to His laws, to look after the spiritual welfare of my fellow-men. From my infancy I had a call to be a priest of Christ's Church. It was my holy vocation. Surely it was no small sorrow to me to be torn from this altar and to come among you in this hall bereft of my priestly functions, but I now feel that I have suffered for the truth, and I shall always preach the Word of God, the glorious principles of the Fatherhood of God and the Brotherhood of Man, even if it be from a platform, a barrel, or the tail of a cart.

I say that I have not insulted the Archbishop and the Pope; but I have criticized their policies and politics. I have given reasons for it. And if they say that in order to be permitted to receive the sacraments of the Catholic Church people must either agree with all their policies and politics, or at least must not be guilty of the indiscretion of publicly disagreeing with them, I say they are grievously misrepresenting Catholic theology and making conditions morally impossible of acceptance not merely by those outside whom they should strive to win, but also by vast numbers inside the Church. And I predict with bitterness of soul, regretting exceedingly that I have so clear a vision of what I am predicting, that in another generation or two, the worst, the bitterest, the most relentless enemies of Catholic authority, of Pope, of bishop, and priest, will not be the children of those old-fashioned English or American Protestants, but will be the children or grandchildren of people who are thronging the Catholic Churches today. And if Rome shall make the accepting of its politics and policies a condition of accepting its creed and its sacraments, then the righteous instincts of men will rebel, then they will refuse to submit to its dogmas and illogically will throw up the whole thing.

It is charity, charity that seeketh not her own, but is prodigal of self in order to win the brother. It was this charity, this love of mankind for God's sake, based upon love of God for His own sake, that converted the world to Christianity, that abolished slavery. And it is only in this spirit that the slavery that we are warring against can ever be abolished.

I should like to do a little toward restoring the glorious word charity to its proper place. Unfortunately, it too often is taken as meaning the mere doling out of alms. Is it not a monstrous injury that is done to the sweet name of charity to so degrade it that its occupation must be gone if there are no more beggars to be fed and clothed?

Charity is a noble virtue, but to make the whole world an almshouse is carrying it to the absurd. The noblest charity is to do justice — not only to procure, at the sacrifice of self, in an unselfish spirit, some improvement in the condition of mankind, but to compel tyrants to do justice to the victims they have wronged.

The supreme moral law, the law of gravitation in the moral order, is justice. Justice is the one thing necessary to hold society together, to give each individual man the proper opportunity of exercising his God-given liberty. Justice must be like Him in whose bosom it finds its eternal resting place, universal — it must prevail throughout the universe of God.

When justice becomes the common atmosphere of human society, then men will take naturally to religion.

There is an old Latin saying, "Let justice be done though the heavens fall." But let justice be done and the heavens will not fall to our ruin. Then the heavens will stoop to the embrace of earth and the earth will be lifted up to the kiss of heaven, and then on earth shall be at last fulfilled the Saviour's Prayer, the prayer that all His children everywhere are reciting with yearning hearts: "Thy kingdom come, Thy will be done on *earth* as it is in heaven."

✪ October 20 ────────────────────────────────

Harriet Starr Cannon

EPISCOPALIAN

May 7, 1823–April 9, 1896

Today, there are dozens of religious orders for women in the Episcopal Church, and almost as many for men. They may not be as widely known as they should be, yet it now seems unlikely that any Episcopalian, or indeed members of most other denominations, would be scandalized to hear of their existence or display the outrage described by one 19th-century witness:

> consternation and ridicule were turned into wrath, and the powers of this world were invoked to overcome the forces of Heaven. Dense ignorance was the parent of intense prejudice, and the fierceness of men and women thus generated knew scarcely any bounds. Clergymen forgot their holy calling in denouncing religious orders and entangling vows. Ladies and gentlemen of the highest social position laid aside their good manners and behaved like barbarians to defenseless sisters, and the general voice and temper of our Church were to the effect that all who sympathized with such extravagancies, not to say follies and wickedness, as entangling vows and a common life based upon spiritual affinities exhibited, must be content to be contemned if not forgotten.

Though Harriet Starr Cannon was orphaned during her first year of life and was moved from South Carolina to the home of an uncle and aunt in Connecticut, where she enjoyed a comfortable upbringing. She was about to move to California with her older, just-married sister, when this last remaining relative also died. Rather than retreat into loneliness, Harriet joined the Sisterhood of the Holy Communion, recently founded by William Augustus Muhlenberg* in New York City. The sisters were not organized according to the traditional model, but it drew together a group of women who served in Muhlenberg's parish as well as the newly created St. Luke's Hospital. For six years, Harriet Cannon remained with them.

But something was still missing. When she went to see Bishop Horatio Potter for guidance, he supported her vision for a new order that would follow more ancient monastic patterns. On the Feast of the Purification, 1865, Bishop Potter received vows of poverty, chastity, and obedience from Cannon and four other women. They called themselves the Community of St. Mary. At first, they worked at houses for "fallen women" and for orphans, but the storm that broke once the bishop's actions became known drove them out of those places. Finding other support, they then established a girls' school and hospital, both of which prospered. Before long, they founded another girls' school in Memphis and still another in Wisconsin. Demand for their services grew beyond their reach, even as the order swelled to nearly 100 professed sisters, novices, and postulants by the end of the century. Until her death, 30 years after the order was established, Harriet

Cannon served as Mother Superior, and by her patience, endurance, wisdom, and faith, she enriched the life of the whole Episcopal Church.

A reading from some of Harriet Starr Cannon's sayings, published with the Rule of the Order

God's will be done whether by life or death.

Thy will, thy blessed will, whatever it may be.

May we so yield ourselves to the operation of the Holy Ghost as in all things to be and to do what he would have us be and do what he would have us do.

I always say, if there exists the need and one has counted the cost as in the sight of God, one must undoubtedly make the venture of faith, believing that the Lord will provide.

We have given ourselves to him; if he calls us we must say, "Lord here am I."

You must have faith to believe that we can learn to do whatever in the providence of God we are asked to do.

We must not regret what we do in his name; our reward is with the Most High.

God is always near us, if only we are always seeking to be near him.

May we all draw near to him through the avenue of trouble.

We know that our discipline comes from God, and we must vindicate God by our acceptance of it.

The grace of humility cannot be ours unless we have humiliations. I try to obey that clause in our Rule that says, "Be thankful for humiliations of whatever kind."

I know and am sure that all is from God, and that his very chastisements are tokens of love.

Our Master marks us for his own when he gives to us a portion of his Cross: and whatever he gives must be our joy.

It is contact with others in the Religious Life which is the golden opportunity of reaching perfection.

Try to excuse in others as far as possible what seems to you so wrong; try to think that more is said than is really meant.

One feels often that the very existence of a Religious Community is a miracle. And one too so often meditates on that first Religious Order, our Lord and his Apostles; one denied him, another betrayed him, and all fled in the hour of trial.

We remember, that knowing all that Judas would do, he allowed him to remain with him to the very last.

If our patron Saint is the *Mater Dolorosa*, our tears must blend with hers.

It is very dark, and we cry, "Lord save us, we perish," but let us rest in him, believing that in due time light will come.

It is only seeming darkness; the light is sure to come.

Things look rather dark; but as a matter of fact things are not really dark. God ruleth over all, and if we feel troubled is it not a want of faith on our part? Just think of our blessings! What are our trials compared to our blessings! I realize that the checks we receive as a Community are blessings in disguise!

I look on the bright side

I hope the sun is shining everywhere and in every corner of every one's heart.

✪ *October 21* _____

Anthony Binga

BAPTIST

June 1, 1843–January 21, 1919

At the end of the Civil War, leadership among African Americans in the south was critically important but, because of the legacy of slavery, had to be supplied in large part by outsiders and, in many cases, by whites. Anthony Binga, one of those outsiders, had the advantage of growing up in Canada, where his parents had fled after escaping from slavery. He was privately tutored in Latin and anatomy because he planned to become a doctor. With a scholarship and what he could earn, he worked his way through King's Institute in Buxton, Canada West, a town founded by a white abolitionist.

After completing his studies in 1865, Binga moved to Kansas to teach school in Atchison but illness forced him to return to Canada. There, at 24, he experienced a religious conversion and was baptized in a Canadian river in February of 1867.

Called again to the United States to serve as a school principal and preacher in Ohio, he discovered that soliciting funds from white philanthropists to support the school required too much travel and interfered with what he felt was his primary work as a preacher. Again he returned to Canada, but in January of 1872 he moved to Richmond, Virginia, as pastor of the First Baptist Church. For a while, he also oversaw the education of black children in Manchester (now a part of Richmond).

As pastor of the First Baptist Church of Richmond, Binga became a leader among black Baptists in the south. He was chosen to be the first chairman of the Foreign Mission Board of the Baptist Foreign Mission Convention in 1880 and helped guide its evolution into the National Baptist Convention. Support for foreign mission was always an important issue for Binga. He proposed smaller, more economical conventions to free funds for work overseas and helped organize a Virginia auxiliary of the Lott Carey* Baptist Foreign Mission Convention. During his 47 years at the First Baptist Church, Binga expanded the voting rights of members and twice oversaw the construction of a larger building to accommodate congregational expansion. His address entitled "Past and Present Social, Moral and Religious Condition of the Colored Baptists of Virginia" is an eloquent summary of his perspective on the years of slavery and its aftermath:

A reading from "Past and Present Social, Moral and Religious Condition of the Colored Baptists of Virginia" by Anthony Binga

We have no book of martyrs in which are recorded the sufferings of colored Baptists in this State, but this is not for the want of facts.

The colored Baptists have suffered by thousands at the stake — if not a stake made deadly by fire — it was one made terrible and bloody by the cruel lash, which tore the quivering flesh from the back of innocent men and women for no other crime than that of worshiping the God of heaven.

Ministers of the gospel of Jesus Christ have suffered imprisonment, and have been taken out of chains, only to receive thirty and nine stripes for preaching the gospel on the Sabbath-day.

Like the Apostle Paul, they could say, "stripes and imprisonment await me in every city," and like him they said, "none of these things move me." They counted not their lives dear, that they might finish their course with joy. Neither the *lash* nor the *law* could prevent them from preaching Christ. So great was their zeal, that ten o'clock at night was not too late to start a journey of ten miles to meet in an humble prayer-meeting and taste that mysterious joy which triumphs over affliction. Their manner of worship was peculiar to themselves — warm and emotional. They were not wholly responsible for the objectionable features about their worship, for they worshiped God the best they knew how, and however much it may have been wanting in form, it was wanting nothing in spirit. The ministers who led these meetings had no scholastic training. . . . But these men, with all their illiteracy, were mighty in the hands of God. Such men as Brother Joseph Abrams and others of his type, wielded a sword that had no fine edge of logic, but like the jawbone which Sampson used, it laid the Philistines in heaps, which shows how God will own and bless the labors of feeble hands which are held up to him in faith. Private houses were chosen as places of meeting, for there they were free from the embarrassing gaze of the "watchman," whose unwanted presence was always necessary to make the worship of God legal.

At other times the colored Baptists met under the same roof with their white Baptist brethren, bathed with the same light, breathed the same air, and listened to the same word of life, but the elevated seats in the gallery, which they were forced to occupy, did not comport with their humble spirits, for they could not bear to feel that they were exalted above their white brethren.

Although they occupied the "uppermost seats in the synagogue," it seems this forbidden place did not bring down upon them the displeasure of the Lord, for their numbers, strange to say, increased rapidly....

There is one thing over which the colored Baptist ministers have cause to rejoice, that is, that they are less fettered by prejudice than their white brethren. While not altogether free from this child of sin, they are yet always found in the lead in extending that Christian courtesy that should adorn Christianity. The colored Baptist churches of Virginia keep no impassible barrier before their pulpit, but fully recognize the fact "that God is no respecter of persons." The colored Baptist minister in extending the courtesy to their white brethren, which is not reciprocated, exemplify much of the spirit of the Great Head of the church. It is quite a graceful thing to lead a minister into your pulpit who can never find room for you in his. This act finds no support in human nature, and the man who can do this graceful thing gives high proof of a new birth.

✪ October 22 _____

Robert G. LeTourneau

CHRISTIAN AND MISSIONARY ALLIANCE

November 30, 1888–June 1, 1969

To drop out of school after eighth grade and elope to Mexico to marry a 17-year-old young woman without her parents' consent is not the best way to start an adult life. After Robert LeTourneau did all that, he and his wife lost their first child, and he was plunged into debt by an inept business partner. Worse still, he broke his neck in a car accident. But LeTourneau was not a quitter, and he knew from his upbringing that there was a God who would welcome sinners. It was just before Christmas, in 1904, at a crusade in Portland, Oregon, that the 16-year-old LeTourneau had made a commitment to Christ. He reports of the event: "What terrified me was that after a week of concentrated singing, and listening to sermons, I didn't feel even a tremor of response." His lack of inner response led him to pray even more. "No bolts of lightning hit me. No great flash of awareness. I just prayed to the Lord to save me, and then I was aware of another presence." But his youthful piety faded. Having dropped out of school to work, he soon discovered life could be a hard road. One of his first jobs was at an iron factory in Portland, where he shoveled sand for a living. The couple of years he spent in the plant gave him great strength and stamina, but also exposed him to a kind of worldliness that was at odds with the faith he had once possessed and that his parents continually prayed he would regain.

Determined, even stubborn, physically large, strong, and energetic, LeTourneau would not give up. He compensated for his lack of formal education with a natural inventiveness. But as important as were his personality traits, even more significant was his return to faith. The death of his child was a moment of awakening for LeTourneau. Recalling his early upbringing, he believed that he and Evelyn had been neglecting God in their marriage. Realizing something was very much amiss in his life, he attended a revival. His humble prayers included: "Lord, if You'll forgive and help me, I'll do anything You want me to do from this day on." At 30, he finally recommitted himself, resolving to tithe even if times were hard. From then on, his labors would all be directed to one goal, the proclamation of the gospel to all who would hear.

LeTourneau's pastor counseled him to remember that God needed businessmen as much as preachers and missionaries. He heard that as a call to put his natural inclinations to work. He began to develop a whole new line of equipment, bigger and more powerful than anything made up to that time. He invented and improved large machinery for ever bigger jobs. Between his first patent granted in 1923 when he was 34, and his last in 1965 when he was 77, LeTourneau acquired almost 300 patents in all. His first was for a scraper, but many other types of scrapers followed, as did the bulldozer, dredgers, rollers, logging devices, and others, including a new type of drilling rig that could be jacked up on three straight legs. Finished at one site, it could be towed to another, thus eliminating the cost of demolishing a more permanent structure, or leaving it as an eyesore in the sea.

He went on to invent earthmovers, transporters, missile launchers, bridgebuilders, and portable offshore drilling rigs. During World War II, LeTourneau provided 70 percent of the heavy equipment used by the Armed Forces. Five colleges granted him honorary doctorates, and numerous industrial awards were bestowed. But his business success did not detract from his enthusiasm for Christian service; rather, it provided the means for him to be effective there also. LeTourneau turned the tithe upside down, giving away 90 percent of his income. He traveled the nation, extolling God and Christianity. As a lay pastor in the Christian and Missionary Alliance, he spoke with conviction about the need for God to be at the heart of each life and every business. He employed three chaplains at his factory. He and his wife rented a house in Chicago for workers in their plant whose housing was inadequate, or who needed to get away from some of the more destructive influences of the city. The couple founded a college in 1946 in Longview, Texas — now known as LeTourneau University — which retains its faith-based foundation and continues to educate new generations of leaders. He funded two agricultural missions in Liberia in West Africa, underwrote work in Peru, South America, and created a foundation to support Christian causes.

One of his favorite enterprises was equipping Christian mission workers with skills to provide practical help in the developing world, such as home-building expertise. He and Evelyn (at her instigation) bought Camp Bethel on Winona Lake on the outskirts of Chicago. Enlisting students from Wheaton College, the facility became a vigorous evangelistic and recreational center. Christian business associations, as one might expect, were high on his list of important groups.

Reluctant to claim too much of his success for himself, LeTourneau said. "I'm just a mechanic that God has blessed, and it seems He wants me to go around telling how He will bless you, too." Not long before the end of his life, he also said: "Everything considered, I've had my share of ups and downs, but thus far my life has been a miracle of God's grace all the way through."

✪ October 23 _____

Samson Occom
PRESBYTERIAN
1723–July 14, 1792

Although conversion of natives was usually one of the principle reasons given for establishing early settlements in America, in practice this seldom happened. Even when efforts were made, they were liable to founder on misunderstandings and controversy. Samson Occom was one of the better-known Native American converts, but his efforts to evangelize others were hamstrung by lack of support from his white sponsors and the continuing intrusion of white settlers into Native American lands.

Occom's mother had been converted to Christianity when he was a young teenager, and when he was 16 years old he, too, was converted. Searching for a school where he could learn to read, he encountered the institution operated by Eleazar Wheelock.* There he not only learned to read English fluently, but also mastered Latin, Greek, and Hebrew. His success encouraged Wheelock to design a school for Native Americans and, eventually, to send Occom off to England to raise funds for the project. During two years in England, Occom preached 300 sermons and raised the substantial sum of over £12,000. Nonetheless, when he returned he found it hard to support himself, and Wheelock, disillusioned by some of his Native American students, had opened his school to white pupils, instead.

Frustrated by the lack of apppreciation for his efforts, Occom strove to found a community for Native Americans in upstate New York, far from European settlements, and in 1785 he finally was able to do so. He served as its spiritual leader, teacher, fund-raiser, and lobbyist until his death in 1792. Occom was an eloquent speaker. A sermon he preached on the execution of a fellow Native American at the convict's request was edited by Jonathan Edwards and widely distributed. Occom also published a collection of hymns and a useful history of the Montauk Indians among whom he served for a number of years as teacher and pastor.

Excerpts from the introduction and sermon preached by Samson Occom at the execution of Moses Paul in New Haven, Connecticut, in 1772

The world is already full of books; and the people of God are abundantly furnished with excellent books upon divine subjects; and it seems altogether unlikely that my performance will be of any great service in the world, since the most excellent writings of worthy and learned men are disregarded. But there are two or three considerations that have induced me to be willing to suffer my broken hints to appear. One is, that the books that are in the world, are written in very high and refined language; and the sermons that are delivered every Sabbath in general, are in a very high and lofty style, so that the common people understand but little of them. But I think they cannot help understanding my talk; it is common, plain, everyday talk; little children may understand me. And poor Negro's may plainly and fully understand my meaning; and that may be of service to them. Again, it may in a particular manner be serviceable to my poor kindred, the Indians. Further, as it comes from an uncommon quarter, it may induce people to read it, because it is from an Indian. Lastly, God works everywhere and when he pleases, and by what instrument he sees fit, and he has used weak and unlikely instruments to bring about his great worth.

O eternity, eternity, eternity! Who can measure it? Who can count the years thereof? Arithmetic must fail, the thoughts of men and angels are drowned in it; how shall we describe eternity? To what shall we compare it? Were it possible to employ a fly to carry off this globe by the small particles thereof, and to carry them to such a distance that it should return once in 10,000 years for another particle, and to continue until it has carried off all this globe, and framed them together in some unknown space, until it has made just such a world as this is; after all, eternity would remain the same unexhausted duration. This must be the unavoidable portion of all impenitent sinners, let them be who they will, great or small, honorable or ignoble, rich or poor, bond or free. Negroes, Indians, English, or of what nations soever, all that die in their sins, must go to hell together, for the wages of sin is death.

My unhappy brother, Moses; as it was your own desire that I should preach to you this last discourse, so I shall speak plainly to you. You are the bone of my bone, and flesh of my flesh. You are an Indian, a despised creature; but you have despised yourself; yea, you have despised God more; you have trodden under foot his authority; you have despised his commands and precepts: and now, as God says, "Be sure your sins will find you out"; so now, poor Moses, your sins have found you out, and they have overtaken for you this day; the day of your death is now; the king of terrors is at hand; you have but a very few moments to breathe in this world. The just laws of man, and holy law of Jehovah, call aloud for the destruction of your mortal life; God says, "Whoso sheddeth man's blood, by man shall his blood be shed." This is the ancient decree of heaven, and it is to be executed by man; nor have you the least gleam of hope of escape, for the unalterable sentence is passed; the terrible day of execution is come; the unwelcome guard is about you; and the fatal instruments of death are now made ready; your coffin and grave, your last lodging, are open ready to receive you.

✪ October 24

Charles Carroll

ROMAN CATHOLIC

September 19, 1737–November 14, 1832

The first settlers in those American colonies that ultimately became the United States were English. Whether members of the "established church" or nonconformists, they considered Roman Catholics to be agents of a foreign power and would not welcome them to the new colonies. Maryland was the exception, since it was established by a royal charter obtained through the influence of Lord Baltimore. Charles Carroll's grandfather came to Maryland under that arrangement, but when Lord Baltimore lost the royal favor, the Church of England was established there as well.

In 1770, Governor Eden imposed certain fees upon the colonists, including ones to establish stipends for the clergy of the Church of England. The jurist Daniel Dulaney defended the government's position in a series of articles in the *Maryland Gazette* under the signature Antillon. Carroll argued that fees were taxes and should not be levied upon the people except by the consent of their representatives. Popular sentiment was decidedly with his four articles. His opposition helped to sway the election of 1773 in favor of the governor's opponents.

Carroll became the only Roman Catholic to sign the Declaration of Independence. With the coming of the American Revolution, Roman Catholics and many Christians of other denominations united in opposition to English rule. Following the Revolution, Carroll served simultaneously in the Maryland legislature and the House of Representatives, then went on to the Senate. When a law was passed that one could not serve in a state legislature and Congress at the same time, Carroll resigned his national office to stay with the Maryland legislature. He was the last surviving signer of the Declaration of Independence.

A reading from a letter of Charles Carroll in defense of religious freedom

In vindication of his conduct, Antillon has not endeavoured to convince the minds of his readers by the force of reason, but "in the favourite method of illiberal calumny, virulent abuse and shameless asseveration to affect their passions" has attempted to render his antagonist ridiculous, contemptible and odious; he has descended to the lowest jests on the person of the Citizen, has expressed the utmost contempt of his understanding, and a strong suspicion of his *political and religious principles*. What connection, Antillon, have the latter with the Proclamation? Attempts to rouse popular prejudices, and to turn the laugh against an adversary, discover the weakness of a cause, or the inabilities of the advocate, who employs ridicule, instead of argument. *"The Citizen's patriotism is entirely feigned";* his reasons must not be considered, or listened to, because his *religious principles* are not to be trusted. Yet if we are to credit Antillon, the Citizen is so little attached to these principles, "That he is most devoutly wishing for the event," which is to free him from their shackles. What my speculative notions on religion may be, this is neither the place nor time to declare; my political principles ought only to be questioned on the present occasion; surely they are constitutional, and have met, I hope, with the approbation of my Countrymen; if so Antillon's aspersions will give me no uneasiness. He asks, who is this Citizen? A man, Antillon, of an independent fortune, one deeply interested in the prosperity of his country: a friend to liberty, a settled enemy to lawless prerogative....

I comprehend fully, Antillon, your threats thrown out against certain religionists; to shew the *greatness of your soul*, and your utter detestation of malice, I shall give the public a translation of your Latin sentence; the sentiment is truly noble, and reflects the highest lustre on its author or adopter; *Eos tamen laedere non exoptemus, qui nos laedere non exoptant*, we would not wish to hurt those who do not wish to hurt us; — in other words, "I cannot wreak my resentment on the Citizen, without involving all of his religion in one common ruin with him; they have not offended me, it is true, but it is better that ninety-nine just should suffer, than one guilty man escape — a thorough paced politician never sticks at the means of accomplishing his ends; why should I, who have so just a claim to the character?" These, Antillon, are the sentiments and threats, couched under your Latin phrase, which *you even* were ashamed to avow in plain English....

The Citizen did not deliver his sentiment only but likewise the sentiment of others. We Catholics, who think we were hardly treated on occasion, *we* still remember the treatment though our resentment hath entirely subsided. It is not in the least surprizing that a man incapable of forming an exalted sentiment, should not readily comprehend the force and beauty of one.... To what purpose was the threat thrown out of enforcing the penal statutes by proclamation? Why am I told that my conduct is very inconsistent with the situation of one, who "owes even the *toleration* he enjoys to the favour of government?" If by instilling prejudices into the Governor, and by every mean and wicked artifice you can rouse the popular resentment against certain religionists, and thus bring on a persecution of them, it will then be known whether the toleration I enjoy, be due to the favour of government or not.

✪ October 25 _____

Justus Falckner

LUTHERAN

November 22, 1672–1723

Providing leadership for small, struggling congregations is still a challenge for church bodies. In the early 18th century, it was more so. Without well developed structures and support systems, and with the kind of inertia that still characterizes so many churches today, newly formed immigrant congregations in the colonies could not count on good leadership. One of the consistent reports we have of frontier congregations of that period concerns the shortage of adequately trained clergy. Such was the case for New World Lutherans in general, and certainly in the Hudson Valley area.

There was a kind of extended parish of Lutherans in this area, many of whom had Dutch roots. Andrew Rudman had been a good pastor to them, but his health was declining, so the parish wondered where they would find a qualified replacement. Justus Falckner eventually became that leader, but he never sought out the role. In fact, the prospect was something of a conflict of conscience for him. As a Swedish pastor, Rudman wrote him, asking, "What shall I do forsaking my little flock? Looking everywhere, I find no one better fitted than you to whom I may safely entrust my sheep." Though complimented, Falckner remained hesitant. He was German, and not fluent in Dutch. He had studied theology, but instead chose to be a land agent and surveyor. He questioned the legitimacy of ordination in the absence of regular church procedures for calling and ordaining new pastors on North American soil. At 31, Falckner was finally convinced that Rudman's request was indeed a true call to ministry. There were Lutheran precedents for what we would now call "presbyteral ordination" — the use of parish clergy to ordain new parish clergy — in the New World. The mission of the church can be hampered by too much rigidity about specific details, especially in times and places that are simply too far removed from the normal apparatus of traditional ecclesiastical structures. Rudman had authorization from his bishop in Sweden to ordain new pastors in the colonies. In addition, Falckner's own inner call began to be irresistible. In a letter to one of his former teachers, he wrote: "After much persuasion, also prompting of heart and conscience, I am staying as a regular preacher with a little Dutch Lutheran congregation, a state of affairs which I had so long avoided."

On November 24, 1703, three Swedes, including Rudman, participated in the ordination of Falckner in Philadelphia. In his book *The World of Justus Falckner*, Delber Wallace Clark describes the event that needed to take into account Swedish, Dutch, German, and American traditions and understandings:

> The arrangements for the ordination were made with a speed, which in those days, was breath-taking. Just three weeks after the acceptance of the call, Rudman had reached Philadelphia and ordained the candidate who was already preparing to leave for New York. There was much to be done in this brief period. The Swedish ministers had to assemble, approve the plan, and settle upon a procedure.
>
> The three-way reference of the act made certain precautions necessary. The ordination must be in a form consistent with Falckner's German tradition and the standards of the Dutch Lutherans to whom he would minister, and it must be the kind the Swedes could validly confer. There were minor questions, such as language, vestments, and even music. They met linguistically upon the common ground of Latin, the learned language. There were just about enough vestments to go around for all involved in the ceremony and some tact had to be used in deciding who should wear which.

Thus began the official ministry of the first Lutheran pastor ordained in what would become the United States.

Falckner proved an able and energetic leader. He studied Dutch to make his preaching to his congregation more meaningful. He traveled the course of the Hudson River in his ministry of visitation to his far-flung parish. He covered an area that took in parts of New York, New Jersey, and Pennsylvania and became known as a missionary and a pastor. He taught, organized, and baptized not just new European immigrants and their children, but also converts within the black and Native American communities. Despite all his pastoral duties, he also found time to develop a manual of Christian teachings and even contribute to the growing body of hymnody.

When a pastor died, others in the area would fill in, covering his duties as best they could until a new pastor could be found. Falckner's own workload expanded until it was no longer possible for one man to fulfill it. He died at 51, during a pastoral visitation journey up the Hudson River. His demise was probably hastened by the previous death of a colleague, the Rev. Joshua von Kocherthal,* which markedly increased his own obligations.

Some of Falckner's records survive. They contain heartfelt prayers following many of the notes of baptisms and other pastoral duties in the course of 20 years of ministry. Although all reference to the date and place of his burial has been lost, his faithfulness keeps his memory alive. A hymn he wrote while still a student in Halle might serve as his epitaph:

> *When His servants stand before Him*
> *Each receiving his reward,*
> *When His saints in light adore Him,*
> *Giving glory to the Lord;*
> *"Victory!" our song shall be*
> *Like the thunder of the sea.*

✪ October 26

Solomon Stoddard

CONGREGATIONAL

September 27, 1643–February 11, 1729

It is said that "God has no grandchildren"; that is, each Christian must come to know him- or herself as a child of God. This relationship cannot be mediated through one's earthly parents, who can teach the faith to their children but cannot experience it for them. Sooner or later, the child must grow into a living relationship — or not. For the Puritan settlers of New England, a conversion experience was critical. Those who made the perilous journey across the Atlantic had that experience in common. But not all their children, though baptized, could make that same profession. What could be done about those who were formally Christian, yet lacked the experience of faith? Gradually, during the latter part of the 17th century a "half-way covenant" became widely accepted: the baptized would be recognized as members and their children could be baptized, but would not have full communicant status. Solomon Stoddard went further still. After many years of debate, he persuaded his congregation in Northampton to make the Lord's Supper available to all who were not leading openly sinful lives. The sacrament would then become a "converting ordinance," a possible means of receiving God's grace and being saved. But Stoddard was not indifferent to the conversion experience of his congregation. He preached conversion constantly and during his years as pastor of the Northampton congregation there were five seasons of revival.

"Stoddardism," as it was called, spread through western New England but remained controversial. Theologians like Increase Mather denounced him for compromising the principles on which Congregationalism was founded. Stoddard, in turn, defended himself with such writings as *The Safety of Appearing at the Day of Judgment in the Righteousness of Christ* (1687); *An Appeal to the Learned* (1709); and *A Guide to Christ* (1714).

Stoddard also challenged the orthodoxy of his day by elevating the power of the pastor above that of the congregation. His critics called him "Pope Stoddard," though his congregation willingly accepted his authority. This pattern became widespread in New England. He served the Northampton congregation for 57 years, but was succeeded by his grandson, Jonathan Edwards, who eventually rejected his grandfather's solution and returned to the requirement of a conversion experience for church membership.

A reading from *The Doctrine of Instituted Churches Explained and Proved from the Word of God* by Solomon Stoddard

Two things are evident in the practise of the Apostles, one is, that they readily admitted such into the Church, as made a profession of the Christian Faith, (Acts 2, Acts 6). We never read that ever they denied Admission to any Man or Woman that made that profession; the other is, that all that were thus received by them, were admitted to the Lords Supper (I Corinthians 10:17, Acts 2:24). They made no distinction of the Adult Members of the Church, into Communicants and Non-Communicants. Those that are commanded by God to participate of the Lords Supper, are to be admitted to the Lords Supper, but all professors that have a good Conversation and Knowledge are commanded by God to participate in the Lords Supper, if Men have not these Qualifications they are not obliged immediately to participate in the Lords Supper, for it would be a sin if they should: But having these Qualifications they are bound, provided they have opportunity. Christ has laid this Law upon Professors, (I Corinthians 11:24, 25).

The persons here commanded are not only true Believers, then none can do it with a good Conscience but those that know themselves to be true Believers; then the Church Authority can require none but true Believers to come, the Persons therefore required to partake are such professors as carry it inoffensively, and if such are bound to come, the Church is bound to receive them, they may not hinder any Man from doing his Duty. There can be no just cause assigned, why such Men should be debarred from coming to the Lords Supper, they are not to be debarred for not giving the highest evidence of sincerity; There never was any such Law in the Church of God, that any should be debarred Church Priviledges because they did not give the highest evidence of sincerity, nor for want of the Exercise of Faith; it is unreasonable to believe Men to be visible Saints from their Infancy till they be forty or fifty years of Age, and yet not capable of coming to the Lords Supper, for want of the Exercise of Faith; they are not to be denied because of the weakness of Grace, they that have the least Grace need to have it Nourished and Cherished.

Such Adult Persons as are worthy to be admitted into the Church, or being in the Church are worthy to be continued without censure, are to be admitted to the Lords Supper; it is utterly unreasonable to deny the Adult Members of the Church, the Lords Supper, and yet not lay them under censure; If they are guilty of any such offence as to be denied the Lords Supper, why are they not censured? If they are not worthy to be censured, why are they kept from the Lords Supper?

✷ *October 27*

James Gibbons

ROMAN CATHOLIC

July 23, 1834–March 24, 1921

He was not an original or creative thinker; he often seemed indecisive; he preferred to avoid controversy; he was not a great administrator, nor did he delegate easily to others. Yet James Gibbons provided exactly the leadership the Roman Catholic Church in America needed at a critical time in its history. During the last half of the 19th century, immigrants from Catholic countries poured into the United States. This influx alarmed many Americans, and the newcomers encountered prejudice and, sometimes, active hostility. The immigrants were divided among themselves and often more interested in preserving their ethnic traditions than in working together to build a church in a new land. The Vatican was deeply concerned about the kind of church they saw emerging across the ocean. As Archbishop of New York, Gibbons faced the unenviable task of mediating Roman Catholicism to Protestant Americans, America to the Vatican, and Roman Catholics to one other. Caution and prudence were essential elements of his approach, which he called "masterly inactivity." A more aggressive program would only have inflamed already strained feelings.

Nevertheless, Gibbons knew how to take a strong stand when needed. Most especially, he could confront the papacy with a passionate defense of American democracy, the rights of organized labor, and the value of separating church from state. He rejoiced in his American citizenship and told the pope, "The Church here enjoys a larger liberty, and more secure position than in any country today where church and state are united. In our country separation is a necessity and Catholics rejoice in it." At his death, the *New York Times* hailed his "wisdom," and the *Baltimore Sun* called him "our Cardinal."

A reading from Cardinal Gibbons's Defense of the Knights of Labor submitted to the Vatican

Scarcely were the United States formed into an independent government when Pius VI, of happy memory, established there the Catholic hierarchy and appointed the illustrious John Carroll first Bishop of Baltimore. Thanks to the fructifying grace of God, the grain of mustard seed then planted has grown to be a large tree, spreading its branches over the length and the width of our fair land. Where only one bishop was found in the beginning of this century, there are now seventy-five serving as many dioceses and vicariates. For their great progress under God and the fostering care of the Holy See we are indebted in no small degree to the civil liberty we enjoy in our enlightened republic.

Our Holy Father, Leo XIII, in his luminous encyclical on the constitution of Christian States, declares that the Church is not committed to any particular form of civil government. She adapts herself to all; she leavens all with the sacred leaven of the Gospel. She has lived under absolute empires; she thrives under constitutional monarchies; she grows and expands under the free republic. She has often, indeed, been hampered in her divine mission and has had to struggle for a footing wherever despotism has cast its dark shadow like the plant excluded from the sunlight of heaven, but in the genial air of liberty she blossoms like the rose!

For myself, as a citizen of the United States, without closing my eyes to our defects as a nation, I proclaim, with a deep sense of pride and gratitude, and in this great capitol of Christendom, that I belong to a country where the civil government holds over us the aegis of its protection without interfering in the legitimate exercise of our sublime mission as ministers of the Gospel of Jesus Christ.

Our country has liberty without license, authority without despotism. Hers is no spirit of exclusiveness. She has no frowning fortifications to repel the invader, for we are at peace with all the world. In the consciousness of her strength and of her good will to all nations she rests secure. Her harbors are open in the Atlantic and Pacific to welcome the honest immigrant who comes to advance his temporal interest and to find a peaceful home.

But, while we are acknowledged to have a free government, we do not, perhaps, receive due credit for possessing also a strong government. Yes, our nation is strong, and her strength lies, under Providence, in the majesty and supremacy of the law, in the loyalty of her citizens to that law, and in the affection of our people for their free institutions.

There are, indeed, grave social problems which are now engaging the earnest attention of the citizens of the United States. But I have no doubt that, with God's blessings, these problems will be solved by the calm judgment and sound sense of the American people without violence, or revolution, or injury to individual right.

✪ October 28 _____

Julia Chester Emery

EPISCOPALIAN

September 24, 1852–January 9, 1922

The demand for equal rights for women found expression in many ways be-fore women's suffrage was finally adopted and the women's movement came of age. During the years before that, there were numerous organizers and many eloquent spokespersons for the cause. But there were also those, like Julia Chester Emery, who worked quietly taking immediate practical steps and pushing persistently — though always politely — for more. As doors swung open, it was those who had gained skills and experience because of such women as Julia Emery who were able to take full advantage of new opportunities.

In 1871, the Episcopal Church decided the time had come to provide a national organization for the women of the church. Julia Emery's older sister, Mary, was hired as the first general secretary of the Woman's Auxiliary to the Board of Missions. Five years later, she married, recommending the 23-year-old Julia for her position. "Julia is young," she told them, "but she can do it." Indeed, Julia could. For the next 40 years, she built up the organization, creating branches in every parish and diocese. Support for missions was its primary focus, and eventually the Woman's Auxiliary was providing as much support for mission as the general budget of the church. Emery realized that firsthand information was necessary to convince donors of the value of their gifts, so she made it her business to be an eyewitness, visiting every diocese and mission district in the United States, as well as Europe and Asia. In China, officials tried to dissuade her from making the dangerous journey up the Yangtse River to visit missionaries, but she was not to be deterred. If there were representatives of the church in that place, she would visit them and learn about their needs.

Julia Emery wrote, spoke, organized, and traveled to transform the church by unleashing the energies of its female members. Only after her death did women move from "auxiliary" positions to leadership at every level in the church's work, but it was Julia Emery who did much to make that transition possible — and necessary.

A reading from the "Fifty-Fifth Annual Report of the Woman's Auxiliary to the Board of Missions: 1916" by Julia Chester Emery

The Auxiliary gratefully acknowledges this unstinted kindness and the friendly appreciation shown it through all these years. And it records with grateful thanks, as well, that approval and personal interest and help on their part of the Bishops of the Church and the parochial clergy and of our missionaries, which have made the establishment of the Auxiliary in diocese and missionary district, in parish and mission, a possibility.

But it is not satisfied with itself nor content to feel that the women of the Church have compassed their capacity for helpfulness. The gain of $29,000 towards the Board's appropriations, largely in response to the Emergent appeal, the suggestions that led to the day of unbroken intercession, now twice kept at the Church Missions House, are by no means a sufficient answer to the Board's latest call. We feel that Board and Bishops and parochial clergy may gain much more from this company of women who stand so ready to cooperate with the men of the Church under their leadership in the widest plans that may be made for the spread of Christ's Kingdom throughout the world.

Therefore, at this time we ask the Board if, in reviewing the Auxiliary' work, it will not hold back its praise, and, instead, give a judicial and constructive help; tell us what it sees not of strength only, but of weakness; not of success, but failure; and set before us some call which shall exercise the very best that not only the women of to-day's Auxiliary, but all the women of the Church can give.

The Woman's Auxiliary has suffered from having been left so largely to its own devisings, which have presented to it tasks entirely incommensurate with its strength. Women whose intelligence is good and cultivated, whose outlook is broad, whose ability is excellent, whose power has never been tried for the Church's service, women who love the Church and devote themselves gladly to her works of love and mercy in their parish lives and rejoice in the beauty of her holiness, would be won to it in increasing numbers, were the limitless possibilities for the winning of this world for Christ set before them in a large and commanding and persuasive way.

Is there no farther work suitable in which they may be enlisted and in the doing of which, under their rectors and Bishops and the organized authorities of the Church, they may realize more fully than they yet have done that they have a valued and valuable contribution to make?

We would ask both the Board and the Auxiliary to consider whether a real gain might be made if we should emphasize the Auxiliary less as an organization but rather as a reminder, a co-operator, and a vehicle by and through which the general missionary interests of the Church might be strengthened in any and every department of parish life.

✪ October 29

Jarena Lee

AFRICAN METHODIST EPISCOPAL

February 11, 1783–?

It was difficult enough for a black man or white woman to become a significant public figure in the 19th century. For a black woman it was almost unprecedented. Jarena Lee had the advantage of being born to free parents in a northern state, but her parents' poverty forced them to hire her out as a servant girl at seven. She didn't see them again for 14 years.

Moving from Cape May to the Philadelphia area, Jarena Lee joined the Bethel African Methodist Church in that city at the age of 21 and had a conversion experience a few weeks later. The next four years were difficult for her. She came to have doubts about her salvation and was depressed almost to the point of suicide. At that point, she encountered the Wesleyan doctrine of sanctification. Lee still believed she had been convicted of sin and justified, but that she had not received "the entire sanctification of the soul to God." Three months after learning this doctrine, however, she received the sanctification she felt she needed. She described it as feeling as if a bolt of lightening had passed through her.

Three more years passed before Lee felt moved to preach. Approaching the church's founding father, Richard Allen,* she was gently but firmly rebuffed. "Methodists," he informed her, "do not call women preachers."

Accepting that judgment for the time being, Jarena married Joseph Lee, the pastor of a small congregation, and gave birth to two children. Six years later, her husband died, and she began holding prayer meetings in her home with Richard Allen's approval. He supported her also when she began to preach, though not as a licensed preacher but as an official traveling exhorter. Slaves often traveled many miles to hear her. More importantly, in 1833, she wrote her autobiography, hoping it would lead others to Christ. Printed at her own cost, it was distributed at camp meetings and quarterly meetings, and even on the street. A second, updated biography was published in 1849. Nothing of her life is known after that point.

A reading from *Religious Experience and Journal of Mrs. Jarena Lee*

I now began to think seriously of breaking up housekeeping, and forsaking all to preach the everlasting Gospel. I felt a strong desire to return to the place of my nativity, at Cape May, after an absence of about fourteen years. To this place, where the heaviest cross was to be met with, the Lord sent me, as Saul of Tarsus was sent to Jerusalem, to preach the same gospel which he had neglected and despised before his conversion. I went by water, and on my passage was much distressed by sea sickness, so much so that I expected to have died, but such was not the will of the Lord respecting me. After I had disembarked, I proceeded on as opportunities offered toward where my mother lived. When within ten miles of that place, I appointed an evening meeting. There were a goodly number came out to hear. The Lord was pleased to give me light and liberty among the people. After meeting, there came an elderly lady to me and said, she believed the Lord had sent me among them: she then appointed me another meeting there two weeks from that night. The next day I hastened forward to the place of my mother, who was happy to see me, and the happiness was mutual between us. With her I left my poor sickly boy while I departed to do my Master's will. In this neighborhood I had an uncle, who was a Methodist and who gladly threw open his door for meetings to be held there. At the first meeting which I held at my uncle's house, there was, with others who had come from curiosity to hear the woman preacher, an old man, who was a Deist, and who said he did not believe the coloured people had any souls — he was sure they had none. He took a seat very near where I was standing, and boldly tried to look me out of countenance. But as I labored on in the best manner I was able, looking to God all the while, though it seemed to me I had but little liberty, yet there went an arrow from the bent bow of the gospel, and fastened in his till then obdurate heart. After I had done speaking, he went out, and called the people around him, said that my preaching might seem a small thing, yet he believed I had the worth of souls at heart. This language was different from what it was a little time before, as he now seemed to admit that coloured people had souls, as it was to these I was chiefly speaking; and unless they had souls, whose good I had in view, his remark must have been without meaning. He now came into the house, and in the most friendly manner shook hands with me, saying, he hoped God had spared him to some good purpose. This man was a great slave holder and had been very cruel, thinking nothing of knocking down a slave with a fence stake, or whatever might come to hand. From this time it was said of him that he became greatly altered in his ways for the better. At that time he was about seventy years old, his head as white as snow; but whether be became a converted man or not, I never heard.

✲ October 30 ——————————————

Henry Highland Garnet

PRESBYTERIAN

1815–February 13, 1882

Born in slavery, Henry Highland Garnet was the great-grandson of an African warrior who had been captured in battle. His father escaped with his family from their home in Maryland to freedom in Pennsylvania and then to New York. Henry sailed as a cabin boy on a ship, but on his return, discovered that his family had been forced to flee again from slave-catchers. The family property had been stolen or destroyed. Garnet moved to Long Island to work on a farm, but injured his leg so severely in a sports contest that it ultimately had to be amputated at the hip. Baptized in a Presbyterian Church, he journeyed to New Hampshire to be enrolled in a school that accepted black students. But the townspeople forced its closure and destroyed the building. Garnet returned to New York and found another school, acceptable to the neighborhood. With the encouragement of a Presbyterian pastor, he continued his education at Princeton Seminary and became the first black graduate of that school. After ordination, he served as pastor of a parish in Troy, New York, traveled for a while in England and Scotland, and spent several years as a missionary in Jamaica for the Scottish Presbyterian Church.

By 1840, Garnet had been drawn into the abolition movement. He began to attend meetings of the American Anti-Slavery Society and, in 1842, became editor of abolitionist newspapers. In 1843, his speech to the National Negro Convention in Buffalo, New York, called on African Americans to take up arms to gain their freedom: "Brethren, arise, arise! Strike for your lives and liberties. Now is the day and the hour. Let every slave throughout the land do this, and the days of slavery are numbered. You cannot be more oppressed than you have been — you cannot suffer greater cruelties than you have already. Rather die freemen than live to be slaves." Garnet was rebuked by Frederick Douglass, among others, for his views, and he then moved toward a more moderate position.

After traveling to England and the West Indies, Garnet returned to the United States before the Civil War, and he took a parish in Washington, DC, where he and Douglass worked to recruit black troops for the Union Army. In February 1865, Congress enacted the bill which became the Thirteenth Amendment. For this occasion, President Lincoln invited Garnet to preach to the House of Representatives and he took this opportunity to exhort the congressmen to complete the work of emancipation. He was made American legate to Liberia in 1872, but died two months after taking the position.

A reading from a sermon preached to the House of Representatives by Henry Highland Garnet in 1865

Honorable Senators and Representatives, illustrious rulers of this great nation! I cannot refrain this day from invoking upon you, in God's name, the blessings of millions who were ready to perish, but to whom a new and better life has been opened by your humanity, justice, and patriotism. You have said, "Let the Constitution of the country be so amended that slavery and involuntary servitude shall no longer exist in the United States, except in punishment for crime." Surely, an act so sublime could not escape Divine notice; and doubtless the deed has been recorded in the archives of heaven. Volumes may be appropriated to your praise and renown in the history of the world. Genius and art may perpetuate the glorious act on canvas and in marble, but certain and more lasting monuments in commemoration of your decision are already erected in the hearts and memories of a grateful people.

The nation has begun its exodus from worse than Egyptian bondage; and I beseech you that you say to the people, "that they go forward." With the assurance of God's favor in all things done in obedience to his righteous will, and guided by day and by night by the pillars of cloud and fire, let us not pause until we have reached the other and safe side of the stormy and crimson sea. Let freemen and patriots mete out complete and equal justice to all men, and thus prove to mankind the superiority of our Democratic, Republican Government.

Favored men, and honored of God as his instruments, speedily finish the work which he has given you to do: Emancipate, Enfranchise, Educate, and give the blessing of the gospel to every American citizen.

> *Hear ye not how, from all high points of Time,*
> *From peak to peak adown the mighty chain*
> *That links the ages — echoing sublime*
> *A Voice Almighty — leaps one grand refrain.*
> *Wakening the generations with a shout,*
> *And trumpet — call of thunder — Come ye out!*
> *Out from old forms and dead idolatries;*
> *From fading myths and superstitious dreams:*
> *From Pharisaic rituals and lies,*
> *And all the bondage of the life that seems!*
> *Out — on the pilgrim path, of heroes trod,*
> *Over earth's wastes, to reach forth after God!*
> *The Lord hath bowed his heaven, and come down!*
> *Now, in this latter century of time,*
> *Once more his tent is pitched on Sinai's crown!*
> *Once more in clouds must Faith to meet him climb!*
> *Once more his thunder crashes on our doubt*
> *And fear and sin — "My people! come ye out!"*
> *From false ambitions and base luxuries;*
> *From puny aims and indolent self-ends;*
> *From cant of faith, and shams of liberties,*
> *And mist of ill that Truth's pure day-beam bends:*
> *Out, from all darkness of the Egypt-land,*
> *Into my sun-blaze on the desert sand!*

✱ *October 31*

Thomas Augustine Judge

ROMAN CATHOLIC

August 23, 1868–November 23, 1933

Thomas Judge was not "practical." He founded a religious order for women, but when the head of that order requested he serve as their spiritual director for life, the archbishop rejected the notion indignantly: "No, never! I would not ask him to be Spiritual Director for life over a kindergarten. I do not believe he is practical." He cited the fact that Judge had left on a recent trip with only 25 cents in his pocket. The nun who had made the request found herself explaining to the archbishop that saints were like that. It was evidence of their trust in God, and Judge's dependence on God had never failed him. The archbishop said it still seemed to him like a lack of good sense.

Thomas Judge had one to do things the way others expected. In his first parish, he annoyed colleagues by going out to visit parishioners in their homes. The other priests saw no need of extra work. Nor did they understand his advocacy for a more active eucharistic life. They complained when he spent extra time hearing confessions. But Thomas Judge liked to listen to his lay people. He drew them together in what he called a "Missionary Cenacle," instructed them, and sent them out two by two to go into homes and schools and workplaces to help alleviate suffering among the poor and those who felt spiritually abandoned. Lay ministry seemed like a novelty to many clergy, but Judge argued that mutual ministry of priest and laity was not "some new spirit invented in modern times," but rather, "the Gospel spirit."

When he was sent to Alabama, some of his lay apostles followed him to help establish a school. He had asked some clergy to accompany him, but they were afraid to visit homes because they felt that prejudice against Roman Catholics in that area made it dangerous. The mission was full of hardships. The teachers lived in quarters with eight in one room, seven in another, and three in a third. They washed in a basin on the porch. Meals were sparse. But Thomas Judge taught them to embrace poverty as an essential element in their ministry.

Other dioceses soon started asking for Judge's lay apostles, and soon there developed one order for men and another for women. Judge told them all: "In the ordinary providence of your everyday lives, you are the Church, you have the grace, you have the capacity, you are conditioned to make yourself responsible for the Catholic church at home in the street car; coming and going to work in your place of employment where you are, there is the Church." The Missionary Servants of the Most Blessed Trinity (women), the Missionary Servants of the Most Holy Trinity (men), and the Missionary Cenacle Apostolate (lay people) continue their work today throughout the United States, and also in Puerto Rico, Mexico, and Costa Rica.

A reading from a 1927 letter by Thomas Judge

We have just returned from a missionary work amongst the most wretched and sadly conditioned people on the island [of Puerto Rico]. Any number of these unfortunates are not baptized. We are surprised when we find any who have made their First Holy Communion. Tonight it was my blessed pleasure to be associated with two priests, three of our Sisters and a Brother, and a little band of University girls who are teaching catechism, and trying to help bring a little multitude to the knowledge, love and fear of God. I never realized as much as I do when I visit those poor, neglected people the catastrophe of the idle hours of our life. Idle hours! What these would mean for the Church and religion if put to a purpose that would bring peace of mind and help to our neighbor! I tell you, my dear children, thousands and thousands of the souls of our little brothers and sisters are going to be lost to God because we have not sacrificed enough.

As for myself, I wish that I might have many lives to give unto these little ones. These people cannot help themselves. There is no reason for us to envy the saints or apostles, for those opportunities are right here today. If we do not take the higher place in heaven, and if many souls are going to be lost, it is because some of us have reason to be disquieted and to beat our breasts in sorrow at those words of our Divine Lord, "He that taketh not up his cross, and followeth me, is not worthy of me" (Mt. 10:38).

When so much good is to be done, and when so many souls are in danger of eternal damnation, this thought comes to me. If so many of our young men and women, because of home ties and attachments cannot, for the love of God and their brother and sister in God, offer themselves to help, how can they separate themselves from all that is dear to them when God's Angel of Death comes and summons them to judgment — summons them, maybe, to answer for the greater good in their lives that has never been done.

The spirit of sacrifice! — do at least pray that we will get more of it. The Cross, Calvary, the Man of Sorrows, the Woman of Sorrows, our thorn-crowned King — these should ever be before us. "He that taketh not up his cross, and followeth me, is not worthy of me" (Mt. 10:38). May we be worthy of Jesus, for what an appalling thing He says of some, that they are not worthy of Him. Let us pray that we will be worthy of Him, that we will show forth in our lives, by the grace of the Holy Spirit, all that those words imply — that we are worthy of Jesus.

November

Channing Moore Williams

EPISCOPALIAN

July 18, 1829–December 2, 1910

"In his meekness and gentleness," wrote a British missionary who knew Channing Moore Williams, "no less than in his devotion to his work, in his deep earnestness and simplicity of life and heart he is truly a worthy successor of the Apostles." An adjective used even more often to describe Williams is "patience." And he had need of that virtue. He had been given an impossible task as bishop of the Episcopal mission in China and Japan: two ancient cultures, suspicious of foreigners and often hostile to them, with cultures mysterious to westerners and difficult languages to master. But Williams was indeed patient and waited for the Lord of the harvest to bring results. He spent seven years in Japan before baptizing the first convert. After 18 years of work, he had scarcely 500 communicants. Yet the foundation had been carefully laid for a church which today, though still small, counts 11 dioceses. "Nippon Seikokai" (Holy Catholic Church of Japan) is an independent and self-governing member of the Anglican Communion.

Williams had gone straight from seminary to serve as a missionary in China and was ordained there to the priesthood. Two years later, when Japan became open to foreign missionaries, he moved to Nagasaki and set out to learn Japanese. Seven years later, when the missionary bishop in China died, Williams was made a bishop and put in charge of the work in both

607

countries. For eight years, he supervised the work in China, making two trips a year to travel around the missions and provide the leadership needed. When that work prospered, he passed it on to other hands and concentrated on Japan.

Faithfully attending to converts and candidates for ordination, Bishop Williams also found time to establish a school and a clinic in Tokyo. St. Paul's/Rikkyo has grown into a large and influential university, while St. Luke's has become a major hospital. Williams hosted his 13 candidates for ordination in his own house until better arrangements could be made and a proper seminary, now the Central Theological College, was established. After more than 20 years as bishop, Williams felt the time had come for new and younger leadership and resigned to return to the missionary work of a parish priest teaching classes and caring for parishes in Kyoto, Osaka, and two other cities. For 20 more years, he continued to serve in Japan until in failing health and not wishing to be a burden, he returned to Virginia, where he died two years later.

The Annual Report of Channing Moore Williams, Missionary Bishop of Yedo (Tokyo) in 1889

Since the last report, an event unique in the history of the world has occurred, which is fraught with far-reaching consequences to Japan. On the 11th of February last, the Emperor, in fulfilment of the promise made several years ago, gave a liberal constitution to the country. This promise was made not through compulsion forced upon him in any way through fear, but simply at the instigation of certain ministers, some of whom had visited America and England, and imbibed liberal opinions. . . .

One article of the constitution materially affects us, as a Church having a mission in the country. The 27th article declares that "Japanese subjects... shall enjoy freedom of religious belief." . . . This may be considered almost as an invitation to Christians to put forth their strength to spread the religion of Christ in this "Land of the Rising Sun," and Christians of many names and divers beliefs — from Greek and Roman on the one side to Quakers and Unitarians on the other — are crowding into the country.

Our Church must settle what part she is to take in the great work of bringing the people of this interesting country to the knowledge of and faith in the Lord Jesus; and what she determines to do must be done without delay. She cannot think that she has, in any sense, come up to the measure of her responsibility. For the truth is the mission has been sadly undermanned from its commencement to the present; and the fact is especially apparent at this time when, by the new treaties, the whole country is to be thrown open to our missionaries to travel and reside where they may please, without restrictions of any kind.

And now when, in view of the new and wider openings, the request for more men is made, the sickening response comes back that the receipts for last year will not justify an appropriation for new men. No blame in the matter is thought to rest on the Board of Managers. They are but acting as the whole Board of Missions directed. There seems no way out of the difficulty at present but to ask that some friends of the mission, to whom God has entrusted large means, or certain churches, would undertake the support of a few men in Japan for a term of years. This plan has been tried and should now be extended. This or some other method must be used to meet the present pressing need. And, as a last request, I earnestly beg that the means may be provided, and the men be sent out to help us with as little delay as possible, and that prayer may be offered for God's rich blessing on the work and the laborers in this land, and that numbers now without God and without hope may be brought by the power of the Holy Spirit to know and love Christ, the Light and Life of the world.

✪ *November 2*

Eliza Edmunds Hewitt

PRESBYTERIAN

June 28, 1851–April 24, 1920

A crippling spinal ailment, possibly related to an injury caused by a careless student, ended Eliza Hewitt's promising career in education. A native of Philadelphia, she had been the valedictorian of her public school class before she set out to become a teacher. Bedridden for long periods, and physically restricted on and off for the rest of her life, Hewitt focused her energy instead on the spiritual life. Neither pain nor immobility could prevent her from studying English literature or writing hymns. Filled with a sense of God's grandeur, she sang and wrote songs in her room.

During the periods when she could be mobile, Hewitt concentrated her efforts on the Sunday School at the Northern Home for Friendless Children and the Church School at the Calvin Presbyterian Church. For a time, her classes exceeded 200 pupils. The majority of her lyrics were written for these classes. She believed music helped communicate the gospel and focused the heart on the eternal joys of the Kingdom, even in times of suffering. She hoped to communicate this to her charges, since her own challenges had strengthened her faith.

John Sweeney, a professor, was among the first to see Hewitt's creations and set them to music. In cooperation with William Kirkpatrick, he and Hewitt published her first hymn. Later, she collaborated with other hymn writers and composers to provide inspiring and instructive songs for her dear young people. Hewitt's close friendship with Fanny Crosby centered around discussions of their latest hymns. A prolific hymn writer herself, Crosby had been blinded by inept medical care in youth. She spent her life singing and writing for others to sing. Upon Crosby's death, Hewitt wrote this poem in remembrance of her:

> *Away to the country of sunshine and song,*
> *Our songbird has taken her flight,*
> *And she who has sung in the darkness so long*
> *Now sings in the beautiful light.*

Hewitt attended Methodist meetings in New Jersey, where she met Emily Wilson, the wife of the district superintendent. Together they produced "When We All Get to Heaven" in 1898.

> *Sing the wondrous love of Jesus,*
> *Sing His mercy and His grace.*
> *In the mansions bright and blessed*
> *He'll prepare for us a place.*
>
> *Refrain*
>
> *When we all get to Heaven,*
> *What a day of rejoicing that will be!*
> *When we all see Jesus,*
> *We'll sing and shout the victory!*
> *While we walk the pilgrim pathway,*
> *Clouds will overspread the sky;*
> *But when traveling days are over,*
> *Not a shadow, not a sigh.*
>
> *Refrain*
>
> *Let us then be true and faithful,*
> *Trusting, serving every day;*
> *Just one glimpse of Him in glory*
> *Will the toils of life repay.*
>
> *Refrain*
>
> *Onward to the prize before us!*
> *Soon His beauty we'll behold;*
> *Soon the pearly gates will open;*
> *We shall tread the streets of gold.*
>
> *Refrain*

These hymns do not embody 21st-century themes or styles, but they brought joy to the Christians of her time. Some of her other lyrics include "More About Jesus," "Stepping in the Light," "There Is Sunshine in My Soul Today," and "Seek Ye First the Kingdom":

> *Seek ye first the kingdom; not the things of earth.*
> *Priceless are the treasures of immortal worth.*

Like a flitting shadow, time will pass away,
But the heav'nly riches change not, nor decay.

Refrain

"Seek ye first the kingdom," 'tis the Master's voice;
In His precious promise evermore rejoice
"All things else," His words are true, "shall be added unto you."
In His precious promise, evermore rejoice.

Seek ye first the kingdom; seek the gift of God.
'Tis the Savior's offer purchased by His blood.
Seek ye first His glory; be it life's sweet aim;
Him to serve and honor, trusting in His Name.

Refrain

A story sweet and wondrous,
Like heav'nly music swells;
In chimings clear to all who will hear,
Ring out the Gospel bells.

For God so loved the world
That He gave His only begotten Son,
That whosoever believeth in Him,
Whosoever believeth in Him
Should not perish,
Should not perish,
But have everlasting life.

When, grieving, brokenhearted,
Because of sin and shame,
We find a joy earth cannot destroy,
Believing on His Name.

Refrain

This love beyond all measure
Of earth or sea or sky,
Could only show its full overflow,
When Jesus came to die.

Refrain

Come, brother, come to Jesus;
His Word was meant for you;
His grace receive, His promise believe,
And sing His praise anew.

Refrain

Hewitt's words were born from her experience of finding hope and confidence in the midst of prolonged pain and disappointment. They were her best gift to the pupils she was called to lead into their own life of faith. In the spirit of Martin Luther, who said "He who sings prays twice," Hewitt gave rhyme and rhythm to the classic Christian lessons she used to equip her charges for a world in need of grace. Even today, her contributions to the American gospel hymn tradition remain staples of numerous hymnals across a variety of denominations and are part of the rich heritage of Christian song.

✪ *November 3*

Ivan Veniaminov

(also known as John, or Ioann,
or his later title, St. Innocent)

ORTHODOX

August 27, 1797–March 31, 1879

Born poor, orphaned early, and brought up in a church boarding school in Russia, Veniaminov nonetheless quickly won recognition for his many talents. His original surname was Popov, but he spent so much time as a young man with a particular monk named Benjamin that he was given the name Veniaminov, meaning "son of Benjamin" in Russian. Along with his academic schooling, he also learned clock-making, a craft he would employ in later years. He married at 20, and was ordained a priest at 24, taking charge of a parish in Siberia. Two years later, in 1824, Veniaminov and his family were stationed in the Aleutian Islands. They lived in an underground hut surrounded by wind, cold, rock, and a people his colleagues back in Russia thought were "savages." In fact, his parish was made up of at least three types of people: Russians, Aleuts, and mixed-race people. Though Veniaminov did not consider himself a scholar, his natural curiosity and detailed observations prompted him to reflect and write about everything around him. He documented details about geology, meteorology, botany, and astronomy. He was also a kind of cultural anthropologist, listening to and learning from the native tribes even as he taught them. He invented an alphabet for the Aleuts and began to translate parts of the Bible, catechisms, and liturgies for them. He was a tireless worker, completing a first draft of Matthew's gospel in Aleut in only two weeks.

Nor were Veniaminov's efforts limited to collecting data or writing. He traveled frequently and far, often in a skin kayak, along the treacherous coast of the islands. With his woodworking skills, he built a house, a church, musical instruments, and clocks. While ministering to the faithful and keeping up with his own spiritual duties, he was always seeking to expand the number of the faithful. His gentle manner and his willingness to become involved in the lives of his parishioners made him an effective missioner. After a decade with the Aleuts, he was transferred to Sitka, on the mainland, to work with the Tlingit people. Again he learned their language, translating Scripture and liturgy into their native tongue. His reputation for wisdom was such that he convinced the tribe to be vaccinated against smallpox — even though their own medicine man said the disease emanated from the Christian priest and his strange religion. Veniaminov even used his talents to build organs for the Spanish missions in California which he had visited in 1836, developing a good relationship with the Jesuits there.

In 1840, after a trip to St. Petersburg (and after the untimely death of his wife back in Alaska), Veniaminov was made an archpriest and became a monk, taking the name Innocent. He was then made an archimandrite, and finally bishop of a new diocese: Kamchatka, the Kurile, and Aleutian Islands. This territory included the Pacific rim of Asia, Canada, Alaska, and what would become the lower 48 United States. Innocent thus became the first Orthodox Bishop of America. As bishop, he continued to travel among his people, preaching the gospel wherever he went. In 1843, he founded a school in Sitka to train indigenous clergy for the diocese. When, in 1848, a cathedral was built there, Innocent made its clock. He became an archbishop, returned to Siberia where, once again, he translated holy works into the native tongue so the Siberians would not have to use Russian or Slavonic for their worship.

In 1867, at 70, Innocent was elected to follow the late Metropolitan Philaret as the Metropolitan of Moscow and All Russia. By the time he died in 1879, he had founded residences for widows and orphans, set up schools, moved the American Vicariate from Sitka to San Francisco, ordained native clergy all around the north Pacific coast, brought English into use in America, and laid the foundations for what would eventually become the Orthodox Church in America.

A reading from the journals of Ivan Veniaminov

July 2. Tuesday. Since there was no hope of any more nomadic people coming here, I invited those here to come see me and then convinced them to listen to me for awhile; they willingly agreed. After evoking the aid of Him, without Whom we are capable of nothing, I spoke to them through an interpreter. I told them that there is no God other than He Whom we and many others worship. I told them about the nature of God and His creation. I explained what serves Him and what does not. Finally, I told them that man was not created for the transient life here, but for eternal life, and [I explained] what one must do to obtain the blessed eternity.

Finally, I asked each in turn whether he would like to enter the ranks of the believers in the true God. They all willingly agreed, with one exception. One of them said to me that he would willingly do so, but that he was a shaman. I, however, told him that he could be included among the believers if he would abandon his shamanism; he consented. After this, I told them the requirements for becoming a believer. Lastly, I told them that they would receive no gifts from me. They replied that they did not require any. Although nothing forbade the carrying out of the sacrament [of baptism], I instructed them to think it over more carefully and give their viewpoints the next day. The one who had not expressed a desire to become a Christian I let depart in peace.

July 3. Since the nomads who had heard me had not changed their intentions, I pitched a tent at the river and baptized them in the river. I required each of them in turn to renounce the devil, and after that I taught them how to pray, and so on.

Here was the first fruit of the seeds of God's word, sown by my unworthy hand in this wild, but fertile land!

✪ November 4 _____

Samuel Seabury

EPISCOPALIAN

November 30, 1729–February 25, 1796

Samuel Seabury might seem an unlikely choice for the first bishop of an independent Anglican Church in the United States since had done all he could to prevent a break from England. Born near New London, Connecticut, where his father served as rector of the Anglican Church, Seabury graduated from Yale at 19 and went to Scotland to study medicine since he was too young to be ordained. A knowledge of medicine was useful to the clergy, who were often relied on for physical as well as spiritual care in those days. In Scotland Episcopalians were severely restricted by the established Presbyterian Church, and Seabury learned something of what it meant to worship in semi-hiding from the authorities.

Ordained in London, Seabury returned to the United States as a missionary and served congregations in New Jersey, Long Island, and New York. When the first Continental Congress met in 1774, Seabury wrote a series of anonymous pamphlets pointing out the legal injustices and economic losses suffered as a result of the rising tension between the colonies and Great Britain. These aroused such anger that a delegation of Connecticut citizens seized him and carried him to New Haven, where he was imprisoned and interrogated for some six weeks before being released. During the Revolutionary War, Seabury served as a chaplain to British forces and his house and farm were repeatedly attacked by bands of patriots.

With the end of the war, Anglican clergy in Connecticut assembled to plan for the future. Believing that episcopal leadership was essential, they chose Samuel Seabury to go to England and be consecrated by English bishops. This turned out to be impossible because bishops had to swear an oath of loyalty to the crown under English law. Remembering the persecuted and disestablished Episcopal Church of Scotland, Seabury traveled north and was consecrated by Scottish bishops in a chapel in the home of one of them.

Returning to the United States, Seabury set out with enormous energy to help reorganize the Anglican Churches in Connecticut and the rest of New England and to play a critical role in the organization of a national structure to serve Episcopalians throughout the new country. English bishops in those days seldom traveled, but Seabury made it his practice to make two long trips a year through his diocese and Rhode Island especially. He would ordain, confirm, and provide pastoral care in a way that became the model for the church in the next century. At his insistence, the newly created Episcopal Church was governed by a bicameral assembly in which bishops met in one house and clergy and laity in the other, with approval of both houses needed for action. Seabury also helped shape the new American Book of Common Prayer by insisting that it include elements of the Scottish Prayer Book. He resisted efforts on the part of some to eliminate the historic creeds. It was said that his funeral was attended mainly by the aged, the halt, the decrepit, and the blind, for Seabury's ministry, faithful to his Lord's example, had always included them.

A prayer of Bishop Seabury for use before receiving communion

Blessed Jesus! Saviour of the world! who hast called me to the participation of these holy mysteries, accept my humble approach to thy sacred table, increase my faith, settle my devotion, fix my contemplation on thy powerful mercy; and while with my mouth I receive the sacred symbols of thy body and blood, may they be the means of heavenly nourishment to prepare my body and soul for that everlasting life which thou hast purchased by thy merits, and promised to bestow on all who believe in and depend on thee. Amen

An extract from Samuel Seabury's diary

On Monday the 20th, [I] went in a post chariot to Newburyport, forty-two miles. At the inn, Dr. Edward Bass, Rector of St. Paul's Church in Newburyport, came to us and conducted us to his house, where we remained till Wednesday.

Wednesday the 22nd, ... we went to Portsmouth, in the State of New Hampshire, with The Reverend Mr. John Cozens Ogden, Rector of St. John's Church in Portsmouth, who had come in a post chariot to Newburyport, to fetch us. In the afternoon we arrived at his house in safety but much fatigued with the violence of the heat.

On the following Sunday, the 26th, being the first Sunday after Trinity, preached to a large congregation and administered confirmation to seventy persons.

Monday the 27th, Dr. Bass and Mr. Robert Fowle, a young gentleman in deacon's orders, who was to be ordained priest for Holderness in New Hampshire, came to us. Wednesday, the 29th, St. Peter's Day, was fixed on for Mr. Fowle's ordination.

Let thy grace, O merciful God, assist me; let thy Holy Spirit direct me in the great duties of that sacred office in the Church of the Redeemer to which thy providence has called me — that I may not rashly lay hands on anyone that neither favour, nor resentment, nor partiality of any kind may influence my conduct; but that the glory of thy name, the honour of the dear Redeemer, the good of thy Holy Church, the salvation of sinners may be the end of all my views, the motives of all my actions. Lord Jesus, to thee all power is committed in heaven and in earth. Thou didst promise to be with thy Apostles to the end of the world: Be with me, Blessed Lord, now about to act under that authority and commission Thou graciously gavest to them. Hear me, Almighty Father; Hear me All gracious Saviour; Hear me most holy and life-giving Spirit — Hear and bless. Amen.

On Tuesday Mr. Fowle was examined. [He] gave the most pleasing hope from his literary attainments, amiable temper and prudent conduct in his Office of Deacon, of his being a worthy and able minister in the higher Order of Priesthood to which he was about to be promoted.

Wednesday, the Festival of St. Peter, the crowd at church was very great. The novelty of the scene (an Episcopal ordination never before having been held in that part of the country) attracted the attendance of some who little regarded the solemnity of the office or the prosperity of the Church. Dr. Bass made the presentation; the sermon was preached by me from St. Matthew 28:18–20. After church several Presbyterian ministers dined and drank tea with us at Mr. Ogden's. All was good humour. That evening, however, I heard some were offended at the sermon and threatened to attack it. Conscious of the soundness of the principles on which it was built, it was a matter of no importance to me whether they attacked or let it pass quietly off.

The next day, Friday, the 30th, we returned early to Newburyport in the stage coach. It ought to have been remarked that confirmation was administered on Wednesday to thirty-three persons.

A prayer for patience (after being maligned)

To bear abuse, and reviling language and misrepresentation, for his sake who bore them all for me is my duty. Enable me, gracious God to bear them with patience and resignation to thy will — in humble dependence on thy grace, in imitation of my dear Redeemer, and in the comfort of thy Holy Spirit. Let me not be discouraged by them from doing my duty in meekness and love; with constancy and perseverance. Have mercy upon and forgive those who persecute me with slanders, and turn their hearts to that charity which rejoiceth in the truth — Hear, O God, and for Christ's sake, forgive them. Amen.

✪ *November 5*

David Abeel

REFORMED

June 12, 1804–September 4, 1846

The 19th century began with an enormous burst of energy as Americans began to explore their western frontier. The Second Great Awakening focused on this expansion, though it did not stop at the western boundaries of the United States, but also looked across the Pacific Ocean. China especially fascinated Americans, as the country with the largest number of non-Christians in the world. David Abeel was one of those who responded to the challenge of China and the Far East. Born in New Brunswick, New Jersey, he went to college at Rutgers, then to the Theological Seminary of the Reformed Church, both located in New Brunswick. His first pastoral charge took him only as far as Athens, New York, but after two years there, he sailed for Asia under the auspices of the Seaman's Friend Society.

Within a year, Abeel had transferred himself to the American Board of Commissioners for Foreign Missions. He spent a year in China studying the language, then visited Java, Singapore, and Siam to assess their opportunities. His health, always uncertain, became worse as a result of his travels, so he decided to return home after four years to recover. His route home took him through Switzerland, France, Holland, England, and other countries in western Europe, urging support for foreign mission at every stop. In particular he called for women to go out and educate their Asian sisters. In England, his efforts led to the organization of a society to support the education of Asian women. Back in the United States, he continued to travel and speak and educate others at every opportunity. He also wrote three books, presenting various aspects of the challenge.

In 1839, feeling somewhat stronger, Abeel returned to Asia, visiting Malacca, Borneo, and other parts of Asia. In 1842, he established a mission at Amoy, but by 1845 his health had failed completely and he returned home to die. His practical vision, organizational skills, and writing left a lasting legacy, and he is remembered as one of the most successful of the early foreign missionaries. He was also a man of deep spirituality of whom it was said that "prayer was the air which he loved to breathe."

A reading from the journal of David Abeel

In China we see a supremacy ... not only taking inalienable rights from man, but presumptuously encroaching on Jehovah's prerogatives, attempting to abrogate his laws, and stigmatizing the religion of Jesus Christ as base and wicked. This supremacy is, we think, about to be broken down, and so much toleration and protection granted, that every man *may* worship God according to the dictates of his own conscience. In view of such prospects, we know that you and all our Christian friends, will anxiously with us watch the progress of events and each opening scene. Amid the distresses and perplexities which have overtaken the inhabitants of this land — by the introduction of opium, by the continuance of war, by inundations, by divisions of councils, by the tumults of the people — God is evidently carrying on His own great designs; and in wrath He will remember mercy, bring order out of confusion, good out of evil, and make even man's wickedness promotive of the Divine glory. His promises are sure, none can stay His hand; the heathen shall be given to His Son, and all the ends of the earth praise Him as Lord of all.

The prospect of soon having access to 400,000,000 of souls, or even to any considerable part of this number, ought to stimulate every true believer in Jesus, to awake to righteousness, to put on strength, and to come up to the Lord's help against the mighty. How great is the work here to be accomplished! How few are the means now in operation!

In our religious services — social and public — the interest hitherto manifested has been continued; but, confined and restricted as we long have been, we ardently desire to enlarge our operations, to increase our labors, and to extend widely the influences of that holy religion, for the propagation of which we have devoted our lives. We hope that great and dreadful evils which now affect this nation will soon be checked. It is painful to see thousands of our fellow-men cut down by the sword — tens of thousands reduced to beggary and death by an insidious poison — and hundreds of millions going mad after their dumb idols. It is impossible to dwell long on such scenes without deep emotion. But who can interpose? Who is able to hush these contending hosts and give peace? Who can stay this flood of poison, and bring in the waters of life? Who can cast down all these idols of wood and stone, and convert these millions of immortal beings to the worship of the living and true God? Awake, put on thy strength, Oh arm of the Lord! Awake! Art not thou it, that shall wound the dragon?

Brethren pray for us — pray for China — pray that God will turn away His wrath, avert these evils, and save the people through the influences of the glorious Gospel of His dear Son.

✪ *November 6*

John Augustine Zahm

ROMAN CATHOLIC

September 14, 1851–November 10, 1921

In the year 2004, the president of Harvard ignited a firestorm of criticism by suggesting that a paucity of women in the sciences might indicate fundamental differences between the brains of men and women. In that perspective, it is remarkable to find a book published almost a century ago that celebrates the achievements of women as scientists. Its author was a Roman Catholic priest, John Augustine Zahm, who noted that whatever had been done for the intellectual advancement of women had been done by their own efforts. Had they had relied on male initiatives, "they would today be in the same condition of ignorance and seclusion and servitude as was the Athenian woman twenty-five centuries ago, and would occupy a status but little above that of the inmates of oriental harems and zenanas."

John Augustus Zahm was the kind of priest who made Vatican authorities nervous about the church in the United States. Born and brought up in the midwest, he was an early graduate of Notre Dame in a class of three, and returned there even before his ordination to teach science and serve as a trustee. Over the following years, Zahm worked hard as professor of chemistry to promote the teaching of science. Eventually, he became its vice president, and he strove to move Notre Dame into the first rank of American universities. His first significant book was a study of the principles of acoustics called *Sound and Music,* but in an era when science and religion seemed increasingly engaged in battle, Zahm inevitably turned his attention to that subject with a series of books entitled *Catholic Science and Catholic Scientists* (1893), *Bible, Science, and Faith* (1894), *Evolution and Dogma* (1896), and *Science and the Church* (1896). Although many in the church saw no reason to include science in a university curriculum, believing it was a threat to faith, Zahm insisted that faith and science ought to support each other in the search for truth. In his study of evolution, he attempted to reconcile Darwin's theory with Christian doctrine rather than condemn it. In words that are still relevant, Zahm criticized "creationism," writing:

> Creationism, then, I repeat, is possible, but there is nothing in a reasonable interpretation of Genesis which makes it at all probable, while all the conclusions of contemporary science render it not only in the highest degree improbable, but also exhibit it as completely discredited and as unworthy of the slightest consideration as a working hypothesis to guide the investigator in the study of Nature and Nature's laws.

But Zahm's careful definition of what he and others called "theistic evolutionism" provoked intense opposition in Rome and calls for it to be condemned. The Vatican did not condemn the book outright, but requested that the author withdraw it from circulation. He complied, and never wrote about science and religion again.

Turning his attention to other fields and traveling widely, Zahm worked hard to develop Notre Dame and other universities founded by his order, the Congregation of the Holy Cross. He became the order's procurator general in Rome (1896–1898) and then its provincial superior in the United States (1898–1906). He also published several books about South America and a noteworthy volume entitled *Woman in Science,* first issued first in 1913 but republished in 1974 and 1991.

A reading from *Woman in Science* by John Augustus Zahm

Woman's long struggle for complete intellectual freedom is almost ended, and certain victory is already in sight. In spite of the sarcasm and ridicule of satirists and comic poets, in spite of the antipathy of philosophers and the antagonism of legislators who persisted in treating women as inferior beings, they are finally in view of the goal toward which they have through so many long ages been bending their best efforts. Moreover, so effective and so concentrated has been their work during recent years that they have accomplished more toward securing complete intellectual enfranchisement than during the previous thirty centuries.

Yes, the world is beginning at last to realize the truth of the proposition which the learned Maria Gaetana Agnesi so eloquently defended nearly two centuries ago — to wit, that nature has endowed the female mind with a capacity for all knowledge, and that, in depriving women of an opportunity of acquiring knowledge, men work against the best interests of the public weal. We are at the long last near that millennium which Emerson had in mind when, in 1822, he predicted "a time when higher institutions for the education of young women would be as needful as colleges for young men" — that millennium for which women have hoped and striven ever since Sappho sang and Aspasia inspired the brightest, the noblest minds of Greece.

The romantic idea of treating woman as a clinging vine, and thus eliminating half the energies of humanity, is rapidly disappearing and giving place to the idea that the strong are for the strong — the intellectually strong; that the evolution of the race will be complete only when men and women shall be associated in perfect unity of purpose, and shall, in fullest sympathy, collaborate for the attainment of the highest and the best. Then, indeed, will man's helpmate become to him and to his children:

> More rich than pearl of Ind or gold of Ophir,
> And in her sex more wonderful and rare.

Then will men and women for the first time fully supplement each other in their aspirations and endeavors and realize somewhat of that oneness of heart and mind which was so beautifully adumbrated in Plato's androgyn. Then will the world witness the return of another Golden Age — the Golden Age of science — the Golden Age of cultured, noble, perfect womanhood.

✪ *November 7*

John Christopher Kunze

LUTHERAN

August 4, 1744–July 24, 1807

A scholar rather than an activist or politician, John Christopher Kunze's contributions to the church mostly involved teaching and academic administration. Few scholars, however, can remain above all the controversies of their time and place. For Kunze, one such issue was whether to use English or German in his church. The Lutherans who came to America did not speak English, and it continued to be a second language for many Germans and Scandinavians, even after several generations, since new immigrants continued to arrive, speaking the languages of the Old World. Love of their native cultures, familiarity with prayers and Bible passages known since childhood, as well as a desire to cling to the traditions of their ancestors made the switch to English a difficult proposition. Yet, if Lutheranism were to function outside the immigrant community, or manage to retain Anglophone children of that community, a change would need to come.

Kunze was not especially good at preaching in English himself, but he understood how important it was for congregations to move in that direction. He helped create an American Ministerium, a collegial network of clergy, scholars, and church leaders who could support and develop Lutheranism on colonial soil. Kunze worked with Henry Melchior Muhlenberg,*, supplementing Muhlenberg's work with his own efforts.

Kunze's life had not been easy. He and his siblings were raised in an orphanage, but education was stressed there, so Kunze was given a good foundation for future studies. He wrote that his zeal for education was partly a result of his need to find a meaningful task in the face of his losses. "Since God had deigned that I make good progress in learning Greek and Latin, the death of my parents, which was as grievous as anyone might imagine, caused me to pursue diligently my studies in the humanities up to the fifty-eighth year of the century." He moved about Germany in his youth, going went from one educational institution to another. Instead of succumbing to self-pity, bitterness, hopelessness, or aimlessness, he found a source of joy, direction, purpose, and commitment.

Before they died, his parents had modeled a simple piety that did not desert him in his grief. He saw those who cared for him after his parents' deaths not as inadequate substitutes, but as gifts from God to show the Creator's love for him. "With the greatest reverence I marvel at the ways of divine providence, at the wisdom which willed me to live by the pure gifts of others." Yet at the same time, he believed he could not put his trust in anyone but God after losing so much so young.

> I had to overcome at the beginning, what privations I had to endure; it came to the point that, when several others went to lunch, in order that I might seem to be summoned to that same meal, I took time for a stroll, praying to God, as earnestly as possible, that he grant me food and clothing. In this way, then, as I freely confess to glorify the most liberal grace of the Lord Jesus Christ, God spared my spirit, like booty snatched from the hand of the enemy, and kept me his own to feed me with more excellent goods.

Kunze's final training was at Halle in Germany. Though he could have chosen to serve in a local congregation or obtained a teaching post, he decided instead to serve fledgling congregations in America. His *Autobiography* was written when he was not quite 26 to raise funds for his trip and to introduce himself to the communities he would encounter upon arrival. His traveling companions were Henry and Fredrick Muhlenberg, sons of the famed Henry Melchior Muhlenberg, both of whom had also studied at Halle and were about to return home to America. They landed in New York on September 22, 1770, then moved on to Philadelphia, where Kunze started his call as an associate pastor to the German congregations in October of 1770. He served also as professor of German at the University of Pennsylvania. He married Margaret Muhlenberg, the sister of Henry and Frederick.

In August of 1784, Kunze moved to New York City to serve the United congregations there. Once again, he was a professor, this time of Oriental languages, at Columbia College. In New York, Kunze began to organize a ministerium of nine pastors who served 18 congregations in New York and New Jersey. He was elected its president for the New York area and served in this capacity until his death. The Ministerium's main tasks were to examine ministerial candidates, license those it judged fit, and provided oversight and discipline for the congregations. Plans for a seminary were also developed. Many of these steps would have eventually been taken out of pressing necessity, but Kunze's leadership and insights were vital catalysts for the emerging Lutheran organization in the colonies. He was sustained by a sense of mission that had remained with him from his days in Germany.

A reading from John Kunze's *Autobiography*

Finally that very thing happened which compels me to compose this biography, and in comparison to which nothing happened in my life which seems more weighty, nothing more important. The most venerable Dr. Knapp, Doctor of Sacred Theology and Ordinary Public Professor in the Academy of Fridericiana of Halle, and Director of the Royal Orphan School at

Glauchau, called me to undertake the responsibility of evangelical ministry at Philadelphia in America.

I prayed long, I long beseeched God, reciting a hundred times or more those words of Samuel: Speak Lord, Thy servant hearkens. Many friends spoke many things for the contrary view, but the path of response to the divine will was open for me to follow and I am compelled to follow God rather than my reason, rather than my fellow man. By Thy Word, O Lord, direct my journey. To my final breath Thine I am, and Thine I shall be into eternity, to the glory of Thy name.

✪ *November 8*

Charles Stelzle

PRESBYTERIAN

June 4, 1869–Feb 27 1941

Charles Stelzle began life in a hard place during hard times. The Bowery of New York in the mid-19th century was a place of scarcity, want, and struggle. As urbanization and industrialization reshaped the American landscape and culture, churches did not always adapt quickly to changing circumstances or respond creatively to problems arising from rural people becoming city workers. At an early age, Stelzle became a laborer in one of the many new factories. As time passed, his talents and passions were channeled into the cause of workers' rights. The Union movement was growing, and Stelzle joined the International Association of Machinists. But this left him spiritually unsatisfied, and he managed to find time to study at the Moody Bible Institute and to be ordained a Presbyterian minister in 1900.

This rather unusual road to ordination enabled Stelzle to bring a wealth of life experience to his ministry. He knew firsthand about labor and the existence of those responsible for the growing output of America's factories. He knew that the fortunes acquired by men who owned and managed companies came from the sweat of their underpaid workers. From his background of poverty and hard work, Stelzle understood that the church might move from simple alms-giving by the privileged to the real work of the social gospel. He was motivated by a sense of empathy and solidarity with those whose life he had shared for so many years.

Stelzle's theology was not inspired by liberalism. His ideas derived from an enthusiastic and warm-hearted evangelical movement. Neither an individualist nor a "spiritualizer," he held that the essence of Christian faith could not be fully embraced apart from an active engagement with the entire church and the wider human community. He believed that spiritual, material, and even political realities intertwined and the church needed to address all of them together in order to fulfill its Great Commission.

Only three years after his ordination, Stelzle began to concentrate his mission on urban laborers. This, in turn, helped Presbyterians become the first denomination to develop a division specifically focused on their problems. In 1910, Stelzle was named the first superintendent of the Presbyterian Department of Church and Labor. He also formed the Labor Temple, a venue for ongoing mission with and for the working people of New York. Later, Stelzle's efforts were plagued by budget cuts, leading to his eventual resignation, but instead of giving up, he simply shifted his base and through the Red Cross and the Council of Churches he was able to persevere in his ministry.

A reading from Charles Stelzle

Must we forever be silent about the hard things that the Church should be doing? What if a few men, or even many men, should be driven away, even from the banquet? The best and strongest will remain, and it may be a good plan to build upon these the foundation of a great superstructure which will stand the test of time.

Here is a chance for the poorest of men to have a part in the building up of the Kingdom of God upon earth, and the rich need not be left out. If the Church is to win the strong men who are to-day offering themselves for hard tasks in other fields, the Church must appeal to the heroic in men. Real men like to do things that demand sacrifice. And when such men are enlisted in the great cause for which the Church stands, then the success of the Church is assured, for even the other kind will follow the strong leaders in the Church.

The Church has been emphasizing the importance of individual salvation. It is time that we talked more about social salvation. We have been saying that we must "build up the Church." We ought to be more deeply interested in "building up the people." It is well to declare that the individual must be saved. But the individual can be saved only as he helps save society.

Institutional work is a very small part of the social gospel. Mere sociability is even less typical of what it implies. The social gospel includes economic justice. It means that underfed women and overworked men must get a square deal. It means that there shall be a more equitable distribution of profits in industry. It carries with it the spirit of true brotherhood and democracy.

The Church must not remain in ignorance of vile sanitary conditions and bad economic relationships. It must study these questions with an open mind and then strike at them with a closed fist. The Church must find out why so many people die of contagious but preventable disease. In former days men said that great epidemics were visitations of divine Providence. To-day they charge it up to the Board of Health. The Church cannot remain out of the fight for health and life. It is too late for the Church to say that it has nothing to do with men's bodies — that it is its business simply to save men's souls.

If the Church does not care for men's bodies, which it has seen, how can it care for men's souls which it has not seen? If Jesus thought it worth His time to heal men's diseases, isn't it worth our while to prevent diseases? And doesn't this mean an interest in sanitation and pure food and good housing? One does not get very far along in the study of social problems before one runs upon a moral principle. Such work *is* religious. It isn't a thing separate and apart. It is vitally related to the deepest spiritual experience.

✪ *November 9*

Dorothy Day
ROMAN CATHOLIC
November 8, 1897–November 29, 1980

Dorothy Day was born in Brooklyn, New York, but grew up in Chicago. She dropped out of college after two years and moved to New York, where she found a job as a reporter for a Socialist newspaper. Even as a child she has been attuned to social justice issues; now she involved herself in efforts to change social conditions. She was arrested and jailed the first time for participating in a demonstration for women's right to vote. Day terminated her first pregnancy with an abortion, but when a second pregnancy produced a child, she felt strongly that the baby should be baptized and she herself was received into the Roman Catholic Church.

Still searching for ways to express her social concerns, she met Peter Maurin,* a radical living a Franciscan kind of life, who persuaded her to start a newspaper. The first edition of the *Catholic Worker* was published on May 1, 1933, and continues to witness against war and injustice. The paper's philosophy promoted creation of a Catholic Worker's hospitality house for the poor and unemployed, and soon, over 30 such houses had been established across the country. Day maintained her pacifist ideals during World War II. She was jailed again for demonstrating against the Cold War, then again in 1973, when she was 75, for demonstrating on behalf of farm workers. She did not want to be considered at saint, fearing that official canonization would be used as a way of dismissing her social witness. Nonetheless, Cardinal O'Connor of New York forwarded her cause to the Vatican in 2000.

A reading from an editorial on "holy poverty" by Dorothy Day

Clarification of thought is the first plank in the Catholic Worker Program.

There can be no revolution without a theory of revolution, Peter Maurin quotes Lenin as saying, "Action must be preceded by thought." There is such a thing as the heresy of good works, "these accursed occupations," as

St. Bernard calls them, which keep people from thinking. To feed the hungry, clothe the naked and shelter the harborless without also trying to change the social order so that people can feed, clothe and shelter themselves, is just to apply palliatives. It is to show a lack of faith in ones fellows, their responsibilities as children of God, heirs of heaven

Of course, "the poor we will always have with us." That has been flung in our teeth again and again, usually with the comment, "so why change things which our Lord said would always be?" But surely He did not intend that there would be quite so many of them. We also have to repeat that line now that war is on and there is plentiful occupation.

"Surely, these men on your breadline, these men living in your house, could get work if they really wanted to?" And again and again we must say, "The poor ye have always with you." These are the lame, the halt, the blind, those injured in industrial accidents and those who have been driven to drink by our industrial order and the refugees and veterans from class, race and international war. There are those, too, who refuse to cooperate in this social order, who prefer to work here with us without salary. We could not do without them.

Yes, the poor have been robbed of the good material things of life, and when they asked for bread, they have been given a stone. They have been robbed of a philosophy of labor. They have been betrayed by their teachers and their political leaders. They have been robbed of their skills and made tenders of the machine. They cannot cook; they have been given the can. They cannot spin or weave or sew — they are urged to go to Klein's and get a dress for four ninety-eight....

The first unit of society is the family. The family should look after its own and, in addition, as the early fathers said, "every home should have a Christ room in it, so that hospitality may be practiced." "The coat that hangs in your closet belongs to the poor." "If your brother is hungry, it is your responsibility."

"When did we see Thee hungry, when did we see Thee naked?" People either plead ignorance or they say "It is none of my responsibility." But we are all members one of another, so we are obliged in conscience to help each other. The parish is the next unit, and there are local councils of the St. Vincent de Paul Society. Then there is the city, and the larger body of charitable groups. And there are the unions, where mutual aid and fraternal charity is also practiced. For those who are not Catholics there are lodges, fraternal organizations, where there is a long tradition of charity. But now there is a dependence on the state. Hospitals once Catholic are subsidized by the state. Orphanages once supported by Catholic charity receive their aid from community chests. And when it is not the state it is bingo parties!

But we must reject it. We must keep on talking about voluntary poverty, and holy poverty, because it is only if we can consent to strip ourselves that we can put on Christ. It is only if we love poverty that we are going to have the means to help others. If we love poverty we will be free to give up a job, to speak when we feel it would be wrong to be silent. We can only talk about voluntary poverty because we believe Christians must be fools for Christ. We can only embrace voluntary poverty in the light of faith.

✪ November 10

Samuel Johnson

EPISCOPALIAN

October 14, 1696–January 6, 1772

The Puritans came to New England with a vision of a like-minded community where their views would prevail. It didn't last. Before long, they had divided into New Lights and Old Lights, Full Covenanters and Half-way Covenanters. By 1722, social harmony was further disrupted on the day after graduation at Yale College. The rector and several other leading members of the Yale faculty suddenly announced that they had come to believe that the ordination they had received as clergy in the Congregational Church was invalid and that they must therefore be ordained by bishops. This shocking event reverberated throughout New England and has gone down in history as "The Dark Day at Yale" when an Anglican understanding of ordination crept back into one of the great citadels of Congregationalism.

Samuel Johnson was a member of a little group that had been meeting together and studying church history. They resolved to follow their quest for the nature of the true church, no matter where it might lead. Not long after that graduation day, Johnson along with several of his colleagues, sailed for England, where they were ordained by the Bishop of London. Their differences with Congregationalism extended well beyond ordination. They also adopted an approach to theology that included tradition and reason as means of understanding God's work in the world and as tools for interpreting scripture. The light of reason became a frequent theme of Johnson's sermons and theological writing.

Returning to New England after his Anglican ordination, Johnson settled in the parish of Stratford, Connecticut, where he served for 30 years. In 1754, he became the first president of Kings College — later, Columbia University. His writings were influential in his own day and mark him out as one of the most important theologians in the history of American Christianity.

A reading from a sermon by Samuel Johnson

Here I begin with the light of nature as the first instance of God the Father's teaching and instruction in order to our coming unto Jesus Christ. The light of nature is that inspiration of the Almighty which gives us understanding, that power of reasoning and knowing and finding out the truth of things, as being what they really are, which God has endowed us with, whereby we are capable of reflecting, knowing, and considering what we ourselves are, what God is, and what relation we stand in to him, and one another and the obligations resulting therefrom. All which we may be properly said to hear and learn of the Father as being the original fountain of all that light and knowledge that we gain by the exercise of the faculties He has given us, upon the objects in nature and Providence that he has set before us.

As to ourselves, a little reflection and consideration will soon teach us that we are feeble, limited, and dependent beings, that in multitudes of cases we have no power of ourselves to help our selves, but all our sufficiency is of God, and this, in a natural, as well as spiritual sense; that we are so fearfully and wonderfully made that our frame and constitution directly points out to us the kind, wise, and powerful hand from whence we are derived, and yet so entirely dependent upon it, that we cannot subsist or enjoy ourselves a moment without its continual agency in supporting us and providing for us; that we are not only very weak, but also very ignorant, and therefore need his instruction to teach us what to do in many cases, as well as his assistance to enable us to perform it. I say, a due contemplation of human nature would lead us to such reflections as these, and in fact has lead many to them, who have had nothing but the light of nature to depend upon. The result of which would be that humility and meekness of spirit, that diffidence of ourselves, that modest and teachable temper, which are those dispositions of mind which directly prepare and qualify us for the reception of the Gospel, and would dispose us gladly to accept of those instructions and assistances which Christ has provided and offers to us therein for our relief and recovery.

Furthermore we learn from reflecting and looking inwards upon ourselves the miserable state of guilt into which sin has brought us. The Father teaches us much by the light of nature of the deformity and odiousness of sin, and its horrid intrinsic baseness, as being entirely beneath the dignity of our nature, and acting a direct violence upon it, and consequently, as what can't fail of being attended with uneasiness, loathing and bitter reflections, and as deserving and exposing us to the hatred and displeasure of our maker and the dire effects of his vengeance and indignation. This is what St. Paul observes of the heathen world, that they show the work of the law written in their hearts, their consciences accusing or excusing (Rom. 2:15). Thus therefore our consciences are as it were a secret whisper from God, inspiring us with a sense of our guilt, and writing bitter things against us, which if we duly hearken and attend to we can't fail of seeing the necessity of a Savior and being earnestly solicitous to come to Christ, as the great atonement for our sins, and the only mediator and intercessor with God for pardon and mercy in our behalf.

✪ *November 11* _____

Obadiah Holmes

BAPTIST

1607–October 15, 1682

A recurring pattern in Christian history is the story of dissidents who separate themselves from larger churches, only to discover they cannot agree among themselves. When Constantine ended the Roman Empire's persecution of Christians, the church found that once it was no longer united by a common adversary, it faced internal conflicts. In the same ways dissenters who fled to New England treated those who did not share their views in much the same way as they had been treated for disagreeing with the established church. Yet out of these experiences, new patterns evolved, establishing greater religious freedom and diversity.

Obadiah Holmes was born in northern England around the year 1607. He grew up in a farm family of eight or nine children and became a glassmaker and a weaver. He seems to have had little interest in religion or books until his mother's last illness caused him to worry that his "disobedient acts caused her death, which forced me to confess the same to her — my evil ways." He married Catherine Hyde two months later and together they "adventured the danger of the seas to come to New England," where they settled in 1639 at Salem, Massachusetts. All went well at first. Holmes helped establish what may have been the first glass factory in North America. He served on juries and took part in community life.

In March of 1640, Obadiah and Catherine joined the Salem Church but soon became uncomfortable with its rigidity. In 1645, Holmes sold his land in Salem and moved to Rehobeth, 40 miles south of Boston, to make a new start. But, again, the new community fell short of the dream. Within five years, the congregation divided with Holmes on one side and Samuel Newman, the minister, on the other. In 1649, the civil government acted to settle the dispute by ordering Holmes and his followers to "to desist, and neither to ordain officers, nor to baptize, nor to break bread together, nor yet to meet upon the first day of the week." As a result, Holmes, who had now received believers' baptism, moved again, this time to Rhode Island.

In Rhode Island, Baptists were safe from the Massachusetts courts, but they were concerned for fellow Baptists who remained in the Boston area. They also worried about the errors of those souls who had not accepted their views. In July of 1651, Holmes and two others journeyed to Lynn to bring spiritual comfort and communion to a blind and aged fellow Baptist, William Witter. They took advantage of the opportunity to proclaim the word, baptize converts, and minister communion in Witter's house, but were interrupted by two constables who placed them under arrest.

Quickly convicted in a proceeding the next day, they were asked to pay fines or be "well whipped." Friends paid the fine for the companions, but Holmes's was larger and he refused to have it paid. His own account of the whipping follows below. After this episode, he returned to Rhode Island, where he succeeded John Clarke* as the second minister of the first Baptist Church in America until his death 30 years later, on October 15, 1682.

The testimony of Obadiah Holmes

I desired to speak a few words, but Mr. Norvel answered, It is not time now to speak: whereupon I took leave, and said, Men, brethren, fathers, and countrymen, I beseech you to give me leave to speak a few words, and the rather because here are many spectators to see me punished, and I am to seal with my blood, if God give me strength, that which I hold and practice in reference to the word of God, and the testimony of Jesus. . . . But in comes Mr. Flint, and saith to the executioner, Fellow, do thine office; for this fellow would but make a long speech to delude the people: so I being resolved to speak, told the people, That which I am to suffer for is the word of God, and testimony of Jesus Christ. . . . Still Mr. Flint calls the man to do his office; so before and in the time of his pulling off my clothes I continued speaking; telling them . . . that the Lord having manifested his love towards me, in giving me repentance towards God and faith in Christ, and so to be baptized in water by a messenger of Jesus, in the name of the Father, Son, and Holy Spirit, wherein I have fellowship with him in his death, burial, and resurrection, I am now come to be baptized in afflictions by your hands, that so I may have further fellowship with my Lord, and am not ashamed of his sufferings, for by his stripes am I healed. And as the man began to lay the strokes on my back, I said to the people, though my flesh should fail, and my spirit should fail, yet God would not fail; so it pleased the Lord to come in and to fill my heart and tongue as a vessel full, and with an audible voice I broke forth, praying the Lord not to lay this sin to their charge, and telling the people that now I found he did not fail me, and therefore now I should trust him for ever who failed me not; for in truth as the strokes fell upon me, I had such a spiritual manifestation of God's presence as I never had before, and the outward pain was so removed from me that I could well bear it, yea, and in a manner felt it not, although it was grievous, as the spectators said, the man striking with all his strength, spitting in his hand three times, with a three-corded whip, giving me therewith thirty strokes. When he had loosed me from the post, having joyfulness in my heart and cheerfulness in my countenance, as the spectators observed, I told the magistrates, You have struck me with roses; and said moreover, although the Lord had made it easy to me, yet I pray God it may not be laid to your charge.

✠ *November 12* ———————————————————————

John Davenport

CONGREGATIONAL

April 1597–March 15, 1669/1670

Dissenters frequently discover that, once they secede from the parent group, they find themselves becoming aware of differences among themselves. John Davenport seems to have moved slowly from the established Church of England to the position of a dissenter. However, after he became settled in his own opinions, he found it increasingly difficult to find common ground with his fellow dissenters.

Financial problems forced Davenport to withdraw from Oxford. At the age of 18, he began to preach in a private chapel. After returning to Oxford to complete his degree, he was appointed in 1619 as a lecturer and curate of St. Lawrence Jewry Church in London. Chosen next to serve as vicar of St. Stephen's, London, he encountered opposition on the grounds that he was a nonconformist but denied the charges and was appointed. Nevertheless, he became increasingly convinced of the Puritan position. When William Laud was appointed Archbishop of Canterbury, Davenport fled first to Holland, then to Massachusetts.

Massachusetts, however, was not the haven he had envisioned. The colony was torn by controversy over Ann Hutchinson* and the antinomians. In addition, Davenport and those who had come with him were dissatisfied with the land they were offered. A new colony was being established in New Haven, so Davenport and his colleague, Theophilus Eaton, moved there in the spring of 1638. Eaton was soon installed as governor, with Davenport as minister. They set out to create a community governed by the Bible. Their land had been purchased from the Native Americans with biblical references used to set prices and wages, even to measure the kegs of ale. Four principles were to govern everything they did: (1) Scripture was to be the perfect rule for government by men in commonwealth, church, and family; (2) They were to be guided by Scripture; (3) They would create a church as soon as God fitted them for it, and (4) they would establish a civil order to implement these articles and ensure prosperity for themselves and their descendants.

The New Haven colony was the first in the New World to profess no allegiance to the mother country. Its colonists planned to be completely independent and self-sufficient. Yet they could not escape the English connection. When Charles II came to the throne and the judges who had condemned Charles I fled to Connecticut, Davenport gave them shelter even, it is said, in his own home. Such independence could not last. The end of the Commonwealth government in England meant the end of New Haven's independence as well. Despite fierce opposition from Davenport, New Haven was forced to unite with the Connecticut colony. Bitterly disappointed, he moved to Boston in 1667, where he was chosen to lead the First Church but died a few months later.

A reading from *God's Call to His People* by John Davenport

Learn . . . that when any Calamity is upon people, or a particular person, to look through it unto sin as the cause of it. Look not only on the outward means, or instruments, or secondary Causes: that which is outward & obvious to our sense, is but the Vial through which Gods wrath is poured forth. *2 Chron.* 12.7. *David* knew that the natural cause of that Famine of three years in Israel, was Drought; but he rested not there, but went to enquire of the Lord, what sin was the cause of it, and received his answer, *2 Sam.* 21.1. This the Lord taught *Joshua* to do, *Josh.* 7.10,11. The people of *Israel* learned it by long continued afflictions, *Lam.* 3.39,40.

Learn hence to look at sin as the most mischievous thing in the world, that you may hate and shun it more perfectly. When men look upon sin abstractively, onely as a thing done, they think it not so dangerous an evil as it is: therefore look at it in the effects of it, and you will see how mischievous it is. If you should know man who is always doing mischief, where ever he comes, he poisons one, stabs another, *&c.* and leaves every where some prints of his villainy, how dreadfull and hatefull would he be to you? Such a thing is Sin: it caused *Ahabs* death, and the dogs licked up his blood, and *Jezabels* also; burnt up *Nadab* and *Abihu;* caused the Earth to open, and swallow up *Corah, Dathan, and Abiram;* struck Ananias and Sapphira dead at Peter's feet. In a word, it blasts the Corn, destroys the fruits of the Trees; brings diseases upon mens bodies; brings in Foreign Enemies upon people; fills the Earth with miseries, and Hell with everlasting torments. . . .

Speedily get sin done away, for the sentence is gone out, as soon as sin is committed, though the execution be deferred for a time, *Eccles.* 8.11,12. and the Decree is in travail before it brings forth, *Zeph.* 2.2. and it may be sin is not finished, *Jam.* 1.15. as Judas, though he was a Thief, was let alone until he had betrayed his Master. See *Zech.* 5.2,3,8,9. Sin may lye like a sleeping debt, which is not demanded for many years, but if the debtor hath not an Acquaintance, the Creditor may call for it when he will, and cast him into prison.

For Comfort to repenting sinners under Affliction: Think not that you shall never be freed from them, but be assured, that if thy heart be humbled, and thy sin mortified, God is as willing as able to remove it. No man is in a hard condition but he that hath an hard heart. See I Pet. 5.6. Humble yourselves therefore under the mighty hand of God, that he may exalt you in due time.

✪ *November 13* _____

John Tracy Ellis

ROMAN CATHOLIC

July 30, 1905–October 16, 1992

The work of historians is crucial to our common life because, through the study of history, society comes to understand itself. Roman Catholics in the late 19th and early 20th centuries had little leisure to ask themselves who they were. Floods of Irish and Italian immigrants were too busy finding their place in the larger American society to stop and ask questions about their identities or how to play their part. Signs that said, "Irish Need Not Apply" and the activities of the Ku Klux Klan taught that they were unwelcome minorities who must create their own institutions and protect themselves in ethnic ghettoes. History for these generations consisted of a chronicle of saints and heroes of past ages whose examples could inspire them to survive in their own times of trial.

John Tracy Ellis began as a student of medieval Catholicism, but when his university needed someone to teach American church history, he switched tracks and found his calling. The history of the American Roman Catholic Church needed to be looked at objectively and a knowledge of history need not, he realized, shield one from contemporary problems. Indeed, by gaining perspective on them, history might be used to promote reform and renewal.

Not everyone shared his outlook. In his autobiography, Ellis recalls visiting a senior member of the hierarchy and coming away with:

> first hand evidence of the spirit and tone in which he and many of the bishops of his generation wished the history of the church to be written. I would say that such was the attitude of a great majority of both bishops and priests who revealed the defensive reaction of men who had grown up in the aftermath of the A.P.A. and the decades of the flourishing Ku Klux Klan. In a word, such a thing as telling the Church's story in an open and honest way was giving consolation to the enemy.... While fully conscious of the attitude of these churchmen, I never allowed it to influence my own writing of church history since I simply did not believe in the validity of their position. I have always preferred the attitude represented by Pope Leo XIII in his letter on historical studies of 1883 where he made his own the words of Job, "God has no need for our lies."

As Ellis continued to discover, many eminent members of the church took extraordinary steps to influence the way history would be written. Cardinal Cushing of Boston burned his papers before his death, while Cardinal O'Connor composed *The Letters of His Eminence William Cardinal O'Connell, Archbishop of Boston*, Volume I, *From College Days 1876 to Bishop of Portland 1901* long after the period at which they were purported to have been written. His nephew and a priest of the diocese spent a long afternoon burning all the volumes they could find when the Cardinal died, but some copies survived and were used in the writing of the *History of the Archdiocese of Boston.* Ellis acquired a copy himself and writes, "I frequently took it to my seminar in later years to show my graduate students and to indicate the critical attitude an historian must always exercise toward the sources he or she employs in their work. One learns the rules of the game, so to speak, in more ways than one!"

Historians do not necessarily feel optimistic about the human condition. Although Ellis valued the spirit of openness that resulted from Vatican II and the evolution of participatory decision-making, he felt the church was facing the ills of American society in the late 1970s — the triumph of secular humanism along with the collapse of the traditional Protestant work ethic and respect for authority. But a Christian historian's perspective is tempered by knowledge of the Lord of history. Ellis knew the church had survived massive changes in the past. He concludes his autobiography with a summation well-tempered by faith:

A reading from the autobiography of John Ellis

It is scarcely exaggerating to say that our current society has brought on widespread anxiety on the part of thoughtful people who sense that a remedy must be found somewhere if, as Palmer phrased it, "continuing deterioration is to be avoided...."

I confess that at the moment I find it difficult to see a light on the horizon of national life, to discern a leader of the caliber and integrity of George Washington, Abraham Lincoln, or Robert E. Lee, for it seems to me it is that type of leadership that the United States desperately needs as the 1980's come to a close. Meanwhile, however, I refuse to succumb to a defeatist attitude, since I recognize and believe that hope is one of the theological virtues ranked with faith and charity. And when I experience momentary discouragement about the future of the United States and the world, I find reassurance in the history of the church whose nearly twenty centuries in this world have borne striking witness through crises infinitely worse than the one through which we are at present passing to the words of the Master, "Know that I am with you always; yes, to the end of time."

✸ *November 14* _____

Conrad Weiser

LUTHERAN

November 2, 1696–July 13, 1760

The Weiser family emigrated from the Rhine Valley to the New York wilderness because Queen Anne of England was looking for Germans to assist the

British in their settlement of the New World. Conrad Weiser was born in Germany and did not begin to learn the language of his adopted country until he was in his teens. But he learned more than English. The new settlers had frequent relationships with the six-nation Iroquois Confederacy, made up of the Mohawk, Oneida, Onondaga, Cayuga, Seneca, and Tuscarora tribes. At 17, Weiser went to live with the Indians for eight months. He absorbed their customs and learned to appreciate their culture. In the inevitable tensions between indigenous people and new settlers, he was often the only European who could speak both languages fluently, and therefore would be called upon to negotiate agreements between the two parties.

In 1729, Weiser married and moved his family to an area of Pennsylvania known as Tulpehocken. He established a large farm there and also practiced his trade as a tanner. His understanding of the Iroquois nations and his skill at finding peaceful solutions to conflicts brought him to the attention of the authorities in Philadelphia, who hired him to be the official liaison between the native and colonials. His role was complicated by the fact that the Indians were not always on friendly terms with each other. The Lenni Lenape of the Delaware region, for example, resisted Iroquois domination. They wanted the right to make treaties independently, while the settlers preferred to deal with the Iroquois, who were stronger and often more amenable. On the European side, the French and British were in competition for the same lands in the New World. Under these difficult conditions, Weiser consistently displayed wisdom in seeking the most peaceful and practical solution.

So effective was his work and so respected his sagacity that Weiser was given the name "Tarachawagon," which can be translated "he who is holding up the heavens." Upon his death, his status among the Indians was summarized by one Iroquois who said: "We are at a great loss and sit in darkness... as since his death we cannot so well understand one another." Weiser served briefly in the militia during the armed conflict between the French with their Indian allies, and the English with theirs, hoping to resolve the violence that was afflicting the countryside. A French and Lenni Lenape pact led to a series of attacks in the eastern part of the state. The Pennsylvanians raised troops to fend off the raiders, and in 1756, Weiser was made a lieutenant colonel in charge of the defense of the area between the Delaware and Susquehanna rivers. By 1758, the French had been pushed out of the state, allowing Weiser to return to his civilian life.

The church was also in upheaval in these early days of colonization. Moravians, Calvinists, Lutherans, Quakers, and others lived in and around the eastern end of Pennsylvania. In many cases, lines of authority were fuzzy or nonexistent. Preachers and overseers shaped local congregational life, often without proper training or clearly defined accountability. A small Lutheran congregation near the Weiser home fell prey to troubles. Some Moravians arrived with the vision of a unified, Spirit-filled Christianity for the New World. Some of the stricter Lutherans objected. The "Tulpehocken

Confusion" as it was called, became bitter and protracted. Weiser's first response was to stay away and avoid the whole situation. He was so distressed at the behavior of the squabbling parties that, for a time, he took up residence in a community called the Cloisters, located at Ephrata. Confused and conflicted, he needed to find a faith he could embrace, but he was not willing simply go his own way. When he left the Cloisters, he aligned with the Moravians for a time, but his Lutheran roots were deep. Eventually, he took the Lutheran side of this congregational debate, and, after attempts to settle the matter with the Moravian bishop failed, he judged in favor of the Lutherans holding control of the church. Then, in 1742, a new Lutheran clergyman disembarked in Philadelphia. His name was Henry Melchior Muhlenberg,* and he was to become the patriarch of American Lutheranism. Later, he married one of Weiser's daughters, cementing the family connection more firmly with the Lutheran tradition. But apart from his personal feelings about denominations, Weiser displayed a solid commitment to a deeply held spiritual orientation in all his work and a controlling concern to bring peace and order to a land filled with tension and upheaval.

Beyond his peacemaking and peacekeeping work with the Native Americans, Weiser was also a trusted judge, and one of the founding fathers of Reading, and later, of Berks County, Pennsylvania. In Reading, he was a founder of First Lutheran Church. But he was never closed to other Christian expressions. He assisted in the establishment of a Dutch Reformed congregation in Reading as well. Weiser's wisdom exercised on behalf of his neighbors, both native and newcomer, stands to this day as an example of faith in action. In the face of so much animosity between European and Native American people across the continent, he labored to avoid bloodshed and to build bridges between cultures. His life is a striking reminder of what one person's dedicated efforts can accomplish.

✠ *November 15*

D. Elton Trueblood

QUAKER

December 12, 1900–December 20, 1994

Because Quakers avoid creedal statements and rely on guidance from an Inner Light, they aroused enormous hostility in the early days of the American colonies. On the other hand, their beliefs are admirably suited to producing practical spiritual leadership that can cut across denominational lines. Elton Trueblood exemplified the possibilities inherent in this tradition. Descended from a long line of Quakers, Trueblood was born on an Iowa farm and educated at a small midwestern college. He went on to acquire a degree in theology from Harvard and a Ph.D. from Johns Hopkins. After teaching at two Quaker colleges, he was made chaplain to Stanford University. There,

Trueblood came in contact with a number of the best known figures of his time and, in particular, former President Herbert Hoover, a close neighbor.

The contacts he had made in his years at Stanford served Trueblood well when, in 1945, he decided to move to a small Quaker institution, Earlham College in Richmond, Indiana, where he was a professor of philosophy. His national reputation helped the college gain a wider recognition. Thanks to his influence, Earlham established a School of Religion to train Quakers for leadership within their denomination. Meanwhile, he produced a steady stream of books that gained a wide readership. In *The Predicament of Modern Man,* he decried "the failure of the power culture" and warned against the dangers of what he called "our cut-flower civilization."

In other books Trueblood proposed the creation of a broadly based ecumenical "fellowship of the committed" that would transcend the differences between Christians and work for the transformation of both churches and society as a whole. He founded the Yokefellow movement, connecting clergy and laity from a number of Christian denominations in a highly decentralized and noncreedal relationship. The movement established Yokefellow retreat houses across America and in several foreign countries and included a special "ministry to prisons," leading to the development of several halfway houses.

Thanks to Trueblood's literary skills, several presidents commissioned him to write presidential proclamations dealing with religion and Thanksgiving Day. He served the Eisenhower administration as chief of religious policy for the U.S. Information Agency, spoke at a national Republican convention, delivered prayers at the opening of various Congressional sessions, and addressed one of the annual presidential prayer breakfasts.

A reading from a sermon entitled "Basic Christianity" by D. Elton Trueblood

Much of our contemporary Christianity fails because all concerned seem vague in their beliefs. We must give our best thinking to an effort to alter this unfortunate situation. The place to start is surely to provide clean answers to three basic questions: "What is God?" "Who is Jesus Christ?" "What is life everlasting?"

What is God? A great part of the effort we put forth to prove the existence of God is wasted, and it is wasted because so many people in the world already believe, in some sense, that God is. There are very few real atheists. The vast majority are believers; they admit that our physical world is not self-explanatory — that it requires something behind it and beyond it to make sense of it — that it could not have come into being of itself. Such a belief is very nearly universal. The difficulty is not in the question whether God is; the difficulty lies in the question what God is or who God is. The problem of the character of God is a much more practical question, certainly in the eyes of students, than the question of the existence of God. We begin our series on this practical question because so many people use the word "God" but mean almost nothing by it. They believe, but their belief is often confused and practically meaningless.

How are we going to know the character of God? The answer is that we cannot know beyond a doubt, but we do have two wonderful ways. One is the way of experience, and this is open to every man and woman. We come to know him not only in what someone else says, but also by what we learn firsthand. Let us say you do not have this experience, that it still seems beyond you. What then? There is another way. The world has had a succession of men and women of wonderful sensitivity and power, those who have given themselves more thoroughly, more logically, and more seriously to the search for the knowledge of God, and these it is reasonable to trust. It is reasonable to trust a well-trained physician in medicine; it is reasonable to trust a disciplined scientist in the laboratory. Individuals become trustworthy because of the quality of their experience and the discipline of their lives. You trust a doctor, not by blind faith, but because he is a disciplined man in a particular field. We have a great succession of men and women in the field of the knowledge of God. These are the ones we have reason to trust, because they are working at the job. They are often simple in the eyes of the world, but also very deep in experience. Amos, Hosea, Micah, Jeremiah are members of a fellowship of verification. Think of the others who have carried on the procession — Saint Francis, Pascal, John Woolman, and so many, many more.

There is no more rationality in trusting the irreligious in religion than there is in trusting the unscientific in science. As we pay attention to the religious experience of disciplined men, from Abraham to Gandhi, we are conscious of a progressive revelation. The change is not in God — the change is in the ability of men to receive. We become more sensitive to what is to be seen all along. Many things are hidden which later become revealed but which were there all the time. Brahms's great Requiem was just as wonderful before any contemporary student learned to appreciate it. Insight comes with growth of power to hear and to see. Now, if we take seriously this lesson of trusting those who give us reason to trust them, we come to something very definite about the nature of God.

✪ *November 16*

Virgil Michel

ROMAN CATHOLIC

June 26, 1890–November 26, 1938

A preoccupation with liturgy can lead some Christians into a rarified world of Gregorian chant and exotic blends of incense, but the word "liturgy" originally meant "public works." Virgil Michel never lost sight of that.

He often said that to separate Christian worship from the social issues of the time was blasphemous. In 1937, in the midst of the Great Depression, Michel wrote

> while many Catholic Christians mind their own business, the injustices suffered by share-croppers, the gross discrimination against Negroes (even at times within the walls of Catholic churches), economic oppression of all sorts, crying court injustices, violent vigilante antics based on the principle that might is right, etc., go on with hardly a prominent Catholic voice raised in protest. How the Church Fathers of old would have made the welkin ring with the righteous indignation of the Lord and with the incessant denunciation on the one hand and the guiding exhortations on the other. They knew of no compromise between Christ and the world.

Michel firmly believed that liturgy provided the means by which Christians could reorient themselves and thus redirect society. He founded a magazine called *Orate Fratres* to propound this vision, and he wrote that "the liturgy is the ordinary school of the development of the true Christian and the very qualities and outlook it develops in him are also those that make for the best realization of a genuine Christian culture."

A man of many talents, Michel was, at various times in his life, an English and philosophy professor, dean of St. John's University, a violinist, a baseball and tennis star, a coach, a translator, and a novelist. But at the center of his life lay a vision of society transformed by a deeper understanding of liturgy. As a graduate student at Catholic University, Michel had studied the views of Orestes Brownson, a 19th-century convert to the Roman Catholic Church, on the relationship between Catholicism and culture. When his order sent him to Europe for further study, he met the leaders of the early liturgical movement there and began to see how it could be an instrument for social transformation and how a proper understanding of the Church as the Body of Christ could counter secularism and individualism in western society.

Returning to St. John's Abbey, Michel shared his vision with others and worked to promote lay participation in the liturgy. He encouraged simplified music so the congregation could join in the singing, frequent reception of communion, the use of homilies to teach people about the liturgy and the liturgical year, and the vernacular in worship. All these ideas were revolutionary for the time. However, they prepared the way for reforms finally called for by the Second Vatican Council 40 years later.

Michel found a ready response to his ideas from Dorothy Day* and other members of the Catholic Worker movement. Michel and Day exchanged frequent visits, encouraging each other as they worked toward common goals in their different ways. Because Michel died at 48, he never saw the fruition of his ideas. Yet his magazine, *Orate Fratres* — renamed *Worship* — and St. John's Abbey continue to advocate his vision of social transformation through liturgy.

Dom Michel writes about "teaching the life in Christ"

Whatever efforts at instruction are made by both teachers and pupils should, as it were, be immersed in the channels of God's graces, in the sacrifice of the altar, the sacraments and the prayer-life of the Church. Thereby they receive not only the added inspiration and motivation found in these, but they are by conscious connection with these official channels of grace elevated to the supernatural efficacy of the energies of Christ which alone can produce the ultimate effect that is being aimed at. In the abundance of our efforts we have indeed planted and watered, but we have almost forgotten the most important of all, that God alone can give the increase. We may have given the divine increase a small opportunity by reciting a prayer in common before beginning the instructions; but we have not thought of giving it a maximum opportunity of operation and attainment by constantly referring all efforts at teaching and study to the divinely established sacramental means of all growth in Christ.

It is not necessary for every Christian to learn how to use a missal at Mass. Some may not have any aptitude for that. But it is necessary to teach children to pray the Mass in some way that is consonant with the nature of the Mass, therefore to participate in it heart and mind in accordance with their intelligence and abilities. It is moreover necessary to teach children to center all the efforts of their life in the altar of God, to unite them there with the sacrifice of Christ, and to derive from the latter, both as sacrifice-oblation and sacrifice-banquet, the help of God that is essential for giving their efforts the needed supernatural efficacy — in other words to coordinate and integrate all their daily efforts, especially their religious endeavors, with the action of Christ unto continued growth in the divine life. Only in that way are habits of Christian life formed in growing children which they can continue to exercise throughout their later years; only in that way can the much needed carry-over from school to later life be achieved, the absence of which in our day has been so detrimental to the growth of the mystical body and the spread of the kingdom of Christ on earth. But for this purpose, to repeat, all efforts at religious education must be centered in the liturgy and in active participation in the liturgy, since the latter is for all the members of Christ the essential way of living the life of their divine Head as long as they are on this earth.

✪ *November 17*

Elizabeth Cady Stanton

EPISCOPALIAN

November 12, 1815–October 26, 1902

Amid the upheavals of the 19th Century, the struggle for women's rights might now seem entirely appropriate, but in those days, even among those who held very progressive views on topics such as workers' rights or racial justice, the legal status of women was not a high priority. In fact, despite liberalizing tendencies during the 1800s, women's issues were considered by many progressive leaders as frivolous, even dangerous. Women could not vote, and even money earned by them or inherited property were controlled by their husbands. If they divorced, their property and children both remained in the husband's custody. Their educational opportunities were limited. Domestic violence was not a crime. They were chattel, belonging to fathers or husbands. Elizabeth Cady Stanton committed her life to changing all that.

Stanton came from an aristocratic background in upstate New York. Educated at home, she became well-read and passionate about the injustices that daily affected most women's lives. She married and raised a family, but still managed to write, travel, and speak throughout the nation on issues related to the rights of women. Stanton was particularly outraged by the oppressive misuse of Christian Scripture in church and society, condoning, or even mandating, the subjugation of women to men, and she produced a feminist interpretation called *The Woman's Bible.*

Her most productive work was for suffrage — granting women the vote. Though she died before women were enfranchised, she never lost hope, laying the foundation for accomplishments in the following century.

A reading from Elizabeth Cady Stanton's first public address to the First Women's Rights Convention at Seneca Falls, New York, July 19, 1848

Among the many important questions which have been brought before the public, there is none that more vitally affects the whole human family than that which is technically called Woman's Rights. Every allusion to the degraded and inferior position occupied by women all over the world has been met by scorn and abuse. From the man of highest mental cultivation to the most degraded wretch who staggers in the streets do we meet ridicule, and coarse jests, freely bestowed upon those who dare assert that woman stands by the side of man, his equal, placed here by her God, to enjoy with him the beautiful earth, which is her home as it is his, having the same sense of right and wrong, and looking to the same Being for guidance and support. So long has man exercised tyranny over her, injurious to himself and benumbing to her faculties, that few can nerve themselves to meet the storm; and so long has the chain been about her that she knows not there is a remedy....

And, strange as it may seem to many, we now demand our right to vote according to the declaration of the government under which we live.... The right is ours. Have it we must. Use it we will. The pens, the tongues, the fortunes, the indomitable wills of many women are already pledged to secure this right. The great truth that no just government can be formed without the consent of the governed, we shall echo and re-echo in the ears of the unjust judge, until by continual coming we shall weary him....

We are assembled to protest against a form of government, existing without the consent of the governed — to declare our right to be free as man is free, to be represented in the government which we are taxed to support, to have such disgraceful laws as give man the power to chastise and imprison his wife, to take the wages she earns, the property she inherits, and, in the case of separation, the children of her love; laws which make her the mere dependent on his bounty. It is to protest against such unjust laws as these that we are assembled today, and to have them, if possible, forever erased from our statute-books, deeming them a shame and a disgrace to a Christian republic in the nineteenth century....

There seems now to be a kind of moral stagnation in our midst. Philanthropists have done their utmost to rouse the nation to a sense of its sins.... Our churches are multiplying on all sides, our missionary societies, Sunday schools, and prayer meetings and innumerable charitable and reform organizations are all in operation, but still the tide of vice is swelling, and threatens the destruction of everything, and the battlements of righteousness are weak against the raging elements of sin and death. Verily, the world waits the coming of some new element, some purifying power, some spirit of mercy and love. The voice of woman has been silenced in the state, the church, and the home, but man cannot fulfill his destiny alone, he cannot redeem his race unaided. There are deep and tender chords of sympathy and love in the heart of the down-fallen and oppressed that woman can touch more skillfully than man... God, in his wisdom has so linked the whole human family together that any violence done at one end of the chain is felt throughout its length, and here, too, is the law of restoration, as in woman all have fallen, so in her elevation shall the race be recreated.

✪ November 18

Harry Hosier

METHODIST

c. 1750–May 1806

"I really believe he is one of the best preachers in the world," said Thomas Coke,* one of the founding bishops of American Methodism, of Harry Hosier. "There is such an amazing power that attends his preaching, though he cannot read; and he is one of the humblest creatures I ever saw." Benjamin Rush* called him "the greatest orator in America," while Henry Boehm, another Methodist preacher, said of him, "Harry was very black, an African of the Africans. He was so illiterate he could not read a word. He would repeat the hymn as if reading it, and quote his text with great accuracy.

His voice was musical, and his tongue as the pen of a ready writer. He was unboundedly popular, and many would rather hear him than the bishops."

Hosier may have possessed great gifts, but he also suffered greater handicaps than most. Growing up in slavery during the 18th century, he never learned to read. Although no one bothered to record the births of slaves, he may have been born in North Carolina. The facts of his conversion were not recorded either, nor how he became acquainted with the major figures in the American Methodist Church of his era. Though Thomas Coke, Francis Asbury, and Freeborn Garrettson recognized Hosier's talents, they never learned to treat him as an equal. When he traveled with these great men, he was their driver and servant until it was time to preach. Yet Francis Asbury acknowledged that crowds were generally more eager to hear Harry than himself. One day at prayer, Freeborn Garrettson had realized that it was not right "to keep his fellow creatures in bondage," so he set his slaves free. Even so, when he traveled with Harry Hosier, he could not bring himself to treat him as a "fellow creature." He always referred to him as "Harry," though he would have addressed a white colleague as "Brother Hosier." Excerpts from Garrettson's diary display his admiration for the man's talents while also revealing his inability to overcome his own sense of superiority:

> ...Harry exhorted after me to the admiration of the people.

> The people of this circuit are amazingly fond of hearing Harry.

> Harry exhorted after me with much freedom.

> ...a large congregation waiting for me. I preached from, "Enoch, walked with God," and I believe good was done. I left Harry to preach another sermon, and went on to the center of the town....

> ...while Harry gave an exhortation some rude people behaved very uncivilly.

> Wednesday, July 28th, I had sent on Harry to supply my afternoon's appointment.

> July 29th, I rode to Hudson, where I found the people very curious to hear Harry. I therefore declined preaching that their curiosity might be satisfied.

> [the next day] as there was a degree of persecution against Harry I thought it expedient to leave him behind.

> I got into Boston and boarded Harry at the master Mason for the Africans, and I took my own lodgings with a private gentleman.

Harry Hosier could preach in mixed company, but when it came time to find accommodations for the night, he was segregated from the white "gentlemen." When American Methodism was organized at the 1784 Christmas Conference, Harry Hosier and Richard Allen* represented other African American members, but were not given a vote. Hosier could not write. While his sermon, "The Barren Fig Tree," at Adam's Chapel, Fairfax County, Virginia, in May of 1781 was the "first recorded Methodist sermon by an African American," this merely means that the occasion, not the contents, was preserved.

His story contains one sad chapter. No saint is perfect; if they had been, they would be useless as models to the rest of us. St. Paul had his "thorn in the flesh;" St. Jerome had a violent temper; St. Augustine put off his conversion indecently long, and Harry Hosier lost a battle with alcohol. As one biographer tells it, "He withstood for years the temptations of extraordinary popularity, but finally... fell by wine [and became] a drunken rag-picker in the streets of Philadelphia." But we may well ask whether the problem grew out of his "extraordinary popularity" or the contrast between the treatment given the white evangelists and his own. Happily, this was not the end of his story. Hosier prayed until his backslidings were healed. "Under a tree, he wrestled with God in prayer" and was delivered from his weakness. Thereafter, he returned to his preaching, though lacking "that pleasing confidence" he had had before. Ironically, he was buried in a free burying ground.

✪ November 19 _____

Peter Christopher Yorke

ROMAN CATHOLIC

August 15, 1864–April 5, 1925

Peter C. Yorke was an immigrant, so his quick wit and combative spirit made him an eloquent and effective advocate for the immigrants in his parish and also for the rising labor unions that championed their cause. The Archbishop of San Francisco had marked him as a potential leader and sent the young priest to the newly established Catholic University, in Washington, DC, for a doctoral program, but Yorke was more interested in issues being fought out in the factories and on the docks, so he returned to San Francisco to involve himself in social causes.

As editor of the diocesan newspaper, *The Monitor,* and chancellor of the diocese, Yorke was able to play a significant role in the teamsters' strike of 1901. As the brutal and bloody strike wore on and the strikers' morale was sinking, Yorke rallied them with a dramatic speech in which he asked, "Shall men for whom Christ died to teach them that they were free men, with free men's rights, be crushed beneath the foot of the least bright of all the angels that fell from heaven, Mammon, the spirit of Greed?" Some people question the appropriateness of clergy taking sides on labor matter, but Yorke answered, "As a priest my duty is with the workingmen, who are struggling for their rights because that is the historical position of the priesthood and because that is the Lord's command." The incident is still remembered as one of the most dramatic moments in the history of the archdiocese.

One of Yorke's biographers called him a "consecrated thunderbolt" because of his fiery outbursts on behalf of his people. Yorke intervened with equal force after the great San Francisco fire. Aged and infirm women from St. Mary's Hospital were transferred to his church, where they had been laid on the floor. While leaders of the relief effort, including an army general and the president's representative, were meeting, Yorke interrupted a speaker to ask whether he could get cots "without unraveling all the red tape in San Francisco." "Mr. Mayor," he said, "you will be held personally responsible if with red tape you strangle American charity." The cots were immediately provided.

But Yorke realized that social action alone did not solve all problems. He wanted to educate his people both to strengthen their faith and to enable them to play an effective role in the larger society. He founded parochial schools, wrote textbooks, and was a leader in the formation of the National Catholic Educational Association. He also took an interest in liturgical renewal long before it became a popular cause and wrote a number of books to help lay people participate intelligently in the liturgy.

A reading from *Ghosts of Bigotry* by Peter C. Yorke

On the laity, too, rests the duty of giving a reason for the faith that is in them. And when the laity are organized, as in this Catholic Truth Society, by the Archbishop of the diocese, who, and who alone, is responsible for the teaching of the faith pure and undefiled, there is no break with the traditions of the church, nothing opposed to Catholic habits of thought.

As I have said, our times have their own advantages and their own drawbacks. It is to make use of one of these advantages that the Catholic Truth Society organized the Catholic laity. In this country men of all creeds meet on the basis of their citizenship. In the ordinary walks of life Catholic and non-Catholic are thrown into close contact. They discuss every question in the heavens above, in the earth beneath and in the waters under the earth. Not the least frequent of these discussions is on the subject of religion. Non-Catholics who would not think of entering a Catholic church or of speaking to a Catholic priest will eagerly question the Catholic laity concerning the teaching and practices of the Catholic Church. Such an opportunity should not be lost. If any one should know about the Catholic Church surely Catholics should. It is not good taste to force religious subjects into a conversation, but it is not good policy to be silent when your Church is under discussion.

The Catholic Church cannot create such a laity, but it can organize it and encourage it. Then, there is a second advantage, as great in its way, if not greater. The American people reads. Perhaps its reading is not deep, but it is wide; moreover, it is impartial. The people will read anything that is readable, no matter what it treats about. Every fad, every humbug, every political measure, every social dream has its expounders, has its readers — why not the old Church that gave printing to the world? We hardly realize what a powerful engine the printing press is. The Church has never despised it; from the beginning she employed it. She employs it now, but in our country not enough. To help in some way to spread Catholic Truth among the people by means of a Catholic literature, this, too, is the end of the Catholic Truth Society.

✪ *November 20* _____

Sarah Patton Boyle

EPISCOPALIAN

May 9, 1906–February 21, 1994

Sarah Patton Boyle's father was an Episcopal priest and director of the American Church Institute for Negroes, an agency of the Episcopal Church, so she wasn't disturbed to be living in a small apartment near the "colored" section of town while her husband studied at the University of Virginia. Besides, she thought, it would be easy to get help with the housework. She was happy when an African American sued successfully to gain admission to the university law school, assuming other well-meaning whites would feel the same. Instead, when her articles on it appeared in national magazines, the White Citizens' Council burned a cross on her lawn while former friends kept their distance. African Americans also seemed less appreciative of her efforts than she had expected. Slowly, Sarah Patton Boyle learned that her assumptions about herself and about others had no real depth. Facing up to the truth about herself, she came to a far deeper understanding of human reality and Christianity. This passage comes toward the end of *The Desegregated Heart*, the widely read story of Boyle's awakening to the realities of Southern life.

A reading from *The Desegregated Heart* by Sarah Patton Boyle

I was slow to know my Divine Companion, but no other labor has rewarded me so well. Despite the near impossibility of such a task, therefore, I shall try to give you glimpses of what I found.

I must begin by saying that all the most trite, silly, and sentimental remarks made about Friendship with Him by the most unschooled and simple folk, to my amazement, turned out to be factual statements. For instance, when they say, "If you jus' got Jesus, you don't need nobody else," it is a piece of exact information, like saying, "If you have an electric blanket, you don't need other blankets...."

Testimony to this effect has been proclaimed and reiterated for twenty centuries, and I was long among the majority who paid not the slightest attention to it. I can think of at least three reasons why we don't.

For one, bringing such a companionship to fruition is a laborious task, like learning to play a difficult instrument, and one who attempts it halfheartedly will succeed only in convincing himself that it is impossible.

For another, man has long exerted his considerable intelligence in finding substitute satisfactions for this hard-to-achieve friendship with God, and has accumulated a large stock pile, ranging from alcohol and tranquilizers through hundreds of distractions and amusements to hundreds of arts and cultures of the mind. He will usually go through quite a lot of this stock pile, trying each item, before he is prepared to concede that nothing has brought him the fulfillment he hoped for, and that his deep longings have been satisfied only briefly, if at all.

A healthy, averagely fortunate person may in easy times go to his grave with his substitute satisfactions (like his illusions) functioning so well that only a few skillful dodges are needed for him to maintain belief that all is well with him. For almost half a century, I certainly made this claim. But having recently had the experience of all actually being well, I look back in wonderment that I could have thought so before.

A third reason why we ignore testimony that Jesus Christ is all we need is that as long as human fellowship is intact, as long as we have dear ones whom we believe in and who believe in us, there usually is much drag against acquiring our Divine Companion. For it appears, though it isn't really so, that we must lose people in order to acquire Christ. Therefore, it usually isn't until we have already lost at least the people we most value, that we will seek Him.

We appear to lose others when we seek Him because we must stop believing that they truly are the lovely images which in fact are dim reflections of Him. Otherwise, we find it hard to isolate Him in the maze of gods and goddesses around us.

For many months one great truth has pursued me at every turn: My relationship with Him is more real, actual, than any other I have known. His presence is more completely *with* me than any human person ever has been. From this mysterious overpowering fact alone I would suspect that here is the Source, that now at last I deal with the basic Substance from which all relationships are made. Moreover, unlike the rest, this One when made transcendant does not dimmish, deaden, or crowd the others out. Rather, It revives, heightens, and includes them all. Love of God is never, I think, a rival to any other love. It is the means by which all loves are made constant, dependable, and strong.

I can't here review the lengthy adventurous drama of my search. Briefly, I sought Him by reading the Gospel stories over and over, studying interpretations of His life and thought, listening to simple hymns, questioning the few who seem to know Him, talking to Him, thinking of Him, doing my housework for Him as though I were His housekeeper, and by many other means.

At first nothing seemed accomplished, but slowly His Personality took definite shape in my mind, and His Presence began to move with me as I moved. Then, quite without warning, one day my fragmentary thoughts about Him drew together and fell into their proper places. For an indescribable moment He was real, present, and living in my midst. My frozenness melted. I had looked upon the Lovable. As I had hoped, the result was love.

✪ *November 21*

John Greenleaf Whittier

QUAKER

December 7, 1807–September 7, 1892

Today John Greenleaf Whittier is probably best remembered as the author of the epic poem *Snow Bound* and the nostalgic portrayer of an agricultural America rapidly fading from experience. In the middle of the 19th century, however, Whittier was considered one of the most important voices of the abolitionist movement. William Lloyd Garrison* thundered against slavery, but Whittier rhymed his protest and the rhymes stuck in people's memories.

An unlikely controversialist, Whittier was born on a small farm and raised in the Society of Friends. He remained a Quaker all his life and saluted others with the sect's "thees" and "thous." Although he had little formal schooling, he began writing poetry as a child and had his first poems published in a local newspaper when he was still in his teens. Whittier's verse attracted the attention of William Lloyd Garrison, who was not much older than he. Through Garrison, he became involved in the abolitionist movement almost from the beginning, writing for various newspapers and magazines in Boston, New York, and Philadelphia. He won wide recognition slowly. *Snow Bound* was published in 1866, when the Civil War was over, and cemented his national reputation.

Though committed to ending slavery, Whittier would never countenance war and believed that it would be better to let the southern states go and learn for themselves the folly of their "mad experiment." "The emancipation that came by military necessity and was enforced by bayonets was not the emancipation for which we worked and prayed," he wrote; but added, "I am glad that the Gospel of freedom was preached, even if by strife and contention."

At the end of his life, Whittier gave his support to the cause of woman's suffrage, saying that the vote "is her right as truly as mine." He called himself "a dreamer with a mission to fulfill,"

> *Making his rustic reed of song*
> *A weapon in the war with wrong.*

A reading from a letter to William Lloyd Garrison, 1866

I look back over thirty years, and call to mind all the circumstances of my journey to Philadelphia in company with thyself and the excellent Dr. Thurston, of Maine, even then, as we thought, an old man, but still living, and true as ever to the good cause. I recall the early gray morning when, with Samuel J. May, our colleague on the committee to prepare a Declaration of Sentiment for the Convention, I climbed to the small upper chamber of a colored friend to hear thee read the first draft of a paper which will live as long as our national history.

I see the members of the Convention, solemnized by the responsibility, rise, one by one, and silently affix their names to that stern pledge of fidelity to freedom. Of the signers, many have passed away from earth, a few have faltered and turned back, but I believe the majority still live to rejoice over the great triumphs of truth and justice, and to devote what remains of time and strength to the cause to which they consecrated their youth and manhood thirty years ago. For while we may well thank God, and congratulate one another on the prospect of the speedy emancipation of the slaves of the United States, we must not for a moment forget that from this hour new and mighty responsibilities devolve upon us to aid, direct, and educate these millions, left free indeed, but bewildered, ignorant, naked, and foodless, in the wild chaos of civil war. We have to undo the accumulated wrongs of two centuries; to remake the manhood that slavery has well-nigh unmade; to see to it that the long-oppressed colored man has a fair field for development and improvement, and to tread under our feet the last vestige of that hateful prejudice which has been the strongest external support of Southern slavery. We must lift ourselves at once to the true Christian altitude where all distinctions of black and white are overlooked in the heart-felt recognition of the brotherhood of man.

I must not close this letter without confessing that I cannot be sufficiently thankful to the Divine Providence which, in a great measure through thy instrumentality; turned me so early away from what Roger Williams calls "the world's great trinity, pleasure, profit, and honor," to take side with the poor and oppressed. I am not insensible to literary reputation; I love, perhaps, too well the praise and good will of my fellow-men; but I set a higher value on my name as appended to the Anti-slavery Declaration of 1833 than on the title page of any book.

Looking over a life marked by many errors and shortcomings, I rejoice that I have been able to maintain the pledge of that signature, and that in the long intervening years:

> *My voice, though not the loudest, has been heard*
> *Wherever Freedom raised her cry of pain.*

✪ *November 22*

Lillias Stirling Horton Underwood

PRESBYTERIAN

1851–1921

Korea and Japan are separated by a narrow sea, and also by a history of hostility dating back to the years in which Korea was occupied by Japan as part of their colonial empire. The two countries have responded to Christianity in remarkably different ways. In Japan, otherwise quick to adopt many aspects of western life, the total Christian population remains at well under 5 percent. In Korea, however, the Christian church now includes well over a quarter of the population, so that they outnumber Buddhists and some of the largest congregations in the world can be found there. Korea was set on this course by a Pentecostal revival in the early years of the 20th century. The beginnings of that revival were carefully chronicled by Lillias Underwood, a medical missionary who had gone to Korea with her husband. Though she found the people curious about many aspects of western culture and Christianity, they were not especially fervent.

Underwood founded a hospital for the destitute and started a school. In the winter of 1893–1894, she was summoned to the palace to explain Christmas to the king and queen. Underwood imagined this might be a political move, intended to strengthen Korean bonds with western nations, because of threats from Japan, but she worked hard to set up a Christmas tree with candles in the palace. The results were disappointing as "their majesties were too impatient to wait till dark to view it." Since there were no drapes to block light from the windows, the effect of the Christmas tree was "quite spoiled" because the "poor little candles flickered in a sickly way in the glaring daylight." When their majesties next requested a demonstration of western ice skating, Underwood felt even more disappointed.

A decade later, she chronicled a conference of Methodist and Presbyterian missionaries who wanted to work together toward a United Korean Church. They pledged to pray daily for an outpouring of the Spirit. Weekly prayer gatherings in many churches increased attendance. "The meetings grew in power," she reports, and then manifestations like the ones at American revivals began to break out. "Awful and overwhelming conviction of sin was its most marked feature. Men wept, groaned, beat their breasts, falling to the ground and writhing in agony." The movement swept through schools and churches, young and old, natives and foreigners. "And now," Underwood asked, "what were the results of this wonderful revival? Was it a mere wave of emotionalism?" Korea had known Christianity for many years but never before had anything been seen like this.

What results can it show as a seal to its divine origin? . . . Here on all sides we see following these revivals, sinners converted, those who had done wrong making confession and restitution of money and goods, the churches crowded to overflowing with inquirers and new believers, the coffers of the Lord's treasury filled, and men of different denominations lovingly joining hands, putting away old jealousies, forwarding the Lord's kingdom shoulder to shoulder.

A reading from Lillias Underwood on the features of the Korean revival

1st. It was preceded ... for a period of three or more years, by a constantly increasing desire and fervent united prayer of missionaries and natives — desire and prayer undoubtedly inspired by Him who intended to give — for the Gift of the Spirit.

2d. It simply fell upon the people waiting before God in insistent, believing prayer, without having been worked up in any way by exciting appeals to emotion.

3d. It came to a people who, during a knowledge of Christianity if some twenty odd years, have never had anything of the kind in their religious life, and have never shown signs of great excitability in their deepest Christian experience.

4th. It was marked, everywhere the same, by a realization of the awful blackness of sin, consequent upon an acute sense of the immediate Presence of the terrible majesty of the Most High and followed by agonizing repentance, confession and restitution.

5th. Wonder and regret have been expressed at the kind of sins confessed by some of these native Christian people. It must be remembered that they were Christians who had come out of heathenism with no previous Christian training and breeding, that they were living surrounded by heathenism, but poorly instructed, and some of them, no doubt, had never been more than intellectually converted.

✖ *November 23*

Elizabeth Ann Seton

ROMAN CATHOLIC

August 28, 1774–January 4, 1821

That God changes lives is a truism, but one seldom as dramatically evident as in the case of Elizabeth Ann Seton. Born Elizabeth Ann Bayley to a prominent New York society family, she was educated to be fluent in French and an excellent horsewoman. She became a popular guest at house parties and entertainments, married well, and lived in a large house on Wall Street, where her husband was involved in the family shipping business. But the tenor of her life became more somber. After the birth of her first two children, her father-in-law died and the family business collapsed. Her husband was threatened with debtor's prison. Seton spent a summer living with her own father, only to see him die of yellow fever. When a doctor suggested a sea voyage for the sake of her husband's deteriorating health, Seton sold her remaining possessions to pay for the voyage. When they arrived in Italy, they were quarantined because of the yellow fever epidemic in New York. They were forced to spend forty days in a stone tower outside Leghorn, where Seton nursed her husband and played skip-rope with the children to offset the bitter cold.

William Seton died two days after Christmas, and Elizabeth attended services with her Italian friends while waiting for a ship to return to New York. Deeply impressed with the liturgy and teaching of Christ's presence in the sacrament, she returned to New York where, in 1805, she became a member of the Roman Catholic Church. To support her family, she opened a boardinghouse for school boys, but opposition from her one-time friends in New York society led her to accept a teaching position at St. Mary's College in Baltimore.

In 1809, Bishop Carroll* gave Elizabeth Seton land in Emmitsburg, Maryland. With her three daughters, two sisters-in-law, and four other young women, she formed the American Sisters of Charity of St. Joseph, the first American religious order for women. Over the next 11 years, two of her daughters and both sisters-in-law died, but nonetheless the order grew. Its progress was never easy. Difficulties arose over their rule of life. They had conflicts with clergy. They faced continual demands for more schools and more sisters to staff them. Seton's letters to her spiritual director recount her suffering, frequent aridity in her prayer life, and dark nights of the soul. She declined slowly and painfully of tuberculosis, and on the night of her death, she had to begin the prayers for the dying herself. In the mid-20th century, the Vatican officially recognized her as the first American saint.

A reading from a letter of Elizabeth Ann Seton concerning her plans for her community, written in 1809

My dear Filicchi,[1] you will think, I fear, that the poor little woman's brain is turned who writes you so often on the same subject, but it is not a matter of choice on my part, as it is my indispensable duty to let you know every particular of a circumstance which has occurred since I wrote you last week relative to the suggestions so strongly indicated in the letters I have written both yourself and your Antonio[2] since my arrival in Baltimore. Some time ago I mentioned to you the conversion of a man of family and fortune in

---

1. Filippo Filicchi, a well-to-do merchant of Leghorn, Italy, had long been a friend of the Seton family. He had assisted and encouraged Mrs. Seton in becoming a Roman Catholic.
2. Antonio was the brother of Filippo Filicchi.

Philadelphia.[3] This conversion is as solid as it was extraordinary, and as *the person* is soon to recieve [*sic*] the Tonsure in our seminary, in making the disposition of his fortune he has consulted our Rd. Mr. Dubourg,[4] the Prest. of the College on the plan of establishing an institution for the advancement of Catholick female children in habits of religion and giving them an education suited to the purpose. He also desires extremely to extend the plan to the reception of the aged and also uneducated persons who may be employed in spinning, knitting, etc., etc., so as to found a Manufactory on a small scale which may be very beneficial to the poor. You see I am bound to let you know the disposition of Providence that you may yourself judge how far you may concur with it. Dr. Matignon[5] of Boston to whom Mr. Cheverus[6] the Bishop elect and Antonio referred me on every Occasion, [*sic*] had suggested this plan for me before the gentleman in question ever thought of it. I have invariably kept in the background and avoided even reflecting voluntarily on anything of the kind, knowing that Almighty God alone could effect it if indeed it will be realized. Father Mr. Dubourg has always said the same, be quiet, God will in his own time discover His intentions, nor will I allow one word of intreaty [*sic*] from my pen. His blessed will be done.

In my former letter I asked you if you could not secure your own property and build something for this purpose on the lot (which is an extensive one) given by Mr. Dubourg. If you will furnish the necessary expenditures for setting us off, and supporting those persons or children who at first will not be able to support themselves. Dr. Matignon will appoint a Director for the establishment which if you knew how many good and excellent souls are sighing for would soon obtain an interest in your breast, so ardently desiring the glory of God. But all is in his hands. If I had a choice and my will would decide in a moment, I would remain silent in his hands. Oh how sweet it is there to rest in perfect confidence, yet in every daily Mass and at communion I beg him to dispose of me and mine in any way which may please him. YOU are Our Father in him, thro your hands we received that new and precious being which is indeed true life.

And may you in your turn be rewarded with the fullness of the divine benediction. Amen a thousand times.

MEA Seton

---

3. Samuel Sutherland Cooper (1769–1843), a convert of means who became a priest gave financial aid to Mother Seton's community in its early years.

4. Louis W. V. Dubourg (1766–1833) was at the time president of St. Mary's College, Baltimore. He died as Archbishop of Besancon.

5. François A. Matignon (1753–1818) was a French-born priest who was pastor of what was soon to become the Cathedral of the Holy Cross in Boston.

6. Jean Cheverus (1768–1836) was the first Bishop of Boston, who died as Cardinal Archbishop of Bordeaux.

✪ *November 24*

John Henry Hobart

EPISCOPALIAN

September 14, 1775–September 12, 1830

At the end of the American Revolution, Anglicans in the United States were a broken and dispirited body. The Church of England had been rejected along with English government, and the new "Episcopal Church" had an anomalous relationship with the Church of England. It was not until a new generation came into positions of leadership that the Episcopal Church began to revive and grow. John Henry Hobart, the Bishop of New York, was a leader in that revival. He traveled by coach, and even on foot, through the newly settled areas in the state's western part to plant new congregations. In one year, he traveled over 4,000 miles within his diocese and confirmed more than 1,900 members. During the 19 years of his episcopate, the number of clergy in his diocese increased from 24 to 140, and the number of congregations grew from 33 to 182. Hobart founded the General Theological Seminary, the first seminary in the Anglican Communion, to prepare men for the ministry. He tirelessly devoted himself to building up the church under the banner of "Evangelical Truth, Apostolic Order."

Unusually for an Episcopalian of that time, he preached without notes and with such ardor and vehemence that he was suspected of Methodist leanings. His infectious warmth and enthusiasm drew people to him. It was said that his presence in a room was like a ray of sunshine. An English clergyman who visited America in 1816 reported of Hobart:

> It was impossible to hear him without becoming sensible of the infinite importance of the Gospel. He warned, counselled, entreated, and comforted, with intense and powerful energy.... He appeared in the pulpit as a father anxious for the eternal happiness of his children — a man of God preparing them for their Christian warfare — a herald from the other world standing between the living and the dead, between heaven and earth, entreating perishing sinners, in the most tender accents, not to reject the message of reconciliation which the Son of the living God so graciously offered for their acceptance.

A reading from a sermon by the Rt. Rev. John Henry Hobart

In uniting us to a visible society, for the purpose of redeeming us from the corruptions of our evil nature and of the world, and for training us for the purity and bliss of a celestial and eternal existence, the Divine Author of our being has not only exercised that sovereign power which makes us in all things dependent on his will, but has mercifully accommodated himself to the social principle which so strongly characterizes us. This, uniform and powerful in its influence, prompts us in *spiritual* as in temporal matters, to mingle with our fellow men our thoughts, our feelings, our pursuits, our hopes. Most conversant as we are, too, with material objects, and most affected by them, what an aid to our conception of spiritual truths, what an excitement to our hopes of spiritual blessings, when they are exhibited as conveyed and pledged by external symbols. Hence the doctrine that the ministrations and ordinances of the church are the means and pledges of salvation to the faithful, to all true believers, is not more enforced by the plainest declarations of sacred writ, than it is conformable to a rational and philosophical view of our nature.

That the church is the body of that divine Lord who gave himself for it, that as members of this body true believers are united in him its head, and thus partake of his fullness of mercy and grace, are truths of the divine word too frequently and too strongly set forth to be denied. But though not denied, how much are they neglected! How much decried, how odiously and contemptuously branded are all researches as to the mode by which, in this divine body of the Redeemer, power is to be derived to minister in, its holy concerns, to dispense its ordinances! And yet, in this spiritual and divine society, no man can minister unless he be called of God by a commission visibly conferred for that purpose; and there can be no commission which is not derived from that Almighty Head of this mystical body, who only possesses all spiritual power, and who, vesting with his apostles the authority of conferring the right of ministering in holy things, pronounced the infallible promise, that this authority should be perpetuated "even to the end of the world." The Bishop of our church on these subjects may prudently and mildly enforce, opinions which boast, in more modern times, of the support of some of the most distinguished names in learning and theology, and which, before papal corruption obscured and deformed them, ranked among their advocates the noble army of martyrs, and the goodly fellowship of apostles. He may enforce them with a spirit which embraces, within the wide spread arms of charity, the sincere, and the pious of every name, and of every nation.

✪ November 25

Washington Gladden

CONGREGATIONAL

February 11, 1836–July 2, 1918

A leader in the Social Gospel movement, Washington Gladden worked as editor of a small-town newspaper, then, as acting editor of a New York newspaper. He helped expose the corruption of the group of politicians known as the "Tweed Ring," who had conspired to plunder the New York City treasury of millions of dollars. Ordained to the ministry of the Congregational Church, Gladden served congregations in Springfield,

Massachusetts, and, for 36 years, in Columbus, Ohio, where he also sat on the city council. In the tradition of American pragmatism, Gladden rejected both Socialism and classical economic theories, attempting instead to apply what he considered the simple and practical nature of the gospel to the problems of society. An early advocate of Christian reunion, Gladden dedicated himself to the realization of the Kingdom of God in this world. His 40-some books exerted a wide influence. Gladden also wrote the well-known hymn, "O Master, let me walk with Thee."

A reading from the *Recollections* of Washington Gladden

The outcry against the Higher Criticism has been feeble compared with the denunciations hurled against the geologists from pulpit and sanctum and platform. Soon, however, it began to be evident to all who could think, that the records plainly written on the rocks by the Creator Himself can be no less veracious than those written upon parchment by human hands; that science gives us the word of God no less authoritatively than revelation; that the infidelity which disputes the truth that God has revealed in his works is quite as heinous as that which questions the truth of a statement in a holy book.

Thus, little by little, the truth began to be dimly apprehended — it is not yet, by any means, fully understood — that God is in his world today as really as He ever was; that the work of creation is not yet finished, and never will be. The work of creation is a continuous process, and so is the work of revelation. All that we call Nature is but the constant manifestation of the divine power; and the Spirit in whose image our spirits are fashioned, and with whom we are made for fellowship, is here, all the while, as close to us as He ever was to any men in any age; as ready to give inspiration and wisdom to us as He has ever been to any of his children. This is the truth which is slowly breaking through the mists of tradition, and is beginning to light up the world with a new sense of the nearness and the reality of the living God.

It is toward this larger faith that the movements of thought have been leading on through all the years of my pilgrimage. It is a far cry from those old legal and mechanical conceptions of the relation of God to the world which prevailed in my youth, to this vital faith in a living God of which I have been trying to tell, and it must not be supposed that the whole church has arrived at these convictions. I have shown where the head of the column is marching; the rest of it is moving along.

These changes in the underlying philosophy of religion are not so obvious to the multitude, but the changes in the popular teaching of the church are evident to all. The message which is spoken today from the most orthodox pulpits is a very different message from that to which I was accustomed to listen in my boyhood. The motive of fear, of terror, was then the leading motive; this motive is not employed now as it was then. It is not a moral motive. It does not appeal to human reason, or human freedom, or human affection; it seeks to overpower the human will. We have found a more excellent way. Mr. Moody was not an advanced thinker, but his appeal had little to do with the old terrorism; love was the motive on which he relied: "by the cords of a man" he drew men to God.

Another change of not less significance is that by which the emphasis is placed more and more upon the altruistic motive. It begins to be evident that that is the strongest motive. When I was a boy, the main reason urged for being a Christian was a selfish reason. It was insurance against loss; it was the personal gain, the personal happiness, the future blessedness of which it put you in possession, that were constantly kept before your mind. That motive has been steadily retreating into the background; the motive of unselfish service has been increasingly emphasized. Because the Christian life is the noblest life; because it is more blessed to give than to receive, and better to minister than to be ministered unto; because the good of life is not found by separating yourself from your fellows, but by identifying yourself with them, — therefore let us be Christians. This is what it means to follow Christ today, as the wisest preachers explain it; and this is an appeal which, when we learn how to use it, will have convincing power.

I am fain to believe that the time is drawing near when the Christian church will be able to discern and declare the simple truth that Religion is nothing but Friendship; friendship with God and with men. I have been thinking much about it in these last days, and I cannot make it mean anything else; so far as I can see, this is all there is to it. Religion is friendship — friendship first with the great Companion, of whom Jesus told us, who is always nearer to us than we are to ourselves, and whose inspiration and help is the greatest fact of human experience. To be in harmony with his purposes, to be open to his suggestions, to be in conscious fellowship with Him, — this is religion on its Godward side.

Then, turning manward, friendship sums it all up. To be friends with everybody; to fill every human relation with the spirit of friendship; is there anything more than this that the wisest and best of men can hope to do? If the church could accept this truth — Religion is Friendship — and build its own life upon it, and make it central and organic to its teaching, should we not see a great revival of religion?

✪ November 26 _____

Anna Julia Haywood Cooper

EPISCOPALIAN

August 10, 1858? — February 27, 1964

Educating freed slaves so they could take their full place in society was an urgent priority at the end of the Civil War, and the Christian churches did much to meet that need. St. Augustine's Normal School and Collegiate Institute in North Carolina was founded by the Episcopal Church for that purpose, and one of its first students was Anna Julia Haywood. Her mother had been a slave and her father was presumed to be her mother's white master. Anna entered St. Augustine's and showed such ability that she was soon tutoring older students. She married George Cooper, an Episcopal priest, when she was 19, but he died two years later. She completed her studies at St. Augustine's, then moved on to Oberlin College to earn both a bachelor's and master's degree.

In Washington, DC, Cooper began her long career as an educator. By 1902 she had become the principal of the only college-preparatory school for African Americans in Washington, but she was dismissed four years later when she refused to reorganize the institution for vocational training rather than liberal arts. After that, she taught for a few years at Lincoln University in Missouri before returning to Washington as a teacher at the same school where she had been principal. Meanwhile, she began studying for a doctorate at Columbia University, then transferred her credits to the University of Paris, completing her dissertation at the Sorbonne in 1925.

Anna Julia Hayward Cooper was a prominent member of the National Association for the Advancement of Colored People and the only woman elected to the American Negro Academy. At 72, she became president of Frelinghuysen University, which had been founded to provide educational opportunities for working adults in Washington's black community. She served in that capacity for 12 years. Throughout her time in Washington, she was an active member of St. Luke's Episcopal Church. She died in 1964, at the age of 105.

A reading from *A Voice from the South* by Anna Julia Cooper

To me, faith means *treating the truth as true.* Jesus *believed* in the infinite possibilities of an individual soul. His faith was a triumphant realization of the eternal development of *the best* in man — an optimistic vision of the human aptitude for endless expansion and perfectibility. This truth to him placed a sublime valuation on each individual sentiency — a value magnified infinitely by reason of its immortal destiny. He could not lay hold of this truth and let pass an opportunity to lift men into nobler living and firmer building. He could not lay hold of this truth and allow his own benevolence to be narrowed and distorted by the trickeries of circumstance or the colorings of prejudice.

Life must be something more than dilettante speculation. And religion (ought to be if it isn't) a great deal more than mere gratification of the instinct for worship linked with the straight-teaching of irreproachable credos. Religion must be *life made true;* and life is action, growth, development — begun now and ending never. And a life made true cannot confine itself — it must reach out and twine around every pulsing interest within reach of its uplifting tendrils.

Do you *believe* that the God of history often chooses the weak things of earth to confound the mighty, and that the Negro race in America has a veritable destiny in His eternal purposes, — then don't spend your time discussing the "Negro Problem" amid the clouds of your fine havanna, ensconced in your friend's well-cushioned arm-chair and with your patent leather boot-tips elevated to the opposite mantel. Do those poor "cowards in the South" need a leader — then get up and lead them! Let go your purse-strings and begin to *live* your creed. Or is it your modicum of truth that God hath made of one blood all nations of the earth; and that all interests which specialize and contract the broad, liberal, cosmopolitan idea of universal brotherhood and equality are narrow and pernicious, then treat that truth as true.

You may have learned that the pole star is twelve degrees from the pole and forbear to direct your course by it — preferring your needle taken from earth and fashioned by man's device. The slave brother, however, from the land of oppression once saw the celestial beacon and dreamed not that it ever deviated from due North. He *believed* that *somewhere* under its beckoning light, lay a far away country where a man's a man. He sets out with his heavenly guide before his face — would you tell him he is pursuing a wandering light? Is he the poorer for his ignorant hope? Are you the richer for your enlightened suspicion?

Yes, I believe there is existence beyond our present experience; that that existence is conscious and culturable; and that there is a noble work here and now in helping men to live *into* it. There are nations still in darkness to whom we owe a light. The world is to be moved one generation forward — whether by us, by blind force, by fate, or by God! If thou believest, all things are possible; and *as* thou believest, so be it unto thee.

✪ November 27 _____

Isabella Graham

PRESBYTERIAN

July 29, 1742–July 27, 1814

A pioneer in founding societies for the relief of the widowed and orphaned and much other good work as well, Isabella Graham grew up in Scotland, married a doctor, and traveled with him to Canada and Antigua, where he died nine years after their marriage. She returned for 15 years to Scotland where she founded a society for the destitute who were also sick, but then emigrated to New York where her children were living. Over the next 25 years, Graham poured her energy into institutions for the relief and assistance of those we now call "marginalized" members of society: the sick, the

poor, widows, orphans, and prisoners. She served as president of several of
these societies herself. She visited hospitals and prisons regularly, distributing Bibles and tracts. She also organized the first missionary society and the
first monthly prayer meeting in the city. Realizing that charity was incomplete until the recipients could provide for themselves, she bought flax and
spinning wheels and loaned them out to women able to work. They would
then pay her for the wheels out of their earnings. Schools were established
for orphans and the children of widows and Graham's society employed
those widows who were capable to teach the children in them. Two Sabbath schools were established, one of which Graham supervised herself and
one of which was directed by her daughter. Feeling that denominational barriers should not be allowed to hinder the work of charity, she involved the
Dutch Reformed, Presbyterian, and Baptist Churches as well. Her closest
colleague, Mrs. Sarah Hoffman, was an Episcopalian.

After her death, a collection of Graham's letters with an account of her
life was published and went through many editions in England, Scotland,
and America.

A reading from *The Power of Faith, exemplified in the Life and Writings of the Late Mrs. Isabella Graham*

February, 1804

A new thing is on the wheel in the city of New York. A Society of ladies,
organized for the purpose of relieving widows with small children, was new
in this country. It is now, by the blessing of God, apparently established. It
was entered upon with prayer, it has been conducted thus far with prayer.
The blessing of God has rested upon it, and much good has been done by
it. Some of us have looked long, and requested of God to open a way by
which the children of these widows might be *instructed and taught to read
his word*, and by his blessing on it, come to the knowledge of the way
of salvation. One means has been attempted of an ordinary kind: twelve
children were last week placed at school with Mrs. L — , to be taught to
read, and some more are to be placed with another of our widows, for the
same purpose. But this indeed is new. A Society of young ladies, the first in
rank in the city, in the very bloom of life, and full of its prospects, engaged
in those pleasures and amusements which tend to engross the mind and
shut out every idea unconnected with them, coming forward and offering,
(not to contribute towards a school,) but *their own personal attendance to
instruct the ignorant*. O Lord, prosper their work. If this be of thee, it shall
prosper, and be productive of much good; but if thou bless not, it will come
to nothing but shame. No good can be done but by thee, for "there is none
good but God"; and what are all thy creatures, but instruments in thy hand,
by which thou bringest to pass the purposes of thy will.... Worldlings also

are thy instruments, by them thou workest and bringest to pass the counsels of thy will; thou puttest into their heart the good thing which thou workest, and girdest them for the purpose: though not the children of thy covenant, they are the instruments of thy providence.

O Lord, take up this matter, gird these young women to this very purpose, and prosper them in the art of teaching these orphans of thy Providence. And, O Lord, hear my more important petition. I am not worthy to be heard. O Lord, I am not worthy to be named in connection with any good done by thee. "I am the chief of sinners," the chief of backsliders, every thing in me, of me, or by me, is vile as far as it is mine. All that is otherwise, all good implanted in me, or done by me, is thine own, it is grace, free grace, the purchase of thine own Anointed, my dear Redeemer, my dying, risen, ascended Savior, and the fruit of the Holy Ghost, "the sent of the Father and of the Son," to set up a kingdom of righteousness in the hearts of the redeemed. Let me, as a sinner saved by grace, to whom thou hast been pleased to give the exceeding great and precious promises; let me, under the sprinkling of the blood of the Covenant, and in entire dependence on my surety-righteousness; let me draw near and present my petition in the name, and for the sake of Him whom thou hearest always. O Lord God Almighty, by this very thing, build up thy Zion. Lay hold of these young creatures, and while they are in the way of thy providence, bring them "to the house of our master's brethren." O thou great Teacher, teach thou teacher and taught. Be found of them who seek thee not, and say with power, "Behold me, behold me, to a people not yet called by thy name," and out of this small thing in thy providence, bring revenues of praise to thy name as the God of grace. Amen.

✪ *November 28*

George Nauman Shuster

ROMAN CATHOLIC

August 27, 1894–January 25, 1977

Many American Christians have concentrated on the differences between the various traditions. George N. Shuster, on the other hand, looked for those things that Christians of various traditions have in common. He knew that his denominational affiliation did not limit his opportunities in the United States. The significant role he played in education, communication, and government were due to his education and talents, and anyone else with the same background and skills ought to have been able to do the same.

> I do not want to be told that I am (like millions of my Catholic fellowmen, of whom I am only an unworthy representative) a fine fellow who served the nation in time of war, and whose forefathers tilled the American soil —

but that such and such an ecclesiastical declaration (the existence of which I do not suspect but which my learned interlocutor naturally knows all about) has damned me in advance. I want to be told whether I can play the American game with the cards I hold in my hand. Catholic men and women have given of their best to American life with a spontaneity, a vigor and a generous ardor that nobody who respects facts will doubt. On the other hand, during these same centuries many Americans of the noblest sort have, after long years of spiritual search, given of their best to the Catholic Church with the same generosity and vigor. There has really been a great exchange of human currency between this nation and this Church, and some of it, at least, has been pure gold.

Educated at Notre Dame and Columbia as well as in France and Germany, Shuster served on the faculties of Notre Dame, Polytechnic Institute, and St. Joseph's College before becoming president of Hunter College, New York, in 1940, then the largest public college for women in the world. As a result of his service in army intelligence in World War I and years of study in Europe, he served on several American and United Nations Commissions in the immediate post–World War II era. Although Shuster admired German culture and had suggested at one point that Hitler's views were "no more commendable for wisdom...than the notions of the average United States Senator," he soon realized the dangers the Fuehrer posed to the world. As early as 1934, he issued warnings about the Nazi assault on individual and religious freedom.

In 1960, Shuster returned to Notre Dame and spent ten years as director of the Center for the Study of Man in Contemporary Society. In a major report on the Roman Catholic educational system, funded by the Carnegie Foundation, Shuster urged a series of radical reforms. These ranged from shifting emphasis from elementary schools to higher education to the suggestion that parochial schools rely on lay teachers rather than members of religious orders or clergy. In 1960, Shuster was the chair of a committee of Roman Catholic scholars who gave a qualified endorsement to the use of contraception and urged that the church's position on birth control be changed.

A reading from *The Catholic Spirit in America* by George N. Shuster

Mankind has needed six thousand brooding years to attain to its present knowledge of matter, and the mystery is not yet cleared up. Meanwhile Christianity had never denied this or any other reality. Its mission has been to affirm — not God only, but also the numberless works of God. In so far as the sciences, arts and philosophies have been affirmations — in so far, that is, as they have been right — they have not conflicted with Christianity, therefore, but have corroborated its testimony. Every thing that exists, every declaration that is true, every flash of the intelligence that is insight, —

all these are part and parcel of the Christian synthesis. The Divine experiment of wedding a soul to an animal, a spirit to a beast, was surely not undertaken for the sake of making the spirit lonely. There must have been an infinite joyful hope on that creative morning that man would warm his hands at every one of countless earthly fires — that he would feel at "home" in the end.

Yet there is a flaw in our natures — the result of some primal tragic failure through which the spirit grew restive and disconsolate. An immemorial shadow has been flung across the hearth of mankind, a death has occurred which we cannot forget. Nevertheless that death was not given to us unwillingly that we might grieve, but eagerly that we might have more abundant life. It was the ultimate heroic sacrifice — made by One who knew that even its infinite worth would not suffice to give all men joy — to save us from despair. After this, pessimism can only be treason. Only those who do not retreat, who do not admit that the "iron of the universe" is greater than the will of God, can truly be followers of Christ. It is not an easy career, certainly. A wilderness, either of nature or of barbarism, is forever covering up the dim footprints of man. Even so there will always be an army to carry on, until the end. "Come, Holy Spirit" will be an unending and unfailing prayer, on the lips of those who know that no art of living is so satisfying...as theirs.

✪ *November 29*

William Passavant

LUTHERAN

October 9, 1821–January 3, 1894

Most religious traditions do some sort of charitable work, and Christians in America have developed far-ranging aid agencies. The largest network of charitable social services in the United States today is Lutheran Social Services. It includes refugee resettlement, adoption services, hospitals, group homes for the mentally retarded, nursing homes, counseling services, and more. William Passavant, one of the builders of this network, stands as a particularly committed laborer in the early days of social ministry and Christian charity in this country.

Passavant attended Jefferson College and Gettysburg Seminary in preparation for Lutheran ministry. His first charge was a parish in Baltimore, where he preached, oversaw Sunday School, and made pastoral visitations and all the usual activities of parochial ministry. But Passavant did not feel this kind of work was his calling. In a letter to his mother, the young pastor reported that the idea of sitting down in one spot and becoming as other ministers, having the same round of duties form week to week and year to year, is to me now as it has always been very melancholy.... I always longed to be a gospel ranger, to go from place to place assisting my companions in labor, or laying a foundation on which others might build.

Pursuing that dream, Passavant moved on to Pittsburgh in 1844, feeling he might be more useful in a less settled part of the country. Upon his arrival, he found a desolate little group of Lutherans, poor, downtrodden, and discouraged. He inspired a new sense of purpose among them. Church revenues went up, Sunday School grew, and the sick and indigent were cared for. Several young men decided to seek ordination due to Passavant's charisma. He also began visiting prisoners, since he hungered to reach out beyond the boundaries of normal parish duties. Around this time, he realized that the growing Lutheran ministries in the Pittsburgh area needed a new synod to focus their work. By 1845, he had established the Pittsburgh Synod of the Evangelical Lutheran Church. Passavant was the primary author of its constitution and the main source of energy in its creation.

The next year, he traveled to Europe and met Theodore Fliedner, another compassionate clergyman who had developed a training program for deaconesses as a way to serve the poor. Passavant was taken with the idea and proposed to duplicate the project in America. By summer of 1848, he had rented a building in Allegheny for use as a Deaconess Hospital. This new facility was for Christian women who felt called to be teachers and nurses for the surrounding community. But months passed and in January of 1849, Passavant reported:

At that time was not a dollar in the treasury and the prospects were gloomy in the extreme. Many doubted the propriety, and more the practicability, of such an undertaking. The general public knew next to nothing of its existence at first; no one applied for admission; and a whole month elapsed before a single patient was admitted.

Things changed with the arrival of a boatload of veterans from the Mexican War. Passavant made arrangements for two injured soldiers to be transported to his hospital, and, with the help of a friend, Asa Waters, nursed the men back to health. From this simple beginning, other invalids came to find healing, comfort, and support. But when a cholera victim was admitted to the Deaconess Hospital, a public furor forced the closing of the institution and all patients were discharged. Those able to manage on their own were sent out with prayer, but the helpless were placed in wagons and taken down the road. With no firm plan and no resources, Passavant managed to acquire a temporarily vacant women's school before the day was out. Working on trust and faith, he guided the fledgling hospital till it became a fully functioning Christian institution. Deaconesses were trained there, money was raised, and programs developed and put into practice. In 1850, Catherine

Louisa Marthens* was set aside as the first American Lutheran deaconess. Passavant's dream of bringing Fliedner's social ministry to America became a reality.

Hospitals, however, despite their best efforts, cannot save all who come to them for care. Parents who died left behind children, often with no means of support. Passavant had seen a fine orphanage in London on his European trip and decided to establish one in Pittsburgh. In 1852, he succeeded and put Louisa Marthens in charge of the children. In order to engage more fully in his charitable endeavors, Passavant resigned his duties as pastor of his congregation in 1855 and journeyed through the upper midwest, helping to create another hospital and to organize and inspire Lutheran settlers there. Not content to have begun a synod, two hospitals, and an orphanage, he next set his sights on Chicago. With the aid of the deaconess community, he was able to offer care to the destitute there in a humble hospital that opened in 1865. Another orphanage was established in upstate New York by 1869, and another hospital in Jacksonville, Illinois, in 1870. In 1872, the first building of what is now Thiel College in Greenville, Pennsylvania, was begun. Passavant's vision and energy were largely responsible for the creation of the Theological Seminary of the Evangelical Lutheran Church at Chicago in 1891.

Through these years of travel, burdens, obstacles, and conflict, Passavant nonetheless managed to stay involved in the doctrinal disputes and organization of the Lutheran Church. He helped ensure that American Lutheranism would be theologically sound and deeply responsive to the needs of the world. His tireless efforts, unfettered optimism, and rock-solid faith resulted in a network of charitable ministries that have brought the healing ministry of the gospel to countless lives.

✱ *November 30* —————————————————————————

Judith Lomax

EPISCOPALIAN

September 25, 1774–January 19, 1828

Like music or art or any other human ability we call a "gift" or "talent," the personal relationship between an individual and God identified as "mystical" emerges unpredictably in every religious tradition. It often finds expression in ecstatic expressions of joy and of love for the divine. Using biblical language, mystics often call their relationship with God a marriage, referring to Christ as the bridegroom. The mystic may attract followers or lead a reclusive life, hardly known to others. Judith Lomax, a native of Virginia who apparently lived her entire life in Fredericksburg and Port Royal, was such a person. In the notebook that she kept, she wrote:

Methinks I hear a voice that says, — Judith prepare thee [to] die! — and shall I not be prepared for the heavenly Bride[-] groom? — I who have no earthly tie! — forbid it thou great Immanuel, — forbid it the triune God! — oh aid me to keep my lamp ready trim'd! let me be the wise Virgin, all in readiness for the heavenly Bridegroom, so shall I win on bouyant step my airy way, seeking the bosom of my Father, and my God!

Familiar in her own community for attending church services of all the local denominations, Lomax sought a wider audience through some small publications, both religious and secular. She dedicated one of them to Thomas Jefferson. However, any local attention her work may have attracted at the time left no enduring reputation. Only recently have scholars begun to reconstruct her writings and her life.

Though Lomax was an Episcopalian, she did not always live near enough to an Episcopal congregation to attend. In any event, she valued the ministry of others and often worshiped at services and taught in the Sabbath Schools of the Baptist and Methodist Churches as well. She wrote in her notebook:

It is sweet to associate with Christians, and to forget the brethren of other denominations bear any other name, save that of Christ. — I must always give a preference to Christians of *my own* denomination, and aid in every way that I can, the institutions in my own Church. — But yet as I think, the probability is, that I may never hear again the sound of the Gospel from an Episcopal Minister, I am determined to extract from *others* all the good I can, — we should be always in the school of Christ, and think ourselves only babes in knowledge, willing to learn, and endeavouring to progress in Christian attainments.

On Christmas Day, 1820, she wrote in her Sabbath journal:

Glorious Epoch! — The Nativity of a Saviour! — may he have lived and died for me! — this day I feel his heavenly presence, this day I feel him in my heart, he fills every avenue of it. — Why is it that clouds and darkness some times shadow my mind, excluding from it the irradiating beams of love and hope? why am I sometimes the victim of doubt respecting my own situation? — away with these fearful foreboding! it is the work of Satan, he seeks to intimidate me, and shake my faith. — When I search my thoughts, my secret wish's, I feel the sacred witness there, feel that I can be none other than the Child of God, born of his spirit! . . . oh let me treasure these things in my mind! let me endeavour to imitate them, and follow after righteousness!. — so shall I "be with him in paradise," I shall be with him even at the right hand of his Father, and be hail'd by kindred spirits in a purer sky. — I sometimes do hope that I love God supremely, — at this time on the natal day of a dear Redeemer, methinks he fills my heart intire. — Absented from all my Relations, and not one person near, who feels any peculiar interest in me, I seem to stand alone in this wide world, as if on earth I had none, no none, to care for me — no not one, — but when I glance my eyes from earth to heaven and view my Saviour there, beholding him as the friend of the friendless, and the Father of the Fatherless. I then feel a happy assurance that *there is one* who careth for me, one who marks my goings out, and my comings in, and who is I trust about my path, and about my bed, who spies out all my ways, who keeps me as the Apple of his eye, and who I trust will never forsake me — oh may he have been born for me! — may he have lived for me, and may he have died for me! — and at the last may I come to his eternal joy, never to sin or sorrow more — hail'd by kindred spirits in a purer sky, oh my I hear the joyful [cry] of "come, ye blessed of my Father, inherit the crown prepared for you from the foundation of the world."

✪ *December 1* _____

William Cameron Townsend

PRESBYTERIAN

July 9, 1896–April 23, 1982

Known by his middle name, Cameron, or more affectionately as "Uncle Cam," William Cameron Townsend was an expert in language and its structure. His passion was the gospel. His contributions to the understanding of ethnically and linguistically isolated people were immense.

Just at the beginning of World War I, Townsend had his first encounter with a foreign culture. He had been considering the problems of delivering Bibles to Central America. He was a member of the National Guard, and the United States had just declared war against Germany; perhaps he should fight for his country. But God's call was stronger. Millions were going to battle; surely a few must be called to bring the Good News to those who had not yet heard it. Townsend and a friend left for California, then went on to Guatemala as Bible salesmen.

Their mission was hampered by difficulties at the beginning. Illness, homesickness, and a struggle to communicate nearly brought an early end to the trip. Spanish language Bibles were of limited use to the native people, whose mother tongue was Cakchiquel. Then the 1918 influenza pandemic hit the region, as did a severe earthquake. But Townsend's faith provided him with the stamina to remain. Out of this stressful environment, a dream began to emerge. What if indigenous people could be offered the Scriptures in their own languages? In 1918, Townsend began to learn the local dialect

668

so he could translate the gospel into it. Until that point, no one had written that language. After eight years, Townsend had analyzed its verb structure, becoming the first to use the internal syntax of a vernacular language to do so. By the end of 1928, the New Testament had been translated.

Townsend and his wife, Elvira, settled in among the native population and set about trying to find a way of coping with the linguistic barriers that divide the human race. Ultimately, they founded the Summer Institute of Linguistics (SIL) to help missionaries translate languages encountered in the field. The Mexican government approved Townsend's scheme to translate every local language in Mexico. As more and more missionaries began using his system, he created a second organization to facilitate their work: the Wycliffe Bible Translators.

Townsend's zeal to make the Bible accessible in every language was matched by his love for the people who used them. He respected native tribes, wanting them to maintain their own sense of particularity and unique tribal culture. Although Townsend wanted to expose them to the Christian gospel, he did not want this exposure to eradicate their existence as a specific ethnic community.

By the end of the 20th century, SIL had developed academic resources with descriptions and analysis for over 1,700 languages and continued work on over a thousand more. Technical advances were always shaped by Townsend's commitment to the people whose languages were being studied. He believed that missionaries needed scientific and academic knowledge about a culture before their gifts could be put to good use for it. He also held that each culture possesses a particular spiritual facet and that addressing social and economic issues as well as spiritual ones was part of the mission. The SIL and WBT did not sponsor a kind of disinterested anthropological research, but an engagement with each unique people in a way that would help them achieve long-term stability.

Townsend built his work slowly. Each year, just a few more students were recruited. Alphabets had to be devised, sounds and structures recorded, grammars printed, teaching methods developed, and coordination with existing government programs maintained. By 1936, Townsend had pairs of students from the United States fanning out into isolated Mexican villages to learn previously unrecorded languages. At the same time, practical assistance was offered: the planting of an orange grove, for example, or teaching women to sew. In concert with official government projects, progress was made. Townsend spent six decades working among the people of Latin America. His friends came from all levels of society, from the simplest peasants to presidents.

Townsend's work attracted the notice of the academic community. In 1942, the University of Oklahoma invited SIL to its campus to offer training. Shortly afterward, so did The University of North Dakota, followed by the universities of Washington, Texas, and Oregon. Courses were opened in

Australia, Brazil, Canada, England, France, Germany, Japan, Mexico, New Zealand, the Republic of South Africa, and Singapore. By 2000, almost 40,000 students had benefited from SIL training, while its staff had grown to nearly 5,000 from over 40 nations. Languages from more than 70 countries are still being studied.

Townsend represented the best combination of intellectual rigor and genuine interest in others. As an organizer, he was nonetheless most at home talking to people and helping them to communicate with each other. His contributions to the world of science and the spread of the gospel will continue to touch lives for years to come. His outlook is captured in these few words: "The greatest missionary is the Bible in the mother tongue. It needs no furlough and is never considered a foreigner."

✪ *December 2* _____

Caroline Friess

ROMAN CATHOLIC

August 21, 1824–July 22, 1892

At a time when American women were only beginning to demand the right to vote, Caroline Friess was already using her executive skills to organize and direct the work of a major institution. She had joined the School Sisters of Notre Dame at the age of 16, and was put in charge of a boarding school before she was 20. When the order decided to branch out to the United States, she was one of the first to volunteer. Arriving from Germany at the age of 23 with a group of five others, she and the other sisters faced hunger and hardship at first, and one soon died. However, Friess was clearly marked for leadership and within three years, she was appointed vicar-general of the order in America. Over the next 42 years, she traveled the length and breadth of the United States and Canada, establishing schools, convents, and orphanages, until by the time of her death at 68, there were 2,000 sisters and 265 schools in 16 states, serving 70,000 children. Friess opened four institutions of higher learning for women in the belief that a solid religious and secular education was essential for those who would take leadership roles in society. Described as "bright, adventurous and with a great love for children," she opened her schools to children of every race and gender but provided that "no sister shall be forced" to work with boys.

Friess was not easily deterred. When a steamship on which she was traveling blew up, killing a good many passengers, she climbed down the side into a rescue ship and went on with her journey. When a newspaper in Milwaukee published an attack on the convent school and the sisters, Friess sued the newspaper for libel and forced it to issue a retraction. Her voluminous correspondence (all in German) covered issues ranging from the health of the sisters (seldom up to her standards), to the mundane details of building and maintenance work, along with her adventures along the way, practical guidance for the order (sisters should be allowed to sleep until 5 a.m.), and spiritual advice.

A reading from a letter of Caroline Friess to the members of her order

Love of God was the motive that prompted each and every one of us to enter Religion. How has this motive manifested itself in our lives to this moment? Has not our first ardor grown tepid and cold? Has not our love of God been checked by shameful self-love which has sullied our hearts and tainted our every thought, word and action? Is it not, therefore, necessary to rekindle the fire of our love — to renew our first fervor? By pronouncing the holy vows of Religion we became the spouses of Jesus Christ, and the "Mortuae estis" proclaimed us dead to the world. At that solemn moment of our consecration — filled with holy enthusiasm for the virtue of mortification, of daily dying to self — we generously placed ourselves in the ranks of the Crucified.

What proofs have we given of our love of mortification and suffering? Have we not often fallen a prey to our passions and bad habits? Is it not our sacred duty to reflect upon the excellence with which the grace of Profession endowed our souls, and to endeavor to preserve or restore this original beauty? As religious, are we not bound to incline our will to good, to persevere energetically in the spiritual combat, and to be faithful and assiduous in prayer that we may ever receive a prompt and generous reply to Deus in adjutorium meum intende? During this holy season we should be more than ever impressed with the words of Jesus, "Sequere me, follow me" — in love and suffering. Let us frequently and earnestly consider how a soul that devotes herself to the love of God is, thereby, enabled to overcome the most obstinate innate faults, to practice heroic virtue and attain the height of perfection.

The love of God inflames our will, effecting a complete overthrow of self-will, eradicating ambition from our hearts and making us zealous promoters of the glory of God — that the burden of our lives be "Ad majorem dei gloriam."

The love of God gives us strength to subject our sensitive, whimsical, sensual, inconstant nature to the control of divine grace.

The love of God makes us generous in bearing the toils and hardships necessarily encountered in the performance of the exercise of works of mercy and strengthens us to persevere in the life of sacrifice which shall, one day, be exchanged for a life of never-ending bliss in heaven.

The love of God enables us to practice the virtues of forbearance, patient endurance, humility, and gentleness which is ever ready to yield to others.

THE LOVE OF GOD aids us in the continual restraint of our senses — regulating the eye, the ear, the tongue, the palate.

THE LOVE OF GOD incites us to conscientious observance of our holy vows, of the Rule and Constitution of the Order, and enables us to fully realize the necessity of holy silence, conventual discipline and religious retirement.

In reflecting upon the points above given, let us not lose sight of the wonders which our Lord is ready to work in us, if with resolute good will, we faithfully correspond to his grace. Let us be courageous and, with childlike confidence, endeavor to satisfy the yearning desire of Jesus.

✪ *December 3*

Peter Williams

EPISCOPALIAN

c. 1780–October 18, 1840

"I have learned," Peter Williams wrote, "that it is a most difficult matter to avoid extremes on subjects of public excitement, without being more censured than those who go to all lengths with either party." He had discovered this through experience. His father, born in slavery, had been able to purchase his freedom and was one of the founders of the African Methodist Zion Church in New York City, but his son joined the Episcopal Church, was ordained a priest after long delays, and founded St. Philip's Church, still a prominent congregation. When the American Anti-Slavery Society began advocating abolition of slavery in 1834, a white mob, aware of Williams's association with it, burned St. Phillip's. The Episcopal Bishop of New York asked Williams to "pursue the prudent course" and resign from the society. "The raging of the sea and the madness of the people," the bishop advised, are equally beyond our control. "Let it be seen that on whatsoever side right may be, St. Philip's Church will be found on the Christian side of meekness, order, and self-sacrifice to common good and the peace of the community. You will be no losers by it, for the God of peace will be to you also a God of all consolation. Let me hear from you or see you soon," the bishop concluded; "I can say better than write all I think."

Williams's lengthy response was printed alongside the bishop's letter in the *New York Spectator.* In it, he expressed his struggle to reconcile his desire to serve as a priest to his people with his longing to be an effective advocate for their freedom. He noted that his relationship with the Anti-Slavery Society had not been of his choosing. He had been appointed to the Board of Managers, but never met with them, except for a few moments at the close of their sessions, and had not spoken even then. He would, therefore, he said, resign from the board as the bishop had requested but without expressing "any opinion respecting the principles on which that society is founded." Williams added that he would have resigned sooner except that he thought he "might exercise a restraining influence upon measures calculated to advance our people faster than they were prepared to be advanced, and the public feeling would bear."

Whether vigorous advocacy or patience and meekness is the more effective course in a given situation is seldom an easy judgment to make. Williams held strong opinions and made them known when he thought it appropriate. An example is this excerpt from a speech he made in 1830 opposing plans to resolve racial conflict by sending freed slaves back to Africa.

A reading from a speech in 1830 by Peter Williams

Those who wish that that vast continent should be *compensated* for the injuries done it, by sending thither the light of the gospel and the arts of civilized life. should aid in sending and supporting well-qualified missionaries, who should be wholly devoted to the work of instruction, instead of sending colonists who would be apt to turn the ignorance of the natives to their own advantage, and do them more harm than good.

Much has also been said by Colonizationists about improving the character and condition of the people of colour of this country by sending them to Africa. This is more inconsistent still. We are to be improved by being sent far from civilized society. This is a novel mode of improvement. What is there in the burning sun, the arid plains, and barbarous customs of Africa, that is so peculiarly favourable to our improvement? What hinders our improving here, where schools and colleges abound, where the gospel is preached at every corner, and where all the arts and sciences are verging fast to perfection? Nothing, nothing but prejudice. It requires no large expenditures, no hazardous enterprises to raise the people of colour in the United States to as highly improved a state as any class of the community. All that is necessary is that those who profess to be anxious for it should lay aside their prejudices and act towards them as they do by others.

We are NATIVES of this country, we ask only to be treated as well as FOREIGNERS. Not a few of our fathers suffered and bled to purchase its independence; we ask only to be treated as well as those who fought against it. We have toiled to cultivate it, and to raise it to its present prosperous condition; we ask only to share equal privileges with those who come from distant lands, to enjoy the fruits of our labour. Let these moderate requests be granted, and we need not go to Africa nor anywhere else to be improved and happy. We cannot but doubt the purity of the motives of those persons who deny us these requests, and would send us to Africa to gain what they might give us at home.

But they say the prejudices of the country against us are invincible; and as they cannot be conquered, it is better that we should be removed beyond their influence. This plea should never proceed from the lips of any man who professes to believe that a just God rules in the heavens.

The African Colonization Society is a numerous and influential body. Would they lay aside their *own* prejudices, much of the burden would be at once removed; and their example (especially if they were as anxious to have *justice done us here* as to send us to Africa) would have such an influence upon the community at large as would soon cause prejudice to hide its deformed head.

But, alas! the course which they have pursued has an opposite tendency. By the *scandalous misrepresentations* which they are continually giving of our character and conduct we have sustained much injury, and have reason to apprehend much more.

✪ December 4 _____

Lucy Jane Rider Meyer

METHODIST

September 9, 1849–March 16, 1922

Chicago in the late 19th century was, like most large American cities, a place of hopeful prospects, but also of want and deprivation. Immigrants from Europe were easily exploited and there were few agencies to help or stand up for them. Churches seldom considered using their female members to address such needs. But this didn't stop Lucy Jane Rider. She began teaching school while still in her teens, first in a high school at Brandon, Vermont, then in a school for freedmen at Greensboro, North Carolina. Later she served as principal of the Troy (Methodist) Conference Academy in Poultney, Vermont, and as a professor of chemistry at McKendree College in Illinois. She wrote a textbook on chemistry for children, and also composed hymns and songs for children, organized Sunday Schools, and attended the World Sunday School Convention in London in 1880. In 1885, she married Josiah S. Meyer, a Methodist Episcopal minister. Together, they opened the Chicago Training School for City, Home, and Foreign Missions, where Lucy Rider Meyer served as principal.

In Germany (1836) and England (1861), the ancient order of deaconesses had been restored. Meyer directed some of her students to begin a ministry of visitation in the tenement neighborhoods of Chicago. Living together, in what came to be called the deaconess home, they went out as had their namesakes in the early church to care for the sick, instruct mothers on child care and homemaking, and provide Christian education. Fundamentalists attacked them, contending that all the teaching women needed was provided in church and Sunday School. Meyer replied that they needed a thorough intellectual preparation to meet the temporal and spiritual challenges of urban America. Conservatives were also unhappy because she taught that the Bible is the work of inspired authors and editors who sometimes assembled older documents to form the current canon. Meyer defended her views, even against her own husband. In 1888, the Methodist Episcopal Church officially recognized the office of deaconess and by the end of her career, Lucy Rider Meyer was being called the "Archbishop of Deaconesses."

A reading from *Deaconesses* by Lucy Rider Meyer

There came a later winter in my life, when all my plans were frustrated, and my future was a blank. I gathered a little class of young men, however, and began teaching them in Sunday-school the best I could. It was only a step from this to preparing Bible Readings for them, and only a step more to writing Bible lessons for children, which came to be accepted and paid for by the Sunday-school papers. But all this required Bible study, and so in the good providence of God I was compelled to study the Bible. What other folks might or might not do, according to inclination or conscience, I had to do for my bread and butter. That is, my private object was bread and butter, but God's object was to train me to be a teacher — a teacher of the Bible. I remember that one year I wrote about four thousand questions on the Sunday-school lessons of the year. God was giving me the details of apprentice work. Then he gave me a drill on Normal Methods, in one of the best secular normal schools in Illinois, and finally sent me out into the field as an employee of the Illinois State Sunday-school Association. In this work it was my duty to attend County Conventions and other Sunday-school gatherings; and there was no kind of detail or general work, it seems to me that did not at times fall to my lot. My program work was to give Bible and Normal lessons, and conduct children's meetings, and this was an invaluable drill, but I remember once arbitrating between two angry men. God was giving me lessons in managing human nature. On another occasion I arrived in a town, an utter stranger, to find every hotel filled, and to be turned from the door of the pastor at eleven o'clock at night. I found a lodging, at last, in a terrible bed over a saloon, and was aroused during the night by the drunken brawls in the room below. God was making me understand what it was, not to have a place to lay my head. In a thousand ways, of grateful interest to me to remember, God tried to prepare me for the work of my life. I ought to be a good teacher to judge by the infinite thoughtfulness of my Divine Tutor, and when I am forced to confess, even with these years of training, to such weakness and imperfection I am constrained to exclaim, "What should I have been but for God's special pains-taking with me!

✪ *December 5*

John Wanamaker
PRESBYTERIAN

July 11, 1838–December 12, 1922

John Wanamaker was an innovator and a "doer" in both faith and business. Born in Philadelphia and living there for most of his life, he became one of the most widely respected and honored men of his time. From rather humble beginnings, Wanamaker entered the world of merchandizing with a men and boy's clothing store. After a sluggish start, the business became successful, so he decided to try something completely novel: he bought an old railroad depot and opened the first department store. It sold both men and women's clothing, along with housewares. Soon he added a restaurant and the world's biggest organ for the musical enjoyment of the patrons. He had a telegraph installed, which made him the first person to hear about the sinking of the *Titanic*. Some of his stores even had Ford dealerships. Wanamaker introduced telephone ordering and refunds on items returned. His advertising was truthful, at a time when manufacturer's claims were not regulated. He introduced price tags, money back guarantees, white sales, and newspaper advertising. His employees received a number of previously rare fringe benefits, including vacations, health care, pensions, life insurance, and payments for further education. Soon, many stores bore Wanamaker's name, making him wealthy and famous.

Faith was the center of his life. A member of the Bethany Presbyterian Church, Wanamaker undertook the establishment of a small Sunday School in 1858, and his little class became one of the world's largest Sunday Schools. He was passionately committed to its welfare. Involvement in the Young Men's Christian Association led to his nomination to be the Y's first salaried national secretary. When the Civil War began, Wanamaker helped found the "Christian Commission," offering medical care to soldiers regardless of their allegiances. His organizational acumen and innovative spirit were sought after in a broad range of fields. For eight years, he was President of the Y.M.C.A. He helped found the Presbyterian Hospital, served as a trustee, and, with Mrs. Wanamaker, donated the Children's Ward of that institution. He also made significant contributions to the University of Pennsylvania Museum. Fascinated by archeology, he underwrote a trip to Alaska in 1916 to further the study of Eskimo life and culture. The list of his concerns continues: he chaired the Citizens Relief Committee to assist the victims of the Irish Famine and sent aid to southerners during a bout of yellow fever and to people affected by a flood along the banks of the Ohio River. Russians and Belgians were recipients of large-scale food shipments spearheaded by Wanamaker during their times of famine early in the 20th century.

Mission work abroad also elicited his support, especially the Allahabad (India) Christian College and Mary Wanamaker High School for Girls in Madras, India, along with Y.M.C.A. work in Seoul, Korea; Kyoto, Japan; Peking, China; Calcutta, India; and a school in Beirut, Lebanon. Wanamaker was president of the World's Sunday School Association and the Pennsylvania State Sabbath School Association. He was also active in politics and was made postmaster general under President Harrison. In the course of four years, he established commemorative stamps; increased free delivery, and established rural delivery. He was responsible for improving the mailing facilities in cities in remote sections of the country, especially the far west.

When word came of Wanamaker's death, Philadelphia lowered its flags, newspapers eulogized his good works, and public schools in his native city were closed for the day of his funeral. His pallbearers included the Governor of Pennsylvania, the mayors of Philadelphia and New York, the chief justice of the Supreme Court, and the inventor, Thomas Edison. Some of Wanamaker's most revealing words are found in a series of prayers he composed for use in his Sunday School classes:

A reading from John Wanamaker

Heavenly Father, to-morrow none of us will be as young as we are to-day. Not to read Thy book aright is to lose another day, and put off our getting into Thy love and knowing Thy plan for our lives. Not to call upon Thee, to-day, in sincere prayer for Thy wisdom and help, is to neglect an opportunity and to risk a certainty on the hazard and the uncertainty of another day that may never come. Thou hast said: "Seek Me early and thou shalt find Me." May our hearts respond gladly to this invitation. With something more than the earnestness of a merely earthly seeking, may we say: "I will give Thee my best strength and bloom of my best years, before the evil days draw nigh, in which I am compelled to say, 'I have no pleasure in them.'" Amen.

We are glad, O God, to be in Thine house, and will sing of Thy mercy. We come to Thee in the Name of Jesus, Thy Son. There are some who disavow the Name of Jesus, but His Name is our plea, the Name chosen of God and precious. Put Thine arms about us. Protect and guide us and give us of Thy grace to supply all our needs according to the riches Thou hast in glory by Christ Jesus, our Lord. Amen.

Most gracious Father, we thank Thee that while sometimes the weeks take us down-hill, yet these blessed Sundays bring us up again to the bright morning. Stop the world's attractions and diversions on this day that our bodies and souls may not be ruined by their curtaining off of the God who will outlive us. May none of us take this life offhand, without carefulness, lest we play with edged tools, and so cut and scar ourselves everlastingly. Grant that we may inherit the rich estate to which we are born through Jesus Christ, Thy Son, the world's Saviour. Amen.

✪ December 6

Anne-Therese Guerin

ROMAN CATHOLIC

October 2, 1798–May 14, 1856

Born and brought up in France, Anne-Therese Guerin became a nun at the age 25 and quickly rose to become the superior of a convent in Rennes. The French government presented her with an award for her work there and for her teaching in Soulianes. In 1830, a French native, Bishop Celestin de la Hailandiere, working in Indiana, needed nuns to serve as missionaries and teachers, and Anne-Therese Guerin (known as Mother Theodore Guerin) was chosen to go with five others to establish this new work.

Reluctantly she saw the coast of France recede in the distance. The reality of the American frontier was beyond her imagination. Her journal provides a vivid picture of her education into life in the New World:

> We entered a thick forest where we saw the most singular kind of road that could be imagined. It was formed of logs, of trees that had been felled to clear the way and then were brought together as though to form a raft [corduroy]. Where some of these logs had become rotten, there were large holes. The coach jolted so terribly as to cause large bumps on one's head. This day, indeed, we danced without a fiddle all the afternoon. The road was really dreadful. Thus jumping and tossing about, we arrived at a farmhouse in the forest, where we decided to spend the night. The kind people gave up to us one room containing three beds, and they took Father Chartier, I know not where. Here we awaited the dawn of that day by whose light we would at length behold the town of Vincennes, towards which we had been journeying so long. . . .
>
> At last we had arrived at Vincennes! Vincennes! The conveyance stopped. We were taken to the Sisters of Charity, who live near the episcopal residence, and who had been requested by the Bishop to take care of us until his return. After partaking of some food and putting on again our religious dress, we begged to be taken to the cathedral. *Ciel!* What a Cathedral! Our barn at Soulaines is better ornamented and more neatly kept. I could not resist this last shock and wept bitterly, which relieved me somewhat. I could not possibly examine this poor church on that day — the following day I did so with more calm. It is a brick building with large windows without curtains; most of the panes of glass are broken; on the roof there is something like the beginning of a steeple, which resembles rather a large chimney fallen into ruins. The interior corresponds perfectly to the exterior: — a poor wooden altar, a railing unfinished and yet seemingly decaying from age. The Bishop's seat is an old red chair which even our peasants would not have in what they consider a nice room. To conclude, I have seen nothing equal to the poverty of the cathedral of Vincennes. I can say nothing of the town except that I doubt whether it will ever grow much on account of its position — solitary, situated in an undeveloped part of the country, on the bank of a little river which is navigable only in winter. . . .

This, then, is what we have for the foundation of a house, which the Bishop foresees will one day be a flourishing institution. No doubt; but we shall have to suffer much. Many things are wanting to us, yet we dare not complain. Shall we not be, and are we not already, in our own little nook? Besides, did we not come here to suffer — we who were so well provided for in France?

Not only were the surroundings unfamiliar — there was "the insupportable pride of the Americans." A servant girl expected to eat at the same table with the nuns. When Guerin suggested she eat with the servants, the American postulants made it clear that such distinctions were not acceptable. Guerin, however, was wise enough to realize that "the spirit of this country is so different from ours that one ought to be acquainted with it before condemning those who know more about it than we do."

Within a few months, Guerin established a boarding school for young girls, the first such school in Indiana and today the College of Our Lady of-the-Woods. Before her death she had established ten other schools throughout Indiana. Eventually the sisters' work extended to other states and even to China. It wasn't easy. The frontier *was* a harsh environment. They were threatened by anti–Roman Catholic agitation. Members of the order died or defected. The bishop tried to change the order's rule and excommunicated Guerin when she opposed his plans. Through it all, her serene confidence kept her on course and inspired others. Eventually, the loyal French woman became an American.

A reading from the journal of Anne-Therese Guerin

We had scarcely passed two days on the steamboat when the spring weather enjoyed at New Orleans was gone. The sweet smelling fruit and flowers were succeeded by majestic trees still bare of foliage. The farther north we went, the lower became the temperature and bleaker the landscape. This severe change was sweet to me, for it meant I was nearing home. Finally on the fifth day, with inexpressible joy I saw once more my Indiana. I would have loved to kiss its soil.

This land was no longer for me the land of exile; it was the portion of my inheritance, and in it I hope to dwell all the days of my life.

✪ December 7 ─────────────────────────

James Otis Sargent Huntington

EPISCOPALIAN

July 23, 1854–June 29, 1935

It was while he was working with immigrants on New York City's lower east side that James Otis Sargent Huntington received a call to monastic life. He founded the first indigenous religious order for men in the Episcopal Church, taking life vows on November 25, 1884. The Order of the Holy Cross grew slowly at first, but eventually settled at West Park, New York, and became one of the best known monastic orders in the Episcopal Church. Fr. Huntington served as the order's superior several times and continued a ministry of preaching, teaching, and spiritual direction until his death in 1935. Huntington was also deeply involved in the social issues of the time and did much to encourage the Episcopal Church's commitment to social ministries. Throughout his life, he called attention to inadequate wages and substandard working conditions of men and women in factories. He said the church should become "the great Anti-Poverty Society" and must be on the side of the poor "if she is going to live at all." He played a leading role in establishing the Church Association for the Advancement of the Interests of Labor, which helped pass legislation abolishing child labor in New York State, investigated conditions in factories and tenements, and arbitrated strikes.

A statement by Fr. Huntington on the nature of the religious life

Has what is known as "The Religious Life" a legitimate place in the Church?

As to that, there are different opinions. To some persons such a life seems to be the fairest burgeoning of Christian discipleship. By others it has been regarded as a perversion of the Christian ideal in a morbid asceticism, and a false, because self-centered, spirituality.

Whatever view may be taken, there is no question but that the Religious Life, as organized in communities, has been found in the historic Church from shortly after the apostolic age. The course of the Christian fellowship has been deeply affected by it, and without it would have had a very different history, in many ages and lands. The Religious Life is a fact to be reckoned with in any comprehensive account of the Church and of civilization.

Two things may, however, be said, in the way of preface, to remove misunderstanding. Prejudice against the monastic state has arisen from the use of the very phrase "The Religious Life." This has been taken to mean that the upholders of this state mean to assert that those who associate themselves in Religious Communities surpass other Christians in piety and moral excellence. That would, of course, be shocking Phariseeism, subversive of all true humility. But the term "Religious" is not used with any such implication. It simply indicates that the duties and obligations of the monk or nun are of a religious character, — worship, prayer, meditation, intercession, etc. That is their business or *metier*. If they sincerely fulfil their vocation they are doing that which will unite the soul with God. That is not true of many useful professions. A man may be a skillful physician and yet live apart from God.

A man may be an honest and upright merchant and yet never say a prayer or exercise faith in God. But a "Religious" cannot discharge the duties of his calling without entering into converse with his Maker. That is why he is said to be in the "Religious State," although, alas, he may have the outward marks of a "Religious" and be secretly unfaithful to all.

The other thing to be said is that the Religious Life is not, in its essentials, alien to the life of the faithful Christian whatever his status and work may be. The virtues of the Religious State are none other than the virtues which all followers of Christ should seek to exercise. Every Christian is called to discipline his body, his mind, and his spirit, that he may advance in the way of holiness. The "Religious" disciplines his body by a life of strictest purity in the celibate state; he disciplines his mind by embracing the condition of poverty, calling nothing his own; he disciplines his spirit by placing himself under the Rule of his Community, and acting in accordance with the will of his superior. In this he is seeking to carry out, under special conditions, the programme incumbent on all Christians. All souls are commanded to seek perfection: the "Religious" vows to use certain means which, he believes, have been indicated by divine instruction and witnessed to through centuries of experience as conducive to that adventure.

✪ *December 8*

Fannie Lou Hamer

BAPTIST

October 6, 1917–March 14, 1977

Fannie Lou Hamer was 44 before she learned that she had a right to vote. She was the 20th child of sharecroppers, and her formal education ended with sixth grade. After that, she had only Bible lessons at her Baptist Church. "Life was very hard," she told an interviewer.

> We never hardly had enough to eat; we didn't have clothes to wear. We had to work real hard, because I started working when I was about six years old. I didn't have a chance to go to school too much, because school would only last about four months at the time when I was a kid going to school. Most of the time we didn't have clothes to wear to that [school]; and then if any work would come up that we would have to do, the parents would take us out of the school to cut stalks and burn stalks or work in dead lands or things like that. It was just really tough as a kid when I was a child.

When organizers for the Student Non-violent Coordinating Committee (SNCC) came to her town to tell people about their right to vote, Hamer decided to try. When she made the first attempt, the landowner told her she would have to leave the place where she was living. After she passed the required test to register, on the third try, she was arrested and beaten.

Then, however, she became a field secretary for the SNCC and traveled around the country encouraging people to register and vote. In 1964, she helped form the Mississippi Freedom Democratic Party and led a delegation to the national Democratic Convention. Although only two of them were seated, they attracted national attention to the number of black people in southern states who were not permitted to vote. In 1969, Hamer founded the Freedom Farm Cooperative, a project that eventually enabled 5,000 people to own collectively 680 acres of land and grow their own food. She also worked for improved living conditions and housing for sharecroppers. In 1971, she helped establish the National Women's Political Caucus, though she was often at odds with white members, feeling they didn't understand the oppression experienced by black women. "But," she said, the white woman's freedom "is shackled in chains to mine, and she realizes that she is not free until I am free."

"Christ," said Fannie Lou Hamer, "was a revolutionary person." She used biblical language in her speeches. Jesus proclaimed that "the things that have been done in the dark will be known on the house tops." Hamer thought her role was to shout from any platform available about injustice and unequal opportunity in the deep south. Like her predecessors, she saw no way to divide her faith from her politics.

A reading from a speech by Fanny Lou Hamer to the NAACP in 1971

I'm not fighting for equal rights. What do I want to be equal to Senator Eastland for? Just tell me that. But we are not only going to liberate ourselves. I think it's a responsibility. I think we're special people. God's children is going to help in the survival of this country if it's not too late. We're a lot sicker than people realize we are. And what we are doing now in the Southern politics, in gaining seats for black people and concerned whites in the state of Mississippi, is going to have an effect on what happens throughout this country. You know, I used to think that if I could go North and tell people about the plight of the black folk in the state of Mississippi, everything would be all right. But traveling around, I found one thing for sure: it's up-South and down-South, and it's no different. The man shoot me in the face in Mississippi, and you turn around he'll shoot you in the back here in New York. We have a problem, folks, and we want to try to deal with the problem in the only way that we can deal with the problem as far as black women. And you know, I'm not hung up on this about liberating myself from the black man, I'm not going to try that thing. I got a black husband, six feet three, two hundred and forty pounds, with a 14 shoe, that I don't want to be liberated from. But we are here to work side by side with this black man: to bring liberation to all people. Sunflower County is one of the poorest counties, one of the poorest counties on earth, while Senator James Eastland — you know, people tells you, don't talk politics, but the air you breathe is polluted air, it's political polluted air. The air you breathe is politics. So you have to be involved in trying to elect people that's going to help do something about the liberation of all people.

✪ *December 9*

Frank Laubach

PRESBYTERIAN

September 2, 1884–June 11, 1970

"In the beginning was the Word," the Gospel of John proclaims. For centuries, information was shared by storytelling before written language opened the way for amazing progress. It seemed to Frank Laubach both an injustice and a sorrow that so many of our brothers and sisters were unable to decipher the printed page. It became his passion and his commitment to do something about the epidemic of illiteracy that engulfed much of the planet.

Laubach was educated at Princeton, Columbia, and Union Theological Seminary. He became a missionary to bring his deep faith to other parts of the world. But his encounters with distant peoples made him aware of the ways in which the inability to read was holding back not just religious knowledge and faith, but many types of progress and hope.

Many others have shared this concern, but few have realized, as Laubach did, how this situation might be remedied. He conceived a plan that empowered a person who had just mastered reading to teach his or her neighbor. His slogan was "Each one teach one." In this way, a single teacher could prepare dozens of local students to teach dozens more to read. Building upon the close-knit communities often found in aboriginal cultures, this method would eliminate the need for an army of highly trained educators to be sent from governments or churches as resources (and willingness) allowed.

Laubach is credited with a system that has taught 100 million people to read — an astounding success. While his focus was not specifically religious, his own faith formed the foundation for this endeavor. Whether the written text is sacred Scripture, instructions for building an irrigation system, a health pamphlet, or a government policy document, the ability to read it opens up possibilities for villages and nations. In the great tradition of the Reformation, which advocated universal access to the Bible, Laubach sought to extend that availability to writing, in general, in the interests of a better life and a better world.

As impressive as his system is, his dedication is even more inspiring. Laubach might easily have taken a cozy parish or teaching post. He could have become the director of an agency advocating literacy. Or, having developed his program, he might then have recruited others to carry it out. Instead, he packed his bags and left the safe surroundings of his own background to go into the poorer sections of the world where need was greatest. Traveling to places most of us will never venture — some of which we may never have heard about — he steadfastly carried on his work, inspired by his vision of universal literacy. This, too, is a kind of Pentecost ministry, enabling everyone to read the Good News of Jesus Christ in his or her own tongue, or, for that matter, the good news of new medications, to read contracts or correspond with one's family, or simply enjoy a newspaper.

Laubach has been called the "Apostle of literacy." The Lord equipped him to bring a particular gift to people barred from modern communication and technology by inadequate education. Thanks to him, the human family is better able to communicate and benefit from the written word.

Readings from Frank Laubach

To be able to look backward and say, "This, this has been the finest year of any life" — that is glorious! But anticipation! To be able to look ahead and say, "The present year can and will be better!" — that is more glorious! I have done nothing but open windows — God has done the rest. There has been a succession of marvelous experiences of the friendship of God. I resolved that I would succeed better this year with my experiment of filling every minute full of the thought of God than I succeeded last year. And I added another resolve — to be as wide open toward people and their need as I am toward God. Windows open outward as well as upward. Windows open especially downward where people need the most!

Submission is the first and last duty of man. That is exactly what I have been needing in my Christian life. Two years ago a profound dissatisfaction led me to begin trying to line up my actions with the will of God about every fifteen minutes or every half hour. Other people to whom I confessed this intention said it was impossible. I judge from what I have said that few people are trying even that. But this year I have started out trying to live all my waking moments in conscious listening to the inner voice, asking without ceasing, "What, Father, do you desire said? What, Father, do you desire done this minute?"

We used to sing a song in the church in Benton which I liked, but which I never really practiced until now. It runs:

> Moment by moment, I'm kept in His love;
> Moment by moment I've life from above;
> Looking to Jesus till glory doth shine;
> Moment by moment, O Lord, I am Thine.

It is exactly that "moment by moment," every waking moment, surrender, responsiveness, obedience, sensitiveness, pliability, "lost in His love," that I now have the mind-bent to explore with all my might. It means two burning passions: First, to be like Jesus. Second, to respond to God as a violin responds to the bow of the master. Open your soul and entertain the glory of God and after a while that glory will be reflected in the world about you and in the very clouds above your head.

✪ *December 10*

William Dwight Porter Bliss

EPISCOPALIAN

August 20, 1856–October 8, 1926

During the last half of the 19th century, the United States moved from a rural to an industrial economy. Once the majority of Americans had lived on farms and led relatively self-sufficient lives, but now, an ever-growing number lived in cities and worked in factories under whatever conditions their employers provided. Women and children often labored 12-hour shifts, six days a week. Men worked in dangerous conditions in coal mines and steel mills. Some deeply committed priests and laypeople joined the growing labor unions to protest against these inhuman conditions. For many, socialism seemed a better alternative to Capitalism.

One of the leading Socialist voices was that of William Dwight Porter Bliss, an Episcopal priest. The son of Congregational missionaries, he too joined the ministry of that church, serving briefly in Colorado and Massachusetts, before becoming an Episcopalian. He had felt an attraction to Anglicanism's catholicity and theological breadth and was also influenced by British Christian Socialists like Charles Kingsley and F. D. Maurice. His first parish was in Lee, Massachusetts, a factory town, and there he saw firsthand the conditions in the factories and confronted the alienation of working people from the church.

In 1890, Bliss founded an experimental inner-city community called the Mission of the Carpenter. Years later Vida Scudder* recalled how they had sung "with special zeal the Magnificat" and "had wonderful suppers, true agape, when the altar at the back of the little room was curtained off and we feasted on ham and pickles and hope of an imminent revolution." But Bliss was neither a wild-eyed zealot nor an impractical dreamer. Throughout his career, he kept in touch with more moderate reformers like Bishop F. D. Huntington and the Church Association for the Advancement of the Interests of Labor and joined the Knights of Labor and titled himself "priest and socialist," but he considered strikes only a necessary evil and thought of Socialism as merely a means to the greater end of awakening the church to its social duty. He wrote:

If we call ourselves Socialists today, it is not because in socialism only do we discover truth, but because it is this social-ism which we believe to be the most needed at this time, and for which we must at present chiefly battle.

Socialism is a via media that would gradually develop the conception of the state and the individual, through and with and beyond the state. True Socialism is not one sided.

Socialism does not claim to reach the ideal at a bound, only to improve gradually upon the present.

Bliss was properly skeptical of simplistic solutions like Communism, secular Socialism, free silver, prohibition, and the single tax. The path of Christian Socialism, he wrote, "is a notoriously straight and a narrow way. . . . The extreme individualist and narrow socialist both will disown us." He was himself a Christocentric realist who knew that salvation came only through Christ's atonement. "No socialism," he wrote, "can be successful unless rooted and grounded in Christ, the Liberator . . . the Head of Humanity." To propagate his views, Bliss traveled, wrote, and organized ceaselessly. An 1879 lecture tour took him to San Francisco, where he filled the city's largest auditorium every day for two weeks, preached from the pulpits of the city's wealthiest Episcopal Churches, and was denounced by the newspapers as an "anarchist, tramp preacher from Boston." Before long he had started an Urban Reform League with chapters in five cities and published a series of pamphlets. A national convention in 1899 brought together Fabian Socialists, Single Taxers, Free Silverites, Prohibitionists, Women's Rights advocates, Populists, and many others. But a wave of prosperity proved fatal to reform, and a new magazine, *Social Unity,* failed after a few issues.

One historian of the era has written that he was "the most tireless of Christian radicals and the most successful organizer. Earnest to the point of fanaticism, incredibly energetic, persistently optimistic, forceful in print and far better informed than most clerical leaders, Bliss was an appropriate spearhead for the left of the social movement." But another historian records that "by and large the Church did not receive the movement in a friendly spirit." The American temperament was pragmatic rather than visionary, but Bliss's outpouring of magazines and pamphlets and his massive *Dictionary of Christian Socialism* did make some impact. The larger church rejected his Socialist principles, but began addressing social injustice. In the generation after Bliss's death the Federal Council of Churches, together with many denominations, condemned systems that showed no concern for their workers. Gradually, changes took place. W. J. Ghent, a younger colleague, said of Bliss:

He is best remembered for his moral force, his passion for justice, his crystalline sincerity and perfect disinterestedness. He believed what he professed; he was a missionary who carried his religion into the workaday world. Unaggressive, yet persistent, he preached his gospel of social salvation to all who would listen or read, and did it with a sheer disregard of personal consequences. He died a poor man.

✪ *December 11*

Dwight Lyman Moody

INDEPENDENT

February 5, 1837–December 22, 1899

Dwight Lyman Moody was baptized in a Unitarian Church, attended Sunday School in a Congregational Church, distributed tracts for a Methodist Church, and was married in a Baptist Church, so it is not surprising that, as an evangelist, he never identified himself with any particular church. Nevertheless, his work was commended by Christians of every sort from Unitarian and Baptist to Roman Catholic.

Moody had little formal education and no seminary training. He began his working life as a clerk in a shoe store, then became a successful businessman. But his interest in the church gradually won him away from the business world so that, at the age of 24, it had become his full-time work. He raised money for the Y.M.C.A. in Chicago and toured the Civil War battlefields, asking the dying, "Are you a Christian?" At 29, he began his own Sunday School in an abandoned railroad car, then in an abandoned saloon. Eventually he built a church that would hold 1,500 to accommodate those who came.

Moody made his first visit to England in 1867 when he was 30 on account of his wife's health. The contacts he established there motivated him to return in 1872 and 1873 to conduct revivals. With Ira Sankey to sing and Moody to preach, they toured the United Kingdom, filling meeting halls with thousands of people, week after week, until two and a half million had heard him preach and thousands had been converted. Moody then came back to America to conduct revivals in Brooklyn and other cities across the country. Sometimes he would give out tickets only to those who were not church members to prevent church members from filling up the seats. Year after year, across America and the United Kingdom, the pattern of revival meetings continued with thousands coming forward to be saved. The hymnal Moody and Sankey published earned over a million dollars in royalties and Moody used the money to establish educational institutions like the Northfield Seminary for Young Woman, the Mount Hermon School for Young Men, and the Chicago school that is today the Moody Bible Institute.

It is said of him that his impact was primarily on middle-class Americans and that he established a pattern of concern for personal salvation with a relative indifference to social change that has continued to be characteristic of evangelical Christianity in America, but he believed social change would take place in the wake of individual conversions. Moody started his last crusade in Kansas City in November 1899, but fell ill a few days later and died the following month.

A reading from a sermon by D. L. Moody

I have met many people who have said to me: "Mr. Moody, I am glad to
see you with such faith; very glad to see you have that child-like trust in
God — very; but I am not so constituted. I can not have it." You believe
it, do you? I believe there is no man in the world so constituted but who
can believe in God's Word. He simply tells you to believe in Him, and He
will save you. Suppose a doctor said to me; "I want you to come to dinner with me to-morrow,. Mr. Moody." "Well," I reply, "I would feel great
pleasure in accepting your invitation, but I don't know how I will feel to-
morrow." "What is the matter?" he asks. "Well, the fact is, I don't know
how I will feel to-morrow," is my reply. "Why, you ain't sick, are you?"
"No, but — ah, the fact is, I am so constituted I can not believe you mean
to invite me." [Laughter]. You laugh at that; but you treat God's invitation
in a similar way. You are under the power of the devil. You can believe it if
you will. There's no ground for your doubting. What we want to do is each
one of us just to take God at His word. He has offered salvation to every
soul here; tell Him you will reach out your hand tonight and accept faith
in Him.

There is another class of people who are always trying to find out the
proper kind of faith. They want to search and discover a particular kind of
faith. Any kind of faith that brings you to Christ is the proper kind of faith;
is the right kind of faith. I remember Mr. Morehouse, while here four years
ago, used an illustration which has fastened itself on my mind. He said,
Suppose you go up the street and meet a man whom you have known for
the last ten years to be a beggar, and you notice a change in his appearance,
and you say, "Hallo, beggar, what's come over you?" "I ain't no beggar.
Don't call me a beggar!" "Why," you say, "I saw you the other day begging
in the street." "Ah, but a change has taken place," he replies. "Is that so;
how did it come about?" you inquire. "Well," he says, "I came out this
morning and got down here, intending to catch the businessmen and get all
the money out of them, when one of them came up to me and said there was
ten thousand dollars deposited for me." "How do you know this is true?"
you say. "I went to the bank and they put the money in my hand." "Are you
sure of that?" you ask "how do you know it was the right kind of a hand?"
But he says, "I don't care whether it was the right kind of a hand or not. I
got the money, and that's all I wanted." And so people are looking to see
if they've got the right kind of a hand before they accept God by it. They
have but to accept His testimony and they are saved, for, as John says, He
that hath received His testimony hath set his seal that God is true. Is there a
man in this assemblage who will receive His testimony and set his seal that
God is true? Proclaim that God speaks the truth. Make yourself a liar, but
make God's testimony truthful. Take Him at His word.

Some time ago I remember reading an incident that occurred between a prince in a foreign land and one of his subjects. This man for rebellion against the government was going to be executed. He was taken to the guillotine block. When the poor fellow reached the place of execution he was trembling with fear, The prince was present and asked him if he wished anything before judgment was carried out. The culprit replied: A glass of water. It was brought to him, but he was so nervous he couldn't drink it. Do not fear, said the prince to him, judgment will not be carried out till you drink that water, and in an instant the glass was dashed to the ground and broken into a thousand pieces. He took that prince at his word.

Oh sinner, take God at His word. He has promised to save you — to save all who trust Him. Now let us put away every false refuge, and just take the Prince of Heaven at His word. Is there a man or woman in this assemblage who will take Him at His word?

✪ *December 12*

Cornelia Hancock

QUAKER

February 8, 1840–December 31, 1927

She was 21 years old when the Civil War began but, although eager for adventure, Cornelia Hancock could not join her two brothers in the Union Army. She could, however, respond to her surgeon brother-in-law's invitation to help him in his medical work.

> A maternal grandmother of whom my father used to say, "No teakettle could pour fast enough to suit her without she tipped it over," was supposed to have supplied my brother and myself with ambition enough to overcome the inertia on the other side of the house, and after the War had been a hideous reality for two years and more, it seemed to me that the teakettle of life was pouring out very slowly indeed its scalding stream of anxiety, woe, and endless waiting. After my only brother and every male relative and friend that we possessed had gone to the War, I deliberately came to the resolution that I, too, would go and serve my country.

Hancock was rejected as an army nurse because of her youth and good looks, but went south on her own anyway. Without training, and within three weeks, she was in charge of the amputees in eight tents. Serving first at Gettysburg, then at the Battle of the Wilderness, she made such a place for herself, both with the army doctors and with her young patients, that she became known as the "Florence Nightingale of North America." She continued to serve in a Second Corps hospital until the fall of Richmond.

Among the problems the army was not prepared to deal with was that of the so-called "contrabands," or escaped Black slaves, who flocked to the Union troops. "Where are the people," Hancock asked in one of her letters home,

> who have been professing such strong abolition proclivity for the last thirty years? — certainly not in Washington laboring with these people whom they have been clamoring to have freed. They are freed now or at least many of them, and herded together in filthy rags, half clothed. And, what is worse than all, guarded over by persons who have not a proper sympathy for them.

"Now I can *see* all the abuses here plainly," she wrote in a other letter, "but to *remedy* them is the trouble."

> Many wise and good people visit here and exclaim, "*this must not be*," go away fully convinced they will do all in their power to rectify matters; go to some *military* functionary, who probably cares as little and less for a contraband than his riding horse. *He* informs them all is done for the contrabands that the government allows; *so* you might go to numerous military men and receive the same answer. I say all is *not* done for contrabands that government allows. The designs of the government are not carried out by subordinate authorities, And the only way ever to get justice done to these people is to separate the whole matter from the military authority, make a separate bureau, have men at the head of this bureau with living souls in them large enough to realize that a contraband is a breathing *human being* capable of being *developed*, if not so now.

Cornelia Hancock was a practical person and her religion was of a very practical sort. She wrote once to her sister, "I am this moment talking to the most silly kind of a Christian. He wishes to know if I have *experienced Religion?*"

After the war, Hancock set to work establishing schools for the freed slaves in the south. One of her achievements was the Laing School in Pleasantville, South Carolina, which is still functioning today. She spent ten years in South Carolina before journeying to England with friends to observe what was being done in London to deal with the growing problem of urban poverty. Returning to Philadelphia, she began to apply what she had learned in the poorer sections of that city. She and her brother, a doctor, created the Society for Organizing Charity, now known as the Family Society of Philadelphia. As a social worker, she became convinced that more must be done for children, so helped to found the Children's Aid Society and Bureau of Information. In the Society's minutes, she wrote:

> We have been anxious not only to do something, but to do it well: to guard the child and to guard society: to help the suffering little one of today, and not, at the same time, to create a pauper for tomorrow. We cannot reconcile it to an enlightened conscientiousness in charity to act without inquiry, blindly trusting that the kind motive will ensure beneficent results.

She had learned that with the army.

Housing also was a concern and she went to work to see what could be done to improve life in a slum area of Philadelphia called Wrightsville. Working with tenants and municipal authorities, she pioneered what might now be called a "holistic" approach that included plans for sanitation, public utilities, the school system, the library, a savings bank, and recreation. By 1914, every tenant had become his or her own landlord. Hancock's goal was always to enable people to help themselves.

✪ *December 13*

William Sloan Coffin, Jr.

PRESBYTERIAN

June 1, 1924–April 12, 2006

One of the most intriguing features of William Sloan Coffin's outspoken criticism of the misuse of American political and economic power is the fact that, for many years, he worked in the middle of that system. The Coffins were educated and prosperous, connected to important businesses and prestigious schools, and patrons of the arts. Young William was fluent in French and studied piano in Paris before World War II. At its outbreak, he returned to the U.S., where he eventually attended Yale and became a friend of George H. W. Bush. Coffin saw the rising Fascist regimes of Europe as dangerous to human freedom and dignity. He eagerly joined the war effort and was chosen by the army to serve as an intelligence officer.

Because of his linguistic skills Coffin became an official interpreter and translator with French and Soviet troops. Later, he joined the CIA during the Korean War in an effort to recruit and train people to undermine Soviet leadership. But Coffin lost faith in the agency in the early 1950s when he realized that it was working to overthrow the Iranian Prime Minister and to depose the leader of Guatemala. He became disheartened by what he saw as America's misuse of her power, especially the CIA as it was functioning then. His uncle, Henry Sloan Coffin,* had been one of the most famous liberal clergymen of the early 1900s. Coffin followed his path and was ordained in the Presbyterian Church. At the height of his professional career, he was the pastor of New York City's Riverside Church.

Coffin was a highly vocal and consistent defender of peace and civil rights. His deep commitment to justice often led him to take part in protests, and on several occasions he was jailed. He also helped organize and train volunteers for the Peace Corps. His orthodox theological understanding of Scripture illuminated his approach to social causes:

"Those who oppress the poor insult their Maker" (Prov. 14:31). But the hard question is, how are the poor to be helped — by charity or by justice, by voluntary contribution or by legislation? In the Book of Acts we read of the first Christian communities: "There was not a needy person among them, for as many as were possessors of lands or houses sold them...and distribution was made to each as any had need" (Acts 2:44–45). It was all voluntary. But those were small communities, charismatic, filled with the Holy Spirit, visited regularly by one apostle or another; their people were poor and far removed from the corrupting seats of power. Should we hold them up as models for the churches? Yes, by all means. Should we hold them up as a model for society at large? Alas, no.

Human nature is sinful, and therefore the virtue of the few will never compensate for the inertia of the many. Rich people and rich nations will not voluntarily open their eyes to see the biblical truth that the poor have ownership rights in their surplus. This they will see only in retrospect, after their surplus is taken away — by legislation hopefully, not by violence. Given human goodness, voluntary contributions are possible, but given human sinfulness, legislation is indispensable. Charity, yes always; but never as a substitute for justice. What we keep forgetting in this country is that people have rights, basic rights; the right to food; the right to decent housing; the right to medical care; the right to education. Food pantries like the one we have here at Riverside, and shelters for the homeless throughout the city, are painful reminders of how the richest country in the world still denies fundamental human rights to the poorest of its citizens.

His arguments for peace were straightforward and eloquent. Coffin opposed not just one particular war, but the whole concept of violence as a means to a better world:

The trouble with violence is that it changes not too much, but too little. Nonviolence is more radical because it is more truthful. Violence always ends up calling on lies to defend it, just as lies call on violence to defend them. By contrast, truth is naked, vulnerable, as Christ, its only weapon Christ's own, God's love. So the very love of God that found oppression, poverty, and corruption intolerable, this same love, rather than inflict suffering — even on those imposing it on the poor — took suffering upon itself. What can only be said cynically of another — "It is better that one man should die than that an entire nation perish." (ah, the demands of national security!) — can be said in utter truthfulness about oneself: "It is better that I should die rather than a single other person perish." That's finally how truth disarms and there is no better way.

Coffin's religious perspective will be sorely missed.

It's comforting to be bitter about evil — not creative, but comforting. It's also easy to blame everything on a tragedy. But in my experience most people give up on life not because of a tragedy, but because they no longer see joys worth celebrating; they do not see that human life, under any circumstances, never ceases to have meaning. Tragedy offers the opportunity to find new meaning and most of all to reevaluate what's important.

✪ December 14

Peter Bohler

MORAVIAN

December 31, 1712–April 27, 1775

A number of Christians have shaped the life and ethos of their respective denominations. It is less common to find one who influenced churches of other traditions as well. Peter Bohler's impact extended far beyond the Moravians he served. A German by birth, he was educated at the University of Jena. Bohler was affected by those leaders of the Pietist movement, Count von Zinzendorf and Johann George Walch. Pietism emphasized a deep, personal response to God's love in Christ. Zinzendorf's first act after being named a Moravian bishop in 1737 was to ordain Peter Bohler to the ministry. Bohler himself later became a bishop and traveled extensively both in England and America. He is responsible for founding several settlements of Moravians, including Nazareth, Pennsylvania.

Bohler strove to educate African Americans and sought out opportunities to evangelize slaves and Native Americans. Many obstacles stood in his way. Sometimes he suffered from fevers that weakened him so that he could not walk. The plantations he visited were far apart, while the slaves rarely had time, much less permission, to move freely from one place to another. The colonial governor, James Oglethorpe, had little interest in the whole endeavor and rebuffed Bohler's suggestions for a mission school in Savannah, forcing him to try to establish one far out from the city, which the children of slaves could reach only with great hardship. Bohler's partner in the work, George Schulius, died in 1739, leaving him with far too broad a territory to cover. He was not paid or reimbursed for expenses — yet another indication of Oglethorpe's resistance to the project. Finally, in January of 1740, Bohler decided to stop seeking official permission and simply go about his God-given task as he saw fit. In spite of all the barriers, he pressed on, founding and running schools and preaching the gospel. Eventually, his efforts bore good fruit.

Earlier in his life, Bohler had had an important meeting with the Wesley brothers. In 1738 he wrote to Zinzendorf:

> I traveled with the two brothers, John and Charles Wesley, from London to Oxford. The elder, John, is a good-natured man; he knew he did not properly believe on the Savior, and was willing to be taught. His brother, with whom you often conversed a year ago, is at present very much distressed in his mind, but does not know how he shall begin to be acquainted with the Savior.

Apparently, at this point, the Wesleys were still trying to earn God's favor. Bohler's evangelical and pietistic training taught him that God's grace was a free gift, which could not be won by works. The three men discussed this. Charles Wesley complained that Bohler was "unloving" and asked,

"Would he rob me of my endeavors? I have nothing else to trust to." As is well known, the Wesleys eventually embraced the liberating doctrine of justification by faith, and went on to establish the Methodist movement, now one of the largest Christian traditions in America.

Bohler's mission was to bring the love of God in Christ to all people in all circumstances. Despite Charles Wesley's initial assessment, there was a gentle pastoral aspect to his teaching. John Wesley, for example, writing in a February 1738 journal entry about his inner struggle to find a meaningful faith, determined that he would "leave off preaching. How can you preach to others, who have not faith yourself?" Many evangelists might agree, advising anyone so conflicted to cease teaching or leading until they found a deeper conviction. But Bohler's advice was of a more pastoral kind and led to a dramatic change in Wesley. He told him to "preach faith until you have it and then, because you have it, you will preach faith." Bohler could tell that Wesley's heart was eager for God and was confident that preaching would not leave him empty, dry, or hypocritical. He was right. Though other issues led Moravians and Methodists on different paths, both remained deeply immersed in the kind of passionate outreach that often flows from strongly held personal conviction and gratitude for God's mercy in Christ.

John Wesley and Peter Bohler remained close friends for the rest of their lives. Their connection may well have enhanced the relationship between the Methodists and the Moravians in the area of Savannah where the Moravians had an important ministry under Augustus Spangenberg,* and where John Wesley paid a visit during his mission to America. Bohler's commitment to be Christ's disciple and share his faith with others never wavered. While small in number, Moravian ministry, still reflecting Bohler's spirit, has touched and shaped countless Christians of other communities.

✸ *December 15* _____

David Low Dodge

PRESBYTERIAN

June 14, 1774–April 23, 1852

When David Low Dodge survived an attack of spotted fever in 1808, he emerged more deeply committed to his faith and regretted that he had not previously made some public witness against war. Until that time, pacifism had been largely the province of Quakers and Mennonites, but Dodge set about to increase its adherents in other denominations. In 1809, he composed a tract entitled "The Mediator's Kingdom not of this World" and attracted sufficient followers so that, by 1812, they were ready to form an interdenominational peace society, but the outbreak of another war made the time seem inauspicious, so they waited till the war was over. The New

York Peace Society, formed in 1815, was probably the first such organization in the world, and Dodge was its president.

David Low Dodge was born on a farm in Connecticut. Although his educational opportunities were limited, he became a schoolteacher when only 19 years of age. A decade later, he was dealing in dry goods in Hartford. Still later, he owned the first cotton factory built in Connecticut, and by 1807 he had started a wholesaling business in New York. He tucked peace tracts into the boxes of goods sent out from his store rooms. Dodge's prosperity enabled him to retire in 1827 to devote himself entirely to his various interests. He was one of the founders of the New York Bible Society and the New York Tract Society. In 1828, the New York Peace Society merged with similar organizations to form the first national peace association, the American Peace Society. Dodge served as its director and was a member of the executive committee until 1836.

Dodge's condemnation of war may have been inspired by the deaths of two half-brothers in the American Revolution, but he took the radical Christian perspective that all war — offensive, or defensive — was contrary to the gospel. Even personal self-defense was wrong. There is no idea more corrupt, more false, or more ruinous, Dodge contended, than doing evil to accomplish a good. "Now if war is in fact an evil," Dodge argued, "and it is prosecuted with a view to attain some good, then going to war is doing evil that good may come. It is therefore doing that which scandalizes Christian character; that which is wholly irreconcilable with the principles of the gospel, and which it is highly criminal for any man or nation to do." He also noted the economic consequences of war with its heavy impact on the poorest members of the community.

A reading from *War Inconsistent with the Religion of Jesus Christ* by David Low Dodge

It is admitted by all that war cannot exist without criminality somewhere, and generally where quarreling and strife are, there is blame on both sides. And how it is that many Christians who manifest a laudable zeal to expose and counteract vice and wickedness in various other forms are silent on the subject of War, silent as to those parts or practices of war which are manifestly and undisputably criminal, is to me mysterious. There has been a noble and persevering opposition against the inhuman and cruel practice of the slave trade; and by the blessing of God the efforts against it have been successful, probably, for the time, beyond the most sanguine expectations. When the lawfulness of this practice was first called in question, it was violently defended as well by professing Christians as by others. Comparatively few Christians fifty years ago doubted the propriety of buying and holding slaves; but now a man advocating the slave trade could hardly hold in this vicinity a charitable standing in any of the churches. But whence has arisen so great a revolution in the minds of the mass of professing Christians on this subject? It has happened not because the spirit or precepts of the gospel have changed, but because they are better understood.

Christians who have been early educated to believe that a doctrine is correct, and who cherish a respect for the instructions of their parents and teachers, seldom inquire for themselves, after arriving at years of maturity, unless something special calls up their attention; and then they are too apt to defend the doctrine they have imbibed before they examine it, and to exert themselves only to find evidence in its favor. Thus error is perpetuated from generation to generation until God, in his providence, raises up some to bear open testimony against it; and as it becomes a subject of controversy, one after another gains light, and truth is at length disclosed and established. Hence it is the solemn duty of every one, however feeble his powers, to bear open testimony against whatever error prevails, for God is able from small means to produce great effects.

There is at present in many of our churches a noble standard lifted up against the abominable sin of intemperance, the greatest evil, perhaps, war excepted, in the land, and this destructive vice has already received a check from which it will never recover unless Christians relax their exertions. But if war is a greater evil than drunkenness, how can Christians remain silent respecting it and be innocent? . . .

Most Christians believe that in the millennial day all weapons of war will be converted into harmless utensils of use, that wars will cease to the ends of the earth, and that the benign spirit of peace will cover the earth as the waters do the seas, But there will be then no new gospel, no new doctrines of peace; the same blessed gospel which we enjoy will produce "peace on earth and good will to men." And is it not the duty of every Christian now to exhibit the same spirit and temper which will be then manifested? If so, let every one "follow the things that make for peace," and the God of peace shall bless him.

✪ *December 16*

Francis Uplegger

LUTHERAN

October 29, 1867–June 19, 1964

Born in Raztosk, Germany, Francis Uplegger came to America at the age of 19 and received his theological education at Concordia Seminary in St. Louis, Missouri. Ordained as a pastor in July 1891 by the Lutheran Church–Missouri Synod, Uplegger's first call was to Saint John's Lutheran Church in Hermansfort, Wisconsin. Many European immigrants of that time came to the New World to pursue stability, success, and prosperity.

For some, however, the opportunity to do well meant also a commitment to do good. Uplegger had a promising career, but felt his calling to be service toward others.

It was actually Uplegger's son who, after ordination, first headed off to the San Carlos reservation in Arizona in 1917 to minister with the Apache. Two years later, the father decided to join his son, and he remained in that ministry until the end of his life. Adept at languages, Uplegger quickly learned to speak and write the Apache language. His native German, his adopted English, and his seminary Latin, Hebrew, and Greek had limited value to his parishioners, but they provided an excellent grounding in the principles of language. Lutherans consider that the living Word of God requires the ability to read and understand both written and spoken Scripture, liturgy, sermons, and songs. One of Uplegger's most important accomplishments was devising a written form of the Apache tongue and the compilation of the first Apache dictionary. He also wrote approximately 25 gospel hymns in Apache and translated several important Lutheran liturgical documents and portions of the Bible into their language.

Uplegger came to be known as The Venerable Missionary (or "Old Man Missionary") by the people on the reservation. He believed that the ministry of the white churches with Native Americans needed to address spiritual matters, not to see itself as primarily social work. Two-week mission trips to patch houses, bring clothes, or set up an infirmary are all worthy ways for wealthier congregations to serve, but people need a full time, fully committed pastoral presence and someone willing to live among them, see them as partners in ministry, and engage with their lives, day after day, year after year. Uplegger was willing to accept this challenge.

In addition to his religious labors, he helped the Apache in 1930 to 1931 to draft a constitution. The document proved useful enough to be used as a model for other indigenous peoples as they, too, drafted their own constitutions. Following Martin Luther's view of the "Two Kingdoms," Uplegger believed that a well-ordered society was as important in its sphere as a strong church and the preaching of the gospel.

Some people of European ancestry considered that the customs of native peoples were uncivilized and it was the duty of clergy and other people who dealt with them to teach them an improved culture, changing their clothing, houses, and language. Uplegger did not share these assumptions. Instead, he learned the native language so that he might tell his parishioners about the Good News. Like Martin Luther in the early 16th century, he wanted to communicate the story of Jesus in a way that indigenous people could grasp. Using their terminology and idioms, he was able to convey the gospel to them in a faithful and engaging way.

This issue is still relevant. Even in places where everyone speaks English, church members too often adopt locutions that impede access to the Good News. Not everyone knows the meaning of "lectionary" or "liturgy."

They do not necessarily understand terms like "Old and New Testament." Increasing numbers of people have almost no familiarity with biblical or religious references or imagery. We fool ourselves if we imagine we have overcome the prejudice of former generations, and often assume that the message of salvation is so precious that people worth their salt will make whatever effort is required to grasp it. We hold this view despite the resistance many of us had to our own religious upbringing, which has presented to us with as few hurdles as possible.

Uplegger understood that, as the emissary of Christ, it was up to him to remove as many impediments as he could from the clear proclamation of God's grace. There are enough unavoidable stumbling blocks to preaching the gospel without adding more. The good will, hard work and total commitment embodied by missionaries like Uplegger capture the spirit of Christ's self-giving ministry. If the gap between American Apaches and a German immigrant seems large, the love of Christ and a heart to serve formed a bridge of affection and mutuality.

The Missouri Synod recognized Uplegger's achievements in 1957 by awarding him a doctor of divinity degree from Concordia Theological Seminary. His pastoral care and steadfast commitment to the people of San Carlos remain a notable sign of Christian witness. He stayed with the people he had served so long, dying in San Carlos in 1964.

✪ *December 17* _____

Mary Lyon

CONGREGATIONAL

February 28, 1797–March 5, 1849

Mary Lyon lived during a tumultuous period in American history. She was a child during the infancy of the United States and grew up within all the excitement, danger, promise, and challenge of that era. Among the hotly debated issues of the emerging social and cultural mix that would become modern America, was the place of women. Very little tradition would survive intact from pre-revolutionary times, nor would a woman's place in the new nation continue as before.

Lyon was blessed with an inquisitive mind and a sturdy Christian upbringing. Born in 1797 in western Massachusetts, the sixth of eight children, her Christian roots went back to the earliest days of the colony. Although poor and raised on a farm — her father died when she was just five — Lyon grew up learning the skills necessary for a girl of her day: spinning, weaving, sewing, and farming. She always had a thirst for knowledge, especially in mathematics and the sciences.

She ferreted out opportunities to learn, studying geology, for example, by questioning a visiting geologist and making her own observations. A willing worker, she kept house for her brother after her mother remarried. In her teens she taught younger children, saving her money so she could continue her own education. At 20, she earned 75 cents a week plus board. Often she would snatch just four hours of sleep each day between work and study.

Although women had demonstrated their lively intellect in many spheres, still the male culture doubted that their intelligence was equipped for higher learning. Women had been running family businesses and farms, in some cases for generations and their skill at keeping these enterprises going was evident to all. But some still asked whether, even if some women were capable of mastering a liberal arts education, they or the larger community would actually benefit from this social change. The movement for greater freedom and inclusion for women in all realms of the new nation was growing; but tilling new ground is hard work in the face of firm resistance.

Lyon herself held several novel ideas. She believed that women should have the benefit of formal education, including college level study in arts, history, languages, sciences, mathematics and theology. A college just for women, she insisted, would bring great benefits to its students and their communities, because it could act as a training ground for them as missionaries to spread the Christian faith. This education should be available not just for those who could easily afford it, but for people of very modest means as well. Lyon's ideas went far beyond the vision of most of her contemporaries.

Furthermore, she possessed the intellect, faith, and perseverance to move ahead with her plans. Of course, even the most radical reformers build on influences from others. One of the schools Lyon had attended was operated by the Rev. Joseph Emerson. He actually "talked to ladies as if they had brains." In an age when women were thought to have second-rate minds, this was a real boost for Mary's morale. Emerson encouraged her to fulfill her dream of founding a school of higher learning for women.

Lyon's vision included providing affordable advanced education for people who were considered by the elite to be "common." Her own journey from a poor farm through higher learning convinced her that others should be given the same opportunity. An institution's costs could be kept down by having the students themselves do much of the physical labor and upkeep. Her primary goal, however, was to nurture the Christian faith of her students. Lyon wanted to inspire her pupils with a willingness to bear witness to their faith, and a commitment to follow whatever calling God, in gracious providence, might give them.

With gifts from Christian contributors, Lyon opened her school but refused suggestions that it should bear her name. America's oldest college for women, Mount Holyoke Female Seminary, opened in South Hadley, Massachusetts, on November 8, 1836. Its motto was taken from Psalm 144:12, "That our daughters may be as cornerstones, polished after the similitude of a palace."

Lyon served as Mt. Holyoke's principal for its first 12 years, providing a model of excellence and Christian living throughout her tenure. Her vision of a world that offered women the same opportunities as men is far from achieved, but Mount Holyoke and all the colleges established through similar convictions have moved us far beyond the limitations her indomitable spirit had to overcome.

A reading from letters by Mary Lyon

When all human help & human wisdom fail, & all knowledge of future events. As connected with present causes, & present actions, seems entirely cut off, how sweet it is to go to the One, who knows all from the beginning to the end — the One who can direct our very thoughts, & who can take us individually by the hand, & lead us in a plain path. Everything appears to me as dark as Egyptian darkness, only as I turn my thoughts to Him, who is the fountain of light. I dare not pray for anything in particular, only that the will of the Lord may be done — that all interested in this new institution may be so humble & so submissive, that his will towards this enterprise may be done, as it is done towards those on whom he smiles, & not as it is done towards those whom he chastens & afflicts. My daily feeling is "Lord thou knowest — not my will but thine be done."

How often have I endeavored to consecrate all the part, all the interests, which God has given me in this complicated institution, most sacredly & solemnly to his service, & how often have I endeavored to pray, that every one, who had any thing to do in building up this institution, may never call aught his own. O that every one, who puts a finger to the work, by giving the smallest contribution of time — of money — or of influence, might feel that this is a work of solemn consecration — a work to be reviewed by the light of eternity. May the Lord so direct all, who shall bear a part in forming the character of this institution, that no considerations, shall have any influence except those which will bear the scrutiny of eternity.

✪ *December 18*

William Reed Huntington

EPISCOPALIAN

September 20, 1838–July 26, 1909

During the latter half of the 19th century, most American churches were preoccupied with expansion on the western frontier and the mission fields overseas. In addition to these concerns, the Episcopal Church was preoccupied with a division between those churchmen who emphasized catholicity and those who identified themselves as evangelicals. William Reed Huntington proposed a broader vision of Christian unity in which the great majority of Americans might come together in an American national church. In an 1870 book, *The Church Idea,* and in other writings and speeches he projected four standards for such a church: "the Bible as, in a special sense, God's book, the faith...of the Apostle's Creed,...the sacraments of Christ's appointment...and a ministry which shall be worth its mint-mark everywhere." The ministry he envisioned as everywhere accepted would be validated through the historic succession of bishops from the time of the apostles. In somewhat modified form, this proposal was adopted by the General Convention of the Episcopal Church in 1886 as a basis for unity with other Christians, and by the Lambeth Conference of the worldwide Anglican Communion in 1888. It continues to provide a focus for ecumenical discussions and relationships.

Huntington was rector for many years at Grace Church in Manhattan and was a leading figure at the General Convention for 36 years. In addition to his work for Christian unity, he is remembered for his social concerns, his efforts to revive the ancient order of deaconesses, and his work toward the first revision of the American Book of Common Prayer. Reestablishing deaconesses in 1889 proved to be an important first step toward the eventual full recognition of women's ordination. The revised Prayer Book, adopted in 1892, provided a flexibility unknown in previous editions.

A reading from a sermon entitled "The Talisman of Unity" preached by William Reed Huntington at the Cathedral of St. John the Divine in New York City in 1899

No ecclesiastical advantage, no historical prestige, no well-fortified quadrilateral will ever make this Church in which you and I believe the reconciling power we long to see her become, until the spirit of sacrifice and of sympathy shall possess her as it has never possessed her yet. In order to fulfill the priest's office to one's fellow-man, one must have learned how to suffer, and until Almighty God shall have disciplined us as a Church out of every slightest remnant of self-sufficiency we need never hope to win the beatitude of them that make peace.

I heard a returned missionary tell, not long ago, of a sermon which he had listened to from the lips of a native preacher. The topic was the wounded side of Christ.

"I believe," said the preacher, "in the wounded side of Christ, for I have seen it, seen it as really as the Apostle Thomas saw it after the resurrection. I saw it the other day as my eyes rested on the countenance of that aged Australian mother who, when told that her two daughters, missionaries in China, had both of them been murdered by a heathen mob, said, 'This decides me; I will go to China now, myself, and try to teach those poor creatures what the love of Jesus means.'"

And these were Methodists, dear friends, Methodists all; there is not an Anglican in the story. And the Methodists you know, are people with whom we, as Churchmen, have ecclesiastically no dealings, no, not any more than the Jews had with the Samaritans. We are not quite sure that they are sound on the question of the undisputed General Councils. All the same, these particular Methodists understood the language in which the angels in heaven talk, and woe be to the cause of church unity in America unless we can all of us learn that dialect.

The old mystics, you remember, used to trace a connection between

> The water and the blood
> From that riven side which flowed,

and the two sacraments which minister to the common life of the Church, and make it organically one; but whether we get at it by inner vision, as the Hindoo preacher did, or sacramentally, with the mystics, let us get at it, for in that wounded side of Christ, lies the talisman of unity.

✪ *December 19* _____

Richard Rust

METHODIST

1815–1906

In 1866, 100 years before the 1960s freedom riders went south, Richard Rust and his companions made the journey to realize a long-held dream: creating a college for African Americans in the heart of the south. They came to Holly Springs, a little town in Mississippi, and started a school in the local Methodist Church. Adults and children alike were accepted for instruction in basic subjects. The next year, the school was able to move to a campus of its own and three years after that, it was chartered by the state of Mississippi. Today, Rust College — named in honor of its founder — is an accredited four-year, co-educational college, and the oldest of 11 historically black colleges and universities related to the United Methodist Church.

Rust understood the value of an education and how difficult it could be to obtain one. Orphaned at the age of nine, he had been apprenticed to a cabinet-maker. Apprenticeships usually lasted seven years, but by saving his earnings, Rust bought out the remaining years of his contract. He enrolled in Phillips Academy, but, inspired by an antislavery lecture, he formed an abolitionist group that offended the school authorities. Expelled from Phillips, he then traveled to New Hampshire and entered Noyes Academy, which was open to both races. Local abolitionists who sponsored the school thought that all young people should have access to an education. Unfortunately, other residents did not. Fearing the possibility of interracial dating, they pulled the building off its foundations and burned it on the village green. The students barely escaped. Rust next moved to Wilbraham, Massachusetts, joining Wesleyan Academy, which was operated by the New England Conference of the Methodist Episcopal Church. Many of its faculty and students were opposed to slavery. He became a Methodist in Wilbraham and went on to Wesleyan University in Middletown, Connecticut. Rust earned money while a student by giving antislavery lectures, and in his junior year, he published *Freedom's Gift,* an anthology of poems and essays by abolitionist writers.

After college, Rust served several congregations in Massachusetts and New Hampshire and became principal of the church's seminary in New Hampshire for a term. But his interests continued to focus on the legacy of slavery. In 1858, he established Wilberforce University in Cincinnati, named for the noted English abolitionist and dedicated to the needs of former slaves. Rust served as chairman of its Board of Trustees, cooperating with the black leadership of both Baptist and Methodist churches. Five years later, the new school was sold to the African Methodist Episcopal Church and Bishop Daniel Payne* became the first African American university president. Rust went on to play a leading role in the founding of some 14 colleges for teachers throughout the south. By 1882, it was estimated that teachers from these schools had taught some three-quarters of a million African American children.

A reading from *The Anti-slavery Enterprise, Its Object and Aims* by Richard Rust

The object of the Anti-Slavery enterprise is to annihilate the bloody system of American Slavery, which is scattering its pestiferous breath ever the brightest prospects of human happiness. It contemplates the complete overthrow of that system, feebly styled by a southern clergyman, "the concocted essence of fraud, tyranny, and cold-hearted avarice." Were this the acme of its injustice it might be endured; but it stops not here. It wages a furious war upon the government of Jehovah, by dragging down man, monarch of the earth, possessor of an immortal nature, to a level with the brute creation; crushes his intellect and whelms him in despair. It forbids millions for whose redemption Christ sweat great drops of blood, to gaze upon the soul-cheering pages of Divine Truth, the lamp given by God to direct man's wayward steps through this world of sin and oppression, up to eternal felicity. It breaks up the sacred and endeared relations of husband and wife, parent and child. Slavery will not permit the child even to sustain the tottering limbs of its aged and infirm parents, nor to wipe away the trickling tear of anguish from the furrowed, care-worn brow of her who gave him existence. It will not permit the husband to protect the companion of his bosom from the base assaults of any heartless, licentious person. He is compelled to endure, without a murmur, the excruciating torture and agony of seeing her, around whom all his affections cluster, insulted, whipped, defiled, and even to have the tender cords of his heart rent asunder, and the purest affections of the soul outraged by an eternal separation.

This is the horrid system which the Abolitionists are attempting to bury in the dark shades of oblivion; and we hope to succeed in heaping such a mountain of disgrace and detestation upon it, that it may never have a resurrection. Shall slavery forever bloom on the soil of the Pilgrims, and fatten on human tears, and groans, and suffering? May Heaven forbid! May the friends of bleeding humanity forbid! May the oceans of blood and tears which slavery has caused, be dried up. Human yokes *must* be burned, and the galling fetters sundered, and the millions of American bondmen shall yet stand forth disenthralled. This enterprise has strong claims upon our sympathy. Man is a creature of sympathy; God created him thus. Sympathy is a sort of mental magnetism, which attracts and blends the different members of the human family, in one *grand brotherhood*. . . . Are the hearts of American Christians, so hard that they cannot be moved by the intense sufferings of our oppressed brethren? Do not the sighs and the groans, which come floating along on the southern breezes, affect the people of the north? Oh that the plantations of the south, drenched with the captive's tears and blood, could break their eternal silence, and thunder forth in your ears, the story of the negroes' wrongs! Oh that the cruel, bloody lash of the slave-driver's whip, could whisper in your ears, the heart-rending sufferings of the slaves! Oh that the crushed and bleeding soul, could depict the unutterable agonies, which slavery has inflicted upon its deathless nature!! We should not be able to endure such overwhelming testimony. We have a faint delineation of "Slavery as it is," by our [Theodore] Weld;* and human nature can scarcely survive the shock. Do not American slaves have strong claims upon our sympathy? If we have hearts so hard, that they cannot feel for others woe, let us tear them out, and let the eagles glut on them; why should we cherish hearts which are as cold and unfeeling as a chilling iceberg!

✠ *December 20*

Iakov Georgevich Netsvetov

ORTHODOX

1802–July 26, 1864

In a span of less than two years, Iakov Netsvetov lost his wife and father and his house burned to the ground with most of his personal possessions. These catastrophes would have been hard to bear under any circumstances. The situation was exacerbated by the fact that Netsvetov was living on a lonely island in the Aleutians. When he asked the Orthodox bishop for permission to enter a monastery in Irkutsk, a substantial community on the Siberian coast of the Sea of Japan, the request was granted contingent on a replacement for his work being found. But who could replace Iakov Netsvetov? He was the only Orthodox priest of mixed Russian and Aleut parentage, invaluable as a translator of Scriptures and liturgy into Aleut languages and dialects. He traveled a vast territory, 2,000 miles long, familiar with the customs of the people and able to make himself understood

Netsvetov remained at his post in Atka for seven more years before his bishop appointed him to the Yukon Delta region as a missionary. There he remained for two decades, enduring the hardships of a desolate frontier. Frequently reduced to subsistence living, he began to suffer from a number of chronic illnesses. Assistants were sent to work with him, but sometimes the assistants caused further problems. One had been sent to America because his Russian abbot wanted him out of the monastery. Before many weeks had passed, the man attacked Netsvetov, first with a pistol and then an ax. He was bound hand and foot and locked away until he could be sent back to his monastery. Another assistant, who was finally declared insane, became convinced that Netsvetov was trying to poison him and made criminal accusations against his supervisor.

Yet Netsvetov faithfully carried on his ministry, building new churches, translating the Scripture and liturgy into new languages and dialects, and working for peace between warring tribes. Impoverished and nearly blind, he died at the age of 62 and was buried near his wife in Sitka. Declared a saint by the Orthodox Church in 1994, he is venerated as "St. Jacob, Enlightener of the Peoples of Alaska."

A reading from the journal of Iakov Georgevich Netsvetov

Hospitality flourishes both amongst the Aleuts and the Kadiaks. The latter (Kadiaks) demonstrate the moral nature of their care for people who may be travelling and who, consequently, might run short if food. Whenever they leave the house the Kadiaks always leave something to eat in the dwelling. The owners are obliged to supply any guest who might arrive with food supplies with which to continue their journey.

But what is especially attractive in both the Aleuts and the Kadiaks is their complete readiness to share their last crust with anyone in need. If, for example, it happens that many people have had bad luck with their hunting and one of them has managed to catch something, then the more fortunate, learning that his neighbors are in need, without waiting for any request on their part, will divide his catch equally with the others and his portion will be no greater than anyone else's; and if it should happen that anyone is accidentally left out during this share-out, then the owner of the catch will give even this person something out of his own share. Such behavior, so worthy of imitation on the part of civilized people, can hardly be ascribed to calculation, to mere self-interest. To us, at least, this seems the appearance of an inner moral law, inscribed in the hearts of men by the Creator of the universe. Both savagery and false civilization cover with a thick skin of sin what is written in the inner recesses of the heart. Take away this skin and the spark of God's truth is visible.

March 25: [1849]

On the Feast Day of the All Holy Theotokos through God's Grace — celebrated the divine services, as is proper, and I performed the Liturgy in the field church, in the tent. In the course of the liturgy the 54 persons who have made confession partook of the Holy Mysteries, and in addition a considerable number of infants. The warm weather permitted me to hold services in the tent without hindrance, but wet snow continued to fall throughout the day, the same as yesterday. At the evening service, I offered the final instruction to the communicants, and then I released [from further obligations] so that they are free to depart home as needed.

Remark:

I am able to say that I finished this engagement with these [people] who fasted with a deep sense of Spiritual joy. First of all, they came in response to my first invitation to prepare themselves for communion, agreed willingly, and commenced to pray, not as it was in the years past. And this, in spite of the fact that nowadays they are especially pressed by their own affairs, that is, the need for daily excursions to forage for subsistence because of the shortage of food. Secondly, in the course of each service they came diligently, in spite of the bad weather, slush, and wetness, which was especially bad on the days of confession and communion. During the services they stood, without any sign of boredom, and listened attentively to the sermon. Throughout the entire morning service and the Liturgy, which were performed in strict observance of the [church] rule.

The Liturgy, consequently, was rather prolonged; they stood in the tent, which due to the heavy wet snow was leaking, and in spite of being dripped on, they remained through the entire service and came to the Holy Mysteries in good order, as is proper, decorously, carrying their infants,

One may say they came with zeal, and accepted everything with understanding which was expressed in their faces. This, this is what makes me joyous! Glory to God for this!

✪ *December 21*

John Woolman

QUAKER

October 19, 1720–October 7, 1772

In the 17th century, Quakers took part in the slave trade as other members of society did, but George Fox began to protest the practice in 1671, and opposition to it grew steadily among the Friends. John Woolman, who led the fight against the slave trade among American Quakers, grew up on a farm in a Quaker family and worked as a clerk in a New Jersey store as a young man. When asked to make out a bill of sale for a slave, he became convinced of the evil of slavery and shortly after that he began to travel up and down the east coast so that he could witness to other Quakers on the matter. He made his journeys on foot whenever possible, wore undyed garments, and avoided, insofar as he could, use of products made by slave labor. Although often called on to help people write their wills, he refused to do so if slaves were to be passed on to the next generation. Often he was able to persuade the owners to amend their wills in this respect and set their slaves free. His journeys spread opposition to slavery through the Society of Friends so that, not long after his death, the practice of slavery had ceased among them. Until the Civil War, they remained the only Christian denomination entirely opposed to slavery.

Woolman also worked to curtail the sale of rum to Native Americans and to develop a more just land policy. At 36, he began to keep a journal, a record of the inner life of the spirit, continuing to make entries until the year he died. It has been said that John Woolman's "purity of motive, breadth of sympathy, and clear spiritual insight" give him "a place among the uncanonized saints of America."

A reading from *The Journal of John Woolman*

Scrupling to do writings relative to keeping slaves has been a means of sundry small trials to me, in which I have so evidently felt my own will set aside that think it good to mention a few of them. Tradesmen and retailers of goods, who depend on their business for a living, are naturally inclined to keep the good will of their customers; nor is it a pleasant thing for young men to be under any necessity to question the judgment or honesty of elderly men, and more especially of such as have a fair reputation. Deep-rooted customs, though wrong, are not easily altered; but it is the duty of all to be firm in that which they certainly know is right for them. A charitable, benevolent man, well acquainted with a negro, may, I believe, under some circumstances, keep him in his family as a servant, on no other motives than the negro's good; but man, as man, knows not what shall be after him, nor hath he any assurance that his children will attain to that perfection in wisdom and goodness necessary rightly to exercise such power; hence it is clear to me, that I ought not to be the scribe where wills are drawn in which some children are made masters over others during life.

About this time an ancient man of good esteem in the neighborhood came to my house to get his will written. He had young negroes, and I asked him privately how he purposed to dispose of them. He told me; I then said, "I cannot write thy will without breaking my own peace," and respectfully gave him my reasons for it. He signified that he had a choice that I should have written it, but as I could not, consistently with my conscience, he did not desire it, and so he got it written by some other person. A few years after, there being great alterations in his family, he came again to get me to write his will. His negroes were yet young, and his son, to whom he intended to give them, was since he first spoke to me, from a libertine become a sober young man, and he supposed that I would have been free on that account to write it. We had much friendly talk on the subject, and then deferred it. A few days after he came again and directed their freedom, and I then wrote his will. . . .

Having found drawings in my mind to visit Friends on Long Island, after obtaining a certificate from our Monthly Meeting, I set off 12th of fifth month, 1756. The Lord, I believe, hath a people in those parts who are honestly inclined to serve him; but many I fear, are too much clogged with the things of this life, and do not come forward bearing the cross in such faithfulness as he calls for.

My mind was deeply engaged in this visit, both in public and private, and at several places where I was, on observing that they had slaves, I found myself under a necessity, in a friendly way, to labor with them on that subject; expressing, as way opened, the inconsistency of that practice with the purity of the Christian religion, and the ill effects of it manifested amongst us.

The latter end of the week their Yearly Meeting began; and in a meeting of ministers and elders way opened for me to express in some measure what lay upon me; and when Friends were met for transacting the affairs of the church, having sat awhile silent, I felt a weight on my mind, and stood up; and through the gracious regard of our Heavenly Father, strength was given fully to clear myself of a burden which for some days had been increasing upon me. . . .

I saw at this time that if I was honest in declaring that which truth opened in me, I could not please all men; and I labored to be content in the way of my duty, however disagreeable to my own inclination;

Until this year, 1756, I continued to retail goods, besides following my trade as a tailor; about which time I grew uneasy on account of my business growing too cumbersome. I had begun with selling trimmings for garments, and from thence proceeded to sell cloths and linens; and at length, having got a considerable shop of goods, my trade increased every year, and the way to large business appeared open but I felt a stop in my mind.

Through the mercies of the Almighty, I had, in a good degree, learned to be content with a plain way of living. I had but a small family; and, on serious consideration, believed truth did not require me to engage much in cumbering affairs. It had been my general practice to buy and sell things really useful. Things that served chiefly to please the vain mind in people, I was not easy to trade in; seldom did it; and whenever I did I found it weaken me.

✪ December 22

Mahalia Jackson

BAPTIST

October 26, 1912–January 27, 1972

The praise of God in song and the proclamation of the gospel in music is one of the Christian church's best gifts to the world. Born in New Orleans, daughter of a Baptist preacher, and living next to a Holiness congregation, Mahalia Jackson knew both the power of the Word and of music. Some of her family were musical entertainers, and the whole culture of her city was rich with rhythms and melodies. Blues, ragtime, jazz and gospel music rang through the air. In her autobiography *Movin' On Up,* Jackson told how she moved to Chicago in 1928. Just 16 at the time, she attended the Greater Salem Baptist Church, which had both a regular choir and a group called the Johnson Gospel Singers. Jackson belonged to both. While she loved her opportunities to sing, she never imagined it might be a way of making a living. Her goal at that time was to become a nurse, but meanwhile she worked to support herself as a cosmetician, eventually opening her own beauty shop. In 1936, she married Isaac Hockenhull, who encouraged her business plans. It did not take him long, however, to realize the potential in Jackson's musical gifts. Though this marriage did not survive, nor did Jackson abandon her gospel roots for more lucrative styles, she moved out from her local parish to a wider audience.

At Hockenhull's urging, she tried out for a part in a Gilbert and Sullivan production and was offered both the role and a recording contract with the Decca label to sing blues professionally. She refused both offers, wanting to sing in the gospel tradition. Even Louis Armstrong encouraged her to consider a high-paying blues career. He is reported to have told her: "Got you a spot with the band, make you some real green, get to move around. You don't have to show me, I know what you can do with the blues." Jackson responded, "I know what I can do with it too, baby, and that's not sing it. Child, I been reborn!"

Gospel music was her love, and she was not at all reluctant to expand her horizons in the field of African American church music. In 1937, Thomas A. Dorsey, the "Father of Gospel Music," became Jackson's musical advisor and accompanist. His tunes and lyrics and her vocal talent were a natural match. He composed — she sang. They were coveted additions to a growing number of church gatherings. Popular music was trying on new styles, and Jackson's soulful performances helped gospel music become part of the wider American cultural landscape. People who never set foot in a church would eagerly listen to her songs about God's love and grace and the believer's peace and joy.

Despite the reluctance of some sophisticated northerners to accept her earthy, vibrant style, Jackson was appointed official soloist to the National Baptist Convention in 1947. She managed to incorporate a more lively, upbeat tempo into the classic hymns of faith so beloved of her tradition. Outside African American houses of worship, audiences clamored to hear gospel music. Along with new arrangements of old favorites and new Dorsey songs, Jackson sang a moving rendition of W. Herbert Brewster's "Move On Up a Little Higher." When she cut a record of it on the Apollo label, it sold over two million copies. Success made it possible for her to seek out other talented composers and to make more frequent public appearances. Titles such as "I Can Put My Trust in Jesus" and "Let the Power of the Holy Ghost Fall On Me" by Kenneth Morris brought international recognition both to her and to the music. Millions of white Americans would delight in both Jackson herself and the music she offered as they sat in front of their television sets watching the Ed Sullivan Show on Sunday nights.

For Jackson, all this attention was not so much about money, fame, or entertainment as about social and political issues. She was a featured singer at the inauguration of John F. Kennedy in 1961. Jackson and Martin Luther King, Jr.,* were also mutual admirers. She gave a powerful performance of "How I Got Over," one of Pastor Brewster's well-known songs, at the 1963 march on Washington, the occasion of King's "I Have a Dream" speech. Her choice of music at many other venues was laced with songs that made the connection between faith and justice. At King's funeral, she paid him the tribute of singing Dorsey's "Precious Lord, Take My Hand." She began adding "We Shall Overcome" to most of her concerts. Her strong support of King's movement and the Southern Christian Leadership Conference (SCLC) added a musical dimension to the rallies that spoken words, even from as evocative a speaker as Dr. King, could not have conveyed.

Jackson's talent and dedication earned her the high praise of a nation and the world. It also provided her with a substantial income. Concerned about the next generation, she founded the Mahalia Jackson Scholarship Foundation, a philanthropy designed to encourage and support young people needing financial help to pay for college. Jackson is one of those fortunate people who could, by doing what she loved, give the combined gifts of music and grace to the world.

✛ *December 23* _____

William Leddra

QUAKER

?–March 24, 1661

The court that condemned him to death confessed that it "found no evil in him," but he was a Quaker: he refused to take off his hat, he used words like "thee" and "thou." For this offensive behavior, he had been several times whipped, imprisoned, and banished. Yet he had returned to Boston after being forbidden to do so. He was the fourth and last Quaker to be hanged for these offences.

Puritans and Quakers didn't mix. The Puritans had been persecuted in England for asserting that the Anglican Reformation had not gone far enough. They had traveled to the New World, enduring great hardship, to establish the purified church for which they had longed. But now they were being visited by the Quakers who insisted on attempting to persuade them that their reformation also had not gone far enough. There was no need, the Quakers argued, for an ordained ministry or an official church or even the Bible. It was enough to be guided by the light within. Christ, they insisted, could be known intimately as a friend without the need of religious rituals. When Quakers arrived by ship in the Massachusetts Bay Colony, they were arrested and sent back, but some of them found a base in Rhode Island from which they could enter Boston easily. With the same determination the Puritans had shown in establishing their colony, the Quakers insisted on bearing witness to their revolutionary doctrine.

How could the Puritans tolerate this deliberate disturbing of their peace? In 1656, they passed the first laws to deal with the problem and explained clearly and reasonably why such laws were necessary:

> Whereas there is a cursed sect of haereticks lately risen up in the world, which are commonly called Quakers, who take uppon them to be immediately sent of God, and infallibly assisted by the spirit to speake and write blasphemouth opinions, despising government and the order of God in church and commonwealth, speaking evill of dignities, reproaching and reviling magistrates and ministers, seeking to turne the people from the faith and gaine proselytes to theire pernicious waies, this Court, taking into serious consideration the premises, and to prevent the like mischiefe as by their meanes is wrought in our native land, doth hereby order, and by the authoritie of this Court be it ordered and enacted, that any commander of a vessel that shall bring into this jurisdiction any knowne Quaker or Quakers, or any other blasphemous haereticks as aforesaid, shall pay the fine of 100 pounds, except it appeare that he wanted true knowledge or information of theire being such; . . . then to give bonds to carry them to the place whence he brought them.
>
> Any Quaker coming into this jurisdiction shall be forthwith committed to the house of correction, and at their entrance to be severely whipt, and by the master thereof to be kept constantly to worke, and none suffered to converse or speak with them during the time of their imprisonment, which shall be no longer than necessitie requireth.

When these laws proved ineffective, sterner measures were taken. Quakers were arrested, beaten, and banished. Some were lashed behind carts, others marched deep into the forest and abandoned, still others branded with "H" for heretic. Some had their tongues bored through with hot irons, while others had their ears cut off. When such severity did not stop them from returning to preach their strange gospel, Governor John Endicott finally saw no alternative to calling for the death penalty. Between 1659 and 1661, four Quakers were hanged in Boston.

Leddra had been banished and told not to return, but human authority could not deny the guidance of the spirit. He returned in 1660, was arrested, and kept in an unheated cell, chained to a log, through the winter. On the morning of March 24, the day appointed for his execution, Leddra wrote a letter to his wife speaking of joy and love:

> Most Dear and Inwardly Beloved,
> The sweet influences of the Morning Star,
> like a Flood distilling into my Innocent Habitation,
> Hath filled me with the joy of [God]
> in the Beauty of Holiness, that my Spirit is,
> as if it did not Inhabit a Tabernacle of Clay....
>
> Oh! My Beloved,
> I have waited as a Dove at the Windows of the Ark,
> and I have stood still in that Watch...,
> wherein my Heart did rejoyce,
> that I might in the Love and Life speak a few Words to you
> sealed with the Spirit of Promise,
> that the Taste thereof might be a Savour of Life
> to your Life, and a Testimony in you,
> of my Innocent Death....

When he was brought out to be hanged, Leddra said, "For bearing my testimony for the Lord against deceivers and the deceived, I am brought here to suffer." And then he said, "Lord Jesus, receive my spirit." When the body was cut down, Robert Harper, a prominent Boston Quaker caught it in his arms. For showing such respect for his dead friend, Harper and his wife were banished themselves. Nevertheless, the Quakers had made their point: perhaps the community could not tolerate their disruptive behavior, but neither could it tolerate such violence toward peaceful citizens. Not long afterward, King Charles II put a stop to the executions.

✪ *December 24*

Phillips Brooks

EPISCOPALIAN

December 13, 1835–January 23, 1893

The most renowned preacher of his day and one of the greatest in the history of the American church, Phillips Brooks is now remembered primarily for his authorship of the popular Christmas carol, "O Little Town of Bethlehem."

For 22 years, he was rector of Trinity Church, Boston, and then for two years at the end of his life he was Bishop of Massachusetts.

Brooks grew up in the evangelical wing of the Episcopal Church, but after his ordination, he led the "Broad Church Movement," a reaction against the growing Anglo-Catholic movement on one hand and the narrowness of evangelical theology on the other. Science, and the theory of evolution in particular, seemed to the Broad Church school to require Christian thinkers to bring the church and the modern world into a creative relationship.

Brooks remained evangelical in many ways, though rejecting much of the dogmatic structure he had inherited. Some accused him of leaning toward Unitarianism, but this was unjust. Although an "apostle of tolerance," he was deeply committed to the basic doctrines of the Christian faith. It seemed to him that true tolerance began with a deeper spirituality, he was impatient with narrowness and the claim that other religions held no truth. He faulted literal interpretations of the Bible, the view that salvation was primarily an escape from eternal punishment, a narrow theory of the atonement, and what he saw as a limited theology of the incarnation and the person of Christ. The truth of the incarnation, beautifully expressed in "O Little Town of Bethlehem," was at the center of his life and thought and preaching. He said his faith was in "not Christianity but Christ; not a doctrine, but a person."

A reading from "The Light of the World," a sermon by Phillips Brooks

Here lies the sublime and beautiful variety of human life. It is as beings come to their reality that they assert their individuality. In the gutter all the poor wretches lie huddled together, one indistinguishable mass of woe; but on the mountain-top each figure stands out separate and clear against the blueness of the sky. The intense variety of Light! The awful monotony of Darkness! Men are various; Christians ought to be various a thousand-fold. Strive for your best, that there you may find your most distinctive life. We cannot dream of what interest the world will have when every being in its human multitude shall shine with his own light and color, and be the child of God which it is possible for him to be, — which he has ever been in the true home-land of his Father's thought.

Do I talk fancies? Do I paint visions upon unsubstantial clouds? If it seem to you that I do, I beg you to come back now, as I close, to those words which I quoted to you at the beginning. "I am the Light of the World," said Jesus. Do you not see now what I meant when I declared that it was in making the world know itself that Christ was primarily the Power of the World's Redemption The Revealer and the Redeemer are not two persons, but only one, — one Saviour.

What then? If Christ can make you know yourself; if as you walk with Him day by day, He can reveal to you your sonship to the Father; if, keeping daily company with Him you can come more and more to know how native is goodness and how unnatural sin is to the soul of man; if, dwelling with Him who is both God and Man, you can come to believe both in God and in Man through Him, then you are saved, — saved from contempt, saved from despair, saved into courage and hope and charity and the power to resist temptation, and the passionate pursuit of perfectness.

It is as simple and as clear as that. Our religion is not a system of ideas about Christ. It is Christ. To believe in Him is what? To say a creed? To join a church? No; but to have a great, strong, divine Master, whom we perfectly love, whom we perfectly trust, whom we will follow anywhere, and who, as we follow Him or walk by His side, is always drawing out in us our true nature and making us determined to be true to Him through everything, is always compelling us to see through falsehood and find the deepest truth, which is, in one great utterance of it, that we are the sons of God, who is thus always "leading us to the Father." The hope of the world is in the ever richer naturalness of the highest life. "The earth shall be full of the knowledge of God as the waters cover the sea." Your hope and mine is the same. The day of our salvation has not come till every voice brings us one message; till Christ, the Light of the world, everywhere reveals to us the divine secret of our life; till everything without joins with the consciousness all alive within, and "the Spirit Itself beareth witness with our spirits that we are the children of God."

✪ December 25 _____

Lottie Moon

BAPTIST

December 12, 1840–December 24, 1912

It may have been her father's death when she was 13 that turned Lottie Moon into a rebellious and defiant teenager, uninterested in the church, but when a friend at college invited her to a missionary meeting, she realized how unattractive her behavior was, spent the night in prayer, and decided to become a missionary. It was the great age of missionary work in China, but there was constant tension with the Chinese authorities who were resisting the colonizing impulses of western powers. Nevertheless, once Lottie Moon made up her mind, she was not to be dissuaded. "If I had a thousand lives, I would give them all for the women of China," she said. And some 40 years later, she did.

After earning one of the first masters degrees given a woman by a southern college, Lottie taught for a few years in a girl's school she helped found in a poor area of Georgia. Southern Baptist policy had prevented single women from missionary work, but as soon as that policy was relaxed, Moon sailed for China arriving in Tonchow, northern China, on October 7, 1873. Suspicious of foreigners, the Chinese rejected her first efforts to break down barriers. When she offered them home-baked cookies, they refused, thinking they were poisoned. So she began to knit and sew for them, and this awakened some interest among the Chinese women. Realizing that women were best approached by others of their sex, she pleaded with the mission board to recruit other women and send them.

Moon began her ministry by teaching in the existing missionary schools, but also journeyed into the countryside whenever she could to evangelize. After 11 years, she was scheduled for a much needed furlough, but just then a group of men from another city arrived on foot and pleaded with her to come to their city where many others wanted to hear the gospel. So Lottie canceled her furlough plans, moved to Pintow, and told people how her life had been changed through her faith. In all the 40 years she spent in China, she only took three furloughs. Finally, in 1885, when she was 45, she gave up teaching and moved into the interior to evangelize full-time, even though the country was torn by plague, famine, revolution, and war.

Lottie was a tireless writer, constantly sending letters and articles to people "back home" to help them understand the missions and support them. She proposed that an annual offering be taken at Christmastime, and in 1888, the first year's offering of over $3,000 made it possible to send three more women. Eventually the "Lottie Moon Offering" became a major Southern Baptist tradition, reached totals of over 20 million dollars and supported half the Southern Baptist mission budget.

During the famine of 1911, Moon shared her meager funds and food with others and had so little left for herself that she was literally starving to death. Fellow workers became alarmed and arranged for her to go on furlough, but she died in Japan en route to America.

A reading from an article by Lottie Moon published in the June 1874 *Foreign Mission Journal*

(*Following a report on various difficulties between the missionaries and the Chinese authorities*)

It is easy to denounce these outrages in no measured terms, but we blush to think they have their counterparts in the justice meted out to the Chinese in San Francisco.

Here in Tungchow, affairs are moving on pretty much as usual. We notice with pleasure an increased attendance on preaching. Another man has been received for baptism. He dates his first convictions to hearing the Christians talk about keeping the Sabbath. He says he never before heard of a Sabbath except at the New Year, & his attention was at once arrested. He has endured firmly a cruel persecution at the hands of his wife.

This city offers a very wide field of usefulness for an active, energetic man, while the surrounding country is full of villages where the gospel has never been preached. Another minister is sadly needed to take some of the burden from Mr. Crawford. What with a regular pastorate, street preaching, itinerating, and instructing a Theological class, making books, and writing hymns, — he is doing the work that ought to be shared. It is too much for one man.

The ladies of the mission are doing what they can to bear the word of life to the people, but the force *is wholly inadequate to the work.* We are already sadly foreboding the departure of one of our most efficient missionaries. In three or four years at most Mrs. Holmes must go home for the education of her son. In the meantime, however, it would seem the part of wisdom that two ladies should be sent out that they may learn the language & thus be prepared to take charge of the girls' boarding school. We say two simply because it would not be desirable or pleasant for a lady to live alone. One of the Presbyterian ladies here is trying this, and she finds it very lonely.

We believe that there are men and women in our Southern Baptist churches who but require to be assured of the pressing demand for more laborers in some specific field, in order to respond, "Send us." We believe; too, that the money needed is in the denomination and that it will be forthcoming. We are convinced that the brethren and sisters at home will not allow these missions which God has blessed so abundantly to languish for want of more laborers or of material support. In this faith we wait: believing we shall hear from home that the needed reinforcements will be sent.

L. Moon.
Tung Chow, March 9, 1874

✪ December 26

Elijah P. Lovejoy

PRESBYTERIAN

November 9, 1802–November 7, 1837

Nothing in the early life of Elijah P. Lovejoy indicated that he would be murdered by an outraged mob before his 35th birthday. He grew up on a farm in Maine, showed remarkable academic ability, graduated at the head of his class from Baptist Waterville College, then headed west, believing that he could be useful as an educator on the new frontier. He settled in St. Louis and founded a private high school but then joined others in establishing a newspaper, the *St. Louis Times,* to support the political philosophy of Henry Clay. He also worked to found a lyceum in the town to discuss ideas for civic improvement. Though active in a tract society that worked against drinking, swearing, and Sabbath breaking, Lovejoy seemed to take no interest in the abolition movement. A conversion experience at the Presbyterian Church in early 1832, however, sent Lovejoy back east to study theology at Princeton Seminary.

Finishing seminary quickly, thanks to his academic ability, Lovejoy was licensed to preach in April 1833 and returned to St. Louis not long afterward to help with another newspaper and deliver sermons in area churches. He thought of himself as a moderate voice on the slavery issue, but the citizens of St. Louis were not ready to hear a fundamental institution of their society criticized. When a free African American killed a deputy sheriff and was lynched by a mob, Lovejoy condemned their lawless behavior and brought the mobs down on himself. When they broke up his printing press, Lovejoy decided to move to Illinois, a free state. He assured the citizens of Alton, Illinois, that he would concentrate on other issues but reserved the right to oppose slavery as a sin. When he went further and began to organize antislavery petitions, mobs formed in Alton as well, stormed his building, broke up the printing press, and threw the pieces in the river.

Lovejoy once again appealed to the community for a free press and free speech, but opposition continued. When a new printing press arrived, the mob once again attacked the building. Defenders fired on the mob, which only increased their anger. When Lovejoy went out to appeal for order, he was shot down and the mob proceeded to a methodical destruction of the printing press. Buried in a simple grave in Alton, Lovejoy became the first martyr of the abolition movement. Former president John Quincy Adams wrote that Lovejoy's death was like an earthquake shock whose reverberations would be felt not only across America, but in the most distant regions of the earth. Abolitionists took his death as proof that proslavery forces could not be reasoned with and that the issue could not be settled without bloodshed.

A reading from the final public speech of Elijah Lovejoy on November 3, 1837

Mr. Chairman — it is not true, as has been charged upon me, that I hold in contempt the feelings and sentiments of this community, in reference to the question which is now agitating it. I respect and appreciate the feelings and opinions of my fellow-citizens, and it is one of the most painful and unpleasant duties of my life, that I am called upon to act in opposition to them. If you suppose, sir, that I have published sentiments contrary to those generally held in this community, because I delighted in differing from them, or in occasioning a disturbance, you have entirely misapprehended me. But, sir, while I value the good opinion of my fellow-citizens, as highly as any one, I may be permitted to say, that I am governed by higher considerations than either the favour or the fear of man. I am impelled to the course I have taken, because I fear God. As I shall answer it to my God in the great day, I dare not abandon my sentiments, or cease in all proper ways to propagate them....

You have, sir, made up, as the lawyers say, a false issue; there are not two parties between whom there can be a compromise. I plant myself, sir, down on my unquestionable rights, and the question to be decided is, whether I shall be protected in the exercise, and enjoyment of those rights — that is the question, sir; — whether my property shall be protected, whether I shall be suffered to go home to my family at night without being assailed, and threatened with tar and feathers, and assassination; whether my afflicted wife, whose life has been in jeopardy, from continued alarm and excitement, shall night after night be driven from a sick bed into the garret to save her life from the brickbats and violence of the mobs; that sir, is the question.

Here, much affected and overcome by his feelings, he burst into tears. Many, not excepting even his enemies, wept — several sobbed aloud, and the sympathies of the whole meeting were deeply excited. He continued:

Forgive me, sir, that I have thus betrayed my weakness. It was the allusion to my family that overcame my feelings. Not, sir, I assure you, from any fears on my part. I have no personal fears, not that I feel able to contest the matter with the whole community, I know perfectly well I am not. I know, sir, that you can tar and feather me, hang me up, or put me into the Mississippi, without the least difficulty. But what then? Where shall I go? I have been made to feel that if I am not safe at Alton, I shall not be safe anywhere. I recently visited St. Charles to bring home my family, and was torn from their frantic embrace by a mob. I have been beset night and day at Alton. And now if I leave here and go elsewhere, violence may overtake me in my retreat, and I have no more claim upon the protection of any other community than I have upon this; and I have concluded, after consultation with my friends, and earnestly seeking counsel of God, to remain at Alton, and here to insist on protection in the exercise of my rights. If the civil authorities refuse to protect me, I must look to God; and if I die, I have determined to make my grave in Alton.

✪ December 27

James Theodore Holly

EPISCOPALIAN

September 25, 1829–March 13, 1911

During the middle years of the 19th century, the position of African Americans in the United States remained unresolved. While white abolitionists battled the institution of slavery, black Americans were divided between the movement advocating a return to Africa and those who demanded freedom on the grounds that so much of this country's development resulted from their own tears and toil. Though James Theodore Holly was born free in the north, it seemed to him that there should be a place where black people could control their own destinies. Since its revolution, Haiti had been an independent black republic, so Holly felt it would be an ideal place for him to work. Though baptized in the Roman Catholic Church, he felt there were no opportunities for him there, so at the age of 33, he became an Episcopalian.

Ordained to the priesthood of the Episcopal Church, Holly served briefly in Bridgeport, Connecticut, and then, after visiting Haiti, took a group of 100 people with him to establish a church there and a center for settlement by American blacks. He established churches, schools, and medical facilities, and in 1874 Holly was consecrated the first black bishop in the Episcopal Church and the second in any major white denomination. Over the remaining years of his life, the church he established as the Orthodox and Apostolic Church of Haiti continued to grow, although slowly. Fire destroyed buildings time and again, frequent revolutions created unstable political conditions, while Roman Catholic opposition made his task particularly difficult. Yet by the time of his retirement, the church he had established had twice as many priests as when he was made bishop and twice as many church members. Abandoning its independence, the Haitian church ultimately became an Episcopal diocese, but the strong foundations Holly had laid served well and it continues to grow so that today it is one of the largest dioceses of the Episcopal Church. Holly argued that the suffering of the "Hamitic race" had prepared it for future greatness in the working out of God's plan.

A reading from "The Divine Plan of Human Redemption, in Its Ethnological Development" by James Theodore Holly

I do not . . . propose to discuss in this article the subject of Human Redemption, nor the details of the Divine Plan by which it is being effected, but shall confine my observations to the Ethnological development of this plan.

If we examine the exact purport of Noah's prophetic curse pronounced against Canaan we will discover another reason for the honored elevation of the Hamitic race. In the millennial age that curse, as defined in the context, is that Canaan should be a servant of servants to his brethren. Now, during the domination of the Gentile empires the place of servitude was and is one of dishonor. But Christ in the Gospel assures us that it shall not be so in His kingdom, but that he that would be the greatest there must be the servant of all. Our Savior assumed the place of servant of servants on the night of the last supper, "when He girded Himself with a towel, poured water into a basin, stooped down and washed the feet of his disciples." The African race has been the servant of servants to their brethren of the other races during all the long and dreary ages of the Hebrew and Christian dispensations. And it is this service that they have so patiently rendered through blood and tears that shall finally obtain for them the noblest places of service in the Coming Kingdom. Thus, what has been a curse to them under Gentile tyranny will become a blessing to them under the mild and beneficent reign of Christ; and thus will be realized the double but adverse significations of the Hebrew word *barak* — which signifies "to bless," and also "to curse," as used in the latter sense by Job's wife when she told her husband to "curse God and die." The curse of Canaan, dooming him to be a servant of servants unto his brethren, which lowered him to a place of dishonor under the earthly governments of men, will turn to a blessing unto him and exalt him to the post of honor under the heavenly government of God.

It will be seen by the ground that I have now gone over that in the development of the Divine Plan of Human Redemption the Semitic race had the formulating, the committing to writing and the primal guardianship of the Holy Scriptures during the Hebrew dispensation. The Japhetic race has had the task committed to them of translating, publishing and promulgating broadcast the same Holy Scriptures as completed by the Canon of the New Testament, during the apostolic phase of the Christian dispensation. But neither the one nor the other of those two races have entered into or carried out the spirit of those Scriptures. This crowning work of the will of God is reserved for the millennial phase of Christianity, when Ethiopia shall stretch out her hands directly unto God.

✪ *December 28*

James Preston Poindexter

BAPTIST

September 25, 1819–February 7, 1907

Few issues in American life have as controversial as the relationship between church and state or politics and religion. It is hardly surprising that that should be the case, since the United States was settled by people for whom that had been an issue even before they reached these shores. New England's first settlers came to avoid what they viewed as the oppression of an established church and quickly established their own version of establishment, driving out all who dissented. Meanwhile, the Virginia colony quickly established the very church New England's settlers had come to avoid. Later immigrants often represented established churches in Sweden, Scotland, and parts of Germany. Others came from dissenting traditions. Conditions in the New World forced everyone to look at things from new perspectives. The New England dissenters quickly became the establishment, while Anglicans in that area learned to live as a tolerated minority. Yet in Virginia, after the Revolution, some of the strongest voices urging separation of church and state came from the heirs of that state's established tradition.

Among black Americans, different forces were at work. African Americans had been converted by both established and nonestablished varieties of Christianity, but they themselves were powerless in society until after the Civil War. With abolition came the opportunity to take part in the political process, but where were their leaders to come from? With few exceptions, the clergy were the best educated members of black communities and therefore, it was only natural that they should take a strong role in political matters.

James Poindexter was one of the most remarkable of the 19th-century generation of black leaders. He seems to have had no formal education and supported himself as a barber, a trade he learned at the age of 10. Married at the age of 18, he moved to Columbus, Ohio, and became involved immediately in the Underground Railroad. He was active also in his church and was called on occasionally to preach. In 1858, he was asked to serve as pastor of the largest black congregation in Columbus but continued to earn his living as a barber so as not to put the burden of his salary on the church. It was said that his ministry was characterized by a "deep earnestness, steadfastness of purpose, fidelity to the cause of Christianity, an uncompromising attitude towards wrong, and a breadth of vision that extended beyond denominational lines."

After the Civil War, as black citizens began to exercise their right to vote, Poindexter began to exercise leadership not only in the black community but in the white community as well. He was nominated for the Ohio House of Delegates, and although he lost the election, his abilities were beginning to be recognized. President-elect Rutherford B. Hayes consulted Poindexter and Frederick Douglass before taking up his office in 1877. Poindexter served as a member and as vice-president of the Columbus City Council and was elected to the School Board, serving, in spite of his lack of formal education, as chair of the textbook and curriculum committee. He advocated integrated schools and through his influence black teachers served side by side with white teachers in the city schools.

The political process necessarily requires compromise, and Poindexter's recognition of that fact was evident when New Orleans planned a World Exposition with a separate department for colored people. At that point in history, he felt it would be better to accept half a loaf than to insist on equal treatment and wind up with nothing. Writing to the *Cleveland Gazette* on the subject, he said,

> Many like myself, and doubtless you are one of them, do not relish anything that draws the line between white and colored citizens, but whether it pleases us or not, a separate department for colored exhibits has been set apart at the World's Fair at New Orleans, and all colored men who love the race will exert every faculty of mind and muscle of body to make the results of that fair a credit to the race. Good sense demands this; love of race enforces this...a sensible view of the matter. Every colored man should arouse himself and

awaken his friends to the responsibility resting upon himself and them. Make the Ohio exhibit one of the best.

In a public address on the subject of the "Pulpit and Politics," Poindexter said:

> Nor can a preacher more than any other citizen plead his religious work or the sacredness of that work as an exemption from duty. Going to the Bible to learn the relation of the pulpit to politics, and accepting the prophets, Christ, and apostles, and the pulpit of their times, and their precepts and examples as the guide of the pulpit to-day, I think that their conclusion will be that wherever there is a sin to be rebuked, no matter by whom committed, and ill to be averted or good to be achieved by our country or mankind, there is a place for the pulpit to make itself felt and heard. The truth is, all the help the preachers and all other good and worthy citizens can give by taking hold of politics is needed in order to keep the government out of bad hands and secure the ends for which governments are formed.

✪ December 29

Thomas Raymond Kelly

QUAKER

June 4, 1893–January 17, 1941

" 'Mystic' and 'Mysticism,' " wrote Evelyn Underhill, "are words ... so vaguely and loosely used that they convey no precise meaning to our minds, and have now come to be perhaps the most ambiguous terms in the whole vocabulary of religion." Underhill's massive study of the subject (*Mysticism*) helped define the terms more fully, but her shorter definition is also helpful: "mysticism is the direct intuition or experience of God, and a mystic is a person who has, to a greater or less degree, such a direct experience." Thomas Raymond Kelly was such a person. He had grown up in the midwest and studied under Rufus Jones* before volunteering for civilian service during World War I. In that capacity, he worked first with the Y.M.C.A. in England, and then, because of his linguistic skill, with German prisoners of war. Returning to the United States, he completed his doctorate and returned to Europe to serve with the American Friends Service Committee and help with the reconstruction of Germany. Back in America again, he taught at Earlham College, then at Wellesley, and once more at Earlham while working on a second doctorate at Harvard. Kelly succeeded Elton Trueblood* as professor of philosophy at Haverford College in 1936, but was turned down for his doctorate at Harvard when his mind went completely blank. He seems to have had a perfectionist streak that kept him from coping well with stress. A similar forgetfulness had occurred at his first doctoral exam, but the examiners on that occasion had been patient and helped him overcome it.

About two months after this upset, he suddenly felt "shaken by the experience of Presence — something that I did not seek, but that sought me." A colleague said that his "fierce academic ambition receded, and a new abandoned kind of fulfillment made its appearance." The following summer, Kelly traveled again to Germany to work with other Friends before Hitler closed the door to outside intervention. He came back deeply distressed by the suffering he had witnessed but enabled by new experiences of divine love to deal with the pain. For weeks afterward, friends heard him exclaim, "I have been literally melted down by the love of God!"

Over the next four years, Kelly spoke and wrote often about his new knowledge of God's love and experience of God's presence. He was a frequent lecturer at the Quaker Pendle Hill conference center. In 1941, however, as he was preparing to meet with editors at Harper and Brothers about publication of some of his work, he suddenly died of a massive heart attack. Douglas Steere, a colleague on the Haverford faculty, completed the preparation of Kelly's writing for publication. *A Testimony of Devotion* has remained in print ever since.

A reading from *The Reality of the Spiritual World* by Thomas Raymond Kelly

One's first experience of the Heavenly Splendour plows through one's whole being, makes one dance and sing inwardly, enthralls one in unspeakable love. Then the world, at first, is all out of focus; we scorn it, we are abstracted, we are drunken with Eternity. We have not yet learned how to live in both worlds at once, how to integrate our life in time fruitfully with Eternity. Yet we are beings whose home is both here and Yonder, and we must learn the secret of being at home in both, all the time. A new level of our being has been opened to us, and lo, it is Immanuel, God with us. The experience of the Presence of God is not something plastered on to our nature; it is the fulfillment of ourselves. The last deeps of humanity go down into the life of God. The stabilizing of our lives, so that we live in God and in time, in fruitful interplay, is the task of maturing religious life.

How do you begin this double mental life, this life at two levels? You begin *now*, wherever you are. Listen to these words outwardly. But, within, deep within you continue steady prayer, offering yourself and all that you are to Him in simple, joyful, serene, unstrained dedication. Practice it steadily. Make it your conscious Intention. Keep it up for days and weeks and years. You will be swept away by rapt attention to the exciting things going on around you. Then catch yourself and bring yourself back. You will forget God for whole hours. But do not waste any time in bitter regrets or self-recriminations. Just begin again. The first weeks and months of such practice are pretty patchy, badly botched. But say inwardly to yourself and to God,

"This is the kind of bungling person I am when I am not wholly Thine. But take this imperfect devotion of these months and transmute it with Thy love." Then begin again. And gradually, in months or in three or four years, the habit of heavenly orientation becomes easier, more established. The times of your wandering become shorter, less frequent. The stability of your deeper level becomes greater. God becomes a more steady background of all your reactions in the time-world. Down in this center you have a Holy Place, a Shekinah, where you and God hold sweet converse. Your outer behavior will be revised and your personal angularities will be melted down, and you will approach the outer world of men with something more like an out-going divine love, directed toward them. You begin to love men, because you live in love toward God. Or the divine love flows out toward men through you and you become His pliant instrument of loving concern.

✪ December 30

Thomas Edward Shields

ROMAN CATHOLIC

May 9, 1862–February 5, 1921

His own education was a disaster, yet Thomas Edward Shields devoted his life to ensuring that other children would be taught to find learning an adventure. In *The Making and the Unmaking of a Dullard*, he wrote that although he was doing long division and fractions at nine, over the next few years he came to be considered unteachable. His parents finally withdrew him from school and set him to work on the farm. At the age of 13, when they sent him back to see if things would go better, the situation grew worse. Older than the other children in the class, he was teased and mocked. He grew afraid of the sound of his own voice and withdrew into silence, trying to avoid speaking to anyone. Then, at 16, he discovered the joy of reading by teaching himself to sound out words. He dreamed of a religious vocation, but when he went to the bishop who asked where he had done his classical studies, he had never heard of them. Using a plot of land his parents had given him, he earned money to pursue his goal, entered college at 20, and completed his undergraduate education in three years.

This slow awakening of his mind convinced him that better methods of education were essential, that rote memorization was a poor way of teaching, and that content needed to be correlated with psychological growth in the student. With John Dewey and other theorists of the time, Shields believed that children learn best by doing and that music and liturgical activity were as important as books and lessons. To persuade others of the value of his approach, he developed a series of religious textbooks and founded the Catholic Education Press and the *Catholic Educational Review* to gain adherents for his ideas. Summer schools were created for nuns who taught in parochial schools, and finally he was instrumental in establishing the Sisters College to provide professional training and appropriate degrees for teachers in the parochial school system and colleges of the church.

"Before his eyes," it was said, "there arose the vision of an educational system wherein all the elements of truth should be harmoniously combined — the knowledge of nature and man leading on to the knowledge of God. In his heart there sprang the hope of a brighter day when religion should vitalize all teaching, all learning, all striving and living — when education should cooperate, in spirit and truth with God's design."

A reading from an article by Thomas Edward Shields in the *Catholic Educational Review*

The first concern of the Catholic Church is to form the character and mould the conduct of her children in accordance with the divine precepts and with the model which, in the person of Jesus Christ, has been set up for the imitation of all who would enter the Kingdom. In fact, the teaching of religion is not satisfactory in her eyes unless it transforms the children of men into the sons of God. Accordingly no method will meet the requirements of the Church that leaves the wellsprings of the child's life unaffected. In the hands of her teachers, religion must purify the imagination, it must strengthen the will, it must ennoble the emotions, as well as link together into unity the fragments of truth that are borne in upon the mind of the child from all nature. The teacher of religion in the Catholic school cannot fulfill his duty by causing the children to memorize a catechism, however well constructed, nor will it suffice to equip the pupil for the adult conflict with error. The immediate duty of the teacher of religion is to render the child committed to his care reverent and obedient, loving and tender, strong to resist temptation, and clear in his perception of God as the central object in all his thinking. Such a teacher must, therefore, draw upon the phenomena of nature and the facts of human history as well as upon the deposit of revealed truth for the material of his instruction, and he must see to it that the food which he ministers to the developing mind and heart of the child is fully assimilated and that it affects the present conduct of the child while at the same time it lays up to him strength against the day of battle. His business is not to load the child's mind with sealed instructions which may or may not declare themselves to his intelligence in after life. All this is borne out by the recent action of the Sovereign Pontiff in allowing the children to approach the Holy Table as soon as they reach the age of reason. The teachers of religion in our Catholic schools are, therefore, called upon to prepare the minds of the little ones for the reception of the Blessed Sacrament by religious instruction which will reach the intelligence of the little ones, touch their imagination, and control their conduct.

✪ December 31 ⎯⎯⎯⎯⎯⎯⎯⎯⎯⎯⎯⎯⎯⎯⎯⎯⎯⎯⎯⎯

William Augustus Muhlenberg

EPISCOPALIAN

September 16, 1796–April 8, 1877

Now that members of many liturgical churches come to communion weekly, and the sacrament is celebrated so often that Roman Catholics and Episcopal liturgists begin to be concerned for the very survival of other forms of worship, it is hard to remember that there was a time when it was considered irreverent to come to communion too often. Not long ago, Roman Catholics seldom received the sacrament more than once a year, Presbyterians had quarterly "communion seasons," and most Episcopal Churches offered Sunday communion only once a month. The thinking behind these practices was that this much time was needed for proper preparation.

William Augustus Muhlenberg (a descendent of Henry Melchior Muhlenberg*) was raised as a Lutheran, but joined the Episcopal Church so he could worship in English. He was among the early advocates of weekly communion as a valuable part of the Christian life. He wrote:

> A good Christian is always fit to partake of the Sacrament; but yet, in order to do it, he will desire to collect himself — to repair himself, as it were — to wipe off the dust and soil of the world, which are forever settling on the soul; just as a good Christian is always prepared to die, while yet he prays against sudden death, in order that he may be actually ready, as well as habitually prepared for the awful change. He would have his lamp not merely burning, but bright, and replenished with oil to light him well as he enters the dark valley. In like manner the communicant, though conscious of having the main qualification for meeting his Lord acceptably at the Holy Table, yet desires to examine it, again and again — to try himself, as the apostle bids him, "whether he be in the faith." Every time he ventures into the presence of the King he endeavors to have his marriage garment cleaner and whiter, more thoroughly purified from the stains of earth. He feels as if he must repent anew — believe anew — love anew — make good resolutions anew, and begin, as it were, his whole Christian life anew. True, the grace which is to enable him to do all this, is the very thing he seeks in going to the Eucharist, yet the grace which he obtains is ever in proportion to that with which he comes.... So oft the grace of which the Eucharist is the means. The more we have to come with, the more we bring away. If none we bring, then none we gain.

To put his ideas into practice, William Augustus Muhlenberg organized a new parish in New York City called the Church of the Holy Communion. He abolished pew rents and celebrated communion every week. He believed that worship should be formal and movingly solemn, not stark and plain. He put flowers on the altar and decorated the church with greens at Christmas. He used traditional vestments and wrote new hymns. He organized a group of women to care for the altar furnishings.

But Muhlenberg was even more concerned for the church's impact on society. To deepen that impact, he promoted the Sunday School movement and founded a boys' school in Flushing, Long Island, that was the inspiration for the New England prep school movement. He created a parish school in the city, established a parish unemployment fund, and organized trips to the country for poor city children. Out of his altar guild came the first American order of deaconesses, which in turn established St Luke's Hospital, still one of the great hospitals in New York City. Not content with that, Muhlenberg founded the Church Industrial Community of St. Johnland, on Long Island, as a home for the aged and for young children, especially cripples.

Muhlenberg believed that the effect of Christianity on the world at large was compromised by its divisions. He persuaded a substantial group of church leaders to join with him in an appeal to the bishops of the Episcopal Church to move toward greater unity with other denominations. The "Muhlenberg Memorial," as it came to be known, asked:

> Whether the Protestant Episcopal Church, with only her present canonical means and appliances, her fixed and invariable modes of public worship, and her traditional customs and usages, is competent to the work of preaching and dispensing the Gospel to all sorts and conditions of men, and so adequate to do the work of the Lord in this land and in this age? This question, your petitioners, for their own part, and in consonance with many thoughtful minds among us, believe must be answered in the negative. Their memorial proceeds on the assumption that our Church confined to the exercise of her present system, is not sufficient to the great purposes of the above-mentioned — that a wider door must be opened for admission to the Gospel ministry, than that through which her candidates for holy orders are now obliged to enter. Besides such candidates among her own members, it is believed that men can be found among the other bodies of Christians around us, who would gladly receive ordination at your hands, could they obtain it, without that entire surrender which would now be required of them, of all the liberty in public worship to which they have been accustomed — men, who could not bring themselves to conform in all particulars to our prescriptions and customs, but yet sound in the faith, and who, having the gifts of preachers and pastors, would be able ministers of the New Testament. . . . Dare we pray the Lord of the harvest, to send forth laborers into the harvest, while we reject all laborers but those of one peculiar type? The extension of orders to the class of men contemplated (with whatever safeguards, not infringing on evangelical freedom, which your wisdom might deem expedient) appears to your petitioners to be a subject supremely worth your deliberations.

This memorial was far ahead of its time, and its influence can be seen in the Episcopal Church's 1886 "Chicago-Lambeth Quadrilateral," which proposes unity among Christians who accept the Bible, the historic creeds, the sacraments of baptism and communion, and ministry in the historic succession of bishops. The Quadrilateral is the basis for full communion between the Lutheran and Episcopal churches, as well as the on-going conversations among "Churches Uniting in Christ."

Muhlenberg called himself an "Evangelical Catholic." As one writer has said, "There was not a significant area of the Church's life, during his ministry that he did not elevate and strengthen by the pureness of his life and the vigor of his consecrated imagination."

ACKNOWLEDGMENTS

Compiling the material for this book has been greatly assisted by a number of individuals, and we are grateful to all of them. We would mention in particular the staff of the ELCA Library in Chicago; the ELCA Archives; the library at the Lutheran Theological Seminary at Philadelphia; the Woodward Library at Emory University; the United States Office of the Lutheran World Federation; the Wycliffe Bible Society; the Lutheran Church–Missouri Synod Archives; Jeffrey H. Kaimowitz, Peter J. Knapp, and Sally S. Dickinson of the Watkinson Library at Trinity College, Hartford; Karen Lesiak, Librarian of the St. Thomas Seminary, Bloomfield, Connecticut; Carolyn Baker, Director of Archives, Shaw University Archives and Special Collections/Records Management Program, Raleigh, North Carolina; Margaret Landon of the Church Historical Society and Steven Sturgeon, Archivist of the Diocese of Utah, for assistance with H. Baxter Liebler; Robert Kim Bingham, Ann Bingham, and Jeffery Rowthorn, for assistance with material on Hiram Bingham IV; Thomas J. Lynch of Boys Town, Nebraska, for assistance with material on Father Flanagan; Ellen Pierce, Director of the Maryknoll Mission Archives, for help with material on Maura Clark and for permission to use unpublished material on Mother Mary Joseph Rogers and the Rev. James A. Walsh; Sister Mary Laurence Hanley, O.S.F., for permission for quotations from *Pilgrimage and Exile,* now published by the University of Hawaii Press; Jody Norman, Archives Supervisor, State Library and Archives of Florida, for permission to use an unpublished interview with Mary McLeod Bethune; Forward Movement, 1959; Mark Gruner for assistance with research on Anthony Binga; Bonnie Shullenberger for assistance with research on Emily Malbone Morgan; Randall Burkett of Emory University for assistance with research on Althea Brown Edmiston; Sheryl Kujawa-Holbrook for allowing us to use material she had collected for her book *Freedom Is a Dream: A Documentary History of Women in the Episcopal Church*; Caroline Grant, Elisabeth Gruner, Peter Tierney, and Frank Peterson for research assistance; Ian Markham of Hartford Seminary, Hartford, Connecticut; Amy Cady of the Cornwall Library, Cornwall, Connecticut; Mother Miriam of the Community of St. Mary; Eleana Silk, Librarian of St. Vladimir's Seminary, Crestwood, New York; La Verne Byrd Smith, Church Historian, First Baptist Church, Richmond, Virginia; Catherine Walsh, Library of St. Joseph's Seminary, Yonkers, New York; and to Pendle Hill Publications for permission to cite Thomas R. Kelly, *Reality of the Spiritual World,* Pendle Hill Pamphlet 21.

THE CALENDAR

Individuals are listed by date of birth if known, otherwise by date of death. Those for whom neither date is known are listed at the end.

January 2, 1889	Mary Ignatia Gavin, Roman Catholic
January 3, 1793	Lucretia Coffin Mott, Quaker
1816	Anne Ayres, Episcopalian
January 4, 1889	Maisie Ward, Roman Catholic
January 5, 1877	Henry Sloan Coffin, Presbyterian
1909	Ileana Hapsburg (Mother Alexandra), Orthodox

born 1864? / died January 5, 1943 – George Washington Carver, Methodist

January 6, 1874	Jean Kenyon Mackenzie, Presbyterian
1940	Penny Lernoux, Roman Catholic
January 8, 1735	John Carroll, Roman Catholic
1867	Emily Greene Balch, Quaker
1885	A. J. Muste, Dutch Reformed, Quaker, and Presbyterian
January 9, 1723/24	Isaac Backus, Baptist
1885	Margaret Louise Keasey, Roman Catholic
January 10, 1862	Louise Cecilia Fleming, Baptist
1887	Adelaide Teague Case, Episcopalian
January 11, 1846	Caroline Louise Darling (Sister Constance), Episcopalian
January 12, 1588	John Winthrop, Congregational
January 13, 1931	Mary Elizabeth (Maura) Clarke, Roman Catholic
January 15, 1811	Abby Kelly Foster, Quaker
1891	Bertha Toni Agnes Carola Paulssen, Lutheran
1906	Gustave Weigel, Roman Catholic
1929	Martin Luther King, Jr., Baptist
January 18, 1868	Eleanor Chestnut, Presbyterian
January 21, 1749	Christian Newcomer, United Brethren
January 22, 1849	Terence Vincent Powderly, Roman Catholic
January 23, 1837	Amanda Berry Devine Smith, African Methodist Episcopal
1838	Marianne Cope, Roman Catholic
January 25, 1863	Rufus Jones, Quaker

January 26, 1963   Mev Puleo, Roman Catholic

January 28, 1860   Charles E. and Augusta Weltner, Lutherans

January 30, 1801   Pierre-Jean De Smet, Roman Catholic

January 31, 1713   Anthony Benezet, Quaker
          1915   Thomas Merton, Roman Catholic

February 1, 1834   Henry McNeal Turner, African Methodist

born 1784? / died February 3, 1882 – Mary Elizabeth Lange, Roman Catholic

February 4, 1790   John Bachman, Lutheran
          1802   Mark Hopkins, Congregational
          1913   Rosa Parks, African Methodist

February 5, 1723   John Witherspoon, Presbyterian
          1837   Dwight L. Moody, Independent
          1877   Michael Williams, Roman Catholic

February 8, 1840   Cornelia Hancock, Quaker
          1835   Nancy Fowler (Nettie) McCormick

February 9, 1834   Kamehameha IV, Episcopalian

February 10, 1909   Paul Chauncey Empie, Lutheran

February 11, 1783   Jarena Lee, African Methodist
          1836   Washington Gladden, Congregationalist

February 13, 1746   Absalom Jones, Episcopalian
          1800   Orange Scott, Free Methodist
          1880   John LaFarge, Roman Catholic
born 1815 / died February 13, 1882 – Henry Highland Garnet, Presbyterian

February 14, 1760   Richard Allen, African Methodist
          1847   Anna Howard Shaw, Methodist

February 15, 1820   Susan B. Anthony, Quaker
          1822   Henry B. Whipple, Episcopalian
          1843   Russell H. Conwell, Baptist

February 17, 1926   John Meyendorff, Orthodox
born 1666 / died February 17, 1713 – Jonas Auren, Lutheran

February 18, 1809   Cyrus McCormick, Presbyterian

February 20, 1805   Angelina Grimké Weld, Quaker

February 23, 1835   Austin Carroll, Roman Catholic

February 24, 1811   Daniel A. Payne, African Methodist
          1867   James Anthony Walsh, Roman Catholic

born 1850 / died February 25, 1921 – Elizabeth Fedde, Lutheran

February 26, 1857   Charles Sheldon, Congregational

February 27, 1897   Marian Anderson, Baptist

February 28, 1757   Joseph Badger, Presbyterian
          1797   Mary Lyon, Congregationalist
          1799   Samuel Simon Schmucker, Lutheran

March 2, 1861   Lucy Whitehead McGill Peabody, Baptist

March 3, 1819   Alexander Crummell, Episcopalian

March 5, 1820   Robert Lewis Dabney, Presbyterian

March 7, 1836   James Mills Thoburn, Methodist

born 1821 / died March 10, 1913 – Harriet Tubman

March 11, 1796   Francis Wayland, Baptist
          1813   Henriette Delille, Roman Catholic
          1926   Ralph David Abernathy, Baptist

March 12, 1758   Jesse Lee, Methodist

March 14, 1808   Narcissa Prentiss Whitman

March 16, 1877   Thomas Wyatt Turner, Roman Catholic
          1885   William Leroy Stidger, Methodist

March 17, 1912   Bayard Rustin, Quaker

March 19, 1748   Elias Hicks, Quaker
          1859   Ellen Gates Starr, Roman Catholic
          1860   William Jennings Bryan

March 20, 1939   Jonathan Myrick Daniels, Episcopalian

March 23, 1812   Stephen Return Riggs, Presbyterian

March 24, 1590   William Bradford, Congregationalist
birth date unknown / died March 24, 1661 – William Leddra, Quaker

March 25, 1783   Luther Rice, Baptist

March 26, 1925   Flannery O'Conner, Roman Catholic

March 27, 1935   Stanley Rother, Roman Catholic

March 28, 1873   Bessie Lee Efner Rehwinkel, Lutheran

March 29, 1840   Isabella Thoburn, Methodist

March 30, 1901   Cordelia Cox, Lutheran

March 31, 1835   John LaFarge, Roman Catholic

April 1, 1855   Agnes Repplier, Roman Catholic

April 4, 1748   William White, Episcopalian
   1802   Dorothea Dix, Congregationalist

April 5, 1780   Edward Hicks, Quaker

April 6, 1830   James Augustine Healy, Roman Catholic
   1851   Martha Gallison Moore Avery, Roman Catholic
born 1904 / died April 6, 1984 – Ruth Youngdahl Nelson, Lutheran

April 7, 1908   Godfrey Diekmann, Roman Catholic

April 8, 1943   Timothy Lull, Lutheran

April 9, 1862   Charles Henry Brent, Episcopalian

April 10, 1882   Frances Perkins, Episcopalian

April 11, 1836   William Porcher DuBose, Episcopalian

April 14, 1802   Horace Bushnell, Congregational
   1854   Lucy Craft Laney, Presbyterian

April 17, 1772   Archibald Alexander, Presbyterian
   1842   Charles H. Parkhurst, Presbyterian

April 18, 1846   Mary C. Collins, Congregationalist

April 20, 1718   David Brainerd, Presbyterian

April 21, 1783   Asahel Nettleton, Congregational
   1891   Georgia Elma Harkness, Methodist
   1897   Aiden Wilson Tozer, Christian and Missionary Alliance

April 22, 1688   Jonathan Dickinson, Presbyterian
   1711   Eleazar Wheelock, Congregational

April 26, 1928   William Stringfellow Episcopalian

April 29, 1792   Matthew Vassar, Baptist

April 30, 1891   James E. Walsh, Roman Catholic

May 1, 1759   Jacob Albright, United Methodist
   1816   Fidelia Fiske, Congregational

May 2, 1740   Elias Boudinot, Presbyterian
   1778   Nathan Bangs, Methodist
   1870   William J. Seymour, Pentecostal
   1879   Nannie Helen Burroughs, Baptist

May 5, 1794   James Osgood Andrews, Methodist

May 6, 1831   Samuel Isaac Joseph Schereschewsky, Episcopalian

May 7, 1823   Harriet Starr Cannon, Episcopalian
   1867   George Washington Truett, Southern Baptist

May 8, 1895	Fulton John Sheen, Roman Catholic

May 9, 1862	Thomas Edward Shields, Roman Catholic
1878	Peter Maurin, Roman Catholic
1906	Sarah Patton Boyle, Episcopalian

May 10, 1778   William Ladd, Congregational

May 11, 1935   Barbara Andrews, Lutheran

May 12, 1823   Catherine FitzGibbon, Roman Catholic

May 13, 1810   Friedrich Konrad Dietrich Wyneken, Lutheran

May 14, 1752   Timothy Dwight, Congregational

May 18, 1834   Sheldon Jackson, Presbyterian

May 20, 1851   Rose Hawthorne Lathrop, Roman Catholic

May 22, 1870   Frederick H. Knubel, Lutheran

May 24, 1877   Mary Madeleva Wolff, Roman Catholic
        1878   Harry Emerson Fosdick, Baptist

May 25, 1865   John Raleigh Mott, Methodist

May 26, 1865   Isabel Alice Hartley Crawford, Baptist

May 27, 1818   Amelia Bloomer, Episcopalian

May 31, 1854   Mary Hannah Fulton, Presbyterian

June 1, 1843   Anthony Binga, Baptist
birth date unknown / died June 1, 1660 – Mary Dyer, Quaker

June 2, 1840   John Lancaster Spalding, Roman Catholic

June 3, 1822   Thomas Gallaudet, Episcopalian

June 4, 1726   Philip William Otterbein, United Brethren
        1869   Charles Stelzle Presbyterian
        1893   Thomas Raymond Kelly, Quaker

June 6, 1843   Elias Benjamin Sanford, Congregational

June 9, 1937   William L. Herzfeld Lutheran

June 12, 1774   Alexander McLeod, Presbyterian
        1804   David Abeel, Reformed
birth date unknown / died June 12, 1902 – Enmegabowh, Episcopalian

June 14, 1774   David Low Dodge, Presbyterian
        1809   Boniface Wimmer, Roman Catholic
        1811   Harriet Beecher Stowe, Episcopalian

June 16, 1862   Fannie Exile Scudder Heck, Baptist

June 18, 1928   John Tietjen, Lutheran

June 21, 1892   Reinhold Niebuhr, Evangelical and Reformed

June 23, 1786   Nathaniel W. Taylor, Congregational

June 24, 1729   Edward Taylor, Congregational
         1797   John Joseph Hughes, Roman Catholic

June 26, 1890   Virgil Michel, Roman Catholic
         1892   Pearl S. Buck Presbyterian

June 27, 1818   James Lloyd Breck, Episcopalian

June 28, 1851   Eliza Edmunds Hewitt, Presbyterian
         1876   Clara Maass, Lutheran

June 29, 1721   John Ettwein, Moravian

June 30, 1897   Paul Hanly Furfey, Roman Catholic
born 1766 / died June 30, 1853 – Pierre Toussaint, Roman Catholic

July 1, 1781   James B. Finley, Methodist

July 9, 1896   William Cameron Townsend, Presbyterian

July 10, 1875   Mary McLeod Bethune, Methodist

July 11, 1767   John Quincy Adams, Congregational
         1838   John Wanamaker, Presbyterian
         1850   Annie Armstrong, Baptist

July 13, 1886   Edward Joseph Flanagan, Roman Catholic

July 15, 1704   August Gottlieb Spangenberg, Moravian
         1850   Frances Xavier Cabrini, Roman Catholic

died July 16, 1792 – Samson Occom, Presbyterian

July 17, 1903

July 17, 1768   Stephen Theodore Badin, Roman Catholic
         1828   Catherine Louisa Marthens, Lutheran
         1903   Hiram Bingham IV, Episcopalian

July 18, 1753   Lemuel Haynes, Congregational
         1829   Channing Moore Williams
         1834   Clara Swain, Methodist

July 23, 1834   James Gibbons, Roman Catholic
         1854   James Otis Sargent Huntington, Episcopalian

July 25, 1823   Benjamin Titus Roberts, Free Methodist

birth date unknown / died July 26, 1864 – Iakov Georgevich Netsvetov, Russian Orthodox

| July 29, 1742 | Isabella Graham, Presbyterian |
| 1912 | Clarence Jordan, Southern Baptist |

| July 30, 1905 | John Tracy Ellis, Roman Catholic |

| July 31, 1604 | John Eliot, Congregational |
| 1861 | Helen Barrett Montgomery, Baptist |

August 1, 1779 — Francis Scott Key, Episcopalian

August 3, 1802 — Sarah Platt Doremus, Reformed

August 4, 1744 — John Christopher Kunze, Lutheran

| August 9, 1788 | Adoniram Judson, Baptist |
| 1866 | Florence Spearing Randolph |

August 10, 1858? — Anna Julia Haywood Cooper, Episcopalian

August 14, 1891 — Garfield Bromley Oxnam, Methodist

August 15, 1601	Johan Campanious, Lutheran
1864	Peter Christopher Yorke, Roman Catholic
1896	Catherine de Hueck Doherty, Roman Catholic

| August 20, 1745 | Francis Asbury, Methodist |
| 1856 | William Dwight Porter Bliss, Episcopalian |

August 21, 1824 — Caroline Friess, Roman Catholic

August 23, 1868 — Thomas Augustine Judge, Roman Catholic

August 26, 1908 — Cynthia Wedel, Episcopalian

August 27, 1772	Gideon Blackburn, Presbyterian
1797	Ivan Veniaminov, Orthodox
1894	George Nauman Shuster, Roman Catholic

| August 28, 1774 | Elizabeth Ann Seton, Roman Catholic |
| 1893 | Georges Florovsky, Orthodox |

August 29, 1782 — Charles Grandison Finney, Presbyterian/Congregational

August 30, 1900 — Franklin Clark Fry, Lutheran

born c. 1846 / died August 31, 1931 – David Pendleton Oakerhater, Episcopalian

September 2, 1884 — Frank Laubach, Presbyterian.

September 3, 1803 — Prudence Crandall, Quaker

September 4, 1802 — Marcus Whitman, Presbyterians

September 6, 1860 — Jane Addams, Presbyterian

| September 9, 1806 | Sarah Mapps Douglass, Quaker |
| 1849 | Lucy Jane Rider Meyer, Methodist |

September 10, 1867   Robert Elliott Speer, Presbyterian

September 11, 1838   John Ireland, Roman Catholic

September 12, 1788   Alexander Campbell, Disciples of Christ
              1904   John Courtney Murray, Roman Catholic

September 14, 1775   John Henry Hobart, Episcopalian
              1851   John Augustine Zahm, Roman Catholic

September 16, 1796   William A. Muhlenberg, Episcopalian
    birth date unknown / died September 16, 1672 – Anne Bradstreet, Congregational

September 17, 1721   Samuel Hopkins, Congregational

September 19, 1737   Charles Carroll, Roman Catholic
              1831   James DeKoven, Episcopalian

September 20, 1838   William Reed Huntington, Episcopalian

September 21, 1915   Stephen G. Cary, Quaker

September 24, 1852   Julia Chester Emery, Episcopalian

September 25, 1774   Judith Lomax, Episcopalian
              1819   James Preston Poindexter, Baptist
              1829   James Theodore Holly, Episcopalian
    born 1785 / died September 25, 1872 – Peter Cartwright, Methodist

September 26, 1786   Jacob Bower, Baptist
              1832   Joanna Moore, Baptist
              1904   Joseph Sittler, Lutheran

September 27, 1643   Solomon Stoddard, Congregational
              1837   Edward McGlynn, Roman Catholic
              1887   Lillian Trasher

September 28, 1839   Frances E. Willard, Methodist

October 2, 1768   John Black, Presbyterian
           1914   Richard McSorley, Roman Catholic
           1798   Anne-Therese Guerin, Roman Catholic

October 4 , 1861   Walter Rauschenbusch, Baptist

October 5, 1703   Jonathan Edwards, Congregational
           1923   Philip Berrigan, Roman Catholic

October 6, 1917   Fannie Lou Hamer, Baptist
    born 1711 / died October 7, 1787 – Henry Melchior Muhlenberg, Lutheran

October 8, 1609   John Clarke, Baptist

October 9, 1821   William Passavant, Lutheran

October 11, 1814   John Baptist Lamy, Roman Catholic

October 14, 1696   Samuel Johnson, Episcopalian

born 1607 / died October 15, 1682 – Obadiah Holmes, Baptist

October 16, 1758   Noah Webster, Congregational

October 17, 1711   Jupiter Hammon, Congregational(?)

born c. 1780 / died October 18, 1840 – Peter Williams, Episcopalian

October 19, 1720   John Woolman, Quaker

born 1807 / died October 20, 1870 – James W. C. Pennington, Presbyterian/
Congregational

October 22, 1910   Emily Gardiner Neal, Episcopalian
born 1749 / died October 22, 1808 – Benjamin Randal, Free Will Baptists

October 26, 1833   Eric Norelius, Lutheran
              1912   Mahalia Jackson

October 27, 1882   Mary Josephine Rogers, Roman Catholic

October 28, 1798   Levi Coffin, Quaker

October 29, 1867   Francis Uplegger, Lutheran
              1924   James Guadalupe Carney, Roman Catholic

October 30, 1815   Elizabeth Leslie Rous Comstock, Quaker

October 31, 1789   John Mason Peck, Baptist
              1796   Walter A. Scott, Disciples of Christ

November 2, 1696   Conrad Weiser, Lutheran

November 3, 1759   Martha Laurens Ramsay, Episcopalian

November 4, 1850   Francis James Grimké

born 1795 / died November 6, 1858 – Samuel Eli Cornish, Presbyterian

November 7, 1763   Benedict Joseph Flaget, Roman Catholic
              1906   Eugene Carson Blake, Presbyterian
born 1793 / died November 7, 1873 – John Christian Frederick Heyer, Lutheran

November 8, 1890   Henry Knox Sherrill, Episcopalian
              1897   Dorothy Day, Roman Catholic

November 9, 1799   Melville B. Cox, Methodist

November 10, 1802   Elijah P. Lovejoy, Presbyterian
born 1780 / died November 10, 1828 – Lott Cary, Baptist

November 12, 1815   Elizabeth Cady Stanton, Episcopalian

November 14, 1803   Jacob Abbott, Congregational

November 18, 1899   Howard Thurman, Baptist

November 19, 1823   Julia A. J. Foote, African Methodist Episcopal Zion

November 20, 1788   Félix Varela, Roman Catholic
1910   Pauli Murray, Episcopalian

November 22, 1672   Justus Falckner, Lutheran

November 23, 1803   Theodore Weld, Quaker

November 24, 1870   Francis Clement Kelley, Roman Catholic

November 25, 1880   Paul Jones, Episcopalian

November 26, 1792   Sarah Grimké, Quaker
1858   Katherine Drexel, Roman Catholic

November 28, 1864   Mary Katherine Jones Bennett, Presbyterian
birth date unknown / died November 28, 1918 – Joseph Hofer

November 30, 1729   Samuel Seabury, Episcopalian
1800   Luther Lee, Methodist
1888   Robert G. LeTourneau, Christian and Missionary Alliance

December 1, 1798   Albert Barnes, Presbyterian

birth date unknown / died December 2, 1918 – Michael Hofer

December 3, 1903   Sophie Koulomzin, Orthodox

December 7, 1807   John Greenleaf Whittier, Quaker
1875   Emma Francis, Lutheran

December 10, 1862   Emily Malbone Morgan, Episcopalian

December 12, 1840   Lottie Moon, Southern Baptist

December 13, 1835   Phillips Brooks, Episcopalian
born 1756 / died December 13, 1837 – Herman of Alaska, Orthodox

December 14, 1900   D. Elton Trueblood, Quaker (from December 12)

December 15, 1843   Albert Benjamin Simpson, Christian and Missionary Alliance
1861   Vida D. Scudder, Episcopalian

December 17, 1875   Althea Brown, Presbyterian

December 18, 1807   Phoebe Worrall Palmer, Methodist

December 19, 1819   Isaac Thomas Hecker, Roman Catholic (from December 18)
1886   William Howard Bishop, Roman Catholic

December 20, 1804   Charles Colcock Jones, Presbyterian

December 22, 1770   Demetrius A. Gallitzin, Roman Catholic

December 23, 1753   Thomas Baldwin, Baptist

December 24, 1745   Benjamin Rush, Presbyterian
              1789   Jackson Kemper, Episcopalian

December 25, 1835   Benjamin Tucker Tanner, African Methodist
              1772   Barton W. Stone, Christian Church (Disciples of Christ)

December 27, 1843   Benajah Carroll, Baptist

December 28, 1797   Charles Hodge, Presbyterian

December 29, 1865   William Adams Brown, Presbyterian
              1937   Thea Bowman, Roman Catholic

December 31, 1812   Peter Bohler, Moravian
              1838   Phineas Bresee, Church of the Nazarene

No specific dates are known for the following:

birth date unknown / died 1597 – John Davenport, Congregational
born 1563? / died 1608 – Robert Hunt, Episcopalian
born 1591 / died 1643 – Anne Hutchinson, Quaker
born 1603 / died between January 27 and March 15, 1683 – Roger Williams, Baptist
born c.1650 / died 1719 / Joshua Kocherthal Lutheran
born 1657/58 / died 1708 – Francis Makemie, Presbyterian
birth date unknown / died 1805 – Peter the Aleut, Orthodox
born 1750 / died May 1806 – Harry Hosier, Methodist
born 1753 / died 1849 – Catherine Livingston Garrettson, Methodist
born 1780 / died 1846 – Daniel Coker, African Methodist
born 1786 / 1866 – Noah Seattle, Roman Catholic
born 1788 / 1873 – Louis Tappan, Presbyterian
born 1797 / died 1847 – Theodore Sedgewick Wright, Presbyterian
born 1797 / 1883 – Sojourner Truth, Baptist
born c. 1800 / died 1866 – Braxton Drayton, Lutheran
born 1803 / died 1879 – Maria W. Stewart, African Baptist
born 1815 / died 1906 – Richard Rust, Methodist
born 1851 / died 1921 – Lillias Stirling Horton Underwood, Presbyterian
born 1890 / died 1971 – Rosa Young, Lutheran

BIBLIOGRAPHY

General Works

American National Biography. Vol. 22. Edited by John A. Garraty and Mark C. Carnes. New York: Oxford University Press, 1999.

Balmer, Randall, and John R. Fitzmier. *The Presbyterians*. Westport, CT: Greenwood Press, 1993.

Chorley, E. Clowes. *Men and Movements in the Episcopal Church*. New York: Charles Scribner's Sons, 1950.

Dictionary of American Biography. Vol. 5. Edited by Allen Johnson and Dumas Malone. New York: Charles Scribner's Sons, 1930.

Dictionary of American Biography. Vol. 13. Edited by Dumas Malone. New York: Charles Scribner's Sons, 1934.

Dictionary of American Biography. Vol. 20. Edited by Dumas Malone. New York: Charles Scribner's Sons, 1936.

Ellsberg, Robert. *All Saints: Daily Reflections on Saints, Prophets, and Witnesses for Our Time* New York: Crossroad, 2004.

George, Timothy, and Denise George, editors. *Baptists and Their Doctrines*. Nashville: Broadman and Holman Publishers, 1995.

Kujawa-Holbrook, Sheryl A. *Freedom Is a Dream: A Documentary History of Women in the Episcopal Church*. New York: Church Publishing, 2002.

Kujawa-Holbrook, Sheryl A., and Frederica Harris Thompsett. *Deeper Joy: Lay Women and Vocation in the 20th Century Episcopal Church*. New York: Church Publishing, 2005.

Marty, Martin. *Pilgrims in Their Own Land*. New York: Penguin Books, 1984.

Nelson, E. Clifford. *The Lutherans in North America*. Philadelphia: Fortress Press, 1975.

20 Centuries of Great Preaching. Vol. 3: *Wesley to Finney, 1703–1875*. Edited by Clyde E. Fant Jr. and William M. Pinson Jr. Waco, TX: Word Books, 1971.

Specific Works

Abbott, Jacob. *Gentle Measures in the Management and Training of the Young, Or, the Principles on Which a Firm Parental Authority May Be Established and Maintained, Without Violence or Anger, and the Right Development of the Moral and Mental Capacities Be Promoted by Methods in Harmony with the Structure and the Characteristics of the Juvenile Mind*. New York: Harper & Brothers, 1872.

———. *Rollo Learning to Read*. Boston: John Allen & Co. 1835.

Adams, Hannah. *A Memoir of Miss Hannah Adams, Written by Herself, with Additional Notices, by a Friend.* Boston: Gray and Bowen, 1832.

Adams, John Quincy. *Letters of John Quincy Adams, to His Son, on the Bible and Its Teachings.* Auburn, NY: J. M. Alden, 1850.

Addams, Jane. *Twenty Years at Hull-House with Autobiographical Notes.* New York: MacMillan, 1912.

Alexander, Archibald. *Practical Directions How to Grow in Grace and Make Progress in Piety.*

Allen, Richard. *The Life Experience and Gospel Labors of the Rt. Rev. Richard Allen to Which is Annexed the Rise and Progress of the African Methodist Episcopal Church in the United States of America; Containing a Narrative of the Yellow Fever in the Year of Our Lord 1793; With an Address to the People of Color in the United States.* Nashville: Abingdon, 1983.

Arden, G. Everett, editor. *The Journals of Eric Norelius: A Swedish Missionary on the American Frontier.* Philadelphia: Fortress Press, 1967.

Asbury, Francis. "The Journal of Francis Asbury, Bishop of the Methodist-Episcopal Church, from March 26, 1772, to April 14, 1773." In *Arminian Magazine* 2 (1790): 401–2.

Avery, Martha Moore, and David Goldstein. *Campaigning for Christ.* Boston: Pilot, 1924.

Bachman, John. *The Doctrine of the Unity of the Human Race Examined on the Principles of Science.* Charleston, SC: C. Canning, 1850.

Backus, Isaac. "Isaac Backus His Writeing Containing Some Particular Account of My Conversion." A manuscript dated August 16, 1751.

Badger, Joseph. *A Memoir of Rev. Joseph Badger; Containing an Autobiography and Selections from His Private Journal and Correspondence.* Hudson, OH: Sawyer, Ingersoll and Company, 1851.

Balch, Emily Greene. "An Exploration of the Infinite." In *The Christian Register of the American Unitarian Association.*

Baldwin, Thomas. *A Sermon, Delivered before His Excellency Caleb Strong, Esq. Governor, the Honorable the Council, Senate, and House of Representatives of the Commonwealth of Massachusetts, May 26, 1802: Being the Day of General Election.* Boston: Young & Minns, 1802.

Bangs, Nathan. *History of the Methodist Episcopal Church from Its Origin in 1776 to the General Conference of 1840.* 4 vols. New York: G. Lane & C. B. Tippett, 1839–42.

Barnes, Albert. *The Church and Slavery.* Philadelphia: Parry & McMillan, 1871.

———. *Lectures on the Evidences of Christianity in the Nineteenth Century.* New York: Harper and Brothers, 1870.

———. *Our Position: A Sermon, Preached before the General Assembly of the Presbyterian Church in the United States in the Fourth Presbyterian Church in the City of Washington, May 20, 1852, by Albert Barnes.* New York: Newman & Ivison, 1852.

Bell, Stephen. *Rebel, Priest, and Prophet: A Biography of Dr. Edward McGlynn.* New York: Devin-Adair, 1937.

Bennett, Mary Katherine Jones (with others). *The Path of Labor.* New York: Council of Women for Home Missions, 1918.

Bethune, Mary McLeod. Unpublished interview from Collection Number M95-2, Biographical records on Mary McLeod Bethune, ca. 1890–1960, State Archives of Florida.

Binga, Anthony. *Sermon and Address: On Past and Present Social, Moral and Religious Conditions of the Colored Baptists of Virginia, Delivered by Appointment of the Shiloh Baptist Association, 1887. II. On the Church and the Sunday School, Delivered before the Sunday School Convention of Virginia, 1881.* Richmond: Johns & Co., 1887.

Bishop, William Howard. *Moving beyond Confined Circles: The Home Mission Writings of William Howard Bishop.* Atlanta: Glenmary Research Center, 1990.

Blake, Eugene Carson. "God, Morality, and Politics." *Theology Today* 36, no. 1 (April 1979).

Bloomer, Amelia. *The Life and Writings of Amelia Bloomer.* Edited by Dexter C. Bloomer. Boston: Arena, 1895.

Boudinot, Elias. *The Life, Public Services, Addresses, and Letters of Elias Boudinot, LL.D.* Edited by J. J.Boudinot. Boston, Houghton, Mifflin, 1896.

Bowman, Thea. *Sister Thea Bowman: Shooting Star.* Edited by Celestine Cepress. Winona, MN: St. Mary's Press, 1993.

Boyd, George Adams. *Elias Boudinot, Patriot and Statesman.* Princeton, NJ: Princeton University Press, 1952.

Bradstreet, Anne. In *Early New England Meditative Poetry,* edited by Charles E. Hambrick-Stowe. New York: Paulist Press, 1988.

Breck, James Lloyd. *The Southern Episcopalian* 1 (November 1854).

Brent, Charles Henry. *Things That Matter: The Best of the Writings of Charles Henry Brent.* Edited by Frederick Ward Kates. New York: Harper & Brothers, 1949.

Brooks, Phillips. *The Light of the World and Other Sermons by the Rt. Rev. Phillips Brooks.* Fifth series. New York: E. P. Dutton, 1899.

Brown, William Adams. *Church and State in Contemporary America: A Study of the Problems They Present and the Principles Which Should Determine Their Relationship.* New York: Scribner's, 1936.

———. *The Church, Catholic and Protestant; A Study of Differences That Matter.* New York: Scribner's, 1935.

Brusher, Joseph. *The Consecrated Thunderbolt: Father Yorke of San Francisco.* Hawthorne, NJ: J. F. Wagner, 1973.

Bushnell, Horace. "Our Gospel a Gift to the Imagination." In *Life and Letters of Horace Bushnell.* New York: Harper & Brothers, 1880.

Buzzell, John. *The Life of Elder Benjamin Randal. Principally Taken from Documents Written by Himself.* Limerick, ME: Hobbs, Woodman & Co., 1827.

Cabrini, Frances Xavier. *Travels of Mother Frances Xavier Cabrini.* Milwaukee: Cuneo Press, 1944.

Carroll, Charles. In *Documents of American Catholic History,* edited by John Tracy Ellis. Milwaukee: Bruce Publishing Co., 1956. Source: Kate Mason Rowland. *The Life of Charles Carroll of Carrollton, 1737–1832, With His Correspondence and Public Papers.* New York: G. P. Putnam's Sons, 1898.

Carroll, John. "First Sermon as Bishop of Baltimore." In *Documents of American Catholic History,* edited by John Tracy Ellis. Milwaukee: Bruce Publishing Co., 2nd ed., 1962. Source: Peter Guilday. *The Life and Times of John Carroll,*

Archbishop of Baltimore, 1735–1815. New York: Encyclopedia Press, 1922, 1:384–85.

Cartwright, Peter. *Autobiography of Peter Cartwright, the Backwoods Preacher.* New York: Carlton A. Porter, 1867.

Carver, George Washington. "How to Search for Truth." In *Carver: In His Own Words,* edited by Gary R. Kremer. Columbia: University of Missouri Press, 1987.

Cary, Stephen G. *Intrepid Quaker: One Man's Quest for Peace.* Edited by Alison Anderson and Jack Coleman. Wallingford, PA: Pendle Hill, 2003.

Cattan, Louise Armstrong. *Lamps Are for Lighting: The Story of Helen Barrett Montgomery and Lucy Waterbury Peabody.* Grand Rapids: Eerdmans, 1972.

Clarke, John. *An Answer to the Question, Why Are You a Christian?* Boston: Apollo Press, 1795.

Coffin, Levi. *Reminiscences of Levi Coffin, the Reputed President of the Underground Railroad; Being a Brief History of the Labors of a Lifetime in Behalf of the Slaves.* Cincinnati: Western Tract Society, 1876.

Coffin, William Sloan. *Credo.* Louisville: Westminster John Knox, 2004.

Coker, Daniel. *A Dialogue between a Virginian and an African Minister.* Baltimore: Benjamin Edes, 1810.

———. *Journal of Daniel Coker, a Descendant of Africa, from the Time of Leaving New York, in the Ship Elizabeth, Capt. Sebor, on a Voyage for Sherbro, in Africa, in Company with Three Agents, and about Ninety Persons of Colour. With an Appendix.* Baltimore: Edward J. Coale, 1820.

Collier-Thomas, Bettye. *Daughters of Thunder: Black Women Preachers and Their Sermons, 1850–1978.* San Francisco: Jossey-Bass, 1997.

Conwell, Russell H. *Acres of Diamonds.* New York: Harper & Brothers, 1915.

Cooper, Anna Julia. *A Voice from the South.* With an Introduction by Mary Helen Washington. New York: Oxford University Press, 1988.

Core, Arthur C. *Philip William Otterbein, Pastor, Ecumenist.* Dayton, OH: Board of Publication, Evangelical United Brethren Church, 1968.

Cox, Melville B. *Remains of Melville B. Cox, Late Missionary to Liberia: With a Memoir.* Boston: Light and Horton, 1835.

Crummell, Alexander. "The Destined Superiority of the Negro," 1877. In Alexander Crummell. *The Greatness of Christ and Other Sermons.* New York: Whitaker, 1882.

Dabney, Robert Lewis. "Our Comfort in Dying: A Sermon." Edited by Michael Bremmer. *www.mbrem.com/life/dab-ser1.htm.*

Davenport, John. *God's Call to His People to Turn unto Him; Together with His Promise to Turn unto Them: Opened and Applied in II Sermons at Two Publick Fasting-Dayes Apointed by Authority.* Boston: John Usher, 1669.

Day, Dorothy. "Holy Poverty." See *www.catholicworker.org/dorothyday/reprint.cfm? TextID=150.*

De Smet, Pierre-Jean, letter to the Editor of the *Catholic Herald* from the Steamboat *Oceana,* Missouri River, May 1, 1841. In *Documents of American Catholic History,* edited by John Tracy Ellis. 2nd ed. Milwaukee: Bruce Publishing Co., 1962. Source: Hiram Martin Chittenden and Alfred Talbot Richardson, editors.

Life, Letters and Travels of Father Pierre-Jean De Smet, S.J., 1801–1873. New York: Francis P. Harper, 1905.

Dickinson, Jonathan. *The Reasonableness of Christianity, in Four Sermons.* Boston: S. Kneeland and T. Green, 1732.

Diekmann, Godfrey. *Come, Let Us Worship.* Baltimore: Helicon Press, 1961.

Doberstein, John W., and Theodore G. Tappert, editors. *The Notebook of a Colonial Clergyman: Condensed from the Journals of Henry Melchior Muhlenberg.* Philadelphia: Fortress Press, 1959.

Dodge, David Low. *War Inconsistent with the Religion of Jesus Christ.* Boston: Ginn, 1905.

Drury, A. W. *History of the Church of the United Brethren in Christ.* Dayton, OH: United Brethren Publishing House, 1924.

Dubois, Ellen Carol, editor. *The Elizabeth Cady Stanton–Susan B. Anthony Reader: Correspondence, Writings, Speeches.* Rev. ed. Boston: Northeastern University Press, 1992.

DuBose, William Porcher. *High Priesthood and Sacrifice.* New York: Longmans, 1908.

Duery, Clifford M. *Marcus and Narcissa Whitman and the Opening of Old Oregon.* Glendale, CA: Arthur Clark, 1973.

Duffy, Consuela Marie. *Katherine Drexel: A Biography.* Cornwells Heights, PA: Sisters of the Blessed Sacrament, 1972.

Eliot, Charles W., editor. *The Journal of John Woolman.* New York: P. F. Collier & Son, 1909.

Eliot, John. *A Brief Narrative of the Progress of the Gospel among the Indians of New England.* Boston, J. K. Wiggin & W. P. Lunt, 1868; reprint of original edition published in London, 1671.

Emery, Julia C. "Forty-Fifth Annual Report of the Woman's Auxiliary to the Board of Missions, 1915–1916." In *Annual Report of the Board of Missions for the Fiscal Year September 1, 1915, to September 30, 1916.* New York: Domestic and Foreign Missionary Society of the Protestant Episcopal Church in the United States of America, 1916.

Finley, James B. *The Autobiography of James B. Finley, or, Pioneer Life in the West.* Edited by W. F. Strickland, Cincinnati: Methodist Book Concern, 1867.

Finney, Charles G. *Finney's Lectures On Systematic Theology.* Edited by J. H. Fairchild. Grand Rapids: Eerdmans, 1953.

Fischer, Robert H., editor. "Franklin Clark Fry: A Palette for a Portrait" *Lutheran Quarterly* 24, supplement, 1972.

Fiske, D. T. *Faith Working by Love, as Exemplified in the Life of Fidelia Fiske.* Boston: Congregational Sabbath School and Publishing Society, 1868.

Flaget, Benedict Joseph. In *Documents of American Catholic History,* edited by John Tracy Ellis. Milwaukee: Bruce Publishing Co., 1956. Source: M. J. Spalding. *Sketches of the Life, Times, and Character of the Rt. Rev. Benedict Joseph Flaget, First Bishop of Louisville.* Louisville, Webb & Levering, 1852.

Foote, Julia A. J. "A Brand Plucked from the Fire: An Autobiographical Sketch." Cleveland: W. F. Schneider, 1879. In *Sisters of the Spirit: Three Black Women's Autobiographies of the Nineteenth Century,* edited by William A. Andrews. Bloomington: Indiana University Press, 1986.

Fosdick, Harry Emerson. "Shall the Fundamentalists Win?" *Christian Work* 102 (June 10, 1922).

Fries, Adelaide L. *The Moravians in Georgia 1735–1740*. Raleigh, NC: Edwards & Broughton, 2003.

Friess, Caroline. *The Letters of Mother Caroline Friess*. Edited by Barbara Brumleve. Winona, MN: St. Mary's Press, 1991.

Furfey, Paul Hanley. *Fire on the Earth*. New York: Macmillan, 1936.

———. *Three Theories of Society*. New York: Macmillan, 1937.

Gaffey, James P. *Francis Clement Kelley and the American Dream*. Bensenville, IL: Heritage Foundation, 1980.

Gallaudet, Thomas. *The Sermon Delivered upon the Occasion of St. Ann's Church for the Deaf-Mutes Commencing Its Services, August 7, 1859, by the Rev. Thomas Gallaudet, Rector*. New York: George F. Nesbitt & Co., 1859.

Gerberding, G. H. *The Life and Letters: W. A. Passavant*. Greenville, PA: Young Lutheran Company, 1906.

Gibbons, James. *Jesus Christ: Our Saviour's Person, Mission, and Spirit*. From the French of the Reverend Father Didon, O.P., edited by the Right Reverend Bernard O'Reilly, with an Introduction by His Eminence James, Cardinal Gibbons, Archbishop of Baltimore. New York: D. Appleton, 1801.

Gilbert, Olive. *Narrative of Sojourner Truth, a Bondswoman of Olden Time, Emancipated by the New York Legislature in the Early Part of the Present Century, with a History of Her Labors and Correspondence Drawn from Her Book of life*. Chicago: Johnson Pub. Co., 1970.

Gladden, Washington. *Recollections*. Cambridge, MA: Houghton Mifflin, 1909.

Graham, Isabella. *The Power of Faith, Exemplified in the Life and Writings of the Late Isabella Graham*. New York: American Tract Society, 1843.

Gray, George A., and Jan V. Bear, editors. *Portraits of the Saints*. Los Angeles: Diocesan Council and Department of Missions, Diocese of the West, Orthodox Church in America, 1994.

Green, Elizabeth Alden. *Mary Lyon and Mount Holyoke: Opening the Gates*. Hanover, NH: University Press of New England, 1979.

Grimké, Angelina. *History of Pennsylvania Hall Which Was Destroyed by a Mob on the 17th of May, 1838*. New York: Negro Universities Press, 1969.

Grimké, Francis James. *The Works of Francis J. Grimké.*, Vol. 1. Edited by Carter G. Woodson. Washington, DC: Associated Publishers, 1942.

Grimké, Sarah. "Letters on the Equality of the Sexes and the Condition of Woman, Addressed to Mary S. Parker, President of the Boston Female Anti-Slavery Society, 1838." In *The Public Years of Sarah and Angelina Grimké: Selected Writings 1835–1839*, edited by Larry Ceplair. New York: Columbia University Press, 1989.

Guerin, Mother Theodore. *Journals and Letters of Mother Theodore Guerin*. Edited by Sister Mary Theodosia Mug. Saint Mary-of-the-Woods, IN: Providence Press, 1937.

Hammon, Jupiter. *The Complete Works of Jupiter Hammon of Long Island*. Edited by Stanley Austin Ransom Jr. Port Washington, NY: Kennikat Press, 1970.

Hancock, Cornelia. *South after Gettysburg: Letters of Cornelia Hancock from the Army of the Potomac, 1863–1865*. Philadelphia: University of Pennsylvania Press, 1937.

Hanley, Mary Laurence, and O. A. Bushnell. *Pilgrimage and Exile: Mother Marianne of Molokai*. Honolulu: University of Hawaii Press, 1991.

Harkness, Georgia. *The Dark Night of the Soul*. New York: Abingdon-Cokesbury Press, 1945.

Harper, Keith, editor. *Rescue the Perishing: Selected Correspondence of Annie Armstrong*. Macon, GA: Mercer University Press, 2004.

Hawkins, Peter. *The Language of Grace*. New York: Church Publishing, 2004.

Haynes, Lemuel. *Black Preacher to White America: The Collected Writings of Lemuel Haynes, 1774–1833*. Edited by Richard Newman. New York: Carlson, 1990.

Hecker, Isaac T. *Romantic Religion in Ante-Bellum America*. Edited by John Farina. New York: Paulist Press, 1998.

Hicks, Edward. *Memoirs of the Life and Religious Labors of Edward Hicks, Late of Newtown, Bucks County, Pennsylvania, Written by Himself*. Philadelphia: Merrihew and Thompson, 1851.

Hobart, John Henry. *The Christian Bishop Approving Himself unto God in Reference to the Present State of the Protestant Episcopal Church in the United States of America. A Sermon by the Rt. Rev. John Henry Hobart*. Philadelphia: Jesper Harding, Printer, 1827.

Hodge, Charles. *Systematic Theology and Other Writings*. See *www.tracts.ukgo.com/charles_hodge.htm*.

Holly, James Theodore. "The Divine Plan of Human Redemption in Its Ethnological Development." *AME Church Review* 1, no. 6 (October 1884).

Hopkins, Mark. *The Law of Love and Love as a Law, or, Moral Science, Theoretical and Practical*. New York: C. Scribner, 1869.

Hopkins, Samuel. "A Discourse upon the Slave Trade and the Slavery of the Africans. Delivered before the Providence Society for Abolishing the Slave Trade, Etc., at Their Annual Meeting, May 17, 1793." In Samuel Hopkins. *Timely Articles on Slavery*. Boston: Congregational Board of Publications, 1854.

———. *An Inquiry into the Nature of True Holiness*. New York: William Durell, 1791.

Hughes, John Joseph, in *Documents of American Catholic History*, edited by John Tracy Ellis. Milwaukee: Bruce Publishing Co., 1956. Source: Henry J. Browne, editor. "The Archdiocese of New York a Century Ago: A Memoir of Archbishop Hughes, 1838–1858." *Historical Records and Studies* 39–40 (1952).

Huntington, James O. S. "Beginnings of the Religious Life for Men in the American Church." *Historical Magazine of the Protestant Episcopal Church* 1 (March 1933).

Huntington, William Reed. *The Church Idea*. New York: Charles Scribner's Sons, 1869.

———. *The Talisman of Unity: A Sermon in Behalf of Church Consolidation Preached in the Crypt of the Cathedral of St. John the Divine, January the Twenty-Second 1899*. New York: Thomas Whittaker, 1899.

Ireland, John. *The Church and Modern Society.* Vol. 1. St. Paul, MN: Pioneer Press, 1905.

James, W. C. *Fannie E. S. Heck: A Study of the Hidden Springs in a Rarely Useful and Victorious Life.* Nashville: Broadman, 1939.

Johnson, Jeff G. *Black Christians: The Untold Story.* St. Louis: Concordia, 1991.

Johnson, Samuel. *Samuel Johnson, President of King's College, His Career and Writings.* Edited by Herbert and Carol Schneider. Vol. 3. New York: Columbia University Press, 1929.

Jones, Absalom. *Thanksgiving Sermon Preached January 1, 1808, in St. Thomas's Church, or the African Episcopal Church, Philadelphia, on Account of the Abolition of the African Slave Trade on That Day by the Congress of the United States.* Philadelphia: Fry and Kammeher, Printers, 1808.

Jones, Charles Colcock. *The Religious Instruction of the Negroes in the United States.* Electronic edition. Chapel Hill: Academic Affairs Library, University of North Carolina, 1999; originally published by Thomas Purse, Savannah, 1842.

Jones, Paul. *Minutes of the House of Bishops.* Wednesday, October 17, 1917.

Jones, Rufus. *Rethinking Quaker Principles.* Wallingford, PA: Pendle Hill, 1940.

Jordan, Clarence. *The Substance of Faith: and Other Cotton Patch Sermons.* Edited by Dallas Lee. New York: Association Press, 1972.

Judson, Adoniram. "Advice to Missionary Candidates." In Edward Judson. *The Life of Adoniram Judson.* New York: Anson D. F. Randolph & Co., 1883.

Judson, Edward. *The Life of Adoniram Judson.* New York: Anson D. F. Randolph & Co., 1883.

Kellersberger, Julia Lake. *A Life for the Congo: The Story of Althea Brown Edmiston.* New York: Fleming H. Revell, 1947.

Kelly, Thomas R. *Reality of the Spiritual World.* Pendle Hill Pamphlet 21. Wallingford, PA: Pendle Hill, 1942.

Kemper, Jackson. "The Duty of the Church with Respect to Missions." *The Spirit of Missions* 6 (December 1841).

Key, Francis Scott. *The Power of Literature and Its Connection with Religion; an Oration delivered at Bristol College, July 23, 1834, before the Philologian Society.* Bristol, PA: Bristol College Press, 1834.

Koulomzin, Sophie. *Many Worlds: A Russian Life,* Crestwood, NY: St. Vladimir's Seminary Press, 1980.

———. *Our Church and Our Children.* Crestwood, NY: St. Vladimir's Seminary Press, 1975.

Ladd, William. *A Solemn Appeal to Christians of All Denominations in Favor of the Cause of Permanent and Universal Peace.* Boston: American Peace Society, 1836.

LaFarge, John. *An American Amen.* New York: Farrar, Straus, and Cudahy, 1958.

LaFarge, John. *A John LaFarge Reader.* Edited by Thurston N. Davis and Joseph Small. New York: America Press, 1956.

Lathrop, Rose Hawthorn. *Selected Writings.* Edited by Diana Culbertson. New York: Paulist Press, 1991.

Lee, Jarena. *Religious Experience and Journal of Mrs. Jarena Lee Giving an Account of Her Call to Preach the Gospel.* Philadelphia, 1849.

Lee, Jesse. *The Substance of a Sermon Preached on the 7th of August, 1814, at the Funeral of Miss Mary Hardy; Daughter of the Rev. William P. Hardy, and Sister to the Rev. Henry Hardy, in Bertie County, North Carolina.* Georgetown: Wm. A. Reid and Co., 1814.

Lee, Luther. *Natural Theology or the Existence, Attributes, and Government of God including the Obligations and Duties of Men, Demonstrated by Arguments Drawn from the Phenomena of Nature.* Syracuse: Wesleyan Methodist Publishing House, 1866.

Lerner, Gerd, editor. *Black Women in White America: A Documentary History.* New York: Vintage Books, 1992.

Lernoux, Penny. *Cry of the People: United States Involvement in the Rise of Fascism, Torture, and Murder and the Persecution of the Catholic Church in Latin America.* Garden City, NY: Doubleday, 1989.

Liebler, H. Baxter. *Boil My Heart for Me.* New York: Exposition Press, 1969.

Lomax, Judith. *The Sabbath Journal of Judith Lomax.* Edited by Laura Hobgood-Oster. Atlanta: Scholars Press, 1999.

Lonnborg, Barbara A., and Thomas J. Lynch. *Father Flanagan's Legacy.* Boys Town, NE: Boys Town Press, 2003.

Merton, Thomas. *The Asian Journal of Thomas Merton.* Edited by Naomi Burton, Patrick Hart, and James Laughlin. New York: New Directions, 1968.

Meyendorff, John. *Living Tradition: Orthodox Witness in the Contemporary World.* Crestwood, NY: St. Vladimir's Seminary Press, 1978.

———. *The Vision of Unity.* Crestwood, NY: St. Vladimir's Seminary Press, 1987.

Michel, Virgil. "Teaching the Life in Christ." *Orate Fratres* 15, no. 1 (December 1, 1940).

Minor, Maria. *Channing Moore Williams: Pioneer Missionary in Japan.* New York: National Council, 1959.

Montgomery, Helen Barrett. *The New Testament in Modern English.* Valley Forge, PA: Judson Press, 1924.

———. *Prayer and Missions.* West Medford, MA: Central Committee on the United Study of Foreign Missions, 1924.

Moody, Dwight Lyman. *New Sermons, Addresses and Prayers.* Chicago: J. W. Goodspeed, 1877.

Moon, Lottie. *Send the Light: Lottie Moon's Letters and Other Writings.* Edited by Keith Harper. Macon, GA: Mercer University Press, 2002.

Moore, Joanna P. *"In Christ's Stead": Autobiographical Sketches.* Chicago: Women's Baptist Home Mission Society, 1902.

Mott, John. *Nobel Prize Lecture. www.nobel.se/peace/laureates/1946/mott-lecture.html.*

Mott, Lucretia. *http://womenshistory.about.com/library/bio/blmott.htm.*

Muhlenberg, William A. *Memorial of Sundry Presbyters of the Protestant Episcopal Church, Presented to the House of Bishops, October 18, 1853.* New York, 1853.

———. *The Weekly Eucharist.*

Muldrey, Mary Hermenia. *Abounding in Mercy: Mother Austin Carroll.* New Orleans: Habersham, 1988.

Murray, John Courtney. "Our Response to the Ecumenical Revolution." In *Bridging the Sacred and the Secular: Selected Writings of John Courtney Murray, S.J.*, edited by James F. Keenan. Washington, DC: Georgetown University Press, 1994.

Murray, Pauli. *Song in a Weary Throat: An American Pilgrimage.* New York: Harper and Row, 1987.

Neal, Emily Gardiner. *The Healing Ministry: A Personal Journal.* New York: Crossroad, 1985.

Nelson, Ruth Youngdahl. *A Grandma's Letters to God.* Minneapolis: Augsburg, 1983.

Nettleton, Asahel. *Asahel Nettleton: Sermons from the Second Great Awakening.* Ames, IA: International Outreach, 1995.

Nevins, Albert J., editor. *The Maryknoll Golden Book: An Anthology of Mission Literature.* New York: Book Treasures, 1956.

Newcomer, Christian. *Christian Newcomer, His Life and Achievements.* Edited by Samuel Hough. Dayton, OH: United Brethren in Christ, 1941.

Nicoloai, Evan P. "Iakov Georgevich Netssvetov: First Aleut-Russian Priest and Missionary to the Native Peoples of the Yukon and Kuskokwim Regions." Dissertation. St. Vladimir's Seminary, 1992.

Niebuhr, Reinhold. *The Essential Reinhold Niebuhr: Selected Essays and Addresses.* Edited by Robert McAfee Brown. New Haven: Yale University Press, 1986.

Occom, Samson. *A Sermon Preached at the Execution of Moses Paul, an Indian, Who Had Been Guilty of Murder, Preached at New Haven, Connecticut, by Samson Occom.* New Haven, 1788.

Osgood, Phillips Endecott. *"Straight Tongue": A Story of Bishop Henry B. Whipple, First Episcopal Bishop of Minnesota.* Minneapolis: T. S. Denison & Company, 1958.

Oursler, Fulton, and Will Oursler. *Father Flanagan of Boys Town.* Garden City, NY: Doubleday, 1972.

Oxnam, Garfield Bromley. *A Testament of Faith.* Boston: Little, Brown, 1958.

Palmer, Phoebe. *The Devotional Writings of Phoebe Palmer.* New York: Garland Publishing, 1985.

Parkhurst, Charles. *My Forty Years in New York.* New York: Macmillan, 1923.

Parks, Rosa. *Quiet Strength.* Grand Rapids: Zondervan, 1994.

Payne, Daniel Alexander. *Recollections of Seventy Years.* Edited by C. S. Smith. Nashville: Publishing House of the A.M.E. Sunday School Union, 1888.

Peabody, Lucy Whitehead McGill. *The Meddlesome Missionary.* New York: Women's Board of Foreign Missions of the Presbyterian Church, 1918.

Peck, John Mason. "Journal of John Mason Peck [microform]." Nashville: Historical Commission, Southern Baptist Convention, 1957 (Ann Arbor: University Microfilms).

Puleo, Mev. *The Struggle Is One: Voices and Visions of Liberation.* Albany: State University of New York Press, 1994.

Powderly, Terence V. *The Path I Trod: The Autobiography of Terence V. Powderly.* New York: Columbia University Press, 1940.

Quinn, Frederick. *Building the "Goodly Fellowship of Faith": A History of the Episcopal Church in Utah, 1867–1996*. Logan: Utah State University Press, 2004.

Ramsay, Martha Laurens. *Memoirs of Martha Laurens Ramsay; Who Died in Charleston, S.C., on the 10th of June, 1811, in the 52nd Year of Her Age: With Extracts from Her Diary, Letters, and Other Private Papers*. Edited by David Ramsay. Philadelphia: American Sunday-School Union, 1845.

Rauschenbusch, Walter. *Walter Rauschenbusch: Selected Writings*. Edited by Winthrop S. Hudson. New York: Paulist Press, 1984.

Rehmer, R. F., editor. *The Distress of the German Lutherans in North America*. Fort Wayne, IN: Concordia Theological Seminary Press, 1982.

Repplier, Agnes. *Points of View*. Boston: Houghton, Mifflin, 1894.

Rice, Luther. *Dispensations of Providence: The Journal and Selected Letters of Luther Rice*. Edited by William H. Brackney. Rochester, NY: American Baptist Historical Society, 1984.

Riggs, Stephen Return. *Mary and I: Forty Years with the Sioux*. Chicago: W. G. Holmes, 1880.

Roberts, Benjamin Titus. *A Symposium on Scriptural Holiness*. Edited by Wilson T. Hogg. Chicago: Free Methodist Publishing House, 1896.

Roelker, William G. *Francis Wayland: A Neglected Pioneer of Higher Education*. Worcester, MA: American Antiquarian Society, 1944.

Rogers, Mary Josephine. "The Maryknoll Spirit." In "Occasional Conferences by Mother Mary Joseph to the Maryknoll Sisters." Unpublished, 1954.

Rush, Benjamin. *The Selected Writings of Benjamin Rush*. Edited by Dagobert D. Runes. New York: Philosophical Library, 1947.

Rust, Richard. *Freedom's Gift or Sentiments of the Free*. Hartford: S. S. Cowles, 1840.

Sanford, Elias B. *Origin and History of the Federal Council of Churches of Christ in America*. Hartford, CT: S. S. Scranton Company, 1916.

Schauinger, Joseph Herman. *Stephen T. Badin: Priest in the Wilderness*. Milwaukee: Bruce Publishing Co., 1956.

Schereschewsky, Samuel Isaac Joseph. "The Rev. Dr. Schereschewsky's Appeal for Funds to Establish a Missionary College in China." *Spirit of Missions* 42 (June 1877).

Schlenther, Boyd Stanley. *The Life and Writings of Francis Makemie, Father of American Presbyterianism*. Lewiston, NY: E. Mellen Press, 1999.

Schmemann, Alexander. *Great Lent*, Crestwood, NY: St. Vladimir's Seminary Press, 1969.

———. *The Orthodox*. Crestwood, NY: St. Vladimir's Seminary Press, 1969.

Schmucker, Samuel Simon. *Fraternal Appeal to the American Churches with a Plan for Catholic Union on Apostolic Principles*. Edited by Frederick K. Wentz. Philadelphia: Fortress Press, 1965.

Seabury, Samuel. "The Journal of Samuel Seabury." Unpublished document in the archives of the Diocese of Hartford, Connecticut.

Shaw, Anna Howard. *Women in the Ministry*. Meadville, PA: T. L. Flood, 1898.

Seller, Maxine Schwartz. *Women Educators in the United States, 1820–1993: A Bio-Bibliographical Sourcebook*. Westport, CT: Greenwood Press, 1994.

Series of Extemporaneous Discourses, Delivered in the Several Meetings of the So-
ciety of Friends, in Philadelphia, Germantown, Abington, Byberry, Newtown,
Falls, and Trenton, by Elias Hicks, A Minister in Said Society. Philadelphia:
Joseph & Edward Parker, 1825.

"A Sermon Delivered by Elias Hicks, at Pine Street Meeting in Philadelphia, December 10, 1826. With Responses to Hicks by Jonathan Evans and Isaac Lloyd,
and Responses to them by Elias Hicks and Willet Hicks." *The Quaker* 1, no. 3
(1827).

Sheen, Fulton J. *Guide to Contentment.* New York: Alba House, 1996.

Sheldon, Charles. *In His Steps.* *www.ssnet.org/bsc/ihs/ihs.html.*

Sherrill, Henry Knox. *Among Friends.* Boston: Little, Brown, 1962.

Shields, Thomas Edward. *Catholic Educational Review* 1 (January–May 1911).

———. *Catholic Educational Review* 19, no. 4 (April 1921).

———. *The Making and Unmaking of a Dullard.* Washington, DC: Catholic
Education Press, 1921.

Sheridan, Robert E. *The Founders of Maryknoll.* Maryknoll, NY: Catholic Foreign
Mission Society of America, 1980.

Shuster, George N. *The Catholic Spirit in America.* New York: Dial Press, 1927.

———. *The Ground I Walked On: Reflections of a College President.* New York:
Farrar, Straus and Cudahy, 1961.

Simpson, A. B. *The Holy Spirit, Or Power from on High: An Unfolding of the Doc-*
trine of the Holy Spirit in the Old and New Testaments. New York: Christian
Alliance Publishing Co., 1896.

Smith, Amanda. *An Autobiography: The Story of the Lord's Dealings with Mrs.*
Amanda Smith the Colored Evangelist. New York: Oxford University Press,
1988.

Smith, Charles, W. F. *Robert Hunt, Vicar of Jamestown.* New York: National
Council, 1957.

Speer, Robert. *The Meaning of Christ to Me.* New York: Fleming H. Revell, 1936.

Stanton, Elizabeth Cady. "Address to the First Women's Rights Convention at Seneca
Falls, N.Y., July 19, 1848." In *The Elizabeth Cady Stanton–Susan B. Anthony*
Reader: Correspondence, Writings, Speeches, edited by Ellen Carol DuBois. Rev.
ed. Boston: Northeastern University Press, 1992.

Starr, Ellen Gates. *On Art, Labor, and Religion.* Edited by Mary Jo Deegan and
Ana-Maria Wahl. New Brunswick, NJ: Transaction Publishers, 2003.

Stelzle, Charles. *The Call of the New Day to the Old Church.* New York: Fleming H.
Revell, 1915.

Stevens, Abel. *Life and Times of Nathan Bangs, D.D.* New York: Carlton & Porter,
1863.

Stewart, Maria. "Lecture Delivered at the Franklin Hall." In *With Pen and Voice:*
A Critical Anthology of Nineteenth-Century African-American Women, edited
by Shirley Wilson Logan. Carbondale: Southern Illinois University Press, 1995.

Stidger, William Leroy. *Personal Power.* Garden City, NY: Doubleday, Doran, 1929.

Stokoe, Mark. *Orthodox Christians in North America, 1794–1994.* Syosset, NY:
Orthodox Christian Publications Center, 1995.

Stoddard, Solomon. *The Doctrine of Instituted Churches Explained and Proved from*
the Word of God. London: Ralph Smith, 1700.

Stokes, George Stewart. *Agnes Repplier: Lady of Letters.* Philadelphia: University of Pennsylvania Press, 1949.

Stowe, Harriet Beecher. *Footsteps of the Master.* New York: J. B. Ford & Company, 1877.

Stringfellow, William. *An Ethic for Christians and Other Aliens in a Strange Land.* Waco, TX: Word, 1973.

Swift, David Everett. *Black Prophets of Justice: Activist Clergy before the Civil War.* Baton Rouge: Louisiana State University Press, 1989.

Taylor, Edward. *Christographia.* Edited by Norman S. Grabo. New Haven: Yale University Press, 1962.

Taylor, J. B. *Biography of Elder Lott Cary, Late Missionary to Africa, With an Appendix on the Subject of Colonization, by J. H. B. Latrobe, Esq., President of the Maryland State Colonization Society.* Baltimore: Armstrong and Berry, 1837.

Taylor, Nathaniel. *Practical Sermons.* New York: Clark, Austin, and Smith, 1859.

Terry, Ellen. *Pierre Toussaint, Apostle of Old New York.* Boston: Pauline Books and Media, 1981.

Thoburn, James M. *The Church of Pentecost.* Calcutta: Methodist Publishing House, 1899.

———. *Life of Isabella Thoburn.* Cincinnati: Jennings and Graham, 1903.

Thurman, Howard. *Mysticism and the Experience of Love.* Wallingford, PA: Pendle Hill, 1965.

Tietjen, John H. "Peter's Confession — and Ours" (Matthew 16:13–16)," a sermon preached at Trinity Lutheran Church, Fort Worth, Texas, on January 18, 2004.

Tonra, Mary. *Led by the Spirit: A Biography of Mother Boniface Keasey.* New York: Gardner Press, 1984.

Trueblood, D. Elton. "Basic Christianity." In *Best Sermons,* edited by G. Paul Butler, New York: McGraw-Hill, 1955.

Truett, George Washington. *www.bibleteacher.org/gwt_4.htm.*

Underwood, Francis H. *John Greenleaf Whittier, a Biography.* Boston: Houghton, Mifflin, 1884.

Varela, Félix. *Letters to Elpido.* Edited by Felipe J. Estévez. New York: Paulist Press, 1989.

Vassar, Matthew. *The Autobiography and Letters of Matthew Vassar.* Edited by Elizabeth Hazelton Haight. New York: Oxford University Press, 1916.

Veniaminov, Ivan. *Journals of the Priest Ioann Veniaminov in Alaska, 1823 to 1836.* Translated by Jerome Kisslinger. Introduction and Commentary by S. A. Mousalimas. Fairbanks: University of Alaska Press, 1993.

Walker, H. Torrey, editor. *Mr. Protestant: An Informal Biography of Franklin Clark Fry.* Edited by the Board of Publication of the United Lutheran Church in America, 1960.

Walsh, James Anthony. "The Spiritual Legacy of James Anthony Walsh." Unpublished.

Wanamaker, John. *Prayers of John Wanamaker.* Edited by A. Gordon MacLennan. New York: Fleming H. Revell, 1923.

Wayland, Francis, and Richard Fuller. *Domestic Slavery Considered as a Scriptural Institution in a Correspondence between the Rev. Richard Fuller of Beaufort,*

S.C., and the Rev. Francis Wayland of Providence, R.I. New York: Lewis Colby & Co., 1847.

Wedel, Cynthia C. *Faith or Fear and Future Shock.* New York: Friendship Press, 1974.

Weekly, Carolyn J. *The Kingdoms of Edward Hicks.* Williamsburg, VA: Harry N. Abrams, 1999.

Weigel, Gustave. *Catholic Theology in Dialogue.* New York: Harper & Brothers, 1960.

———. *Faith and Understanding in America.* New York: Macmillan, 1959.

Weld, Theodore. *The Bible against Slavery: A Inquiry into the Patriarchal and Mosaic Systems on the Subject of Human Rights.* Pittsburgh: United Presbyterian Board of Publication, 1864.

West, Robert Frederick. *Alexander Campbell and Natural Religion.* New Haven: Yale University Press, 1948.

Wheelock, Eleazar. *A Plain and Faithful Narrative of the Original Design, Rise, Progress and Present State of the Indian Charity-School at Lebanon, in Connecticut.* Boston: R. and S. Draper, 1763.

Whipple, Henry B. *Light and Shadows of a Long Episcopate.* New York: Macmillan, 1899.

White, William. *The Past and the Future: A Charge on Events Connected with the Organization of the Protestant Episcopal Church in the United States America, and the Lessons They Inculcate.* Philadelphia: By Order of the Convention, 1834.

Willard, Frances E. *Writing Out My Heart: Selections from the Journal of Frances E. Willard, 1855–96.* Edited by Carolyn De Swarte Gifford. Urbana: University of Illinois Press, 1995.

Williams, Channing Moore. "Annual Report of the Missionary Bishop of Yedo." *Spirit of Missions* 54 (October 1889).

Williams, Roger. *The Bloudy Tenent of Persecution for Cause of Conscience Discussed.* London: J. Haddon, 1848.

Williamson, G. R. *Memoir of the Rev. David Abeel, D.D., Late Missionary to China.* New York: Robert Carter, 1848.

Wolf, M. Madeleva. *Addressed to Youth.* Paterson, NJ: Saint Anthony Guild Press, 1944.

Woodson, Carter G. *Negro Orators and Their Orations.* Washington, DC: Associated Publishers, 1925.

Woolman, John. *The Journal of John Woolman.* Edited by Charles W. Eliot. New York: P. F. Collier & Son, 1909.

Yorke, Peter Christopher. *The Ghosts of Bigotry.* San Francisco: Text Book Publishing Co., 1913.

Zahm, John Augustus. *Woman in Science.* Notre Dame, IN: University of Notre Dame Press, 1991; published under the name H. J. Mozans.

INDEX